THE LOEB CLASSICAL LIBRARY

FOUNDED BY JAMES LOEB, LL.D.

EDITED BY

† T. E. PAGE, C.H., LITT.D.

† E. CAPPS, PH.D., LL D.   † W. H. D. ROUSE, LITT.D.

L. A. POST, L.H.D.   E. H. WARMINGTON, M.A., F.R.HIST.SOC.

MINOR ATTIC ORATORS

I

MINOR ATTIC ORATORS

IN TWO VOLUMES

I

ANTIPHON
ANDOCIDES

WITH AN ENGLISH TRANSLATION BY

K. J. MAIDMENT, M.A.

FELLOW AND CLASSICAL TUTOR OF MERTON COLLEGE, OXFORD

LONDON
WILLIAM HEINEMANN LTD
CAMBRIDGE, MASSACHUSETTS
HARVARD UNIVERSITY PRESS
MCMLX

First printed 1941
Reprinted 1953, 1960

Printed in Great Britain

MINOR ATTIC ORATORS

IV. The Third Tetralogy

Introductory Note . . 118

Text and Translation . . 120

V. On the Murder of Herodes—

Analysis . . 155

Text and Translation . .

CONTENTS OF VOLUME I

v

CONTENTS

PREFACE

THE text upon which the present translation is based
is that of I. Bekker (1822) ; but I have not hesitated
to introduce such alterations and corrections as the
fresh manuscript evidence and detailed linguistic
study of the last hundred years have made necessary
or probable. The critical apparatus, while by no
means exhaustive, will, I hope, prove full enough to
enable the reader to appreciate for himself the relative value of the principal sources from which the
text of Antiphon and Andocides derives. Of the
surviving fragments all those are printed which
possess any historical or literary importance. It
appeared beyond the scope of the present volume to
include isolated words quoted by the ancient lexicographers as grammatical rarities. These are readily
accessible in existing editions of the two authors and
are of no interest to the general reader. In regard
to the translation itself I need say only that I have
aimed at being both accurate and readable, but am
fully conscious that I have too often failed to be
either. I should, however, like to take this opportunity of thanking many friends for their suggestions and advice, particularly the present Warden
of Merton, Sir John Miles, whose critical acumen
and long experience of comparative law have repeatedly saved me from error; Mr. R. G. C. Levens,

my former tutor, who has put me still further in his debt by reading much of the translation in proof and offering valuable criticisms; and Professor H. T. Wade-Gery, who has always been ready with advice upon the many historical problems presented by Antiphon. I must also express my gratitude to the proprietors of the Bibliotheca Teubneriana for their courteous permission to reprint, as it stands, Thalheim's text of the first four columns of the papyrus fragments of Antiphon's Περὶ τῆς μεταστάσεως, together with his critical apparatus.

K. J. MAIDMENT

August 1940

THE MANUSCRIPTS

ANTIPHON.—When Bekker published his edition of the Attic Orators in 1822, he relied upon four manuscripts for the reconstruction of the text of Antiphon. These manuscripts were :

(1) Crippsianus (Brit. Mus. Burneianus 95), thirteenth century . . . A
(2) Laurentianus, fifteenth century . . B
(3) Marcianus, fifteenth century . . L
(4) Vratislaviensis, sixteenth century . . Z

The contents of all four were the same, viz. : Andocides, Isaeus, Dinarchus, Antiphon, and Lycurgus, together with a number of short pieces attributed to Gorgias, Alcidamas, and others. While regarding A, the earliest, as of the first importance, Bekker held that B, L, and Z represented an independent, if inferior, tradition, and they consequently occupy a prominent place in his critical apparatus. In 1829 Dobson collated yet another MS. from the British Museum, the fifteenth century Burneianus 96 (M), and attempted to show that it must rank at least as high as Bekker's B, L, and Z. It has since been conclusively proved, however, that B, L, Z, and M derive from one another in the order B L M Z, and that B itself is wholly dependent upon A.[a] All four there-

[a] Cf. *Jahrb. f. Phil.* 1877, p. 673, *Hermes*, xvii., p. 385, and *Rhein. Mus.* xl., p. 387.

fore lose their claim to the respect shown them by their early editors. But the supremacy of A itself has been seriously challenged since attention was drawn by Maetzner in 1838 to an Oxford ms. of the late thirteenth or early fourteenth century, now known as N (Bodl. Misc. 208). N, it is clear, is independent of A, though closely related to it—both, in fact, may be descended directly from a common archetype—and is of equal importance for the determination of the text. In the present edition the evidence of both mss. has been allowed full weight; neither shows a marked superiority over the other, and the choice, not infrequently offered, between two equally acceptable variants, must depend less upon the ms. in which each occurs than upon the intuition of the editor and his conception of what Antiphon could or could not have written. Both mss. have been corrected by more than one hand. A contains corrections both by the copyist himself (A corr.), which generally find confirmation in N and are clearly derived from a common archetype, and also by a second hand (A corr.²). These last are not so certainly based upon ms. authority and cease abruptly at § 84 of the *De Caede Herodis*. In N the corrections are of the same twofold character. The copyist has himself revised his work from the original (N corr.), while here and there a later hand or hands can also be detected at work (N corr.²); these later corrections in N, however, are the merest conjectures and can be of little use in the reconstruction of the text.

ANDOCIDES.—Here again the edition of Bekker rested upon A, B, L, and Z, with the addition of Ambrosianus D 42 sup. (Q), a fourteenth century paper manuscript containing the last two speeches

of Andocides and the first two of Isaeus. Q, while
independent of A, must be ranked below it. It is
occasionally of use in supplying an omission in A, and
is valuable as in the main confirming A's readings ;
but it has suffered from well meant attempts to
smooth out the roughness of Andocides' style at the
cost of accuracy and contains frequent lacunae. In
effect, then, A remains our principal authority for the
De Pace and *In Alcibiadem*, and our sole authority for
the *De Mysteriis* and the *De Reditu*. Once again it
seems possible to distinguish the work of two cor-
rectors. The first is clearly the copyist himself. The
second, who uses a slightly darker ink, but is otherwise almost identical with the first, differs from the
A corr.[2] of Antiphon in that he is clearly making his
corrections from the same original as the copyist. In
view of the close correspondence between the two
hands, both will be referred to without distinction
as A corr.

ANTIPHON

LIFE OF ANTIPHON

ANTIPHON was born either shortly before or shortly after the year 480.[a] He died at about the age of seventy in 411. Thus, like his younger contemporaries, Thucydides and Socrates, he saw the swift growth of the Athenian empire, its brief brilliance, its inevitable decline; and, like them, he was influenced profoundly by the release of those energies of the spirit and the intellect which, even in his lifetime, made Athens the focus of Hellenic culture. Of his family little is known; but the fact that his grandfather had been a devoted supporter of the Peisistratidae [b] is significant of the political traditions which he was brought up to respect. The statement that his father, Sophilus, was a sophist [c] can hardly be more than an unlucky guess, as he must have been an old man before the full force of the

[a] Sources for life of Antiphon: Thucyd. viii. 68, [Plutarch], *Vit. X Or.*, Philostratus, *Vit.* i. 15, Photius, cod. 259. Of these the two last are derived from the Pseudo-Plutarch, who drew in his turn upon Caecilius of Calactê writing in the Augustan period. Many of the statements of the Pseudo-Plutarch, Philostratus, and Photius are vitiated by the confusion which existed in ancient times between Antiphon the orator, Antiphon the sophist, Antiphon the tragic poet, and a fourth Antiphon put to death by the Thirty Tyrants.

[b] Περὶ τῆς μεταστάσεως, fragment 1.

[c] [Plutarch], § 2.

2

sophistic movement was felt at Athens ; and when
we are told in addition that Alcibiades was among his
pupils, it is hard not to believe that he has been
confused with Socrates.   Antiphon himself, however,
must early have become interested in the new culture
which made its first appearance with the visit of
Protagoras of Abdera to Athens c. 450 and thrust its
roots ever deeper during the succeeding generation.
But his gifts were not those of a Hippias or Prodicus;
he was no encyclopaedist.   He concerned himself
solely with the possibility of reducing the rules of
effective speaking to an ordered system ; and it is
thus with the Sicilians, Corax, Teisias and Gorgias,
that he has the closest affinity.   We hear of a Τέχνη
or rhetorical handbook written by him [a] ; and, if the
evidence of Plato is to be trusted,[b] he opened a school
in Athens, where those who wished to succeed in the
courts or Assembly could benefit by his experience
and research.

How soon Antiphon began to win a reputation for
himself in this field is not known.[c]   It is likely enough
that he became prominent before the beginning of
the Peloponnesian War.   But more important is the
fact that he was at the same time composing speeches
for others to deliver in both the law-courts and the
Assembly ; for it is in his activity as the first of the
λογογράφοι [d] that the explanation of the vast, but
subterranean, influence which he later came to exert

[a] See fragments, p. 308.

[b] *Menexenus* 236 A.

[c] The reference to his φιλαργυρία in the *Peisander* of Plato
Comicus ([Plut.] § 16) would seem to show that he had gained
notoriety for high fees by *circa* 420 at the latest, but is
otherwise of no help.

[d] [Plut.] § 4, Diod. ap. Clem. Alex. *Strom.* i. 365.

3

in Athenian politics is largely to be sought. By upbringing and predilection he was an uncompromising opponent of democracy ; and his oratorical genius was always at the service of that compactly organized minority which, though it seldom came into the open, strove ceaselessly to undermine the supremacy of the Demos. All too little is known of the activities of the oligarchic ἑταιρεῖαι before their brief triumph in 411 ; but it is at least clear that they made a practice of championing the subject-states of the Empire against the oppression of the democratic imperialists, and lost no opportunity of exposing the shortcomings of the popular government in its domestic administration. It is thus of some significance that among the lost speeches of Antiphon there should occur two in which he defends allied states against Athens,[a] and that among those which survive, one, the *Choreutes*, should give prominence to the corruption of the officials of the democracy, and a second, the *Herodes*, should attempt to clear a native of Lesbos of the charge of murdering an Athenian citizen.

But it was during the critical period which followed the defeat of the Sicilian expedition that Antiphon's great opportunity came. In the spring of 411 Peisander arrived in Athens from the army at Samos with the news that Alcibiades would secure the support of Persia against Sparta on condition that the popular government was suppressed. Antiphon's plans were laid and his organization was perfected. The democrats, on the other hand, were in despair and their inability to resist was assured by the

[a] *On the Tribute of Samothrace, On the Tribute of Lindus.*
See fragments, pp. 290-292.

4

news that the army at Samos was in favour of accepting the Persian terms. Without violence and without bloodshed the existing Council and Assembly were superseded by a new Council of Four Hundred and a purely nominal Assembly of Five Thousand, and Athens was completely under the control of the oligarchs. At last the end for which Antiphon had worked so long and so patiently was achieved; but he was destined to benefit but little by his success. Not only had Peisander and his associates already lost their hold over the army at Samos, but a serious split occurred within the Council of Four Hundred itself between the extremists, among whom Antiphon was prominent, and the moderates, led by Theramenes and Aristocrates. Finally, in May the extremists were forced to appeal to Sparta for help; and a delegation left Athens consisting of Phrynichus, Antiphon, and ten others. The result of the appeal is not known; but popular feeling in Athens was by now thoroughly outraged, and on the return of the delegates Phrynichus was assassinated and the Four Hundred deposed. Most of the extremists fled for their lives; but three stood their ground, among them Antiphon. He was a disillusioned and a bitterly disappointed man; the work of years had gone for nothing; and he could expect little mercy from a government which counted him among its most dangerous enemies. Yet when facing the court with his companions on a charge of treason,[a] he delivered the greatest defence made within living memory by a

---

[a] The decree of the Boulê, committing Antiphon, Archeptolemus and Onomacles for trial, has been preserved by the Pseudo-Plutarch, as has the official text of their condemnation. Both will be found printed in full on pp. 314-317.

man on trial for his life.[a] Of that defence we have
the merest fragments ; but they are enough to show
that even at this last hour that proved mastery of
device and expression of which Thucydides speaks [b]
did not desert him.   In spite, however, of his attempt
to justify his conduct, he was found guilty and
condemned to death.   The Eleven executed the
sentence ; burial was refused to his corpse ; and his
house was rased to the ground.

[a] Thucyd. viii. 68.   [b] Ibid.

I

PROSECUTION OF THE STEP-
MOTHER FOR POISONING

INTRODUCTION

THE facts with which the *Prosecution for Poisoning* is concerned may be summarized as follows. A certain Philoneos entertained a friend to dinner at his house in Peiraeus. His mistress served them both with wine after the meal. The wine, it seems, was poisoned; and Philoneos died instantaneously, while his friend fell violently ill and died three weeks later. The woman, who was a slave, was arrested, tortured for information, and executed.

The occasion of the present speech was the re-opening of the case some years afterwards by an illegitimate son of the friend.[a] In obedience to his father's dying command (ἐπίσκηψις), he charges the father's wife, his own stepmother, with the murder of her husband and of Philoneos. The stepmother's defence is conducted by her own sons, the prosecutor's half-brothers. The line of attack chosen by the prosecution is that the mistress of Philoneos was merely an accessory to the crime: the principal had been the stepmother, who had previously made

---

[a] The stress laid upon the prosecutor's extreme youth (§§ 1, 30) makes it impossible to suppose that he is the legitimate son of an earlier marriage. He has brought the case as soon as he was eligible to do so; and had his half-brothers been younger than he, they would have been debarred by their age from appearing for the defence.

a similar, but ineffectual, attempt to murder her husband.

It has been suggested that the speech was never intended for actual delivery in a court of law, but that it is simply an academic exercise in the manner of the *Tetralogies*. The reasons advanced for this are the complete inadequacy of the prosecution's case from a practical point of view, the absence of witnesses, and the seemingly fictitious character of the proper names which occur. However, a brief consideration of the structure and contents will perhaps be enough to show that we have here what is almost certainly a genuine piece of early pleading.

The case for the prosecution rests upon two things: a carefully elaborated narrative of the planning and execution of the murders, and the development of a single argument to the detriment of the defence, the argument that the accused must be guilty, because the defence has refused to allow the family slaves to be questioned under torture about the previous attempt to poison the husband. The refusal, it is assumed, means that the stepmother was guilty of that attempt, and this fact furnishes in its turn a strong presumption, if not proof, of her guilt in the present instance.

This is quite unlike the *Tetralogies*, where no emphasis is laid on the narrative, the minimum of fact is given, and the writer obviously regards the speeches for the prosecution and defence as an opportunity for demonstrating the possibilities of *a priori* reasoning and sophistry when a case has to be presented to a jury. It is scarcely credible that the present speech, if composed for the same purpose, should contain so circumstantially detailed a narrative, and at the same time be limited to but a single argument in favour of the prosecution. On the other hand, its peculiar meagreness becomes intelligible if it is assumed that the case was historical but, owing to the circumstances which set it in motion, extremely weak.

Thus, a man lies dying from the effects of the wine which he drank when dining with a friend ; the fact that his friend died instantaneously convinces him that they have both been poisoned. He has been on bad terms with his wife for some time, and only recently caught her placing something in his drink. He suspected her at the time of trying to poison him ; but she avowed that it was merely a love-philtre. The incident remains in his mind, and the fact that his wife is acquainted with the girl who served his friend and himself with wine at dinner leads him to conclude that she has made a second attempt upon his life, this time with success. He therefore summons his son and solemnly enjoins him to prosecute the wife for murder. The son is bound to carry out the command ; but unfortunately there is not a scrap of evidence to show that his stepmother was concerned in his father's death. The one possible source of information was the supposed accomplice who administered the poison ; and no amount of pressure had induced her to say anything to incriminate any second person whatsoever. Hence he has to make what play he can with the imaginary account of the planning of the crime given him by his father. He tries to shift attention to the earlier attempt at poisoning which failed ; but the defence refuses to let him question the family slaves about the facts. Thus he is reduced to emphasizing as strongly as possible the damning implications of the refusal. That is why the speech necessarily takes its present unsatisfactory form. On the assumption that the prosecution was set in motion entirely in deference to the father's ἐπί-σκηψις, both its unconvincing argumentation and the absence of witnesses become intelligible.

If this is the truth, there is a strong probability that the stepmother is innocent. Had she been implicated in any way, it is difficult to believe that the παλλακή of Philoneos would not have tried to shift the blame on to her when faced with torture and death. The refusal of the defence to allow an examination of the slaves is not in itself evidence of guilt : slaves could not be relied upon to adhere to the truth under pressure ; and to refuse to hand them over was the obvious course, in spite of its drawbacks.

The evidence of the proper names which occur in the speech does not affect the above interpretation. There are only two : Philoneos and Clytemnestra. Philoneos is well authenticated as an Attic name by inscriptions ranging from the fifth century to the third and by a reference in the ᾿Αθ. Πολ.[a] to an Archon so called in the age of Peisistratus. The fact that the Philoneos of this speech lived in Peiraeus [b] and may thus have had some connexion with shipping is an intelligible coincidence. Clytemnestra (§ 17) occurs in a corrupt passage which should almost certainly be emended to give it a purely metaphorical sense.

If, then, the speech was more than an academic exercise, before what court was it delivered ? Probably the Areopagus, which tried cases of wilful murder. Admittedly, the defendant was charged,

[a] ᾿Αθ. Πολ. xvii. 1. For a list of the inscriptions referred to cf. Kirschner's *Prosopographia*, *s.v.*
[b] See note on § 16.

ANTIPHON

not as having caused her husband's death immediately, but as having procured it through the agency of an accomplice ; and the law of homicide, as we know it in the last quarter of the fourth century,[a] distinguished between πρᾶξις and βούλευσις, assigning πρᾶξις to the cognizance of the Areopagus, βούλευσις to that of the Palladium. But this proves nothing of fifth century procedure ; and the evidence of the speech itself, which treats the defendant, no less than the παλλακή, as a φονεύς,[b] suggests rather that contemporary practice made no distinction between principal and agent.

There remains the question of authorship. Ancient tradition unanimously regarded the speech as the work of Antiphon ; and it is supported by the evidence of language and style. Here there are none of those peculiarities of diction which must make the authorship of the *Tetralogies* a matter of doubt ; and, although such evidence cannot be stressed, the recurrence in both the *Herodes* and the *Choreutes* of a form of argument used in the present speech [c] points likewise to a common origin for all three. Critics who follow Schmitt [d] in treating the *Prosecution for Poisoning* as apocryphal rest their case almost entirely upon the intuitive conviction that it is unworthy of Antiphon. But, as he himself would remark, αὐτὸς ἕκαστος τούτου κρατεῖ. The crudity of the speech, no less than its Gorgian assonances and rhythms,[e] are better explained by the assumption that it is a product of Antiphon's early years.

---

[a] 'Αθ. Πολ. lvii. 3. [b] *e.g.* §§ 2, 6, 20, *et passim.*
[c] Compare §§ 11-12 with *Her.* § 38 and *Chor.* § 27.
[d] *De oratione in novercam quae Antiphontis fertur*, Fulda, 1853. [e] *Cf.* §§ 5 *sub fin.*, 22, 27 *init.*

ANALYSIS

§§ 1-4. Appeal to the jury for sympathy.
§§ 5-13. Conclusions to be drawn from the fact
          that the defence had refused to hand
          over their slaves for examination.
§§ 14-20. Narrative of the crime.
§§ 21-31. Largely a repetition of the arguments used
          in §§ 1-13. The half-brother who is con-
          ducting the defence is bitterly attacked
          for his behaviour, and fresh emphasis is
          laid on the guilt of the stepmother. There
          is, strictly speaking, no formal peroration.

ΦΑΡΜΑΚΕΙΑΣ ΚΑΤΑ ΤΗΣ ΜΗΤΡΥΙΑΣ

1 Νέος μὲν καὶ ἄπειρος δικῶν ἔγωγε ἔτι, δεινῶς δὲ
καὶ ἀπόρως ἔχει μοι περὶ τοῦ πράγματος, ὦ ἄνδρες,
τοῦτο μὲν εἰ ἐπισκήψαντος τοῦ πατρὸς ἐπεξελθεῖν
τοῖς αὐτοῦ φονεῦσι μὴ ἐπέξειμι, τοῦτο δὲ εἰ ἐπεξιόντι ἀναγκαίως ἔχει οἷς ἥκιστα ἐχρῆν ἐν διαφορᾷ
καταστῆναι, ἀδελφοῖς ὁμοπατρίοις καὶ μητρὶ ἀδελ-
2 φῶν. ἡ γὰρ τύχη καὶ αὐτοὶ οὗτοι ἠνάγκασαν ἐμοὶ
πρὸς τούτους αὐτοὺς τὸν ἀγῶνα καταστῆναι, οὓς
εἰκὸς ἦν τῷ μὲν τεθνεῶτι τιμωροὺς γενέσθαι, τῷ
δ' ἐπεξιόντι βοηθούς. νῦν δὲ τούτων τἀναντία γε-
γένηται· αὐτοὶ γὰρ οὗτοι καθεστᾶσιν ἀντίδικοι καὶ
φονῆς, ὡς καὶ ἐγὼ καὶ ἡ γραφὴ λέγει.

3 Δέομαι δ' ὑμῶν, ὦ ἄνδρες, ἐὰν ἐπιδείξω ἐξ ἐπιβουλῆς καὶ προβουλῆς τὴν τούτων μητέρα φονέα
οὖσαν τοῦ ἡμετέρου πατρός, καὶ μὴ ἅπαξ ἀλλὰ καὶ
πολλάκις ἤδη ληφθεῖσαν τὸν θάνατον τὸν ἐκείνου
ἐπ' αὐτοφώρῳ μηχανωμένην, τιμωρῆσαι πρῶτον

---

[a] *i.e.* the charge as formally registered with the βασιλεύς
(*cf. Choreutes,* §§ 38, 41 ff.). The action itself was of course
a δίκη φόνου.

PROSECUTION OF THE STEPMOTHER FOR POISONING

Not only am I still too young to know anything of courts of law, gentlemen; but I am also faced with a terrible dilemma. On the one hand, how can I disregard my father's solemn injunction to bring his murderers to justice? On the other hand, if I obey it, I shall inevitably find myself ranged against the last persons with whom I should quarrel, my half-brothers and their mother. Circumstances for which the defence have only themselves to blame have made it necessary that my charge should be directed against them, and them alone. One would have expected them to seek vengeance for the dead and support the prosecution; but as it is, the opposite is the case: they are themselves my opponents and the murderers, as both I and my indictment [a] state.

Gentlemen, I have one request. If I prove that my opponents' mother murdered our father by malice aforethought, after being caught not merely once, but repeatedly, in the act of seeking his life,[b] then first

---

[b] A natural rhetorical exaggeration. The proof does not in fact occur as promised; but there is no good reason for supposing that the speech is therefore incomplete. In the circumstances outlined in the Introduction such a proof would have been impossible.

[112] μὲν τοῖς νόμοις τοῖς ὑμετέροις, οὓς παρὰ τῶν
θεῶν καὶ τῶν προγόνων διαδεξάμενοι κατὰ τὸ αὐτὸ
ἐκείνοις περὶ τῆς καταψηφίσεως δικάζετε, δεύτερον δ᾽ ἐκείνῳ τῷ τεθνηκότι, καὶ ἅμα ἐμοὶ μόνῳ
4 ἀπολελειμμένῳ βοηθῆσαι. ὑμεῖς γάρ μοι ἀναγ-
καῖοι. οὓς γὰρ ἐχρῆν τῷ μὲν τεθνεῶτι τιμωροὺς
γενέσθαι, ἐμοὶ δὲ βοηθούς, οὗτοι τοῦ μὲν τεθνεῶτος
φονῆς γεγένηνται, ἐμοὶ δ᾽ ἀντίδικοι καθεστᾶσι.
πρὸς τίνας οὖν ἔλθῃ τις βοηθούς, ἢ ποῖ τὴν κατα-
φυγὴν ποιήσεται ἄλλοθι ἢ πρὸς ὑμᾶς καὶ τὸ
δίκαιον;

5 Θαυμάζω δ᾽ ἔγωγε καὶ τοῦ ἀδελφοῦ, ἥντινά ποτε
γνώμην ἔχων ἀντίδικος καθέστηκε πρὸς ἐμέ, καὶ
εἰ νομίζει τοῦτο εὐσέβειαν εἶναι, τὸ τὴν μητέρα μὴ
προδοῦναι. ἐγὼ δ᾽ ἡγοῦμαι πολὺ ἀνοσιώτερον
εἶναι ἀφεῖναι τοῦ τεθνεῶτος τὴν τιμωρίαν, ἄλλως
τε καὶ τοῦ μὲν ἐκ προβουλῆς ἀκουσίως ἀποθανόντος,
6 τῆς δὲ ἑκουσίως ἐκ προνοίας ἀποκτεινάσης. καὶ
οὐ τοῦτό γ᾽ ἐρεῖ,[1] ὡς εὖ οἶδεν ὅτι οὐκ[2] ἀπέκτεινεν
ἡ μήτηρ αὐτοῦ τὸν πατέρα τὸν ἡμέτερον· ἐν οἷς
μὲν γὰρ αὐτῷ ἐξουσία ἦν σαφῶς εἰδέναι παρὰ τῆς
βασάνου, οὐκ ἠθέλησεν· ἐν οἷς δ᾽ οὐκ ἦν πυθέσθαι,
τοῦτ᾽ αὐτὸ προυθυμήθη. καίτοι αὐτὸ τοῦτο ἐχρῆν,
ὃ καὶ ἐγὼ προυκαλούμην, προθυμηθῆναι, ὅπως τὸ
7 πραχθὲν ᾖ ἀληθῶς[3] ἐπεξελθεῖν. μὴ γὰρ ὁμολογούν-
των τῶν ἀνδραπόδων οὗτός τ᾽ εὖ εἰδὼς ἂν ἀπ-
ελογεῖτο καὶ ἀντέσπευδε πρὸς ἐμέ, καὶ ἡ μήτηρ
αὐτοῦ ἀπήλλακτο ἂν ταύτης τῆς αἰτίας. ὅπου
δὲ μὴ ἠθέλησεν ἔλεγχον ποιήσασθαι τῶν πεπραγμένων, πῶς περὶ γ᾽ ὧν οὐκ ἠθέλησε πυθέσθαι,
ἐγχωρεῖ αὐτῷ περὶ τούτων εἰδέναι; [πῶς οὖν περὶ

avenge the outrage against your laws, that heritage from the gods and your forefathers which enables you to sentence the guilty even as they did ; and secondly avenge the dead man, and in so doing give me, a lonely orphan, your aid. For you are my kin ; those who should have avenged the dead and supported me are his murderers and my opponents. So where is help to be sought, where is a refuge to be found, save with you and with justice ?

I am at a loss indeed to understand the feelings which have led my brother to range himself against me. Does he imagine that his duty as a son consists simply in loyalty to his mother ? To my mind, it is a far greater sin to neglect the avenging of the dead man ; and the more so since he met his doom as the involuntary victim of a plot, whereas she sent him to it by deliberately forming that plot. Further, it is not for my brother to say that he is quite sure his mother did not murder our father ; for when he had the chance of making sure, by torture, he refused it ; he showed readiness only for those modes of inquiry which could yield no certainty. Yet he ought to have been ready to do what I in fact challenged him to do, so that an honest investigation of the facts might have been possible ; because then, if the slaves had admitted nothing, he would have confronted me with a vigorous defence based on certainty, and his mother would have been cleared of the present charge. But after refusing to inquire into the facts, how can he possibly be certain of what he refused to find out ? [How, then, is it to be

---

[1] καίτοι τοῦτό γ' ἐρεῖ Thalheim, coll. §§ 8 et 28.
[2] ὅτι οὐκ Cobet: ὅτι γ' οὐκ codd.
[3] ἀληθῶς scripsi, auct. Thalheim: ἀληθὲς codd. Alii alia.

τούτων, ὦ δικάζοντες, αὐτὸν εἰκὸς εἰδέναι, ὧν γε
τὴν ἀλήθειαν οὐκ εἴληφε;[1]]

8 Τί ποτε ἀπολογήσεσθαι μέλλει μοι; ἐκ μὲν γὰρ
τῆς τῶν ἀνδραπόδων βασάνου εὖ ᾔδει ὅτι οὐχ οἷόν
τ' ἦν αὐτῇ σωθῆναι, ἐν δὲ τῷ μὴ βασανισθῆναι
ἡγεῖτο τὴν σωτηρίαν εἶναι· τὰ γὰρ γενόμενα ἐν
τούτῳ ἀφανισθῆναι ᾠήθησαν. πῶς οὖν εὔορκα
ἀντομωμοκὼς ἔσται φάσκων εὖ εἰδέναι, ὃς οὐκ
ἠθέλησε σαφῶς πυθέσθαι ἐμοῦ ἐθέλοντος τῇ δι-
καιοτάτῃ βασάνῳ χρήσασθαι περὶ τούτου τοῦ
9 πράγματος; τοῦτο μὲν γὰρ ἠθέλησα μὲν[2] τὰ τούτων ἀνδράποδα βασανίσαι, ἃ συνῄδει καὶ πρότερον
τὴν γυναῖκα ταύτην, μητέρα δὲ τούτων, τῷ πατρὶ
τῷ ἡμετέρῳ θάνατον μηχανωμένην φαρμάκοις,
καὶ τὸν πατέρα εἰληφότα ἐπ' αὐτοφώρῳ, ταύτην
τε οὐκ οὖσαν ἄπαρνον, πλὴν οὐκ ἐπὶ θανάτῳ φάσ-
10 κουσαν διδόναι ἀλλ' ἐπὶ φίλτροις. διὰ οὖν ταῦτα
ἐγὼ βάσανον τοιαύτην ἠθέλησα ποιήσασθαι περὶ
αὐτῶν, γράψας ἐν γραμματείῳ ἃ ἐπαιτιῶμαι τὴν
γυναῖκα ταύτην. βασανιστὰς δὲ αὐτοὺς τούτους
ἐκέλευον γίγνεσθαι ἐμοῦ παρόντος, ἵνα μὴ ἀναγκαζόμενοι ἃ ἐγὼ ἐπερωτῴην[3] λέγοιεν—ἀλλ' ἐξήρκει
μοι τοῖς ἐν τῷ γραμματείῳ χρῆσθαι· καὶ αὐτό
μοι τοῦτο τεκμήριον δίκαιον γενέσθαι,[4] ὅτι ὀρθῶς
καὶ δικαίως μετέρχομαι τὸν φονέα τοῦ πατρός—εἰ
δὲ ἄπαρνοι γίγνοιντο ἢ λέγοιεν μὴ ὁμολογούμενα,

---

[1] πῶς οὖν . . . εἴληφε secl. Schoell, qui alterius esse recen-
sionis vestigium coniecit. πῶς . . . εἰδέναι om. N.

[2] ἠθέλησα μὲν Bake: ἠθελήσαμεν codd.

[3] ἐπερωτῴην Jernstedt: ἐπερωτῶ μὴ codd.

[4] γενέσθαι Jernstedt, coll. Chor. § 27: ἔσται codd.

* See critical note.

18

expected, gentlemen of the jury, that he should be sure of facts about which he has not learnt the truth ? [a]]

What reply does he mean to make to me ? He was fully aware that once the slaves were examined under torture his mother was doomed ; and he thought that her life depended upon the avoiding of such an examination, as he and his companions imagined that the truth would in that event be lost to sight. How, then, is he going to remain true to his oath as defendant,[b] if he claims to be in full possession of the facts after refusing to make certain of them by accepting my offer of a perfectly impartial investigation of the matter by torture ? In the first place, I was ready to torture the defendants' slaves, who knew that this woman, my opponents' mother, had planned to poison our father on a previous occasion as well, that our father had caught her in the act, and that she had admitted everything—save that it was not to kill him, but to restore his love that she alleged herself to be giving him the potion. Owing, then, to the nature of the slaves' evidence, I proposed to have their story tested under torture after making a written note of my charges against this woman ; and I told the defence to conduct the examination themselves in my presence, so that the slaves might not give forced answers to questions put by me. I was satisfied to have the written questions used ; and that in itself should afford a presumption in my favour that my search for my father's murderer is honest and impartial. Should the slaves resort to denial or make

[b] A curiously loose expression. The oath taken by both parties in cases of murder was always a διωμοσία (cf. § 28), never, as here, an ἀντωμοσία.

⟨ἡ βάσανος⟩¹ ἀναγκάζοι τὰ γεγονότα κατηγορεῖν·
αὕτη γὰρ καὶ τοὺς τὰ ψευδῆ παρεσκευασμένους
λέγειν τἀληθῆ κατηγορεῖν ποιήσει.

11 Καίτοι εὖ οἶδά γ᾿, εἰ οὗτοι πρὸς ἐμὲ ἐλθόντες,
ἐπειδὴ τάχιστα αὐτοῖς ἀπηγγέλθη ὅτι ἐπεξίοιμι
τοῦ πατρὸς τὸν φονέα, ἠθέλησαν τὰ ἀνδράποδα ἃ
ἦν αὐτοῖς παραδοῦναι, ἐγὼ δὲ μὴ ἠθέλησα παρα-
λαβεῖν, αὐτὰ ἂν ταῦτα μέγιστα τεκμήρια παρ-
είχοντο ὡς οὐκ ἔνοχοί εἰσι τῷ φόνῳ. νῦν δ᾿,
ἐγὼ γάρ εἰμι τοῦτο μὲν ὁ θέλων αὐτὸς βασανιστὴς
γενέσθαι, τοῦτο δὲ τούτους αὐτοὺς κελεύων ἀντ᾿
ἐμοῦ βασανίσαι, ἐμοὶ δήπου εἰκὸς ταὐτὰ ταῦτα
12 τεκμήρια εἶναι ὡς εἰσὶν ἔνοχοι τῷ φόνῳ. εἰ γὰρ
τούτων ἐθελόντων διδόναι εἰς βάσανον ἐγὼ μὴ
ἐδεξάμην, τούτοις ἂν ἦν ταῦτα τεκμήρια. τὸ αὐτὸ
οὖν τοῦτο καὶ ἐμοὶ γενέσθω, εἴπερ ἐμοῦ θέλοντος
ἔλεγχον λαβεῖν τοῦ πράγματος αὐτοὶ μὴ ἠθέλησαν
δοῦναι. δεινὸν δ᾿ ἔμοιγε δοκεῖ εἶναι, εἰ ὑμᾶς μὲν
ζητοῦσιν αἰτεῖσθαι ὅπως αὐτῶν μὴ καταψηφίσησθε,
αὐτοὶ δὲ σφίσιν αὐτοῖς οὐκ ἠξίωσαν δικασταὶ
γενέσθαι δόντες βασανίσαι τὰ αὑτῶν ἀνδράποδα.

13 Περὶ μὲν οὖν τούτων οὐκ ἄδηλον ὅτι αὐτοὶ
ἔφευγον τῶν πραχθέντων τὴν σαφήνειαν πυθέσθαι·
ᾔδεσαν γὰρ οἰκεῖον σφίσι τὸ κακὸν ἀναφανησό-
μενον, ὥστε σιωπώμενον καὶ ἀβασάνιστον αὐτὸ
[113] ἐᾶσαι ἐβουλήθησαν. ἀλλ᾿ οὐχ ὑμεῖς γε, ὦ ἄνδρες,
ἔγωγ᾿ εὖ οἶδα, ἀλλὰ σαφὲς ποιήσετε. ταῦτα μὲν
οὖν μέχρι τούτου· περὶ δὲ τῶν γενομένων πειράσομαι ὑμῖν διηγήσασθαι τὴν ἀλήθειαν· δίκη δὲ
κυβερνήσειεν.

---

¹ ἡ βάσανος add. Baiter et Sauppe : ἡ δίκη Aldina. Nonnihil excidisse patet.

inconsistent statements, my intention was that the torture should force from them the charges which the facts demanded : for torture will make even those prepared to lie confine their charges to the truth.

I am quite sure, though, that had the defence approached me with an offer of their slaves directly they learned that I intended to proceed against my father's murderer, only to meet with a refusal of the offer, they would have produced that refusal as affording the strongest presumption of their innocence of the murder. As it is, it was I who in the first place volunteered to conduct the examination personally, and in the second told the defence to conduct it themselves in my stead. Surely, then, it is only logical that this corresponding offer and refusal should afford a presumption in my favour that they are guilty of the murder. Had I refused an offer of theirs to hand over their slaves for torture, the refusal would have afforded a presumption in their favour. The presumption, then, should similarly be in my favour, if I was ready to discover the truth of the matter, while they refused to allow me to do so. In fact, it is amazing to me that they should try to persuade you not to find them guilty, after refusing to decide their case for themselves by handing over their slaves for torture.

In the matter of the slaves, then, it is quite clear that the defence were themselves anxious to avoid ascertaining the facts. The knowledge that the crime would prove to lie at their own door made them desirous of leaving it wrapped in silence and uninvestigated. But you will not do this, gentlemen, as I know full well ; you will bring it into the light. Enough, though ; I will now try to give you a true statement of the facts : and may justice guide me.

14 Ὑπερῷόν τι ἦν τῆς ἡμετέρας οἰκίας, ὃ εἶχε
Φιλόνεως ὁπότ᾽ ἐν ἄστει διατρίβοι, ἀνὴρ καλός τε
κἀγαθὸς καὶ φίλος τῷ ἡμετέρῳ πατρί· καὶ ἦν αὐτῷ
παλλακή, ἣν ὁ Φιλόνεως ἐπὶ πορνεῖον ἔμελλε καταστῆσαι.   ταύτην οὖν [πυθομένη]¹ ἡ μήτηρ τοῦ
15 ἀδελφοῦ ἐποιήσατο φίλην. αἰσθομένη δ᾽ ὅτι ἀδικεῖσθαι ἔμελλεν ὑπὸ τοῦ Φιλόνεω, μεταπέμπεται,
καὶ ἐπειδὴ ἦλθεν, ἔλεξεν αὐτῇ ὅτι καὶ αὐτὴ ἀδι-
κοῖτο ὑπὸ τοῦ πατρὸς τοῦ ἡμετέρου· εἰ οὖν ἐθέλει
πείθεσθαι, ἔφη ἱκανὴ εἶναι ἐκείνη τε τὸν Φιλόνεων
φίλον ποιῆσαι καὶ αὑτῇ τὸν ἐμὸν πατέρα, εἶναι
φάσκουσα αὑτῆς μὲν τοῦτο εὕρημα, ἐκείνης δ᾽
16 ὑπηρέτημα. ἠρώτα οὖν αὐτὴν εἰ ἐθελήσει δια-
κονῆσαί οἱ, καὶ ἣ ὑπέσχετο τάχιστα, ὡς οἶμαι.

Μετὰ ταῦτα ἔτυχε τῷ Φιλόνεῳ ἐν Πειραιεῖ ὄντα
ἱερὰ Διὶ Κτησίῳ, ὁ δὲ πατὴρ ὁ ἐμὸς εἰς Νάξον
πλεῖν ἔμελλεν. κάλλιστον οὖν ἐδόκει εἶναι τῷ
Φιλόνεῳ τῆς αὐτῆς ὁδοῦ ἅμα μὲν προπέμψαι εἰς
τὸν Πειραιᾶ τὸν πατέρα τὸν ἐμὸν φίλον ὄντα
ἑαυτῷ, ἅμα δὲ θύσαντα τὰ ἱερὰ ἑστιᾶσαι ἐκεῖνον.
17 ἡ οὖν παλλακὴ τοῦ Φιλόνεω ἠκολούθει τῆς θυσίας
ἕνεκεν. καὶ ἐπειδὴ ἦσαν ἐν τῷ Πειραιεῖ, οἷον
εἰκός, ἔθυεν.² καὶ ἐπειδὴ αὐτῷ ἐτέθυτο τὰ ἱερά,
ἐντεῦθεν ἐβουλεύετο ἡ ἄνθρωπος ὅπως ἂν αὐτοῖς
τὸ φάρμακον δοίη, πότερα πρὸ δείπνου ἢ ἀπὸ δείπνου. ἔδοξεν οὖν αὐτῇ βουλευομένῃ βέλτιον εἶναι
μετὰ δεῖπνον δοῦναι, τῆς Κλυταιμνήστρας ταύτης³

---

¹ πυθομένη seccl. Dobree. Glossema esse videtur verbo
αἰσθομένη quod sequitur olim adscriptum : πιστουμένη Weber.
² ἔθυεν Orelli : ἔθυον codd.

22

There was an upper room in our house occupied by Philoneos, a highly respected friend of our father's, during his visits to Athens. Now Philoneos had a mistress[a] whom he proposed to place in a brothel. My brother's mother made friends with her ; and on hearing of the wrong intended by Philoneos, she sends for her, informing her on her arrival that she herself was also being wronged by our father. If the other would do as she was told, she said, she herself knew how to restore Philoneos' love for her and our father's for herself. She had discovered the means ; the other's task was to carry out her orders. She asked if she was prepared to follow her instructions, and, I imagine, received a ready assent.

Later, Philoneos happened to have a sacrifice to perform to Zeus Ctesius[b] in Peiraeus, while my father was on the point of leaving for Naxos. So Philoneos thought that it would be an excellent idea to make one journey of it by seeing my father as far as Peiraeus, offering the sacrifice, and entertaining his friend. Philoneos' mistress accompanied him to attend the sacrifice. On reaching Peiraeus, Philoneos of course carried out the ceremony. When the sacrifice was over, the woman considered how to administer the draught : should she give it before or after supper ? Upon reflection, she decided that it would be better to give it afterwards, thereby carrying out the suggestion

[a] Clearly a slave, as Philoneos has complete control over her, and she was later on tortured and summarily executed.
[b] Zeus as god of the household. Hence the sacrifice takes place at Philoneos' private residence.

---

[3] τῆς Κλυταιμνήστρας ταύτης ταῖς ὑποθήκαις Gernet: alii alia. τῆς Κλ. τῆς τούτου μητρὸς ὑποθήκαις N : τῆς Κλ. τοῖς τούτου μητρὸς ὑποθ. A : ταῖς Κλ. τῆς κτλ. A corr.[2]

[τῆς τούτου μητρὸς] ταῖς ὑποθήκαις ἅμα δια-
18 κονοῦσαν. καὶ τὰ μὲν ἄλλα μακρότερος ἂν εἴη
λόγος περὶ τοῦ δείπνου ἐμοί τε διηγήσασθαι ὑμῖν
τ᾽ ἀκοῦσαι· ἀλλὰ πειράσομαι τὰ λοιπὰ ὡς ἐν βραχυ-
τάτοις ὑμῖν διηγήσασθαι, ὡς γεγένηται ἡ δόσις
τοῦ φαρμάκου.

Ἐπειδὴ γὰρ ἐδεδειπνήκεσαν, οἷον εἰκός, ὁ μὲν
θύων Διὶ Κτησίῳ κἀκεῖνον ὑποδεχόμενος, ὁ δ᾽
ἐκπλεῖν τε μέλλων καὶ παρ᾽ ἀνδρὶ ἑταίρῳ αὑτοῦ
δειπνῶν, σπονδάς τ᾽ ἐποιοῦντο καὶ λιβανωτὸν ὑπὲρ
19 αὑτῶν ἐπετίθεσαν. ἡ δὲ παλλακὴ τοῦ Φιλόνεω
τὴν σπονδὴν ἅμα ἐγχέουσα ἐκείνοις εὐχομένοις ἃ
οὐκ ἔμελλε τελεῖσθαι, ὦ ἄνδρες, ἐνέχει τὸ φάρμακον. καὶ ἅμα οἰομένη δεξιὸν ποιεῖν πλέον
δίδωσι τῷ Φιλόνεῳ, ἴσως ⟨ὡς⟩,[1] εἰ δοίη πλέον,
μᾶλλον φιλησομένη ὑπὸ τοῦ Φιλόνεω· οὔπω γὰρ
ᾔδει ὑπὸ τῆς μητρυιᾶς τῆς ἐμῆς ἐξαπατωμένη,
πρὶν ἐν τῷ κακῷ ἤδη ἦν· τῷ δὲ πατρὶ τῷ ἡμετέρῳ
20 ἔλασσον ἐνέχει. καὶ ἐκεῖνοι ἐπειδὴ ἀπέσπεισαν,
τὸν ἑαυτῶν φονέα μεταχειριζόμενοι ἐκπίνουσιν
ὑστάτην πόσιν. ὁ μὲν οὖν Φιλόνεως εὐθέως παραχρῆμα ἀποθνήσκει, ὁ δὲ πατὴρ ὁ ἡμέτερος εἰς
νόσον ἐμπίπτει, ἐξ ἧς καὶ ἀπώλετο εἰκοσταῖος.
ἀνθ᾽ ὧν ἡ μὲν διακονήσασα καὶ χειρουργήσασα[2]
ἔχει τὰ ἐπίχειρα ὧν ἀξία[3] ἦν, οὐδὲν αἰτία οὖσα—τῷ
γὰρ δημοκοίνῳ τροχισθεῖσα παρεδόθη—, ἡ δ᾽ αἰτία

_____
[1] ὡς add. Pahle.

24

of this Clytemnestra[a] here. Now it would take too long for me to furnish or for you to listen to a detailed description of the meal; so I shall try to give you as brief an account as I can of the administration of the poison which followed.

After supper was over, the two naturally set about pouring libations and sprinkling some frankincense to secure the favour of heaven, as the one was offering sacrifice to Zeus Ctesius and entertaining the other, and his companion was supping with a friend and on the point of putting out to sea. But Philoneos' mistress, who poured the wine for the libation, while they offered their prayers—prayers never to be answered, gentlemen—poured in the poison with it. Thinking it a happy inspiration, she gave Philoneos the larger draught; she imagined perhaps that if she gave him more, Philoneos would love her the more: for only when the mischief was done did she see that my stepmother had tricked her. She gave our father a smaller draught. So they poured their libation, and, grasping their own slayer, drained their last drink on earth. Philoneos expired instantly; and my father was seized with an illness which resulted in his death twenty days later. In atonement, the subordinate who carried out the deed has been punished as she deserved, although the crime in no sense originated from her: she was broken on the wheel and handed over to the executioner; and the woman from whom it did originate, who was guilty

[a] For the metaphorical use of the name cf. Andoc. *Myst.* § 129 τίς ἂν εἴη οὗτος; Οἰδίπους, ἢ Αἴγισθος;

[2] καὶ χειρουργήσασα huc transposuit Blass: post ἐνθυμηθεῖσα habent codd.
[3] ἀξία] ἄξια Blass: οὐκ ἀξία Reutzel.

25

τε ἤδη καὶ ἐνθυμηθεῖσα ἕξει, ἐὰν ὑμεῖς τε καὶ οἱ
θεοὶ θέλωσιν.

21 Σκέψασθε οὖν ὅσῳ δικαιότερα ὑμῶν δεήσομαι
ἐγὼ ἢ ὁ ἀδελφός. ἐγὼ μέν γε τῷ τεθνεῶτι
ὑμᾶς κελεύω καὶ τῷ ἠδικημένῳ τὸν ἀίδιον χρόνον
τιμωροὺς γενέσθαι· οὗτος δὲ τοῦ μὲν τεθνεῶτος
πέρι οὐδὲν ὑμᾶς αἰτήσεται, ὃς ἄξιος καὶ ἐλέου καὶ
βοηθείας καὶ τιμωρίας παρ' ὑμῶν τυχεῖν, ἀθέως
καὶ ἀκλεῶς πρὸ τῆς εἱμαρμένης ὑφ' ὧν ἥκιστα
22 ἐχρῆν τὸν βίον ἐκλιπών, ὑπὲρ δὲ τῆς ἀποκτεινάσης
δεήσεται ἀθέμιτα καὶ ἀνόσια καὶ ἀτέλεστα καὶ
ἀνήκουστα καὶ θεοῖς καὶ ὑμῖν, δεόμενος ὑμῶν ⟨μὴ
τιμωρῆσαι⟩[1] ἃ αὐτὴ ἑαυτὴν οὐκ ἔπεισε μὴ κακο-
τεχνῆσαι. ὑμεῖς δ' οὐ τῶν ἀποκτεινάντων ἐστὲ
βοηθοί, ἀλλὰ τῶν ἐκ προνοίας ἀποθνησκόντων, καὶ
ταῦτα ὑφ' ὧν ἥκιστα ἐχρῆν αὐτοὺς ἀποθνήσκειν.
ἤδη οὖν ἐν ὑμῖν ἐστι τοῦτ' ὀρθῶς διαγνῶναι, ὃ καὶ
ποιήσατε.

23 Δεήσεται δ' ὑμῶν οὗτος μὲν ὑπὲρ τῆς μητρὸς
τῆς αὐτοῦ ζώσης, τῆς ἐκεῖνον διαχρησαμένης
ἀβούλως τε καὶ ἀθέως, ὅπως δίκην μὴ δῷ, ἂν
ὑμᾶς πείθῃ, ὧν ἠδίκηκεν· ἐγὼ δ' ὑμᾶς ὑπὲρ τοῦ
πατρὸς τοὐμοῦ[2] τεθνεῶτος αἰτοῦμαι, ὅπως παντὶ
τρόπῳ δῷ· ὑμεῖς δέ, ὅπως διδῶσι δίκην οἱ ἀδι-
κοῦντες, τούτου γε ἕνεκα καὶ δικασταὶ ἐγένεσθε
24 καὶ ἐκλήθητε. καὶ ἐγὼ μὲν ἐπεξέρχομαι [λέγων],[3]
ἵνα δῷ δίκην ὧν ἠδίκηκε καὶ τιμωρήσω τῷ τε

---

[1] μὴ τιμωρῆσαι add. Thalheim.
[2] τοὐμοῦ Franke: μου codd.
[3] λέγων secl. Gernet.

---

[a] αἰτία must here have the meaning of "ultimately re-

26

of the design, shall receive her reward also, if you and heaven so will.[a]

Now mark the justice of my request as compared with my brother's. I am bidding you avenge once and for all time him who has been wrongfully done to death ; but my brother will make no plea for the dead man, although he has a right to your pity, your help, and your vengeance, after having had his life cut short in so godless and so miserable a fashion by those who should have been the last to commit such a deed. No, he will appeal for the murderess ; he will make an unlawful, a sinful, an impossible request, to which neither heaven nor you can listen. He will ask you to refrain from punishing a crime which the guilty woman could not bring herself to refrain from committing. But you are not here to champion the murderers : you are here to champion the victims wilfully murdered, murdered moreover by those who should have been the last to commit such a deed. Thus it now rests with you to reach a proper verdict ; see that you do so.

My brother will appeal to you in the name of his mother who is alive and who killed her husband without thought and without scruple ; he hopes that if he is successful, she will escape paying the penalty for her crime. I, on the other hand, am appealing to you in the name of my father who is dead, that she may pay it in full ; and it is in order that judgement may come upon wrongdoers for their misdeeds that you are yourselves constituted and called judges. I am prosecuting to ensure that she pays for her crime and

sponsible " rather than "guilty." That the παλλακή was to some extent guilty is implicitly acknowledged in the statement that she deserved her punishment.

27

πατρὶ τῷ ἡμετέρῳ καὶ τοῖς νόμοις τοῖς ὑμετέροις·
ταύτῃ καὶ ἄξιόν μοι βοηθῆσαι ὑμᾶς ἅπαντας, εἰ
ἀληθῆ λέγω· οὗτος δὲ τἀναντία, ὅπως ἡ τοὺς
νόμους παριδοῦσα μὴ δῷ δίκην ὧν ἠδίκηκε, ταύτῃ
25 βοηθὸς καθέστηκε. καίτοι πότερον δικαιότερον τὸν
ἐκ προνοίας ἀποκτείναντα δοῦναι δίκην ἢ μή; καὶ
πότερον δεῖ[1] οἰκτεῖραι μᾶλλον τὸν τεθνεῶτα ἢ τὴν
ἀποκτείνασαν; ἐγὼ μὲν οἶμαι τὸν τεθνεῶτα· καὶ
γὰρ ⟨ἂν⟩[2] δικαιότερον καὶ ὁσιώτερον καὶ πρὸς
θεῶν καὶ πρὸς ἀνθρώπων γίγνοιτο ὑμῖν. ἤδη οὖν
ἐγὼ ἀξιῶ, ὥσπερ κἀκεῖνον ἀνελεημόνως καὶ ἀν-
οικτίστως αὕτη ἀπώλεσεν, οὕτω καὶ αὐτὴν ταύτην
26 ἀπολέσθαι ὑπό τε ὑμῶν καὶ τοῦ δικαίου. ἡ μὲν
γὰρ ἑκουσίως καὶ βουλεύσασα τὸν θάνατον ⟨ἀπέ-
κτεινεν⟩,[3] ὁ δ' ἀκουσίως καὶ βιαίως ἀπέθανε. πῶς
γὰρ οὐ βιαίως ἀπέθανεν, ὦ ἄνδρες; ὅς γ' ἐκπλεῖν
ἔμελλεν ἐκ τῆς γῆς τῆσδε, παρά τε ἀνδρὶ φίλῳ
αὐτοῦ εἱστιᾶτο· ἡ δὲ πέμψασα τὸ φάρμακον καὶ
κελεύσασα ἐκείνῳ δοῦναι πιεῖν ἀπέκτεινεν ἡμῶν
τὸν πατέρα. πῶς οὖν ταύτην ἐλεεῖν ἄξιόν ἐστιν
ἢ αἰδοῦς τυγχάνειν παρ' ὑμῶν ἢ ἄλλου του; ἥτις
αὐτὴ οὐκ ἠξίωσεν ἐλεῆσαι τὸν ἑαυτῆς ἄνδρα, ἀλλ'
27 ἀνοσίως καὶ αἰσχρῶς ἀπώλεσεν. οὕτω δέ τοι καὶ
ἐλεεῖν ἐπὶ τοῖς ἀκουσίοις παθήμασι μᾶλλον προσήκει ἢ τοῖς ἑκουσίοις καὶ ἐκ προνοίας ἀδικήμασι
καὶ ἁμαρτήμασι. καὶ ὥσπερ ἐκεῖνον αὕτη[4] οὔτε
θεοὺς οὔθ' ἥρωας οὔτ' ἀνθρώπους αἰσχυνθεῖσα οὐδε[5]
δείσασ' ἀπώλεσεν, οὕτω καὶ αὐτὴ ὑφ' ὑμῶν καὶ
τοῦ δικαίου ἀπολομένη, καὶ μὴ τυχοῦσα μήτ'
αἰδοῦς μήτ' ἐλέου μήτ' αἰσχύνης μηδεμιᾶς παρ'
ὑμῶν, τῆς δικαιοτάτης ἂν τύχοι τιμωρίας.

---

[1] δεῖ Jernstedt: δικαιότερον codd.   [2] ἂν add. Dobree.

28

to avenge our father and your laws : wherein you
should support me one and all, if what I say is true.
My brother, on the contrary, is defending this
woman to enable one who has broken the laws to
avoid paying for her misdeeds. Yet which is the more
just : that a wilful murderer should be punished, or
that he should not ? Which has a better claim to pity,
the murdered man or the murderess ? To my mind,
the murdered man : because in pitying him you
would be acting more justly and more righteously in
the eyes of gods and men. So now I ask that just as
this woman put her husband to death without pity
and without mercy, so she may herself be put to death
by you and by justice ; for she was the wilful murderess who compassed his death : he was the victim
who involuntarily came to a violent end. I repeat,
gentlemen, a violent end ; for he was on the point of
sailing from this country and was dining under a friend's
roof, when she, who had sent the poison, with orders
that a draught be given him, murdered our father.
What pity, then, what consideration, does a woman
who refused to pity her own husband, who killed him
impiously and shamefully, deserve from you or anyone
else ? Involuntary accidents deserve such pity : not
deliberately planned crimes and acts of wickedness.
Just as this woman put her husband to death without respecting or fearing god, hero, or human being,
so she would in her turn reap her justest reward were
she herself put to death by you and by justice, without finding consideration, sympathy, or respect.

---

[3] ἀπέκτεινεν add. Reiske : τὸν θάνατον del. Franke.
[4] αὕτη Reiske : αὐτὴ codd.
[5] οὐδὲ Maetzner : οὔτε N, αἰσχυνθεῖσα οὔτε om. A.

28 Θαυμάζω δὲ ἔγωγε τῆς τόλμης τοῦ ἀδελφοῦ καὶ
τῆς διανοίας, τὸ διομόσασθαι ὑπὲρ τῆς μητρὸς εὖ
εἰδέναι μὴ πεποιηκυῖαν¹ ταῦτα. πῶς γὰρ ἄν τις
εὖ εἰδείη οἷς μὴ παρεγένετο αὐτός; οὐ γὰρ δήπου
μαρτύρων γ᾽ ἐναντίον οἱ ἐπιβουλεύοντες τοὺς θανά-
τους τοῖς πέλας μηχανῶνταί τε καὶ παρασκευά-
ζουσιν, ἀλλ᾽ ὡς μάλιστα δύνανται λαθραιότατα καὶ
29 ὡς ἀνθρώπων μηδένα εἰδέναι· οἱ δ᾽ ἐπιβουλευό-
μενοι οὐδὲν ἴσασι, πρίν γ᾽ ἤδη ἐν αὐτῷ ὦσι τῷ
κακῷ καὶ γιγνώσκωσι τὸν ὄλεθρον ἐν ᾧ εἰσί. τότε
δέ, ἐὰν μὲν δύνωνται καὶ φθάνωσι πρὶν ἀποθανεῖν,
καὶ φίλους καὶ ἀναγκαίους τοὺς σφετέρους ⟨αὐτῶν⟩²
καλοῦσι καὶ μαρτύρονται, καὶ λέγουσιν αὐτοῖς
ὑφ᾽ ὧν ἀπόλλυνται, καὶ ἐπισκήπτουσι τιμωρῆσαι
30 σφίσιν αὐτοῖς ἠδικημένοις· ἃ κἀμοὶ παιδὶ ὄντι
ὁ πατήρ, τὴν ἀθλίαν καὶ τελευταίαν νόσον νοσῶν,
ἐπέσκηπτεν. ἐὰν δὲ τούτων ἁμαρτάνωσι, γράμματα
γράφουσι, καὶ οἰκέτας τοὺς σφετέρους αὐτῶν ἐπι-
καλοῦνται μάρτυρας, καὶ δηλοῦσιν ὑφ᾽ ὧν ἀπόλ-
λυνται.³ κἀκεῖνος ἐμοὶ νέῳ ἔτι ὄντι ταῦτα ἐδήλωσε
καὶ ἐπέστειλεν, ὦ ἄνδρες, οὐ τοῖς ἑαυτοῦ δούλοις.
31 Ἐμοὶ μὲν οὖν διήγηται καὶ βεβοήθηται τῷ τεθνεῶτι καὶ τῷ νόμῳ· ἐν ὑμῖν δ᾽ ἐστὶ σκοπεῖν τὰ
λοιπὰ πρὸς ὑμᾶς αὐτοὺς καὶ δικάζειν τὰ δίκαια.
οἶμαι δὲ καὶ τοῖς θεοῖς τοῖς κάτω μέλειν οἷ⁴
ἠδίκηνται.

¹ πεποιηκυῖαν Cobet : πεποιηκέναι codd.
² αὐτῶν add. Hirschig.

30

I am astounded at the shameless spirit shown by my brother. To think that he swore in his mother's defence that he was sure of her innocence ! How could anyone be sure of what he did not witness in person ? Those who plot the death of their neighbours do not, I believe, form their plans and make their preparations in front of witnesses ; they act as secretly as possible and in such a way that not a soul knows ; while their victims are aware of nothing until they are already trapped and see the doom which has descended upon them. Then, if they are able and have time before they die, they summon their friends and relatives, call them to witness, tell them who the murderers are, and charge them to take vengeance for the wrong ; just as my father charged me, young as I was, during his last sad illness. Failing this, they make a statement in writing, call their slaves to witness, and reveal their murderers to them. My father told me, and laid his charge upon me, gentlemen, not upon his slaves, young though I still was.

I have stated my case ; I have championed the dead man and the law. It is upon you that the rest depends ; it is for you to weigh the matter and give a just decision. The gods of the world below are themselves, I think, mindful of those who have been wronged.[a]

[a] *i.e.* a curse will fall upon the living, unless justice is done to the dead. *Cf. Tetral.* Gen. Introd. pp. 38-39.

---

[3] ἀπόλλυνται Bekker : ἂν ἀπολοῦνται A pr. N, ἀπόλωνται Α corr.   [4] οἷ] οἱ' Boekmeijer.

II, III, IV
THE TETRALOGIES

GENERAL INTRODUCTION

OF all that has come down to us under the name of Antiphon nothing presents a more interesting or a more difficult problem than the three groups of four short speeches each, which are known as the *Tetralogies*. Each group deals with a case of homicide, the first with wilful murder, the second with what to-day would be described as death by misadventure, and the third with homicide in self-defence; and each consits of two speeches for the prosecution and two corresponding speeches for the defence. In all three the purpose of the author is to show how far it is possible to establish the guilt or innocence of the accused by means of purely general reasoning; he is concerned with what Aristotle calls πίστεις ἔντεχνοι, "artificial proofs," as distinct from πίστεις ἄτεχνοι, proofs based on evidence. Hence although the cases which he selects for treatment would in practice be settled largely by the citation of witnesses and the application of specific laws, he keeps both witnesses and laws in the background as far as possible and concentrates instead upon logical subtleties and *a priori* inferences.[a]

---

[a] *A priori* inferences in general are known as εἰκότα, probable conclusions based on known facts. These evidentiary facts are called τεκμήρια (a different thing from μαρτυρίαι, the evidence of witnesses). A third term, σημεῖα, also occurs. The meaning of this can be gathered from an extant fragment

Now, as is well known, the first attempts to develop an "art of persuasion" were made during the fifth century. They had their origins in the sophistic movement which came into being in the generation after the Persian Wars, to meet the needs of an age of growing intellectual activity and political self-consciousness. The aim of the sophists was educational; they systematized the knowledge and acquirements necessary to the man who was seeking to become an enlightened and efficient member of society, and for a fee would instruct all comers. In the main they interpreted efficiency as the ability to present a point of view in a convincing fashion, whether in the Assembly, the law-courts, or general conversation; and sophists from Protagoras to Thrasymachus devoted a great deal of thought to the formulation of the basic principles of argument and the most effective method of presenting a case. It is in this setting that tradition places the *Tetralogies*. Antiphon himself is known to have taught rhetoric and to have written upon the subject; and so it was only natural that he should have published a number of model speeches for the benefit of pupils. Furthermore, it is known that the type of situation proposed for discussion in the *Tetralogies* was a favourite one with the sophists of the fifth century. Pericles, for instance, argued with Protagoras over the hypothetical case of the boy who was accidentally killed by a javelin in the gymnasium,[a] precisely the problem treated in the second *Tetralogy*; and in Plato's *Phaedrus* there is a still more striking parallel.[b]

of Antiphon's own Τέχνη (Fr. 74, *infra*, p. 308): τὰ μὲν παροιχόμενα σημείοις πιστοῦσθαι, τὰ δὲ μέλλοντα τεκμηρίοις.

[a] Plutarch, *Per.* 36.   [b] *Phaedrus* 273 A.

35

Socrates is discussing the methods of argument advocated by Antiphon's predecessor, Teisias, in his handbook on rhetoric. Teisias, he says, lays it down that " if
a man who was courageous but physically weak gave
a hiding to a strong man who was a coward, because
he had been robbed by him of his cloak or something
similar, and was prosecuted in consequence, neither
of the two must speak the truth. The coward must
allege that the courageous man did not give him the
hiding unaided, while the other must seek to establish
the fact that the two of them were alone, and then
go on to make play with the argument: ' How could
a man such as I have attacked a man such as he ? '
The prosecutor, on the other hand, will not admit his
own cowardice, but will endeavour to produce some
false statement by means of which he may perhaps
refute his opponent." Here again we have precisely
the methods of argument illustrated at length in the
first *Tetralogy*.

Thus far the evidence suggests that we are dealing
with what is genuinely the work of Antiphon, the
work perhaps of his younger days when he had not
as yet made his reputation as a λογογράφος and was
still obliged to teach for a living. But such a consideration is hardly supported, if the style and
language of the *Tetralogies* be compared with that
of the *Herodes* and *Choreutes*. It was Herwerden [a]
who first called attention to their peculiarities of
vocabulary and grammar. Words like ἀναγιγνώσκειν for ἀναπείθειν (I. β. 7), καταδοκεῖν for ὑποπτεύειν
(I. γ. 7), καταλαμβάνειν for καταψηφίζεσθαι (III. δ. 9),
constructions like πειρασόμεθα ἐλέγχοντες (I. γ. 1),
and the use of the passive ἀπελογήθη for the usual

[a] *Mnemosyne*, N.S. 9, p. 201, 11, p. 203.

ἀπελογήσατο (I. γ. 1, III. γ. 1) are found nowhere else
in Antiphon ; the first three verbs mentioned are, in
fact, pure Ionic. To these one might add such rarities
as ἀνατροπεύς (I. β. 2), ἐλεγκτήρ (I. δ. 3), συμπράκτωρ
(II. δ. 6), ἀδυνάτως (III. γ. 3), θανασίμως (III. γ. 4),
ἀπολύσιμος, καταλήψιμος (III. δ. 9), and poetical
expressions like γηραιὸς τελευτή (III. a. 2). Some
of these do not occur again in Greek literature ; none
can be paralleled in Antiphon himself. If, then, the
Tetralogies are his work, how comes it that they
show such peculiarities of grammar and diction ?
The difficulty is no trifling one. Admittedly, academic exercises of the type which we are considering
will differ considerably from speeches composed by
the same author for delivery in a court of law. They
will be more concise, probably a good deal more
closely argued, and certainly less ornate. But that
they should exhibit a language entirely peculiar to
themselves is strange. It is hard to see how the man
who wrote the *Herodes*, an Athenian born and bred,
could have sprinkled his pages with Ionicisms in his
earlier days.

If an examination of their language points to the
conclusion that the *Tetralogies* are not the work of
Antiphon, is the same true of the evidence to be
obtained from what may conveniently be called their
general background ? This is a far harder question.
It has already been pointed out that the author is
clearly at some pains to give as little prominence as
possible to πίστεις ἄτεχνοι, proofs based on specific
laws, on the evidence of witnesses, and on other
matters of fact, because his intention is to reveal the
scope of general reasoning in forensic pleading. But
reasoning, however general, cannot develop *in vacuo* ;

it must proceed from premises of a kind ; and if the *Tetralogies* discard the premises afforded by particular laws, they can do so only by substituting the universal principles from which those laws derive. This is in fact what happens ; and before proceeding further, we must briefly consider the conception of blood-guilt upon which the entire argument of the *Tetralogies* rests.

The central fact for the author is that, unlike ordinary crimes, the taking of life, whether wilfully or by accident, is an ἀσέβημα, an act of impiety,[a] which upsets the existing harmony between man and those superhuman forces which surround him, and brings upon him a μίασμα or defilement.[b] This μίασμα, also spoken of as a κηλίς,[c] is described at times in terms which suggest a literal stain of blood (*cf.* II. γ. 8, θεία κηλὶς τῷ δράσαντι προσπίπτει ἀσεβοῦντι). It rests primarily upon the slayer himself ; but in a wider sense his family and the entire community to which he belongs are infected with it,[d] possibly because of their contact with him,[e] but more probably because of the persistence of the primitive notion that the true unit of existence is the tribe or the πόλις, the members of which have no separate individuality. This μίασμα will continue until due expiation has been made ; and the expiation should, strictly speaking, consist in the death of the slayer ; he has taken the life of another, and his own life must be taken in return. The *Tetralogies* recognize, however, the possible alternative of exile, the permanent exclusion of the offender from his community being regarded

---

[a] I. a. 3, I. a. 9.
[b] I. a. 3, I. a. 10, II. a. 2, III. γ. 6.
[c] II. γ. 11.   [d] I. a. 3, II. a. 2.   [e] I. a. 10.

as itself equivalent to death. Unless expiation of
the one sort or the other is forthcoming, the dead
man will remain ἐνθύμιος τοῖς ζῶσιν,[a] *i.e.* the conscience of the living will be burdened with guilt, and
the unseen powers of vengeance which have been
awakened by the shedding of blood will work their
will. Upon the criminal himself they will bring
destruction ; upon the state famine and disaster.[b]
Generally these powers of vengeance are called
ἀλιτήριοι [c]; but here and there a different word
is used to describe them—προστρόπαιοι [d]—a word
which lets us see something more of their nature.
They are the vaguely conceived personification of
eternal justice " turned to " in mute appeal by him
who has been wronged.[e] They will hear his appeal,
and until reparation has been made will ceaselessly
haunt the guilty.

Much that is curious in the argument of the *Tetralogies* follows directly from these presuppositions.
Tetralogy II, for example, is concerned with the case
of a boy who was accidentally killed by a javelin-
cast in the gymnasium. Now it might be expected
that the only method of treating the situation open
to the author would be to make the prosecution take
the line that the victim met his death as the result of
a deliberate intention to kill on the part of the defend-

[a] I. γ. 10. Sometimes he is said to leave an ἐνθύμιον
behind him. *Cf.* II. a. 2, II. δ. 9.
[b] I. a. 10.
[c] III. a. 4, III. β. 8, III. δ. 10.
[d] III. a. 4.
[e] Sometimes the dead man is himself spoken of as προστρόπαιος, "turning in appeal." *Cf.* I. γ. 10, and see
Murray's *Rise of the Greek Epic*, 4th ed., p. 88, n. 2, for a
slightly different interpretation of the word.

39

ant, or else as the result of criminal negligence ;
while the defendant would reply by trying to prove
that death occurred by misadventure. But instead
both sides admit from the start that death was
purely accidental, because for the writer it makes
no difference. A life has been lost by violence.
Therefore an unexpiated μίασμα may still rest upon
the community. If the boy was himself to blame
for running into the path of the javelin, all is
well ; but if the fault rested with its thrower, the
blood-guilt arising from the deed still remains, and
he will have to make reparation with his life. From
this springs the involved argument as to which of the
two parties was guilty of ἁμαρτία, with its series of
sophistries so wearisome to modern taste. For the
author it represents the one means, however imperfect
that may be, of discovering whether or not satisfaction
is still owing to the powers of vengeance for the blood
which has been shed.

It is hardly necessary to point out how extra-
ordinarily primitive are the beliefs which lie behind
this conception of blood-guilt. They have their roots
in a dim past when the life of man was felt to be
at the mercy of mysterious δαίμονες, spiritual forces
which surround him on every side and manifest themselves in the endless processes of nature, forces of
which none knew the limits or precise character, but
which might be rendered benevolent by due propitia-
tion. It was in an animistic world of this kind that
the worship known as Chthonic took shape. The
spirits of the dead below the ground were themselves
thought to influence the lives of those upon the earth
which they had quitted. They too were δαίμονες,
and malignant ones, starved ghosts potent for evil,

unless appeased with food and drink and the performance of the ritual proper to them. And most malignant of all was the spirit of the man whose life had been taken from him by violence. He demanded blood, the blood of his slayer; and until he had received satisfaction, his curse lay upon the living.

Beliefs of this kind, woven into the very fabric of life, provide in themselves an inarticulate code of law; and with the development of a more complex social system, while some will pass into oblivion, others will receive explicit formulation as being fundamental to society's existence. They will become νόμοι πάτριοι whose authority is unquestioned —not so much because the superstitions and taboos from which they originated still persist, but because they have proved their worth in practice and have become accepted as part of the nature of things. We have seen how the author of the *Tetralogies* takes such a body of primitive law as his material; it now remains to ascertain whether this is in any way related to the Athenian legal code in so far as that code is concerned with φόνος.

Homicide in all its forms was dealt with at Athens under the laws first put into writing by Draco in the seventh century, but with origins in a far remoter past. The basic principle upon which they were framed was the principle with which we have already met in the *Tetralogies*, namely, that the shedding of blood involves a defilement which can only be removed by making due reparation to the dead. But closely related to this was a second principle, of which the *Tetralogies* take no account, the principle that there are degrees of blood-guilt and that therefore the reparation in a given case of φόνος must depend upon

41

the nature of that case. Homicide, in fact, under the Draconian code could take one of two main forms, φόνος ἑκούσιος and φόνος ἀκούσιος; and according as it was the one or the other, so the penalty to be inflicted upon the offender was death (with the recognized alternative of exile for life) or exile for a specified period, probably not more than a year (ἀπενιαυτισμός). In addition there was a third form, φόνος δίκαιος, which might be ἑκούσιος or ἀκούσιος, but which at the same time embodied a legal principle that the other two did not. How early these momentous distinctions were drawn is not known; but there can be no doubt that it was long before the days of Draco, as already in his time special courts were in existence for the trial of different kinds of φόνος. These courts were five in number. The first, and probably the most ancient, was the Areopagus, which sat to try cases of φόνος ἑκούσιος, wilful murder. The second was the court which met in the precincts of the Palladium (τὸ ἐπὶ Παλλαδίῳ δικαστήριον), to try cases of φόνος ἀκούσιος, homicide committed without intent to kill. The third met in the precincts of the temple of Apollo Delphinius (τὸ ἐπὶ Δελφινίῳ δικ.), to try cases of φόνος δίκαιος, homicide where the defendant pleaded justification. The fourth met in the precincts of the Prytaneum, the ancient Council-Hall (τὸ ἐπὶ τῷ Πρυτανείῳ δικ.), to try cases where the slayer was unknown or where death had been caused by an inanimate object. The fifth sat at Phreatto, a part of Peiraeus on the seashore, (τὸ ἐν Φρεαττοῖ δικ.) and tried cases where a person already in exile for φόνος ἀκούσιος was charged with having taken life a second time before leaving the country; Phreatto was chosen to enable the defendant to plead from a boat, and thereby avoid setting foot on the soil from which his previous crime had debarred him. The same jury, the fifty-one Ephetae, sat in all these courts save the Areopagus, which was composed of ex-Archons.

Of two of the five courts, the Areopagus and the Palladium, something more should be added. As already stated, the Draconian code recognized the existing distinction between φόνος ἑκούσιος and φόνος ἀκούσιος. Now such a distinction can only be made after it has become clear that the law must take into account not only facts but intentions. But from this it is only a step to a further principle. Cases sometimes occur where A plans an act and B carries it out at A's suggestion in ignorance of the effects which will follow. In such cases the βούλευσις and the πρᾶξις, which are usually indissolubly connected, are divided between A and B. It follows that the responsibility for the act must also be divided ; and at once there emerges the principle τὸν βουλεύσαντα ἐν τῷ αὐτῷ ἐνέχεσθαι καὶ τὸν τῇ χειρὶ ἐργασάμενον [a] ; and this will apply not only to φόνος ἑκούσιος but also to φόνος ἀκούσιος. B may perform an act at the instigation of A which results in the death of C. Neither A nor B foresaw such a consequence ; yet the act was deliberately performed. A is therefore guilty of βούλευσις φόνου ἀκουσίου, and in the eyes of the law must make precisely the same reparation as B. When this principle first received explicit formulation is not known. Possibly it is as early as Draco or earlier. In any case by the fifth century βούλευσις φόνου ἑκουσίου came within the jurisdiction of the

---

[a] Andocides, *Myst.* § 94.

Areopagus and βούλευσις φόνου ἀκουσίου within that of the Palladium.

It was into the framework of the five courts that Draco fitted his laws relating to φόνος. Of the character of that code enough has been said to show that it represents a relatively advanced stage of development; the instinctive sanctions of a more rudimentary society have been modified by the emergence of consciously articulated legal principles. But in spite of the rational analysis to which the act of homicide has been subjected, the primitive conception of blood-guilt persists and forms the basis of the Draconian code. Homicide was still held to involve defilement, and was for that reason placed in a category of its own. This is abundantly clear from known details of procedure in trials for homicide during the fifth century. Thus as soon as a charge of φόνος had been registered with the Basileus, a proclamation was made, forbidding the accused access to the Agora and temples as being suspected of defilement.[a] Anyone who came into contact with him or even spoke to him was liable to be infected with the same μίασμα; while the court which eventually tried the case sat in the open air to avoid sharing a roof with him.[b] There could be no better evidence that the old conception of blood-guilt had never lost its hold. Homicide was still an ἀσέβημα rather than an ἀδίκημα, an act of impiety rather than a crime against the community.

It is plain from this that, in taking the view which he did of the nature of blood-guilt, the author of the *Tetralogies* was doing nothing more than accepting an assumption recognized as fundamental by

[a] See *Choreutes*, Introd. p. 240.   [b] *Herodes*, § 11.

44

Athenian law itself. At the same time he diverges noticeably in his treatment of particular cases from the lines laid down in Draco's code. One of the features of that code was its recognition of the fact that φόνος ἀκούσιος cannot be treated as a crime of the same order as φόνος ἑκούσιος ; and it even went so far as to acknowledge that in certain circumstances φόνος ἀκούσιος was no crime at all ; thus the man who accidentally takes the life of another ἐν ἄθλοις is expressly absolved from blame, and it is held that he has incurred no defilement. The second *Tetralogy*, however, which deals with a case of homicide in almost these circumstances, pays no attention to this. It replaces Draco's law with another, which is less of a νόμος, though it is spoken of as such, than a general principle : homicide, whatever the circumstances in which it is committed, is punishable with death.[a] Again, the Draconian code recognized that homicide in self-defence is in certain cases justified ; it laid down, for instance, that the man who kills a thief in the effort to protect his goods is guiltless. But the third *Tetralogy*, which would have provided an excellent opportunity for exhibiting the principle implicit in such a law, is taken up with argument along different lines.

Does this divergence mean that the author of the *Tetralogies* was ignorant of Athenian law on the subject of homicide, and that his conception of blood-guilt as involving defilement agrees with that embodied in the Draconian code only by chance ? The evidence does not admit of a certain answer. But it is significant that while the *Tetralogies* do not openly recognize the existence of the Draconian code, each

[a] II. β. 9.

ANTIPHON

of them deals with one of the three types of φόνος distinguished by it : the first is concerned with φόνος ἑκούσιος, the second with φόνος ἀκούσιος, and the third with φόνος δίκαιος. Further, passing references to laws other than those of homicide certainly seem to indicate a knowledge of the Athenian legal system as a whole. Thus κλοπὴ ἱερῶν χρημάτων is punishable by fine after being made the subject of a γραφή[a]; slaves can only give evidence under torture[b]; a citizen convicted of ψευδομαρτυρία is fined and disfranchised[c]; no blame attaches to a physician, if a patient dies while under his care.[d] And in addition to this it must always be remembered that the author is not trying to show how the cases which he selects would be argued in a court of law; as has already been pointed out, he is confining himself as far as possible to purely general reasoning. In view of such facts it seems more probable that he was purposely neglecting the details of the Draconian code than that he was ignorant of them altogether.

The evidence of background, then, suggests, if anything, that the writer of the *Tetralogies* was acquainted with Attic law. That he was Antiphon, or indeed a native Athenian at all, it is not easy to believe, when the peculiarities of language are taken into account.[e] We are left with the possibility that he was a foreigner who had spent time enough in Athens to gain a knowledge of her legal system and write Attic of a kind. On this assumption the *Tetra-*

[a] I. a. 6.
[b] I. β. 7.
[c] I. δ. 7, cf. Andoc. *Myst.* § 74.
[d] III. γ. 5.
[e] The evidence which suggests that the *Tetralogies* are spurious, while cogent, is not absolutely conclusive. They have therefore been printed as Antiphon's in the present edition.

46

logies will stand as the relic of a literature long since dust and shadows ; for the naïve ingenuity of their thought and the archaic balance of their language alike suggest that they are the work of a sophist of the age of Corax, Teisias, and Gorgias, rather than the forgery of a later time. If this is so, we may regret the namelessness of their author ; but we must count it fortunate that we possess a perfect specimen of that τέχνη ῥητορική which held the young Pericles engrossed, while it invited the scorn of Aristophanes and Plato.

II

THE FIRST TETRALOGY

INTRODUCTORY NOTE

THE situation presupposed by the first *Tetralogy* is a simple one. X is found dead in a deserted spot. His attendant, a slave, lies mortally wounded at his side and dies shortly after the pair are discovered, but not before stating that he had recognized Y among the assailants. The family of X now prosecute Y for wilful murder. This clearly affords an admirable field for argument ἐκ τῶν εἰκότων on the side of prosecution and defence alike, as the evidence of the slave cannot be tested under torture and has to be accepted or rejected as the probabilities dictate. In fact the whole purpose of this particular *Tetralogy* is to show how far *a priori* methods of proof can be pushed.

The prosecution opens with an attempt to establish the guilt of the accused by elimination. Next this negative argument is buttressed by the positive evidence of Y's past relations with X ; the known fact that X was threatening Y with a serious lawsuit at the time of his death proves that Y had a peculiarly strong motive for committing the murder. Finally the statement of the slave is produced.

Y replies by showing that the method of elimination employed by the prosecution is logically unsound, that the evidence of the slave was given in such circumstances as to render it untrustworthy, that his presence at the scene of the crime is in any event improbable *a priori*, and finally that the suggested motive is inadequate.

The two remaining speeches break no new ground, but consist of further argument on the lines followed in the first two. A touch of realism is added in the final speech for the defence. The speaker states that he will prove from the evidence of his slaves that he was at home and in bed on the night of the Diipoleia, when the crime was committed. This may well be a practical hint on the part of the author to indicate the most effective moment for the introduction of important evidence. Coming where it does, the prosecution has no opportunity of replying to it.

ΤΕΤΡΑΛΟΓΙΑ Α

α

ΚΑΤΗΓΟΡΙΑ ΦΟΝΟΥ ΑΠΑΡΑΣΗΜΟΣ

1 Ὁπόσα μὲν τῶν πραγμάτων ὑπὸ τῶν ἐπιτυχόντων ἐπιβουλεύεται, οὐ χαλεπὰ ἐλέγχεσθαί ἐστιν·
ἂν δ' οἱ ἱκανῶς μὲν πεφυκότες, ἔμπειροι δὲ τῶν
πραγμάτων ὄντες, ἐν δὲ τούτῳ τῆς ἡλικίας καθ-
εστῶτες ἐν ᾧ κράτιστοι φρονεῖν αὐτῶν εἰσι,
πράσσωσι, χαλεποὶ καὶ γνωσθῆναι καὶ ἐλεγχθῆναί[1]
2 εἰσι· διὰ γὰρ τὸ μέγεθος τοῦ κινδύνου ἐκ πολλοῦ
τὴν ἀσφάλειαν ὧν ἐπιβουλεύουσι σκοποῦντες, οὐ
πρότερον ἐπιχειροῦσιν ἢ πάσης ὑποψίας φυλακὴν
ποιήσωνται. γιγνώσκοντας οὖν ὑμᾶς χρὴ ταῦτα,
κἂν ὁτιοῦν εἰκὸς παραλάβητε, σφόδρα πιστεύειν
αὐτῷ. ἡμεῖς δ' οἱ ἐπεξερχόμενοι τὸν φόνον οὐ
3 τὸν αἴτιον ἀφέντες τὸν ἀναίτιον διώκομεν· σαφῶς
γὰρ οἴδαμεν ὅτι πάσης τῆς πόλεως μιαινομένης
ὑπ' αὐτοῦ, ἕως ἂν διωχθῇ, τό τ' ἀσέβημα ἡμέτερον
γίγνεται, τῆς θ' ὑμετέρας ἁμαρτίας ἡ ποινὴ εἰς
ἡμᾶς τοὺς μὴ δικαίως διώκοντας ἀναχωρεῖ. ἅπαν-
τος δὲ τοῦ μιάσματος ἀναχωροῦντος εἰς ἡμᾶς, ὡς

---

[1] ἐλεγχθῆναι Kayser: δειχθῆναι codd.

THE FIRST TETRALOGY

I

ANONYMOUS PROSECUTION FOR MURDER

WHEN a crime is planned by an ordinary person, it is not hard to expose; but to detect and expose criminals who are naturally able, who are men of experience, and who have reached an age when their faculties are at their best, is no easy matter. The enormous risk makes them devote a great deal of thought to the problem of executing the crime in safety, and they take no steps until they have completely secured themselves against suspicion. With these facts in mind, you must place implicit confidence in any and every indication from probability[a] presented to you. We, on the other hand, who are seeking satisfaction for the murder, are not letting the guilty escape and bringing the innocent into court; we know very well that as the whole city is defiled by the criminal until he is brought to justice, the sin becomes ours and the punishment for your error falls upon us, if our prosecution is misdirected. Thus, as the entire defilement falls upon

---

[a] εἰκός, εἰκότως, and τὰ εἰκότα cannot properly be rendered by any single English equivalent. I have made use of "natural," "logical," "probable," "to be expected," etc., according to the requirements of the context.

53

ANTIPHON

ἂν δυνώμεθα σαφέστατα ἐξ ὧν γιγνώσκομεν πειρασόμεθα ὑμῖν δηλοῦν ὡς ἀπέκτεινε τὸν ἄνδρα.

4 ⟨Οὔτε γὰρ κακούργους εἰκὸς ἀποκτεῖναι τὸν
ἄνθρωπον⟩[1]· οὐδεὶς γὰρ ἂν τὸν ἔσχατον κίνδυνον
περὶ τῆς ψυχῆς κινδυνεύων ἑτοίμην καὶ κατειργασ-
μένην τὴν ὠφέλειαν ἀφῆκεν· ἔχοντες γὰρ [ἂν][2] τὰ
ἱμάτια ηὑρέθησαν. οὐ μὴν οὐδὲ παροινήσας οὐδεὶς
διέφθειρεν αὐτόν· ἐγιγνώσκετο γὰρ ἂν ὑπὸ τῶν
συμποτῶν. οὐδὲ μὴν οὐδ᾽ ἐκ λοιδορίας· οὐ γὰρ
⟨ἂν⟩[3] ἀωρὶ τῶν νυκτῶν οὐδ᾽ ἐν ἐρημίᾳ ἐλοιδο-
ροῦντο. οὐδὲ μὴν ἄλλου στοχαζόμενος ἔτυχε τού-
του· οὐ γὰρ ἂν σὺν τῷ ἀκολούθῳ διέφθειρεν αὐτόν.

5 Ἀπολυομένης δὲ τῆς ὑποψίας ἁπάσης αὐτὸς ὁ
θάνατος ἐξ ἐπιβουλῆς ἀποθανόντα μηνύει αὐτόν.
ἐπιθέσθαι δὲ τινα μᾶλλον εἰκός ἐστιν ἢ τὸν μεγάλα
μὲν κακὰ προπεπονθότα, ἔτι δὲ μείζονα ἐπίδοξον
ὄντα πάσχειν; ἔστι δ᾽ ὁ διωκόμενος οὗτος· ἐκ
παλαιοῦ γὰρ ἐχθρὸς ὢν αὐτοῦ πολλὰς μὲν καὶ
6 μεγάλας γραφὰς διώξας οὐδεμίαν εἷλεν, ἔτι δὲ
μείζους καὶ πλείους διωχθεὶς οὐδεπώποτ᾽ ἀπο-
φυγὼν ἱκανὸν μέρος τῶν ὄντων ἀποβέβληκε, τὰ δ᾽

---

[1] οὔτε . . . ἄνθρωπον add. Ald.
[2] ἂν secl. Reiske.
[3] ἂν add. Dobree. Cf. δ, § 5.

---

[a] Inserted in the Aldine edition to fill a probable lacuna in
the ms. text; some reference to κακοῦργοι is clearly wanted.
The term κακοῦργος (cf. δ, §§ 5, 6) is a generic one compris-
ing various species of criminal: κλέπται, τοιχωρύχοι, βαλλαντιο-
τόμοι, etc. The "malefactors" here referred to are doubtless

us, we shall try to show you as conclusively as our knowledge allows that the defendant killed the dead man.

⟨Malefactors are not likely to have murdered him,⟩[a] as nobody who was exposing his life to a very grave risk would forgo the prize when it was securely within his grasp ; and the victims were found still wearing their cloaks. Nor again did anyone in liquor kill him : the murderer's identity would be known to his boon-companions. Nor again was his death the result of a quarrel ; they would not have been quarrelling at the dead of night or in a deserted spot. Nor did the criminal strike the dead man when intending to strike someone else ; he would not in that case have killed master and slave together.

As all grounds for suspecting that the crime was unpremeditated are removed, it is clear from the circumstances of death themselves that the victim was deliberately murdered.[b] Now who is more likely to have attacked him than a man who had already suffered cruelly at his hands and who was expecting to suffer more cruelly still ? That man is the defendant. He was an old enemy of the other, and indicted him on several serious charges without success. On the other hand, he has himself been indicted on charges still more numerous and still more grave, and not once has he been acquitted, with the result that he has lost a good deal of his property. Further, he had recently been indicted by the dead man for

λωποδύται "footpads." For a further discussion of κακοῦργοι see *Herodes*, Introd.

[b] Here, as elsewhere in the *Tetralogies*, the Greek has to be expanded in translating in order to make the connexion of thought clear. For an explanation of the words αὐτὸς ὁ θάνατος, "circumstances of death," see p. 60, note *b*.

ANTIPHON

ἄγχιστα ἱερῶν κλοπῆς δυοῖν ταλάντοιν γεγραμμένος ὑπ' αὐτοῦ, συνειδὼς μὲν αὐτῷ τὸ ἀδίκημα, ἔμπειρος δ' ὢν τῆς τούτου δυνάμεως, μνησικακῶν δὲ τῶν ἔμπροσθεν, εἰκότως μὲν ἐπεβούλευσεν, εἰκότως δ' ἀμυνόμενος τὴν ἔχθραν ἀπέκτεινε τὸν 7 ἄνδρα. ἥ τε γὰρ ἐπιθυμία τῆς τιμωρίας ἀμνήμονα τῶν κινδύνων καθίστη αὐτόν, ὅ τε φόβος τῶν ἐπιφερομένων κακῶν ἐκπλήσσων θερμότερον ἐπιχειρεῖν ἐπῆρεν. ἤλπιζέ τε τάδε μὲν δράσας καὶ λήσειν ἀποκτείνας αὐτὸν καὶ ἀποφεύξεσθαι τὴν 8 γραφήν· οὐδὲ[1] γὰρ ἐπεξιέναι οὐδένα, ἀλλ' ἐρήμην αὐτὴν ἔσεσθαι· εἴ τε καὶ ἁλοίη, τιμωρησαμένῳ κάλλιον ἔδοξεν αὐτῷ ταῦτα πάσχειν, ἢ ἀνάνδρως μηδὲν ἀντιδράσαντα ὑπὸ τῆς γραφῆς διαφθαρῆναι. σαφῶς δ' ᾔδει ἁλωσόμενος αὐτήν· οὐ γὰρ ἂν τόνδε τὸν ἀγῶνα ἐνόμισεν ἀσφαλέστερον εἶναι.

9 Τὰ μὲν βιασάμενα ταῦτά ἐστιν ἀσεβῆσαι αὐτόν. μάρτυρες δ' εἰ μὲν πολλοὶ παρεγένοντο, πολλοὺς ἂν παρεσχόμεθα· ἑνὸς δὲ τοῦ ἀκολούθου παραγενομένου, οἳ τούτου ἤκουον μαρτυρήσουσιν. ἔμπνους γὰρ ἔτι ἀρθείς, ἀνακρινόμενος ὑφ' ἡμῶν, τοῦτον μόνον ἔφη γνῶναι τῶν παιόντων[2] αὐτούς.

Ἐξελεγχόμενος δ' ὑπό τε τῶν εἰκότων ὑπό τε τῶν παραγενομένων, οὐδενὶ τρόπῳ οὔτε δικαίως 10 οὔτε συμφερόντως ἀπολύοιτ' ἂν ὑφ' ὑμῶν. οἵ τε γὰρ ἐπιβουλεύοντες ἀνεξέλεγκτοι ἂν εἶεν, εἰ μήθ' ὑπὸ τῶν παραγενομένων μήθ' ὑπὸ τῶν εἰκότων

---

[1] οὐδὲ Reiske: οὔτε codd.
[2] παιόντων ci. Bekker, coll. δ, § 4: παρόντων codd.

---

[a] ἱερῶν κλοπή (embezzlement of sacred monies of which the person concerned was in charge) is to be distinguished from ἱεροσυλία (temple-robbery), for which see *Herodes*, § 10. The
56

embezzling sacred monies,[a] the sum to be recovered
being assessed at two talents ; he knew himself to be
guilty, experience had taught him how powerful his
opponent was, and he bore him a grudge for the past ;
so he naturally plotted his death : he naturally sought
protection against his enemy by murdering him.
Thirst for revenge made him forget the risk, and the
overpowering fear of the ruin which threatened him
spurred him to all the more reckless an attack. In
taking this step he hoped not only that his guilt
would remain undiscovered, but that he would also
escape the indictment [b] ; nobody, he thought, would
proceed with the suit, and judgement would go by
default ; while in the event of his losing his case after
all, he considered it better to have revenged himself
for his defeat than, like a coward, to be ruined by the
indictment without retaliating. And he knew very
well that he would lose it, or he would not have
thought the present trial the safer alternative.

Such are the motives which drove him to sin as he
did. Had there been eyewitnesses in large numbers,
we should have produced them in large numbers ;
but as the dead man's attendant was alone present,
those who heard his statement will give evidence ;
for he was still alive when picked up, and in reply to
our questions stated that the only assailant whom he
had recognized was the defendant.

Inferences from probability and eyewitnesses have
alike proved the defendant's guilt : so both justice
and expediency absolutely forbid you to acquit him.
Not only would it be impossible to convict deliberate
criminals if they are not to be convicted by eye-

penalty for ἱερῶν κλοπή was the repayment of ten times the
sum embezzled (Dem. *In Timocr.* §§ 111, 112).

[b] Or possibly : " be acquitted on the indictment."

ΑΝΤΙΦΩΝ

ἐξελέγχονται· ἀσύμφορόν θ᾽ ὑμῖν ἐστι τόνδε μιαρὸν
καὶ ἄναγνον ὄντα εἰς ⟨τε⟩[1] τὰ τεμένη τῶν θεῶν
εἰσιόντα μιαίνειν τὴν ἁγνείαν αὐτῶν, ἐπί τε τὰς
αὐτὰς τραπέζας ἰόντα συγκαταπιμπλάναι τοὺς ἀναι-
τίους· ἐκ γὰρ τούτων αἵ τ᾽ ἀφορίαι γίγνονται
11 δυστυχεῖς θ᾽ αἱ πράξεις καθίστανται. οἰκείαν οὖν
χρὴ τὴν τιμωρίαν ἡγησαμένους, αὐτῷ τούτῳ τὰ
τούτου ἀσεβήματα ἀναθέντας, ἰδίαν μὲν τὴν συμφοράν, καθαρὰν δὲ τὴν πόλιν καταστῆσαι.

β

ΑΠΟΛΟΓΙΑ ΕΙΣ ΤΟ ΑΥΤΟ ΠΡΑΓΜΑ

1 Οὔ μοι δοκῶ ἁμαρτάνειν ἀτυχέστατον ἐμαυτὸν
ἡγούμενος εἶναι τῶν πάντων ἀνθρώπων. τῶν μὲν
γὰρ ἄλλων οἱ δυστυχοῦντες, ὁπόταν μὲν ὑπὸ χειμῶνος πονῶσιν, εὐδίας γενομένης παύονται· ὅταν
δὲ νοσήσωσιν, ὑγιεῖς γενόμενοι σῴζονται· ἐὰν δέ
τις ἄλλη συμφορὰ καταλαμβάνῃ αὐτούς, τὰ ἐναντία
2 ἐπιγιγνόμενα ὀνίνησιν. ἐμοὶ δὲ ζῶν τε ἄνθρωπος
ἀνατροπεὺς τοῦ οἴκου ἐγένετο, ἀποθανών τε, κἂν
ἀποφύγω, ἱκανὰς λύπας καὶ φροντίδας προσ-
βέβληκεν. εἰς τοῦτο γὰρ βαρυδαιμονίας ἥκω
ὥστε οὐκ ἀρκοῦν μοί ἐστιν ἐμαυτὸν ὅσιον καὶ
δίκαιον παρέχοντα μὴ διαφθαρῆναι, ἀλλὰ κἂν μὴ
τὸν ἀποκτείναντα εὑρὼν ἐξελέγξω, ὃν οἱ τιμωροῦν-
τες αὐτῷ ἀδύνατοι εὑρεῖν εἰσιν, αὐτὸς καταδοχθεὶς
φονεὺς εἶναι ἀνοσίως ἁλώσομαι.

[1] τε add. Blass.

58

witnesses and by such inferences : but it is against all your interests that this polluted wretch should profane the sanctity of the divine precincts by setting foot within them, or pass on his defilement to the innocent by sitting at the same tables as they.[a] It is this that causes dearth and public calamity. And so you must hold the avenging of the dead a personal duty ; you must visit the defendant with retribution for the sin which was his alone ; you must see that none but he suffers, and that the stain of guilt is removed from the city.

II

REPLY TO THE SAME CHARGE

I am not far wrong, I think, in regarding myself as the most unlucky man alive. Others meet with misfortune. They may be buffeted by a tempest ; but calm weather returns and they are buffeted no longer. They may fall ill ; but they recover their health and are saved. Or some other mishap may overtake them ; but it is followed by its opposite which brings relief. With me this is not so. Not only did this man make havoc of my house during his lifetime : but he has caused me distress and anxiety in plenty since his death, even if I escape sentence ; for so luckless is my lot that a godfearing and an honest life is not enough to save me. Unless I also find and convict the murderer, whom the dead man's avengers cannot find, I shall myself be deemed guilty of murder and suffer an outrageous sentence of death.

[a] *Cf.* the disabilities involved in τὸ εἴργεσθαι τῶν νομίμων, *Choreutes*, §§ 34 *sqq.*

ANTIPHON

3 Καὶ ἐμὲ ὡς δεινὸν μὲν παγχάλεπόν φασιν ἐλέγχεσθαι εἶναι, ὡς δ' ἠλίθιον ἐξ αὐτῶν ὧν ἔπραξα
φανερὸν εἶναι ἐργασάμενον τὸ ἔργον. εἰ γὰρ νῦν
διὰ τῆς ἔχθρας τὸ μέγεθος εἰκότως ὑφ' ὑμῶν κατα-
δοκοῦμαι, πρὶν ἐργάσασθαι εἰκότερον ἦν προειδότα[1]
τὴν νῦν ὑποψίαν εἰς ἐμὲ ἰοῦσαν,[2] καὶ τῶν ἄλλων
εἴ τινα ἔγνων ἐπιβουλεύοντα αὐτῷ, διακωλύειν
μᾶλλον ἢ αὐτὸν ἐργασάμενον εἰς ἑκουσίους καὶ
προδήλους ὑποψίας ἐμπεσεῖν· ἔκ τε γὰρ αὐτοῦ τοῦ
ἔργου φανερὸς γενόμενος ἀπωλλύμην, λαθών τε
σαφῶς ἤδη τήνδε τὴν ὑποψίαν εἰς ἐμὲ ἰοῦσαν.

4 Ἄθλια μὲν οὖν πάσχω μὴ ἀπολογεῖσθαι μόνον
βιαζόμενος, ἀλλὰ καὶ τοὺς ἀποκτείναντας φανε-
ροὺς καταστῆσαι· ὅμως δὲ καὶ τοῦτο ἐπιχειρητέον·
οὐδὲν γὰρ πικρότερον τῆς ἀνάγκης ἔοικεν εἶναι.
ἔχω δὲ οὐδαμῶς ἄλλως ἐλέγχειν ἢ ἐξ ὧν τοὺς
ἄλλους ὁ κατήγορος ἀπολύων αὐτὸν τὸν θάνατόν
φησι μηνύειν ἐμὲ τὸν φονέα ὄντα. εἰ γὰρ τούτων
ἀναιτίων δοκούντων εἶναι ἐν ἐμοὶ τἀδίκημα φανεῖ-

---

[1] προειδότα Kayser: τὸν εἰδότα codd.
[2] ἰοῦσαν Reiske: οὖσαν codd.

---

[a] Or possibly: "If on the one hand I was detected in
the act of committing the crime . . ." The speaker is endeavouring to prove that he did not commit the murder by
showing that his knowledge of the consequences to himself,
even in the event of his escaping detection, must necessarily
have deterred him. The sentence must therefore be regarded
as explaining not the whole of that preceding, but only
αὐτὸν . . . ἐμπεσεῖν.

[b] An exceedingly difficult sentence to render clearly in
English. The speaker means that he too is obliged from the

Now the prosecution allege that it is very difficult to prove my guilt because of my astuteness. Yet in maintaining that my actions themselves prove me to be the criminal, they are assuming me to be a simpleton. For if the bitterness of my feud is a natural ground for your deeming me guilty to-day, it was still more natural for me to foresee before committing the crime that suspicion would settle upon me as it has done. I was more likely to go to the length of stopping anyone else whom I knew to be plotting the murder than deliberately to incur certain suspicion by committing it myself; for if, on the one hand, the crime in itself showed that I was the murderer,[a] I was doomed : while if, on the other hand, I escaped detection, I knew very well that suspicion would fall on me as it has done.

My plight is indeed hapless : I am forced not only to defend myself, but to reveal the criminals as well. Still, I must attempt this further task ; nothing, it seems, is more relentless than necessity. I can expose the criminals, I may say, only by following the principle used by my accuser, who establishes the innocence of every one else and then asserts that the circumstances of death in themselves show the murderer to be me.[b] If the apparent innocence of every one else is to fasten the crime upon me, it is

nature of the case to resort to proof by elimination. The prosecution had argued (a, §§ 4, 5) that death could not have been due to footpads, a drunken quarrel, or a mistaken assault, *i.e.* it cannot have been unpremeditated ; therefore, since the circumstances showed it to have been violent, not natural (this is the point of αὐτὸς ὁ θάνατος in a, § 5), it was premeditated ; and the defendant was alone likely to have planned such a crime. Here the defendant recapitulates this, actually quoting the words αὐτὸς ὁ θάνατος, which had formed part of the argument of the prosecution.

ται, τούτων ὑπόπτων ὄντων ἐγὼ εἰκότως ⟨ἂν⟩¹
καθαρὸς δοκοίην εἶναι.

Ἔστι δὲ οὐκ ἀπεικός, ὡς οὗτοί φασιν, ἀλλὰ
εἰκὸς ἀωρὶ τῶν νυκτῶν πλανώμενον ἐπὶ τοῖς
ἱματίοις διαφθαρῆναι. τὸ γὰρ μὴ ἐκδυθῆναι οὐδὲν
σημεῖόν ἐστιν· εἰ γὰρ μὴ ἔφθησαν περιδύσαντες
αὐτόν, ἀλλά τινας προσιόντας φοβηθέντες ἀπέλιπον,
ἐσωφρόνουν καὶ οὐκ ἐμαίνοντο τὴν σωτηρίαν τοῦ
6 κέρδους προτιμῶντες. εἰ δὲ μὴ καὶ ἐπὶ τοῖς
ἱματίοις διεφθάρη, ἀλλ' ἑτέρους ἰδὼν ἄλλο τι
κακὸν ποιοῦντας, ἵνα μὴ μηνυτὴς τοῦ ἀδικήματος
γένηται, ἀπέθανεν ὑπ' αὐτῶν, τίς οἶδε; τοὺς δὲ
μὴ πολὺ ἧσσον ἐμοῦ μισοῦντας αὐτόν—ἦσαν δὲ
πολλοί—πῶς οὐκ εἰκὸς ἦν ἐμοῦ μᾶλλον διαφθεῖραι
αὐτόν; ἐκείνοις μὲν γὰρ φανερὰ ἦν ἡ ὑποψία εἰς
ἐμὲ ἰοῦσα, ἐγὼ δὲ ὑπὲρ ἐκείνων ὑπαίτιος ἐσόμενος
σαφῶς ἤδη.

7 Τοῦ δὲ ἀκολούθου ἡ μαρτυρία πῶς ἀξία πι-
στεύεσθαί ἐστιν; ὑπό τε γὰρ τοῦ κινδύνου ἐκ-
πεπληγμένον αὐτὸν οὐκ εἰκὸς ἦν τοὺς ἀποκτείναντας γνῶναι, ὑπό τε τῶν κυρίων ἀναγιγνωσκόμενον
ἐπινεῦσαι ἦν εἰκός. ἀπιστουμένων δὲ καὶ τῶν
ἄλλων δούλων ἐν ταῖς μαρτυρίαις—οὐ γὰρ ἂν
ἐβασανίζομεν αὐτούς—πῶς δίκαιον τούτῳ μαρ-
8 τυροῦντι πιστεύσαντας διαφθεῖραί με; εἰ δέ τις
τὰ εἰκότα ἀληθέσιν ἴσα ἡγεῖται καταμαρτυρῆσαί
μου, ταὐτὸν² ἀντιλογισάσθω ὅτι με εἰκότερον ἦν

¹ ἂν add. Blass: δ' εἰκότως A, δικαίως N.
² τοὔργον Blass: τοῦτ' αὖ Gernet: alii alia. Codicum tamen
fidem vindicat Thalheim, collato Platonis *Phileb.* 37 D.

ª ἀναγιγνώσκειν in the sense of "persuade," which it must
bear here, is found elsewhere only in Herodotus. "Masters"

only logical for me to be held guiltless, should others
be brought under suspicion.

It is not, as the prosecution maintain, unlikely that
a man wandering about at the dead of night should
be murdered for his clothing ; nothing is more likely.
The fact that he was not stripped indicates nothing.
If the approach of passers-by startled his assailants
into quitting him before they had had time to strip
him, they showed sense, not madness, in preferring
their lives to their spoils. Further, he may not in
fact have been murdered for his clothing : he may
have seen others engaged in some quite different
outrage and have been killed by them to prevent
his giving information of the crime : who knows ?
Again, were not those who hated him almost as much
as I did—and there were a great many—more likely
to have murdered him than I ? It was plain to them
that suspicion would fall on me ; while I knew very
well that I should bear the blame for them.

Why, moreover, should the evidence of the attendant be allowed any weight ? In his terror at the
peril in which he stood, there was no likelihood of his
recognizing the murderers. On the other hand, it
was likely enough that he would obediently confirm
any suggestions made by his masters.[a] We distrust
the evidence of slaves in general, or we should not
torture them ; so what justification have you for
putting me to death on the evidence of this one ?
Further, whoever allows probability the force of fact
when it testifies to my guilt must on the same
principle bear the following in mind as evidence of

implies that the passers-by who found the slave were members
of the dead man's own family, although this fact is nowhere
explicitly mentioned by the prosecution.

τὴν ἀσφάλειαν τῆς ἐπιβουλῆς τηροῦντα φυλάξασθαι
καὶ μὴ παραγενέσθαι τῷ ἔργῳ μᾶλλον ἢ τοῦτον
σφαττόμενον ὀρθῶς γνῶ ᾳ.

9 Ὡς δὲ τόνδε¹ τὸν κίνδυνον οὐκ ἀσφαλέστερον
τοῦ ἀπὸ τῆς γραφῆς ἡγούμην εἶναι, ἀλλὰ πολλα-
πλάσιον, εἰ μὴ παρεφρόνουν, διδάξω. ἁλοὺς μὲν
γὰρ τὴν γραφὴν τῆς μὲν οὐσίας ἤδη ἐκστησόμενος,
τοῦ δὲ σώματος καὶ τῆς πόλεως² οὐκ ἀπεστερούμην,
περιγενόμενος δὲ καὶ λειφθείς, κἂν ἔρανον παρὰ
τῶν φίλων συλλέξας, οὐκ ἂν εἰς τὰ ἔσχατα κακὰ
ἦλθον· ἐὰν δὲ νῦν καταληφθεὶς ἀποθάνω, ἀνόσια
ὀνείδη τοῖς παισὶν ὑπολείψω, ἢ φυγὼν γέρων καὶ
ἄπολις ὢν ἐπὶ ξενίας πτωχεύσω.

10 Οὕτω μὲν ἃ κατηγόρηταί μου, πάντα ἄπιστά
ἐστιν· ἀπολύεσθαι δὲ ὑφ᾽ ὑμῶν, εἰ καὶ εἰκότως μὲν
ὄντως δὲ μὴ ἀπέκτεινα τὸν ἄνδρα, πολὺ μᾶλλον
δίκαιός εἰμι. ἐγώ τε γὰρ φανερὸν ὅτι μεγάλα
ἀδικούμενος ἠμυνόμην³· οὐ γὰρ ἂν εἰκότως ἐδόκουν
ἀποκτεῖναι αὐτόν· τούς τε ἀποκτείναντας καὶ οὐ
τοὺς αἰτίαν ἔχοντας ἀποκτεῖναι ὀρθῶς ἂν κατα-
λαμβάνοιτε.

11 Ἐκ δὲ παντὸς τρόπου ἀπολυόμενος τῆς αἰτίας
ἔγωγε οὔτε εἰς τὰ τεμένη εἰσιὼν τὴν ἁγνείαν τῶν

¹ τόνδε Dobree : οὐδὲ codd.
² τοῦ δὲ σώματος καὶ τῆς πόλεως N : τῆς δὲ π. καὶ τοῦ σ. A.
³ ἠμυνόμην Kayser : ἠμυνάμην codd.

ᵃ ἔρανον συλλέγειν. Cf. infra § 12, ἐρανίζειν. The reference in both cases is to a sum of money advanced without
interest by friends who each contributed a portion. ἔρανος
later came to have the more specialized sense of a club formed
for the purpose of lending money without interest to any of
its members. Each member paid a subscription (also called
ἔρανος) : and such clubs often acquired landed property.
They grew political in character as time went on.

my innocence : it was more likely that, with an eye to carrying out my plot in safety, I should take the precaution of not being present at the scene of the crime than that the slave should recognize me distinctly just as his throat was being cut.

I will now show that, unless I was mad, I must have thought the danger in which I now stand far greater, instead of less, than the danger to be expected from the indictment. If I was convicted on the indictment, I knew that I should be stripped of my property ; but I did not lose my life or civic rights. I should still have been alive, still left to enjoy those rights ; and even though I should have had to obtain a loan of money from my friends,[a] my fate would not have been the worst possible. On the other hand, if I am found guilty to-day and put to death, my children will inherit from me an insufferable disgrace ; if instead I go into exile, I shall become a beggar in a strange land, an old man without a country.

Thus not one of the charges brought against me has any foundation. But even if the probabilities, as distinct from the facts, point to me as the murderer, it is acquittal that I deserve from you far more than anything else : since first, it is clear that if I struck back, it was only because I was being deeply wronged : had that not been so, it would never have been thought likely that I was the murderer : and secondly, it is the murderers, not those accused of the murder, whom it is your duty to convict.[b]

As I am completely cleared of the charge, it is not I who will profane the sanctity of the gods when I set

[b] *i.e.* (1) Even if he can be proved guilty, there are extenuating circumstances which will make it impossible to condemn him. (2) But he cannot be proved guilty in any case.

θεῶν μιανῶ, οὔτε ὑμᾶς πείθων ἀπολῦσαί με ἀνόσια
πράσσω. οἱ δὲ διώκοντες μὲν ἐμὲ τὸν ἀναίτιον,
τὸν δ' αἴτιον ἀφιέντες, τῆς τε ἀφορίας αἴτιοι
γίγνονται, ὑμᾶς τε ἀσεβεῖς εἰς τοὺς θεοὺς πείθοντες
καταστῆναι πάντων ὧν ἐμὲ ἄξιόν φασι παθεῖν
εἶναι δίκαιοί εἰσι τυγχάνειν.

12 Τούτους μὲν οὖν τούτων ἀξίους ὄντας ἀπίστους
ἡγεῖσθε· ἐμὲ δὲ ἔκ γε¹ τῶν προειργασμένων γνώσεσθε οὔτε ἐπιβουλεύοντα οὔτε τῶν οὐ προσηκόντων ὀρεγόμενον, ἀλλὰ τἀναντία τούτων πολλὰς μὲν
καὶ μεγάλας εἰσφορὰς εἰσφέροντα, πολλὰ δὲ
τριηραρχοῦντα, λαμπρῶς δὲ χορηγοῦντα, πολλοῖς²
δὲ ἐρανίζοντα, μεγάλας δὲ ὑπὲρ πολλῶν ἐγγύας
ἀποτίνοντα, τὴν δὲ³ οὐσίαν οὐ δικαζόμενον ἀλλ'
ἐργαζόμενον κεκτημένον, φιλοθύτην δὲ καὶ νόμιμον
ὄντα. τοιούτου δὲ ὄντος μου μηδὲν ἀνόσιον μηδὲ
αἰσχρὸν καταγνῶτε.

13 Εἰ δὲ ὑπὸ ζῶντος ἐδιωκόμην, οὐκ ἂν μόνον ὑπὲρ
ἐμαυτοῦ ἀπελογούμην, ἀλλ' αὐτόν τε τοῦτον καὶ
τοὺς τούτῳ μὲν βοηθοῦντας, παρ' ἐμοῦ δὲ ὠφελεῖσθαι ζητοῦντας ἐφ' οἷς κατηγορεῖταί⁴ μου,

---

¹ ἔκ γε Franke : ἔκ τε codd.
² πολλοῖς Salmasius (cf. Dem. 999. 24): πολλοὺς codd.
³ τὴν δὲ Schaefer : τήν τε codd.
⁴ κατηγορεῖται Vulg.: κατηγορεῖτε AN.

ᵃ The εἰσφορά was an extraordinary property-tax levied
on citizens and metics in time of war.

ᵇ One of the most important liturgies or public services
which the richer members of the community were obliged to
undertake from time to time. The τριήραρχος served for a year
as the commander of a trireme; and although the State

foot within their precincts, any more than it is I who am sinning against them in urging you to acquit me. It is those who are prosecuting an innocent man like myself, while they let the criminal escape, to whom dearth is due: it is they who deserve in full the penalty which they say should be inflicted upon me, for urging you to become guilty of impiety.

If this is the treatment which the prosecution deserve, you must put no faith in them. I myself, on the other hand, as you will see by examining my past life, do not form plots or covet what does not belong to me. On the contrary, I have made several substantial payments to the Treasury,[a] I have more than once served as Trierarch,[b] I have furnished a brilliant chorus,[c] I have often advanced money to friends, and I have frequently paid large sums under guarantees given for others; my wealth has come not from litigation, but from hard work[d]; and I have been a religious and law-abiding man. If my character is such as this, you must not deem me guilty of anything sinful or dishonourable.

Were my enemy alive and prosecuting me, I should not be resting content with a defence; I should have shown what a scoundrel he was himself and what scoundrels are those who, while professedly his champions, seek in fact to enrich themselves at

furnished rigging, etc., and pay for the crew, the trierach was frequently forced to expend large sums on repairs and to make up shortages in the payment of his men from his own pocket. The average cost of a Trierarchy was 50 minae.

[c] *i.e.* as Choregus he had paid for the training and equipment of a chorus at one of the dramatic or choral festivals so frequent at Athens and throughout Greece in general.

[d] The Greek is a deliberate jingle, which cannot be rendered convincingly in English. Perhaps ". . . not from litigation, but from application" might serve.

ANTIPHON

ἀπέδειξα¹ ἂν ἀδικοῦντας. ταῦτα μὲν οὖν ἐπιεικέσ-
τερον ἢ δικαιότερον παρήσω· δέομαι δ' ὑμῶν, ὦ
ἄνδρες, τῶν μεγίστων κριταὶ καὶ κύριοι, ἐλεήσαντας
τὴν ἀτυχίαν μου ἰατροὺς γενέσθαι αὐτῆς, καὶ μὴ
συνεπιβάντας τῇ τούτων ἐπιθέσει περιιδεῖν ἀδίκως
καὶ ἀθέως διαφθαρέντα με ὑπ' αὐτῶν.

γ

ΕΚ ΚΑΤΗΓΟΡΙΑΣ Ο ΥΣΤΕΡΟΣ

1 Ἥ τε ἀτυχία ἀδικεῖται ὑπ' αὐτοῦ, ἣν προϊστά-
μενος τῆς κακουργίας ἀφανίσαι τὴν αὐτοῦ μιαρίαν
ζητεῖ· ὑπό τε ὑμῶν οὐκ ἄξιος ἐλεεῖσθαί ἐστιν,
ἀκούσιον μὲν τῷ παθόντι περιθεὶς τὴν συμφοράν,
ἑκουσίως δὲ αὐτὸς εἰς τοὺς κινδύνους καταστάς.
ὡς μὲν οὖν ἀπέκτεινε τὸν ἄνδρα, ἐν τῷ προτέρῳ
λόγῳ ἀπεδείξαμεν· ὡς δὲ οὐκ ὀρθῶς ἀπελογήθη,
νῦν πειρασόμεθα ἐλέγχοντες.

2 Εἴτε γὰρ προσιόντας τινὰς προϊδόντες οἱ ἀποκτείναντες αὐτοὺς ἀπολιπόντες ᾤχοντο φεύγοντες
πρότερον ἢ ἀπέδυσαν, οἱ ἐντυχόντες ἂν αὐτοῖς,²
εἰ καὶ τὸν δεσπότην τεθνεῶτα ηὗρον, τόν γε θερά-

¹ ἀπέδειξα A : ἐπέδειξα N.   ² αὐτοῖς Reiske : αὐτῷ codd.

ᵃ Implying that the defendant's property would be confiscated upon his conviction and a percentage given to the
prosecution. See *Herodes*, § 79, for a similar complaint.
ᵇ The ἀτυχία and ἐλεεῖσθαι of course echo the ἐλεήσαντας
τὴν ἀτυχίαν μου at the close of the preceding speech for the
defence.
ᶜ It is important to distinguish between the various
meanings of ἀκούσιος. Whereas ἑκούσιος is always " willing "
or " voluntary," ἀκούσιος can mean one of three things:
68

my expense over the charge which I am facing.[a]
However, more out of decency than in fairness to
myself, I shall refrain.   Instead, I entreat you,
gentlemen, you who are empowered to decide the
most critical of issues : take pity on my misfortune
and remedy it : do not join my opponents in their
attack : do not allow them to make an end of me
without regard to justice or the powers above.

III

SECOND SPEECH FOR THE PROSECUTION

It is an outrage to "misfortune" that he should use
it to cloak his crime, in the hope of concealing his
defilement.   Neither does he deserve your "pity"[b];
he did not consult his victim's wishes[c] in bringing
doom upon him : whereas he did consult his own
before exposing himself to danger.   We proved in
our first speech that he is the murderer ; we shall now
endeavour to show by examination that his defence
was unsound.

Assume that the murderers hurried off, leaving
their victims before they had stripped them, because
they noticed the approach of passers-by.   Then even
if the persons who came upon them found the master
dead, they would have found the slave still conscious,

(a) "unwilling," (b) "accidental" or "involuntary," (c) "non-
voluntary."   In (a) I do or suffer something against my
will; in (b) I do or suffer something voluntarily, but the
consequences are other than I willed them to be ; in (c) I
do or suffer something unconsciously or in entire ignorance
(e.g. I may be hypnotized and unknowingly commit murder,
or I may be the unsuspecting victim of sudden death, as
here): my will does not enter into the matter at all.

ποντα, ὃς ἔμπνους ἀρθεὶς ἐμαρτύρει¹, ἔτι ἔμφρονα
εὑρόντες, σαφῶς ἀνακρίναντες τοὺς ἐργασαμένους
ἤγγειλαν ἂν ἡμῖν, καὶ οὐχ οὗτος ἂν τὴν αἰτίαν εἶχεν·
εἴτε ἄλλοι τινὲς ἕτερόν τι τοιοῦτον κακουργοῦντες
ὀφθέντες ὑπ' αὐτῶν, ἵνα μὴ γνωσθῶσι διέφθειραν
αὐτούς, ἅμα τῷ τούτων φόνῳ τὸ κακούργημα ἂν
ἐκηρύσσετο καὶ εἰς τούτους ἂν ἡ ὑποψία ἧκεν.

3 Οἵ τε ἧσσον κινδυνεύοντες τῶν μᾶλλον ἐν φόβῳ
ὄντων οὐκ οἶδ' ὅπως ἂν μᾶλλον ἐπεβούλευσαν
αὐτῷ· τοὺς μὲν γὰρ ὅ τε φόβος ἥ τε ἀδικία ἱκανὴ
ἦν παῦσαι τῆς προμηθίας, τοῖς δὲ ὅ τε κίνδυνος ἥ
τε αἰσχύνη μείζων οὖσα τῆς διαφορᾶς, εἰ καὶ
διενοήθησαν ταῦτα πρᾶξαι, ἀρκοῦσα ἦν σωφρονίσαι
τὸ θυμούμενον τῆς γνώμης.

4 Οὐκ ὀρθῶς δὲ τὴν τοῦ ἀκολούθου μαρτυρίαν
ἄπιστον λέγουσιν εἶναι. οὐ γὰρ ἐπὶ ταῖς τοιαύταις
μαρτυρίαις βασανίζονται, ἀλλ' ἐλεύθεροι ἀφίενται·
ὁπόταν δὲ ἢ κλέψαντες ἀπαρνῶνται ἢ συγκρύπτωσι
τοῖς δεσπόταις, τότε βασανίζοντες ἀξιοῦμεν τἀληθῆ²
λέγειν αὐτούς.

5 Οὐδὲ μὴν ἀπογενέσθαι ἢ παραγενέσθαι εἰκότερον
αὐτόν ἐστιν. εἰ γὰρ ἀπεγένετο, τὸν μὲν κίνδυνον

¹ Verba ὃς ἔμπνους ἀρθεὶς ἐμαρτύρει delent nonnulli ut quae
ex a. 9 per errorem irrepserint.
² τἀληθῆ Weidner : ἀληθῆ codd.

ᵃ The evidence of slaves was accepted only under torture.
But the torture could not be inflicted without the consent
of the owner. Hence there are instances of the purchase of
slaves solely for the purpose of extorting evidence from
them (see *Herodes*, § 47, for a case in point). The last half
of the present paragraph envisages a similar purchase in
order to obtain evidence against the slave's former owner.
On the other hand, a slave who defended his master's life at
the risk of his own would more often than not be rewarded
with his freedom; and once he was free, he could not be

as he was picked up alive and gave evidence. They would have questioned him closely and have informed us who the criminals were : so that the defendant would not have been accused. Or assume, on the other hand, that others, who had been seen by the two committing some similar outrage, had murdered them to keep the matter dark. Then news of that outrage would have been published at the same time as the news of the present murder, and suspicion would have fallen on those concerned in it.

Again, how persons whose position was not so serious should have plotted against the dead man sooner than persons who had more to fear, I fail to understand. The fears and sense of injury of the second were enough to put an end to caution ; whereas with the first the risk and disgrace involved, to which their resentment could not blind them, were sufficient to sober the anger in their hearts, even if they had intended to do the deed.

The defence are wrong when they say that the evidence of the slave is not to be trusted ; where evidence of this sort is concerned, slaves are not tortured : they are given their freedom. It is when they deny a theft or conspire with their masters to keep silence that we believe them to tell the truth only under torture.[a]

Again, the probabilities are not in favour of his having been absent from the scene of the crime rather than present at it. In remaining absent he was going

tortured : he gave his evidence in a court of law in the ordinary way. Thus the argument in the present passage is : the dying slave was virtually a free man, as he had given his life for his master ; hence there is no ground whatever for maintaining, as the defendant is doing, that his evidence cannot be accepted in court because it was not given under torture.

τὸν αὐτὸν ἔμελλε καὶ παρὼν κινδυνεύειν—πᾶς γὰρ
αὐτῶν ληφθεὶς τοῦτον ἂν τὸν ἐπιβουλεύσαντα
ἤλεγχεν ὄντα—τὸ δ᾽ ἔργον ἧσσον πράσσειν· οὐδεὶς
γὰρ ὅστις τῶν παρόντων οὐκ ἂν ὀκνηρότερος εἰς
τὴν πρᾶξιν ἦν.

6 Ὡς δ᾽ οὐκ ἐλάσσω ἀλλὰ πολὺ μείζω τὸν ἀπὸ τῆς
γραφῆς κίνδυνον ἢ τόνδε ἡγεῖτο εἶναι, διδάξω.
τὸ μὲν ἁλῶναι καὶ ἀποφυγεῖν ἀμφοτέρας τὰς
διώξεις ἐν ἴσαις ἐλπίσι θῶμεν αὐτῷ εἶναι. μὴ
παραχθῆναι δὲ τὴν γραφὴν οὐδεμίαν ἐλπίδα εἶχε
τούτου γε ζῶντος· οὐ γὰρ ἂν ἐπείθετο αὐτῷ· εἰς
δὲ τόνδε τὸν ἀγῶνα¹ ἥξειν οὐκ ἤλπισε· λήσειν γὰρ
ἐδόκει ἀποκτείνας αὐτόν.

7 Ἀξιῶν δὲ διὰ τὸ φανερὰν εἶναι τὴν ὑποψίαν
αὐτῷ μὴ καταδοκεῖσθαι ὑφ᾽ ὑμῶν, οὐκ ὀρθῶς ἀξιοῖ.
εἰ γὰρ² τοῦτον ἐν τοῖς μεγίστοις κινδύνοις ὄντα
ἱκανὴ ἦν ἡ ὑποψία ἀποτρέψαι³ τῆς ἐπιθέσεως,
οὐδείς γ᾽ ἂν⁴ ἐπεβούλευσεν αὐτῷ· πᾶς γὰρ ἄν τις
τῶν ἧσσον κινδυνευόντων, τὴν ὑποψίαν μᾶλλον
τοῦ κινδύνου φοβούμενος, ἧσσον ἢ οὗτος ἐπέθετο⁵
αὐτῷ.

8 Αἱ δ᾽ εἰσφοραὶ καὶ χορηγίαι εὐδαιμονίας μὲν
ἱκανὸν σημεῖόν ἐστι, τοῦ δὲ μὴ ἀποκτεῖναι τὰ-
ναντία· περὶ γὰρ αὐτῆς τῆς εὐδαιμονίας τρέμων
μὴ ἀποστερηθῇ, εἰκότως μὲν ἀνοσίως δὲ ἀπέκτεινε

¹ ἀγῶνα N : κίνδυνον A.
² εἰ γὰρ Reiske : οὐ γὰρ codd.
³ ἀποτρέψαι Reiske : ἀποστρέψαι codd.
⁴ γ᾽ ἂν Reiske : γὰρ codd.
⁵ ἐπέθετο Maetzner, quem dubitanter secutus sum : ἡγεῖτο
codd.   Fortasse exciderunt nonnulla post αὐτῷ.

---

a i.e. that his position in both suits was completely hope-
less.

72

to run the same risks as he would run if present, as any of his confederates if caught would have shown that it was he who had originated the plot. And not only that : he was going to dispatch the business on hand less satisfactorily, as not one of the criminals taking part would have felt the same enthusiasm for the deed.

Further, he did not believe the danger threatened by the indictment to be less serious than that in which he now stands, but much more so, as I will prove to you. Let us assume that his expectations of conviction or acquittal were the same in the one suit as in the other.[a] Now he had no hope of the indictment being dropped as long as his enemy was alive ; his entreaties would never have been listened to. But he did not, on the other hand, expect to be involved in the present trial, as he thought that he could commit the murder without being found out.

Again, in claiming an acquittal on the ground that he could foresee that he would be suspected, he is arguing falsely. If the defendant, whose position was desperate, could be deterred from violence by the knowledge that suspicion would fall on himself, nobody at all would have planned the crime. Every one who stood in less danger than he would have been more frightened by the certainty of being suspected than by that danger, and would therefore have been less ready than he to use violence.

His contributions to the Treasury and his provision of choruses may be satisfactory evidence of his wealth ; but they are anything but evidence of his innocence. It was precisely his fear of losing his wealth which drove him to commit the murder : though an unscrupulous crime, it was to be expected

73

τὸν ἄνδρα. φάσκων δὲ οὐ τοὺς εἰκότως ἀλλ' ὄντως[1]
ἀποκτείναντας φονέας εἶναι, περὶ μὲν τῶν ἀποκτεινάντων ὀρθῶς λέγει, εἴπερ ἐγένετο φανερὸν
ἡμῖν τίνες ἦσαν οἱ ἀποκτείναντες αὐτόν· μὴ δεδη-
λωμένων δὲ τῶν ἀποκτεινάντων, ὑπὸ τῶν εἰκότων
ἐλεγχόμενος οὗτος ἂν καὶ οὐδεὶς ἕτερος ⟨ὁ⟩[2]
[119] ἀποκτείνας αὐτὸν εἴη. οὐ γὰρ ἐπὶ[3] μαρτύρων ἀλλὰ
κρυπτόμενα πράσσεται τὰ τοιαῦτα.

9   Οὕτω δὲ φανερῶς ἐκ τῆς αὐτοῦ ἀπολογίας ἐλεγ-
χθεὶς διαφθείρας αὐτόν, οὐδὲν ἕτερον ὑμῶν δεῖται
ἢ τὴν αὐτοῦ μιαρίαν εἰς ὑμᾶς αὐτοὺς ἐκτρέψαι.
ἡμεῖς δὲ ὑμῶν δεόμεθα μὲν οὐδέν, λέγομεν δ' ὑμῖν,
εἰ μήτε ἐκ τῶν εἰκότων μήτε ἐκ τῶν μαρτυρου-
μένων οὗτος νῦν ἐλέγχεται, οὐκ ἔστιν ἔτι τῶν
10 διωκομένων ἔλεγχος οὐδείς. σαφῆ μὲν γὰρ τὸν
θάνατον γιγνώσκοντες, φανερῶς δὲ τὰ ἴχνη τῆς
ὑποψίας εἰς τοῦτον φέροντα, πιστῶς δὲ τοῦ ἀκολούθου μαρτυροῦντος, πῶς ἂν δικαίως ἀπολύοιτε
αὐτόν; ἀδίκως δ' ἀπολυομένου τούτου ὑφ' ὑμῶν,
ἡμῖν μὲν προστρόπαιος ὁ ἀποθανὼν οὐκ ἔσται, ὑμῖν
11 δὲ ἐνθύμιος γενήσεται.[4] ταῦτα οὖν εἰδότες βοηθεῖτε μὲν τῷ ἀποθανόντι, τιμωρεῖσθε δὲ τὸν ἀποκτείναντα, ἁγνεύετε δὲ τὴν πόλιν. τρία γὰρ ἀγαθὰ
πράξετε· ἐλάσσους μὲν τοὺς ἐπιβουλεύοντας καταστήσετε, πλείους δὲ τοὺς τὴν εὐσέβειαν ἐπιτηδεύον-
τας, ἀπολύσεσθε[5] δ' αὐτοὶ τῆς ὑπὲρ τούτου
μιαρίας.

---

[1] ἀλλ' ὄντως Funkhänel : ἀλλὰ τοὺς codd.
[2] ὁ add. Weidner.   [3] ἐπὶ Ald. : ὑπὸ codd.
[4] ἀδίκως . . . γενήσεται huc transposuit Jernstedt : ante
σαφῆ μὲν γὰρ . . . habent codd.
[5] ἀπολύσεσθε Sauppe : ἀπολύεσθε codd.

of him. He objects that murderers are not those who were to be expected to commit murder, but those who actually did so. Now he would be quite right, provided that those who did commit it were known to us; but as they are not, proof must be based on what was to be expected: and that shows that the defendant, and the defendant alone, is the murderer. Crimes of this kind are committed in secret, not in front of witnesses.

As he has been proved guilty of the murder so conclusively from his own defence, he is simply asking you to transfer his own defilement to yourselves. We make no requests: we merely remind you that if neither inferences from probability nor the evidence of witnesses prove the defendant guilty to-day, there remains no means of proving any defendant guilty. As you see, there is no doubt about the circumstances of the murder: suspicion points plainly to the defendant [a]: and the evidence of the slave is to be trusted; so how can you in fairness acquit him? And if you acquit him unfairly, it is not upon us that the dead man's curse will lie: it is upon you that he will bring disquiet.[b] So with this in mind come to the victim's aid, punish his murderer, and cleanse the city. Do this, and you will do three beneficial things: you will reduce the number of deliberate criminals; you will increase that of the godfearing; and you will yourselves be rid of the defilement which rests upon you in the defendant's name.

[a] Lit.: "the tracks left by suspicion lead in the direction of the defendant." ὑποψία is half personified and regarded as itself moving towards the person upon whom it is to settle. Cf. τὰ ἴχνη τοῦ φόνου in δ, § 10.

[b] See Introduction, p. 39.

δ

ΕΞ ΑΠΟΛΟΓΙΑΣ Ο ΥΣΤΕΡΟΣ

1 Ἰδοὺ ἐγὼ τῇ τε ἀτυχίᾳ, ἣν οὐ δικαίως αἰτιῶμαι,
ὡς οὗτοί φασιν, ἑκὼν ἐμαυτὸν ἐγχειρίζω, τῇ τε
τούτων ἔχθρᾳ, δεδιὼς μὲν τὸ μέγεθος τῆς διαβολῆς
αὐτῶν, πιστεύων δὲ τῇ ὑμετέρᾳ γνώμῃ τῇ τε
ἀληθείᾳ τῶν ἐξ ἐμοῦ πραχθέντων. ἀποστερού-
μενος δὲ ὑπ᾽ αὐτῶν μηδὲ τὰς παρούσας ἀτυχίας
ἀνακλαύσασθαι πρὸς ὑμᾶς, ἀπορῶ εἰς ἥντινα
2 ἄλλην σωτηρίαν χρή με καταφυγεῖν. καινότατα
γὰρ δή, εἰ χρὴ καινότατα μᾶλλον ἢ κακουργότατα
εἰπεῖν, διαβάλλουσί με. κατήγοροι γὰρ καὶ τιμωροὶ
φόνου προσποιούμενοι εἶναι, ὑπεραπολογούμενοι
τῆς ἀληθοῦς ὑποψίας ἁπάσης, διὰ τὴν ἀπορίαν τοῦ
ἀποκτείναντος αὐτόν, ἐμὲ φονέα φασὶν εἶναι· δρῶντες δὲ τἀναντία ὧν προστέτακται αὐτοῖς, φανερὸν
ὅτι ἀδίκως ἐμὲ μᾶλλον ἀποκτεῖναι ζητοῦσιν ἢ τὸν
3 φονέα τιμωρεῖσθαι. ἐμὲ δὲ προσῆκεν οὐδὲν ἄλλο
ἢ πρὸς τὴν μαρτυρίαν τοῦ ἀκολούθου ἀπολογηθῆναι·
οὐ γὰρ μηνυτὴς οὐδ᾽ ἐλεγκτὴρ τῶν ἀποκτεινάντων
εἰμί, ἀλλὰ διωκόμενος ἀποκρίνομαι. ὅμως δὲ
περιεργαστέον, ἵνα ἐκ παντὸς τρόπου τούτους τε
ἐπιβουλεύοντάς μοι ἐμαυτόν τε ἀπολυόμενον ἐπι-
4 δείξω τῆς ὑποψίας. τὴν μὲν οὖν ἀτυχίαν ᾗ με
διαβάλλουσιν, εἰς εὐτυχίαν αἰτοῦμαι μεταστῆναι·
ἀξιῶ δ᾽ ὑμᾶς ἀπολύσαντάς με μακαρίσαι μᾶλλον
ἢ καταλαβόντας ἐλεῆσαι.

Φασὶ δὲ τῶν μὲν ἐντυχόντων παιομένοις αὐτοῖς
οὐδένα ὅντινα οὐκ εἰκότερον εἶναι σαφῶς πυθό-

IV

SECOND SPEECH FOR THE DEFENCE

See, I have chosen to place myself at the mercy of the misfortune which you have been told that I blame unfairly, and at the mercy of my enemies here ; for much as I am alarmed by their wholesale distortion of the facts, I have faith in your judgement and in the true story of my conduct ; though if the prosecution deny me even the right of lamenting before you the misfortunes which have beset me, I do not know where to fly for refuge, so utterly startling—or should I say villainous ?—are the methods which are being used to misrepresent me. They pretend that they are prosecuting to avenge a murder; yet they defend all the true suspects, and then assert that I am a murderer because they cannot find the criminal. The fact that they are flatly disregarding their appointed duty shows that their object is not so much to punish the murderer as to have me wrongfully put to death. I myself ought simply to be replying to the evidence of the attendant, for I am not here to inform you of the murderers or prove them guilty : I am answering a charge which has been brought against me. However, in order to make it completely clear that the prosecution have designs upon my life and that no suspicion can attach itself to me, I must, quite unnecessarily, go further. I ask only that my misfortune, which is being used to discredit me, may turn to good fortune ; and I call upon you to acquit and congratulate me rather than condemn and pity me.

According to the prosecution, those who came up during the assault were one and all more likely to

μενον τοὺς διαφθείραντας αὐτοὺς εἰς οἶκον ἀγγεῖ-
5 λαι ἢ ἀπολιπόντα οἴχεσθαι. ἐγὼ δὲ οὐδένα οὕτω
θερμὸν καὶ ἀνδρεῖον ἄνθρωπον εἶναι δοκῶ, ὅντινα
οὐκ ἂν ἀωρὶ τῶν νυκτῶν[1] νεκροῖς ἀσπαίρουσι συν-
τυχόντα πάλιν ὑποστρέψαντα φεύγειν μᾶλλον ἢ
πυνθανόμενον τοὺς κακούργους περὶ τῆς ψυχῆς
κινδυνεῦσαι. τούτων δὲ μᾶλλον ἃ εἰκὸς ἦν δρασάν-
των, οἱ μὲν ἐπὶ τοῖς ἱματίοις διαφθείραντες αὐτοὺς
οὐκ ἂν ἔτι εἰκότως ἀφίοιντο, ἐγὼ δὲ ἀπήλλαγμαι
τῆς ὑποψίας.

6 Εἰ δὲ ἐκηρύσσοντο ἢ μὴ ἄλλοι τινὲς κακοῦργοι
ἅμα τῷ τούτων φόνῳ, τίς οἶδεν; οὐδενὶ γὰρ ἐπι-
μελὲς ἦν σκοπεῖν ταῦτα. ἀφανοῦς δὲ ὄντος τοῦ
κηρύγματος, οὐδὲ ὑπὸ τούτων τῶν κακούργων
ἄπιστον διαφθαρῆναι αὐτόν.

7
[120] Τοῦ δὲ θεράποντος πῶς χρὴ πιστοτέραν τὴν
μαρτυρίαν ἢ τῶν ἐλευθέρων ἡγεῖσθαι; οἱ μὲν γὰρ
ἀτιμοῦνταί τε καὶ χρήμασι ζημιοῦνται, ἐὰν μὴ
τἀληθῆ δοκῶσι μαρτυρῆσαι· ὁ δὲ οὐκ ἔλεγχον
παρασχὼν οὐδὲ βάσανον—ποῦ[2] δίκην δώσει; ἢ τίς[3]
ἔλεγχος ἔσται; ἀκινδύνως τε οὗτός γε μέλλων

---

[1] τῶν νυκτῶν N : τῆς νυκτὸς A.
[2] ποῦ Reiske : οὐ A : τι οὐ N pr., τινα οὐ N corr.[2]
[3] ἢ τίς Reiske : εἴ τις codd.

---

[a] Immediately intended as an answer to γ, § 2 *init.*, where
it is maintained that if the murder was the work of footpads,
the passers-by who appeared on the scene would have
obtained information about their identity from the victims.
The reply here given is: (*a*) if a group of footpads had in
fact been engaged in the murder, the passers-by would have
run away. (*b*) The passers-by would in that case have been
unable to supply information about the identity of the
criminals. (*c*) As no passer-by has come forward with such
information, all the passers-by must have run away. (*d*) It
follows from (*a*) that the murderers must have been a group

inquire exactly who the murderers were and carry the news to the victims' home than to take to their heels and leave them to their fate. But I, for my part, do not believe that there exists a human being so reckless or so brave that, on coming upon men writhing in their death agony in the middle of the night, he would not turn round and run away rather than risk his life by inquiring after the malefactors responsible. Now since it is more likely that the passers-by behaved in a natural manner, you cannot logically continue to treat the footpads who murdered the pair for their clothing as innocent, any more than suspicion can still attach itself to me.[a]

As to whether or not proclamation of some other outrage was made at the time of the murder, who knows? Nobody felt called upon to inquire; and as the question is an open one, it is quite possible to suppose that the malefactors concerned in such an outrage committed the murder.

Why, moreover, should the evidence of the slave be thought more trustworthy than that of free men?[b] Free men are disfranchised and fined, should their evidence be considered false; whereas this slave, who gave us no opportunity of either cross-examining or torturing him—when can he be punished? Nay, when can he be cross-examined? He could make a state-

of footpads. A portentous *petitio principii*, which of course entirely neglects the fact that passers-by had come forward with very different information.

[b] Or " of the free men." A puzzling sentence which has been treated by some as evidence of the incompleteness of this *Tetralogy* in its present form. No " free men " have given evidence in favour of the defence, and we can hardly suppose that the speaker is referring to himself. I have taken the words in a purely general sense, although I feel it to be unsatisfactory.

μαρτυρεῖν, οὐδὲν θαυμαστὸν ἔπαθεν ὑπὸ τῶν κυρίων
ἐχθρῶν μοι ὄντων πεισθεὶς καταψεύδεσθαί μου·
ἐγώ τε ἀνόσι᾽ ἂν πάσχοιμι, εἰ μὴ πιστῶς κατα-
μαρτυρηθεὶς διαφθαρείην ὑφ᾽ ὑμῶν.

8 Μὴ παραγενέσθαι δέ με τῷ φόνῳ ἀπιστότερον ἢ
παραγενέσθαι φασὶν εἶναι. ἐγὼ δ᾽ οὐκ ἐκ τῶν
εἰκότων ἀλλ᾽ ἔργῳ δηλώσω οὐ παραγενόμενος.
ὁπόσοι γὰρ δοῦλοί μοι ἢ δοῦλαί εἰσι, πάντας παρα-
δίδωμι βασανίσαι· καὶ ἐὰν μὴ φανῶ ταύτῃ τῇ
νυκτὶ ἐν οἴκῳ καθεύδων ἢ ἐξελθών ποι,[1] ὁμολογῶ
φονεὺς εἶναι. ἡ δὲ νὺξ οὐκ ἄσημος· τοῖς γὰρ
Διιπολείοις ὁ ἀνὴρ ἀπέθανε.

9 Περὶ δὲ τῆς εὐδαιμονίας, ἧς ἕνεκα τρέμοντά μέ
φασιν εἰκότως ἀποκτεῖναι αὐτόν, πολὺ τἀναντία
ἐστί. τοῖς μὲν γὰρ ἀτυχοῦσι νεωτερίζειν[2] συμφέρει·
ἐκ γὰρ τῶν μεταβολῶν ἐπίδοξος ἡ δυσπραγία
μεταβάλλειν αὐτῶν ἐστι· τοῖς δ᾽ εὐτυχοῦσιν ἀτρεμί-
ζειν καὶ φυλάσσειν τὴν παροῦσαν εὐπραγίαν.
μεθισταμένων γὰρ τῶν πραγμάτων δυστυχεῖς ἐξ
εὐτυχούντων καθίστανται.

10 Ἐκ δὲ τῶν εἰκότων προσποιούμενοί με ἐλέγχειν,
οὐκ εἰκότως ἀλλ᾽ ὄντως φονέα μέ φασι τοῦ ἀνδρὸς
εἶναι. τὰ δὲ εἰκότα ἄλλα πρὸς ἐμοῦ μᾶλλον ἀποδέδεικται ὄντα. ὅ τε γὰρ καταμαρτυρῶν μου
ἄπιστος ἐλήλεγκται ὤν, ὅ τε ἔλεγχος οὐκ ἔστι· τά

---

[1] ποι Reiske: που codd.
[2] ἀτυχοῦσι νεωτερίζειν Ald.: ἀτυχοῦσιν ἑταιρίζειν codd.

---

[a] A festival in honour of Zeus, celebrated in the first week
of June.

[b] The ἄλλα is answered by ὅ τε γὰρ, which explains away
the one fact which might have been unfavourable to the de-

ment in perfect safety; so it is only natural that he was induced to lie about me by his masters, who are enemies of mine. On the other hand, it would be nothing short of impious were I put to death by you on evidence which was untrustworthy.

According to the prosecution, it is harder to believe that I was absent from the scene of the crime than that I was present at it. But I myself, by using not arguments from probability but facts, will prove that I was not present. All the slaves in my possession, male or female, I hand over to you for torture; and if you find that I was not at home in bed that night, or that I left the house, I agree that I am the murderer. The night can be identified, as the murder was committed during the Diipoleia.[a]

As regards my wealth, my fears for which are said to have furnished a natural motive for the murder, the facts are precisely the opposite. It is the unfortunate who gain by arbitrary methods, as they expect changes to cause a change in their own sorry plight. It pays the fortunate to safeguard their prosperity by living peaceably, as change turns their good fortune into bad.

Again, although the prosecution pretend to base their proof of my guilt on inferences from probability, they assert not that I am the probable, but that I am the actual murderer. Moreover, those inferences[b] have in fact been proved to be in my favour rather than theirs—for not only has the witness for the prosecution been proved untrustworthy, but he cannot

fence. The connexion of thought is: "The inferences are all in my favour; and, after all, it is only inferences that we have to consider in this case. There can be no question of evidence of fact, as the one possible witness has been proved prejudiced." The construction is thus elliptical.

τε τεκμήρια ἐμά, οὐ τούτων¹ ὄντα ἐδήλωσα· τά τε
ἴχνη τοῦ φόνου οὐκ εἰς ἐμὲ φέροντα, ἀλλ' εἰς τοὺς
ἀπολυομένους ἀποδέδεικται ὑπ' αὐτῶν. πάντων
δὲ τῶν κατηγορηθέντων ἀπίστων ἐλεγχθέντων, οὐκ
ἐὰν ἀποφύγω οὐκ ἔστιν ἐξ ὧν ἐλεγχθήσονται οἱ
κακουργοῦντες, ἀλλ' ἐὰν καταληφθῶ,² οὐδεμία ἀπολογία τοῖς διωκομένοις ἀρκοῦσά ἐστιν.

11 Οὕτω δὲ ἀδίκως διώκοντές με, αὐτοὶ μὲν ἀνοσίως
ἀποκτεῖναι ζητοῦντες καθαροί φασιν εἶναι, ἐμὲ δέ,
ὃς εὐσεβεῖν ὑμᾶς πείθω, ἀνόσια δρᾶν λέγουσιν. ἐγὼ
δὲ καθαρὸς ὢν πάντων τῶν ἐγκλημάτων ὑπὲρ
⟨μὲν⟩³ ἐμαυτοῦ ἐπισκήπτω αἰδεῖσθαι τὴν τῶν μηδὲν ἀδικούντων εὐσέβειαν, ὑπὲρ δὲ τοῦ ἀποθανόντος
ἀναμιμνήσκων τὴν ποινὴν παραινῶ ὑμῖν μὴ τὸν
ἀναίτιον καταλαβόντας τὸν αἴτιον ἀφεῖναι· ἀποθανόντος γὰρ ἐμοῦ οὐδεὶς ἔτι τὸν αἴτιον ζητήσει.

12 ταῦτα οὖν σεβόμενοι ὁσίως καὶ δικαίως ἀπολύετέ
με, καὶ μὴ μετανοήσαντες τὴν ἁμαρτίαν γνῶτε·
ἀνίατος γὰρ ἡ μετάνοια τῶν τοιούτων ἐστίν.

---

¹ τούτων Jernstedt : τούτου codd.
² καταληφθῶ Spengel : ἐλεγχθῶ codd.
³ μὲν add. Bekker.

ᵃ τεκμήρια are here distinguished from εἰκότα ; but the distinction is hardly observed by Antiphon in practice.

be cross-examined. Similarly, I have shown that the presumptions [a] are in my favour and not in favour of the prosecution ; and the trail of guilt has been proved to lead not to me, but to those whom the prosecution are treating as innocent. Thus the charges made against me have been shown without exception to be unfounded. But it does not follow that there is no way of convicting criminals, if I am acquitted; it does follow that there is no way of effectively defending persons accused, if I am sentenced.

You see how unjustifiably my accusers are attacking me. Yet notwithstanding the fact that it is they who are endeavouring to have me put to death in so impious a fashion, they maintain that they themselves are guiltless ; according to them, it is I who am acting impiously—I, who am urging you to show yourselves godfearing men. But as I am innocent of all their charges, I adjure you on my own behalf to respect the righteousness of the guiltless, just as on the dead man's behalf I remind you of his right to vengeance and urge you not to let the guilty escape by punishing the innocent ; once I am put to death, no one will continue the search for the criminal. Respect these considerations, and satisfy heaven and justice by acquitting me. Do not wait until remorse proves to you your mistake ; remorse in cases such as this has no remedy.

III

THE SECOND TETRALOGY

INTRODUCTORY NOTE

THE second *Tetralogy* is concerned not with establishing facts but with interpreting them. X was practising with the javelin in the gymnasium. Y ran in front of the target just as X was making a cast, and was killed. Y's father prosecutes X for accidentally causing his son's death.

To understand the case as developed in the four speeches made by the prosecution and defence, it is necessary to bear in mind the oddly inelastic conception of blood-guilt upon which they are based. Homicide, whether wilful or not, involves blood-guilt ; and that blood-guilt must rest upon someone ; in the last resort it may even be assumed to rest upon the inanimate instrument of death. Here, then, the question at issue is not whether X is guilty of wilful murder or manslaughter, nor again whether Y met his end by misadventure. It is acknowledged from the start that Y's death was purely accidental. The point is that a life has been lost ; and as only two persons, X and Y, were concerned, the blood-guilt must rest upon the one or the other. If it can be shown to rest upon Y himself, due atonement has already been made, as Y has paid with his life. If, however, it proves to rest upon X, X must be punished. Otherwise X's defilement will bring down divine vengeance not only upon himself but upon the community at large.

SECOND TETRALOGY

Since an accident involves ἁμαρτία on the part of the person responsible, the object of the prosecution and defence throughout is to prove that the ἁμαρτία lay with the other side. ἁμαρτία is the failure to perform an act as one intended to perform it, owing to circumstances outside of one's control; it is " error." But owing to the conception of blood-guilt mentioned, a ἁμάρτημα which results in another's death carries a certain moral responsibility with it. It was only the fact that the agent was performing the act at all that made it possible for the error to occur : and so he must bear the blame. In γ, § 8 it is implied that at least in some cases a ἁμάρτημα is due to the direct intervention of heaven ; the agent has committed a sin, and the divine Nemesis takes the form of his being so blinded that he becomes guilty of a ἁμάρτημα, for which he is punished ; it is the familiar notion of ὕβρις and ἄτη thinly disguised. Presumably in other cases the ἁμαρτία is due simply to τύχη ; but the author of the *Tetralogy* is not concerned to work out the theory in detail.

ΤΕΤΡΑΛΟΓΙΑ Β

α

ΚΑΤΗΓΟΡΙΑ ΦΟΝΟΥ ΑΚΟΥΣΙΟΥ

1   Τὰ μὲν ὁμολογούμενα τῶν πραγμάτων ὑπό τε
τοῦ νόμου κατακέκριται ὑπό τε τῶν ψηφισαμένων,
οἳ κύριοι πάσης τῆς πολιτείας εἰσίν· ἐὰν δέ τι
ἀμφισβητήσιμον ᾖ, τοῦτο ὑμῖν, ὦ ἄνδρες πολῖται,
προστέτακται διαγνῶναι. οἶμαι μὲν οὖν οὐδὲ
ἀμφισβητήσειν πρὸς ἐμὲ τὸν διωκόμενον· ὁ γὰρ
παῖς μου ἐν γυμνασίῳ ἀκοντισθεὶς διὰ τῶν πλευρῶν
[121] ὑπὸ τούτου τοῦ μειρακίου παραχρῆμα ἀπέθανεν.
2 ἑκόντα μὲν οὖν οὐκ ἐπικαλῶ ἀποκτεῖναι, ἄκοντα
δέ. ἐμοὶ δὲ οὐκ ἐλάσσω τοῦ ἑκόντος ἄκων τὴν
συμφορὰν κατέστησε. τῷ δὲ ἀποθανόντι αὐτῷ μὲν
οὐδὲν ἐνθύμιον, τοῖς δὲ ζῶσι προσέθηκεν. ὑμᾶς
δὲ ἀξιῶ ἐλεοῦντας μὲν τὴν ἀπαιδίαν τῶν γονέων,
οἰκτίροντας δὲ τὴν ἄωρον τοῦ ἀποθανόντος τελευ-
τήν, εἴργοντας ὧν ὁ νόμος εἴργει τὸν ἀποκτείναντα
μὴ περιορᾶν ἅπασαν τὴν πόλιν ὑπὸ τούτου μι-
αινομένην.

PROSECUTION FOR ACCIDENTAL HOMICIDE

CASES in which the facts are agreed upon are settled in advance either by the law or by the statutes of the Assembly, which between them control every branch of civic life. But should matter for dispute occur, it is your task, gentlemen, to give a decision. However, I do not imagine that any dispute will in fact arise between the defendant and myself. My son was struck in the side by a javelin thrown by yonder lad in the gymnasium, and died instantly. I accuse him not of killing my son deliberately, but of killing him by accident—though the loss which I have suffered is not thereby lessened. But if he has not caused the dead boy himself disquiet, he has caused disquiet to the living [a]; and I ask you to pity that dead boy's childless parents : to show your sorrow for his own untimely end : to forbid his slayer to set foot where he is forbidden to set foot by the law [b] : and to refuse to allow him to defile the whole city.

[b] See *Choreutes*, Introd. §§ 34 *sqq.* for the meaning of εἴργεσθαι τῶν νομίμων.

β

ΑΠΟΛΟΓΙΑ ΦΟΝΟΥ ΑΚΟΥΣΙΟΥ

1 Νῦν δὴ φανερόν μοι ὅτι αὐταὶ αἱ συμφοραὶ καὶ
χρεῖαι τούς τε ἀπράγμονας εἰς ἀγῶνας ⟨κατα-
στῆναι⟩[1] τούς τε ἡσυχίους τολμᾶν τά τε ἄλλα
παρὰ φύσιν λέγειν καὶ δρᾶν βιάζονται. ἐγὼ γὰρ
ἥκιστα τοιοῦτος ὢν καὶ βουλόμενος εἶναι, εἰ μὴ
πολύ γε ἔψευσμαι, ὑπ' αὐτῆς τῆς συμφορᾶς ἠναγ-
κάσθην νῦν παρὰ τὸν ἄλλον τρόπον ὑπὲρ πραγμάτων ἀπολογεῖσθαι, ὧν ἐγὼ χαλεπῶς μὲν τὴν
ἀκρίβειαν ἔγνων, ἔτι δὲ ἀπορωτέρως διάκειμαι ὡς
2 χρὴ ὑμῖν ἑρμηνεῦσαι ταῦτα. ὑπὸ δὲ σκληρᾶς
ἀνάγκης βιαζόμενος, καὶ αὐτὸς εἰς τὸν ὑμέτερον
ἔλεον, ὦ ἄνδρες δικασταί, καταπεφευγὼς δέομαι
ὑμῶν, ἐὰν ἀκριβέστερον ἢ ὡς σύνηθες ὑμῖν δόξω
εἰπεῖν, μὴ διὰ τὰς προειρημένας τύχας ⟨δυσχερῶς⟩[2]
ἀποδεξαμένους μου τὴν ἀπολογίαν δόξῃ καὶ μὴ
ἀληθείᾳ τὴν κρίσιν ποιήσασθαι· ἡ μὲν γὰρ δόξα
τῶν πραχθέντων πρὸς τῶν λέγειν δυναμένων ἐστίν,
ἡ δὲ ἀλήθεια πρὸς τῶν δίκαια καὶ ὅσια πρασ-
σόντων.

3 Ἐδόκουν μὲν οὖν[3] ἔγωγε ταῦτα παιδεύων τὸν
υἱὸν ἐξ ὧν μάλιστα τὸ κοινὸν ὠφελεῖται, ἀμφοῖν τι
ἡμῖν ἀγαθὸν ἀποβήσεσθαι· συμβέβηκε δέ μοι πολὺ
παρὰ γνώμην τούτων. τὸ γὰρ μειράκιον οὐχ ὕβρει
οὐδὲ ἀκολασίᾳ, ἀλλὰ μελετῶν μετὰ τῶν ἡλίκων

---

[1] καταστῆναι add. Maetzner.   [2] δυσχερῶς add. Gebauer.
[3] μὲν οὖν edd.: μὲν Α, γοῦν Ν.

---

[a] For τολμᾶν used absolutely in this sense cf. γ. 2.

II

REPLY TO A CHARGE OF ACCIDENTAL HOMICIDE

I now see that sheer misfortune and necessity can force those who hate litigation to appear in court and those who love peace to show boldness[a] and generally belie their nature in word and deed; for I myself, who, unless I am sorely mistaken, am very far from finding or wanting to find such a task congenial, have to-day been forced by sheer misfortune to depart from my habits and appear as defendant in a case in which I found it hard enough to arrive at the exact truth, but which leaves me still more perplexed when I consider how I should present it to you. I am driven by pitiless necessity : and I, like my opponents, gentlemen of the jury, seek refuge in your sympathy. I beg of you : if my arguments appear more subtle than those generally presented to you, do not allow the circumstances already mentioned[b] so to prejudice you against my defence as to make you base your verdict upon apparent fact instead of upon the truth ; apparent fact puts the advantage with the clever speaker, but truth with the man who lives in justice and righteousness.

In training my son in those pursuits from which the state derives most benefit I imagined that both of us would be rewarded ; but the result has sadly belied my hopes. For the lad—not from insolence or wantonness, but while at javelin-practice in the gymnasium

[b] *i.e.* the fact that he was not accustomed to appearing in courts of law, which should make it *a priori* probable that he is a simple and straightforward man who would not resort to subtleties of argument if his case were a sound one.

91

ἀκοντίζειν ἐν[1] τῷ γυμνασίῳ ἔβαλε μέν, οὐκ ἀπέκτεινε δὲ οὐδένα κατά γε τὴν ἀλήθειαν ὧν ἔπραξεν, ἄλλου δ' εἰς αὑτὸν ἁμαρτόντος εἰς ἀκουσίους αἰτίας ἦλθεν.

4 Εἰ μὲν γὰρ τὸ ἀκόντιον ἔξω τῶν ὅρων τῆς αὑτοῦ πορείας ἐπὶ τὸν παῖδα ἐξενεχθὲν ἔτρωσεν αὐτόν, οὐδεὶς ⟨ἂν⟩[2] ἡμῖν λόγος ὑπελείπετο μὴ φονεῦσιν[3] εἶναι· τοῦ δὲ παιδὸς ὑπὸ τὴν τοῦ ἀκοντίου φορὰν ὑποδραμόντος καὶ τὸ σῶμα προστήσαντος, ⟨ὃ μὲν ἐκωλύθη⟩[4] τοῦ σκοποῦ τυχεῖν, ὃ δὲ ὑπὸ τὸ ἀκόντιον ὑπελθὼν ἐβλήθη, καὶ τὴν αἰτίαν οὐχ 5 ἡμετέραν οὖσαν προσέβαλεν ἡμῖν. διὰ δὲ τὴν ὑποδρομὴν βληθέντος τοῦ παιδός, τὸ μὲν μειράκιον οὐ δικαίως ἐπικαλεῖται, οὐδένα γὰρ ἔβαλε τῶν ἀπὸ τοῦ σκοποῦ ἀφεστώτων· ὁ δὲ παῖς εἴπερ ἑστὼς φανερὸς ὑμῖν ἐστι μὴ βληθείς, ἑκουσίως ⟨δ'⟩[5] ὑπὸ τὴν φορὰν τοῦ ἀκοντίου ὑπελθών, ἔτι σαφεστέρως δηλοῦται διὰ τὴν αὑτοῦ ἁμαρτίαν ἀποθανών· οὐ γὰρ ἂν ἐβλήθη ἀτρεμίζων καὶ μὴ διατρέχων.

6 Ἀκουσίου δὲ τοῦ φόνου ἐξ ἀμφοῖν ὑμῖν ὁμολογουμένου γενέσθαι, ἐκ τῆς ἁμαρτίας, ὁποτέρου αὐτῶν ἐστιν, ἔτι γε[6] σαφέστερον ⟨ἂν⟩[7] ὁ φονεὺς

---

[1] ἐν Bekker : ἐπὶ codd. [2] ἂν add. Dobree.
[3] φονεῦσιν Bekker : φονεὺς codd.
[4] ὃ μὲν ἐκωλύθη add. Reiske.
[5] δ' add. Blass.
[6] ἔτι γε Sauppe : ἔτι δὲ codd. δὲ del. Dobree.
[7] ἂν add. Dobree.

---

[a] Two interpretations of the text as it stands in the mss. are possible: (1) "He threw (his spear), it is true, but killed no one"; (2) "He struck (someone), it is true, but did not kill him." (1) gives good sense; but elsewhere in the *Tetralogy* βάλλειν means "to hit," not "to throw." (2) avoids

with his fellows—made a hit, it is true, but killed no one, if one considers his true part in the matter[a] : he accidentally[b] incurred the blame for the error of another which affected that other's own person.

Had the boy been wounded because the javelin had travelled in his direction outside the area appointed for its flight, we should be left unable to show that we had not caused his death. But he ran into the path of the javelin and placed his person in its way. Hence my son was prevented from hitting the target : while the boy, who moved into the javelin's path, was struck, thereby causing us to be blamed for what we did not do. It was because he ran in front of the javelin that the boy was struck. The lad is therefore accused without just cause, as he did not strike anyone standing clear of the target. At the same time, since it is plain to you that the boy was not struck while standing still, but was struck only after deliberately moving into the path of the javelin, you have still clearer proof that his death was due to an error on his own part. Had he stood still and not run across, he would not have been struck.

Both sides are agreed, as you see, that the boy's death was accidental ; so by discovering which of the two was guilty of error, we should prove still more

this difficulty; but it has been urged (*e.g.* by Blass, who favours emendation) that the words τὸν μὲν βαλόντα καὶ ἀποκτείναντα οὔτε τρῶσαι οὔτε ἀποκτεῖναί φησι in γ. 5 (*cf.* also γ. 6 *sub fin.*) prove that the speaker in the present passage had not admitted that X struck Y. The contradiction, however, is only apparent. The speaker here is saying in effect that the responsibility for the blow must rest with Y, although X dealt it; in γ. 5 and 6 his opponents argue that the responsibility must rest with X, because X dealt it.

[b] For ἀκουσίως *cf.* p. 68, note *c.*

ANTIPHON

ἐλεγχθείη. οἵ τε γὰρ ἁμαρτάνοντες ὡς[1] ἂν ἐπι-
νοήσωσί τι[2] δρᾶσαι, οὗτοι πράκτορες τῶν ἀκουσίων
εἰσίν· οἵ τε[3] ἑκούσιόν τι δρῶντες ἢ πάσχοντες, οὗτοι
τῶν παθημάτων αἴτιοι γίγνονται.

7   Τὸ μὲν τοίνυν μειράκιον περὶ οὐδένα οὐδὲν ἥμαρτεν. οὔτε γὰρ ἀπειρημένον ἀλλὰ προστεταγμένον
ἐξεμελέτα, οὔτε ἐν γυμναζομένοις ἀλλ' ἐν τῇ τῶν
ἀκοντιζόντων τάξει ἠκόντιζεν, οὔτε τοῦ σκοποῦ
ἁμαρτών, εἰς τοὺς ἀφεστῶτας ἀκοντίσας, τοῦ
παιδὸς ἔτυχεν, ἀλλὰ πάντα ὀρθῶς ὡς ἐπενόει δρῶν
ἔδρασε μὲν οὐδὲν ἀκούσιον, ἔπαθε δὲ διακωλυθεὶς
[122]   τοῦ σκοποῦ τυχεῖν.

'Ο δὲ παῖς βουλόμενος προδραμεῖν, τοῦ καιροῦ[4]
8   διαμαρτὼν ἐν ᾧ διατρέχων οὐκ ἂν ἐπλήγη, περι-
έπεσεν οἷς οὐκ ἤθελεν, ἀκουσίως δὲ ἁμαρτὼν εἰς
ἑαυτὸν οἰκείαις συμφοραῖς κέχρηται, τῆς δ' ἁμαρτίας τετιμωρημένος ἑαυτὸν ἔχει τὴν δίκην, οὐ
συνηδομένων μὲν οὐδὲ συνεθελόντων ἡμῶν, συν-
αλγούντων δὲ καὶ συλλυπουμένων.

Τῆς δὲ ἁμαρτίας εἰς τοῦτον[5] ἡκούσης, τό ⟨τ'⟩[6]
ἔργον οὐχ ἡμέτερον ἀλλὰ τοῦ ἐξαμαρτόντος ἐστί,
τό τε πάθος εἰς τὸν δράσαντα ἐλθὸν ἡμᾶς μὲν
ἀπολύει τῆς αἰτίας, τὸν δὲ δράσαντα δικαίως ἅμα
τῇ ἁμαρτίᾳ τετιμώρηται.

[1] ὡς Wilamowitz : ὢν codd.
[2] ὢν . . . [τι] δρᾶσαι Maetzner.   [3] τε Spengel : δὲ codd.
[4] καιροῦ Spengel : χώρου codd.
[5] τοῦτον Reiske : τοῦτο codd.   [6] τ' add. Spengel.

---

[a] The argument is : (1) It is agreed that death was accidental. (2) But accidents are always due to ἁμαρτία on the
part of someone. (3) Therefore if the person guilty of
ἁμαρτία is discovered, we have eo ipso discovered the person
responsible for the boy's death.

conclusively who killed him. For it is those guilty of error in carrying out an intended act who are responsible for accidents [a] : just as it is those who voluntarily do a thing or allow it to be done to them who are responsible for the effects suffered.

Now the lad, on his side, was not guilty of error in respect of anyone : in practising he was not doing what he was forbidden but what he had been told to do, and he was not standing among those engaged in gymnastics when he threw the javelin, but in his place among the other throwers : nor did he hit the boy because he missed the target and sent his javelin instead at those standing clear. He did everything correctly, as he intended ; and thus he was not the cause of any accident, but the victim of one, in that he was prevented from hitting the target.

The boy, on the other hand, who wished to run forward, missed the moment at which he could have crossed without being hit, with results which he by no means desired. He was accidentally guilty of an error which affected his own person, and has thus met with a disaster for which he had himself alone to thank. He has punished himself for his error, and is therefore duly requited ; not that we rejoice at or approve of it—far from it : we feel both sympathy and sorrow.

It is thus the dead boy who proves to have been guilty of error ; so the act which caused his death is to be attributed not to us, but to him, the party guilty of error : just as the recoiling of its effects upon the agent not only absolves us from blame, but has caused the agent to be punished as he deserved directly his error was committed.

9 Ἀπολύει δὲ καὶ ὁ νόμος ἡμᾶς, ᾧ πιστεύων, εἴργοντι μήτε ἀδίκως μήτε δικαίως ἀποκτείνειν, ὡς φονέα με διώκει. ὑπὸ μὲν γὰρ τῆς αὐτοῦ τοῦ τεθνεῶτος ἁμαρτίας ὅδε ἀπολύεται μηδὲ ἀκουσίως ἀποκτεῖναι αὐτόν· ὑπὸ δὲ τοῦ διώκοντος οὐδ' ἐπικαλούμενος ὡς ἑκὼν ἀπέκτεινεν, ἀμφοῖν ἀπολύεται τοῖν ἐγκλημάτοιν, ⟨μήτ' ἄκων⟩[1] μήθ' ἑκὼν ἀποκτεῖναι.

10 Ἀπολυόμενος δὲ ὑπό τε τῆς ἀληθείας τῶν πραχθέντων ὑπό τε τοῦ νόμου καθ' ὃν διώκεται, οὐδὲ τῶν ἐπιτηδευμάτων ἕνεκα δίκαιοι τοιούτων κακῶν ἀξιοῦσθαί ἐσμεν. οὗτός τε γὰρ ἀνόσια πείσεται τὰς οὐ προσηκούσας φέρων ἁμαρτίας, ἐγώ τε μᾶλλον μὲν οὐδέν, ὁμοίως δὲ τούτῳ ἀναμάρτητος ὤν, εἰς πολλαπλασίους τούτου συμφορὰς ἥξω· ἐπί τε γὰρ τῇ τούτου διαφθορᾷ ἀβίωτον τὸ λειπόμενον τοῦ βίου διάξω, ἐπί τε τῇ ἐμαυτοῦ ἀπαιδίᾳ ζῶν ἔτι κατορυχθήσομαι.[2]

11 Ἐλεοῦντες οὖν τοῦδε μὲν τοῦ νηπίου τὴν ἀναμάρτητον συμφοράν, ἐμοῦ δὲ τοῦ γηραιοῦ καὶ ἀθλίου τὴν ἀπροσδόκητον κακοπάθειαν, μὴ καταψηφισάμενοι δυσμόρους ἡμᾶς καταστήσητε, ἀλλ' ἀπολύοντες εὐσεβεῖτε. ὅ τε γὰρ ἀποθανὼν συμφοραῖς περιπεσὼν οὐκ ἀτιμώρητός ἐστιν, ἡμεῖς τε οὐ δίκαιοι τὰς τούτων ἁμαρτίας συμφέρειν

12 ἐσμέν. τήν τε οὖν εὐσέβειαν τούτων τῶν πραχθέντων καὶ τὸ δίκαιον αἰδούμενοι ὁσίως καὶ δικαίως ἀπολύετε ἡμᾶς, καὶ μὴ ἀθλιωτάτω δύο,

---

[1] μήτ' ἄκων add. Ald.

Furthermore, our innocence is attested by the law upon which my accuser relies in charging me with the boy's death, the law which forbids the taking of life whether wrongfully or otherwise. For the fact that the victim himself was guilty of error clears the defendant here of having killed him by accident: while his accuser does not even suggest that he killed him deliberately. Thus he is cleared of both charges, of killing the boy by accident and of killing him deliberately.

Not only do the true facts of the case and the law under which he is being prosecuted attest my son's innocence ; but our manner of life is equally far from justifying such harsh treatment of us. Not only will it be an outrage, if my son is to bear the blame for errors which he did not commit ; but I myself, who am equally innocent, though assuredly not more so, will be visited with woes many times more bitter. Once my son is lost, I shall pass the rest of my days longing for death : once I am left childless, mine will be a life within the tomb.

Have pity, then, on this child, the victim of calamity, though guilty of no error : and have pity on me, an old man in distress, stricken thus suddenly with sorrow. Do not bring a miserable fate upon us by condemning us : but show that you fear God by acquitting us. The dead boy is not unavenged for the calamity which befell him : nor ought we ourselves to share the responsibility for errors due to our accusers. So respect the righteousness which the facts before you have revealed : respect justice : and acquit us as godly and just men should. Do not bring upon a father and a son, two of the most

---

[2] ἔτι κατορυχθήσομαι Reiske : ἐπικατορ. codd.

πατέρα καὶ παῖδα, ἀώροις συμφοραῖς περιβάλητε.[1]

γ
ΕΚ ΚΑΤΗΓΟΡΙΑΣ Ο ΥΣΤΕΡΟΣ

1 Ὅτι μὲν αὐτὴ ἡ χρεία παρὰ φύσιν καὶ λέγειν καὶ
δρᾶν ἅπαντας ἀναγκάζει, ἔργῳ καὶ οὐ λόγῳ δοκεῖ
μοι σημαίνειν οὗτος· ἥκιστα γὰρ ἔν γε τῷ ἔμπροσθεν χρόνῳ ἀναιδὴς καὶ τολμηρὸς ὤν, νῦν
ὑπ' αὐτῆς τῆς συμφορᾶς ἠνάγκασται λέγειν οἷα
2 οὐκ ἄν ποτε ᾤμην ἐγὼ τοῦτον εἰπεῖν. ἐγώ τε γὰρ
πολλῇ ἀνοίᾳ χρώμενος οὐκ ἂν ὑπέλαβον τοῦτον
ἀντειπεῖν· οὐδὲ γὰρ ἂν ἕνα λόγον ἀντὶ δυοῖν[2] λέξας
τὸ ἥμισυ τῆς κατηγορίας ἐμαυτὸν ἂν ἀπεστέρησα·
οὗτός τε μὴ τολμῶν οὐκ ἂν προεῖχε τῷ διπλασίῳ
μου, ἕνα μὲν πρὸς ἕνα λόγον ἀπολογηθείς, ἃ δὲ
κατηγόρησεν ἀναποκρίτως εἰπών.
3 Τοσοῦτον δὲ προέχων ἐν τοῖς λόγοις ἡμῶν, ἔτι
δὲ ἐν οἷς ἔπρασσε πολλαπλάσια τούτων, οὗτος μὲν
οὐχ ὁσίως δεῖται ὑμῶν εὐμενῶς[3] τὴν ἀπολογίαν
ἀποδέχεσθαι αὐτοῦ· ἐγὼ δὲ δράσας[4] μὲν οὐδὲν

---

[1] περιβάλητε N, περιβάλοιτε A.
[2] ἀντὶ δυοῖν Reiske: ἀντιδοὺς ἢ codd.
[3] εὐμενῶς Reiske: συχνῶς codd.
[4] δὲ δράσας Reiske: δ' ἔδρασα codd.

---

[a] I take the speaker to mean : " The case seemed so
simple that instead of developing any argument in my first
speech for the prosecution, I merely stated the bare facts.
The defendant, however, has made an elaborate reply, and
will doubtless do the same again in his second speech ; this
is equivalent to his making two speeches to my one. Further,
he will be able to use his second speech to answer my one

98

wretched of beings, sorrows which the years of
neither can well bear.

III

SECOND SPEECH FOR THE PROSECUTION

That sheer necessity can force all men to belie their
nature in both word and deed is a fact of which the
defendant seems to me to be giving very real proof.
Whereas in the past he was the last to show impudence or audacity, his very misfortune has to-day
forced him to say things which I for one would never
have expected of him. I, in my great folly, imagined
that he would not reply ; otherwise I would not
have deprived myself of half of my opportunities
as prosecutor by making only one speech instead
of two ; and he, but for his audacity, would not
have had the twofold advantage over me of using one
speech to answer the one speech for the prosecution
and making his accusations when they could not be
answered.[a]

With his great advantage over us in the matter
of the speeches, and with the far greater one
which his methods have given him in addition,[b] it
is outrageous that the accused should entreat you to
listen kindly to his defence. I myself, on the other

serious speech for the prosecution (ἕνα πρὸς ἕνα λόγον ἀπολογηθείς) ; while I cannot effectively answer the attack
which he made upon me in his first speech (ἃ κατηγόρησεν
ἀναποκρίτως εἰπών), because, as prosecutor, I must now devote
myself to attacking him."

[b] Referring apparently to the artifices employed by the
defence for working upon the feelings of the court (cf. β. 1 ff.).

κακόν, παθὼν δὲ ἄθλια καὶ δεινά, καὶ νῦν ἔτι
δεινότερα τούτων, ἔργῳ καὶ οὐ λόγῳ εἰς τὸν ὑμέτερον ἔλεον καταπεφευγὼς δέομαι ὑμῶν, ὦ ἄνδρες
ἀνοσίων ἔργων τιμωροί, ὁσίων δὲ διαγνώμονες, μὴ
⟨παρ'⟩[1] ἔργα φανερὰ ὑπὸ πονηρᾶς λόγων ἀκριβείας
πεισθέντας ψευδῆ τὴν ἀλήθειαν τῶν πραχθέντων
4 ἡγήσασθαι· ἡ μὲν γὰρ πιστότερον ἢ ἀληθέστερον
σύγκειται, ἡ δ' ἀδολώτερον καὶ ἀδυνατώτερον
λεχθήσεται.

Τῷ μὲν οὖν δικαίῳ πιστεύων ὑπερορῶ τῆς ἀπο-
λογίας· τῇ δὲ σκληρότητι τοῦ δαίμονος ἀπιστῶν
ὀρρωδῶ μὴ οὐ μόνον τῆς χρείας τοῦ παιδὸς ἀπο-
[123] στερηθῶ, ἀλλὰ καὶ αὐθέντην προσκαταγνωσθέντα
5 ὑφ' ὑμῶν ἐπίδω αὐτόν. εἰς τοῦτο γὰρ τόλμης καὶ
ἀναιδείας ἥκει, ὥστε τὸν μὲν βαλόντα καὶ ἀποκτείναντα οὔτε τρῶσαι οὔτε ἀποκτεῖναί φησι, τὸν
δὲ οὔτε ψαύσαντα τοῦ ἀκοντίου οὔτε ἐπινοήσαντα
ἀκοντίσαι, ἁπάσης μὲν γῆς ἁμαρτόντα, πάντων δὲ
σωμάτων, διὰ τῶν ἑαυτοῦ πλευρῶν διαπῆξαι τὸ
ἀκόντιον λέγει. ἐγὼ δὲ ἑκουσίως κατηγορῶν ἀποκτεῖναι αὐτὸν πιστότερος ἄν μοι δοκῶ εἶναι ἢ
οὗτος, ⟨ὃς⟩[2] μήτε βαλεῖν μήτε ἀποκτεῖναί φησι τὸ
μειράκιον.

6 Ὁ μὲν γὰρ ἐν τούτῳ τῷ καιρῷ κελευόμενος[3] ὑπὸ
τοῦ παιδοτρίβου, ὃς ὑπεδέχετο τοῖς ἀκοντίζουσι
τὰ ἀκόντια, ἀναιρεῖσθαι, διὰ τὴν τοῦ βαλόντος
ἀκολασίαν πολεμίῳ τῷ τούτου βέλει περιπεσών,
οὐδὲν οὐδ' εἰς ἕν'[4] ἁμαρτών, ἀθλίως ἀπέθανεν· ὁ δὲ

---

[1] παρ' addidi : παρὰ τὰ Gernet : alii alia.   [2] ὃς add. Ald.
[3] κελευόμενος scripsi : καλούμενος codd. ex δ. 4. Verba ὃς
ὑπεδέχετο κτλ. potius corrupta esse plerique arbitrantur. Sic
ὡς ὑπεδέχοιτο Blass, ᾧ ὑπεδέχετο Thalheim.   ἀναιρεῖσθαι secl.
Franke.   [4] ἕν' Franke : ἕν codd.

hand, far from causing any harm, have been the victim of cruel affliction, and am to-day being treated still more cruelly. It is as one who seeks more than a pretended refuge in your sympathy that I make my own request of you. You who take vengeance for unrighteous deeds and determine wherein is righteousness, do not, I beg of you, let worthless subtleties of speech induce you to disregard plain facts and treat the truth as false; for such subtleties result in a tale more plausible than true, whereas the truth, when told, will be less guileful and therefore less convincing.

My faith in justice, then, enables me to despise his defence. Yet my distrust of the pitiless will of fate makes me fear that I may not only lose the benefit of my child, but that I may see him convicted by you of taking his own life in addition. For the defendant has had the audacity and shamelessness to say that he who struck and killed neither wounded nor killed, whereas he who neither touched the javelin nor had any intention of throwing it missed every other point on earth and every other person, and pierced his own side with the javelin. Why, I should myself sound more convincing, I think, were I accusing the lad of wilful murder, than does the defendant in claiming that the lad neither struck nor killed.

My son was bidden at that moment by the master in charge, who was taking the javelins of the throwers into his keeping, to pick them up; but thanks to the wantonness of him who cast it, he was greeted by yonder lad's cruel weapon; though guilty of error in respect of no single person, he died a piteous death. The lad, on the other hand,

101

περὶ τὸν τῆς ἀναιρέσεως καιρὸν πλημμελήσας, οὐ
τοῦ σκοποῦ τυχεῖν ἐκωλύθη, ἀλλ' ἄθλιον καὶ πικρὸν
σκοπὸν ἐμοὶ ἀκοντίσας, ἑκὼν μὲν οὐκ ἀπέκτεινεν,
μᾶλλον δὲ ἑκὼν ἢ οὔτ' ἔβαλεν οὔτ' ἀπέκτεινεν.

7 Ἀκουσίως δὲ οὐχ ἧσσον ἢ ἑκουσίως ἀποκτείναντες[1] μου τὸν παῖδα, τὸ παράπαν δ' ἀρνούμενοι[2]
μὴ ἀποκτεῖναι αὐτόν, οὐδ' ὑπὸ τοῦ νόμου καταλαμβάνεσθαί φασιν,[3] ὃς ἀπαγορεύει μήτε δικαίως
μήτε ἀδίκως ἀποκτείνειν. ἀλλὰ τίς ὁ βαλών; εἰς
τίν' ὁ φόνος ἀνήκει;[4] εἰς τοὺς θεωμένους ἢ εἰς
τοὺς παιδαγώγους, ὧν οὐδεὶς οὐδὲν κατηγορεῖ;
οὐ γὰρ ἀφανὴς ἀλλὰ καὶ λίαν φανερὸς ἔμοιγε
αὐτοῦ ὁ θάνατός ἐστιν. ἐγὼ δὲ τὸν νόμον ὀρθῶς
ἀγορεύειν φημὶ τοὺς ἀποκτείναντας κολάζεσθαι·
ὅ τε γὰρ ἄκων ἀποκτείνας ἀκουσίοις κακοῖς περιπεσεῖν δίκαιός ἐστιν, ὅ τε διαφθαρεὶς οὐδὲν ἧσσον
ἀκουσίως ἢ ἑκουσίως βλαφθεὶς ἀδικοῖτ' ἂν ἀτιμώρητος γενόμενος.

8 Οὐ δίκαιος δὲ ἀποφυγεῖν ἐστι διὰ τὴν ἀτυχίαν
τῆς ἁμαρτίας. εἰ μὲν γὰρ ὑπὸ μηδεμιᾶς ἐπιμελείας
τοῦ θεοῦ ἡ ἀτυχία γίγνεται, ἁμάρτημα οὖσα τῷ
ἁμαρτόντι συμφορὰ δικαία γενέσθαι ἐστίν· εἰ
δὲ αὖ θεία[5] κηλὶς τῷ δράσαντι προσπίπτει ἀσε-

---

[1] ἀποκτείναντες Blass : -αντος A pr. N : ἀπέκτεινε A corr.[2]
[2] ἀρνούμενοι Blass : ἀρνουμένου A pr. N : -μενος A corr.[2]

who mistook the moment at which the javelins were being picked up, was not prevented from making a hit. To my bitter sorrow, he struck a target; and although he did not kill my son deliberately, there are better grounds for maintaining that he did than for asserting that he neither struck nor killed.

Although it was by accident that they killed my son, the effects were the same as those of wilful murder. Yet they deny that they killed him at all, and even maintain that they are not amenable to the law which forbids the taking of life whether wrongfully or otherwise. Then who did throw the javelin? To whom is the boy's death in fact to be attributed? To the spectators or the masters in charge—whom no one accuses at all? The circumstances of my son's death are no mystery: to me, for one, they are only too clear; and I maintain that the law is right when it orders the punishment of those who have taken life; not only is it just that he who killed without meaning to kill should suffer punishment which he did not mean to incur; but it would also be an injustice to the victim, whose injury is not lessened by being accidental, were he deprived of vengeance.

Nor does he deserve acquittal because of his misfortune in committing the error which he did. If, on the one hand, the misfortune is not due to any dispensation of heaven, then, as an error pure and simple, it is right that it should prove disastrous to him who was guilty of it; and if, on the other hand, a defilement from heaven has fallen upon the slayer by

---

[3] φασιν Blass: φησιν codd.

[4] τίς ὁ βαλών; ἐς τίν' ὁ φόνος ἀνήκει Bekker: τίς ὁ βάλλων ἐστίν; ὁ φόνος ὃν ἀνήκει codd.: βαλὼν A corr.[2]

[5] εἰ δὲ αὖ θεία Jernstedt: ἡ δὲ ἀλήθεια A pr. N: ἡ δὲ θεία A corr.[2]

βοῦντι, οὐ δίκαιον τὰς θείας προσβολὰς διακωλύειν
γίγνεσθαι.

9 Ἔλεξαν δὲ καὶ ὡς οὐ πρέπει χρηστὰ ἐπιτηδεύον-
τας αὐτοὺς κακῶν ἀξιοῦσθαι· ἡμεῖς δὲ πῶς ἂν
πρέποντα πάσχοιμεν, εἰ μηδὲν ὑποδεέστερα τούτων
μελετῶντες θανάτῳ ζημιούμεθα;

Φάσκων δὲ ἀναμάρτητος εἶναι, καὶ ἀξιῶν τὰς
συμφορὰς τῶν ἁμαρτόντων εἶναι καὶ μὴ εἰς τοὺς
ἀναμαρτήτους ἐκτρέπεσθαι, ὑπὲρ ἡμῶν λέγει. ὅ
τε γὰρ παῖς μου εἰς οὐδένα οὐδὲν ἁμαρτών, ὑπὸ
τούτου τοῦ μειρακίου ἀποθανών, ἀδικοῖτ' ἂν
ἀτιμώρητος γενόμενος· ἐγώ τε τοῦδε μᾶλλον
ἀναμάρτητος ὢν δεινὰ πείσομαι, ἃ ὁ νόμος ἀπο-
δίδωσί μοι μὴ τυχὼν παρ' ὑμῶν.

10 Ὡς δὲ οὐδὲ τῆς ἁμαρτίας οὐδὲ τοῦ[1] ἀκουσίως
ἀποκτεῖναι, ἐξ ὧν αὐτοὶ λέγουσιν, ἀπολύεται, ἀλλὰ
κοινὰ ἀμφότερα ταῦτα ἀμφοῖν αὐτοῖν ἐστι, δηλώσω.
εἴπερ ὁ παῖς διὰ τὸ ὑπὸ τὴν φορὰν τοῦ ἀκοντίου
ὑπελθεῖν καὶ μὴ ἀτρέμας ἑστάναι φονεὺς αὐτὸς
αὑτοῦ δίκαιος εἶναί ἐστιν, οὐδὲ τὸ μειράκιον καθαρὸν τῆς αἰτίας ἐστίν, ἀλλ' εἴπερ τούτου μὴ ἀκοντί-
ζοντος ἀλλ' ἀτρέμα ἑστῶτος ἀπέθανεν ὁ παῖς. ἐξ
ἀμφοῖν δὲ τοῦ φόνου γενομένου, ὁ μὲν παῖς εἰς αὑτὸν
ἁμαρτὼν μᾶλλον ἢ κατὰ τὴν ἁμαρτίαν ἑαυτὸν τε-

[1] οὐδὲ τοῦ Sauppe : τοῦδε τοῦ A pr. N : τοῦδε τῷ A corr.[2]

---

[a] i.e. it might be argued that the lad was ἀτυχής in committing the ἁμαρτία which he did, and therefore deserves
acquittal. But the prosecution produce a dilemma : (a) If
the ἀτυχία was a piece of divine retribution for some past
offence, he deserves punishment all the more, as it is God's
will that he should be punished. (b) If it is not due to God,
then to say that the lad was the victim of ἀτυχία is only a more

reason of some act of sin, then it is wrong for us to impede the visitation of God.[a]

They also maintained that it is wrong for those who have lived as honourably as they to be treated with severity. But what of us ? Should we be treated aright, if we are punished with death when our life has been as praiseworthy as theirs ?

When he argues that he is not guilty of error and claims that the consequences must be borne by those who are, instead of being diverted to the innocent, he is pleading our case for us. Not only would it be an injustice to my son, who was killed by yonder lad, though guilty of error in respect of no one, were he deprived of vengeance ; but it will be an outrage, if I myself, who am even more guiltless than he, fail to obtain from you the recompense which the law assigns me.

Further, the defence's own statements show that the accused cannot be acquitted either of error or of accidentally taking life, but that he and my son are equally guilty of both ; I will prove this.[b] Assume that because my son moved into the path of the javelin instead of standing still, he deserves to be treated as his own slayer. Then the lad is not free from blame either ; he is only innocent if he was standing still and not throwing his javelin when the boy was killed. The boy's death was therefore due to both of them. Now the boy, whose error affected his own person, has punished himself even

---

polite way of saying that he was guilty of ἁμαρτία (ἁμάρτημα οὖσα), and we are back where we started.

[b] An attempt to show the two-edged character of the arguments used by the defence. " If," say the prosecution, " the dead boy has been proved guilty by the defence, then *eo ipso* the lad has been proved guilty too."

τιμώρηται, τέθνηκε γάρ, ὁ δὲ συλλήπτωρ καὶ
κοινωνὸς εἰς τοὺς οὐ προσήκοντας τῆς ἁμαρτίας
γενόμενος πῶς δίκαιος ἀζήμιος ἀποφυγεῖν ἐστιν;

11 Ἐκ δὲ τῆς αὐτῶν τῶν ἀπολογουμένων ἀπολογίας
μετόχου τοῦ μειρακίου τοῦ φόνου ὄντος, οὐκ ἂν
δικαίως οὐδὲ ὁσίως ἀπολύοιτε αὐτόν. οὔτε γὰρ
ἡμεῖς, οἱ διὰ τὴν τούτων ἁμαρτίαν διαφθαρέντες,
αὐθένται καταγνωσθέντες ὅσια ἀλλ' ἀνόσι' ἂν
πάθοιμεν ὑφ' ὑμῶν· οὔθ' οἱ θανατώσαντες ἡμᾶς μὴ
εἰργόμενοι τῶν προσηκόντων †εὐσεβοῖντ' ἂν†[1] ὑπὸ
τῶν ἀπολυσάντων τοὺς ἀνοσίους.

Πάσης δ' ὑπὲρ πάντων τῆς κηλῖδος εἰς ὑμᾶς
ἀναφερομένης, πολλὴ εὐλάβεια[2] ὑμῖν τούτων ποιητέα
ἐστί· καταλαβόντες μὲν γὰρ αὐτὸν καὶ εἴρξαντες
ὧν ὁ νόμος εἴργει καθαροὶ τῶν ἐγκλημάτων ἔσεσθε,
12 ἀπολύσαντες δὲ ὑπαίτιοι καθίστασθε. τῆς οὖν
[124] ὑμετέρας εὐσεβείας ἕνεκα καὶ τῶν νόμων ἀπάγοντες τιμωρεῖσθε αὐτόν, ⟨καὶ⟩[3] αὐτοί τε μὴ
μεταλάβητε τῆς τούτου μιαρίας, ἡμῖν τε τοῖς
γονεῦσιν, οἳ ζῶντες κατορωρύγμεθα[4] ὑπ' αὐτοῦ,
δόξῃ γοῦν ἐλαφροτέραν τὴν συμφορὰν καταστή-
σατε.

---

[1] Verba εὐσεβοῖντ' ἂν ut corrupta obelis inclusi.
[2] εὐλάβεια A corr.[2]: εὐσέβεια A pr. N.
[3] καὶ add. Blass.
[4] κατορωρύγμεθα Ald.: κατωρύγμεθα codd.

---

[a] The passive of εὐσεβεῖν, while exceedingly rare (it occurs
otherwise only at [Plato,] *Axiochus* 4, as far as I know), might
be supported here by the parallel use of the passive of ἀσεβεῖν
in the phrase τοὺς ἄνω θεοὺς ἀσεβεῖσθαι, [Lys.] ii. 7. But
εὐσεβοῖντ' ἂν could only mean " would be reverenced "; and
that clearly gives an impossible sense to the passage, which

more harshly than that error warranted : for he has
lost his life. So what right has his accomplice, who
joined him in committing his unfortunate error, to
escape unpunished ?

The accused have themselves proved by their
defence that the lad had a share in the slaying. So,
as just and godfearing men, you cannot acquit him.
If we, who have lost our life through the defendants'
error, were found guilty of having taken it ourselves,
it would be an act not of righteousness but of wickedness on your part : and if those responsible for our
death were not prohibited from setting foot where
they should not, [it would be an outrage against
heaven :]ᵃ you would have acquitted persons stained
with guilt.

As the whole of the defilement, upon whomsoever
it rests, is extended to you, you must take the
greatest care. If you find him guilty and prohibit
him from setting foot where the law forbids him to
set foot, you will be free of the charges brought to-day ;
but if you acquit him, you become liable to them. So
satisfy the claims of heaven and the laws by taking
him and punishing him. Do not share his blood-guilt
yourselves : but let me, the parent whom he has sent
to a living death, at least appear to have had my
sorrow lightened.

requires something like " would be rendered εὐσεβεῖς," or
" would be treated as εὐσέβεια requires," if it is to be intelligible. Conceivably there is a lacuna before εὐσεβοῖντ' ἄν,
which might be filled by τὰ ἄξια ἂν φέροιντο τῆς αὐτῶν
ἁμαρτίας· οὐδὲ αὖ αὐτοὶ οἱ θεοὶ or something similar, giving
εὐσεβοῖντ' ἄν the subject it requires. But this would destroy
the balance of the two halves of the sentence as they stand
in the MSS.; and it is more probable that the words
εὐσεβοῖντ' ἄν are themselves corrupt.

δ

ΕΞ ΑΠΟΛΟΓΙΑΣ Ο ΥΣΤΕΡΟΣ

1 Τοῦτον μὲν εἰκὸς πρὸς τὴν ἑαυτοῦ κατηγορίαν
προσέχοντα τὸν νοῦν μὴ μαθεῖν τὴν ἀπολογίαν μου·
ὑμᾶς δὲ χρή, γιγνώσκοντας[1] ὅτι ἡμεῖς μὲν οἱ ἀντίδικοι κατ᾽ εὔνοιαν κρίνοντες τὸ πρᾶγμα εἰκότως
δίκαια ἑκάτεροι αὑτοὺς οἰόμεθα λέγειν, ὑμᾶς δὲ
2 ὁσίως ὁρᾶν προσήκει τὰ πραχθέντα· ἐκ τῶν λεγομένων γὰρ ἡ ἀλήθεια σκεπτέα αὐτῶν ἐστίν. ἐγὼ
δέ, εἰ μέν τι ψεῦδος εἴρηκα, ὁμολογῶ καὶ τὰ ὀρθῶς
εἰρημένα προσδιαβάλλειν ἄδικα εἶναι· εἰ δὲ ἀληθῆ
μέν, λεπτὰ δὲ καὶ ἀκριβῆ, οὐκ ἐγὼ ὁ λέγων ἀλλ᾽
ὁ πράξας τὴν ἀπέχθειαν αὐτῶν δίκαιος φέρεσθαί
ἐστι.
3 Θέλω δὲ ὑμᾶς πρῶτον μαθεῖν, ὅτι οὐκ ἐάν
τις φάσκῃ ἀποκτεῖναι, τοῦτ᾽ ἔστιν, ἀλλ᾽ ἐάν τις
ἐλεγχθῇ. οὗτος δὲ ὁμολογῶν τὸ ἔργον ὡς ἡμεῖς
λέγομεν γενέσθαι, ὑπὲρ τοῦ ἀποκτείναντος ἀμφισ-
βητεῖ, ὃν ἀδύνατον ἀλλαχόθεν ἢ ἐκ τῶν πραχθέν-
4 των δηλοῦσθαι. σχετλιάζει δὲ κακῶς ἀκούειν
φάσκων τὸν παῖδα, εἰ μήτε ἀκοντίσας μήτ᾽ ἐπι-
νοήσας αὐθέντης ὢν ἀποδέδεικται, καὶ οὐ πρὸς τὰ
λεγόμενα ἀπολογεῖται. οὐ γὰρ ἀκοντίσαι οὐδὲ
βαλεῖν αὐτόν φημι τὸν παῖδα, ἀλλ᾽ ὑπὸ τὴν πληγὴν

---

[1] γινώσκοντας A pr. N : γινώσκειν A corr.[2]

[a] The addition of this sentence is necessary for a proper
understanding of the connexion of thought. The γάρ is
explanatory of the words ὑμᾶς δὲ χρή in l. 3.

108

IV

SECOND SPEECH FOR THE DEFENCE

While it is only to be expected that the pre-occupation of my opponent with his speech for the prosecution should prevent his understanding my defence, the same is not true of yourselves. You should bear in mind that while we, the interested parties, take a biassed view of the case, each naturally thinking that his own version of it is fair, your duty is to consider the facts conscientiously; and so you must give your attention to me as much as you did to him[a]: as it is in what is said that the true facts are to be sought. For my part, if I have told any falsehoods, I am content that you should treat the truth which I have spoken as itself a piece of equally dishonest pleading. On the other hand, if my arguments have been honest, but close and subtle, it is not I who used them, but he whose conduct made them necessary, upon whom the displeasure which they have caused should properly fall.

I would have you understand to begin with that it requires not mere assertion, but proof, to show that someone has killed someone else. Now our accuser agrees with us as to how the accident happened, but disagrees as to the person responsible; yet it is only from what happened that that person can be deter-mined. He complains bitterly, because, according to him, it is a slur upon his son's memory that he should have been proved a slayer when he neither threw the javelin nor had any intention of so doing. That com-plaint is not an answer to my arguments. I am not maintaining that his son threw the javelin or struck

109

τοῦ ἀκοντίου ὑπελθόντα οὐχ ὑπὸ τοῦ μειρακίου
ἀλλ' ὑφ' ἑαυτοῦ διαφθαρῆναι· οὐ γὰρ ἀτρεμίζων
ἀπέθανε. τῆς δὲ διαδρομῆς αἰτίας ταύτης γιγνο-
μένης, εἰ μὲν ὑπὸ τοῦ παιδοτρίβου καλούμενος
διέτρεχεν, ὁ παιδοτρίβης ἂν ἀποκτείνας αὐτὸν εἴη,
εἰ δ' ὑφ' ἑαυτοῦ πεισθεὶς ὑπῆλθεν, αὐτὸς ὑφ'
ἑαυτοῦ διέφθαρται.

5 Θέλω δὲ μὴ πρότερον ἐπ' ἄλλον λόγον ὁρμῆσαι,
ἢ τὸ ἔργον ἔτι φανερώτερον καταστῆσαι, ὁποτέρου
αὐτῶν ἐστί. τὸ μὲν μειράκιον οὐδενὸς μᾶλλον τῶν
συμμελετώντων ἐστὶ τοῦ σκοποῦ ἁμαρτόν, οὐδὲ
τῶν ἐπικαλουμένων τι διὰ τὴν αὐτοῦ ἁμαρτίαν
δέδρακεν· ὁ δὲ παῖς οὐ ταὐτὰ τοῖς συνθεωμένοις
δρῶν, ἀλλ' εἰς τὴν ὁδὸν τοῦ ἀκοντίου ὑπελθών,[1]
σαφῶς δηλοῦται παρὰ τὴν αὐτοῦ ἁμαρτίαν περισ-
σοτέροις ἀτυχήμασι[2] τῶν ἀτρεμιζόντων περιπεσών.
ὁ μὲν γὰρ ἀφεὶς οὐδὲν ἂν ἥμαρτε, μηδενὸς ὑπὸ τὸ
βέλος ὑπελθόντος αὐτῷ· ὁ δ' οὐκ[3] ἂν ἐβλήθη μετὰ
τῶν θεωμένων ἑστώς.

6 Ὡς δ' οὐδενὸς μᾶλλον τῶν συνακοντιζόντων
μέτοχός ἐστι τοῦ φόνου, διδάξω. εἰ γὰρ διὰ τὸ
τοῦτον ἀκοντίζειν ὁ παῖς ἀπέθανε, πάντες ἂν οἱ
συμμελετῶντες συμπράκτορες εἶεν τῆς αἰτίας·

---

[1] ὑπελθών N : ἐπελθών A.
[2] ἀτυχήμασι A corr.[2] : ἁμαρτήμασι A pr. N.
[3] αὐτῷ· ὁ δ' οὐκ Blass : ὑπελθόντος· αὐτὸς δ' οὐκ codd.

---

[a] It is at first sight odd that so little is made of the part
played by the παιδοτρίβης, who would be a vitally important
witness, were the case being tried in a modern court of law.
But it should not be forgotten that the writer is throughout
endeavouring to exhibit the possibilities of the πίστις ἔντεχνος
as such.   See Gen. Introd. p. 34.

[b] A highly artificial piece of sophistry.   (1) The lad did

110

himself. I am maintaining that since he moved
within range of the javelin, his death was due not to
the lad, but to himself ; for he was not killed standing
in his place. As this running across was his undoing, it
follows that if it was at his master's summons that he
ran across, the master would be the person responsible
for his death [a] ; but if he moved into the way of his
own accord, his death was due to himself.

Before proceeding to any further argument, I
wish to show still more clearly which of the two was
responsible for the accident. The lad no more missed
the target than any of those practising with him [b] :
nor has he rendered himself guilty of any of the acts
with which he is charged owing to error on his own
part. On the other hand, the boy did not do the
same as the other onlookers ; he moved into the
javelin's path. And this is clear proof that it was
through his own error that he met with a disaster
which those who stood still did not. The thrower
would not have been guilty of an error in any
respect,[c] had no one moved into the path of his
spear : while the boy would not have been hit, had
he remained in his place among the onlookers.

Further, my son was not more concerned in the
boy's death than any one of those throwing javelins
with him, as I will show. If it was owing to the fact
that my son was throwing a javelin that the boy was
killed, then all those practising with him must share
in the guilt of the deed, as it was not owing to their

exactly the same as the other throwers : so, as they did not
miss the target, neither can he have done. (2) On the
other hand, the boy did *not* do the same as the other spectators ; and so he is *not* blameless, as they are.

[c] A curious admission that the μειράκιον was guilty of
ἁμαρτία to at least some extent.

οὗτοι γὰρ οὐ διὰ τὸ μὴ ἀκοντίζειν οὐκ ἔβαλον
αὐτόν, ἀλλὰ διὰ τὸ μηδενὶ[1] ὑπὸ τὸ ἀκόντιον ὑπ-
ελθεῖν· ὁ δὲ νεανίσκος οὐδὲν περισσότερον[2] τούτων
ἁμαρτών, ὁμοίως τούτοις οὐκ ἂν ἔβαλεν αὐτὸν
ἀτρέμα σὺν τοῖς θεωμένοις ἑστῶτα.

7 Ἔστι δὲ οὐδὲ τὸ ἁμάρτημα τοῦ παιδὸς μόνον,
ἀλλὰ καὶ ἡ ἀφυλαξία. ὁ μὲν γὰρ οὐδένα ὁρῶν
διατρέχοντα, πῶς ἂν ἐφυλάξατο μηδένα βαλεῖν; ὁ
δ' ἰδὼν τοὺς ἀκοντίζοντας εὐπετῶς ἂν ἐφυλάξατο
μὴ διαδραμεῖν[3]· ἐξῆν γὰρ αὐτῷ ἀτρέμα ἑστάναι.

8 Τὸν δὲ νόμον ὃν παραφέρουσιν, ἐπαινεῖν δεῖ.
ὀρθῶς γὰρ καὶ δικαίως τοὺς ἀκουσίως ἀποκτείναντας ἀκουσίοις παθήμασι κολάζει. τὸ μὲν οὖν μειράκιον ἀναμάρτητον ὂν οὐκ ἂν δικαίως ὑπὲρ τοῦ
ἁμαρτόντος κολάζοιτο· ἱκανὸν γὰρ αὐτῷ ἐστι τὰς
αὑτοῦ ἁμαρτίας φέρειν· ὁ δὲ παῖς ταῖς αὑτοῦ
ἁμαρτίαις διαφθαρείς, ἅμα ἥμαρτέ τε καὶ ὑφ' ἑαυτοῦ ἐκολάσθη. κεκολασμένου δὲ τοῦ ἀποκτείναντος, οὐκ ἀτιμώρητος ὁ φόνος ἐστίν.

9 Ἔχοντός γε δὴ τὴν δίκην τοῦ φονέως,[4] οὐκ ἐὰν
[125] ἀπολύσητε ἡμᾶς, ἀλλ' ἐὰν καταλάβητε, ἐνθύμιον
ὑπολείψεσθε. ὁ μὲν γὰρ[5] αὐτὸς τὰς αὑτοῦ ἁμαρτίας
φέρων, οὐδενὶ οὐδὲν προστρόπαιον καταλείπει· ὁ δὲ
καθαρὸς τῆς αἰτίας ὢν[6] ἐὰν διαφθαρῇ, τοῖς κατα-
λαμβάνουσι μεῖζον τὸ ἐνθύμιον γενήσεται.

---

[1] μηδενὶ Reiske: μηδένα codd.
[2] περισσότερον Sakorraphos, coll. Plat. *Ap.* 20 c (cf. § 5. supra): περισσὸν codd.
[3] μὴ διαδραμεῖν Wilamowitz: μὴ βληθῆναι Kayser: μηδένα μὴ βαλεῖν codd.
[4] Verba ἔχοντος . . . φονέως huc rettulit Jernstedt. Prae-cedentibus adiungunt codd.
[5] γὰρ om. N.   [6] ὢν Scheibe: ὃς δὲ NA.

failure to throw that they did not strike him, but owing to the fact that he did not move into the path of the javelin of any one of them. Similarly the young man, who was no more guilty of error than they, would not have hit the boy any more than they did, had the boy stood still with the onlookers.

Again, not only was the boy guilty of the error committed ; he was also to blame for the failure to take due precautions. My son saw no one running across, so how could he have taken precautions against striking anyone ? The boy, on the other hand, upon seeing the throwers, might easily have guarded against running across, as he was quite at liberty to remain standing still.

The law which they quote is a praiseworthy one ; it is right and fair that it should visit those who have killed without meaning to do so with chastisement which they did not mean to incur. But the lad is not guilty of error ; and it would therefore be unjust that he should suffer for him who is. It is enough that he should bear the consequences of his own errors. On the other hand, the boy, who perished through his own error, punished himself as soon as he had committed that error. And as the slayer has been punished, the slaying has not gone unavenged.

The slayer has paid the penalty ; so it is not by acquitting us, but by condemning us that you will leave a burden upon your consciences. The boy, who is bearing the consequence of his own error, will leave behind him nothing that calls for atonement from anyone ; but if my son, who is innocent, is put to death, the conscience of those who have condemned him will be more heavily burdened than ever.

Εἰ δὲ αὐθέντης ἐκ τῶν λεγομένων ἐπιδείκνυται,
οὐχ ἡμεῖς αὐτῷ οἱ λέγοντες αἴτιοί ἐσμεν, ἀλλ' ἡ
10 πρᾶξις τῶν ἔργων. ὀρθῶς δὲ τῶν ἐλέγχων ἐλεγ-
χόντων τὸν παῖδα αὐθέντην ὄντα, ὁ νόμος ἀπολύων
ἡμᾶς τῆς αἰτίας τὸν ἀποκτείναντα καταλαμβάνει.
μήτε οὖν ἡμᾶς εἰς μὴ προσηκούσας συμφορὰς
ἐμβάλητε, μήτε αὐτοὶ ταῖς τούτων ἀτυχίαις βοη-
θοῦντες ἐναντία τοῦ δαίμονος γνῶτε, ἀλλ' ὥσπερ
ὅσιον καὶ δίκαιον, μεμνημένοι τοῦ πάθους, ὅτι διὰ
τὸν ὑπὸ τὴν φορὰν τοῦ ἀκοντίου ὑπελθόντα ἐγένετο,
ἀπολύετε ἡμᾶς· οὐ γὰρ αἴτιοι τοῦ φόνου ἐσμέν.

If the arguments put forward prove the dead boy his own slayer, it is not we who have stated them whom he has to thank, but the fact that the accident happened as it did. Since examination proves beyond doubt that the boy was his own slayer, the law absolves us from blame, and condemns him who was guilty. See, then, that we are not plunged into woes which we do not deserve, and that you yourselves do not defy the powers above by a verdict succouring my opponents in their misfortunes. Remember, as righteousness and justice require you to do, that the accident was caused by him who moved into the javelin's path. Remember, and acquit us; for we are not guilty of his death.

IV
THE THIRD TETRALOGY

INTRODUCTORY NOTE

THE third *Tetralogy* treats of φόνος in yet another of its aspects, that of homicide in self-defence. As in the second *Tetralogy*, the facts are not disputed; the problem is one of interpretation. An old man, X, quarrels with a young one, Y, as they sit drinking. They come to blows : and X is seriously injured in consequence. He receives medical attention, but ultimately dies. The relatives of X prosecute Y for wilful murder. He, however, pleads provocation and attempts to show that he was acting in self-defence.

The argumentation is considerably more involved than in the second *Tetralogy*, where the issue resolved itself immediately into the question whether the ἁμαρτία committed lay with X or Y. Here the original charge is wilful murder, and the prosecution make some effort to sustain it throughout. On the other hand, the defence meet it by attempting to prove justifiable homicide ; while it is simultaneously suggested that death was entirely due to the incompetence of the medical attention received. Besides this, the possibility that death was purely accidental is admitted, and both sides use arguments similar to those developed at greater length in *Tetralogy II* to show that the ἁμαρτία committed must rest with their opponents.

In spite of the complication of the issue, the object

of the author is clearly to exhibit the lines along which a plea of justifiable homicide should be supported or attacked. On the side of the defence it is argued that the responsibility for the fatal blow must be thrust back beyond the striker to the aggressor, because Y, the striker, was acting under compulsion. On the side of the prosecution it is urged that responsibility for a given act must remain with the agent himself; Y struck the blow which caused death, therefore Y is to blame for it. This principle is forgotten, however, when the physician comes under discussion. The question of his competence is treated as irrelevant, and it is maintained that the responsibility for death must be thrust back to Y, whose blows made medical attention necessary in the first place. But the inconsistency is intelligible, if it is remembered that the purpose of the *Tetralogy* as a whole is to illustrate the opportunities offered the advocate by a pseudo-philosophical analysis of the terms, motive and will.

A touch of realism is added in δ, where it is stated that the accused has taken advantage of his right to throw up the case half-way through. The last speech is delivered by his friends on his behalf.

ΤΕΤΡΑΛΟΓΙΑ Γ

a

ΚΑΤΗΓΟΡΙΑ ΦΟΝΟΥ ΚΑΤΑ ΤΟΥ ΛΕΓΟΝΤΟΣ ΑΜΥΝΑΣΘΑΙ

1 Νενόμισται μὲν ὀρθῶς τὰς φονικὰς δίκας περὶ
πλείστου τοὺς κρίνοντας ποιεῖσθαι διώκειν τε καὶ
μαρτυρεῖν κατὰ τὸ δίκαιον, μήτε τοὺς ἐνόχους
ἀφιέντας μήτε τοὺς καθαροὺς εἰς ἀγῶνα καθισ-
2 τάντας. ὅτε¹ γὰρ ⟨ὁ⟩² θεὸς βουλόμενος ποιῆσαι τὸ
ἀνθρώπινον φῦλον³ τοὺς πρώτους⁴ γενομένους ἔφυσεν
ἡμῶν, τροφέας τε καὶ ⟨σωτῆρας⟩⁵ παρέδωκε τὴν
γῆν καὶ τὴν θάλασσαν, ἵνα μὴ σπάνει τῶν ἀναγκαίων προαποθνήσκοιμεν τῆς γηραιοῦ τελευτῆς.
ὅστις οὖν, τούτων ὑπὸ τοῦ θεοῦ ἀξιωθέντος τοῦ
βίου ἡμῶν, ἀνόμως τινὰ ἀποκτείνει, ἀσεβεῖ μὲν
περὶ τοὺς θεούς, συγχεῖ δὲ τὰ νόμιμα τῶν ἀνθρώ-
3 πων. ὅ τε γὰρ ἀποθανών, στερόμενος ὧν ὁ θεὸς
ἔδωκεν αὐτῷ, εἰκότως θεοῦ τιμωρίαν ὑπολείπει
τὴν τῶν ἀλιτηρίων δυσμένειαν, ἣν οἱ παρὰ τὸ

---

¹ ὅτε Spengel : ὅ τε codd.
² ὁ add. Thalheim, coll. § 3, β. 7, 8.
³ φῦλον N : γένος A.
⁴ πρώτους N : πρῶτον A.

120

THE THIRD TETRALOGY

I

PROSECUTION FOR MURDER OF ONE WHO PLEADS THAT HE WAS ACTING IN SELF-DEFENCE

It is very rightly laid down that in cases of murder prosecutors must take especial care to observe justice in making their charge and presenting their evidence : they must neither let the guilty escape nor bring the innocent to trial. For when God was minded to create the human race and brought the first of us into being, he gave us the earth and sea to sustain and preserve us, in order that we might not die for want of the necessaries of life before old age brought us to our end. Such being the value placed upon our life by God, whoever unlawfully slays his fellow both sins against the gods and confounds the ordinances of man. For the victim, robbed of the gifts bestowed by God upon him, naturally leaves behind him the angry spirits of vengeance,[a] God's instruments of punishment, spirits which they who prosecute and

[a] For the ἀλιτήριοι see General Introduction, p. 39.

---

[5] σωτῆρας add. Thalheim. Nonnihil huiusmodi videtur excidisse.

δίκαιον κρίνοντες ἢ μαρτυροῦντες, συνασεβοῦντες
τῷ ταῦτα δρῶντι, οὐ προσῆκον μίασμα εἰς τοὺς
4 ἰδίους οἴκους εἰσάγονται· ἡμεῖς τε οἱ τιμωροὶ τῶν
διεφθαρμένων, εἰ δι᾽ ἄλλην τινὰ ἔχθραν τοὺς ἀν-
αιτίους διώκοιμεν, τῷ μὲν ἀποθανόντι οὐ τιμω-
ροῦντες δεινοὺς ἀλιτηρίους ἕξομεν τοὺς τῶν ἀποθανόντων προστροπαίους, τοὺς δὲ καθαροὺς ἀδίκως
ἀποκτείνοντες ἔνοχοι τοῦ φόνου τοῖς ἐπιτιμίοις
ἐσμέν, ὑμᾶς δὲ[1] ἄνομα δρᾶν πείθοντες καὶ τοῦ
ὑμετέρου ἁμαρτήματος ὑπαίτιοι γιγνόμεθα.
5 Ἐγὼ μὲν οὖν δεδιὼς ταῦτα, εἰς ὑμᾶς παράγων
τὸν ἀσεβήσαντα καθαρὸς τῶν ἐγκλημάτων εἰμί·
ὑμεῖς δὲ ἀξίως τῶν προειρημένων τῇ κρίσει προσ-
έχοντες τὸν νοῦν, ἀξίαν δίκην τοῦ πάθους τῷ εἰργασμένῳ ἐπιθέντες,[2] ἅπασαν τὴν πόλιν καθαρὰν τοῦ
6 μιάσματος καταστήσετε. εἰ μὲν γὰρ ἄκων ἀπέκτεινε τὸν ἄνδρα, ἄξιος ἂν ἦν συγγνώμης τυχεῖν
τινός· ὕβρει δὲ καὶ ἀκολασίᾳ παροινῶν εἰς ἄνδρα
πρεσβύτην, τύπτων τε καὶ πνίγων ἕως τῆς ψυχῆς
ἀπεστέρησεν αὐτόν, ὡς μὲν ἀποκτείνας τοῦ φόνου
τοῖς ἐπιτιμίοις ἔνοχός ἐστι, ὡς δὲ συγχέων ἅπαντα
τῶν γεραιοτέρων τὰ νόμιμα οὐδενὸς ἁμαρτεῖν, οἷς
οἱ τοιοῦτοι κολάζονται, δίκαιός ἐστιν.
7 Ὁ μὲν τοίνυν νόμος ὀρθῶς ὑμῖν τιμωρεῖσθαι
παραδίδωσιν αὐτόν· τῶν δὲ μαρτύρων ἀκηκόατε, οἳ
παρῆσαν παροινοῦντι αὐτῷ. ὑμᾶς δὲ χρὴ τῇ τε
ἀνομίᾳ τοῦ παθήματος ἀμύνοντας, τήν τε ὕβριν

---

[1] δὲ Schaefer : τε codd.
[2] ἀξίαν δίκην τῶν εἰργασμένων ἐπιθ. **A pr.**

testify without giving heed to justice bring into their own homes, defiling them with the defilement of another, because they share in the sin of him who did the deed. And similarly, should we, the avengers of the dead, accuse innocent persons because of some private grudge, not only will our failure to avenge the murdered man cause us to be haunted by dread demons to whom the dead will turn for justice, but by wrongfully causing the death of the innocent we are liable to the penalties prescribed for murder, and because we have persuaded you to break the law, the responsibility for your mistake also becomes ours.

For my part, my fear of such consequences has led me to bring the true sinner before you, and thus the stain of none of the charges which I am making rests upon me; and if you yourselves give that attention to the trial which the considerations I have put before you demand, and inflict upon the criminal a punishment proportionate to the injury which he has done, you will cleanse the entire city of its defilement. Had he killed his victim accidentally, he would have deserved some measure of mercy. But he wantonly committed a brutal assault upon an old man when in his cups; he struck him and throttled him until he robbed him of life. So for killing him he is liable to the penalties prescribed for murder: and for violating every right to respect enjoyed by the aged he deserves to suffer in full the punishment usual in such cases.

Thus the law rightly hands him over to you for punishment; and you have listened to the witnesses who were present during his drunken assault. It is your duty to take vengeance for the injury which he so lawlessly inflicted: to punish such brutal violence

123

κολάζοντας ἀξίως τοῦ πάθους, τὴν βουλεύσασαν
ψυχὴν ἀνταφελέσθαι αὐτόν.

β

[126] ΑΠΟΛΟΓΙΑ ΦΟΝΟΥ, ΩΣ ΑΜΥΝΟΜΕΝΟΣ
ΑΠΕΚΤΕΙΝΕΝ

1 Ὅτι μὲν βραχεῖς τοὺς λόγους ἐποιήσαντο, οὐ
θαυμάζω αὐτῶν· οὐ γὰρ ὡς μὴ πάθωσιν ὁ κίνδυνος
αὐτοῖς ἐστιν, ἀλλ᾽ ὡς ἐμὲ μὴ δικαίως δι᾽ ἔχθραν
διαφθείρωσιν. ὅτι δ᾽ ἐξισοῦν τοῖς μεγίστοις ἐγ-
κλήμασιν ἤθελον τὸ πρᾶγμα, οὗ ὁ ἀποθανὼν αὐτῷ
αἴτιος καὶ μᾶλλον ἢ ἐγὼ ἐγένετο, εἰκότως ἂν ἀγανακτεῖν μοι δοκῶ. ἄρχων γὰρ χειρῶν ἀδίκων, καὶ
παροινῶν εἰς ἄνδρα πολὺ αὐτοῦ σωφρονέστερον,
οὐχ αὑτῷ μόνον τῆς συμφορᾶς, ἀλλὰ καὶ ἐμοὶ
αἴτιος τοῦ ἐγκλήματος γέγονεν.

2 Οἶμαι μὲν οὖν ἔγωγε οὔτε δίκαια τούτους οὔθ᾽
ὅσια δρᾶν ἐγκαλοῦντας ἐμοί. τὸν γὰρ ἄρξαντα τῆς
πληγῆς, εἰ μὲν σιδήρῳ ἢ λίθῳ ἢ ξύλῳ ἠμυνάμην
αὐτόν, ἠδίκουν μὲν οὐδ᾽ οὕτως—οὐ γὰρ ταὐτὰ ἀλλὰ
μείζονα καὶ πλείονα δίκαιοι οἱ ἄρχοντες ἀντιπάσχειν εἰσίν·—ταῖς δὲ χερσὶ τυπτόμενος ὑπ᾽ αὐτοῦ,
ταῖς χερσὶν ἅπερ ἔπασχον ἀντιδρῶν, πότερα
ἠδίκουν;[1]

---

[1] πότερα ἂν ἠδίκουν A pr. N: ἂν in A erasum.

124

as harshly as the harm which it has caused requires : to deprive him in his turn of a life which was used to plot another's death.

II

REPLY TO A CHARGE OF MURDER, ARGUING THAT THE ACCUSED KILLED IN SELF-DEFENCE

The fact that their speech was brief does not surprise me : because for them the danger is, not that they may come to some harm, but that they may fail to gratify their animosity by sending me to a death which I do not deserve. On the other hand, that they should want to treat the present matter, in which the victim had himself to blame more than me, as a case of the greatest gravity, gives me, I think, some excuse for indignation. By resorting to violence as he did and making a drunken assault upon a man far more in control of himself than he, he was responsible not only for the disaster which befell himself, but for the accusation which has been brought against me.

In my opinion, the prosecution are setting both God and man at defiance in accusing me. He was the aggressor ; and even if I had used steel or stone or wood to beat him off, I was acting within my rights ; an aggressor deserves to be answered with, not the same, but more and worse than he gave. Actually, when he struck me with his fists, I used my own to retaliate for the blows which I received. Was that unjustified ?

ANTIPHON

3 Εἶεν· ἐρεῖ δέ, "ἀλλ' ὁ νόμος εἴργων μήτε δικαίως μήτε ἀδίκως ἀποκτείνειν ἔνοχον τοῦ φόνου τοῖς ἐπιτιμίοις ἀποφαίνει σε ὄντα· ὁ γὰρ ἀνὴρ τέθνηκεν." ἐγὼ δὲ δεύτερον καὶ τρίτον οὐκ ἀποκτεῖναί φημι. εἰ μὲν γὰρ ὑπὸ τῶν πληγῶν ὁ ἀνὴρ παραχρῆμα ἀπέθανεν, ὑπ' ἐμοῦ μὲν δικαίως δ' ἂν ἐτεθνήκει— οὐ γὰρ ταὐτὰ ἀλλὰ μείζονα καὶ πλείονα οἱ ἄρξαντες

4 δίκαιοι ἀντιπάσχειν εἰσί·—νῦν δὲ πολλαῖς ἡμέραις ὕστερον μοχθηρῷ[1] ἰατρῷ ἐπιτρεφθεὶς διὰ τὴν τοῦ ἰατροῦ μοχθηρίαν καὶ οὐ διὰ τὰς πληγὰς ἀπέθανε. προλεγόντων γὰρ αὐτῷ τῶν ἄλλων ἰατρῶν, εἰ ταύτην τὴν θεραπείαν θεραπεύσοιτο, ὅτι ἰάσιμος ὢν διαφθαρήσοιτο, δι' ὑμᾶς τοὺς συμβούλους διαφθαρεὶς ἐμοὶ ἀνόσιον ἔγκλημα[2] προσέβαλεν.

5 Ἀπολύει δέ με καὶ ὁ νόμος καθ' ὃν διώκομαι. τὸν γὰρ ἐπιβουλεύσαντα κελεύει φονέα εἶναι.[3] ἐγὼ μὲν οὖν πῶς ἂν ἐπιβουλεύσαιμι αὐτῷ ὅ τι μὴ[4] καὶ ἐπεβουλεύθην ὑπ' αὐτοῦ; τοῖς γὰρ αὐτοῖς ἀμυνόμενος αὐτὸν καὶ τὰ αὐτὰ δρῶν ἅπερ ἔπασχον, σαφὲς ὅτι τὰ αὐτὰ ἐπεβούλευσα καὶ ἐπεβουλεύθην.

6 Εἰ δέ τις ἐκ τῶν πληγῶν τὸν θάνατον οἰόμενος γενέσθαι φονέα με αὐτοῦ ἡγεῖται εἶναι, ἀντιλογισάσθω ὅτι διὰ τὸν ἄρξαντα αἱ πληγαὶ γενόμεναι τοῦτον αἴτιον τοῦ θανάτου καὶ οὐκ ἐμὲ ἀποφαίνουσιν ὄντα· οὐ γὰρ ἂν ἠμυνάμην μὴ τυπτόμενος ὑπ' αὐτοῦ.

---

[1] μοχθηρῷ N: πονηρῷ A.　　[2] ἔγκλημα om. N.
[3] εἶναι om. N.　　[4] ὅτι μὴ Schoell: εἰ μὴ codd.

126

Well and good. "But," he will object, "the law which forbids the taking of life whether justifiably or not shows you to be liable to the penalty prescribed for murder; for the man is dead." I repeat for a second and a third time that I did not kill him. Had the man died on the spot from the blows which he received, his death would have been due to me, not but what I would have been justified—an aggressor deserves to be answered with not the same, but more and worse than he gave;—but in fact he died several days later, after being placed under an incompetent physician. His death was due to the incompetence of the physician, and not to the blows which he received. The other physicians warned him that though he was not beyond cure, he would die if he followed this particular treatment. Thanks to your advice, he did die, and thereby caused an outrageous charge to be brought against myself.

Further, the very law under which I am being accused attests my innocence; it lays down that the guilt of a murder shall rest upon that party which acted from design. Now what designs could I have on his life which he did not also have on mine? I resisted him with his own weapons, and returned him blow for blow; so it is clear that I only had the designs upon his life which he had on mine.

Furthermore, if anyone thinks that his death was the result of the blows which he received and that therefore I am his murderer, let him set against that the fact that it was the aggressor who was the cause of those blows, and that they therefore point to him, not to me, as the person responsible for his death; I would not have defended myself unless I had been struck by him.

Ἀπολυόμενος δὲ ὑπό τε τοῦ ⟨νόμου ὑπό τε τοῦ⟩[1]
ἄρξαντος τῆς πληγῆς, ἐγὼ μὲν οὐδενὶ τρόπῳ
φονεὺς αὐτοῦ εἰμι, ὁ δὲ ἀποθανών, εἰ μὲν ἀτυχίᾳ
τέθνηκεν, τῇ ἑαυτοῦ ἀτυχίᾳ κέχρηται—ἠτύχησε
γὰρ ἄρξας τῆς πληγῆς—εἰ δ᾽ ἀβουλίᾳ τινί, τῇ ἑαυτοῦ
ἀβουλίᾳ διέφθαρται· οὐ γὰρ εὖ φρονῶν ἔτυπτέ με.

7 Ὡς μὲν οὖν οὐ δικαίως κατηγοροῦμαι, ἐπι-
δέδεικταί μοι· ἐθέλω δὲ τοὺς κατηγοροῦντάς μου
πᾶσιν οἷς ἐγκαλοῦσιν ἐνόχους αὐτοὺς[2] ὄντας ἀποδεῖξαι. καθαρῷ μέν μοι τῆς αἰτίας ὄντι φόνον
ἐπικαλοῦντες,[3] ἀποστεροῦντες δέ με τοῦ βίου ὃν ὁ
θεὸς παρέδωκέ μοι, περὶ τὸν θεὸν ἀσεβοῦσιν·
ἀδίκως δὲ θάνατον ἐπιβουλεύοντες τά τε νόμιμα
συγχέουσι φονῆς τέ μου γίγνονται· ἀνοσίως δ᾽
ἀποκτεῖναι ὑμᾶς με πείθοντες καὶ τῆς ὑμετέρας
εὐσεβείας †αὐτοὶ φονῆς†[4] εἰσί.

8 Τούτοις μὲν οὖν ὁ θεὸς ἐπιθείη τὴν δίκην· ὑμᾶς
δὲ χρὴ τὸ ὑμέτερον σκοποῦντας ἀπολῦσαί με μᾶλλον ἢ καταλαβεῖν βούλεσθαι. ἀδίκως μὲν γὰρ
[127] ἀπολυθείς, διὰ τὸ μὴ ὀρθῶς ὑμᾶς διδαχθῆναι
ἀποφυγών, τοῦ μὴ διδάξαντος καὶ οὐχ ὑμέτερον
τὸν προστρόπαιον τοῦ ἀποθανόντος καταστήσω· μὴ
ὀρθῶς δὲ καταληφθεὶς ὑφ᾽ ὑμῶν, ὑμῖν καὶ οὐ τούτῳ
τὸ μήνιμα τῶν ἀλιτηρίων προστρέψομαι.[5]

9 Ταῦτ᾽ οὖν εἰδότες, τουτοισὶ τὸ ἀσέβημα τοῦτο

---

[1] νόμου ὑπό τε τοῦ add. Reiske.   [2] αὐτοὺς om. N.
[3] ἐπικαλοῦντες Kayser: ἐπιβουλ(-βολ-)εύοντες codd.
[4] Obelis inclusi. αὐτοὶ φονῆς Blass: ἀνατροπῆς ci. Thalheim.
[5] προστρέψομαι Gernet, coll. Plat. Leg. ix. 866 в: προσ-
τρίψομαι codd.

---

[a] See note on γ. 4, ad fin.
[b] The ms. text is clearly corrupt here. αὐτοὶ cannot be
right; and φονῆς is hardly tolerable after the φονῆς of the

Thus my innocence is attested both by the law and by the fact that my opponent was the aggressor ; in no way am I his murderer. As to the dead man, if his death was due to mischance, he had himself to thank for that mischance : for it consisted in his taking the offensive.[a] Similarly, if his death was due to a loss of self-control it was through his own loss of self-control that he perished : for he was not in his right mind when he struck me.

I have now proved that I am unjustly accused. But I wish to prove also that my accusers are themselves exposed to all the charges which they are bringing against me. By accusing me of murder when I am free from guilt, and by robbing me of the life which God bestowed upon me, they are sinning against God ; by seeking to compass my death wrongfully, they are confounding the laws of man and becoming my murderers ; and by urging you to commit the sin of taking my life, [they are murdering your consciences also].[b]

May God visit them with the punishment which they deserve. You on your side must look to your own interests and be more disposed to acquit than to condemn me. If I am acquitted unjustly, if I escape because you have not been properly informed of the facts, then it is he who failed to inform you, not you, whom I shall cause to be visited by the spirit who is seeking vengeance for the dead. But if I am wrongfully condemned by you, then it is upon you, and not upon my accuser, that I shall turn the wrath of the avenging demons.

In this knowledge, make the prosecution bear the

previous sentence. No satisfactory emendation has yet been proposed.

ἀναθέντες, αὐτοί τε καθαροὶ τῆς αἰτίας γένεσθε,
ἐμέ τε ὁσίως καὶ δικαίως ἀπολύετε· οὕτω γὰρ ἂν
καθαρώτατοι πάντες οἱ πολῖται εἴημεν.

γ

ΕΚ ΚΑΤΗΓΟΡΙΑΣ Ο ΥΣΤΕΡΟΣ

1 Τοῦτόν τε οὐ θαυμάζω ἀνόσια δράσαντα ὅμοια
οἷς εἴργασται λέγειν, ὑμῖν τε συγγιγνώσκω βουλομένοις τὴν ἀκρίβειαν τῶν πραχθέντων μαθεῖν
τοιαῦτα ἀνέχεσθαι ἀκούοντας αὐτοῦ, ἃ ἐκβάλλεσθαι
ἄξιά ἐστι. τὸν γὰρ ἄνδρα ὁμολογῶν τύπτειν τὰς
πληγὰς ἐξ ὧν ἀπέθανεν, αὐτὸς μὲν τοῦ τεθνηκότος
οὔ φησι φονεὺς εἶναι, ἡμᾶς δὲ τοὺς τιμωροῦντας
αὐτῷ ζῶν τε καὶ βλέπων φονέας αὐτοῦ φησιν εἶναι.
θέλω δὲ καὶ τἆλλα παραπλήσια ἀπολογηθέντα
τούτοις ἐπιδεῖξαι αὐτόν.

2 Εἶπε δὲ πρῶτον μέν, εἰ καὶ ἐκ τῶν πληγῶν ἀπέθανεν ὁ ἀνήρ, ὡς οὐκ ἀπέκτεινεν αὐτόν· τὸν γὰρ
ἄρξαντα τῆς πληγῆς, τοῦτον αἴτιον τῶν πραχθέντων γενόμενον καταλαμβάνεσθαι ὑπὸ τοῦ νόμου,
ἄρξαι δὲ τὸν ἀποθανόντα. μάθετε δὴ πρῶτον μὲν
ὅτι ἄρξαι καὶ παροινεῖν τοὺς νεωτέρους τῶν πρεσ-
βυτέρων εἰκότερόν ἐστι· τοὺς μὲν γὰρ ἥ τε μεγαλοφροσύνη τοῦ γένους ἥ τε ἀκμὴ τῆς ῥώμης[1] ἥ τε
ἀπειρία τῆς μέθης ἐπαίρει τῷ θυμῷ χαρίζεσθαι,

---

[1] ῥώμης A corr. N : ὡ..ς (sc. ὥρας) A pr.

---

[a] ἥ μεγαλοφροσύνη τοῦ γένους ought to mean "pride of
birth": but the speaker is not limiting his remarks to

consequences of their sin ; cleanse yourselves of
guilt : and acquit me as righteousness and justice
require you to do. Thus may all of us citizens
best avoid defilement.

III

SECOND SPEECH FOR THE
PROSECUTION

I am not surprised that the defendant, who has
committed so outrageous a crime, should speak as he
has acted ; just as I pardon you, who are desirous
of discovering the facts exactly, for tolerating such
utterances from his lips as deserve to be greeted
with derision. Thus, he admits that he gave the
man the blows which caused his death ; yet he not
only denies that he himself is the dead man's murderer, but asserts, alive and well though he is, that
we, who are seeking vengeance for the victim, are
his own murderers. And I wish to show that the
remainder of his defence is of a similar character.

To begin with, he said that even if the man did
die as a result of the blows, he did not kill him : because it is the aggressor who is to blame for what
happens : it is he whom the law condemns ; and the
aggressor was the dead man. First, let me tell you
that young men are more likely to be the aggressors
and make a drunken assault than old. The young
are incited by their natural arrogance,[a] their full
vigour, and the unaccustomed effects of wine to give
free play to anger : whereas old men are sobered by

young aristocrats. γένος must be used in the sense of
" class " or " type."

131

τοὺς δὲ ἥ τε ἐμπειρία τῶν παροινουμένων[1] ἥ τε
ἀσθένεια τοῦ γήρως ἥ τε δύναμις τῶν νέων φοβοῦσα
σωφρονίζει.

3 Ὡς δὲ οὐδὲ τοῖς αὐτοῖς ἀλλὰ τοῖς ἐναντιωτάτοις
ἠμύνατο αὐτόν, αὐτὸ τὸ ἔργον σημαίνει. ὁ μὲν
γὰρ ἀκμαζούσῃ τῇ ῥώμῃ τῶν χειρῶν χρώμενος
ἀπέκτεινεν· ὁ δὲ ἀδυνάτως τὸν κρείσσονα ἀμυνόμενος, οὐδὲ σημεῖον οὐδὲν ὧν ἠμύνατο ὑπολιπών,[2]
ἀπέθανεν. εἰ δὲ ταῖς χερσὶν ἀπέκτεινε καὶ οὐ
σιδήρῳ, ὅσον αἱ χεῖρες τοῦ σιδήρου οἰκειότεραι
τούτῳ εἰσί, τοσούτῳ μᾶλλον φονεύς ἐστιν.

4 Ἐτόλμησε δὲ εἰπεῖν ὡς ὁ ἄρξας τῆς πληγῆς καὶ
μὴ διαφθείρας μᾶλλον τοῦ ἀποκτείναντος φονεύς
ἐστι· τοῦτον γὰρ βουλευτὴν τοῦ θανάτου φησὶ
γενέσθαι. ἐγὼ δὲ πολὺ τἀναντία τούτων φημί.
εἰ γὰρ αἱ χεῖρες ἃ διανοούμεθα ἑκάστῳ ἡμῶν
ὑπουργοῦσιν, ὁ μὲν πατάξας καὶ μὴ ἀποκτείνας
τῆς πληγῆς βουλευτὴς ἐγένετο, ὁ δὲ θανασίμως
τύπτων τοῦ θανάτου· ἐκ γὰρ ὧν ἐκεῖνος διανοηθεὶς
ἔδρασεν, ὁ ἀνὴρ τέθνηκεν.

Ἔστι δὲ ἡ μὲν ἀτυχία τοῦ πατάξαντος, ἡ δὲ
συμφορὰ τοῦ παθόντος. ὁ μὲν γὰρ ἐξ ὧν ἔδρασεν
ἐκεῖνος διαφθαρείς, οὐ τῇ ἑαυτοῦ ἁμαρτίᾳ ἀλλὰ τῇ
τοῦ πατάξαντος χρησάμενος ἀπέθανεν[3]· ὁ δὲ μείζω

---

[1] παροινουμένων Reiske : παρανομουμένων codd.
[2] ὧν ἠμύνατο ὑπολείπων N : ὑπολιπὼν ὧν ἠμύνατο A.
[3] ἀπέθανεν A : ἔπαθεν N.

their experience of drunken excesses, by the weakness of age, and by their fear of the strength of the young.

Further, it was not with the same, but with vastly different weapons that the accused withstood him, as the facts themselves show. The one used hands which were in the fullness of their strength, and with them he slew; whereas the other defended himself but feebly against a stronger man, and died without leaving any mark of that defence behind him. Moreover, if it was with his hands and not with steel that the defendant slew, then the fact that his hands are more a part of himself than is steel makes him so much the more a murderer.

He further dared to assert that he who struck the first blow, even though he did not slay, is more truly the murderer than he who killed; for it is to the aggressor's wilful act that the death was due, he says. But I maintain the very opposite. If our hands carry out the intentions of each of us, he who struck without killing was the wilful author of the blow alone: the wilful author of the death was he who struck and killed: for it was as the result of an intentional act on the part of the defendant that the man was killed.

Again, while the victim suffered the ill-effect of the mischance, it is the striker who suffered the mischance itself; for the one met his death as the result of the other's act, so that it was not through his own mistake, but through the mistake of the man who struck him, that he was killed; whereas the other did more than he meant to do, and he had only himself to blame for the mischance

ὧν ἤθελε πρᾶξαι, τῇ ἑαυτοῦ ἀτυχίᾳ ὃν οὐκ ἤθελεν
ἀπέκτεινεν.

5 Ὑπὸ δὲ τοῦ ἰατροῦ φάσκων αὐτὸν ἀποθανεῖν,
θαυμάζω ὅτι [οὐχ]¹ ὑφ᾽ ἡμῶν τῶν συμβουλευσάντων
ἐπιτρεφθῆναί φησιν αὐτὸν διαφθαρῆναι. καὶ γὰρ
ἂν εἰ μὴ ἐπετρέψαμεν, ὑπ᾽ ἀθεραπείας ἂν ἔφη
διαφθαρῆναι αὐτόν. εἰ δέ τοι καὶ ὑπὸ τοῦ ἰατροῦ
ἀπέθανεν, ὡς οὐκ ἀπέθανεν, ὁ μὲν ἰατρὸς οὐ φονεὺς
αὐτοῦ ἐστιν, ὁ γὰρ νόμος ἀπολύει αὐτόν, διὰ δὲ
τὰς τούτου πληγὰς ἐπιτρεψάντων ἡμῶν αὐτῷ, πῶς
ἂν ἄλλος τις ἢ ὁ βιασάμενος ἡμᾶς χρῆσθαι αὐτῷ
φονεὺς εἴη ἄν;

6 Οὕτω δὲ φανερῶς ἐκ παντὸς τρόπου ἐλεγχόμενος
ἀποκτεῖναι τὸν ἄνδρα, εἰς τοῦτο τόλμης καὶ ἀναιδείας ἥκει, ὥστ᾽ οὐκ ἀρκοῦν αὐτῷ ἐστιν ὑπὲρ τῆς

---

¹ οὐχ del. Hemstege. Cf. β. 4.

ᵃ A reply to the arguments of the defence in β. 6. The
terms ἀτυχία, ἁμαρτία, and συμφορά represent the logically
distinguishable elements which constitute an "unfortunate
accident." Owing to ἀτυχία the agent commits an error
(ἁμαρτία), *i.e.* performs an act which he either had no intention of performing at all or intended to perform differently,
and the result is a συμφορά, which may fall either upon the
agent himself or upon some second person. In the present
paragraph it is assumed for the moment, as it had been
assumed by the defence in β. 6, that death was purely accidental. Blood-guilt will still rest upon one of the two parties:
but it will rest upon the party guilty of ἁμαρτία (*cf. Tetralogy
II*). Now the defence had argued in β. 6 that X, the aggressor,
had been responsible for the ἁμαρτία; it had consisted in his
taking the offensive: and he was ἀτυχής in doing so. The
resultant συμφορά had fallen on himself. The prosecution
here reply that while the συμφορά indeed fell on X, the ἀτυχία
and the ἁμαρτία lay with Y, because Y had given a harder
blow than he intended.

ᵇ If the οὐχ of the mss. is retained, we have a flat con-

whereby he killed a man whom he did not mean to slay.[a]

I am surprised that, in alleging the man's death to have been due to the physician,[b] he should assign the responsibility for it to us, upon whose advice it was that he received medical attention ; for had we failed to place him under a physician, the defendant would assuredly have maintained that his death was due to neglect. But even if his death was due to the physician, which it was not, the physician is not his murderer, because the law absolves him from blame. On the other hand, as it was only owing to the blows given by the defendant that we placed the dead man under medical care at all, can the murderer be anyone save him who forced us to call in the physician ?

Although it has been proved so clearly and so completely that he killed the dead man, his impudence and shamelessness are such that he is not content with defending his own act of wickedness : he

tradiction of β. 4, where the defence do in fact accuse the prosecution of having caused the man's death. Further, the argument of the present paragraph becomes exceedingly elliptical. It will presumably run thus : " The defendant accuses the physician ; but he ought logically to accuse us instead. He would undoubtedly have accused us of having been responsible for the man's death through neglect, had we not sought medical aid at all ; so he should similarly accuse us of murder, if we sent the patient to a bad physician instead of to a good one." If the οὐχ is deleted, we get consistency with β. 4, and the argument is as in the text. οὐχ was probably inserted by a reader who thought that the first sentence of § 5 was self-contradictory. Note that this first sentence (ὑπὸ δὲ . . . διαφθαρῆναι) does not imply merely that the defence have contradicted themselves by accusing first the physician and then the prosecution ; this is clear from the καὶ γὰρ ἂν κτλ. which follows, giving the true reason for the speaker's surprise.

ANTIPHON

αὐτοῦ ἀσεβείας ἀπολογεῖσθαι, ἀλλὰ καὶ ἡμᾶς, οἱ
[128] τὸ τούτου μίασμα ἐπεξερχόμεθα, ἀθέμιστα καὶ
ἀνόσια δρᾶν φησι.

7 Τούτῳ μὲν οὖν πρέπει καὶ ταῦτα καὶ ἔτι τούτων
δεινότερα λέγειν, τοιαῦτα δεδρακότι· ἡμεῖς δὲ τόν
⟨τε⟩[1] θάνατον φανερὸν ἀποδεικνύντες, τήν τε
πληγὴν ὁμολογουμένην ἐξ ἧς ἀπέθανε, τόν τε νόμον
εἰς τὸν πατάξαντα τὸν φόνον ἀνάγοντα, ἀντὶ τοῦ
παθόντος ἐπισκήπτομεν ὑμῖν, τῷ τούτου φόνῳ τὸ
μήνιμα τῶν ἀλιτηρίων ἀκεσαμένους πᾶσαν τὴν
πόλιν καθαρὰν τοῦ μιάσματος καταστῆσαι.

δ

ΕΞ ΑΠΟΛΟΓΙΑΣ Ο ΥΣΤΕΡΟΣ

1 Ὁ μὲν ἀνήρ, οὐ καταγνοὺς αὐτὸς αὑτοῦ, ἀλλὰ
τὴν σπουδὴν τῶν κατηγόρων φοβηθείς, ὑπαπέστη·
ἡμῖν δὲ τοῖς φίλοις ζῶντι ἢ ἀποθανόντι εὐσεβέσ-
τερον ἀμύνειν αὐτῷ. ἄριστα μὲν οὖν αὐτὸς ἂν
ὑπὲρ αὑτοῦ ἀπελογεῖτο· ἐπεὶ δὲ τάδε ἀκινδυνότερα
ἔδοξεν εἶναι, ἡμῖν,[2] οἷς μέγιστον ἂν πένθος γένοιτο
στερηθεῖσιν αὐτοῦ, ἀπολογητέον.

2 Δοκεῖ δέ μοι περὶ τὸν ἄρξαντα τῆς πληγῆς τὸ
ἀδίκημα εἶναι. ὁ μὲν οὖν διώκων οὐκ εἰκόσι
τεκμηρίοις χρώμενος τοῦτον τὸν ἄρξαντά φησιν
εἶναι. εἰ μὲν γὰρ ὥσπερ βλέπειν μὲν τοῖν ὀφθαλ-
μοῖν, ἀκούειν δὲ τοῖς ὠσίν, οὕτω κατὰ φύσιν ἦν

[1] τε add. Blass.   [2] εἶναι, ἡμῖν Hirschig : ἡμῖν εἶναι codd.

[a] A touch of realism. It was recognized that the defendant in a δίκη φόνου had the right of withdrawing into exile

136

actually accuses us, who are seeking expiation of the defilement which rests upon him, of acting like unscrupulous scoundrels.

Assertions as outrageous as this, or even more so, befit one guilty of such a crime as he. We, on our side, have clearly established how the death took place : we have shown that there are no doubts about the blow which caused it : and we have proved that the law fixes the guilt of the murder upon him who gave that blow. So in the name of the victim we charge you to appease the wrath of the spirits of vengeance by putting the defendant to death, and thereby cleanse the whole city of its defilement.

IV

SECOND SPEECH FOR THE DEFENCE

The defendant, not because he has judged himself guilty, but because he was alarmed by the vehemence of the prosecution, has withdrawn.[a] As to us, his friends, we are discharging our sacred duty to him more fitly by aiding him while he is alive than by aiding him after he is dead. Admittedly, he himself would have pleaded his own case best ; but since the present course appeared the safer, it remains for us, to whom his loss would be a very bitter grief, to defend him.

To my mind, it is with the aggressor that the blame for the deed rests. Now the presumptions from which the prosecution argues that the defendant was the aggressor are unreasonable. If brutal violence on the part of the young and self-control on the part of the old were as natural as seeing with the eyes and

half-way through the trial, if he saw no hope of an acquittal. *Cf. Herodes,* Introd.

ὑβρίζειν μὲν τοὺς νέους, σωφρονεῖν δὲ τοὺς γέροντας, οὐδὲν ἂν τῆς ὑμετέρας κρίσεως ἔδει· αὐτὴ γὰρ ⟨ἂν⟩[1] ἡ ἡλικία τῶν νέων κατέκρινε· νῦν δὲ πολλοὶ μὲν νέοι σωφρονοῦντες, πολλοὶ δὲ πρεσβῦται παροινοῦντες, οὐδὲν μᾶλλον τῷ διώκοντι ἢ τῷ φεύγοντι τεκμήριον γίγνονται.

3 Κοινοῦ δὲ τοῦ τεκμηρίου ἡμῖν ὄντος ⟨καὶ⟩[2] τούτῳ, τῷ παντὶ προέχομεν· οἱ γὰρ μάρτυρες τοῦτόν φασιν ἄρξαι τῆς πληγῆς. ἄρξαντος δὲ τούτου, καὶ τῶν ἄλλων ἁπάντων ⟨τῶν⟩[3] κατηγορουμένων ἀπολύεται τῆς αἰτίας. εἴπερ[4] γὰρ ὁ πατάξας, διὰ τὴν πληγὴν βιασάμενος ὑμᾶς ἐπιτρεφθῆναι ἰατρῷ, μᾶλλον τοῦ ἀποκτείναντος φονεύς ἐστιν, ὁ ἄρξας τῆς πληγῆς φονεὺς γίγνεται. οὗτος γὰρ ἠνάγκασε τόν τε ἀμυνόμενον ἀντιτύπτειν τόν τε πληγέντα ἐπὶ τὸν ἰατρὸν ἐλθεῖν. ἀνόσια γὰρ ⟨ἂν⟩[5] ὁ[6] διωκόμενος πάθοι, εἰ μήτε ἀποκτείνας ὑπὲρ[7] τοῦ ἀποκτείναντος μήτε ἄρξας ὑπὲρ τοῦ ἄρξαντος φονεὺς ἔσται.

4 Ἔστι δὲ οὐδὲ ὁ ἐπιβουλεύσας οὐδὲν μᾶλλον ὁ διωκόμενος τοῦ διώκοντος. εἰ γὰρ ὁ μὲν ἄρξας τῆς πληγῆς τύπτειν καὶ μὴ ἀποκτείνειν διενοήθη, ὁ δὲ ἀμυνόμενος ἀποκτεῖναι, οὗτος ἂν ὁ ἐπιβουλεύσας εἴη. νῦν δὲ καὶ ὁ ἀμυνόμενος τύπτειν καὶ οὐκ ἀποκτεῖναι διανοηθεὶς ἥμαρτεν, εἰς ἃ οὐκ 5 ἐβούλετο πατάξας. τῆς μὲν οὖν πληγῆς βουλευτὴς

---

[1] ἂν probat Blass.
[2] καὶ add. Blass.   [3] τῶν add. Bekker.
[4] εἴπερ Ignatius : εἴτε codd.
[5] ἂν add. Sauppe.   [6] ὁ Reiske : ὅτε A pr. N, ὅ γε A corr.
[7] ὑπὲρ A corr.[2] : ὑπὸ A pr. N.

---

[a] τοῦ ἀποκτείναντος is of course the physician.

hearing with the ears, then there would be no need for you to sit in judgement ; the young would stand condemned by their mere age. In fact, however, many young men are self-controlled, and many old men are violent in their cups ; and so the presumption which they furnish favours the defence no less than the prosecution.

As the presumption supports us as much as it does the dead man, the balance is in our favour ; for according to the witnesses, it was he who was the aggressor. This being so, the defendant is cleared of all the other charges brought against him as well. For once it is argued that, because it was only the blow given by the striker which obliged you to seek medical attention at all, the murderer is the striker rather than the person immediately responsible for the man's death,[a] it follows that the murderer was he who struck the very first blow of all : because it was he who compelled both his adversary to strike back in self-defence and the victim struck to go to the physician. It would be outrageous, were the defendant, who was neither slayer nor aggressor, to be held a murderer in place of the true slayer and the true aggressor.

Nor again is the intention to kill to be attributed to the accused rather than to his accuser. If it had been the case that, whereas he who struck the first blow had meant not to kill, but to strike, he who was defending himself had meant to kill, then it would have been this last who was guilty of the intention to kill. As it was, he who was defending himself like-wise intended to strike, not to kill ; but he committed an error, and struck where he did not mean to strike. He was thus admittedly the wilful author of the blow ;

ANTIPHON

ἐγένετο, τὸν δὲ θάνατον πῶς ἂν ἐπεβούλευσεν, ὅς γε[1] ἀκουσίως ἐπάταξεν;

Οἰκεῖον δὲ καὶ τὸ ἁμάρτημα τῷ ἄρξαντι μᾶλλον ἢ τῷ ἀμυνομένῳ ἐστίν. ὁ μὲν γὰρ ἃ ἔπασχεν ἀντιδρᾶν ζητῶν, ὑπ᾽ ἐκείνου βιαζόμενος ἐξήμαρτεν· ὁ δὲ διὰ τὴν αὑτοῦ ἀκολασίαν πάντα δρῶν καὶ πάσχων, καὶ τῆς ἑαυτοῦ[2] καὶ τῆς ἐκείνου ἁμαρτίας ⟨αἴτιος ὤν⟩[3] δίκαιος φονεὺς εἶναί ἐστιν.

6 Ὡς δὲ οὐδὲ κρεισσόνως[4] ἀλλὰ πολὺ ὑποδεεστέρως ὢν ἔπασχεν ἠμύνετο, διδάξω. ὁ μὲν ὑβρίζων καὶ παροινῶν πάντ᾽ ἔδρα καὶ οὐδὲν ἠμύνατο· ὁ δὲ μὴ πάσχειν ἀλλὰ ἀπωθεῖσθαι ζητῶν, ἅ τε ἔπασχεν ἀκουσίως ἔπασχεν, ἅ τ᾽ ἔδρασε τὰ παθήματα βουλόμενος διαφυγεῖν ἐλασσόνως ἢ κατ᾽ ἀξίαν τὸν ἄρξαντα ἠμύνετο, καὶ οὐκ ἔδρα.

7 Εἰ δὲ κρείσσων ὢν τὰς χεῖρας κρεισσόνως ἠμύνετο ἢ ἔπασχεν, οὐδ᾽ οὕτω δίκαιος ὑφ᾽ ὑμῶν καταλαμβάνεσθαί ἐστι. τῷ μὲν γὰρ ἄρξαντι πανταχοῦ μεγάλα ἐπιτίμια ἐπίκειται, τῷ δὲ ἀμυνομένῳ οὐδαμοῦ οὐδὲν ἐπιτίμιον γέγραπται.

8 Πρὸς δὲ τὸ μήτε δικαίως μήτε ἀδίκως ἀποκτείνειν ἀποκέκριται· οὐ γὰρ ὑπὸ τῶν πληγῶν ἀλλ᾽ ὑπὸ τοῦ ἰατροῦ ὁ ἀνὴρ ἀπέθανεν, ὡς οἱ μάρτυρες

---

[1] ὅς γε Sauppe: ὃν γε codd.   [2] καὶ τῆς ἑαυτοῦ om. N.
[3] αἴτιος ὤν add. Maetzner: ἁμ. δίκαιος φορεὺς tentavit Thalheim.   [4] κρεισσόνως Reiske: κρεῖσσον (-ων) ὢν codd.

140

but how can he have killed wilfully, when he struck otherwise than he intended ?

Further, it is with the aggressor rather than with him who was defending himself that the responsibility for the error itself rests. The one was seeking to retaliate for the blows which he was receiving, when he committed his error : he was being forced to act by his attacker ; whereas with the other, it was his own lack of self-control which caused him to give and receive the blows which he did : and so, since he is responsible both for his own error and for his victim's, he deserves the name of murderer.

Again, his defence was not more vigorous than the attack made upon him, but much less so : as I will show. The one was truculent, drunken, and violent ; he took the offensive throughout, and was never on the defensive at all. The other was seeking to avoid his blows and repel him ; the blows which he received, he received from no choice of his own : and the blows which he gave were given in defence of himself against the aggressor, and much less vigorously than that aggressor deserved, because his only object was to avoid the hurt which was being done him ; he did not take the offensive at all.

Even supposing that his defence was more vigorous than the attack made upon him, because there was more vigour in his hands, you cannot justly condemn him. Heavy penalties are invariably provided for the aggressor : whereas no penalty is ever prescribed for him who defends himself.

The objection that the taking of life, whether justifiably or not, is forbidden, has been answered ; it was not to the blows, but to the physician, that the man's death was due, as the witnesses state in their

141

μαρτυροῦσιν. ἔστι δὲ καὶ ἡ τύχη τοῦ ἄρξαντος
καὶ οὐ τοῦ ἀμυνομένου. ὁ μὲν γὰρ ἀκουσίως πάντα
δράσας καὶ παθὼν ἀλλοτρίᾳ τύχῃ κέχρηται· ὁ δὲ
[129] ἑκουσίως πάντα πράξας, ἐκ τῶν αὑτοῦ ἔργων τὴν
τύχην προσαγόμενος,[1] τῇ αὑτοῦ ἀτυχίᾳ ἥμαρτεν.
9 Ὡς μὲν οὖν[2] οὐδενὶ ἔνοχος τῶν κατηγορημένων
ὁ διωκόμενός ἐστιν, ἀποδέδεικται. εἰ δέ τις κοινὴν
μὲν τὴν πρᾶξιν, κοινὴν δὲ τὴν ἀτυχίαν αὐτῶν
ἡγούμενος εἶναι, μηδὲν ἀπολύσιμον μᾶλλον ἢ κατα-
λήψιμον ἐκ τῶν λεγομένων γιγνώσκει αὐτὸν ὄντα,
καὶ οὕτως ἀπολύειν μᾶλλον ἢ καταλαμβάνειν δίκαιός[3] ἐστι. τόν τε γὰρ διώκοντα οὐ δίκαιον καταλαμβάνειν, μὴ σαφῶς διδάξαντα ὅτι ἀδικεῖται· τόν
τε φεύγοντα ἀνόσιον ἁλῶναι, μὴ φανερῶς ἐλεγ-
χθέντα ἃ ἐπικαλεῖται.
10 Οὑτωσὶ δὲ ἐκ παντὸς τρόπου τῶν ἐγκλημάτων
ἀπολυομένου τοῦ ἀνδρός, ἡμεῖς ὁσιώτερον ὑμῖν
ἐπισκήπτομεν ὑπὲρ αὐτοῦ, μὴ τὸν φονέα ζητοῦντας
κολάζειν τὸν καθαρὸν ἀποκτείνειν. ὅ τε γὰρ
†ἀποκτείνας τοῦ ἀποθανόντος†[4] οὐδὲν ἧσσον τοῖς
αἰτίοις προστρόπαιος ἔσται,[5] οὗτός τε ἀνοσίως
διαφθαρεὶς διπλάσιον καθίστησι τὸ μίασμα[6] τῶν

---

[1] προσαγόμενος Reiske: προαγόμενος codd.
[2] οὖν om. N.   [3] δίκαιος N: δίκαιον A.
[4] Locus vix sanus: ἀλιτήριος pro ἀποκτείνας Thalheim,
fortasse recte.
[5] ἔσται Kayser: ἐστιν codd.   [6] μίασμα] μήνιμα Briegleb.

---

[a] There is clearly some corruption here. Some reference
is wanted to the spirits of vengeance who will continue to

evidence. Further, it is the aggressor, and not he who was defending himself, who was responsible for the accident. The one gave and received the blows which he did from no choice of his own, and therefore the accident in which he had a part was not of his own causing. The other did what he did of his own free will, and it was by his own actions that he brought the accident upon himself ; hence he had himself to blame for the mischance whereby he committed his error.

It has been shown, then, that not one of the charges made concerns the defendant; and even if both parties are thought equally responsible alike for the actual crime and for the mischance which led to it, and it is decided from the arguments put forward that there is no more reason for acquitting the defendant than for condemning him, he still has a right to be acquitted rather than condemned. Not only is it unjust that his accuser should secure his conviction without clearly showing that he has been wronged : but it is a sin that the accused should be sentenced, if the charges made against him have not been proved conclusively.

As the defendant has been cleared so completely of the charges made, we lay upon you in his name a more righteous behest than did our opponents : in seeking to punish the murderer, do not put him who is blameless to death. If you do, [the slayer no less than the slain will bring the wrath of heaven upon the guilty :][a] and if the defendant is put to death without scruple, he causes the defilement brought upon his slayers by the spirits of vengeance to become

haunt the guilty until due reparation has been made to the dead. See *app. crit.*

ANTIPHON

11 ἀλιτηρίων τοῖς ἀποκτείνασιν αὐτόν. ταῦτα οὖν δεδιότες, τὸν μὲν καθαρὸν ὑμέτερον ἡγεῖσθε[1] εἶναι ἀπολύειν τῆς αἰτίας, τὸν δὲ μιαρὸν τῷ χρόνῳ ἀποδόντες φῆναι τοῖς ἔγγιστα τιμωρεῖσθαι ὑπολείπετε· οὕτω γὰρ ἂν[2] δικαιότατα καὶ ὁσιώτατα πράξαιτ' ἄν.

---

[1] ἡγεῖσθε A corr.[2]: ἡγεῖσθαι A pr. N.   [2] ἂν om. A.

---

[a] Briegleb's μήνιμα is unnecessary. It is clear from a. 3 sub fin. that the writer felt the δυσμένεια τῶν ἀλιτηρίων and

144

twofold.[a] Hold that defilement in fear : and consider
it your duty to absolve him who is guiltless. Him
upon whom the stain of blood rests you may let time
reveal, even as you may leave his punishment to
his victim's kin. It is thus that you will best
observe justice and the will of heaven.

the μίασμα φόνου to be complementary aspects of one and the
same thing. The ἀλιτήριοι were the positive forces which
gave effect to the μίασμα. Hence such a phrase as μίασμα
τῶν ἀλιτηρίων in the present passage is perfectly orthodox ;
it is the "pollution to which the spirits of vengeance give
expression."

V

ON THE MURDER OF HERODES

INTRODUCTION

ANCIENT criticism regarded the *Murder of Herodes* as one of the most notable products of Antiphon's period of maturity. The year in which it was delivered cannot be determined with absolute accuracy : but it was not much earlier or much later than 415 ; thus we learn that the revolt of Lesbos (428–427) had occurred when the speaker was still a mere child, and he has now just reached manhood (§ 74) : while it is clear that the Athenian disaster in Sicily is still a thing of the future (§ 81). The facts are as follows.

A wealthy young Mytilenean, Euxitheus,*a* and an Athenian, Herodes—probably one of the Cleruchs settled in Lesbos after the revolt—embarked together at Mytilene for Aenus on the Thracian coast. They were unfortunate enough to meet with bad weather before completely rounding Lesbos and were forced to run for a bay on the north coast of the island near Methymna. Other ships had done the same ; and Herodes, Euxitheus, and their fellow-passengers took the opportunity of sheltering from the rain on one bound for Mytilene, as their own vessel was open to the sky. A convivial evening followed ; and in the course of it Herodes, who had drunk more than was good for him, went ashore. From that moment he was never seen again. A search was made in the

---

a *Cf.* Sopater, *ap. Rhet. Graeci*, iv. 316.

neighbourhood and a message sent back to Mytilene in the hope that he had made his way thither; but both were without result. Finally, he was given up for lost, and the remainder of the passengers resumed their voyage to Aenus in the original vessel.

The family of Herodes, who had been informed of his disappearance, were convinced that he had been the victim of foul play, and suspected Euxitheus; so directly the boat which Herodes had left so strangely reached Mytilene, they boarded it to make investigations for themselves. Some bloodstains came to light; but they turned out to be due to a sacrifice. A member of the crew [a] was examined under torture; but he stoutly maintained that Euxitheus had remained on board throughout the night in question. A second member of the crew, a slave, was purchased from his owners for similar examination. However, before he had been tortured, a note was discovered purporting to be a message from Euxitheus to a certain Lycinus to the effect that Euxitheus had murdered Herodes. Then the slave was examined, and the confession wrung from him that he had helped Euxitheus to commit the murder. He alleged that Euxitheus had struck Herodes on the head with a stone, the pair of them had carried the body down to a boat, and then he himself had rowed out to sea and thrown it overboard. In consequence of this admission the accusers put the slave to death as a party to the crime. They next seem to have obtained authority for the arrest of Euxitheus by lodging an information against him, whether locally or with the Eleven at Athens; and, in accordance with the warrant, he was taken to Athens and

[a] See further, note, p. 180.

thrown into prison to await trial, bail being refused.

At the trial Euxitheus adopts two main lines of defence. First, he maintains that the case should have taken the form of a δίκη φόνου instead of an ἀπαγωγή for κακουργία ; and secondly he shows that the evidence of his guilt produced by the prosecution is self-contradictory. In connexion with this second line of argument he examines the case against Lycinus, who, it had been suggested, had paid him to commit the murder, and endeavours to rehabilitate his own father, whose supposed anti-Athenian activities during the past dozen years had been used to prejudice the court.

The main problem presented by the speech is that of the validity of the objection raised by the defendant to the action of his accusers in prosecuting him as a κακοῦργος before a Heliastic court, instead of as a φονεύς before the Areopagus. The procedure generally followed in cases of murder was that of the δίκη φόνου, which had remained unchanged since the days of Draco. The form which it took is known from the *Choreutes.*[a] The prosecution had first to register their charge with the Basileus (ἀπογράφεσθαι τὴν δίκην). If he consented to admit it, the accused was *ipso facto* debarred from the Agora and from all temples—was forbidden in fact to take any part whatsoever in the public and religious life of the community ; and proclamation was made to this effect by his prosecutors (πρόρρησις). No one who was under suspicion of having the blood of another on his hands could be allowed to contaminate his fellows or defile sacred buildings. Next the Basileus issued

[a] See *Choreutes*, Introd. p. 238.

writs to secure the attendance of the accused and the necessary witnesses. There followed a preliminary inquiry (προδικασία), which opened with the administration of a peculiarly solemn oath to the prosecutor, defendant, and witnesses by the court official known as the ὁρκώτης. A goat, a ram, and a bull were sacrificed, and all had to lay their hands on the offerings and swear, ἐξωλείαν αὐτοῖς καὶ γένει καὶ οἰκίᾳ ἐπαρώμενοι,[a] to tell nothing but the truth and to confine themselves to the question at issue. Two other προδικασίαι were held within the three months following the registration of the charge, and it was not until the fourth month that the case came before the Areopagus. At the trial proper each side spoke twice, and the penalty upon conviction was death. However, the defendant had the right to throw up his case and withdraw into exile after making his first speech.

Clearly this was a cumbersome procedure; and it became lengthier still if the Basileus had less than three months of office left when the prosecutor applied for permission to register the charge. As he was forbidden by tradition to hand over the case half-finished to his successor, the entire proceedings had to be postponed to the next archonship. But what if the accused were not an Athenian citizen? Could the δίκη φόνου operate at all? Direct evidence is lacking; but it seems most doubtful. The δίκη φόνου was essentially a local institution. It was the instrument whereby the community of archaic Attica had sought to rid itself of the pollution brought upon it by the blood-guilt of one of its

[a] "Invoking utter destruction upon themselves, their family, and their house."

members. Hence the elaborate precautions to insure that none came into contact with the accused. But if the φονεύς had no part in the πόλις of the victim, his blood-guilt lost this social importance; what now required satisfaction was the wrong done to a member of the community by one outside it. And for such a purpose the δίκη φόνου had never been intended.

It would seem likely *a priori* that some alternative procedure should appear to meet this difficulty, particularly after the growth of her empire forced Athens to some definition of the legal status of her subjects in relation to herself; and the methods used against Euxitheus meet it admirably. An alien, or at least, an alien from a subject-state, charged with the murder of an Athenian citizen can be treated as a κακοῦργος; and a charge of κακουργία allows the summary arrest of the accused and his close confinement until the day of his trial. When that day arrives, he is brought before an ordinary Heliastic court and tried as a "malefactor," his particular malefaction being murder.

This is, I think, the reasonable conclusion from (*a*) the fact that the δίκη φόνου was parochial in its operation, and (*b*) the definite statement of Euxitheus that he was being tried as a κακοῦργος before the Heliaea, instead of as a φονεύς before the Areopagus. But we must be wary of identifying the use here made of ἔνδειξις and ἀπαγωγή with their use in certain other cases of φόνος; if a common legal principle can be detected at work, it was a fluid one, as a brief examination will show.

There are three such instances : (1) Lysias, *In*

ON THE MURDER OF HERODES

Agoratum. Here Dionysius arrests Agoratus for causing the death of his brother, Dionysodorus, under the Thirty by turning informer. Dionysius proceeds by lodging an information against Agoratus with the Eleven. They, however, refuse to permit his arrest until Dionysius has added the qualification ἐπ᾽ αὐτο-φώρῳ ληφθείς[a] to his formal charge of murder. The case is tried before a Heliastic court and the penalty upon conviction is death. (2) Demosthenes, *In Aristocratem* (§§ 641 ff.). Here there is a detailed description of the five courts competent to try the various forms of homicide, followed by the statement that there was a sixth means of proceeding against a murderer in cases where none of the others was possible or convenient. This was by ἀπαγωγή. If the criminal was seen in the Agora or in a temple, he could be arrested at sight and thrown into prison to await trial. Should he be found guilty, the penalty was death. (3) Lycurgus, *In Leocratem* (§ 112). The friends of Phrynichus arrest and imprison his murderers. A clear case of ἀπαγωγή, although the absence of further details makes it impossible to say under what head the accused were tried.

Originally ἀπαγωγή was limited in its application to crimes of violence where the criminal was caught *in flagrante delicto*. For judicial purposes these crimes formed a single group and were known as κακουργή-ματα. Thieves, footpads, cutpurses, temple-robbers, kidnappers, were all κακοῦργοι, and, if caught in the act (ἐπ᾽ αὐτοφώρῳ), could be summarily arrested and in most cases punished by the Eleven on their own authority. If the crime was too serious to fall within

[a] *i.e.* " taken in the act."

153

the jurisdiction of the Eleven, however, they kept the prisoner in close confinement until his trial before a Heliastic court.

Now it is clear from Lysias that Agoratus, who was charged with murder, was similarly subjected to ἀπαγωγή ; and the fact that his arrest was authorized by the Eleven only on the condition that the clause ἐπ' αὐτοφώρῳ ληφθείς was added to the written ἔνδειξις presented to them by the prosecutor, makes it reasonably certain that by the end of the fifth century murder itself could be treated as a κακούργημα, provided that the criminal was taken ἐπ' αὐτοφώρῳ. Agoratus, it is important to remember, had some sort of civic rights, in spite of the statement to the contrary in § 64 of Lysias' speech. The allegation that he was "a slave and of slave parentage" is a rhetorical exaggeration which is tacitly acknowledged as false in the next paragraph, where we are told that Agoratus had made a living as a συκοφάντης and had been very heavily fined for it. No slave could have conducted prosecutions in this fashion.

The case mentioned by Demosthenes, on the other hand, is somewhat different. It is true that the criminal is in a sense taken ἐπ' αὐτοφώρῳ ; he is caught in the act of entering the Agora or a temple when his defilement has deprived him of the right to do so. But he is not arrested qua κακοῦργος, because he is not caught in the act of committing the murder which has brought about his defilement. The justification for his ἀπαγωγή must be sought elsewhere. Now it is highly probable, if not certain, that ἀπαγωγή was permissible, if a person against whom proceedings were being instituted for murder before the Basileus disobeyed the formal πρόρρησις of his

accuser which forbade him to frequent public places ;
and it is here that we must look for the origin of the
type of ἀπαγωγή described in the *In Aristocratem*.
It looks as though the πρόρρησις had been dispensed
with by the middle of the fourth century, allowing the
use of ἀπαγωγή without any of the preliminaries before the Archon.   In fact, it is a convenient, because
quicker, alternative to the δίκη φόνου from which it had
been evolved.   It must have emerged after 400 B.C.,
as τὸ ἐπ᾽ αὐτοφώρῳ λαβεῖν is still the one condition of
the ἀπαγωγή of murderers in the time of Agoratus.
No doubt it quickly superseded this older form of
ἀπαγωγή, which treated the φονεύς as a κακοῦργος and
required him to be caught ἐπ᾽ αὐτοφώρῳ, because of
its wider application.

It remains to determine the relation between the
arrest of Agoratus and that of Euxitheus.   Both were
apparently κακοῦργοι in the eyes of the law.   But
whereas it was necessary in the case of Agoratus that
he should be taken ἐπ᾽ αὐτοφώρῳ, no such condition
was observed in the case of Euxitheus.   Now Euxitheus was a ξένος from Lesbos, a subject-state ;
Agoratus had civic rights of some kind and lived in
Athens.   Clearly the conclusion is that ἀπαγωγή was
permissible in the case of Athenians only if they were
caught ἐπ᾽ αὐτοφώρῳ; while ξένοι suspected of murder
could be arrested as κακοῦργοι, even if they were not
so caught, for the reason that ἀπαγωγή was found to
be the only practicable method of bringing them to
trial.

A second difficulty in connexion with the objections raised by Euxitheus to the procedure of the
prosecution is the statement in § 10 that the case
was τιμητός, *i.e.* that in the event of a verdict of guilty,

155

alternative penalties would be proposed by the prosecution and defence, and the court would decide between them. In § 10 it is stated that this penalty would take the form of a fine. Later in the speech, however, the only penalty envisaged is death (*e.g.* §§ 59, 71, etc.).

We cannot treat Euxitheus' words in § 10 as a piece of sheer falsehood. Both he and the jury must have known whether or not the case was τιμητός, and if it was not, if the penalty was fixed at death, Euxitheus would hardly have been so ingenuous as to imagine that he could talk his hearers into forgetting the fact. He must mean what he says; and the explanation would appear to be this. In the case of a citizen there were various courts to try the various kinds of homicide which he might commit, and the penalties which each was empowered to impose differed in severity according to the seriousness of the offence with which the court in question dealt. But these courts were largely unsuited to try ξένοι, and the alternative procedure of ἀπαγωγή followed by a trial before a Heliastic court seems frequently to have replaced them. The various types of offence were here all tried in identical fashion; and as no common penalty was possible, the difficulty must have been surmounted by treating any case of homicide tried by the Heliaea as an ἀγὼν τιμητός which admitted of an adjustment of the penalty to suit circumstances.

The further fact that Euxitheus contradicts himself later in the speech by treating the penalty as fixed at death is intelligible if it is remembered that he is arguing in § 10 for the transference of the case to the Areopagus. As there was never any alternative to death as the penalty for conviction before the

Areopagus, Euxitheus gives great emphasis to the possibility of his merely being fined by the Heliaea in order to prove the incompetence of such a court to try his case as it should be tried ; that the prosecution have in fact determined upon the death penalty is carefully kept in the background at this stage.

The fact that bail was refused cannot be accounted for with absolute certainty owing to the incompleteness of the evidence as to ἔνδειξις and ἀπαγωγή. It is clear from § 17 that the right of furnishing sureties (ἐγγυηταί) was recognized by law in certain cases, probably in the case of citizens only. The Eleven very likely had powers of discretion when the prisoner was an alien, and if the accuser could show good reason for supposing that the accused would default if allowed his liberty, bail would be refused.

ANALYSIS

ΠΕΡΙ ΤΟΥ ΗΡΩΙΔΟΥ ΦΟΝΟΥ

1 Ἐβουλόμην μέν, ὦ ἄνδρες, τὴν δύναμιν τοῦ
λέγειν καὶ τὴν ἐμπειρίαν τῶν πραγμάτων ἐξ ἴσου
μοι καθεστάναι τῇ τε συμφορᾷ καὶ τοῖς κακοῖς
τοῖς γεγενημένοις· νῦν δὲ τοῦ μὲν πεπείραμαι πέρα
τοῦ προσήκοντος, τοῦ δὲ ἐνδεής εἰμι μᾶλλον τοῦ
2 συμφέροντος. οὗ μὲν γάρ με ἔδει κακοπαθεῖν τῷ
σώματι μετὰ τῆς αἰτίας τῆς οὐ προσηκούσης,
ἐνταυθοῖ οὐδέν με ὠφέλησεν ἡ ἐμπειρία· οὗ δέ με
δεῖ σωθῆναι μετὰ τῆς ἀληθείας εἰπόντα τὰ γενόμενα, ἐν τούτῳ με βλάπτει ἡ τοῦ λέγειν ἀδυνασία.[1]
3 πολλοὶ μὲν[2] γὰρ ἤδη τῶν οὐ δυναμένων λέγειν,
ἄπιστοι γενόμενοι τοῖς ἀληθέσιν, αὐτοῖς τούτοις
ἀπώλοντο, οὐ δυνάμενοι δηλῶσαι αὐτά· πολλοὶ δὲ
τῶν λέγειν δυναμένων[3] πιστοὶ γενόμενοι τῷ ψεύδεσθαι, τούτῳ ἐσώθησαν, διότι ἐψεύσαντο. ἀνάγκη
οὖν, ὅταν τις ἄπειρος ᾖ τοῦ ἀγωνίζεσθαι, ἐπὶ τοῖς
τῶν κατηγόρων λόγοις εἶναι μᾶλλον ἢ ἐπ’ αὐτοῖς
τοῖς ἔργοις καὶ τῇ ἀληθείᾳ τῶν πραγμάτων.

4 Ἐγὼ οὖν, ὦ ἄνδρες, αἰτήσομαι[4] ὑμᾶς, οὐχ ἅπερ

---

[1] ἀδυνασία Sauppe ex Bekker An. i. 345: ἀδυναμία codd.
[2] μὲν om. A.
[3] δυναμένων add. A corr.[2]: τῶν δεινῶν λέγειν Fuhr: alii alia.
[4] αἰτήσομαι δὲ N: δὲ erasum in A.

---

[a] τῶν πραγμάτων refers especially to the workings of the law,
and is picked up by οὐ μὲν γάρ με ἔδει . . . ἐμπειρία. The

160

ON THE MURDER OF HERODES

I COULD have wished, gentlemen, that my powers of
speech and my experience of the world [a] were as
great as the misfortune and the severities with which
I have been visited. Instead, I know more of the last
two than I should, and am more wanting in the first
than is good for me. When I had to submit to the
bodily suffering which this unwarranted charge
brought with it, experience afforded me no help; while
now that my life depends upon my giving a truthful
account of the facts, my case is being prejudiced by my
inability to speak. Poor speakers have often before
now been disbelieved because they spoke the truth,
and the truth itself has been their undoing because
they could not make it convincing : just as clever
speakers have often gained credit with lies, and have
owed their lives to the very fact that they lied. Thus
the fate of one who is not a practised pleader inevitably depends less upon the true facts and his actual
conduct than upon the version of them given by his
accusers.

I shall therefore ask you, gentlemen, not indeed

speaker means that had he been less ignorant in such matters,
he might have effectively protested against the employment
of ἔνδειξις and ἀπαγωγή, which involved the close confinement
of the defendant before his trial, instead of the more regular
δίκη φόνου before the Areopagus. See Introd. p. 150.

οἱ πολλοὶ τῶν ἀγωνιζομένων ἀκροᾶσθαι σφῶν αὐτῶν αἰτοῦνται, σφίσι μὲν αὐτοῖς ἀπιστοῦντες, ὑμῶν
δὲ προκατεγνωκότες ἄδικόν τι—εἰκὸς γὰρ ἐν
ἀνδράσι γε ἀγαθοῖς καὶ ἄνευ τῆς αἰτήσεως τὴν
ἀκρόασιν ὑπάρχειν τοῖς φεύγουσιν, οὗπερ καὶ οἱ
5 διώκοντες ἔτυχον ἄνευ αἰτήσεως·—τάδε δὲ[1] δέομαι
ὑμῶν, τοῦτο μὲν ἐάν τι τῇ γλώσσῃ ἁμάρτω, συγγνώμην ἔχειν μοι,[2] καὶ ἡγεῖσθαι ἀπειρίᾳ αὐτὸ μᾶλλον ἢ ἀδικίᾳ ἡμαρτῆσθαι, τοῦτο δὲ ἐάν τι ὀρθῶς
εἴπω, ἀληθείᾳ μᾶλλον ἢ δεινότητι εἰρῆσθαι. οὐ
γὰρ δίκαιον οὔτ' ἔργῳ ἁμαρτόντα διὰ ῥήματα
[130] σωθῆναι, οὔτ' ἔργῳ ὀρθῶς πράξαντα διὰ ῥήματα
ἀπολέσθαι· τὸ μὲν γὰρ ῥῆμα τῆς γλώσσης ἁμάρ-
6 τημά ἐστι, τὸ δ' ἔργον τῆς γνώμης. ἀνάγκη δὲ
κινδυνεύοντα περὶ αὑτῷ καί πού τι καὶ ἐξαμαρτεῖν.
οὐ γὰρ μόνον τῶν λεγομένων ἀνάγκη ἐνθυμεῖσθαι,
ἀλλὰ καὶ τῶν ἐσομένων· ἅπαντα γὰρ τὰ ἐν ἀδήλῳ
ἔτ' ὄντα ἐπὶ τῇ τύχῃ μᾶλλον ἀνάκειται ἢ τῇ
προνοίᾳ. ταῦτ' οὖν ἔκπληξιν πολλὴν παρέχειν
7 ἀνάγκη ἐστὶ τῷ κινδυνεύοντι. ὁρῶ γὰρ ἔγωγε καὶ
τοὺς πάνυ ἐμπείρους τοῦ ἀγωνίζεσθαι πολλῷ χεῖ-
ρον ἑαυτῶν λέγοντας, ὅταν ἔν τινι κινδύνῳ ὦσιν·
ὅταν δ' ἄνευ κινδύνων τι διαπράσσωνται, μᾶλλον
ὀρθουμένους.
8 Ἡ μὲν οὖν αἴτησις, ὦ ἄνδρες, καὶ νομίμως καὶ
ὁσίως ἔχουσα, καὶ ἐν τῷ ὑμετέρῳ δικαίῳ οὐχ
ἧσσον ἢ ἐν τῷ ἐμῷ· περὶ δὲ τῶν κατηγορημένων
ἀπολογήσομαι καθ' ἕκαστον.

Πρῶτον μὲν οὖν, ὡς παρανομώτατα καὶ βιαιό-

for a hearing, as do the majority of those on trial, who lack confidence in themselves and presume you to be biassed; for with an honest jury the defence is naturally assured of a hearing even without appealing for it, seeing that that same jury accorded the prosecution a hearing unasked—no, my request of you is this. If, on the one hand, I make any mistake in speaking, pardon me and treat it as due to inexperience rather than dishonesty; and if, on the other hand, I express a point well, treat it as due to truthfulness rather than skill. For it is no more right that mere words should be the undoing of a man who is in fact innocent than that they should be the salvation of a man who is in fact guilty; the tongue is to blame for a word: whereas the will is to blame for an act. Moreover, a man in personal danger is sure to make some mistake; he cannot help thinking of his fate as well as of his argument, as the decision of an issue which is still in doubt always depends more upon chance than upon human effort. Hence a man in danger is bound to be not a little distraught. Even speakers with a long experience of the courts are far from being at their best, I notice, when in any danger; they are more successful when conducting a case in safety.

So much for my request, gentlemen; it breaks no law, human or divine: and it takes into account what you have a right to expect from me as much as what I have a right to expect from you. And now for the charges made, which I will answer one at a time.

To begin with, I shall prove to you that the methods

---

¹ δὲ om. A pr. N: add. A corr.²
² συγγνώμην ἔχειν μοι ante τοῦτο μὲν codd.: huc transtulit Baiter.

τατα εἰς τόνδε τὸν ἀγῶνα καθέστηκα, τοῦτο ὑμᾶς
διδάξω, οὐ τῷ φεύγειν ἂν τὸ πλῆθος τὸ ὑμέτερον,
ἐπεὶ κἂν ἀνωμότοις ὑμῖν καὶ μὴ κατὰ νόμον μηδένα ἐπιτρέψαιμι περὶ τοῦ σώματος τοῦ ἐμοῦ δια-
ψηφίσασθαι, ἕνεκά γε τοῦ πιστεύειν ἐμοί τε μηδὲν
ἐξημαρτῆσθαι εἰς τόδε τὸ πρᾶγμα καὶ ὑμᾶς γνώσεσθαι τὰ δίκαια, ἀλλ' ἵνα ᾖ τεκμήρια ὑμῖν[1] καὶ
τῶν ἄλλων πραγμάτων [καὶ][2] τῶν εἰς ἐμὲ ἡ τούτων
βιαιότης καὶ παρανομία.

9 Πρῶτον μὲν γὰρ κακοῦργος ἐνδεδειγμένος φόνου
δίκην φεύγω, ὃ οὐδεὶς πώποτ' ἔπαθε τῶν ἐν τῇ
γῇ ταύτῃ. καὶ ὡς μὲν οὐ κακοῦργός εἰμι οὐδ'
ἔνοχος τῷ τῶν κακούργων νόμῳ, αὐτοὶ οὗτοι
τούτου γε μάρτυρες γεγένηνται. περὶ γὰρ τῶν
κλεπτῶν καὶ λωποδυτῶν ὁ νόμος κεῖται, ὧν οὐδὲν
ἐμοὶ προσὸν ἀπέδειξαν. οὕτως εἴς γε ταύτην τὴν
ἀπαγωγὴν νομιμωτάτην καὶ δικαιοτάτην πεποιή-
10 κασιν ὑμῖν τὴν ἀποψήφισίν μου. φασὶ δὲ αὖ τό
γε[3] ἀποκτείνειν μέγα κακούργημα εἶναι, καὶ ἐγὼ
ὁμολογῶ μέγιστόν γε, καὶ τὸ ἱεροσυλεῖν καὶ τὸ
προδιδόναι τὴν πόλιν· ἀλλὰ χωρὶς περὶ αὐτῶν
ἑκάστου οἱ νόμοι κεῖνται. ἐμοὶ δὲ πρῶτον μέν,
οὗ τοῖς ἄλλοις εἴργεσθαι προαγορεύουσι τοῖς τοῦ
φόνου φεύγουσι τὰς δίκας, ἐνταυθοῖ πεποιήκασι τὴν
κρίσιν, ἐν τῇ ἀγορᾷ· ἔπειτα τίμησίν μοι ἐποίησαν,
ἀνταποθανεῖν τοῦ νόμου κειμένου τὸν ἀποκτείναντα,

---

[1] ὑμῖν A corr. N : ἐμοὶ A pr.   [2] καὶ del. Sauppe.
[3] αὖ τό γε Sauppe : αὖ τό τε codd.

---

[a] For the meaning of this and the following paragraph
see Introd.
[b] A deliberate ambiguity. τῶν ἐν τῇ γῇ ταύτῃ can mean

used to involve me in to-day's proceedings were entirely illegal and arbitrary. Not that I wish to evade trial before a popular court ; as far as my belief in my innocence of the present charge and in the justice of your verdict is concerned, I would place my life in your hands even if you were not on oath and I were being tried under no particular law. No, my object is to let the arbitrary and illegal behaviour of the prosecution furnish you with a presumption as to the character of the rest of their case against me.

First,[a] whereas an information has been lodged against me as a malefactor, I am being tried for murder : a thing which has never before happened to anyone in this country.[b] Indeed, the prosecution have themselves borne witness to the fact that I am not a malefactor and cannot be charged under the law directed against malefactors, as that law is concerned with thieves and footpads, and they have omitted to prove my claim to either title. Thus, as far as this arrest of mine goes, they have given you every right and justification to acquit me. They object, however, that murder is a malefaction, and a grave one. I agree, a very grave one ; so is sacrilege ; so is treason ; but the laws which apply to each of them differ. In my case the prosecution have first of all caused the trial to be held in the one place from which those charged with murder are always debarred by proclamation, the Agora : and secondly, although it is laid down by law that a murderer shall pay with his life, they have entered a claim for damages[c]

(a) Athenian citizens, (b) persons who happen to be in Attica. Taken in sense (a) the statement is true. Taken in sense (b) it is probably false.

[c] For an explanation of the phrase τίμησιν ποιεῖν see Introd. pp. 155-156.

165

οὐ τοῦ ἐμοὶ συμφέροντος ἕνεκα, ἀλλὰ τοῦ σφίσιν
αὐτοῖς λυσιτελοῦντος, καὶ ἐνταῦθα ἔλασσον ἔνειμαν¹
τῷ τεθνηκότι τῶν ἐν τῷ νόμῳ κειμένων· οὗ δ᾽
ἕνεκα, γνώσεσθε προϊόντος τοῦ λόγου.

11 Ἔπειτα δέ, ὃ πάντας οἶμαι ὑμᾶς ἐπίστασθαι,
ἅπαντα τὰ δικαστήρια ἐν ὑπαίθρῳ δικάζει τὰς δίκας τοῦ φόνου, οὐδενὸς ἄλλου ἕνεκα ἢ ἵνα τοῦτο
μὲν οἱ δικασταὶ μὴ ἴωσιν εἰς τὸ αὐτὸ τοῖς μὴ
καθαροῖς τὰς χεῖρας, τοῦτο δὲ ὁ διώκων τὴν δίκην
τοῦ φόνου ἵνα μὴ ὁμωρόφιος γίγνηται τῷ αὐθέντῃ.
σὺ δὲ τοῦτο μὲν παρελθὼν τοῦτον τὸν νόμον τοὐναντίον τοῖς ἄλλοις πεποίηκας· τοῦτο δὲ δέον σε
διομόσασθαι ὅρκον τὸν μέγιστον καὶ ἰσχυρότατον,
ἐξώλειαν σαυτῷ² καὶ γένει καὶ οἰκίᾳ τῇ σῇ ἐπαρώ-
μενον, ἦ μὴν μὴ ἄλλα κατηγορήσειν ἐμοῦ ἢ εἰς
αὐτὸν τὸν φόνον, ὡς ἔκτεινα, ἐν ᾧ οὔτ᾽ ἂν κακὰ
πολλὰ εἰργασμένος ἡλισκόμην ἄλλῳ ἢ αὐτῷ τῷ
πράγματι, οὔτ᾽ ἂν πολλὰ ἀγαθὰ εἰργασμένος τού-
12 τοις ἂν ἐσῳζόμην τοῖς ἀγαθοῖς· ἃ σὺ παρελθών,³
αὐτὸς σεαυτῷ νόμους ἐξευρών, ἀνώμοτος μὲν αὐτὸς
ἐμοῦ κατηγορεῖς, ἀνώμοτοι δὲ οἱ μάρτυρες κατα-
μαρτυροῦσι, δέον αὐτοὺς τὸν αὐτὸν ὅρκον σοὶ
διομοσαμένους καὶ ἁπτομένους τῶν σφαγίων κατα-
μαρτυρεῖν ἐμοῦ. ἔπειτα κελεύεις τοὺς δικαστὰς
ἀνωμότοις πιστεύσαντας τοῖς μαρτυροῦσι φόνου
δίκην καταγνῶναι, οὓς σὺ αὐτὸς ἀπίστους κατ-

¹ ἔνειμαν A corr² : ἂν ἔνειμαν ἂν A pr. : ἔνειμαν ἂν N.
² σαυτῷ N : αὐτῷ A.   ³ σὺ παρελθών A : συμπαρελθών N.

ᵃ A promise which is never adequately fulfilled. The
only further reference to the subject is § 79, *ad fin.*
ᵇ The διωμοσία, or preliminary oath, taken by the prose-

—not as a kindness to me, but for their own benefit —and by so doing they have grudged the dead man his lawful due. Their motives you will learn in the course of my speech.[a]

Secondly, as of course you all know, every court judges cases of murder in the open air, and for good reasons : first, that the jurors may avoid entering the same building as those whose hands are unclean : and secondly, that he who is conducting the prosecution for murder may avoid being under the same roof as the murderer. No one but yourself has ever dreamed of evading this law. And not only that : you should, as a preliminary, have taken the most solemn and binding oath known,[b] swearing, under pain of causing yourself, your kin, and your house to perish from the earth, that you would accuse me only in connexion with the murder itself, to the effect that I committed it ; whereby, however numerous my crimes, I could have been condemned only on the charge before the court, and however numerous my good deeds, none of those good deeds could have gained me an acquittal. This requirement you have evaded. You have invented laws to suit yourself. You, the prosecutor, are not on oath ; nor are the witnesses, who are giving evidence against me which they should have given only after taking the same preliminary oath as yourself, their hands on the sacrifice as they did so. You bid the court, moreover, believe your witnesses, in spite of their not being on oath, and pass sentence for murder—

cutor, the defendant, and the witnesses of each, was peculiar to the δίκη φόνου ; the equivalent elsewhere was the ἀντωμοσία taken by both plaintiff and defendant at the ἀνάκρισις before the Archon. From this witnesses were exempt.

ἔστησας παρελθὼν τοὺς κειμένους νόμους, καὶ ἡγῇ[1]
χρῆναι αὐτοῖς τὴν σὴν παρανομίαν κρείσσω γενέσθαι αὐτῶν τῶν νόμων.

13 Λέγεις δὲ ὡς οὐκ ἂν παρέμεινα εἰ ἐλελύμην,
ἀλλ' ᾠχόμην ἂν ἀπιών,[2] ὡσπερεὶ ἄκοντά με ἀναγκάσας εἰσελθεῖν εἰς τὴν γῆν ταύτην. καίτοι ἐμοὶ
εἰ μηδὲν διέφερε στέρεσθαι τῆσδε τῆς πόλεως, ἴσον
[131] ἦν μοι καὶ προσκληθέντι μὴ ἐλθεῖν, ἀλλ' ἐρήμην
ὀφλεῖν τὴν δίκην,[3] τοῦτο δ' ἀπολογησαμένῳ τὴν
προτέραν ἐξεῖναι ἐξελθεῖν· ἅπασι γὰρ τοῦτο κοινόν
ἐστι. σὺ δέ, ὃ τοῖς ἄλλοις Ἕλλησι κοινόν ἐστιν,
ἰδίᾳ ζητεῖς με μόνον ἀποστερεῖν, αὐτὸς σαυτῷ
νόμον θέμενος.

14 Καίτοι τούς γε νόμους οἳ κεῖνται περὶ τῶν τοιούτων, πάντας ἂν οἶμαι ὁμολογῆσαι κάλλιστα νόμων
ἁπάντων κεῖσθαι καὶ ὁσιώτατα. ὑπάρχει μέν γε
αὐτοῖς ἀρχαιοτάτοις εἶναι ἐν τῇ γῇ ταύτῃ, ἔπειτα
τοὺς αὐτοὺς ἀεὶ περὶ τῶν αὐτῶν, ὅπερ μέγιστόν
ἐστι σημεῖον νόμων καλῶς κειμένων· ὁ γὰρ χρόνος
καὶ ἡ ἐμπειρία τὰ μὴ καλῶς ἔχοντα ἐκδιδάσκει
τοὺς ἀνθρώπους. ὥστε οὐ δεῖ ὑμᾶς[4] ἐκ τῶν τοῦ
κατηγόρου λόγων τοὺς νόμους καταμανθάνειν, εἰ
καλῶς ὑμῖν κεῖνται ἢ μή, ἀλλ' ἐκ τῶν νόμων τοὺς

---

[1] ἡγῇ Dryander: εἴ γε A, ἤ γε N.
[2] ἂν ἀπιών A corr.[2]: ἀνάπτων A pr. N.
[3] τὴν δίκην om. N.   [4] ὑμᾶς A: ἡμᾶς N.

---

[a] i.e. the prosecution justify their choice of an ἀπαγωγή rather
than a δίκη φόνου by claiming that only thus could the defendant be prevented from slipping through their fingers. The
defendant objects to this on two grounds : (a) The prosecution have no reason to assume that he would not have faced a
δίκη φόνου if left at liberty. In fact, he cut himself off from

when your own evasion of the laws of the land has destroyed the trustworthiness of those witnesses. Yes, you imagine that, in the eyes of the court, the laws themselves should have less authority than your own actions in defiance of them.

You reply that if I had been allowed my freedom, I should have made off without awaiting my trial—as though you had forced me to enter this country against my will. Yet if I attached no importance to being debarred from Athens for the future, it was equally open to me either to disregard the summons to appear in court and so lose the case by default, or to avail myself of the right given to every one of leaving the country after making the first speech for the defence.[a] You, however, for purely personal reasons, are trying to rob me, and me alone, of a privilege accorded to every Greek, by framing a law to suit yourself.

Yet it would be unanimously agreed, I think, that the laws which deal with cases such as the present are the most admirable and righteous of all laws. Not only have they the distinction of being the oldest in this country, but they have changed no more than the crime with which they are concerned ; and that is the surest token of good laws, as time and experience show mankind what is imperfect. Hence you must not use the speech for the prosecution to discover whether your laws are good or bad : you must use the laws to discover whether or not the speech

Athens by so defaulting, and that was a strong deterrent. (b) In any case, it was recognized that the defendant in a δίκη φόνου had the right of withdrawing into exile either before or during the trial. The speaker is of course careful not to remind the court that he is an alien, whose position is not necessarily the same as that of an Athenian citizen charged with murder.

τοῦ κατηγόρου λόγους, εἰ ὀρθῶς καὶ νομίμως ὑμᾶς διδάσκουσι[1] τὸ πρᾶγμα ἢ οὔ.

15 Οὕτως οἵ γε νόμοι κάλλιστα κεῖνται οἱ περὶ φόνου, οὓς οὐδεὶς πώποτε ἐτόλμησε κινῆσαι· σὺ δὲ μόνος δὴ τετόλμηκας γενέσθαι νομοθέτης ἐπὶ τὰ πονηρότερα,[2] καὶ ταῦτα παρελθὼν ζητεῖς με ἀδίκως ἀπολέσαι. ἃ δὲ σὺ παρανομεῖς, αὐτὰ ταῦτά μοι μέγιστα μαρτύριά[3] ἐστιν· εὖ γὰρ ᾔδεις ὅτι οὐδεὶς ἂν ἦν σοι ὃς ἐκεῖνον τὸν ὅρκον διομοσάμενος ἐμοῦ κατεμαρτύρησεν.

16 Ἔπειτα δὲ οὐχ ὡς πιστεύων τῷ πράγματι ἀναμφισβητήτως ἕνα τὸν ἀγῶνα περὶ τοῦ πράγματος ἐποιήσω, ἀλλὰ ἀμφισβήτησιν καὶ λόγον ὑπελίπου ὡς καὶ τοῖσδε τοῖς[4] δικασταῖς ἀπιστήσων. ὥστε μηδέν μοι ἐνθάδε [μηδὲ][5] πλέον εἶναι μηδ᾽ ἀποφυγόντι, ἀλλ᾽ ἐξεῖναί σοι λέγειν ὅτι κακοῦργος ἀπέφυγον, ἀλλ᾽ οὐ τοῦ φόνου τὴν δίκην· ἑλὼν δ᾽ αὖ ἀξιώσεις[6] με ἀποκτεῖναι ὡς τοῦ φόνου τὴν δίκην ὠφληκότα. καίτοι πῶς ἂν εἴη τούτων δεινότερα μηχανήματα, εἰ ὑμῖν μὲν ἅπαξ τουτουσὶ πεῖσαι κατείργασται ἃ βούλεσθε, ἐμοὶ δ᾽ ἅπαξ ἀποφυγόντι ὁ αὐτὸς κίνδυνος ὑπολείπεται;

17 Ἔτι δὲ μάλ᾽ ἐδέθην, ὦ ἄνδρες, παρανομώτατα ἁπάντων ἀνθρώπων. ἐθέλοντος γάρ μου ἐγγυητὰς τρεῖς καθιστάναι κατὰ τὸν νόμον, οὕτως οὗτοι

---

[1] διδάσκουσι Reiske: διδάξουσι A: διδάξει N.

[2] πονηρότερα N: πονηρότατα A.

[3] μαρτύρια A: μαρτυρία N (μεγίστη N corr.²).

[4] τοῖσδε τοῖς Pahle: τοῖς τότε codd.: κἂν τοῖς τότε δικασταῖς ἀμφισβητήσων Sauppe.

[5] μηδὲ del. Reiske.

[6] αὖ ἀξιώσεις Bekker: ἂν ἀξιώσεις A corr.²: ἂν ἀξιώσῃς A pr. N.

for the prosecution is giving you a correct and lawful interpretation of the case.[a]

The laws concerned with the taking of life are thus excellent, and no one has ever before ventured to interfere with them. You alone have had the audacity to turn legislator and substitute worse for better ; and the object of this arbitrary behaviour of yours is to have me put to death without just cause. In fact, your infringement of the law is itself decisive evidence in my favour, because you well knew that you would find no one to testify to my guilt once he had taken that preliminary oath.

Furthermore, instead of acting like a man confident of his case and arranging that it should be tried once and indisputably, you have left yourself grounds for dispute and argument, as though you proposed to show your distrust of even the present court. The result is that even if I am acquitted to-day, I am no better off ; you can say that it was as a malefactor that I was acquitted, not on a charge of murder. On the other hand, if you win your case, you will claim my life, on the ground that it is on a charge of murder that I have been tried and found guilty. Could anything more unfair be devised ? You and your associates have only to convince this court once, and your object is gained ; whereas I, if I am acquitted once, am left in the same peril as before.

Then again, gentlemen, my imprisonment was an act of illegality quite without parallel. I was ready to furnish the three sureties required by law ; yet

---

[a] This paragraph reappears in *Choreutes*, § 2 (*cf.* §§ 87-89 and *Chor.* §§ 3-4). The employment of such *loci communes* was frequent, and there is no reason to suspect the genuineness of the present passage.

διεπράξαντο τοῦτο ὥστε μὴ ἐγγενέσθαι μοι[1] ποιῆσαι.
τῶν δὲ ἄλλων ξένων ὅστις πώποτε ἠθέλησε καταστῆσαι ἐγγυητάς, οὐδεὶς πώποτ' ἐδέθη. καίτοι οἱ
ἐπιμεληταὶ τῶν κακούργων τῷ αὐτῷ χρῶνται νόμῳ
τούτῳ. ὥστε καὶ οὗτος κοινὸς τοῖς ἄλλοις πᾶσιν
ὢν ἐμοὶ μόνῳ ἐπέλιπε μὴ ἀπολῦσαι τοῦ δεσμοῦ.[2]

18 τούτοις γὰρ ἦν τοῦτο συμφέρον, πρῶτον μὲν
ἀπαρασκευότατον γενέσθαι με, μὴ δυνάμενον δια-
πράσσεσθαι αὐτὸν τἀμαυτοῦ πράγματα, ἔπειτα
κακοπαθεῖν τῷ σώματι, τούς τε φίλους προθυμο-
τέρους ἔχειν τοὺς ἐμαυτοῦ τούτοις τὰ ψευδῆ μαρτυρεῖν ἢ ἐμοὶ τἀληθῆ λέγειν, διὰ τὴν τοῦ σώματος
κακοπάθειαν. ὄνειδός τε αὐτῷ τε[3] ἐμοὶ περιέθεσαν
καὶ τοῖς ἐμοῖς προσήκουσιν εἰς τὸν βίον ἅπαντα.

19 Οὑτωσὶ μὲν δὴ πολλοῖς ἐλασσωθεὶς[4] τῶν νόμων
τῶν ὑμετέρων καὶ τοῦ δικαίου καθέστηκα εἰς τὸν
ἀγῶνα· ὅμως μέντοι γε καὶ ἐκ τούτων πειράσομαι
ἐμαυτὸν ἀναίτιον ἐπιδεῖξαι. καίτοι χαλεπόν γε
τὰ ἐκ πολλοῦ κατεψευσμένα καὶ ἐπιβεβουλευμένα,
ταῦτα παραχρῆμα ἀπελέγχειν· ἃ γάρ τις μὴ προσ-
εδόκησεν, οὐδὲ φυλάξασθαι ἐγχωρεῖ.

20 Ἐγὼ δὲ τὸν μὲν πλοῦν ἐποιησάμην ἐκ τῆς
Μυτιλήνης, ὦ ἄνδρες, ἐν τῷ πλοίῳ πλέων ᾧ
Ἡρῴδης οὗτος, ὅν φασιν ὑπ' ἐμοῦ ἀποθανεῖν·
ἐπλέομεν δὲ εἰς τὴν Αἶνον, ἐγὼ μὲν ὡς τὸν πατέρα

---

[1] μοι A : με N.
[2] ἀπολῦσαι τοῦ δεσμοῦ Thalheim : ὠφελῆσαι τοῦδε κόσμου
A pr. N : ὠφελεῖσθαι τοῦδε τοῦ νόμου A corr.[2]
[3] τε Reiske : γε codd.
[4] ἐλασσωθεὶς A pr. N : ἔλος σωθεὶς A corr. : ἔλος σωθεὶς
deteriores.

---

[a] i.e. the Eleven, who were the magistrates concerned in

172

the prosecution took steps to ensure that I should be prevented from doing so. Hitherto no alien willing to furnish sureties has ever been imprisoned ; and, moreover, the law concerned applies to the custodians of malefactors *a* as it does to others. Here again, then, we have a law by which everyone benefits : and it has failed to release me, and me alone, from confinement. The reason was that it was to the prosecution's advantage, first, that I should be prevented from looking after my interests in person, and so be quite unable to prepare for my trial : and secondly, that I should undergo bodily suffering, and by reason of that bodily suffering find my friends readier to tell lies as witnesses for the prosecution than the truth as witnesses for the defence.*b* In addition to which, lifelong disgrace has been brought upon me and mine.

Such are the manifold respects in which I have had to submit to a loss *c* of the rights accorded me by your laws and by justice before appearing in court. However, in spite of that disadvantage, I will try to prove my innocence : although it is hard to refute at a moment's notice false charges so carefully framed, as one cannot prepare oneself against the unexpected.

I sailed from Mytilene, gentlemen, as a passenger on the same boat as this Herodes whom, we are told, I murdered. We were bound for Aenus, I to visit my

the ἔνδειξις of a κακοῦργος and who were responsible for his safe custody pending trial.

b Apparently on the assumption that the rats will leave a sinking ship.

c From the reading ἕλος σωθείς of the inferior mss. the writer of a (late) Argument, which is found prefixed to the speech in A and N, made the curious deduction that the speaker's name was Ἕλος.

ANTIPHON

—ἐτύγχανε γὰρ ἐκεῖ ὢν τότε—ὁ δ᾽ Ἡρῴδης ἀνδράποδα Θρᾳξὶν ἀνθρώποις ἀπολύσων. συνέπλει δὲ
τά τε ἀνδράποδα ἃ ἔδει αὐτὸν ἀπολῦσαι, καὶ οἱ
Θρᾷκες οἱ λυσόμενοι. τούτων δ᾽ ὑμῖν τοὺς μάρτυρας παρέξομαι.

21 Ἡ μὲν πρόφασις ἑκατέρῳ τοῦ πλοῦ αὕτη· ἐτύ-
χομεν δὲ χειμῶνί τινι χρησάμενοι, ὑφ᾽ οὗ ἠναγκάσθημεν κατασχεῖν εἰς τῆς Μηθυμναίας τι χωρίον, οὗ τὸ πλοῖον ὥρμει τοῦτο εἰς ὃ μετεκβάντα¹
φασὶν ἀποθανεῖν αὐτόν [, τὸν Ἡρῴδην].²

[132] Καὶ πρῶτον μὲν αὐτὰ ταῦτα σκοπεῖτε, ὅτι ⟨οὐ
τῇ ἐ⟩μῇ προνοίᾳ³ μᾶλλον ἐγίγνετο ἢ τύχῃ. οὔτε
γὰρ πείσας τὸν ἄνδρα οὐδαμοῦ ἀπελέγχομαι σύμ-
πλουν μοι γενέσθαι, ἀλλ᾽ αὐτὸς καθ᾽ αὑτὸν⁴ τὸν

22 πλοῦν πεποιημένος ἕνεκα πραγμάτων ἰδίων· οὔτ᾽
αὖ ἐγὼ ἄνευ προφάσεως ἱκανῆς φαίνομαι τὸν
πλοῦν ποιησάμενος εἰς τὴν Αἶνον, οὔτε κατα-
σχόντες εἰς τὸ χωρίον τοῦτο ἀπὸ παρασκευῆς οὐδεμιᾶς, ἀλλ᾽ ἀνάγκῃ χρησάμενοι· οὔτ᾽ αὖ ἐπειδὴ
ὡρμισάμεθα, ἡ μετέκβασις⁵ ἐγένετο εἰς τὸ ἕτερον
πλοῖον οὐδενὶ μηχανήματι οὐδ᾽ ἀπάτῃ, ἀλλ᾽
ἀνάγκῃ καὶ τοῦτο ἐγίγνετο. ἐν ᾧ μὲν γὰρ ἐπλέομεν, ἀστέγαστον ἦν τὸ πλοῖον, εἰς ὃ δὲ μετέβημεν,
ἐστεγασμένον· τοῦ δὲ ὑετοῦ ἕνεκα ταῦτ᾽ ἦν. τούτων δ᾽ ὑμῖν μάρτυρας⁶ παρέξομαι.

---

¹ μετεκβάντα A corr. N : μεταβάντα A.
² τὸν Ἡρῴδην secl. Reiske.
³ ὅτι οὐ τῇ ἐμῇ πρ. Jebb : ὅτι οὐ προνοίᾳ Maetzner : ὅτι μὴ
προνοίᾳ codd.
⁴ καθ᾽ αὑτὸν Stephanus : κατ᾽ αὐτὸν codd.
⁵ μετέκβασις A corr. N : μετάβασις A.
⁶ μάρτυρας Reiske : μαρτυρίας codd.

174

father, who happened to be there just then, and Herodes to release some slaves [a] to certain Thracians. The slaves whom he was to release were also passengers, as were the Thracians who were to purchase their freedom. I will produce witnesses to satisfy you of this.

Witnesses

Such were our respective reasons for making the voyage. In the course of it, we happened to meet with a storm which forced us to put in at a place within the territory of Methymna, where the boat on to which Herodes transhipped, and on which the prosecution maintain that he met his end, lay at anchor.

Now consider these circumstances in themselves to begin with ; they were due to chance, not to any design on my part. It has nowhere been shown that I persuaded Herodes to accompany me ; on the contrary, it has been shown that I made the voyage independently on business of my own. Nor again, as is clear, was I making my voyage to Aenus without good reason. Nor did we put in at this particular spot by prearrangement of any sort ; we were forced to do so. And the transhipment after coming to anchor was similarly forced upon us, and not part of any plot or ruse. The boat on which we were passengers had no deck, whereas that on to which we transhipped had one ; and the rain was the reason for the exchange. I will produce witnesses to satisfy you of this.

[a] Probably prisoners of war who were being ransomed by their relatives. It is surprising that no attempt is made to throw suspicion on one of these Thracians, as a motive would have been easy to find.

23 Ἐπειδὴ δὲ μετεξέβημεν¹ εἰς τὸ ἕτερον πλοῖον,
ἐπίνομεν. καὶ ὁ μέν ἐστι φανερὸς ἐκβὰς ἐκ τοῦ
πλοίου καὶ οὐκ εἰσβὰς πάλιν· ἐγὼ δὲ τὸ παράπαν
οὐκ ἐξέβην ἐκ² τοῦ πλοίου τῆς νυκτὸς ἐκείνης. τῇ
δ' ὑστεραίᾳ, ἐπειδὴ ἀφανὴς ἦν ὁ ἀνήρ, ἐζητεῖτο οὐδέν
τι μᾶλλον ὑπὸ τῶν ἄλλων ἢ καὶ ὑπ' ἐμοῦ· καὶ εἴ
τῳ τῶν ἄλλων ἐδόκει δεινὸν εἶναι, καὶ ἐμοὶ ὁμοίως.
καὶ εἴς τε τὴν Μυτιλήνην ἐγὼ αἴτιος ἦ πεμφθῆναι
24 ἄγγελον, καὶ τῇ ἐμῇ γνώμῃ ἐπέμπετο. καὶ ἄλλου
οὐδενὸς ἐθέλοντος βαδίζειν, οὔτε τῶν ἀπὸ τοῦ
πλοίου οὔτε τῶν αὐτῷ τῷ Ἡρώδῃ συμπλεόντων,
ἐγὼ τὸν ἀκόλουθον τὸν ἐμαυτοῦ πέμπειν ἕτοιμος
ἦ· καίτοι οὐ δήπου γε κατ' ἐμαυτοῦ μηνυτὴν ἔπεμπον εἰδώς. ἐπειδὴ δὲ ὁ ἀνὴρ οὔτε ἐν τῇ Μυτιλήνῃ
ἐφαίνετο ζητούμενος οὔτ' ἄλλοθι οὐδαμοῦ, πλοῦς
τε ἡμῖν ἐγίγνετο, καὶ τἆλλ' ἀνήγετο πλοῖα ἅπαντα,
ᾠχόμην κἀγὼ πλέων. τούτων δ' ὑμῖν τοὺς μάρτυρας παρασχήσομαι.

25 Τὰ μὲν γενόμενα ταῦτ' ἐστίν· ἐκ δὲ τούτων ἤδη
σκοπεῖτε τὰ εἰκότα. πρῶτον μὲν γὰρ πρὶν ἀνάγεσ-
θαί με εἰς τὴν Αἶνον, ὅτε ἦν ἀφανὴς ὁ ἀνήρ, οὐδεὶς
ᾐτιάσατό με ἀνθρώπων, ἤδη πεπυσμένων τούτων
τὴν ἀγγελίαν· οὐ γὰρ ἄν ποτε ᾠχόμην πλέων.
ἀλλ' εἰς μὲν τὸ παραχρῆμα κρεῖσσον ἦν τὸ ἀληθὲς
καὶ τὸ γεγενημένον τῆς τούτων αἰτιάσεως, καὶ
ἅμα ἐγὼ ἔτι ἐπεδήμουν· ἐπειδὴ δὲ ἐγώ τε ᾠχόμην

---

¹ μετεξέβημεν Α : μετέβημεν Ν.   ² ἐκ om. Ν.

Witnesses

After crossing into the other boat, we fell to drinking. Now whereas it is established that Herodes quitted the boat and did not board it again, I did not leave the boat at all that night. Next day, when Herodes was missing, I joined in the search as anxiously as any ; if anyone considered the matter serious, I did. Not only was I responsible for the dispatch of a messenger to Mytilene, that is to say, it was upon my suggestion that it was decided to send one, but when none of the passengers or the personal companions of Herodes volunteered to go, I offered to send my own attendant ; and I hardly imagine that I was deliberately proposing to send someone who would inform against me. Finally, when the search had failed to reveal any trace of Herodes either at Mytilene or anywhere else and, with the return of fair sailing-weather, the rest of the boats began standing out to sea, I likewise took my departure. I will produce witnesses to prove these statements to you.

Witnesses

Those are the facts ; now draw the logical conclusions. First, in the interval before I put to sea for Aenus, when Herodes was missing, not a soul accused me, although the prosecution had already heard the news ; otherwise I should never have taken my departure. For the moment the true facts of the matter were too much for any charge which they could bring ; and, moreover, I was still on the island. It was not until I had resumed my voyage, and the

πλέων καὶ οὗτοι ἐξ ἐπιβουλῆς συνέθεσαν ταῦτα
καὶ ἐμηχανήσαντο κατ᾽ ἐμοῦ, τότε ᾐτιάσαντο.

26 Λέγουσι δὲ ὡς ἐν μὲν τῇ γῇ ἀπέθανεν ὁ ἀνήρ,
κἀγὼ λίθον αὐτῷ ἐνέβαλον[1] εἰς τὴν κεφαλήν, ὃς οὐκ
ἐξέβην τὸ παράπαν ἐκ τοῦ πλοίου. καὶ τοῦτο μὲν
ἀκριβῶς οὗτοι ἴσασιν. ὅπως δ᾽ ἠφανίσθη ὁ ἀνήρ,
οὐδενὶ λόγῳ εἰκότι δύνανται ἀποφαίνειν. δῆλον
γὰρ ὅτι ἐγγύς που τοῦ λιμένος εἰκὸς ἦν τοῦτο[2]
γίγνεσθαι, τοῦτο μὲν μεθύοντος τοῦ ἀνδρός, τοῦτο
δὲ νύκτωρ ἐκβάντος ἐκ τοῦ πλοίου· οὔτε γὰρ αὐτοῦ[3]
κρατεῖν ἴσως ἂν ἐδύνατο, οὔτε τῷ ἀπάγοντι νύκτωρ
μακρὰν ὁδὸν ἡ πρόφασις ἂν εἰκότως ἐγίγνετο·

27 ζητουμένου δὲ τοῦ ἀνδρὸς δύο ἡμέρας καὶ ἐν
τῷ λιμένι καὶ ἄπωθεν τοῦ λιμένος, οὔτε ὀπτὴρ
οὐδεὶς ἐφάνη οὔθ᾽ αἷμα οὔτ᾽ ἄλλο σημεῖον οὐδέν.
κᾆτ᾽ ἐγὼ συγχωρῶ τῷ τούτων λόγῳ, παρεχό-
μενος μὲν τοὺς μάρτυρας ὡς οὐκ ἐξέβην ἐκ τοῦ
πλοίου· εἰ δὲ καὶ ὡς μάλιστα ἐξέβην ἐκ τοῦ
πλοίου, οὐδενὶ τρόπῳ εἰκὸς ἦν ἀφανισθέντα λαθεῖν
τὸν ἄνθρωπον, εἴπερ γε[4] μὴ πάνυ πόρρω ἀπῆλθεν
ἀπὸ τῆς θαλάσσης.

28 Ἀλλ᾽ ὡς κατεποντώθη λέγουσιν. ἐν τίνι πλοίῳ;
δῆλον γὰρ ὅτι ἐξ αὐτοῦ τοῦ λιμένος ἦν τὸ πλοῖον.
πῶς ἂν οὖν οὐκ ἐξηυρέθη; καὶ μὴν εἰκός γε ἦν
καὶ σημεῖόν τι γενέσθαι ἐν τῷ πλοίῳ ἀνδρὸς τεθνεώ-

---

[1] αὐτῷ ἐνέβαλον Ν : ἐνέβαλον αὐτῷ Α.
[2] τοῦτο Α : αὐτὸ Ν.
[3] αὐτοῦ Taylor : αὐτοῦ codd.
[4] γε om. Α.

---

[a] These "witnesses" are not specifically referred to again.
If they are included in those cited at the end of the paragraph, it is strange that nothing more is made of their
evidence. In all probability the speaker is alluding to the

prosecution had conspired to form this plot of theirs upon my life, that they made their accusation.

Their story is that it was on shore that Herodes was killed, and that I, who did not leave the boat at all, struck him upon the head with a stone. Yet while they have detailed information of this, they cannot give any plausible account of how the man came to disappear. Clearly, the probabilities suggest that the crime was committed somewhere in the neighbourhood of the harbour. On the one hand, Herodes was drunk; and on the other hand, it was at night that he left the boat. He probably would not have been in a condition to control his own movements, nor could anyone who wished to take him a long way off by night have found any plausible excuse for doing so. Yet in spite of a two days' search both in the harbour and at a distance from it, no eyewitness, no blood-stain, and no clue of any other description was found. But I will go further. I accept the prosecution's story. I can indeed produce witnesses to prove that I did not quit the boat.[a] But suppose as much as you please that I did quit it; it is still utterly improbable that the man should have remained undiscovered after his disappearance, if he did not go very far from the sea.

However, we are told that he was thrown into the sea. From what boat? Clearly, the boat came from the harbour itself; and in that case, why should it not have been identified? For that matter, we should also have expected to find some traces in the boat, seeing that a dead man had been placed in it

[a] witness for the prosecution who sturdily maintained that Euxitheus remained on board all night. See § 42.

τος ⟨ἐντιθεμένου⟩[1] καὶ ἐκβαλλομένου νύκτωρ. νῦν δὲ ἐν ᾧ μὲν ἔπινε πλοίῳ καὶ ἐξ οὗ ἐξέβαινεν, ἐν τούτῳ φασὶν εὑρεῖν σημεῖα, ἐν ᾧ αὐτοὶ μὴ ὁμολογοῦσιν ἀποθανεῖν τὸν ἄνδρα· ἐν ᾧ δὲ κατεποντώθη, οὐχ ηὗρον οὔτ᾽ αὐτὸ τὸ πλοῖον οὔτε σημεῖον οὐδέν. τούτων δ᾽ ὑμῖν τοὺς μάρτυρας παρασχήσομαι.[2]

MΑΡΤΥΡΕΣ

29 Ἐπειδὴ δὲ ἐγὼ μὲν φροῦδος ἦ πλέων εἰς τὴν Αἶνον, τὸ δὲ πλοῖον ἧκεν εἰς τὴν Μυτιλήνην ἐν ᾧ
[133] ἐγὼ καὶ ὅ[3] Ἡρῴδης ἐπίνομεν,[4] πρῶτον μὲν εἰσβάντες εἰς τὸ πλοῖον ἠρεύνων, καὶ ἐπειδὴ τὸ αἷμα[5] ηὗρον, ἐνταῦθα ἔφασαν τεθνάναι τὸν ἄνδρα· ἐπειδὴ δὲ αὐτοῖς τοῦτο οὐκ ἐνεχώρει, ἀλλ᾽ ἐφαίνετο τῶν[6] προβάτων ὂν αἷμα, ἀποτραπόμενοι τούτου τοῦ λόγου συλλαβόντες ἐβασάνιζον τοὺς ἀνθρώπους.
30 καὶ ὃν μὲν τότε παραχρῆμα ἐβασάνισαν, οὗτος μὲν

---

[1] ἐντιθεμένου add. Blass.
[2] παρασχήσομαι Bekker: παραστήσομαι codd.
[3] ὅ om. A.   [4] ἐπίνομεν Weil: ἐπλέομεν codd.
[5] τι αἷμα Ald.   [6] τῶν del. Reiske.

---

[a] Weil's emendation is certain. Herodes and Euxitheus took shelter for the night on a boat bound for Mytilene. After the storm was over, the passengers returned to their own vessel.

[b] τὸ αἷμα (cf. τῶν προβάτων), because it had already been mentioned in the preceding evidence. Similarly with τοὺς ἀνθρώπους (infr.); they had been referred to in the speech for the prosecution.

[c] The references in the course of the speech to the two witnesses for the prosecution are confusing. The relevant passages are §§ 29, 42, 49, and 52. From § 49 it is clear that one was a slave and the other a free man, although he cannot

180

and thrown overboard in the dark. The prosecution claim, indeed, to have found traces—but only in the boat on board of which he was drinking and which he quitted, the one boat on which they themselves agree that he was not murdered. The boat from which he was thrown into the sea they have not discovered; they have found neither it itself nor any trace of it. I will produce witnesses to prove these statements to you.

Witnesses

After I had departed for Aenus and the boat on which Herodes and I had been drinking [a] had reached Mytilene, the prosecution first of all went on board and conducted a search. On finding the bloodstains,[b] they claimed that this was where Herodes had met his end. But the suggestion proved an unfortunate one, as the blood turned out to be that of the animals sacrificed. So they abandoned that line, and instead seized the two men and examined them under torture.[c] The first, who was tortured there and then,

have been a Greek, as he was subjected to torture by the prosecution (*ibid.*). § 29 suggests that the two were members of the crew of the homeward bound vessel on which Euxitheus and Herodes sheltered from the rain, and that after the storm they continued their voyage to Mytilene, where the relatives of Herodes immediately came aboard and took them into custody. This is supported by § 52, which implies that Euxitheus parted from the men after the storm, he proceeding to Aenus, and they to Mytilene. § 42, however, offers a difficulty. Euxitheus there says with reference to the free man: "he sailed in the same boat as myself, and was present and in my company throughout," a statement which on the face of it should mean that he travelled with Euxitheus from Mytilene to Aenus. There seems to be only one explanation of the inconsistency. Euxitheus must have been intentionally misrepresenting the facts in § 42, as it was

οὐδὲν εἶπε περὶ ἐμοῦ φλαῦρον· ὃν δ᾽ ἡμέραις ὕστερον
πολλαῖς ἐβασάνισαν, ἔχοντες παρὰ σφίσιν αὐτοῖς
τὸν πρόσθεν χρόνον, οὗτος ἦν ὁ πεισθεὶς ὑπὸ τούτων καὶ καταψευσάμενος ἐμοῦ. παρέξομαι δὲ
τούτων τοὺς μάρτυρας.

MΑΡΤΥΡΕΣ

31 Ὡς μὲν ὕστερον τοσούτῳ[1] χρόνῳ ὁ ἀνὴρ ἐβα-
σανίσθη, μεμαρτύρηται ὑμῖν· προσέχετε δὲ τὸν
νοῦν αὐτῇ τῇ βασάνῳ, οἷα γεγένηται. ὁ μὲν γὰρ
δοῦλος, ᾧ ἴσως οὗτοι τοῦτο μὲν ἐλευθερίαν ὑπ-
έσχοντο, τοῦτο δ᾽ ἐπὶ τούτοις ἦν παύσασθαι κακού-
μενον αὐτόν, ἴσως ὑπ᾽ ἀμφοῖν πεισθεὶς κατεψεύσατό
μου, τὴν μὲν ἐλευθερίαν ἐλπίσας οἴσεσθαι, τῆς δὲ
βασάνου εἰς τὸ παραχρῆμα βουλόμενος ἀπηλλάχθαι.
οἶμαι δ᾽ ὑμᾶς ἐπίστασθαι τοῦτο, ὅτι ἐφ᾽ οἷς ἂν τὸ
32 πλεῖστον μέρος τῆς βασάνου, πρὸς τούτων εἰσὶν
οἱ βασανιζόμενοι λέγειν ὅ τι ἂν[2] ἐκείνοις μέλλωσι
χαριεῖσθαι· ἐν τούτοις γὰρ αὐτοῖς ἐστιν ἡ ὠφέλεια,
ἄλλως τε κἂν μὴ παρόντες τυγχάνωσιν ὧν ἂν
καταψεύδωνται. εἰ μὲν γὰρ ἐγὼ[3] ἐκέλευον αὐτὸν
στρεβλοῦν ὡς οὐ τἀληθῆ λέγοντα, ἴσως ἂν ἐν αὐτῷ
τούτῳ ἀπετρέπετο μηδὲν κατ᾽ ἐμοῦ καταψεύδεσθαι·
νῦν δὲ αὐτοὶ[4] ἦσαν καὶ βασανισταὶ καὶ ἐπιτιμηταὶ
τῶν σφίσιν αὐτοῖς συμφερόντων.

[1] τοσούτῳ Reiske: τούτῳ τῷ codd.
[2] ὅ τι ἂν Ald.: ὅταν codd.
[3] εἰ μὲν γὰρ ἐγὼ Gebauer: εἰ γὰρ ἐγὼ μὲν A pr. N: μὲν del.
A corr.
[4] αὐτοὶ Blass: αὑτοὶ codd.

important to show that the favourable evidence of this
182

said nothing to damage me. The second was tortured several days later, after being in the prosecution's company throughout the interval. It was he who was induced by them to incriminate me falsely. I will produce witnesses to confirm these facts.

Witnesses

You have listened to evidence for the length of the delay before the man's examination under torture; now notice the actual character of that examination. The slave was doubtless promised his freedom: it was certainly to the prosecution alone that he could look for release from his sufferings. Probably both of these considerations induced him to make the false charges against me which he did; he hoped to gain his freedom, and his one immediate wish was to end the torture. I need not remind you, I think, that witnesses under torture are biassed in favour of those who do most of the torturing; they will say anything likely to gratify them. It is their one chance of salvation, especially when the victims of their lies happen not to be present. Had I myself proceeded to give orders that the slave should be racked for not telling the truth, that step in itself would doubtless have been enough to make him stop incriminating me falsely. As it was, the examination was conducted by men who also knew what their own interests required.

witness was based upon a personal acquaintance with his movements and general behaviour. If so, it seems not unlikely that the man was actually in the pay of Euxitheus. Can he have been the ἀκόλουθος of § 24, sent back to Mytilene by E. and there detained by the family of Herodes?

183

ANTIPHON

33 Ἕως μὲν οὖν μετὰ χρηστῆς[1] ἐλπίδος ἐγίγνωσκέ
μου καταψευσάμενος, τούτῳ διϊσχυρίζετο τῷ λόγῳ·
ἐπειδὴ δὲ ἐγίγνωσκεν ἀποθανούμενος, ἐνταῦθ' ἤδη
τῇ ἀληθείᾳ ἐχρῆτο, καὶ ἔλεγεν ὅτι πεισθείη ὑπὸ
τούτων ἐμοῦ καταψεύδεσθαι. διαπειραθέντα δ'
αὐτὸν τὰ ψευδῆ λέγειν, ὕστερον δὲ[2] τἀληθῆ λέγοντα,
34 οὐδέτερα ὠφέλησεν,[3] ἀλλ' ἀπέκτειναν ἄγοντες τὸν
ἄνδρα, τὸν μηνυτήν, ᾧ πιστεύοντες ἐμὲ διώκουσι,
τοὐναντίον ποιήσαντες ἢ οἱ ἄλλοι ἄνθρωποι. οἱ
μὲν γὰρ ἄλλοι τοῖς μηνυταῖς τοῖς μὲν ἐλευθέροις
χρήματα διδόασι, τοὺς δὲ δούλους ἐλευθεροῦσιν·
οὗτοι δὲ θάνατον τῷ μηνυτῇ τὴν δωρεὰν ἀπέδοσαν,
ἀπαγορευόντων τῶν φίλων τῶν ἐμῶν μὴ ἀπο-
35 κτείνειν τὸν ἄνδρα πρὶν [ἂν][4] ἐγὼ ἔλθοιμι. δῆλον
οὖν ὅτι οὐ τοῦ σώματος αὐτοῦ[5] χρεία ἦν αὐτοῖς,
ἀλλὰ τῶν λόγων· ζῶν μὲν γὰρ ὁ ἀνὴρ διὰ τῆς
αὐτῆς βασάνου ἰὼν ὑπ' ἐμοῦ κατήγορος ἂν ἐγίγνετο τῆς τούτων ἐπιβουλῆς, τεθνεὼς δὲ τὸν μὲν
ἔλεγχον τῆς ἀληθείας ἀπεστέρει δι' αὐτοῦ τοῦ
σώματος ἀπολλυμένου, τοῖς δὲ λόγοις τοῖς ἐψευσ-
μένοις ὑπ' ἐκείνου ὡς ἀληθέσιν οὖσιν ἐγὼ ἀπόλλυμαι. τούτων δὲ μάρτυράς μοι κάλει.

⟨ΜΑΡΤΥΡΕΣ⟩[6]

36 Ἐχρῆν μὲν[7] γὰρ αὐτούς, ὡς ἐγὼ νομίζω, ἐνθάδε
παρέχοντας τὸν μηνυτὴν αὐτὸν ἀπελέγχειν ἐμέ,
καὶ αὐτῷ τούτῳ χρῆσθαι ἀγωνίσματι, ἐμφανῆ

---

[1] χρηστῆς N : χρηστῆς τῆς A.
[2] δὲ A corr. N : μὲν A pr.
[3] ὠφέλησεν Reiske : ὠφέλησαν codd.
[4] ἂν secl. Dobree : πρὶν ἐγὼ ἀνέλθοιμι Ignatius.
[5] αὐτοῦ om. A pr.
[6] Titulum inseruit Reiske.
[7] μὲν om. N.

184

Now as long as he believed that he had something to gain by falsely incriminating me, he firmly adhered to that course ; but on finding that he was doomed, he at once reverted to the truth and admitted that it was our friends here who had induced him to lie about me. However, neither his persevering attempts at falsehood nor his subsequent confession of the truth helped him. They took him, took the man upon whose disclosures they are resting their case against me, and put him to death,[a] a thing which no one else would have dreamed of doing. As a rule, informers are rewarded with money, if they are free, and with their liberty, if they are slaves. The prosecution paid for their information with death, and that in spite of a protest from my friends that they should postpone the execution until my return. Clearly, it was not his person, but his evidence, which they required ; had the man remained alive, he would have been tortured by me in the same way, and the prosecution would be confronted with their plot : but once he was dead, not only did the loss of his person mean that I was deprived of my opportunity of establishing the truth, but his false statements are assumed to be true and are proving my undoing. Call me witnesses to confirm these facts.

⟨*Witnesses*⟩

In my opinion, they should have produced the informer himself in court, if they wished to prove me guilty. That was the issue to which they should have

---

[a] It should be noted that the witness was a slave who had been purchased by the prosecution (*cf.* previous note and § 47, *init.*).

ANTIPHON

παρέχοντας τὸν ἄνδρα καὶ κελεύοντας βασανίζειν,
ἀλλὰ μὴ ἀποκτεῖναι. φέρε γὰρ δὴ ποτέρῳ νῦν
χρήσονται τῶν λόγων; πότερα ᾧ πρῶτον εἶπεν
ἢ ᾧ ὕστερον; καὶ πότερ' ἀληθῆ ἐστιν, ὅτ' ἔφη
37 με εἰργάσθαι τὸ ἔργον ἢ ὅτ' οὐκ ἔφη; εἰ μὲν
γὰρ ἐκ τοῦ εἰκότος ἐξετασθῆναι δεῖ τὸ πρᾶγμα,
οἱ ὕστεροι λόγοι ἀληθέστεροι φαίνονται. ἐψεύ-
δετο μὲν γὰρ ἐπ' ὠφελείᾳ τῇ ἑαυτοῦ, ἐπειδὴ δὲ
τῷ¹ ψεύδεσθαι ἀπώλλυτο, ἡγήσατο τἀληθῆ κατει-
πὼν διὰ τοῦτο² σωθῆναι ἄν. τῆς μὲν οὖν ἀληθείας
οὐκ ἦν αὐτῷ τιμωρὸς οὐδείς· οὐ γὰρ παρὼν ἐγὼ
ἐτύγχανον, ᾧπερ σύμμαχος ἦν ἡ ἀλήθεια τῶν
ὑστέρων λόγων· τοὺς δὲ προτέρους λόγους τοὺς
κατεψευσμένους ἦσαν οἱ ἀφανιοῦντες, ὥστε μηδέ-
38 ποτε εἰς τὸ ἀληθὲς καταστῆναι. καὶ οἱ μὲν
ἄλλοι καθ' ὧν ἂν μηνύῃ³ τις, οὗτοι⁴ κλέπτουσι
τοὺς μηνύοντας, κᾆτ' ἀφανίζουσιν· αὐτοὶ δὲ οὗτοι
[134] οἱ ἀπάγοντες καὶ ζητοῦντες τὸ πρᾶγμα τὸν κατ'
ἐμοῦ μηνυτὴν ἠφάνισαν. καὶ εἰ μὲν ἐγὼ τὸν ἄνδρα
ἠφάνισα ἢ μὴ ἤθελον ἐκδοῦναι τούτοις ἢ ἄλλον
τινὰ ἔφευγον ἔλεγχον, αὐτοῖς ἂν⁵ τούτοις ἰσχυροτάτοις εἰς τὰ πράγματα ἐχρῶντο, καὶ ἦν ταῦτα
αὐτοῖς μέγιστα τεκμήρια κατ' ἐμοῦ· νῦν δέ, ὁπότε
αὐτοὶ οὗτοι προκαλουμένων τῶν φίλων τῶν ἐμῶν
ταῦτ' ἔφυγον, ἐμοὶ δήπου κατὰ τούτων εἶναι χρὴ

---

¹ τῷ A corr. ²: τὸ A pr. N.
² τοῦτο A pr. N: τούτου A corr.²

186

brought the case. Instead of putting the man to death, they ought to have produced him in the flesh and challenged me to examine him under torture. As it is, which of his statements will they use, may I ask : his first or his second ? And which is true : the statement that I committed the murder or the statement that I did not ? If we are to judge from probability, it is obviously the second which is the truer ; he was lying to benefit himself, but on finding that those lies were proving fatal, he thought that he would be saved by telling the truth. However, he had no one to stand up for the truth, as I, who was vindicated by his second, true statement, was unfortunately not present ; while there were those who were ready to put his first, his false one, beyond all reach of future correction. As a rule, it is the victim who quietly seizes an informer and then makes away with him. In this case, it is the very persons who arrested the slave in order to discover the truth who have done so ; and it is the very person who had supplied information against myself with whom they have made away. Had I myself been responsible for his disappearance, had I refused to surrender him to the prosecution or declined to establish the truth in some other way, they would have treated that very fact as most significant : it would have furnished the strongest presumption in their favour that I was guilty. So now that they themselves have declined to submit to an inquiry, in spite of a challenge from my friends to do so, that fact should in the same way

---

³ ἂν μηνύῃ N : μηνύῃ ἄν A.
⁴ οὗτοι Reiske : αὐτοὶ codd.
⁵ αὐτοῖς ἂν Spengel : αὐτοὶ δὴ codd.

ταὐτὰ ταῦτα[1] τεκμήρια, ὡς οὐκ ἀληθῆ τὴν αἰτίαν
ἐπέφερον ἦν ᾐτιῶντο.[2]

39 Ἔτι δὲ καὶ τάδε λέγουσιν, ὡς ὡμολόγει[3] ὁ ἄνθρωπος βασανιζόμενος συναποκτεῖναι τὸν ἄνδρα.
ἐγὼ δέ φημι ταῦτα μὲν οὐ λέγειν αὐτόν, ὅτι δὲ
ἐξαγάγοι[4] ἐμὲ καὶ τὸν ἄνδρα ἐκ τοῦ πλοίου, καὶ
ὅτι ἤδη τεθνεῶτα αὐτὸν ὑπ᾽ ἐμοῦ συνανελὼν[5]
40 καὶ ἐνθεὶς εἰς τὸ πλοῖον καταποντώσειε. καίτοι
σκέψασθε ὅτι πρῶτον μέν, πρὶν ἐπὶ τὸν τροχὸν
ἀναβῆναι, ὁ ἀνὴρ μέχρι τῆς ἐσχάτης ἀνάγκης τῇ
ἀληθείᾳ ἐχρῆτο καὶ ἀπέλυέ με τῆς αἰτίας· ἐπειδὴ
δὲ ἐπὶ τὸν τροχὸν ἀνέβη, τῇ ἀνάγκῃ χρώμενος
ἤδη κατεψεύδετό μου, βουλόμενος ἀπηλλάχθαι
41 τῆς βασάνου. ἐπειδὴ δὲ ἐπαύσατο βασανιζόμενος,
οὐκέτι ἔφη με τούτων εἰργάσθαι οὐδέν, ἀλλὰ τὸ
τελευταῖον ἀπώμωξεν ἐμέ τε καὶ αὑτὸν ὡς ἀδίκως
ἀπολλυμένους, οὐ χάριτι τῇ ἐμῇ — πῶς γάρ; ὅς
γε κατεψεύσατο, — ἀλλ᾽ ἀναγκαζόμενος ὑπὸ τοῦ
ἀληθοῦς καὶ βεβαιῶν τοὺς πρώτους λόγους ὡς
ἀληθεῖς εἰρημένους.

42 Ἔπειτα δὲ ὁ ἕτερος ἄνθρωπος, ὁ ἐν τῷ αὐτῷ
πλοίῳ πλέων καὶ παρὼν διὰ τέλους καὶ συνών μοι,
τῇ αὐτῇ βασάνῳ βασανιζόμενος τοῖς μὲν πρώτοις
καὶ τοῖς ὕστερον λόγοις τοῖς τοῦ ἀνθρώπου συνεφέρετο ὡς ἀληθέσιν οὖσι, διὰ τέλους γάρ με ἀπέλυε,
τοῖς δ᾽ ἐπὶ τοῦ τροχοῦ λεγομένοις, οὓς ἐκεῖνος

---

[1] ταὐτὰ ταῦτα Fuhr: ταῦτα τὰ codd. Cf. i. 11., vi. 27.
[2] ᾐτιῶντο Dobree: ᾤοντο codd.
[3] ὡμολόγει A: ὁμολογεῖ N.
[4] ἐξαγάγοι Baiter: ἐξάγει codd. (-οι A corr.).
[5] συνανελὼν Maetzner: συνελὼν N: συνελὼν καὶ om. A.

[a] Cf. Stepmother, § 11, and Choreutes, § 27, for a similar
line of argument.

furnish a presumption in my favour that the charge which they are bringing is a false one.[a]

They further allege that the slave admitted under torture that he had been my accomplice in the murder. I maintain that he did not say this ; what he said was that he conducted Herodes and myself off the boat, and that after I had murdered him, he helped me pick him up and put him in the boat ; then he threw him into the sea. Also let me point out to you that at the start, before being placed on the wheel, in fact, until extreme pressure was brought to bear, the man adhered to the truth and declared me innocent. It was only when on the wheel, and when driven to it, that he falsely incriminated me, in order to put an end to the torture. When it was over, he ceased affirming that I had had any part in the crime ; indeed, at the end he bemoaned the injustice with which both I and he were being sent to our doom : not that he was trying to do me a kindness—hardly that, after falsely accusing me as he had done ; no, the truth left him no choice : he was confirming as true the declaration which he had made to begin with.

Then there was the second man.[b] He had travelled on the same boat as I : had been present throughout the voyage : and had been constantly in my company. When tortured in the same way, he confirmed the first and last statements of the other as true ; for he declared me innocent from start to finish. On the other hand, the assertions made by the other upon the wheel, made not because they were the truth,

---

[b] The ἐλεύθερος of § 49. Since he is tortured, he cannot have been born a Greek. For further details as to both witnesses see p. 180, note c.

ἀνάγκῃ μᾶλλον ἢ ἀληθείᾳ ἔλεγε, τούτοις δὲ δι-
εφέρετο. ὁ μὲν γὰρ ἐκβάντα μ' ἔφη ἐκ τοῦ πλοίου
ἀποκτεῖναι τὸν ἄνδρα, καὶ αὐτὸς ἤδη τεθνεῶτα
συνανελεῖν[1] μοι· ὁ δὲ τὸ παράπαν ἔφη οὐκ ἐκβῆναί
43 με ἐκ τοῦ πλοίου. καίτοι τὸ εἰκὸς σύμμαχόν μοί
ἐστιν. οὐ γὰρ δήπου οὕτω κακοδαίμων ἐγώ, ὥστε
τὸ μὲν ἀποκτεῖναι τὸν ἄνδρα προὐνοησάμην μόνος,
ἵνα μοι μηδεὶς συνειδείη, ἐν ᾧ μοι ὁ πᾶς κίνδυνος
ἦν, ἤδη δὲ πεπραγμένου μοι τοῦ ἔργου μάρτυρας
44 καὶ συμβούλους ἐποιούμην. καὶ ἀπέθανε μὲν ὁ[2]
ἀνὴρ οὑτωσὶ[3] ἐγγὺς τῆς θαλάσσης καὶ τῶν
πλοίων, ὡς ὁ τούτων λόγος ἐστίν· ὑπὸ δὲ ἑνὸς
ἀνδρὸς ἀποθνήσκων οὔτε ἀνέκραγεν οὔτ' αἴσθησιν
οὐδεμίαν ἐποίησεν οὔτε τοῖς ἐν τῇ γῇ οὔτε
τοῖς ἐν τῷ πλοίῳ; καὶ μὴν πολλῷ ⟨ἐπὶ⟩[4] πλέον
γε ἀκούειν[5] ἔστι νύκτωρ ἢ μεθ' ἡμέραν, ἐπ' ἀκτῆς
ἢ κατὰ πόλιν· καὶ μὴν ἔτι ἐγρηγορότων φασὶν
ἐκβῆναι τὸν ἄνδρα ἐκ τοῦ πλοίου.
45 Ἔπειτα ἐν τῇ γῇ μὲν ἀποθανόντος, ἐντιθεμένου
δὲ εἰς τὸ πλοῖον, οὔτε ἐν τῇ γῇ σημεῖον οὐδὲ αἷμα
ἐφάνη οὔτε ἐν τῷ πλοίῳ, νύκτωρ μὲν ἀναιρεθέντος,
νύκτωρ δ' ἐντιθεμένου εἰς τὸ πλοῖον. ἢ δοκεῖ ἂν
ὑμῖν ἄνθρωπος δύνασθαι ἐν τοιούτῳ πράγματι ὢν
τά τ' ἐν τῇ γῇ ὄντα ἀναξύσαι καὶ τὰ ἐν τῷ πλοίῳ
ἀποσπογγίσαι,[6] ἃ οὐδὲ μεθ' ἡμέραν ⟨ἂν⟩[7] τις οἷός

---

[1] συνανελεῖν A: συνελεῖν N. [2] ὁ om. A.
[3] οὑτωσὶ Blass: οὑτοσὶ codd.
[4] ἐπὶ add. Schoemann.
[5] γε ἀκούειν Schoemann: γεγωνεῖν Cobet: γε ἀγνοεῖν codd.
[6] ἀποσπογγίσαι A: ἀνασπογγίσαι N.
[7] ἂν add. Baiter.

---

[a] If the ms. reading is retained, this sentence will be the
supposed answer of the prosecution to the question just put

but because they were wrung from him, he contradicted. Thus, while the one said that it was not until I had left the boat that I killed Herodes, and that he had himself helped me to remove the body after the murder, the other maintained that I did not leave the boat at all. And indeed, the probabilities are in my favour; I hardly imagine myself to have been so benighted that after planning the murder on my own to ensure that no one was privy to it—for there lay my one great danger—I proceeded to furnish myself with witnesses and confederates once the crime had been committed. Furthermore, Herodes was murdered very close to the sea and the boats, or so we are told by the prosecution. Was a man who was struck down by but one assailant not going to shout out or attract the attention of those on shore or on board? Moreover, sounds can be heard *a* over much greater distances by night than by day, on a beach than in a city. Moreover, it is admitted that the passengers were still awake when Herodes left the boat.

Again, he was murdered on shore and placed in the boat; yet no trace or bloodstain was found either on shore or in the boat, in spite of the fact that it was at night that he was picked up and at night that he was placed in the boat. Do you think that any human being in such circumstances would have been able to smooth out the traces on shore and wipe away the marks on the boat, clues which a calm and

by the defence; but the introductory καὶ μὴν makes against such an interpretation. In view of the frequent mis-copying of perfectly common words elsewhere in the MSS., it is less likely that γε ἀγνοεῖν arose through ignorance from the rarity γεγωνεῖν than that it replaced γε ἀκούειν through carelessness.

τ' ἐγένετο, ἔνδον ὢν αὐτοῦ καὶ μὴ πεφοβημένος,
τὸ παράπαν ἀφανίσαι; ταῦτα, ὦ ἄνδρες, πῶς
εἰκότα ἐστίν;

46 ῝Ο δὲ ⟨δεῖ⟩[1] καὶ μάλιστα ἐνθυμεῖσθαι,—καὶ μή
μοι ἄχθεσθε, ἂν ὑμᾶς πολλάκις ταὐτὰ[2] διδάξω.
μέγας γὰρ ὁ κίνδυνός ἐστι, καθ' ὅ τι δ' ἂν ὑμεῖς
ὀρθῶς γνῶτε, κατὰ τοῦτο σῴζομαι, καθ' ὅ τι δ'
ἂν ψευσθῆτε τἀληθοῦς, κατὰ τοῦτο ἀπόλλυμαι—μὴ
οὖν ἐξέληται[3] τοῦτο ὑμῶν μηδείς, ὅτι τὸν μηνυτὴν
ἀπέκτειναν, καὶ διετείναντο αὐτὸν μὴ εἰσελθεῖν εἰς
ὑμᾶς, μηδ' ἐμοὶ ἐγγενέσθαι παρόντι ἄξαι τὸν ἄνδρα
47 καὶ βασανίσαι αὐτόν. καίτοι πρὸς τούτων ἦν
τοῦτο. νῦν δὲ πριάμενοι τὸν ἄνδρα, ἰδίᾳ ἐπὶ σφῶν
αὐτῶν ἀπέκτειναν, τὸν μηνυτήν, οὔτε τῆς πόλεως
[135] ψηφισαμένης, οὔτε αὐτόχειρα ὄντα τοῦ ἀνδρός.
ὃν ἐχρῆν δεδεμένον αὐτοὺς φυλάσσειν, ἢ τοῖς φίλοις
τοῖς ἐμοῖς ἐξεγγυῆσαι, ἢ τοῖς ἄρχουσι τοῖς ὑμετέροις παραδοῦναι, καὶ ψῆφον περὶ αὐτοῦ γενέσθαι.
νῦν δὲ αὐτοὶ καταγνόντες τὸν θάνατον τοῦ ἀνδρὸς
ἀπεκτείνατε· ὃ οὐδὲ πόλει ἔξεστιν, ἄνευ Ἀθηναίων
οὐδένα θανάτῳ ζημιῶσαι. καὶ τῶν μὲν ἄλλων

---

[1] δεῖ hic add. Thalheim: ὁ δὲ καὶ μάλιστα ἐνθυμεῖσθε N: ὁ
δὲ καὶ μάλιστα ἐνθυμεῖσθαι A pr.: δεῖ post μάλιστα add. A corr.[2]
[2] ταὐτὰ Reiske: ταῦτα codd.
[3] ἐξέληται A corr.[2]: ἐξελεῖται A pr. N.

---

[a] Since, if his statements were true, he would adhere to
them when examined by Euxitheus, and the prosecution
would be able to make play with the fact in court.
[b] The evidence of inscriptions confirms this. Decrees
regulating the relations between Athens and certain members
of her confederacy have survived, from which it would seem
that while the σύμμαχοι were left with a limited civil jurisdiction of their own, criminal cases were transferred to the
Athenian courts. Thus the Erythraean Decree (*I.G.* i[2].

collected man could not have removed successfully even by daylight ? What probability is there in such a suggestion, gentlemen ?

One thing above all you must remember, and I hope that you will forgive me for repeatedly stressing the same point ; but my danger is great, and only if you form a right judgement, am I safe ; if you are misled, I am doomed. I repeat, let no one cause you to forget that the prosecution put the informer to death, that they used every effort to prevent his appearance in court and to make it impossible for me to take him and examine him under torture on my return; although to allow me to do so was to their own advantage.[a] Instead, they bought the slave and put him to death, entirely on their own initiative—put the informer himself to death, without any official sanction, and without the excuse that he was guilty of the murder. They should of course have kept him in custody, or surrendered him to my friends on security, or else handed him over to the magistrates of Athens in order that his fate might be decided by a court. As it was, you sentenced him to death on your own authority and executed him, when even an allied state is denied the right of inflicting the death-penalty in such fashion without the consent of the Athenian people.[b] You thought fit to let the present court

10 ff.) enacts that all cases of treason involving capital punishment shall be tried at Athens, the Chalcidian Decree (*I.G.* i². 39) that cases arising from the εὔθυναι of a magistrate and involving exile, death, or ἀτιμία, shall likewise be tried at Athens, while the Milesian Decree (*I.G.* i². 22) allows the local courts a jurisdiction extending only to cases which do not involve a penalty of more than 100 drachmas.

It should be borne in mind, however, that although the trial of Euxitheus himself took place at Athens, the choice of such a forum was not necessarily determined by a similar

λόγων τῶν ἐκείνου τουτουσὶ κριτὰς ἠξιώσατε
γενέσθαι, τῶν δὲ ἔργων αὐτοὶ δικασταὶ γίγνεσθε.
48 καίτοι οὐδὲ οἱ τοὺς δεσπότας ἀποκτείναντες, ἐὰν
ἐπ᾽ αὐτοφώρῳ ληφθῶσιν, οὐδ᾽ οὗτοι ἀποθνήσκουσιν
ὑπ᾽ αὐτῶν τῶν προσηκόντων, ἀλλὰ παραδιδόασιν
αὐτοὺς τῇ ἀρχῇ κατὰ νόμους ὑμετέρους πατρίους.
εἴπερ γὰρ καὶ μαρτυρεῖν ἔξεστι δούλῳ κατὰ τοῦ
ἐλευθέρου τὸν φόνον, καὶ τῷ δεσπότῃ, ἂν δοκῇ,
ἐπεξελθεῖν ὑπὲρ τοῦ δούλου, καὶ ἡ ψῆφος ἴσον
δύναται τῷ δοῦλον ἀποκτείναντι καὶ τῷ[1] ἐλεύθερον,
εἰκός τοι καὶ ψῆφον γενέσθαι περὶ αὐτοῦ ἦν, καὶ
μὴ ἄκριτον ἀποθανεῖν αὐτὸν ὑφ᾽ ὑμῶν. ὥστε
πολλῷ ἂν ὑμεῖς δικαιότερον κρίνοισθε[2] ἢ ἐγὼ νῦν
φεύγω ὑφ᾽ ὑμῶν ἀδίκως.
49 Σκοπεῖτε δή, ὦ ἄνδρες, καὶ ἐκ τοῖν λόγοιν τοῖν
ἀνδροῖν ἑκατέροιν τοῖν βασανισθέντοιν τὸ δίκαιον
καὶ τὸ εἰκός. ὁ μὲν γὰρ δοῦλος δύο λόγω ἔλεγε·
τοτὲ μὲν ἔφη με εἰργάσθαι τὸ ἔργον, τοτὲ δὲ οὐκ
ἔφη· ὁ δὲ ἐλεύθερος οὐδέπω νῦν εἴρηκε περὶ ἐμοῦ
φλαῦρον οὐδέν, τῇ αὐτῇ βασάνῳ βασανιζόμενος.
50 τοῦτο μὲν γὰρ οὐκ ἦν αὐτῷ ἐλευθερίαν προτείναντας[3] ὥσπερ τὸν ἕτερον πεῖσαι· τοῦτο δὲ μετὰ τοῦ
ἀληθοῦς ἐβούλετο κινδυνεύων πάσχειν ὅ τι δέοι,

---

[1] τῷ Reiske: τὸν codd.
[2] κρίνοισθε vulg.: κρίνεσθε AN.
[3] προτείναντας Reiske: προτείνοντας codd.

---

decree transferring the criminal jurisdiction of the Mytilenean
courts to Athens. Such a decree doubtless existed; but
those which have survived appear to envisage only those
cases in which the parties were both members of a subject-
state, and it is very probable, though nowhere explicitly
stated, that Herodes was not a native Lesbian, but an
Athenian citizen resident in Lesbos as a cleruch. If so,

decide the merits of his statements ; but you pass judgement on his acts yourselves. Why, even slaves who have murdered their masters and been caught red-handed are not put to death by the victim's own relatives ; they are handed over to the authorities as the ancient laws of your country ordain. If it is a fact that a slave is allowed to give evidence that a free man is guilty of murder, if a master can seek vengeance for the murder of his slave, should he see fit, and if a court can sentence the murderer of a slave as effectively as it can the murderer of a free man,[a] it follows at once that the slave in question should have had a public trial, instead of being put to death by you without a hearing. Thus it is you who deserve to be on trial far rather than I, who am being accused this day so undeservedly.

And now, gentlemen, consider further the statements of the two witnesses tortured. What are the fair and reasonable conclusions to be drawn from them ? The slave gave two accounts : at one time he maintained that I was guilty, at another that I was not. On the other hand, in spite of similar torture, the free man has not even yet said anything to damage me. He could not be influenced by offers of freedom, as his companion had been ; and at the same time he was determined to cling to the truth,

there is nothing to prevent our supposing that the trial would have taken place in Athens in any event. *Cf.* pp. 151-152.

[a] *i.e.* (1) The slave could have been cited as a witness in court. (2) It is a criminal offence to put to death a slave belonging to someone else. (3) Anyone who commits such an act can be prosecuted for murder.

(2) is of course a deliberate distortion of the facts, as the slave in question had become the property of the prosecution by purchase (§ 47); and with it (3) loses its force.

ἐπεὶ τό γε συμφέρον καὶ οὗτος ἠπίστατο, ὅτι τότε
παύσοιτο¹ στρεβλούμενος, ὁπότε εἴποι τὰ τούτοις
δοκοῦντα. ποτέρῳ οὖν εἰκός ἐστι πιστεῦσαι, τῷ
διὰ τέλους τὸν αὐτὸν ἀεὶ λόγον λέγοντι, ἢ τῷ τοτὲ
μὲν φάσκοντι τοτὲ δ' οὔ; ἀλλὰ καὶ ἄνευ βασάνου
τοιαύτης οἱ τοὺς αὐτοὺς αἰεὶ περὶ τῶν αὐτῶν²
λόγους λέγοντες πιστότεροί εἰσι τῶν διαφερομένων
σφίσιν αὐτοῖς.

51 Ἔπειτα δὲ καὶ ἐκ τῶν λόγων τῶν τοῦ ἀνθρώπου
μερὶς ἑκατέροις³ ἴση ἂν εἴη,⁴ τούτοις⁵ μὲν τὸ φάσκειν,
ἐμοὶ δὲ τὸ μὴ φάσκειν· [ἔκ τε ἀμφοῖν τοῖν ἀνδροῖν
τοῖν βασανισθέντοιν· ὁ μὲν γὰρ ἔφησεν, ὁ δὲ διὰ
τέλους ἔξαρνος ἦν.]⁶ καὶ μὲν δὴ τὰ ἐξ ἴσου γενόμενα τοῦ φεύγοντός ἐστι μᾶλλον ἢ τοῦ διώκοντος,
εἴπερ γε καὶ τῶν ψήφων ὁ ἀριθμὸς ἐξ ἴσου γενό-
μενος⁷ τὸν φεύγοντα μᾶλλον ὠφελεῖ ἢ τὸν διώκοντα.

52 Ἡ μὲν βάσανος, ὦ ἄνδρες, τοιαύτη ἐγένετο,⁸ ᾗ
οὗτοι πιστεύοντες εὖ εἰδέναι φασὶν ὑπ' ἐμοῦ ἀποθανόντα τὸν ἄνδρα. καίτοι τὸ παράπαν ἔγωγ' ἂν
εἴ τι συνῄδη ἐμαυτῷ καὶ εἴ τί μοι⁹ τοιοῦτον εἴρ-
γαστο, ἠφάνισ' ἂν τὼ ἀνθρώπω, ὅτε ἐπ' ἐμοὶ ἦν

---

¹ παύσοιτο Madvig : παύσαιτο codd.
² αὐτῶν A corr. N : ἄλλων A pr.
³ ἑκατέροις Weidner : ἑκατέρῳ codd.
⁴ ἴση ἂν εἴη Thalheim : ἴσον εἰ N : ἴσον εἴ(η?) A.
⁵ τούτοις μὲν τὸ A corr.² : τούτων μέντοι A pr. N.
⁶ Verba ἔκ τε . . . ἦν secl. Hirschig.
⁷ γενόμενος A : γιγνόμενος N.
⁸ ἐγένετο A : γεγένηται N.
⁹ εἴ τί μοι A corr.² : εἴ τ' ἐμοὶ A pr. N.

cost what it might. Of course, as far as his own advantage was concerned, he knew, like the other, that the torture would be over as soon as he corroborated the prosecution. Which, then, have we more reason to believe : the witness who firmly adhered to the same statement throughout, or the witness who affirmed a thing at one moment, and denied it at the next ? Why, quite apart from the torture employed, those who consistently keep to one statement about one set of facts are more to be trusted than those who contradict themselves.

Then again, of the slave's statements half are in favour of one side, half in favour of the other : his affirmations support my accusers, and his denials support me. [Similarly with the combined statements of both the witnesses examined: the one affirmed, and the other consistently denied.]ᵃ But I need not point out that any equal division is to the advantage of the defence rather than the prosecution, in view of the fact that an equal division of the votes of the jury similarly benefits the defence rather than the prosecution.

Such was the examination under torture on which the prosecution rely, gentlemen, when they say that they are convinced that I am the murderer of Herodes. Yet if I had had anything whatsoever on my conscience, if I had committed a crime of this kind, I should have got rid of both witnesses while I had the opportunity, either by taking them with me

---

ᵃ Clearly an addition by a reader who thought that the argument ought to be pushed still further. The syntax is harsh and the reasoning itself unsound ; B had denied throughout, it is true ; but A, as we have just heard, spent half his time denying, and the other half affirming ; so he cannot be set against B.

τοῦτο μὲν εἰς τὴν Αἶνον ἀπάγειν[1] ἅμα ἐμοί, τοῦτο
δὲ εἰς τὴν ἤπειρον διαβιβάσαι, καὶ μὴ ὑπολείπεσθαι
μηνυτὰς κατ᾽ ἐμαυτοῦ τοὺς συνειδότας.

53 Φασὶ δὲ γραμματείδιον εὑρεῖν ἐν τῷ πλοίῳ, ὃ
ἔπεμπον ἐγὼ Λυκίνῳ, ὡς ἀποκτείναιμι τὸν ἄνδρα.
καίτοι τί ἔδει με γραμματείδιον πέμπειν, αὐτοῦ
συνειδότος τοῦ τὸ γραμματείδιον φέροντος;[2] ὥστε
τοῦτο μὲν σαφέστερον αὐτὸς[3] ἔμελλεν ἐρεῖν[4] ὁ εἰργασμένος, τοῦτο δὲ οὐδὲν ἔδει κρύπτειν αὐτόν[5]· ἃ
γὰρ μὴ οἷόν τε εἰδέναι τὸν φέροντα, ταῦτ᾽ ἄν τις
54 μάλιστα συγγράψας πέμψειεν. ἔπειτα δὲ ὅ τι μὲν
μακρὸν εἴη πρᾶγμα, τοῦτο[6] μὲν ἄν τις ἀναγκασθείη
γράψαι τῷ μὴ διαμνημονεύειν τὸν ἀπαγγέλλοντα
ὑπὸ πλήθους. τοῦτο δὲ βραχὺ ἦν ἀπαγγεῖλαι,
ὅτι τέθνηκεν ὁ ἀνήρ. ἔπειτα ἐνθυμεῖσθε ὅτι
διάφορον[7] ἦν τὸ γραμματείδιον τῷ βασανισθέντι,
διάφορος δ᾽ ὁ ἄνθρωπος τῷ γραμματειδίῳ. ὁ μὲν
γὰρ βασανιζόμενος αὐτὸς ἔφη ἀποκτεῖναι, τὸ δὲ
γραμματείδιον ἀνοιχθὲν ἐμὲ τὸν ἀποκτείναντα
55 ἐμήνυεν. καίτοι ποτέρῳ χρὴ πιστεῦσαι; τὸ μὲν
γὰρ πρῶτον οὐχ ηὗρον ἐν τῷ πλοίῳ ζητοῦντες τὸ
γραμματείδιον, ὕστερον δέ. τότε μὲν γὰρ οὔπω
οὕτως ἐμεμηχάνητο αὐτοῖς. ἐπειδὴ δὲ ὁ ἄνθρωπος
ὁ πρότερος βασανισθεὶς οὐδὲν ἔλεγε κατ᾽ ἐμοῦ,
τότε εἰσβάλλουσιν εἰς τὸ πλοῖον τὸ γραμματείδιον,
[136] ἵνα ταύτην ἔχοιεν ἐμοὶ τὴν αἰτίαν ἐπιφέρειν·
56 ἐπειδὴ δ᾽ ἀνεγνώσθη τὸ γραμματείδιον καὶ ὁ

---

[1] ἀπάγειν A corr.[2]: ἀπάγων A pr. N.
[2] Sequuntur in codd.: τίνος γε δὴ ἕνεκα . . . κἀκείνῳ, quae
nunc ad § 57 init. leguntur auct. Ald.
[3] αὐτὸς Reiske: αὐτοῖς codd.
[4] ἐρεῖν A: εὑρεῖν N.
[5] αὐτὸν Ald.: αὐτὰ codd.

to Aenus or by shipping them to the mainland.[a] I should not have left the men who knew the truth behind to inform against me.

The prosecution further allege that they discovered on board a note stating that I had killed Herodes, which I had intended to send to Lycinus. But what need had I to send a note, when the bearer himself was my accomplice ? Not only would he, as one of the murderers, have told the story more clearly in his own words, but it would have been quite unnecessary to conceal the message from him, and it is essentially messages which cannot be disclosed to the bearer that are sent in writing. Then again, an extensive message would have had to be written down, as its length would have prevented the bearer remembering it. But this one was brief enough to deliver—" The man is dead." Moreover, bear in mind that the note contradicted the slave tortured, and the slave the note. The slave stated under torture that he had committed the murder himself,[b] whereas the note when opened revealed the fact that I was the murderer. Which are we to believe ? The prosecution discovered the note on board only during a second search, not during their first one ; they had not hit on the idea at the time. It was not until the first witness had said nothing to incriminate me when tortured that they dropped the note in the boat, in order to have that, if nothing else, as a ground for accusing me. Then, once the note had been read

---

[a] *i.e.* to Asia Minor.
[b] The speaker forgets that he denied this in §

---

[6] τοῦτο A corr.[2]: τούτου A pr. N.
[7] διάφορον Reiske: διαφέρον codd.

199

ANTIPHON

ὕστερος βασανιζόμενος οὐ συνεφέρετο τῷ γραμματειδίῳ, οὐκέθ᾽ οἷόν τ᾽ ἦν ἀφανίσαι τὰ ἀναγνωσθέντα. εἰ γὰρ ἡγήσαντο τὸν ἄνδρα πείσειν ἀπὸ πρώτης καταψεύδεσθαί μου, οὐκ ἄν ποτ᾽ ἐμηχανήσαντο τὰ ἐν τῷ γραμματειδίῳ. καί μοι μάρτυρας τούτων κάλει.

ΜΑΡΤΥΡΕΣ

57 Τίνος γε δὴ ἕνεκα τὸν ἄνδρα ἀπέκτεινα; οὐδὲ[1] γὰρ ἔχθρα οὐδεμία ἦν ἐμοὶ κἀκείνῳ. λέγειν δὲ τολμῶσιν ὡς ἐγὼ χάριτι τὸν ἄνδρα ἔκτεινα. καὶ τίς πώποτε χαριζόμενος ἑτέρῳ τοῦτο εἰργάσατο; οἶμαι μὲν γὰρ οὐδένα, ἀλλὰ δεῖ μεγάλην τὴν ἔχθραν ὑπάρχειν τῷ τοῦτο μέλλοντι ποιήσειν, καὶ τὴν πρόνοιαν ἐκ πολλῶν[2] εἶναι φανερὰν ἐπιβουλευομένην.

58 ἐμοὶ δὲ κἀκείνῳ οὐκ ἦν ἔχθρα οὐδεμία. εἶεν, ἀλλὰ δείσας περὶ ἐμαυτοῦ μὴ αὐτὸς παρ᾽ ἐκείνου τοῦτο πάθοιμι; καὶ γὰρ ἂν τῶν τοιούτων ἕνεκά τις ἀναγκασθείη τοῦτο ἐργάσασθαι. ἀλλ᾽ οὐδέν μοι τοιοῦτον ὑπῆρκτο εἰς αὐτόν. ἀλλὰ χρήματα ἔμελλον λήψεσθαι ἀποκτείνας αὐτόν; ἀλλ᾽ οὐκ ἦν

59 αὐτῷ.[3] ἀλλὰ σοὶ μᾶλλον ἐγὼ τὴν πρόφασιν ταύτην ἔχοιμ᾽ ἂν εἰκότως μετὰ τῆς ἀληθείας ἀναθεῖναι, ὅτι χρημάτων ἕνεκα ζητεῖς ἐμὲ ἀποκτεῖναι, μᾶλλον ἢ σὺ ἐμοὶ[4] ἐκεῖνον· καὶ πολὺ ἂν δικαιότερον ἁλοίης σὺ φόνου[5] ἐμὲ ἀποκτείνας ὑπὸ τῶν ἐμοὶ προσηκόντων, ἢ ἐγὼ ὑπὸ σοῦ καὶ τῶν ἐκείνου ἀναγκαίων. ἐγὼ μὲν γὰρ σοῦ[6] φανερὰν τὴν πρόνοιαν

---

[1] οὐδὲ Ald. : οὔτε codd.
[2] πολλῶν] πολλοῦ nonnulli auct. Pahle.
[3] Verba ἀλλὰ χρήματα . . . αὐτῷ quae ante εἶεν habent codd. huc transtulit Dobree.

and the second witness, when tortured, persisted in disagreeing with the note, it was impossible to spirit away the message read from it. Needless to say, had the prosecution supposed that they would induce the slave to lie about me immediately, they would never have devised the message contained in the note. Call me witnesses to confirm these facts.

Witnesses

Now what was my motive in murdering Herodes? For there was not even any bad feeling between us. The prosecution have the audacity to suggest that I murdered him as a favour. But who has ever turned murderer to oblige a friend? No one, I am sure. The bitterest feeling has to exist before murder is committed, while the growth of the design is always abundantly manifest. And, as I said, between Herodes and myself there was no bad feeling. Well and good. Then was it that I was afraid of being murdered by him myself? A motive of that kind might well drive a man to the deed. No, I had no such fears with regard to him. Then was I going to enrich myself by the murder? No, he had no money. Indeed, it would be more intelligible and nearer the truth for me to maintain that money was at the bottom of your own attempt to secure my death than it is for you to suggest it as my motive in murdering Herodes. You yourself deserve to be convicted of murder by my relatives for killing me far more than I by you and the family of Herodes. Of your designs on my life I have clear proof: whereas

---

⁴ σὺ ἐμοὶ A corr.: σὺν ἐμοὶ A pr. N.
⁵ σὺ φόνου Maetzner: τοῦ φόνου codd.
⁶ σοῦ Blass: σοι codd.

εἰς ἐμὲ ἀποδείκνυμι, σὺ δ' ἐμὲ¹ ἐν ἀφανεῖ λόγῳ
ζητεῖς ἀπολέσαι.

60 Ταῦτα μὲν ὑμῖν λέγω, ὡς αὐτῷ μοι πρόφασιν
οὐδεμίαν εἶχε τἀποκτεῖναι² τὸν ἄνδρα· δεῖ δέ με καὶ
ὑπὲρ Λυκίνου ἀπολογήσασθαι, ὡς ἔοικεν, ἀλλ' οὐχ
ὑπὲρ αὐτοῦ μόνον, ὡς οὐδ' ἐκεῖνον εἰκότως αἰτιῶνται. λέγω τοίνυν ὑμῖν ὅτι ταὐτὰ ὑπῆρχεν αὐτῷ
εἰς ἐκεῖνον ἅπερ ἐμοί· οὔτε γὰρ χρήματα ἦν αὐτῷ
ὁπόθεν ἂν ἔλαβεν ἀποκτείνας ἐκεῖνον, οὔτε κίνδυνος αὐτῷ ὑπῆρχεν οὐδεὶς ὅντινα διέφευγεν ἀπο-
61 θανόντος ἐκείνου. τεκμήριον δὲ μέγιστον ὡς οὐκ
ἐβούλετο αὐτὸν ἀπολέσαι. ἐξὸν γὰρ αὐτῷ ἐν
ἀγῶνι καὶ κινδύνῳ μεγάλῳ καταστήσαντι μετὰ
τῶν νόμων τῶν ὑμετέρων ἀπολέσαι ἐκεῖνον, εἴπερ
προωφείλετο αὐτῷ κακόν, καὶ τό τε ἴδιον τὸ αὐτοῦ διαπράξασθαι καὶ τῇ πόλει τῇ ὑμετέρᾳ χάριν
καταθέσθαι, εἰ ἐπέδειξεν ἀδικοῦντα ἐκεῖνον, οὐκ
ἠξίωσεν, ἀλλ' οὐδ' ἦλθεν ἐπὶ τοῦτον. καίτοι καλλίων γε ἦν ὁ κίνδυνος αὐτῷ . . .

¹ δ' ἐμὲ Blass: δέ με codd.
² εἶχε τἀποκτεῖναι Kayser: ἔχει ἀποκτεῖναι codd.
³ Nonnulla deesse videntur, quae sic e.g. suppleri pos-
sint: ἐν ἀγῶνι καταστήσαντι κεῖνον ἢ δι' ἐμοῦ βιαίως ἀπολέ-
σαντι. καί μοι μάρτυρας τούτων κάλει.

ᵃ The occurrence of the rubric ΜΑΡΤΥΡΕΣ immediately
after the words ὁ κίνδυνος αὐτῷ in the mss. has led the majority
of edd. to suppose that one of the usual formulae introducing
witnesses has dropped out. But there are grounds for suspecting a larger lacuna. If the words καίτοι καλλίων γε ἦν ὁ
κίνδυνος αὐτῷ form a complete sentence in themselves, they
are both obscure and ambiguous. κίνδυνος might refer (a) to
κινδύνῳ μεγάλῳ six lines above and bear the meaning "the

you, in seeking to make an end of me, produce only a tale of which proof is impossible.

I assure you that I personally can have had no motive for murdering Herodes ; but I must apparently clear Lycinus as well as myself by showing the absurdity of the charge in his case also. I assure you that his position with regard to Herodes was the same as my own. He had no means of enriching himself by the murder ; and there was no danger from which the death of Herodes released him. Further, the following consideration indicates most strikingly that he did not desire his death : had redress for some old injury been owing to Lycinus, he could have brought Herodes into court on a charge which endangered his life, and have enlisted the help of your laws in making an end of him. By proving him a criminal he could have gained both his own object and your city's gratitude. This he did not trouble to do : he did not even attempt to institute proceedings against him, in spite of the fact that he was running a more honourable risk ⟨by bringing Herodes into court than by engaging me to murder him. Call me witnesses to confirm these facts.⟩[a]

---

danger into which L. would bring H. by prosecuting him." The gist of the sentence would then be "to endanger H.'s life by legal methods was a more creditable course for L. than to murder him." On the other hand, it might refer (b) to the risk (of failing to gain a verdict and so being fined) run by L. himself in prosecuting H. The speaker would then be saying in effect " it was more creditable for L. to risk losing a case at law against H. than to risk murdering him." Of the two alternatives (b) is the more probable. But Antiphon is not in the habit of being terse to the point of obscurity; and it is hard to believe that the sentence as he wrote it ended at αὐτῷ. For a suggested supplement see crit. note 3.

62 Ἀλλὰ γὰρ ἐνταῦθα μὲν ἀφῆκεν αὐτόν· οὗ δὲ[11]
ἔδει κινδυνεύειν αὐτὸν περί τε αὐτοῦ καὶ περὶ[2] ἐμοῦ,
ἐνταῦθα δ' ἐπεβούλευεν, ἐν ᾧ γνωσθεὶς ἂν ἀπεστέρει μὲν ἐμὲ τῆς πατρίδος, ἀπεστέρει δὲ αὐτὸν
ἱερῶν καὶ ὁσίων καὶ τῶν ἄλλων ἅπερ μέγιστα καὶ
περὶ πλείστου ἐστὶν ἀνθρώποις.

Ἔπειτα δ' εἰ καὶ ὡς μάλιστα ἐβούλετο αὐτὸν
ὁ Λυκῖνος τεθνάναι — εἶμι γὰρ καὶ ἐπὶ τὸν τῶν
κατηγόρων λόγον, — οὗ αὐτὸς οὐκ ἠξίου αὐτόχειρ
γενέσθαι, τοῦτο τὸ ἔργον ἐγώ ποτ' ἂν ἐπείσθην
63 ἀντ' ἐκείνου ποιῆσαι; πότερα ὡς ἐγὼ μὲν ἢ τῷ
σώματι ἐπιτήδειος διακινδυνεύειν, ἐκεῖνος δὲ χρήμασι τὸν ἐμὸν κίνδυνον ἐκπρίασθαι; οὐ δῆτα· τῷ
μὲν γὰρ οὐκ ἦν χρήματα, ἐμοὶ δὲ ἦν[3]· ἀλλ' αὐτὸ τὸ
ἐναντίον[4] ἐκεῖνος τοῦτο θᾶσσον ἂν ὑπ' ἐμοῦ ἐπείσθη
κατά γε τὸ εἰκὸς ἢ ἐγὼ ὑπὸ τούτου, ἐπεὶ ἐκεῖνός
γ' ἑαυτὸν οὐδ' ὑπερήμερον γενόμενον ἑπτὰ μνῶν
δυνατὸς ἦν λύσασθαι, ἀλλ' οἱ φίλοι αὐτὸν ἐλύσαντο.
καὶ μὲν δὴ καὶ τῆς χρείας τῆς ἐμῆς καὶ τῆς
Λυκίνου τοῦτο ὑμῖν μέγιστον τεκμήριόν ἐστιν, ὅτι
οὐ σφόδρα ἐχρώμην ἐγὼ Λυκίνῳ φίλῳ, ὡς πάντα
ποιῆσαι ἂν τὰ ἐκείνῳ δοκοῦντα· οὐ γὰρ δήπου
ἑπτὰ μὲν μνᾶς οὐκ ἀπέτεισα ὑπὲρ[5] αὐτοῦ δεδεμένου
καὶ λυμαινομένου, κίνδυνον δὲ τοσοῦτον ἀράμενος
ἄνδρα ἀπέκτεινα δι' ἐκεῖνον.

---

[1] οὐ δὲ Blass: οὐδὲ N: οὐ γὰρ A.
[2] περὶ om. A.
[3] Verba τῷ μὲν γὰρ . . . ἦν post ὑπὸ τούτου infra collocavit
Reiske: del. Dobree.

204

Witnesses

So we are to understand that Lycinus left Herodes in peace as far as an action at law was concerned, and instead chose the one course which was bound to endanger both himself and me, that of plotting his death, notwithstanding the fact that, if discovered, he would have deprived me of my country and himself of his rights before heaven and mankind, and of all that men hold most sacred and most precious.

I will go further : I will adopt the standpoint of the prosecution : I will admit as readily as you like that Lycinus did desire the death of Herodes. Does it follow that I should ever have been induced to perform in his stead a deed which he refused to commit with his own hand ? Was I, for instance, in a position to risk my life, and he in a position to hire me to do so ? No, I had money, and he had none. On the contrary, the probabilities show that he would have been induced to commit the crime by me sooner than I by him ; for even after suffering an execution for a debt of seven minae, he could not release himself from prison : his friends had to purchase his release. In fact, this affords the clearest indication of the relations between Lycinus and myself ; it shows that my friendship with him was hardly close enough to make me willing to satisfy his every wish. I cannot suppose that I braved the enormous risk which murder involved to oblige him, after refusing to pay off seven minae for him when he was suffering the hardships of imprisonment.

---

[4] αὐτὸ τὸ ἐναντίον A corr.[2] : αὐτὸ τοῦτο ἐναντίον A pr. N.
[5] ὑπὲρ Meier : περὶ codd.

64 Ὡς μὲν οὖν οὐκ αὐτὸς αἴτιός εἰμι τοῦ πράγματος
[137] οὐδὲ ἐκεῖνος, ἀποδέδεικται καθ᾽ ὅσον ἐγὼ δύναμαι
μάλιστα. τούτῳ δὲ χρῶνται πλείστῳ ⟨τῷ⟩[1] λόγῳ
οἱ κατήγοροι, ὅτι ἀφανής ἐστιν ὁ ἀνήρ, καὶ ὑμεῖς
ἴσως περὶ τούτου αὐτοῦ ποθεῖτε ἀκοῦσαι. εἰ μὲν
οὖν τοῦτο εἰκάζειν με δεῖ, ἐξ ἴσου τοῦτό ἐστι καὶ
ὑμῖν καὶ ἐμοί· οὔτε γὰρ ὑμεῖς αἴτιοι τοῦ ἔργου ἐστὲ
οὔτε ἐγώ· εἰ δὲ δεῖ τοῖς ἀληθέσι χρῆσθαι, τῶν
εἰργασμένων τινὰ ἐρωτώντων· ἐκείνου γὰρ ἄριστ᾽
65 ἂν[2] πύθοιντο. ἐμοὶ μὲν γὰρ τῷ μὴ εἰργασμένῳ
τοσοῦτον τὸ μακρότατον[3] τῆς ἀποκρίσεώς ἐστιν, ὅτι
οὐκ εἴργασμαι· τῷ δὲ ποιήσαντι ῥᾳδία ἐστὶν ἡ
ἀπόδειξις, καὶ μὴ ἀποδείξαντι εὖ εἰκάσαι. οἱ μὲν
γὰρ πανουργοῦντες ἅμα τε πανουργοῦσι καὶ πρόφασιν εὑρίσκουσι τοῦ ἀδικήματος· τῷ δὲ μὴ
εἰργασμένῳ[4] χαλεπὸν περὶ τῶν ἀφανῶν εἰκάζειν.
οἶμαι δ᾽ ἂν καὶ ὑμῶν ἕκαστον, εἴ τίς τινα ἔροιτο ὅ
τι μὴ τύχοι εἰδώς, τοσοῦτον ἂν εἰπεῖν, ὅτι οὐκ
οἶδεν. εἰ δέ τις περαιτέρω τι κελεύοι[5] λέγειν, ἐν
66 πολλῇ ἂν ἔχεσθαι ὑμᾶς ἀπορίᾳ δοκῶ. μὴ τοίνυν
ἐμοὶ νείμητε τὸ ἄπορον τοῦτο, ἐν ᾧ μηδ᾽ ἂν αὐτοὶ
εὐποροῖτε· μηδ᾽ ἐὰν εὖ εἰκάζω, ἐν τούτῳ μοι
ἀξιοῦτε τὴν ἀπόφευξιν εἶναι, ἀλλ᾽ ἐξαρκείτω μοι
ἐμαυτὸν ἀναίτιον ἀποδεῖξαι τοῦ πράγματος. ἐν
τούτῳ οὖν ἀναίτιός εἰμι, οὐκ ἐὰν [μὴ][6] ἐξεύρω ὅτῳ
τρόπῳ ἀφανής ἐστιν ἢ ἀπόλωλεν ἀνήρ,[7] ἀλλ᾽ εἰ μὴ
προσήκει μοι μηδὲν ὥστ᾽ ἀποκτεῖναι αὐτόν.
67 Ἤδη δ᾽ ἔγωγε καὶ πρότερον ἀκοῇ ἐπίσταμαι

---

[1] τῷ add. Frohberger.
[2] ἄριστ᾽ ἂν Hirschig : ἄριστα codd.
[3] μακρότατον N : μακρότερον A.
[4] εἰργασμένῳ A : ἐργασαμένῳ N.

I have proved, then, to the best of my ability that both Lycinus and I are innocent. However, the prosecution make endless play with the argument that Herodes has disappeared ; and doubtless it is a fact which you want explained. Now if it is conjecture which is expected of me, you are just as capable of it as I am—we are both alike innocent of the crime ; on the other hand, if it is the truth, the prosecution must ask one of the criminals : he would best be able to satisfy them. The utmost that I who am not guilty can reply is that I am not guilty ; whereas the criminal can easily reveal the facts, or at least make a good guess. Criminals no sooner commit a crime than they invent an explanation to suit it [a] ; on the other hand, an innocent man can scarcely guess the answer to what is a mystery to him. Each of you yourselves, I am sure, if asked something which he did not happen to know, would simply reply to that effect ; and if told to say more, you would find yourselves, I think, in a serious difficulty. So do not present me with a difficulty which you yourselves would not find easy of solution. Furthermore, do not make my acquittal depend on my making plausible conjectures. Let it be enough for me to prove my innocence of the crime ; and that depends not upon my discovering how Herodes disappeared or met his end, but upon my possessing no motive whatever for murdering him.

As I know from report, there have been similar

[a] *i.e.* a culprit is the first to suggest that someone else is to blame.

---

⁵ κελεύοι Reiske : κελεύει codd.
⁶ μὴ del. Reiske.   ⁷ ἀνήρ Sauppe : ἀνήρ codd.

γεγονός, τοῦτο μὲν τοὺς ἀποθανόντας, τοῦτο δὲ
τοὺς ἀποκτείναντας οὐχ εὑρεθέντας· οὔκουν ἂν
καλῶς ἔχοι, εἰ τούτων δέοι τὰς αἰτίας ὑποσχεῖν
τοὺς συγγενομένους. πολλοὶ δέ γ᾽ ἤδη σχόντες
ἑτέρων πραγμάτων αἰτίας, πρὶν τὸ σαφὲς αὐτῶν
68 γνωσθῆναι, προαπώλοντο. αὐτίκα Ἐφιάλτην τὸν
ὑμέτερον πολίτην οὐδέπω νῦν ηὕρηνται οἱ ἀποκτεί-
ναντες· εἰ οὖν τις ἠξίου τοὺς συνόντας ἐκείνῳ εἰκάζειν οἵτινες ἦσαν οἱ ἀποκτείναντες [Ἐφιάλτην],[1]
εἰ δὲ μή, ἐνόχους εἶναι τῷ φόνῳ, οὐκ ἂν καλῶς
εἶχε τοῖς συνοῦσιν. ἔπειτα οἵ γε Ἐφιάλτην ἀποκτείναντες οὐκ ἐζήτησαν τὸν νεκρὸν ἀφανίσαι, οὐδ᾽
ἐν τούτῳ κινδυνεύειν μηνῦσαι τὸ πρᾶγμα, ὥσπερ
οἵδε φασὶν ἐμὲ τῆς μὲν ἐπιβουλῆς οὐδένα κοινωνὸν
ποιήσασθαι τοῦ θανάτου, τῆς δ᾽ ἀναιρέσεως.

69   Τοῦτο δ᾽ ἐντὸς οὐ πολλοῦ χρόνου παῖς ἐζήτησεν
οὐδὲ δώδεκα ἔτη γεγονὼς τὸν δεσπότην ἀποκτεῖναι.
καὶ εἰ μὴ φοβηθείς, ὡς ἀνεβόησεν, ἐγκαταλιπὼν
τὴν μάχαιραν ἐν[2] τῇ σφαγῇ ᾤχετο φεύγων, ἀλλ᾽
ἐτόλμησε μεῖναι, ἀπώλοντ᾽ ἂν οἱ ἔνδον ὄντες[3] ἅπαν-
τες· οὐδεὶς γὰρ ἂν ᾤετο τὸν παῖδα τολμῆσαί ποτε
τοῦτο· νῦν δὲ συλληφθεὶς αὐτὸς ὕστερον κατεῖπεν
αὐτοῦ.

Τοῦτο δὲ περὶ χρημάτων αἰτίαν ποτὲ σχόντες
οὐκ οὖσαν, ὥσπερ ἐγὼ νῦν, οἱ Ἑλληνοταμίαι οἱ

---

[1] Ἐφιάλτην del. Dobree.   [2] ἐν om. A.
[3] ὄντες om. A.

---

[a] The murder had been committed some forty-five years
before (first half of 461). Ephialtes was an extreme radical,
and in conjunction with Pericles was responsible for the violent
attack made upon the prerogatives of the Areopagus in 462.
His assassination was the result. Aristotle states that the crime

208

cases in the past, when sometimes the victim, sometimes the murderer, has not been traced ; it would be unfair, were those who had been in their company held responsible. Many, again, have been accused before now of the crimes of others, and have lost their lives before the truth became known. For instance, the murderers of one of your own citizens, Ephialtes,[a] have remained undiscovered to this day ; it would have been unfair to his companions to require them to conjecture who his assassins were under pain of being held guilty of the murder themselves. Moreover, the murderers of Ephialtes made no attempt to get rid of the body, for fear of the accompanying risk of publicity—unlike myself, who, we are told, took no one into my confidence when planning the crime, but then sought help for the removal of the corpse.

Once more, a slave, not twelve years old, recently attempted to murder his master. Had he had the courage to stay where he was, instead of taking to his heels in terror at his victim's cries, leaving the knife in the wound, the entire household[b] would have perished, as no one would have dreamed him capable of such audacity. As it was, he was caught, and later confessed his own guilt.

Then again, your Hellenotamiae[c] were once accused of embezzlement, as wrongfully as I am

was committed by Aristodicus of Tanagra, employed for the purpose by Ephialtes' enemies. This may well be true, as it suited Antiphon's requirements here to assume that the mystery had never been satisfactorily solved. Cf. 'Αθ. Πολ. xxv. 5, Diod. xi. 77. 6, Plut. Per. 10.

[b] i.e. of slaves.

[c] Nothing further is known of the incident. The Hellenotamiae were ten in number and administered the funds of the Delian League.

ὑμέτεροι, ἐκεῖνοι μὲν ἅπαντες ἀπέθανον[1] ὀργῇ μᾶλλον ἢ γνώμῃ, πλὴν ἑνός, τὸ δὲ πρᾶγμα ὕστερον
70 καταφανὲς ἐγένετο. τοῦ δ' ἑνὸς τούτου—Σωσίαν
ὄνομά φασιν αὐτῷ εἶναι—κατέγνωστο μὲν ἤδη
θάνατος, ἐτεθνήκει δὲ οὔπω· καὶ ἐν τούτῳ ἐδηλώθη
τῷ τρόπῳ ἀπωλώλει τὰ χρήματα, καὶ ὁ ἀνὴρ
ἀπήχθη ὑπὸ τοῦ δήμου τοῦ ὑμετέρου παραδεδομένος ἤδη τοῖς ἕνδεκα, οἱ δ' ἄλλοι ἐτέθνασαν οὐδὲν
71 αἴτιοι ὄντες. ταῦθ' ὑμῶν αὐτῶν ἐγὼ οἶμαι μεμνῆσθαι τοὺς πρεσβυτέρους, τοὺς δὲ νεωτέρους
πυνθάνεσθαι ὥσπερ ἐμέ.

Οὕτως ἀγαθόν ἐστι μετὰ τοῦ χρόνου βασανίζειν
τὰ πράγματα. καὶ τοῦτ' ἴσως ἂν[2] φανερὸν γένοιτ'
ἂν ὕστερον, ὅτῳ τρόπῳ τέθνηκεν ὁ ἄνθρωπος. μὴ
οὖν ὕστερον τοῦτο γνῶτε, ἀναίτιόν με ὄντα ἀπολέσαντες, ἀλλὰ πρότερόν γ' εὖ βουλεύσασθε, καὶ μὴ
μετ'[3] ὀργῆς καὶ διαβολῆς, ὡς τούτων οὐκ ἂν
72 γένοιντο ἕτεροι πονηρότεροι σύμβουλοι. οὐ γὰρ
ἔστιν ὅ τι ἂν[4] ὀργιζόμενος ἄνθρωπος εὖ γνοίη· αὐτὸ
γὰρ ᾧ[5] βουλεύεται, τὴν γνώμην, διαφθείρει τοῦ
ἀνθρώπου. μέγα τοι ἡμέρα παρ' ἡμέραν γιγνομένη[6] γνώμην, ὦ ἄνδρες, ἐξ ὀργῆς μεταστῆσαι[7]
καὶ τὴν ἀλήθειαν εὑρεῖν τῶν γεγενημένων.

[138]
73 Εὖ δὲ ἴστε ὅτι ἐλεηθῆναι ὑφ' ὑμῶν ἄξιός εἰμι
μᾶλλον ἢ δίκην δοῦναι· δίκην μὲν γὰρ εἰκός ἐστι
διδόναι τοὺς ἀδικοῦντας, ἐλεεῖσθαι δὲ τοὺς ἀδίκως
κινδυνεύοντας. κρεῖσσον δὲ[8] χρὴ γίγνεσθαι ἀεὶ τὸ
ὑμέτερον δυνάμενον ἐμὲ δικαίως σῴζειν ἢ τὸ τῶν

---

[1] ἀπέθανον A corr.[2]: ἀποθανόντες A pr. N.
[2] ἂν om. N.   [3] μὴ μετ' vulg.: μήτε μετ' AN.
[4] ἂν add. Stobaeus, *Flor.* xx. 44, qui verba οὐ γὰρ ἔστιν . . .
διαφθείρει τοῦ ἀνθρώπου affert. Idem εὖ γνοίη: ἂν γνοίη codd.
[5] ᾧ] ὃ Stobaeus.

accused to-day. Anger swept reason aside, and they were all put to death save one. Later the true facts became known. This one, whose name is said to have been Sosias, though under sentence of death, had not yet been executed. Meanwhile it was shown how the money had disappeared. The Athenian people rescued him from the very hands of the Eleven [a] : while the rest had died entirely innocent. You older ones remember this yourselves, I expect, and the younger have heard of it like myself.

Thus it is wise to let time help us in testing the truth of a matter. Perhaps the circumstances of Herodes' death will similarly come to light hereafter ; so do not discover that you have put an innocent man to death when it is too late. Weigh the matter carefully while there is yet time, without anger and without prejudice : for they are the worst of counsellors ; it is impossible for an angry man to make a right decision, as anger destroys his one instrument of decision, his judgement. The lapse of one day after another, gentlemen, has a wondrous power of liberating the judgement from the sway of passion and of bringing the truth to light.

Remember too that it is pity which I deserve from you, not punishment. Wrongdoers should be punished : those wrongfully imperilled should be pitied. You must never let your power to satisfy justice by saving my life be overridden by my

---

[a] The accusation must have taken the form of an impeachment (εἰσαγγελία) before the Assembly. The task of the Eleven was to supervise the execution of the sentence.

---

6 ἡμέρα . . . γιγνομένη Stephanus: ἡμέραν . . . γιγνομένην codd.

7 μεταστῆσαι Stephanus: μεταστήσειν codd.

8 δὲ A : δὴ N.

ἐχθρῶν βουλόμενον ἀδίκως με ἀπολλύναι. ἐν μὲν
γὰρ τῷ ἐπισχεῖν ἔστι καὶ τὰ δεινὰ ταῦτα ποιῆσαι
ἃ οὗτοι κελεύουσιν· ἐν δὲ τῷ παραχρῆμα οὐκ ἔστιν
ἀρχὴν¹ ὀρθῶς βουλεύεσθαι.

74 Δεῖ δέ με καὶ ὑπὲρ τοῦ πατρὸς ἀπολογήσασθαι.
καίτοι γε πολλῷ μᾶλλον εἰκὸς ἦν ἐκεῖνον ὑπὲρ ἐμοῦ
ἀπολογήσασθαι, πατέρα ὄντα· ὁ μὲν γὰρ πολλῷ
πρεσβύτερός ἐστι τῶν ἐμῶν πραγμάτων, ἐγὼ δὲ
πολλῷ νεώτερος τῶν ἐκείνῳ πεπραγμένων. καὶ εἰ
μὲν ἐγὼ τούτου ἀγωνιζομένου κατεμαρτύρουν ἃ μὴ
σαφῶς ᾔδη, ἀκοῇ δὲ ἠπιστάμην, δεινὰ ἂν ἔφη
75 πάσχειν ὑπ᾽ ἐμοῦ· νῦν δὲ ἀναγκάζων ἐμὲ ἀπολογεῖσθαι ὧν ἐγὼ πολλῷ νεώτερός εἰμι καὶ λόγῳ
οἶδα, ταῦτα οὐ δεινὰ ἡγεῖται εἰργάσθαι. ὅμως
μέντοι καθ᾽ ὅσον ἐγὼ οἶδα, οὐ προδώσω τὸν
πατέρα κακῶς ἀκούοντα ἐν ὑμῖν ἀδίκως. καίτοι
τάχ᾽ ἂν σφαλείην, ἃ ἐκεῖνος ὀρθῶς ἔργῳ ἔπραξε,
ταῦτ᾽ ἐγὼ λόγῳ μὴ ὀρθῶς εἰπών· ὅμως δ᾽ οὖν
κεκινδυνεύσεται.²

76 Πρὶν μὲν γὰρ τὴν ἀπόστασιν τὴν Μυτιληναίων³
γενέσθαι, ἔργῳ τὴν εὔνοιαν ἐδείκνυε τὴν εἰς ὑμᾶς·
ἐπειδὴ δὲ ἡ πόλις ὅλη κακῶς ἐβουλεύσατο ἀποστᾶσα καὶ ἥμαρτε [τῆς ὑμετέρας γνώμης],⁴ μετὰ
τῆς πόλεως ὅλης ἠναγκάσθη συνεξαμαρτεῖν. τὴν
μὲν οὖν γνώμην ἔτι καὶ ἐν ἐκείνοις ὅμοιος ἦν εἰς
ὑμᾶς, τὴν δ᾽ εὔνοιαν οὐκέτι ἦν ἐπ᾽ ἐκείνῳ τὴν

¹ ἀρχὴν Ald.: ἀρχὴ ἢ codd.
² κεκινδυνεύσεται A corr.²: καὶ κινδυνεύσεται A pr. N.
³ τὴν Μυτ. Blass: τῶν Μυτ. codd.
⁴ τῆς ὑμετέρας γνώμης del. Hirschig, qui ἀποστᾶσα quoque damnat.

ᵃ Mytilene had revolted from Athens some ten years
previously, in 428.

enemies' desire to outrage it by putting me to death.
A delay will still allow you to take the awful step
which the prosecution urge upon you ; whereas haste
will make a fair consideration of the case quite
impossible.

I must also defend my father ; although, as my
father, it would have been far more natural for him
to be defending me. He is far older than I, and
knows what my life has been : whereas I am far
younger than he, and cannot know what his has
been. If my accuser were on trial, and I were giving
evidence against him based on hearsay instead of
certain knowledge, he would protest that he was
being treated monstrously ; yet he sees nothing
monstrous in forcing me to explain occurrences with
which I am far too young to be acquainted save from
hearsay. However, as a loyal son, I will use what
knowledge I have to defend my father against the
unwarranted abuse to which you have been listening.
Possibly indeed I may fail. I may describe but
faultily a life which was without fault. But none
the less, I will accept that risk.

Before the revolt of Mytilene [a] my father gave
visible proof of his devotion to your interests.
When, however, the city as a whole was so ill-
advised as to commit the blunder of revolting,[b] he
was forced to join the city as a whole in that blunder.
Not but what even then his feelings towards you
remained unchanged : although he could no longer

---

[b] Although the τῆς ὑμετέρας γνώμης of the mss., if retained
and taken with ἥμαρτε, would give the sense "failed in what
you expected of them," an expression for which there are
parallels, συνεξαμαρτεῖν requires ἥμαρτε alone to balance it,
and the repetition of γνώμη two lines later is harsh in the
extreme.

αὐτὴν εἰς ὑμᾶς παρέχειν. οὔτε γὰρ ἐκλιπεῖν τὴν
πόλιν εὐρόπως[1] εἶχεν αὐτῷ· ἱκανὰ γὰρ ἦν τὰ ἐνέχυρα
ἃ εἴχετο αὐτοῦ, οἵ τε παῖδες καὶ τὰ χρήματα·
τοῦτο δ᾽ αὖ μένοντι πρὸς τὴν πόλιν αὐτῷ ἀδυνάτως
77 εἶχεν ἰσχυρίζεσθαι. ἐπεὶ δ᾽ ὑμεῖς τοὺς αἰτίους
τούτων ἐκολάσατε, ἐν οἷς οὐκ ἐφαίνετο ὢν ὁ ἐμὸς
πατήρ, τοῖς δ᾽ ἄλλοις Μυτιληναίοις ἄδειαν ἐδώκατε
οἰκεῖν τὴν σφετέραν αὐτῶν, οὐκ ἔστιν ὅ τι ὕστερον
αὐτῷ ἡμάρτηται [τῷ ἐμῷ πατρί],[2] οὐδ᾽ ὅ τι οὐ
πεποίηται τῶν δεόντων, οὐδ᾽ ἧς τινος λῃτουργίας
ἡ πόλις ἐνδεὴς γεγένηται, οὔτε ἡ ὑμετέρα οὔτε ἡ
Μυτιληναίων, ἀλλὰ καὶ χορηγίας χορηγεῖ[3] καὶ τέλη
78 κατατίθησιν.[4] εἰ δ᾽ ἐν Αἴνῳ χωροφιλεῖ, τοῦτο ⟨ποιεῖ⟩[5]
οὐκ ἀποστερῶν γε τῶν εἰς τὴν πόλιν ἑαυτὸν οὐδενὸς
οὐδ᾽ ἑτέρας πόλεως πολίτης γεγενημένος, ὥσπερ
ἑτέρους ὁρῶ, τοὺς μὲν εἰς τὴν ἤπειρον ἰόντας καὶ
οἰκοῦντας ἐν τοῖς πολεμίοις τοῖς ὑμετέροις, ⟨τοὺς
δὲ⟩[6] καὶ δίκας ἀπὸ ξυμβόλων ὑμῖν δικαζομένους,

[1] εὐρόπως A corr.[2]: εὐρ᾽ ὅπως A pr. N.
[2] τῷ ἐμῷ πατρί secl. Dobree.
[3] χορηγεῖ Blass: ἐχορήγει codd.
[4] κατατίθησιν N: κατετίθει A.
[5] ποιεῖ add. Reiske.   [6] τοὺς δὲ add. Reiske.

───────

[a] See Thuc. iii. 50. The walls of Mytilene were rased,
her fleet taken from her, and the entire island, except for
Methymna, divided among Athenian cleruchs. These drew
a fixed rent from the inhabitants, who continued to work
the land.

[b] The choruses mentioned were of course local, and performed at the Mytilenean festivals. The "services to Athens"
amount to nothing more than the payment of τέλη (? harbour-
dues). Professor Wade-Gery suggests to me that the εἰκοστή
may be meant, a 5% impost which replaced the tribute early
in 413 (Thuc. vii. 28). If so, the date of the speech must fall
between the spring of 413 and the autumn, when news of the
Sicilian disaster arrived (cf. p. 148).

display his devotion in the old way. It was not easy
for him to leave the city, as the ties which bound
him, his children, and his property, were strong ones ;
nor yet could he set it at defiance as long as he
remained there. But from the moment that you
punished the authors of the revolt—of whom my
father was not found to be one —and granted the
other citizens of Mytilene an amnesty which allowed
them to continue living on their own land,[a] he has
not been guilty of a single fault, of a single lapse from
duty. He has failed neither the city of Athens nor
that of Mytilene, when a public service was demanded
of him ; he regularly furnishes choruses, and always
pays the imposts.[b] If Aenus is his favourite place of
resort, that fact does not mean that he is evading any
of his obligations towards Athens,[c] or that he has
become the citizen of another city, like those others,
some of whom I see crossing to the mainland and
settling among your enemies, while the rest actually
litigate with you under treaty [d] ; nor does it mean

[c] Or possibly Mytilene.
[d] The ms. text is clearly unsound here. (1) The μὲν in the
fourth line of § 78 has no answering δὲ. (2) The sense of the
passage as it stands is in any case unsatisfactory. σύμβολα (l. 6)
were special treaties regulating the settlement of private dis-
putes, generally commercial in character, between the citizens
of different states. Fragments of two such treaties have survived : Athens-Phaselis (*I.G.* i². 16 ff.) and Athens-Mytilene
(*I.G.* i². 60 ff.) ; and in the first of these there is a reference
to a third, Athens-Chios. It is quite certain, however, that
agreements of this sort did not extend to enemy states, as the
passage would suggest if the ms. reading be accepted.
Various corrections have been proposed. A. Fraenkel and
Wilamowitz suppose a considerable lacuna which contained
the words τοὺς δ᾽ ἐς πόλιν συμμαχίδα διοικιζομένους, or the like.
The objection to such a solution is that καὶ δίκας ἀπὸ συμβόλων
ὑμῖν δικαζομένους in l. 6 becomes otiose, as it is known that

215

οὐδὲ φεύγων τὸ πλῆθος τὸ ὑμέτερον, τοὺς δ᾽ οἴους
ὑμεῖς μισῶν συκοφάντας.

79 ῝Α μὲν οὖν μετὰ τῆς πόλεως ὅλης ἀνάγκῃ μᾶλλον
ἢ γνώμῃ ἔπραξεν, τούτων οὐ δίκαιός ἐστιν ὁ ἐμὸς
πατὴρ ἰδίᾳ¹ δίκην διδόναι. ἅπασι γὰρ Μυτιληναίοις
ἀείμνηστος ἡ τότε ἁμαρτία γεγένηται· ἠλλάξαντο
μὲν γὰρ πολλῆς εὐδαιμονίας πολλὴν κακοδαι-
μονίαν, ἐπεῖδον δὲ τὴν ἑαυτῶν πατρίδα ἀνάστατον
γενομένην. ἃ δὲ ἰδίᾳ οὗτοι διαβάλλουσι τὸν ἐμὸν
πατέρα, μὴ πείθεσθε²· χρημάτων γὰρ ἕνεκα ἡ πᾶσα
παρασκευὴ γεγένηται ἐπ᾽ ἐμοί³ κἀκείνῳ. πολλὰ δ᾽
ἐστὶ τὰ συμβαλλόμενα τοῖς βουλομένοις τῶν ἀλλοτρίων ἐφίεσθαι. γέρων μὲν ἐκεῖνος ὥστ᾽ ἐμοὶ⁴
βοηθεῖν, νεώτερος δ᾽ ἐγὼ πολλῷ ἢ ὥστε δύνασθαι
80 ἐμαυτῷ τιμωρεῖν ἱκανῶς. ἀλλ᾽ ὑμεῖς βοηθήσατέ
μοι, καὶ μὴ διδάσκετε τοὺς συκοφάντας μεῖζον
ὑμῶν αὐτῶν δύνασθαι. ἐὰν μὲν γὰρ εἰσιόντες εἰς
ὑμᾶς ἃ βούλονται πράσσωσι, δεδειγμένον ἔσται τούτους μὲν πείθειν, τὸ δ᾽ ὑμέτερον πλῆθος φεύγειν·
ἐὰν δὲ εἰσιόντες εἰς ὑμᾶς πονηροὶ μὲν αὐτοὶ δοκῶσιν
εἶναι, πλέον δ᾽ αὐτοῖς μηδὲν γένηται, ὑμετέρα ἡ
τιμὴ καὶ ἡ δύναμις ἔσται, ὥσπερ καὶ τὸ δίκαιον
ἔχει. ὑμεῖς οὖν ἐμοί τε βοηθεῖτε καὶ τῷ δικαίῳ.

[139]
81 ῞Οσα μὲν οὖν ἐκ τῶν ἀνθρωπίνων τεκμηρίων
καὶ μαρτυριῶν οἷά τε ἦν ἀποδειχθῆναι, ἀκηκόατε·

¹ ἰδίᾳ om. A pr.   ² πείθεσθαι N pr.
³ ἐπ᾽ ἐμοὶ A : ὑπ᾽ ἐμοὶ N.
⁴ ὥστ᾽ ἐμοὶ Bekker : ὥστε μοι codd.

σύμβολα already existed between Athens and Mytilene.
Better is Reiskes's τοὺς δὲ. We then have a contrast between
Euxitheus' father, who is a loyal citizen of Mytilene under
Athenian rule, and other Mytileneans who, since the revolt
of Lesbos ten years previously, have either (a) shown their

that he desires to be beyond the reach of the Athenian courts. It means that he shares your own hatred of those who thrive on prosecution.

The act which my father joined his whole city in committing, which he committed not from choice but under compulsion, affords no just ground for punishing him individually. The mistake then made will live in the memory of every citizen of Mytilene. They exchanged great prosperity for great misery, and saw their country pass into the possession of others. Nor again must you be influenced by the distorted account of my father's conduct as an individual with which you have been presented. Nothing but money is at the bottom of this elaborate attack upon him and myself ; and unfortunately there are many circumstances which favour those who seek to lay hands on the goods of others ; my father is too old to help me : and I am far too young to be able to avenge myself as I should. You must help me : you must refuse to teach those who make a trade of prosecution to become more powerful than yourselves. If they achieve their purpose when they appear before you, it will be a lesson to their victims to compromise with them and avoid open court ; but if by appearing before you they succeed only in gaining an evil reputation for themselves, you will enjoy the honour and the power which it is right that you should. So give me and give justice your support.

Proof as complete as the presumptions and the evidence supplied by things human could make it has

hostility to Athens passively by settling on the Asiatic coast in towns under Persian control or (b) shown it actively by remaining in Lesbos and initiating an unending series of lawsuits against the Athenian cleruchs who have become their landlords.

χρὴ δὲ καὶ τοῖς ἀπὸ τῶν θεῶν σημείοις γενομένοις εἰς τὰ τοιαῦτα οὐχ ἥκιστα τεκμηραμένους
ψηφίζεσθαι. καὶ γὰρ τὰ τῆς πόλεως κοινὰ τούτοις
μάλιστα πιστεύοντες ἀσφαλῶς διαπράσσεσθε, τοῦτο
μὲν τὰ εἰς τοὺς κινδύνους ἥκοντα, τοῦτο δὲ [εἰς]¹
τὰ ἔξω τῶν κινδύνων. χρὴ δὲ καὶ εἰς τὰ ἴδια ταῦτα
82 μέγιστα καὶ πιστότατα ἡγεῖσθαι. οἶμαι γὰρ ὑμᾶς
ἐπίστασθαι ὅτι πολλοὶ ἤδη ἄνθρωποι μὴ καθαροὶ
⟨τὰς⟩² χεῖρας ἢ ἄλλο τι μίασμα ἔχοντες συνεισ-
βάντες εἰς τὸ πλοῖον συναπώλεσαν μετὰ τῆς αὑτῶν
ψυχῆς τοὺς ὁσίως διακειμένους τὰ πρὸς τοὺς θεούς·
τοῦτο δὲ ἤδη ἑτέρους ἀπολομένους μὲν οὔ, κιν-
δυνεύσαντας δὲ τοὺς ἐσχάτους κινδύνους διὰ τοὺς
τοιούτους ἀνθρώπους· τοῦτο³ δὲ ἱεροῖς παραστάν-
τες πολλοὶ δὴ καταφανεῖς ἐγένοντο οὐχ ὅσιοι
ὄντες, [καὶ]⁴ διακωλύοντες τὰ ἱερὰ μὴ γίγνεσθαι
83 τὰ νομιζόμενα. ἐμοὶ τοίνυν ἐν πᾶσι τούτοις τὰ
ἐναντία ἐγένετο. τοῦτο μὲν γὰρ ὅσοις συνέπλευσα,
καλλίστοις ἐχρήσαντο πλοῖς· τοῦτο δὲ ὅπου ἱεροῖς
παρέστην, οὐκ ἔστιν ὅπου οὐχὶ κάλλιστα τὰ ἱερὰ
ἐγένετο. ἃ ἐγὼ ἀξιῶ μεγάλα μοι τεκμήρια εἶναι
τῆς αἰτίας, ὅτι οὐκ ἀληθῆ μου οὗτοι κατηγοροῦσι.
⟨εἰσὶ δέ μοι καὶ⟩⁵ τούτων μάρτυρες.

MΑΡΤΥΡΕΣ

84 Ἐπίσταμαι δὲ καὶ τάδε, ὦ ἄνδρες δικασταί, ὅτι
εἰ μὲν ἐμοῦ κατεμαρτύρουν οἱ μάρτυρες, ὥς τι

¹ εἰς del. Bekker.   ² τὰς add. Fuhr.
³ τοῦτο δὲ A : τοῦ δὲ N.   ⁴ καὶ del. Sauppe.
⁵ εἰσὶ δέ μοι καὶ add. Reiske.

ᵃ The fact that an argument of this kind could be ad-

218

now been presented to you. But in cases of this nature the indications furnished by heaven must also have no small influence on your verdict.[a] It is upon them that you chiefly depend for safe guidance in affairs of state, whether in times of crisis or tranquillity ; so they should be allowed equal prominence and weight in the settlement of private questions. I hardly think I need remind you that many a man with unclean hands or some other form of defilement who has embarked on shipboard with the righteous has involved them in his own destruction.[b] Others, while they have escaped death, have had their lives imperilled owing to such polluted wretches. Many, too, have been proved to be defiled as they stood beside a sacrifice, because they prevented the proper performance of the rites. With me the opposite has happened in every case. Not only have fellow-passengers of mine enjoyed the calmest of voyages : but whenever I have attended a sacrifice, that sacrifice has invariably been successful. I claim that these facts furnish the strongest presumption in my favour that the charge brought against me by the prosecution is unfounded ; I have witnesses to confirm them.

Witnesses

I know furthermore, gentlemen of the jury, that if the witnesses were testifying against me that my pres-

vanced in a court of law, shows, like the popular agitation over the mutilation of the Hermae, that the average Athenian of the time was far from being a rationalist.

[b] Oddly reminiscent of Aeschylus, *Septem* 602 ff. :

$$\text{ἢ γὰρ ξυνεισβὰς πλοῖον εὐσεβὴς ἀνὴρ}$$
$$\text{ναύταισι θερμοῖς καὶ πανουργίᾳ τινὶ}$$
$$\text{ὄλωλεν ἀνδρῶν σὺν θεοπτύστῳ γένει.}$$

ἀνόσιον γεγένηται ἐμοῦ παρόντος ἐν πλοίῳ ἢ ἐν
ἱεροῖς, αὐτοῖς γε τούτοις ἰσχυροτάτοις ἂν ἐχρῶντο,
καὶ πίστιν τῆς αἰτίας ταύτην σαφεστάτην ἀπέφαινον, τὰ σημεῖα τὰ ἀπὸ τῶν θεῶν· νῦν δὲ τῶν
τε σημείων ἐναντίων¹ τοῖς τούτων λόγοις γιγνομένων,² τῶν τε μαρτύρων ἃ μὲν ἐγὼ λέγω μαρτυρούντων ἀληθῆ εἶναι, ἃ δ' οὗτοι κατηγοροῦσι ψευδῆ,
τοῖς μὲν μαρτυροῦσιν ἀπιστεῖν ὑμᾶς κελεύουσι,
τοῖς δὲ λόγοις οὓς αὐτοὶ λέγουσι πιστεύειν ὑμᾶς
φασι χρῆναι. καὶ οἱ μὲν ἄλλοι ἄνθρωποι τοῖς
ἔργοις τοὺς λόγους ἐλέγχουσιν, οὗτοι δὲ τοῖς λόγοις
τὰ ἔργα ζητοῦσιν ἄπιστα καθιστάναι.

85 Ὅσα μὲν οὖν ἐκ τῶν κατηγορηθέντων μέμνημαι,
ὦ ἄνδρες, ἀπολελόγημαι· οἶμαι δὲ καὶ³ ὑμῶν ⟨αὐτῶν
ἕνεκα δεῖν ὑμᾶς μου⟩⁴ ἀποψηφίσασθαι. ταῦτα⁵ γὰρ
ἐμέ τε σῴζει, καὶ ὑμῖν νόμιμα καὶ εὔορκα γίγνεται.
κατὰ γὰρ τοὺς νόμους ὠμόσατε δικάσειν· ἐγὼ δὲ
καθ' οὓς μὲν ἀπήχθην, οὐκ ἔνοχός εἰμι τοῖς νόμοις,
ὧν δ' ἔχω τὴν αἰτίαν, ἀγών μοι νόμιμος ὑπολείπεται. εἰ δὲ δύο ἐξ ἑνὸς ἀγῶνος γεγένησθον, οὐκ
ἐγὼ αἴτιος, ἀλλ' οἱ κατήγοροι. καίτοι οὐ δήπου
οἱ μὲν ἔχθιστοι οἱ ἐμοὶ δύο ἀγῶνας περὶ ἐμοῦ
πεποιήκασιν, ὑμεῖς δὲ οἱ τῶν δικαίων ἴσοι κριταὶ
προκαταγνώσεσθέ μου⁶ ἐν τῷδε τῷ ἀγῶνι⁷ τὸν
86 φόνον. μὴ ὑμεῖς γε, ὦ ἄνδρες· ἀλλὰ δότε τι καὶ
τῷ χρόνῳ, μεθ' οὗ ὀρθότατα εὑρίσκουσιν οἱ τὴν
ἀκρίβειαν ζητοῦντες τῶν πραγμάτων. ἠξίουν μὲν

---

¹ ἐναντίων A corr.² N : ἐναντίον A pr.
² γιγνομένων A corr.² N : γιγνομένοις A pr.
³ καὶ om. N.
⁴ Nonnulla excidisse videntur : sensum suppl. Schoemann.
⁵ ταῦτα Bekker : ταὗτα codd.
⁶ μου A : με N.
⁷ ἀγῶνι Maetzner : λόγῳ codd.

ence on shipboard or at a sacrifice had been the occasion of some unholy manifestation, the prosecution would be treating that fact as supremely significant ; they would be showing that here, in the signs from heaven, was to be found the clearest confirmation of their charge. As, however, the signs have contradicted their assertions, and the witnesses testify that what I say is true and that what the prosecution say is not, they urge you to put no credence in the evidence of those witnesses ; according to them, it is their own statements which you should believe. Whereas every one else uses the facts to prove the worth of mere assertion, they use mere assertion for the purpose of discrediting the facts.

All the charges which I can remember, gentlemen, I have answered ; and for your own sakes I think that you should acquit me. A verdict saving my life will alone enable you to comply with the law and your oath ; for you have sworn to return a lawful verdict ; and while the crime with which I am charged can still be tried legally, the laws under which I was arrested do not concern my case.[a] If two trials have been made out of one, it is not I, but my accusers, who are to blame ; and I cannot suppose that if my bitterest enemies have involved me in two trials, impartial ministers of justice like yourselves will prematurely find me guilty of murder in the present one. Beware of such haste, gentlemen ; give time its opportunity ; it is time which enables those who seek the truth to find it with certainty. In fact,

[a] Another reference to the argument that his case could be properly tried only by a δίκη φόνου before the Areopagus. The " laws under which I was arrested " are of course the νόμοι τῶν κακούργων defining the scope of ἀπαγωγή for κακουργία.

γὰρ ἔγωγε περὶ τῶν τοιούτων, ὦ ἄνδρες, εἶναι
τὴν δίκην κατὰ τοὺς νόμους, κατὰ μέντοι ⟨τού-
τους⟩[1] τὸ δίκαιον ὡς πλειστάκις ἐλέγχεσθαι.
τοσούτῳ γὰρ ἄμεινον ἂν ἐγιγνώσκετο· οἱ γὰρ
πολλοὶ ἀγῶνες τῇ μὲν ἀληθείᾳ σύμμαχοί εἰσι, τῇ
87 δὲ διαβολῇ πολεμιώτατοι. φόνου γὰρ δίκη καὶ
μὴ ὀρθῶς γνωσθεῖσα ἰσχυρότερον τοῦ δικαίου καὶ
τοῦ ἀληθοῦς ἐστιν· ἀνάγκη γάρ, ἐὰν ὑμεῖς μου
καταψηφίσησθε, καὶ μὴ ὄντα φονέα μηδ' ἔνοχον
τῷ ἔργῳ χρῆσθαι τῇ δίκῃ καὶ τῷ νόμῳ· καὶ οὐδεὶς
ἂν τολμήσειεν οὔτε τὴν δίκην τὴν δεδικασμένην
παραβαίνειν, πιστεύσας αὑτῷ ὅτι οὐκ ἔνοχός ἐστιν,
οὔτε ξυνειδὼς αὑτῷ τοιοῦτον ἔργον εἰργασμένῳ μὴ
οὐ χρῆσθαι τῷ νόμῳ· ἀνάγκη δὲ τῆς ⟨τε⟩ δίκης νικᾶσθαι παρὰ τὸ ἀληθές, αὐτοῦ τε τοῦ ἀληθοῦς, καὶ
88 ἄλλως τε καὶ ἐὰν μὴ ᾖ ὁ τιμωρήσων. αὐτῶν δὲ
τούτων ἕνεκα[2] οἵ τε νόμοι καὶ αἱ διωμοσίαι καὶ τὰ
τόμια καὶ αἱ προρρήσεις, καὶ τἄλλ' ὁπόσα[3] γίγνεται
τῶν δικῶν ἕνεκα τοῦ φόνου, πολὺ διαφέροντά ἐστιν
ἢ καὶ ἐπὶ τοῖς ἄλλοις, ὅτι καὶ αὐτὰ τὰ πράγματα,

---

[1] τούτους addidit Sauppe.
[2] ἕνεκα A : εἴνεκα N.   [3] ὁπόσα A : ὅσα N.

---

[a] §§ 87-89 appear, with slight modifications, in the *Choreutes*
(§§ 3-6). It is clear that we have here one of those *loci communes* which were part of the stock in trade of every λογόγραφος
and could easily be adapted to different contexts (*cf. Her.*
§§ 14 f., *Chor.* § 2 : *Stepm.* §§ 12 f., *Her.* §§ 38 f., *Chor.* § 27 :
and Andocides, *Mysteries*, §§ 1, 6, 7, 9, where see note).
The present passage stresses the gravity and the finality of a
δίκη φόνου, a theme which was likely to find a place in most
φονικοὶ λόγοι. Here, however, it is introduced a little awk-
wardly. The words δίκη φόνου (§ 87 *init.*) refer, not to the
present trial, which is an ἔνδειξις, but to the trial before the
Areopagus which Euxitheus hopes will follow ; and the word

gentlemen, I for one have always maintained that, while a case of this kind should certainly be tried according to law, the rights of the matter should be established as many times as the law will permit, since they would thus be the better understood; the repeated trial of a case is a good friend of the truth and the deadly foe of misrepresentation. In a trial for murder,[a] even if judgement is wrongly given against the defendant, justice and the facts cannot prevail against that decision. Once you condemn me, I must perforce obey your verdict and the law, even if I am not the murderer or concerned in the crime. No one would venture either to disregard the sentence passed upon him because he was sure that he had had no part in the crime, or to disobey the law if he knew in his heart that he was guilty of such a deed. He has to submit to the verdict in defiance of the facts, or submit to the facts themselves, as the case may be, above all if his victim has none to avenge him.[b] The laws, the oaths, the sacrifices, the proclamations, in fact the entire proceedings in connexion with trials for murder[c] differ as profoundly as they do from the proceedings elsewhere simply because it is of supreme importance that the

ὑμεῖς in the third line of § 87 is used in the same general sense as in § 90 (cf. note ad loc.).

[b] The speaker is here thinking of the master who has killed his slave; the slave has no family to institute proceedings on his behalf (cf. Chor. §§ 4 ad fin. and 5). The argument of § 87 as a whole sounds odd to modern ears; but it should be remembered that at Athens the defendant in a δίκη φόνου always had the option of going into voluntary exile before the court passed sentence. Hence it was possible to speak of " disregarding the sentence imposed."

[c] See Introduction, p. 150.

περὶ ὧν οἱ κίνδυνοι, περὶ πλείστου ἐστὶν ὀρθῶς
γιγνώσκεσθαι· ὀρθῶς μὲν γὰρ γνωσθέντα τιμωρία
[140] ἐστὶ τῷ ἀδικηθέντι, φονέα δὲ τὸν μὴ αἴτιον ψηφισθῆναι ἁμαρτία καὶ ἀσέβειά ἐστιν εἴς τε τοὺς
89 θεοὺς καὶ εἰς τοὺς νόμους. καὶ οὐκ ἴσον ἐστὶ τόν
τε διώκοντα μὴ ὀρθῶς αἰτιάσασθαι[1] καὶ ὑμᾶς τοὺς
δικαστὰς μὴ ὀρθῶς γνῶναι. ἡ μὲν γὰρ τούτων
αἰτίασις οὐκ ἔχει τέλος, ἀλλ' ἐν ὑμῖν ἐστι καὶ τῇ
δίκῃ· ὅ τι δ' ἂν ὑμεῖς ἐν αὐτῇ τῇ δίκῃ μὴ ὀρθῶς
γνῶτε, τοῦτο οὐκ ἔστιν ὅποι ἄν τις ἀνενεγκὼν[2] τὴν
ἁμαρτίαν ἀπολύσαιτο.

90   Πῶς ἂν οὖν ὀρθῶς δικάσαιτε[3] περὶ αὐτῶν; εἰ
τούτους τε ἐάσετε τὸν νομιζόμενον ὅρκον διομοσαμένους κατηγορῆσαι, κἀμὲ περὶ αὐτοῦ τοῦ πράγματος ἀπολογήσασθαι. πῶς δὲ ἐάσετε; ἐὰν νυνὶ
ἀποψηφίσησθέ μου. διαφεύγω γὰρ οὐδ' οὕτω τὰς
ὑμετέρας γνώμας, ἀλλ' ὑμεῖς ἔσεσθε οἱ κἀκεῖ[4] περὶ
ἐμοῦ διαψηφιζόμενοι. καὶ φεισαμένοις[5] μὲν ὑμῖν
ἐμοῦ νῦν ἔξεστι τότε χρῆσθαι ὅ τι ἂν βούλησθε,[6]
ἀπολέσασι δὲ[7] οὐδὲ βουλεύσασθαι ἔτι περὶ ἐμοῦ
ἐγχωρεῖ.

91   Καὶ μὴν εἰ δέοι ἁμαρτεῖν τι, τὸ[8] ἀδίκως ἀπολῦσαι ὁσιώτερον ἂν εἴη[9] τοῦ[10] μὴ δικαίως ἀπολέσαι·

---

¹ αἰτιάσασθαι A corr. N : αἰτιᾶσθαι A pr.
² ἀνενεγκὼν A corr. N : ἐνεγκὼν A pr.
³ δικάσαιτε Bekker : δικάσητε codd.
⁴ κἀκεῖ Ald. : κακοί codd.
⁵ φεισαμένοις N : ψηφισαμένοις A.
⁶ ὅ τι ἂν βούλησθε Dobree : ὅ τι ἃ δὴ βούλεσθαι A corr. N :
βούλεσθε A pr.
⁷ ἀπολέσασι δὲ Dobree : ἀπολογήσασθαι codd.
⁸ τι, τὸ Maetzner : ἐπὶ τῷ codd. : τι ἁμαρτεῖν τὸ Stobaeus,
qui verba εἰ δέοι . . . ἀσέβημα, memoriter fortasse, sic affert,
Flor. xlvi. 19 : εἰ δέοι τι ἁμαρτεῖν, τὸ ἀδ. ἀπολῦσαι ὁσιώτερον

facts at issue, upon which so much turns, should themselves be rightly interpreted. Such a right interpretation means vengeance for him who has been wronged; whereas to find an innocent man guilty of murder is a mistake, and a sinful mistake, which offends both gods and laws. Nor is it as serious for the prosecutor to accuse the wrong person as it is for you jurors to reach a wrong verdict. The charge brought by the prosecutor is not in itself effective ; whether it becomes so, depends upon you, sitting in judgement. On the other hand if you yourselves, when actually sitting in judgement, return a wrong verdict, you cannot rid yourselves of the responsibility for the mistake by blaming someone else for that verdict.

Then how can you decide the case aright ? By allowing the prosecution to bring their charge only after taking the customary oath, and by allowing me to confine my defence to the question before the court. And how will you do this ? By acquitting me to-day. For I do not escape your sentence even so : you will be the judges at the second hearing also.[a] If you spare me now, you can treat me as you will then ; whereas once you put me to death, you cannot even consider my case further.

Indeed, supposing that you were bound to make some mistake, it would be less of an outrage to acquit me unfairly than to put me to death without just

[a] True only in a general sense. The present jury was composed of ordinary Heliasts; whereas the jury at a δίκη φόνου would consist of ex-Archons, sitting as members of the Areopagus. Euxitheus is speaking as an alien, and by ὑμεῖς means " you Athenians."

τοῦ ἀδίκως ἀπολέσαι· τὸ μὲν γὰρ ἁμ. ἐστι, τὸ δὲ ἀδίκως ἀποκτεῖναι ἀσεβῆμα.   9 ἂν εἴη Dobree: ἂν ᾖ codd. : om. Stobaeus.
10 τοῦ Stobaeus, Ald.: τὸ codd.

τὸ μὲν γὰρ ἁμάρτημα μόνον ἐστί, τὸ δὲ ἕτερον καὶ
ἀσέβημα. ἐν ᾧ χρὴ πολλὴν πρόνοιαν ἔχειν, μέλλοντας ἀνήκεστον[1] ἔργον ἐργάζεσθαι. ἐν μὲν γὰρ
ἀκεστῷ[2] πράγματι καὶ ὀργῇ χρησαμένους καὶ διαβολῇ πιθομένους[3] ἔλαττόν ἐστιν ἐξαμαρτεῖν· μετα-
γνοὺς γάρ ⟨τις⟩[4] ἔτι ἂν ὀρθῶς βουλεύσαιτο· ἐν δὲ
τοῖς ἀνηκέστοις πλέον βλάβος τὸ μετανοεῖν καὶ
γνῶναι ἐξημαρτηκότας. ἤδη δέ τισιν ὑμῶν καὶ
μετεμέλησεν ἀπολωλεκόσι. καίτοι ὅπου[5] ὑμῖν τοῖς
ἐξαπατηθεῖσι μετεμέλησεν, ᾗ[6] καὶ πάνυ τοι χρῆν[7]
τούς γε ἐξαπατῶντας ἀπολωλέναι.

92 Ἔπειτα δὲ τὰ μὲν ἀκούσια τῶν ἁμαρτημάτων
ἔχει συγγνώμην, τὰ δὲ ἑκούσια οὐκ ἔχει. τὸ μὲν
γὰρ[8] ἀκούσιον ἁμάρτημα, ὦ ἄνδρες, τῆς τύχης ἐστί,
τὸ δὲ ἑκούσιον τῆς γνώμης.[9] ἑκούσιον δὲ πῶς ἂν
εἴη μᾶλλον ἢ εἴ τις, ὧν βουλὴν ποιοῖτο, ταῦτα
παραχρῆμα ἐξεργάζοιτο;[10] καὶ μὴν τὴν ἴσην γε
δύναμιν ἔχει, ὅστις τε ἂν τῇ χειρὶ ἀποκτείνῃ ἀδίκως
καὶ ὅστις τῇ ψήφῳ.

93 Εὖ δ' ἴστε ὅτι οὐκ ἄν ποτ' ἦλθον εἰς τὴν πόλιν,
εἴ τι ξυνῄδη ἐμαυτῷ τοιοῦτον· νῦν δὲ πιστεύων τῷ
δικαίῳ, οὗ πλέονος οὐδέν ἐστιν ἄξιον ἀνδρὶ
συναγωνίζεσθαι, μηδὲν αὑτῷ συνειδότι ἀνόσιον
εἰργασμένῳ μηδ'[11] εἰς τοὺς θεοὺς ἠσεβηκότι· ἐν γὰρ
τῷ τοιούτῳ ἤδη καὶ τὸ σῶμα ἀπειρηκὸς ἡ ψυχὴ
συνεξέσωσεν, ἐθέλουσα ταλαιπωρεῖν διὰ τὸ μὴ
ξυνειδέναι ἑαυτῇ. τῷ δὲ ξυνειδότι τοῦτο αὐτὸ

---

[1] ἀνήκεστον Stephanus : ἀνηκέστερον codd.
[2] ἀκεστῷ Stephanus : ἑκάστῳ codd.
[3] πιθομένους Cobet : πειθομένους codd.
[4] τις add. Bohlmann.
[5] ὅπου Leo : οὔπω codd.
[6] ἦ Leo : εἰ codd.
[7] χρῆν Blass : χρὴ codd.
[8] γὰρ om. N.
[9] ἐστίν post γν. habet N.

cause ; for the one thing is a mistake and nothing more : the other is a sin in addition. You must exercise the greatest caution in what you do, because you will not be able to reconsider your action. In a matter which admits of reconsideration a mistake, whether made through giving rein to the feelings or through accepting a distorted account of the facts, is not so serious ; it is still possible to change one's mind and come to a right decision. But when reconsideration is impossible, the wrong done is only increased by altering one's mind and acknowledging one's mistake. Some of you yourselves have in fact repented before now of having sent men to their death ; but when you, who had been misled, felt repentance, most assuredly did those who had misled you deserve death.

Moreover, whereas involuntary mistakes are excusable, voluntary mistakes are not ; for an involuntary mistake is due to chance, gentlemen, a voluntary one to the will. And what could be more voluntary than the immediate putting into effect of a carefully considered course of action ? Furthermore, the wrongful taking of life by one's vote is just as criminal as the wrongful taking of life by one's hand.

Rest assured that I should never have come to Athens, had such a crime been on my conscience. I am here, as it is, because I have faith in justice, the most precious ally of the man who has no deed of sin upon his conscience and who has committed no transgression against the gods. Often at such an hour as this, when the body has given up the struggle, its salvation is the spirit, which is ready to fight on in the conscience that it is innocent. On the other

---

¹⁰ ἐξεργάζοιτο N : ἐργάζοιτο A.
¹¹ μηδ' Franke : μήτ' codd.

πρῶτον πολέμιόν ἐστιν· ἔτι γὰρ καὶ τοῦ σώματος
ἰσχύοντος ἡ ψυχὴ προαπολείπει, ἡγουμένη τὴν
τιμωρίαν οἱ ἥκειν ταύτην τῶν ἀσεβημάτων[1]· ἐγὼ
δ᾽ ἐμαυτῷ τοιοῦτον οὐδὲν ξυνειδὼς ἥκω εἰς ὑμᾶς.

94 Τὸ δὲ[2] τοὺς κατηγόρους διαβάλλειν οὐδέν ἐστι
θαυμαστόν. τούτων γὰρ ἔργον τοῦτο, ὑμῶν δὲ τὸ
μὴ πείθεσθαι τὰ μὴ δίκαια. τοῦτο μὲν γὰρ ἐμοὶ
πειθομένοις ὑμῖν[3] μεταμελῆσαι ἔστιν, καὶ τούτου
φάρμακον τὸ αὖθις κολάσαι, τοῦ δὲ τούτοις πειθομένους ἐξεργάσασθαι ἃ οὗτοι βούλονται οὐκ ἔστιν
ἴασις. οὐδὲ χρόνος πολὺς ὁ διαφέρων, ἐν ᾧ ταῦτα
νομίμως πράξεθ᾽[4] ἃ[5] νῦν ὑμᾶς παρανόμως πείθουσιν
οἱ κατήγοροι ψηφίσασθαι. οὔ τοι τῶν ἐπειγο-
μένων ἐστὶ τὰ πράγματα, ἀλλὰ τῶν εὖ βουλευο-
μένων. νῦν μὲν οὖν γνωρισταὶ γίγνεσθε τῆς δίκης,
τότε δὲ δικασταὶ [τῶν μαρτύρων][6]· νῦν μὲν δοξα-
σταί, τότε δὲ κριταὶ τῶν ἀληθῶν.

95 Ῥᾷστον δέ τοί[7] ἐστιν ἀνδρὸς περὶ θανάτου φεύγοντος τὰ ψευδῆ καταμαρτυρῆσαι. ἐὰν γὰρ τὸ
παραχρῆμα μόνον πείσωσιν ὥστε ἀποκτεῖναι, ἅμα
τῷ σώματι καὶ ἡ τιμωρία ἀπόλωλεν. οὐδὲ γὰρ οἱ
φίλοι ἔτι θελήσουσιν ὑπὲρ ἀπολωλότος τιμωρεῖν·
ἐὰν δὲ καὶ βουληθῶσιν, τί ἔσται πλέον τῷ γε

96 ἀποθανόντι; νῦν μὲν οὖν ἀποψηφίσασθέ μου· ἐν
δὲ τῇ τοῦ φόνου δίκῃ οὗτοί τε τὸν νομιζόμενον

---

[1] ἀσεβημάτων N : ἀσεβηκότων A.
[2] τὸ δὲ Ald. : τῶ A, τῷ N.   [3] ὑμῖν N : ἡμῖν A.
[4] πράξεθ᾽ A pr. : πράξεσθ᾽ A corr. N.
[5] ἃ A : ἂν N.
[6] τῶν μαρτύρων secl. Jernstedt : post δοξασταὶ transp.
Sauppe.

hand, he whose conscience is guilty has no worse enemy than that conscience; for his spirit fails him while his body is still unwearied, because it feels that what is approaching him is the punishment of his iniquities. But it is with no such guilty conscience that I come before you.

There is nothing remarkable in the fact that the prosecution are misrepresenting me. It is expected of them; just as it is expected of you not to consent to do what is wrong. I say this because if you follow my advice, it is still open to you to regret your action, and that regret can be remedied by punishing me at the second trial: whereas if you obediently carry out the prosecution's wishes, the situation cannot be righted again. Nor is there a question of a long interval before the law will allow you to take the step to which the prosecution are to-day urging you to consent in defiance of it. It is not haste, but discretion which triumphs; so take cognizance of the case to-day: pass judgement on it later [a]; form an opinion as to the truth to-day: decide upon it later.

It is very easy, remember, to give false evidence against a man on a capital charge. If you are persuaded only for an instant to put him to death, he has lost his chance of redress with his life. A man's very friends will refuse to seek redress for him once he is dead; and even if they are prepared to do so, what good is it to one who has lost his life? Acquit me, then, to-day; and at the trial for murder the prose-

---

[a] τῶν μαρτύρων is clearly an unintelligent gloss, added by a reader who felt that a genitive was needed to correspond to τῆς δίκης.

---

[7] ῥᾷστον δέ τοι Dobree: ἀραῖς τῶν δέτοι A, om. N., qui lacunam hic habet.

ANTIPHON

ὅρκον διομοσάμενοι ἐμοῦ κατηγορήσουσι, καὶ ὑμεῖς
περὶ ἐμοῦ κατὰ τοὺς κειμένους νόμους διαγνώ-
σεσθε, καὶ ἐμοὶ οὐδεὶς λόγος ἔσται[1] ἔτι, ἐάν τι
[141] πάσχω, ὡς παρανόμως[2] ἀπωλόμην.

Ταῦτά τοι δέομαι ὑμῶν, οὔτε τὸ ὑμέτερον εὐσε-
βὲς παριεὶς[3] οὔτε ἐμαυτὸν ἀποστερῶν τὸ δίκαιον· ἐν
δὲ τῷ ὑμετέρῳ ὅρκῳ καὶ ἡ ἐμὴ σωτηρία ἔνεστι.
πειθόμενοι δὲ τούτων ὅτῳ βούλεσθε, ἀποψηφίσασθέ
μου.

---

[1] ἔσται A : ἐστὶ N.
[2] παρανόμως Reiske : παράνομος codd.
[3] παριεὶς Fuhr : παρεὶς codd.

230

cution shall take the traditional oath before accusing
me : you shall decide my case by the laws of the
land : and I, if I am unlucky, shall have no grounds
left for complaining that I was sentenced to death
illegally.

That is my request ; and in making it I am not
forgetting your duty as godfearing men or depriving
myself of my rights, as my life is bound up with your
oath.   Respect which you will, and acquit me.

VI
ON THE CHOREUTES

INTRODUCTION

THERE has been a considerable divergence of opinion as to the date of the *Choreutes*. It is clear from internal evidence that it was delivered one autumn, following the impeachment of a certain Philinus in the previous April (§ 12 *et pass.*); but the year within which the two speeches fell has been, and still is, a matter for dispute. On the one side we have a fragment of the Κατὰ Φιλίνου, also the work of Antiphon, which consists of the words " to make all the Thetes hoplites " (τούς τε θῆτας ἅπαντας ὁπλίτας ποιῆσαι); and it has been urged that such a measure could have been suggested only during the period of domestic demoralization which followed the Athenian defeat in Sicily in 413 B.C. Hence the *Philinus* is to be assigned to April, 412, and the *Choreutes* to the closing months of the same year. Confirmation of this date is sought in the political colouring of the *Choreutes* itself; the man who delivered it, it is argued, is clearly someone of oligarchic sympathies who is being attacked by his political enemies in revenge for his having exposed some months previously the corruption and jobbery rife among the officials of the popular government; and such attempts as his to discredit democrats and democracy fall most naturally within the twelve months which preceded the oligarchic revolution of 411. These

arguments are not entirely convincing, however. In
the first place, the evidence of the *Philinus* fragment
is by no means conclusive. Apart from the fact
that we are completely ignorant of the context in
which the words which survive occurred, Thucydides
in his account of the situation at the close of 413 and
the beginning of 412 implies very clearly that the
scarcity felt was not one of heavy infantry but of
rowers for the navy [a] ; and it is not easy to believe
that at such a moment it can have been proposed
to train as hoplites the one class of citizens who
were traditionally the source of man-power for the
fleet. Nor again can overmuch weight be attached
to the argument from the political situation of 412.
Oligarchs were never slow to seize an opportunity
of discrediting their opponents, and there is no
reason to presume that the incidents referred to in
the *Choreutes* could not have taken place at any
time during the last half of the fifth century. More
suggestive perhaps of a date somewhere in the
region of 412 is the style of the speech itself, which
is far less stiff than that of the *Herodes* and in which
the artificialities of Gorgias and the older generation
of rhetoricians are far less apparent. Recently,
however, attention has been called to evidence of
date of a rather different kind.[b] The *Choreutes*
contains certain references to the Athenian calendar,
which, when related to what is otherwise known of
the system of intercalation in use in the last quarter
of the fifth century, suggest that the speech must
have been delivered in 419 B.C., *i.e.* before the *Herodes*.

---

[a] Thucyd. viii. 1. 2 οὐχ ὁρῶντες . . . ὑπηρεσίας ταῖς ναυσίν.
[b] See B. D. Meritt, *The Athenian Calendar in the Fifth
Century*, pp. 121, 122.

It is impossible to examine this evidence in any detail here ; but in brief it is as follows. §§ 44-45 of the *Choreutes* contain two indications of time : (*a*) the speaker was formally accused of φόνος before the Basileus on the fifty-first day after the latter took up office, *i.e.* on the 21st of Metageitnion, the second month of the Attic year : (*b*) he was Prytanis for the whole of the first Prytany of the year save two days (the implication being that he was forced to resign before completing his term of office, because of the charge of φόνος lodged against him with the Basileus). Now as in the latter part of the fifth century the opening Prytanies of a given year are known to have consisted of 37 days, the speaker must have held office for 35 ; and this gives the equation : Prytany I. 35 = Metageitnion 21 : or, in other words, Prytany I. 1 = Hecatombaeon 16. The Council therefore assumed office in this particular year sixteen days after the commencement of the civil year, an occurrence which was common enough, as the civil and conciliar years rarely coincided. It remains to discover in which years this particular discrepancy of sixteen days made its appearance ; and the epigraphical evidence [a] makes it clear that only 419 B.C. will meet the case. This is admittedly unsatisfactory in view of the marked difference in style between the *Choreutes* and *Herodes* ; but the systematic variations in the Attic calendar have been convincingly demonstrated from the plentiful data available, and unless we are inclined to resort to

[a] Meritt's calculations are based upon data furnished by *I.G.* i². 324, a fragmentary inscription containing detailed accounts of monies borrowed by the state from Athena Polias, Athena Nicê, Hermes, and the " Other Gods " during the years 426–422 B.C.

arbitrary alteration of the figures contained in the MSS. of the *Choreutes*, we must rest content with the earlier date. It will be best, then, to assume, in default of further evidence, that the speech was delivered in the autumn of 419 B.C.

Although its language shows a considerable advance on the *Herodes* in suppleness and force, the argumentation of the *Choreutes* is less satisfactory. The issues with which it deals are far more complex, and much of the fact underlying it is assumed to be too familiar to the jury to need detailed repetition ; thus even the narrative of the death of the boy Diodotus breaks off before the actual circumstances of the accident have been described. In addition to this, there is evidence that the concluding paragraphs are incomplete as we have them, and further references to certain important facts, which in the present speech receive a surprisingly brief mention, may well have been lost. The following is a reconstruction of the events leading up to the trial in so far as they can be ascertained from the speech.

Early in 419 an Athenian, whose name is unknown, but who probably belonged to the anti-democratic party which was to enjoy a short period of supremacy after the revolution of 411, discovered that the clerk to the Thesmothetae, in conjunction with three private citizens—Ampclinus, Aristion, and Philinus, was systematically embezzling public monies. He at once impeached all four before the Boulê ; and it was arranged that the case should be heard during the last week in April. Meanwhile this same man had been selected as Choregus for the Thargelia, a festival held about the first of May, the chief feature of which was a competition between choruses of boys. He recruited a chorus and set aside a room in his own house for training purposes; and as he was himself too preoccupied with his approaching lawsuit to be able to supervise the boys in person, he appointed his son-in-law, Phanostratus, and three others as deputies. All went well until a week or so before the festival, when one of the Choreutae, Diodotus, was given some kind of mixture to improve his voice. It unfortunately proved poisonous, and he died after drinking it.

It was fully recognized by every one concerned that the death of Diodotus had been a pure accident. However, Philinus and his associates, whose trial was to begin three days later, saw at once that they could turn it to their own advantage. By putting pressure upon Philocrates, the boy's brother, they induced him to go to the Basileus without delay and enter a formal charge of homicide against the Choregus. This would of course have the effect of depriving him of the right to frequent public places until his case had been tried, and he would consequently be unable to proceed with his impeachment. Unfortunately, however, they had overlooked the fact that a δίκη φόνου had to be preceded by three preliminary inquiries, conducted by the Basileus and spread over a period of three months: and the same official had to conduct all three. It was now the last week of April; and as the Basileus went out of office on the twenty-first of June, he had no time for three inquiries. He therefore refused to register the charge.

The four were not yet defeated. Philocrates was persuaded to appear before a Heliastic court without loss of time and there publicly avow that the Choregus had been responsible for his brother's death. The purpose of this move is not absolutely clear ; it was probably a final effort to proclaim the fact that the Choregus was defiled and therefore debarred from conducting a prosecution ; it was certainly not a second attempt to enter a charge of homicide, as that could not be done by merely appearing before a court in session. The Choregus retorted by pointing out to the court why Philocrates was attacking him in this fashion ; and when Philocrates reappeared next day, the day fixed for the trial of the other four, and declared once more—very probably to the jury which was about to try them—that the Choregus was guilty of homicide and had no right to prosecute, he challenged him to an examination of the witnesses of the accident and offered to hand over his slaves for torture. Philocrates could do no more. He withdrew ; and the trial took place. All four defendants were convicted and heavily fined.

No sooner was the trial over than Philocrates changed his tone. He apologized for his behaviour, and went so far as to ask for a formal reconciliation. His motives are not hard to discover. Not only had he had some kind of connexion with Philinus and the other three, as is clear from his readiness to oblige them, but he was involved in similar activities on a far greater scale elsewhere ; and it was obviously in his interests to remain on friendly terms with a man who had shown how merciless he was prepared to be in exposing public corruption. The Choregus consented to a reconciliation ; and for a month or so all was well. On July 7th, however, he became a member of the Boulê, and from July to August acted as Prytanis. During this period it came to his notice that members of no less than three boards of finance-officers, the Poristae, the Practores, and the Poletae, together with their clerks, were systematically embezzling monies over which they had control, and that certain private citizens—Philocrates among them—were enjoying a share in the profits. He immediately brought the matter before the Boulê and demanded an investigation.

The culprits acted quickly. If we are to believe the statement of the Choregus himself, a substantial bribe was offered to Philocrates as an inducement to reopen the matter of the death of Diodotus ; but he probably needed little encouragement. He approached the new Basileus, and this time had no difficulty in registering his charge. The usual πρόρρησις followed, debarring the Choregus from intercourse with his fellow men until such time as his case should be tried ; and on the 10th of August, while still a Prytanis, he was obliged to resign from the Boulê and withdraw from public life. However, Philocrates had struck too late ; attention had been called to the criminals, and an inquiry into their activities was held, as a result of which they were put on trial and convicted.

Naturally this did not quash the charge made against the Choregus. After the requisite προδικασίαι he appeared for trial in the following November, probably before the court which sat ἐπὶ Παλλαδίῳ.[a] Antiphon composed his defence ; and we have the first of the two speeches delivered. The final verdict is unknown, although it is hard to believe that the defendant was not acquitted.

One problem remains : what was the charge

[a] See Gen. Introd. to *Tetr.*, p. 42.

brought against the Choregus by Philocrates ? Such evidence as there is is to be found in §§ 16, 17, and 19, where the following statements occur : (i) § 16 διωμόσαντο δὲ οὗτοι μὲν ἀποκτεῖναί με Διόδοτον βουλεύσαντα τὸν θάνατον, ἐγὼ δὲ μὴ ἀποκτεῖναι, μήτε χειρὶ ἐργασάμενος μήτε βουλεύσας. (ii) § 17 αἰτιῶνται δὲ οὗτοι μὲν ἐκ τούτων, ὡς αἴτιος ὃς ἐκέλευσε πιεῖν τὸν παῖδα τὸ φάρμακον ἢ ἠνάγκασεν ἢ ἔδωκεν. (iii) § 19 πρῶτον μὲν αὐτοὶ οἱ κατήγοροι ὁμολογοῦσι μὴ ἐκ προνοίας μηδ᾽ ἐκ παρασκευῆς γενέσθαι τὸν θάνατον τῷ παιδί. To take (i) first : it is clear that βουλεύσαντα τὸν θάνατον is directly contrasted with χειρὶ ἐργασάμενος, and that therefore the Choregus is charged with having been in some sense the principal concerned in the death of Diodotus. On the other hand (iii) indicates that the prosecution were not bringing a charge of wilful murder ; if the accusation was one of βούλευσις φόνου, it was βούλευσις φόνου ἀκουσίου. This, then, is a different type of βούλευσις from that envisaged in Antiphon's first speech, on the *Stepmother.* There we have βούλευσις in its simplest and most readily intelligible form. A. who wishes to murder C, procures B to perform an act which will result in C's death. B may or may not know that the act will have this result. Whichever is the case, the responsibility must rest jointly with B and A. This became a recognized legal principle at an early date, although there are no grounds for supposing that at the time of the speech against the *Stepmother* it was felt necessary to draw a distinction in kind between the part played by the principal and that played by the accessory : both alike are φονεῖς, and the prosecutor argues throughout that his stepmother

has committed murder. φόνος ἀκούσιος was analysed
in the same fashion. If A incites B to perform an
act which unexpectedly results in the death of C,
A and B are equally guilty of homicide. And it is
clearly this principle which is invoked to prove that
the Choregus was concerned in the death of Diodotus.
Here too it is doubtful whether any clear distinction
as yet exists between βούλευσις and πρᾶξις ; the prosecution appears to be trying to prove that the
accused was a φονεὺς ἀκούσιος in much the same way
as the stepson appeared to be trying to prove his
stepmother guilty of φόνος ἑκούσιος in the earlier
speech. But however that may be, we may conclude
that Diodotus died as the result of the voluntary act
of someone who performed that act in pursuance of
certain general instructions given by the Choregus ;
Phanostratus, say, deliberately gave him a certain
mixture to drink because he had been given orders
to make the boys' voices as perfect as possible. So
far this is intelligible enough. But there is a difficulty in § 17 (ii *supra*) ; there it is stated that the
prosecution argue the Choregus to be guilty because
the responsibility for the boy's death must lie with
the person who ordered him to drink the poison,
forced him to drink it, or gave it to him to drink.
This suggests that they accused the defendant of
having been immediately, instead of indirectly, responsible for the accident ; and the Choregus assumes
this to be so, when he replies that he was not even
in the room when it happened. The explanation is
probably to be found in the ambiguous phraseology
of the charge and the natural desire of the prosecution to make as much play with it as possible. In
actual fact, the defendant was accused of having

given certain general instructions which, as interpreted by a second person, accidentally led to the death of a third. Is it surprising that his accusers should at some point in their speech have argued as though the responsibility was directly, instead of indirectly, his? Diodotus was dead, poisoned. He had been forced to drink the poison. Who had forced him to drink it? The accused, because it was in accordance with the instructions of the accused that measures were taken to improve his voice. It must be remembered that Philocrates was driven to prosecute, and had to make as strong a case as he could out of somewhat unpromising material; the Choregus had certainly been indirectly concerned in his brother's death, but the more confused the court became over the precise extent of his responsibility, the better.

Unfairness of infanticide

is used

§§ 10-13. Narrative of the events which led up to the death of the boy Diodotus.

§§ 14-19. Refutation of the immediate charge. The defendant proves with the help of witnesses that he was not even present when the poison was administered.

§§ 20-24. Account of the first attempt of Philocrates to replace a charge of homicide with the Basileus. Its bearing upon the impending trial of Aristion, Philinus, and Ampelinus explained. The refusal of Philocrates to accept the challenge of the speaker to cross-examine those who witnessed the death of Diodotus and to question his slaves under torture.

§§ 25-26. Digression on the surest methods of

ANALYSIS

eliciting the truth from witnesses. The defendant's πρόκλησις had made it possible for the prosecution to employ these methods.

§§ 27-32. The witnesses are one and all agreed upon the innocence of the defendant; the importance of this fact is emphasized at length.

§§ 33-40. Further and more detailed explanation of the attempt of Philocrates to debar the Choregus from proceeding against Aristion and the other two, by registering a charge of homicide.

§§ 41-46. Refutation of the suggestion that the Basileus refused to register the charge because he had been tampered with by the speaker.

§ 47-51. Reason for the second and successful attempt of Philocrates to register his charge against the Choregus. The speech then closes abruptly without the usual Epilogos.

ΠΕΡΙ ΤΟΥ ΧΟΡΕΥΤΟΥ

1 Ἥδιστον μέν, ὦ[1] ἄνδρες δικασταί, ἀνθρώπῳ ὄντι μὴ γενέσθαι μηδένα κίνδυνον περὶ τοῦ σώματος, καὶ εὐχόμενος ἄν τις ταῦτα εὔξαιτο· εἰ ⟨δ'⟩[2] ἄρα τις καὶ ἀναγκάζοιτο κινδυνεύειν, τοῦτο γοῦν ὑπάρχειν, ὅπερ[3] μέγιστον ἐγὼ νομίζω ἐν πράγματι τοιούτῳ, αὐτὸν ἑαυτῷ συνειδέναι μηδὲν ἐξημαρτηκότι, ἀλλ' εἴ τις καὶ συμφορὰ γίγνοιτο, ἄνευ κακότητος καὶ αἰσχύνης γίγνεσθαι, καὶ τύχῃ μᾶλλον ἢ ἀδικίᾳ.

2 Καὶ τοὺς μὲν νόμους οἳ κεῖνται περὶ τῶν τοιούτων πάντες ἂν ἐπαινέσειαν[4] κάλλιστα νόμων κεῖσθαι καὶ ὁσιώτατα. ὑπάρχει μὲν γὰρ αὐτοῖς ἀρχαιοτάτοις εἶναι ἐν τῇ γῇ ταύτῃ, ἔπειτα τοὺς αὐτοὺς αἰεὶ περὶ τῶν αὐτῶν, ὅπερ μέγιστον σημεῖον νόμων καλῶς κειμένων· ὁ χρόνος γὰρ καὶ ἡ[5] ἐμπειρία τὰ μὴ καλῶς ἔχοντα διδάσκει τοὺς ἀνθρώπους. ὥστ' οὐ δεῖ ὑμᾶς ἐκ τῶν λόγων τοῦ κατηγοροῦντος τοὺς νόμους μαθεῖν εἰ καλῶς ἔχουσιν ἢ μή, ἀλλ' ἐκ τῶν νόμων τοὺς τούτων λόγους, εἰ ὀρθῶς ὑμᾶς καὶ νομίμως διδάσκουσιν ἢ οὔ.

3 Ὁ μὲν οὖν ἀγὼν ἐμοὶ μέγιστος τῷ κινδυνεύοντι

---

[1] ὦ om. N. [2] δ' add. Ald. [3] ὅπερ N : ὁ A.
[4] ἐπαινέσειαν A : ἐπαινέσειεν N. [5] ἡ om. N.

246

ON THE CHOREUTES

TRUE happiness for one who is but human, gentlemen, would mean a life in which his person is threatened by no peril : and well might that be the burden of our prayers. But well too might we pray that if we must perforce face danger, we may have at least the one consolation which is to my mind the greatest of blessings at such an hour, a clear conscience ; so that if disaster should after all befall us, it will be due to no iniquity of ours and bring no shame : it will be the result of chance rather than of wrongdoing.

It would be unanimously agreed, I think, that the laws which deal with cases such as the present are the most admirable and righteous of laws. Not only have they the distinction of being the oldest in this country, but they have changed no more than the crime with which they are concerned ; and that is the surest token of good laws, as time and experience show mankind what is imperfect. Hence you must not use the speech for the prosecution to discover whether your laws are good or bad : you must use the laws to discover whether or not the speech for the prosecution is giving you a correct and lawful interpretation of the case.[a]

The person whom to-day's proceedings concern

---

[a] *Cf. Herodes*, § 14.

καὶ διωκομένῳ· ἡγοῦμαι μέντοι γε καὶ ὑμῖν τοῖς
δικασταῖς περὶ πολλοῦ εἶναι τὰς φονικὰς δίκας
ὀρθῶς διαγιγνώσκειν, μάλιστα μὲν τῶν θεῶν
ἕνεκα καὶ τοῦ εὐσεβοῦς, ἔπειτα δὲ καὶ ὑμῶν αὐτῶν.
ἔστι μὲν γὰρ περὶ τοῦ τοιούτου [αὐτοῦ][1] μία δίκη·
αὕτη δὲ μὴ ὀρθῶς καταγνωσθεῖσα ἰσχυροτέρα
4 ἐστὶ τοῦ δικαίου καὶ τοῦ ἀληθοῦς. ἀνάγκη γάρ,[2]
ἐὰν ὑμεῖς καταψηφίσησθε, καὶ μὴ ὄντα φονέα μηδ᾽
ἔνοχον τῷ ἔργῳ χρήσασθαι τῇ δίκῃ, καὶ νόμῳ
εἴργεσθαι πόλεως, ἱερῶν, ἀγώνων, θυσιῶν, ἅπερ
μέγιστα καὶ παλαιότατα τοῖς ἀνθρώποις. τοσαύτην
γὰρ ἀνάγκην ὁ νόμος ἔχει, ὥστε καὶ ἄν τις κτείνῃ
τινὰ ὧν αὐτὸς κρατεῖ καὶ μὴ ἔστιν ὁ τιμωρήσων,
τὸ νομιζόμενον καὶ τὸ θεῖον δεδιὼς ἁγνεύει τε
ἑαυτὸν καὶ ἀφέξεται ὧν εἴρηται ἐν τῷ νόμῳ,
5 ἐλπίζων οὕτως ἂν ἄριστα πρᾶξαι.[3] ἔστι μὲν γὰρ
τὰ πλείω τοῖς ἀνθρώποις τοῦ βίου ἐν ταῖς ἐλπίσιν·
ἀσεβῶν δὲ καὶ παραβαίνων τὰ εἰς τοὺς θεοὺς καὶ
αὐτῆς ἂν τῆς ἐλπίδος, ὅπερ ἐστὶ μέγιστον ἀνθρώποις[4]
ἀγαθόν, αὐτὸς αὑτὸν ἀποστεροίη. καὶ οὐδεὶς
ἂν τολμήσειεν οὔτε τὴν[5] δίκην τὴν δεδικασμένην[6]
παραβαίνειν, πιστεύσας ὅτι οὐκ ἔνοχός ἐστι τῷ
ἔργῳ, οὔτ᾽ αὖ συνειδὼς αὐτὸς αὑτῷ ἔργον εἰργασμένος τοιοῦτον μὴ οὐ χρῆσθαι τῷ νόμῳ· ἀνάγκη δὲ τῆς τε δίκης νικᾶσθαι παρὰ τὸ ἀληθές,
αὐτοῦ τε τοῦ ἀληθοῦς, κἂν μὴ ὁ τιμωρήσων ᾖ.

    [1] αὐτοῦ del. Maetzner.
    [2] γάρ A corr. N : δέ A pr.
    [3] πρᾶξαι Dobree : πράξειν codd.
    [4] ἀνθρώποις A : τοῖς ἀνθρ. N.
    [5] οὔτε τὴν A : οὔτ᾽ ἂν τὴν N.
    [6] δεδικασμένην Stephanus ex Her. § 87 : δεδοκισμασμένην A :
    δεδοκιμασμένην N.

most of all is myself, because I am the defendant and in danger. Nevertheless, it is also, I think, of great importance to you who are my judges that you should reach a correct verdict in trials for murder, first and foremost because of the gods and your duty towards them, and secondly for your own sakes. A case of this kind can be tried only once [a]; and if it is wrongly decided against the defendant, justice and the facts cannot prevail against that decision. Once you condemn him, a defendant must perforce accept your verdict, even if he was not the murderer or concerned in the crime. The law banishes him from his city, its temples, its games, and its sacrifices, the greatest and the most ancient of human institutions; and he must acquiesce. So powerful is the compulsion of the law, that even if a man slays one who is his own chattel and who has none to avenge him, his fear of the ordinances of god and of man causes him to purify himself and withhold himself from those places prescribed by law, in the hope that by so doing he will best avoid disaster. Most of the life of man rests upon hope; and by defying the gods and committing transgressions against them, he would rob himself even of hope, the greatest of human blessings. No one would venture either to disregard the sentence passed upon him because he was sure that he had had no part in the crime, or to disobey the law if he knew in his heart that he was guilty of such a deed. He has to submit to the verdict in defiance of the facts, or submit to the facts themselves, as the case may be, even if his victim has none to avenge him. The laws, the

---

[a] Cf. *Herodes*, §§ 87-89.

6 αὐτῶν δὲ τούτων ἕνεκα οἵ τε νόμοι καὶ αἱ διωμο-
σίαι¹ καὶ τὰ τόμια καὶ αἱ προρρήσεις, καὶ τἆλλ'
ὅσα γίγνεται τῶν δικῶν τοῦ φόνου ἕνεκα, πολὺ
[142] διαφέροντά ἐστιν ἢ ἐπὶ τοῖς ἄλλοις, ὅτι καὶ
αὐτὰ τὰ² πράγματα, περὶ ὧν οἱ κίνδυνοι, περὶ πλείστου ἐστὶν ὀρθῶς γιγνώσκεσθαι· ὀρθῶς μὲν γὰρ³
γνωσθέντα τιμωρία ἐστὶν ὑπὲρ τοῦ ἀδικηθέντος,
φονέα δὲ τὸν μὴ αἴτιον ψηφισθῆναι ἁμαρτία καὶ
ἀσέβεια εἴς τε τοὺς θεοὺς καὶ τοὺς νόμους. καὶ
οὐκ ἴσον ἐστὶ τόν τε διώκοντα μὴ ὀρθῶς ⟨αἰτιά-
σασθαι καὶ ὑμᾶς τοὺς δικαστὰς μὴ ὀρθῶς⟩⁴ γνῶναι.
ἡ μὲν γὰρ τούτου αἰτίασις οὐκ ἔχει [νῦν]⁵ τέλος,
ἀλλ' ἐν ὑμῖν ἐστι καὶ τῇ δίκῃ· ὅ τι δ' ἂν ὑμεῖς μὴ
ὀρθῶς γνῶτε, τοῦτο οὐκ ἔστιν ὅποι ἂν ἀνενεγκών⁶
τις τὴν αἰτίαν ἀπολύσαιτο.

7 Ἐγὼ δέ, ὦ ἄνδρες, οὐ τὴν αὐτὴν γνώμην ἔχω
περὶ τῆς ἀπολογίας ἥνπερ οἱ κατήγοροι περὶ τῆς
κατηγορίας. οὗτοι γὰρ τὴν μὲν δίωξιν εὐσεβείας
ἕνεκά φασι ποιεῖσθαι καὶ τοῦ δικαίου, τὴν δὲ κατηγορίαν ἅπασαν πεποίηνται διαβολῆς ἕνεκα καὶ
ἀπάτης, ὅπερ ἀδικώτατόν ἐστι τῶν ἐν ἀνθρώποις·
καὶ οὐκ ἐλέγξαντες, εἴ τι⁷ ἀδικῶ, δικαίως με βούλονται τιμωρεῖσθαι, ἀλλὰ διαβαλόντες,⁸ καὶ εἰ
μηδὲν ἀδικῶ, ζημιῶσαι καὶ ἐξελάσαι ἐκ τῆς γῆς
8 ταύτης. ἐγὼ δὲ ἀξιῶ πρῶτον μὲν περὶ αὐτοῦ τοῦ

¹ διωμοσίαι A : δημοσίαι N.
² αὐτὰ τὰ Ald. ex Her. § 88 : αὐτὰ ταῦτα codd.
³ γὰρ om. N.
⁴ Verba αἰτιάσασθαι . . . μὴ ὀρθῶς add. Ald. ex Her. § 89.
⁵ νῦν seclusit Reiske, coll. Her. § 89.
⁶ ἂν ἀνενεγκών Reiske: ἂν ἐνεγκών codd. Cf. Her. § 89.
250

oaths, the sacrifices, the proclamations, in fact the whole of the proceedings in connexion with trials for murder differ as profoundly as they do from the proceedings elsewhere simply because it is of supreme importance that the facts at issue, upon which so much turns, should themselves be rightly interpreted. Such a right interpretation means vengeance for him who has been wronged ; whereas to find an innocent man guilty of murder is a mistake, and a sinful mistake, which offends both gods and laws. Nor is it as serious for the prosecutor to accuse the wrong person as it is for you judges to reach a wrong verdict. The charge brought by the prosecutor is not in itself effective ; whether it becomes so, depends upon you, sitting in judgement. On the other hand, if you yourselves arrive at a wrong verdict, you cannot rid yourselves of the responsibility for so doing by blaming someone else for that verdict.

My own attitude to my defence, gentlemen, is very different from that of my accusers to their prosecution. They, on their side, allege that their object in bringing this action is to discharge a sacred duty and to satisfy justice ; whereas they have in fact treated their speech for the prosecution as nothing but an opportunity for malicious falsehood, and such behaviour is the worst travesty of justice humanly possible. Their aim is not to expose any crime I may have committed in order to exact the penalty which it deserves, but to blacken me, even though I am entirely innocent, in order to have me punished with exile from this country. I, on the other hand, con-

---

7 εἴ τι Bekker : εἰ γ᾽ codd.
8 διαβαλόντες Baiter : διαβάλλοντες codd.

251

πράγματος ἀποκρίνεσθαι,[1] καὶ διηγήσασθαι ἐν ὑμῖν
τὰ γενόμενα πάντα· ἔπειτα περὶ τῶν ἄλλων ὧν
οὗτοι κατηγοροῦσιν, ἐὰν ὑμῖν ἡδομένοις, βουλήσο-
μαι ἀπολογήσασθαι. ἡγοῦμαι γὰρ ἐμοὶ[2] τιμὴν καὶ
ὠφέλειαν αὐτὰ οἴσειν, τοῖς δὲ κατηγόροις καὶ τοῖς
ἐπηρεάζουσιν αἰσχύνην· ἐπεί τοί γε καὶ δεινόν, ὦ
9 ἄνδρες· ἵνα μὲν ἐξῆν[3] αὐτοῖς, εἴ τι ἠδίκουν ἐγὼ τὴν
πόλιν ἢ ἐν χορηγίᾳ ἢ ἐν ἄλλοις τισίν, ἀποφήνασι
καὶ ἐξελέγξασιν ἄνδρα τε ἐχθρὸν τιμωρήσασθαι[4]
καὶ τὴν πόλιν ὠφελῆσαι, ἐνταῦθα μὲν οὐδεὶς πώποτε οἷός τε ἐγένετο αὐτῶν οὔτε μικρὸν οὔτε μέγα
ἐξελέγξαι[5] ἀδικοῦντα τόνδε τὸν ἄνδρα τὸ πλῆθος τὸ
ὑμέτερον· ἐν δὲ τούτῳ τῷ ἀγῶνι, φόνου διώκοντες
καὶ τοῦ νόμου οὕτως ἔχοντος, εἰς αὐτὸ τὸ πρᾶγμα
κατηγορεῖν, μηχανῶνται ἐπ' ἐμοὶ[6] λόγους ψευδεῖς
συντιθέντες καὶ διαβάλλοντες τὰ εἰς τὴν πόλιν. καὶ
τῇ μὲν πόλει, εἴπερ[7] ἀδικεῖται, κατηγορίαν ἀντὶ
τιμωρίας ἀπονέμουσιν, αὐτοὶ δὲ οὓ[8] τὴν πόλιν φασὶν ἀδικεῖσθαι, τούτου ἰδίᾳ[9] ἀξιοῦσι δίκην λαμβά-
10 νειν. καίτοι αὗται αἱ κατηγορίαι οὔτε χάριτος ἄξιαι
οὔτε πίστεως. οὔτε γὰρ δὴ οὗ ἡ πόλις ἐλάμβανεν
ἂν δίκην εἴ τι ἠδίκητο, ἐνταῦθα τὴν κατηγορίαν ποιεῖται, ὥστε χάριτος ἄξιον εἶναι τῇ πόλει·

---

[1] ἀποκρίνεσθαι Reiske: κρίνεσθαι codd.
[2] ἐμοὶ Rosenthal: μοι N, om. A pr.
[3] ἐξῆν Ald.: ἐξῇ codd.
[4] τιμωρήσασθαι Ald.: τιμωρήσεσθαι codd.
[5] ἐξελέγξαι N: ἐλέγξαι A.
[6] ἐπ' ἐμοὶ Blass, coll. §§ 36, 48: ἐπ' ἐμὲ codd.
[7] εἴπερ Blass: εἰ μὲν codd.
[8] οὓ Thalheim: ᾧ A, ᾧ N.
[9] τούτου ἰδίᾳ Bekker: τουτουὶ δὴ A corr. N: τούτου εἰ δεῖ A pr.

[a] This promise is never directly fulfilled, but §§ 33 ff. deal
with the general conduct of the prosecution.

252

sider that my first duty is to reply to the charge
before the court by giving you a complete account of
the facts. Afterwards, if you so desire, I shall be
pleased to answer the remaining accusations made,[a]
as they will, I feel, turn to my own credit and advantage, and to the discomfiture of my opponents to whose
impudence they are due. For it is indeed a strange
fact, gentlemen : when they had the opportunity of
avenging themselves on an enemy and doing the state
a service by exposing and bringing home to me any
public offence of which I had been guilty, as Choregus
or otherwise, not one of them was able to prove that
I had done your people any wrong, great or small.[b]
Yet at to-day's trial, when they are prosecuting for
murder and are obliged by the law to confine that
prosecution to the charge before the court,[c] they are
seeking to achieve my downfall with a tissue of lies
calculated to bring my public life into disrepute. If
the state has in fact been wronged, they are com-
pensating it, not with redress, but with a mere accusation; while they are themselves demanding that
reparation for a wrong which has been suffered by the
state should be made to them in person. Indeed,
they deserve to win neither gratitude nor credence
with these charges of theirs. The circumstances in
which they are prosecuting are not such as to allow
the state to obtain satisfaction if really wronged,
and only so would they be entitled to its gratitude;

[b] This is presumably a reference to the speaker's δοκιμασία
when elected a member of the βουλή in the preceding
June. All magistrates had to submit to an inquiry into
their general fitness to assume public office before they were
installed.

[c] Cf. Herodes, § 11. There it is stated more explicitly
that the διωμοσία ensured against irrelevant charges.

οὔτε ὅστις [οὐκ]¹ ἄλλα κατηγορεῖ ἢ ἃ διώκει ἐν
πράγματι τοιούτῳ, πιστεῦσαι δήπου αὐτῷ ἀξιώ-
τερόν ἐστιν ἢ ἀπιστῆσαι. ἐγὼ δὲ σχεδὸν ἐπίσταμαι
τὴν ὑμετέραν γνώμην, ὅτι οὔτ᾽² ἂν καταψηφίσαισθε³
οὔτ᾽ ἂν ἀποψηφίσαισθε⁴ ἑτέρου τινὸς ἕνεκα μᾶλλον
ἢ αὐτοῦ τοῦ πράγματος· ταῦτα γὰρ καὶ δίκαια καὶ
ὅσια. ἄρξομαι δὲ ἐντεῦθεν.

11   Ἐπειδὴ χορηγὸς κατεστάθην εἰς Θαργήλια καὶ
ἔλαχον⁵ Παντακλέα διδάσκαλον καὶ Κεκροπίδα
φυλὴν πρὸς τῇ ἐμαυτοῦ, [τουτέστι τῇ Ἐρεχθῇδι,]⁶
ἐχορήγουν ὡς ἄριστα ἐδυνάμην καὶ δικαιότατα.
καὶ πρῶτον μὲν διδασκαλεῖον ⟨ᾗ⟩⁷ ἦν ἐπιτηδειό-
τατον τῆς ἐμῆς οἰκίας κατεσκεύασα, ἐν ᾧπερ καὶ
Διονυσίοις ὅτε ἐχορήγουν ἐδίδασκον· ἔπειτα τὸν
χορὸν συνέλεξα ὡς ἐδυνάμην ἄριστα, οὔτε ζημιώσας
οὐδένα οὔτε ἐνέχυρα βίᾳ φέρων οὔτ᾽ ἀπεχθανό-
μενος οὐδενί, ἀλλ᾽ ὥσπερ ἂν ἥδιστα καὶ ἐπιτηδειό-

¹ οὐκ seclusit Taylor: εἰς Leo ex § 9.
² οὔτ᾽ Baiter et Sauppe: οὐκ codd.
³ καταψηφίσαισθε Bekker: καταψηφίσεσθε A pr. N, -ίσησθε
A corr.
⁴ ἀποψηφίσαισθε Bekker: ἀποψηφίσησθε codd.
⁵ ἔλαχον A: ἔλεγχον N.
⁶ Verba τουτέστι τῇ Ἐρεχθῇδι ut scholium ex § 13 secl.
Reiske.
⁷ ᾗ add. Bekker.

ᵃ The χορηγία was one of the λῃτουργίαι, or public duties,
imposed upon the richer citizens by the state. A Choregus
had to equip and train a chorus for one of the annual festivals,
in this case the Thargelia, held in honour of Apollo and
celebrated on the 7th of Thargelion (May 1st) by a competition between choirs of boys selected from the ten tribes,
which were grouped in pairs for the purpose.

while the prosecutor who refuses to confine himself to the charge before the court in an action such as the present does not so much deserve to be believed as to be disbelieved. I myself know well enough what your own feelings are ; nothing save the facts immediately at issue would lead you either to condemn or to acquit, because only thus can the claims of heaven and of justice be satisfied. So with those facts I will begin.

When I was appointed Choregus for the Thargelia,[a] Pantacles[b] falling to me as poet and the Cecropid as the tribe that went with mine [that is to say the Erechtheïd],[c] I discharged my office as efficiently and as scrupulously as I was able. I began by fitting out a training-room in the most suitable part of my house, the same that I had used when Choregus at the Dionysia.[d] Next, I recruited the best chorus that I could, without inflicting a single fine, without extorting a single pledge,[e] and without making a single enemy. Just as though nothing could have been

[b] Probably this is the Pantacles who appears as a lyric poet in a choregic inscription of the period (*I.G.* i². 771). Aristophanes also refers jokingly to a Pantacles who got into difficulties with his helmet at the Panathenaic procession on one occasion (*Frogs* 1036: first staged in 405); but it is not certain that he was the poet.

[c] See critical note 6.

[d] *i.e.* the Great Dionysia (τὰ ἐν ἄστει Διονύσια), celebrated every March with a procession, choruses of boys, and tragic and comic performances. The speaker had undertaken the training of a chorus for the festival in some previous year.

[e] The Choregus was empowered to inflict fines upon parents who refused to allow their sons to perform without good reason. The " pledges " mentioned would presumably be exacted from parents who did proffer some excuse. If the excuse proved unsatisfactory, they would forfeit their money.

τατα ἀμφοτέροις ἐγίγνετο, ἐγὼ μὲν ἐκέλευον καὶ
ἠτούμην,[1] οἱ δ᾽ ἑκόντες καὶ βουλόμενοι ἔπεμπον.

12 Ἐπεὶ δὲ ἧκον οἱ παῖδες, πρῶτον μέν μοι ἀσχολία
ἦν παρεῖναι καὶ ἐπιμελεῖσθαι· ἐτύγχανε γάρ μοι
πράγματα ὄντα πρὸς Ἀριστίωνα καὶ Φιλῖνον, ἃ
ἐγὼ περὶ πολλοῦ ἐποιούμην, ἐπειδήπερ εἰσήγγειλα,
ὀρθῶς καὶ δικαίως ἀποδεῖξαι τῇ βουλῇ καὶ τοῖς
ἄλλοις Ἀθηναίοις. ἐγὼ μὲν οὖν τούτοις προσ-
εῖχον τὸν νοῦν, κατέστησα δὲ ἐπιμελεῖσθαι, εἴ τι
δέοι τῷ χορῷ, Φανόστρατον, δημότην μὲν τουτωνὶ
τῶν διωκόντων, κηδεστὴν δ᾽ ἐμαυτοῦ, ᾧ ἐγὼ
δέδωκα τὴν θυγατέρα, καὶ ἠξίουν αὐτὸν ⟨ὡς⟩[2]

13 ἄριστα ἐπιμελεῖσθαι· ἔτι δὲ πρὸς τούτῳ δύο
ἄνδρας, τὸν μὲν Ἐρεχθῆδος Ἀμεινίαν,[3] ὃν αὐτοὶ
[143] οἱ φυλέται ἐψηφίσαντο συλλέγειν καὶ ἐπιμελεῖσθαι
τῆς φυλῆς ἑκάστοτε, δοκοῦντα χρηστὸν εἶναι, τὸν
δ᾽ ἕτερον[4] . . ., τῆς Κεκροπίδος, ὅσπερ ἑκάστοτε
εἴωθεν ταύτην τὴν φυλὴν συλλέγειν· ἔτι δὲ τέταρ-
τον Φίλιππον, ᾧ προσετέτακτο ὠνεῖσθαι καὶ ἀνα-
λίσκειν εἴ τι φράζοι ὁ διδάσκαλος ἢ ἄλλος τις
τούτων, ὅπως ⟨ὡς⟩[5] ἄριστα χορηγοῖντο οἱ παῖδες
καὶ μηδενὸς ἐνδεεῖς εἶεν διὰ τὴν ἐμὴν ἀσχολίαν.

14 Καθεστήκει μὲν ἡ χορηγία οὕτω. καὶ τούτων
εἴ τι ψεύδομαι προφάσεως ἕνεκα, ἔξεστι τῷ κατ-
ηγόρῳ ἐξελέγξαι ἐν τῷ ὑστέρῳ λόγῳ ὅ τι ἂν
βούληται [εἰπεῖν].[6] ἐπεί τοι οὕτως ἔχει, ὦ ἄνδρες·

---

[1] ἠτούμην Bekker: ἡγούμην codd.
[2] ὡς add. Blass.
[3] Ἀμεινίαν, ὃν Jernstedt: ἀμηνιανὸν AN: Ἀμυννίαν, ὃν vulg.
[4] Post ἕτερον nomen excidisse censuerunt Baiter et Sauppe.
[5] ὡς add. Blass.
[6] εἰπεῖν del. Dobree: εἰπών Sauppe: καὶ ante ὅ τι add.
Thalheim.

more satisfactory or better suited to both parties, I
on my side would make my demand or request, while
the parents on theirs would send their sons along without demur, nay, readily.

For a while after the arrival of the boys I had no
time to look after them in person, as I happened to
be engaged in suits against Aristion and Philinus,[a]
and was anxious to lose no time after the impeachment in sustaining my charges in a just and
proper manner before the Council and the general
public. Being thus occupied myself, I arranged that
the needs of the chorus should be attended to by
Phanostratus, a member of the same deme as my
accusers here and a relative of my own (he is my
son-in-law) ; and I told him to perform the task
with all possible care. Besides Phanostratus I appointed two others. The first, Ameinias, whom I
thought a trustworthy man, belonged to the Erech-
theïd tribe and had been officially chosen by it to
recruit and supervise its choruses at the various festivals; while the second, . . ., regularly recruited the
choruses of the Cecropid tribe, to which he belonged,
in the same way. There was yet a fourth, Philippus,
whose duty it was to purchase or spend whatever
the poet or any of the other three told him. Thus I
ensured that the boys should receive every attention
and lack nothing owing to my own preoccupation.

Such were my arrangements as Choregus. If I am
lying as regards any of them in order to exonerate
myself, my accuser is at liberty to refute me on any
point he likes in his second speech. For this is how

• For embezzlement of public monies. See § 35.

πολλοὶ τῶν περιεστώτων τούτων τὰ μὲν πράγματα
ταῦτα πάντα ἀκριβῶς ἐπίστανται, καὶ τοῦ ὁρκωτοῦ
ἀκούουσι, καὶ ἐμοὶ προσέχουσι τὸν νοῦν ἄττα ἐγὼ
ἀποκρίνομαι, οἷς ἐγὼ βουλοίμην[1] ἂν δοκεῖν αὐτός
τε εὔορκος εἶναι καὶ ὑμᾶς τἀληθῆ λέγων πεῖσαι
ἀποψηφίσασθαί μου.

15 Πρῶτον μὲν οὖν ἀποδείξω ὑμῖν ὅτι οὔτ᾽ ἐκέλευσα
πιεῖν τὸν παῖδα τὸ φάρμακον οὔτ᾽ ἠνάγκασα οὔτ᾽
ἔδωκα καὶ οὐδὲ[2] παρῆ ὅτ᾽ ἔπιεν. καὶ οὐ τούτου
ἕνεκα ταῦτα σφόδρα λέγω, ὡς ἐμαυτὸν ἔξω αἰτίας
καταστήσω, ἕτερον δέ τινα εἰς αἰτίαν ἀγάγω· οὐ
δῆτα ἔγωγε, πλήν γε τῆς τύχης, ἥπερ οἶμαι καὶ
ἄλλοις πολλοῖς ἀνθρώπων αἰτία ἐστὶν ἀποθανεῖν· ἣν
οὔτ᾽ ἂν ἐγὼ οὔτ᾽ ἄλλος οὐδεὶς οἷός τ᾽ ἂν εἴη ἀποτρέψαι[3] μὴ οὐ γενέσθαι ἥντινα δεῖ ἑκάστῳ. . . .[4]

16 Μεμαρτύρηται μὲν οὖν, ὦ ἄνδρες, περὶ τοῦ πράγματος ἃ ἐγὼ ὑμῖν ὑπεσχόμην· ἐξ αὐτῶν δὲ τούτων
χρὴ σκοπεῖν ἅ τε οὗτοι διωμόσαντο καὶ ἃ ἐγώ,
πότεροι ἀληθέστερα καὶ εὐορκότερα. διωμόσαντο
δὲ οὗτοι μὲν ἀποκτεῖναί με Διόδοτον βουλεύσαντα
τὸν θάνατον, ἐγὼ δὲ μὴ ἀποκτεῖναι,[5] μήτε χειρὶ
ἐργασάμενος[6] μήτε βουλεύσας.

17 Αἰτιῶνται δὲ οὗτοι μὲν ἐκ τούτων, ὡς αἴτιος ὅς[7]

---

[1] βουλοίμην Dobree: ἐβουλόμην codd.
[2] οὐδὲ Reiske: οὔτε codd.
[3] ἀποτρέψαι Dobree: ἀποστρέψαι codd.
[4] Lacunam statuit Blass, coll. *Her.* § 61.
[5] μὴ ἀποκτεῖναι A: ἀποκτεῖναί με N.
[6] ἐργασάμενος Dobree ex Andoc. i. 94: ἀράμενος codd.
[7] αἴτιος ὅς Sauppe: οὗτος codd.

it is, gentlemen: many of the spectators here present are perfectly familiar with every one of these facts, the voice of the officer who administered the oath is in their ears, and they are giving my defence their close attention ; I would like them to feel that I am respecting that oath, and that if I persuade you to acquit me, it was by telling the truth that I did so.

In the first place, then, I will prove to you that I did not tell the boy to drink the poison, compel him to drink it, give it to him to drink, or even witness him drinking it. And I am not insisting on these facts in order to incriminate someone else once I have cleared myself ; no indeed—unless that someone else be Fortune ; and this is not the first time, I imagine, that she has caused a man's death. Fortune neither I nor any other could prevent from fulfilling her destined part in the life of each of us. . . .[a]

Witnesses

The facts have been confirmed by evidence as I promised, gentlemen ; and you must let that evidence help you to decide which of the two sworn statements made,[b] the prosecution's or my own, reveals more respect for truth and for the oath by which it was preceded. The prosecution swore that I was responsible for the death of Diodotus as having instigated the act which led to it [c] ; whereas I swore that I did not cause his death, whether by my own act or by instigation.

Further, in making their charge, the prosecution

[a] Some such phrase as καί μοι μάρτυρας τούτων κάλει seems to have been lost. Cf. Herodes, § 61.

[b] For the διωμοσία cf. Herodes, § 11.

[c] That βουλεύσαντα τὸν θάνατον is not to be taken in the sense of " wilfully caused his death " is clear from § 19.

ἐκέλευσε[1] πιεῖν τὸν παῖδα τὸ φάρμακον ἢ ἠνάγκασεν ἢ ἔδωκεν· ἐγὼ δὲ ἐξ αὐτῶν τούτων ὧν αἰτιῶνται οὗτοι ἀποφανῶ ὅτι οὐκ ἔνοχός εἰμι· οὔτε
γὰρ ἐκέλευσα οὔτ' ἠνάγκασα οὔτ' ἔδωκα[2]· καὶ ἔτι
προστίθημι[3] αὐτοῖς ὅτι οὐ παρεγενόμην πίνοντι.
καὶ εἴ φασιν ἀδικεῖν εἴ τις ἐκέλευσεν,[4] ἐγὼ οὐκ
ἀδικῶ· οὐ γὰρ ἐκέλευσα. καὶ εἴ φασιν ἀδικεῖν εἴ
τις ἠνάγκασεν, ἐγὼ οὐκ ἀδικῶ· οὐ γὰρ ἠνάγκασα.
καὶ εἰ τὸν δόντα τὸ φάρμακόν φασιν αἴτιον εἶναι,
ἐγὼ οὐκ αἴτιος· οὐ γὰρ ἔδωκα.

18 Αἰτιάσασθαι μὲν οὖν καὶ καταψεύσασθαι ἔξεστι
τῷ βουλομένῳ· αὐτὸς γὰρ ἕκαστος τούτου κρατεῖ·
γενέσθαι μέντοι τὰ μὴ γενόμενα καὶ ἀδικεῖν τὸν
μὴ ἀδικοῦντα οὐκ ἐν τοῖς τούτων λόγοις ἡγοῦμαι
εἶναι, ἀλλ' ἐν τῷ δικαίῳ καὶ τῷ ἀληθεῖ. ὁπόσα
μὲν γὰρ λάθρᾳ πράττεται καὶ ἐπὶ θανάτῳ βουλευ-
θέντα, ὧν μή εἰσι μάρτυρες, ἀνάγκη περὶ τῶν
τοιούτων ἐξ αὐτῶν τῶν λόγων τῶν τε τοῦ κατηγόρου καὶ τοῦ ἀποκρινομένου τὴν διάγνωσιν ποιεῖσθαι καὶ θηρεύειν καὶ ἐπὶ σμικρὸν ὑπονοεῖν τὰ
λεγόμενα, καὶ εἰκάζοντας μᾶλλον ἢ σάφα εἰδότας
19 ψηφίζεσθαι περὶ τῶν πραγμάτων· ὅπου δὲ πρῶτον
μὲν αὐτοὶ οἱ κατήγοροι ὁμολογοῦσι μὴ ἐκ προνοίας
μηδ' ἐκ παρασκευῆς γενέσθαι τὸν θάνατον τῷ
παιδί, ἔπειτα τὰ πραχθέντα φανερῶς ἅπαντα πραχ-

---

[1] ἐκέλευσε Baiter: κελεύσειε codd.
[2] οὔτ' ἦν. οὔτ' ἔδ. Dobree: οὔτ' ἔδ. οὔτ' ἦν. codd.
[3] ἔτι προστίθημι Ald.: ἐπιπροστίθημι codd.
[4] Verba ἐκέλευσεν . . . ἀδικεῖν εἴ τις om. N.

invoke the principle that the responsibility rests with
whoever told the boy to drink the poison, forced him
to drink it, or gave it to him to drink. By that very
principle, however, I will myself prove that I am
innocent : for I neither told the boy to drink the
poison, nor forced him to drink it, nor gave it to him
to drink. I will even go a step further than they
and add that I did not witness him drink it. If the
prosecution say that it was a criminal act to tell him
to drink it, I am no criminal : I did not tell him to
drink it. If they say that it was a criminal act to
force him to drink it, I am no criminal : I did not
force him to drink it. And if they say that the
responsibility rests with the person who gave him the
poison, I am not responsible : I did not give it to him.

Now accusations and lies can be indulged in at
will, as they are at the command of each one of
us. But that what never happened should be transformed into fact, that an innocent man should be
transformed into a criminal is not, I feel, a matter
which depends upon the eloquence of the prosecution ;
it is a question of what is right and what is true.
Admittedly, with a deliberately planned murder,
carried out in secret and with none to witness it, the
truth can only be determined from the accounts given
by the prosecutor and the defendant, and from them
alone ; their statements must be followed up with care
and suspected on the slightest grounds and the final
verdict must necessarily be the result of conjecture
rather than certain knowledge. But in the present
instance, the prosecution themselves admit to begin
with that the boy's death was not due to premedi-
tation or design : and secondly, everything which
happened happened publicly and before numerous

θῆναι καὶ ἐναντίον μαρτύρων πολλῶν, καὶ ἀνδρῶν
καὶ παίδων, καὶ ἐλευθέρων καὶ δούλων, ἐξ ὧνπερ
καὶ εἴ τίς τι ἠδίκηκε, φανερώτατος ἂν[1] εἴη, καὶ
εἴ τις μὴ ἀδικοῦντα αἰτιῷτο, μάλιστ' ἂν[2] ἐξελέγχοιτο.

20 Ἄξιον δ' ἐνθυμηθῆναι, ὦ ἄνδρες, ἀμφότερα καὶ
τῆς γνώμης τῶν ἀντιδίκων καὶ οἴῳ τρόπῳ ἔρχονται
ἐπὶ τὰ πράγματα. ἐξ ἀρχῆς γὰρ οὐδὲν ὁμοίως
οὗτοί τε πρὸς ἐμὲ πράττουσι καὶ ἐγὼ πρὸς τού-
21 τους. ἔλεξε μὲν γὰρ Φιλοκράτης οὑτοσὶ ἀναβὰς
εἰς τὴν ἡλιαίαν[3] τὴν τῶν θεσμοθετῶν, τῇ ἡμέρᾳ ᾗ
ὁ παῖς ἐξεφέρετο, ὅτι ἀδελφὸν αὐτοῦ ἀποκτείναιμι
ἐγὼ ἐν τῷ χορῷ, φάρμακον ἀναγκάσας πιεῖν.
ἐπειδὴ δὲ οὗτος ταῦτ' ἔλεγεν, ἀναβὰς ἐγὼ εἰς τὸ
δικαστήριον τοῖς αὐτοῖς δικασταῖς ἔλεξα ὅτι τὸν
μὲν νόμον οὐ δικαίως μου προκαθισταίη[4] Φιλοκράτης κατηγορῶν καὶ διαβάλλων εἰς τὸ δικαστήριον, μελλόντων ἔσεσθαί μοι ἀγώνων πρὸς
Ἀριστίωνα καὶ Φιλῖνον αὔριον καὶ[5] ἔνη,[6] ὧνπερ
[144]
22 ἕνεκα τοὺς λόγους τούτους λέγοι[7]· ἃ μέντοι αἰτιῷτο
καὶ διαβάλλοι, ῥᾳδίως ἐξελεγχθήσοιτο ψευδόμενος.
εἶεν[8] γὰρ οἱ συνειδότες πολλοί, καὶ ἐλεύθεροι καὶ
δοῦλοι, καὶ νεώτεροι καὶ πρεσβύτεροι, σύμπαντες
πλείους ἢ πεντήκοντα, οἳ τούς τε λόγους τοὺς
λεχθέντας περὶ τῆς πόσεως τοῦ φαρμάκου καὶ τὰ
πραχθέντα καὶ τὰ γενόμενα[9] πάντα ἐπίσταιντο.[10]
23 Καὶ εἶπόν τε ταῦτα ἐν τῷ δικαστηρίῳ, καὶ προὔ-

---

[1] ἂν A : τ' ἂν N.   [2] μάλιστ' ἂν Sauppe : μάλιστα codd.
[3] ἡλιαίαν Taylor : ἡλιακὴν codd.
[4] οὐ δικαίως μου προκαθισταίη Thalheim : οὐ δίκαιον οὐ
προκαθῆσθαι εἰ A : οὐ δίκαιον οὐ προκάθισται ἢ N.
[5] καὶ Maetzner : τῇ codd.
[6] ἔνη Taylor : ἔννη A, ἔνῃ N.

witnesses, men and boys, free men and slaves, who would have ensured the complete exposure of the criminal, had there been one, and the instant refutation of anyone who accused an innocent person.[a]

Both the spirit shown by my opponents and the way in which they set to work are worth noticing, gentlemen ; for their behaviour towards me has been very different from mine towards them from the outset. Philocrates yonder presented himself before the Heliaea of the Thesmothetae[b] on the very day of the boy's burial, and declared that I had murdered his brother, a member of the chorus, by forcing him to drink poison. At that, I presented myself before the court in my turn. I told the same jury that Philocrates had no right to place legal impediments in my way by coming to court with his outrageous charge, when I was bringing suits against Aristion and Philinus on the following day and the day after : for that was his only reason for making such allegations. However, I said, there would be no difficulty in proving his monstrous accusation a lie, as there were plenty of witnesses, slave and free, young and old, in fact, over fifty in all, who knew how the drinking of the poison had been accounted for and were in complete possession of the facts and circumstances.

Not only did I make this declaration before the

---

[a] § 19 in the Greek consists of an intricate dependent clause without a main verb to complete the grammatical construction. By the time ἐξελέγχοιτο has been reached, the initial ὅπου has been forgotten.

[b] i.e. before an ordinary Heliastic court (δικαστήριον).

---

7 λέγοι N : λέγει A.   8 εἰ ἒν N : εἰσὶ A.

9 γενόμενα Reiske : λεγόμενα codd.

10 ἐπίσταιντο Maetzner : ἠπίσταντο codd.

καλούμην αὐτὸν εὐθὺς τότε, καὶ αὖθις τῇ ὑστεραίᾳ
ἐν τοῖς αὐτοῖς δικασταῖς, καὶ ἰέναι ἐκέλευον λα-
βόντα μάρτυρας ὁπόσους βούλοιτο ἐπὶ τοὺς παραγενομένους, λέγων αὐτῷ ὀνόματι ἕκαστον, τούτους
ἐρωτᾶν καὶ ἐλέγχειν, τοὺς μὲν ἐλευθέρους ὡς χρὴ
τοὺς ἐλευθέρους, οἳ σφῶν ⟨τ' αὐτῶν⟩[1] ἕνεκα καὶ
τοῦ δικαίου ἔφραζον ἂν τἀληθῆ καὶ τὰ γενόμενα,
τοὺς δὲ δούλους, εἰ μὲν αὐτῷ ἐρωτῶντι[2] τἀληθῆ
δοκοῖεν λέγειν, εἰ δὲ μή, ἕτοιμος εἴην[3] διδόναι
βασανίζειν τούς τε ἐμαυτοῦ πάντας, καὶ εἴ τινας
τῶν ἀλλοτρίων κελεύοι,[4] ὡμολόγουν πείσας τὸν
δεσπότην παραδώσειν αὐτῷ βασανίζειν τρόπῳ ὁ-
24 ποίῳ βούλοιτο. καὶ ταῦτα ἐμοῦ προκαλουμένου καὶ
λέγοντος ἐν τῷ δικαστηρίῳ, οὗ καὶ αὐτοὶ οἱ δικασταὶ καὶ ἕτεροι ἰδιῶται πολλοὶ μάρτυρες παρῆσαν,
οὔτε τότε παραχρῆμα οὔτε ὕστερον ἐν παντὶ τῷ
χρόνῳ οὐδεπώποτε ἠθέλησαν ἐλθεῖν ἐπὶ τοῦτο
τὸ δίκαιον, εὖ εἰδότες ὅτι οὐκ ἂν τούτοις κατ'
ἐμοῦ ἔλεγχος ἐγίγνετο οὗτος, ἀλλ' ἐμοὶ κατὰ
τούτων, ὅτι οὐδὲν δίκαιον οὐδ' ἀληθὲς ᾐτιῶντο.
25 Ἐπίστασθε δέ, ὦ ἄνδρες, ὅτι αἱ ἀνάγκαι αὗται
ἰσχυρόταται καὶ μέγισταί εἰσι τῶν ἐν ἀνθρώποις,
καὶ ἔλεγχοι ἐκ τούτων σαφέστατοι καὶ πιστότατοι
περὶ τοῦ δικαίου, ὅπου εἶεν μὲν ἐλεύθεροι πολλοὶ οἱ
συνειδότες, εἶεν δὲ δοῦλοι, καὶ ἐξείη μὲν τοὺς
ἐλευθέρους ὅρκοις καὶ πίστεσιν ἀναγκάζειν, ἃ τοῖς
ἐλευθέροις μέγιστα καὶ περὶ πλείστου ἐστίν, ἐξείη

---

[1] τ' αὐτῶν add. Sauppe.
[2] διδόναι post ἐρωτῶντι hab. codd. : om. Ald.
[3] εἴην Taylor : εἶεν A, εἰμι N.
[4] κελεύοι Bekker : κελεύει codd.

264

court, but I offered Philocrates a challenge there and
then, and repeated it the following day in the presence
of the same jury. Let him take with him as many
witnesses as he liked : let him go to the persons who
had been present at the accident (I specified them by
name) : and let him interrogate and cross-examine
them. Let him question the free men as befitted free
men ; for their own sakes and in the interests of
justice, they would give a faithful account of what had
occurred. As to the slaves, if he considered that they
were answering his questions truthfully, well and
good; if he did not, I was ready to place all my
own at his disposal for examination under torture,
and should he demand any that did not belong to
me, I agreed to obtain the consent of their owner
and hand them over to him to examine as he liked.
That was the challenge which I addressed to him
before the court ; and not only the jurors themselves
but numbers of private persons also were there to
witness it. Yet the prosecution refused to bring
the case to this issue at the time, and have persist-
ently refused ever since. They knew very well that
instead of supplying them with proof of my guilt,
such an inquiry would supply me with proof that
their own charge was totally unjust and unfounded.

You do not need to be reminded, gentlemen, that
the one occasion when compulsion is as absolute and
as effective as is humanly possible, and when the rights
of a case are ascertained thereby most surely and
most certainly, arises when there is an abundance of witnesses, both slave and free, and it is possible to put pressure upon the free men by exacting
an oath or word of honour, the most solemn and
the most awful form of compulsion known to free

δὲ τοὺς δούλους ἑτέραις ἀνάγκαις, ὑφ' ὧν καὶ ἦν
μέλλωσιν ἀποθανεῖσθαι κατειπόντες, ὅμως ἀναγκά-
ζονται τἀληθῆ λέγειν· ἡ γὰρ παροῦσα ἀνάγκη
ἑκάστῳ ἰσχυροτέρα ἐστὶ τῆς μελλούσης ἔσεσθαι.

26 Εἰς πάντα[1] τοίνυν ἐγὼ ταῦτα προὐκαλεσάμην
τούτους, καὶ ἐξ ὧν γε[2] χρὴ ἄνθρωπον ὄντα τἀληθῆ
καὶ τὰ δίκαια πυνθάνεσθαι, ἐξῆν αὐτοῖς πυνθάνεσθαι, καὶ πρόφασις οὐδεμία ὑπελείπετο. καὶ ἐγὼ
μὲν ὁ τὴν αἰτίαν ἔχων καὶ ἀδικῶν, ὡς οὗτοί φασιν,
ἕτοιμος ἦ αὐτοῖς κατ' ἐμαυτοῦ παρέχειν ἔλεγχον
τὸν δικαιότατον· οἱ δ' αἰτιώμενοι καὶ φάσκοντες
ἀδικεῖσθαι αὐτοὶ ἦσαν οἱ οὐκ ἐθέλοντες ἐλέγχειν εἴ

27 τι ἠδικοῦντο. καὶ εἰ μὲν ἐγὼ τούτων προκαλουμένων μὴ ἠθέλησα τοὺς παραγενομένους ἀποφῆναι,
⟨ἢ⟩[3] θεράποντας ἐξαιτοῦσι μὴ ἤθελον ἐκδιδόναι, ἢ
ἄλλην τινὰ πρόκλησιν ἔφευγον, αὐτὰ ἂν ταῦτα
μέγιστα τεκμήρια κατ' ἐμοῦ ἐποιοῦντο ὅτι ἀληθὴς
ἦν ἡ[4] αἰτία· ἐπεὶ δ' ἐμοῦ προκαλουμένου οὗτοι ἦσαν
οἱ φεύγοντες τὸν ἔλεγχον, ἐμοὶ δήπου δίκαιον κατὰ
τούτων τὸ αὐτὸ τοῦτο τεκμήριον γενέσθαι ὅτι οὐκ
ἀληθὴς [ἦν][5] ἡ αἰτία ἦν[6] αἰτιῶνται κατ' ἐμοῦ.

28 Ἐπίσταμαι δὲ καὶ τάδε, ὦ ἄνδρες, ὅτι εἰ μὲν
τούτοις ἐμοῦ κατεμαρτύρουν οἱ μάρτυρες οἱ παραγενόμενοι, αὐτοῖς ἂν τούτοις ἰσχυροτάτοις ἐχρῶντο

---

[1] πάντα Blass : πᾶν codd.　　　[2] γε Ald. : σε codd.
[3] ἢ add. Bekker.　　　[4] ἡ om. A.
[5] ἦν del. Jernstedt.　　　[6] ἦν A : ἣν N.

---

[a] A difficult sentence. Literally : "The compulsion which
is present has more influence over each than that which is
to come." The meaning seems to be: the torture which they
are suffering at the moment (ἡ παροῦσα ἀνάγκη) forces them
to speak in spite of the fact that they will inevitably be
put to death in consequence of their disclosures (ἡ μέλλουσα
ἀνάγκη). ἀνάγκη is used in two slightly different senses

men, and upon the slaves by other devices, which will force them to tell the truth even if their revelations are bound to cost them their lives, as the compulsion of the moment has a stronger influence over each than the fate which he will suffer by compulsion afterwards.[a]

It was to this, then, and nothing less that I challenged the prosecution. Every means which mortal man finds it necessary to use in order to discover the true rights of a matter, they had the opportunity of using; not the vestige of an excuse was left them. I, the defendant, the alleged criminal, was ready to give them the chance of proving my guilt in the fairest possible way; it was they, the prosecutors, the professedly injured party, who refused to obtain proof of such injury as they had sustained. Suppose that the offer had come from them. Then had I refused to disclose who the eyewitnesses were: had I refused to hand over my servants at their request: or had I been afraid to accept some other challenge, they would be claiming that those facts in themselves afforded to my detriment the strongest presumption of the truth of their charge. Instead, it was I who issued the challenge, and the prosecution who evaded the test. So it is surely only fair that this same fact should afford me a presumption to their detriment that the charge which they have made against me is untrue.

Further, I am certain, gentlemen, that if the witnesses present at the accident were testifying in the prosecution's favour and against me, the prosecution would be treating them as supremely important:

—(1) of torture: that which leaves a man no choice but to speak.   (2) Of a death which is certain.

καὶ πίστιν ταύτην σαφεστάτην ἀπέφαινον, τοὺς
μάρτυρας τοὺς καταμαρτυροῦντας· τῶν αὐτῶν δὲ
τούτων μαρτυρούντων,[1] ἃ μὲν ἐγὼ λέγω, ἀληθῆ
εἶναι, ἃ δὲ οὗτοι λέγουσιν, οὐκ ἀληθῆ, τοῖς μὲν
μάρτυσι τοῖς ⟨ἐμοὶ⟩[2] μαρτυροῦσιν ἀπιστεῖν ὑμᾶς
διδάσκουσι, τοῖς δὲ λόγοις οἷς αὐτοὶ λέγουσι πιστεύειν ὑμᾶς φασι χρῆναι, οὓς ἐγὼ εἰ ἔλεγον ἄνευ
29 μαρτύρων, ψευδεῖς ἂν κατηγόρουν εἶναι. καίτοι
δεινὸν εἰ οἱ αὐτοὶ μάρτυρες τούτοις μὲν ἂν μαρτυροῦντες πιστοὶ ἦσαν, ἐμοὶ δὲ μαρτυροῦντες ἄ-
πιστοι ἔσονται. καὶ εἰ μὲν πάνυ μὴ παρεγένοντο
μάρτυρες, ἐγὼ δὲ παρειχόμην,[3] ἢ τοὺς παραγενομένους μὴ παρειχόμην, ἑτέρους δέ τινας, εἰκότως
ἂν οἱ τούτων λόγοι πιστότεροι ἦσαν τῶν ἐμῶν
μαρτύρων· ὅπου δὲ μάρτυράς τε ὁμολογοῦσι παραγενέσθαι, καὶ ἐγὼ τοὺς παραγενομένους παρέχομαι,
⟨καὶ⟩[4] εὐθὺς ἀπὸ τῆς πρώτης ἡμέρας καὶ αὐτὸς ἐγὼ
καὶ οἱ μάρτυρες ἅπαντες φανεροί ἐσμεν λέγοντες
ἅπερ νυνὶ πρὸς ὑμᾶς, πόθεν χρή, ὦ ἄνδρες, ἢ
[145] τἀληθῆ πιστὰ ἢ τὰ μὴ ἀληθῆ ἄπιστα ποιεῖν ἄλ-
30 λοθεν ἢ ἐκ τῶν τοιούτων; ὅπου μὲν γὰρ λόγῳ
τις διδάσκοι περὶ τῶν πραχθέντων, μάρτυρας δὲ μὴ
παρέχοιτο, μαρτύρων ἄν τις τοὺς λόγους τούτους
ἐνδεεῖς φαίη εἶναι· ὅπου δὲ μάρτυρας μὲν παρέχοιτο,[5] τεκμήρια δὲ αὖ τοῖς[6] μαρτυροῦσιν ὅμοια
μὴ ἀποφαίνοι,[7] ταῦτα[8] ἄν τις ἔχοι εἰπεῖν, εἰ βούλοιτο.
31 ἐγὼ τοίνυν τούς τε λόγους ὑμῖν εἰκότας ἀποφαίνω,
καὶ τοῖς λόγοις τοὺς μάρτυρας ὁμολογοῦντας καὶ

---

[1] μαρτυρούντων A pr.: καταμαρτυρούντων A corr. N.
[2] ἐμοὶ add. Reiske.
[3] παρειχόμην Stephanus: παρεσχόμην codd.
[4] καὶ add. Reiske.
[5] παρέχοιτο N corr.: παρέχοιτο A N pr.

they would be showing that such unfavourable evidence was proof conclusive. As, however, these same witnesses are testifying that what I say is true and that what the prosecution say is not, they urge that the evidence of those witnesses in my favour is untrustworthy ; according to them, it is their own statements which you should believe, statements which they would be attacking as false, were I making them myself without witnesses to support me. Yet it is strange that the witnesses who would be trustworthy, were their evidence favourable to the prosecution, are to be untrustworthy when it is favourable to me. Were I producing eyewitnesses when there had been none, or were I not producing the true eyewitnesses, there would be some ground for treating the statements of the prosecution as more trustworthy than my witnesses. But the prosecution admit that witnesses were actually present : I am producing those witnesses : and both I and all my witnesses are well known to have maintained from the very first day what we are repeating to you now. So what other means than these are to be employed to confirm what is true and to disprove what is not ? If a bare statement of the facts were made, but not supported by the evidence of witnesses, it might well be criticized for the absence of that support ; and if witnesses were forthcoming, only to conflict with the presumptions furnished by the pleader, his opponent might well pass a corresponding criticism, should he so wish. Now in my own case, you are being presented with an account which is reasonable, with evidence

---

⁶ αὖ τοῖς Reiske: αὐτοῖς codd.
⁷ ἀποφαίνοι Reiske: ἀποφαίνοιτο N, ἀποφαίνοιντο A.
⁸ ταὐτὰ Reiske: ταῦτα codd.

τοῖς μάρτυσι τὰ ἔργα, καὶ τεκμήρια ἐξ αὐτῶν τῶν
ἔργων, καὶ ἔτι πρὸς τούτοις δύο τὼ μεγίστω καὶ
ἰσχυροτάτω, τούτους μὲν αὐτούς τε ὑπὸ σφῶν
αὐτῶν ἐξελεγχομένους καὶ ὑπ' ἐμοῦ, ἐμὲ δὲ ὑπό τε
32 τούτων καὶ ὑπὸ ἐμαυτοῦ ἀπολυόμενον· ὅπου γὰρ
ἐθέλοντος ἐλέγχεσθαι ἐμοῦ περὶ ὧν ᾐτιῶντο οὗτοι[1]
μὴ ἤθελον ἐλέγχειν ⟨εἴ τι⟩[2] ἠδικοῦντο, ἐμὲ μὲν
δήπου ἀπέλυον, αὐτοὶ δὲ κατὰ σφῶν αὐτῶν μάρτυρες ἐγένοντο, ὅτι οὐδὲν δίκαιον οὐδ' ἀληθὲς
ᾐτιῶντο. καίτοι εἰ πρὸς τοῖς ἐμαυτοῦ μάρτυσι
τοὺς ἀντιδίκους αὐτοὺς μάρτυρας παρέχομαι, ποῖ
ἔτι ἐλθόντα δεῖ ἢ πόθεν ἀποδείξαντα τῆς αἰτίας
ἀπολελύσθαι;

33 Ἡγοῦμαι μὲν οὖν καὶ ἐκ τῶν εἰρημένων καὶ
ἀποδεδειγμένων, ὦ ἄνδρες, δικαίως ἄν μου ἀποψηφίσασθαι ὑμᾶς, καὶ ἐπίστασθαι ἅπαντας ὅτι
οὐδέν μοι προσήκει τῆς αἰτίας ταύτης. ἵνα δ' ἔτι
καὶ ἄμεινον μάθητε, τούτου ἕνεκα πλείω λέξω, καὶ
ἀποδείξω ὑμῖν τοὺς κατηγόρους τούτους ἐπιορκοτάτους ὄντας καὶ ἀσεβεστάτους ἀνθρώπων, καὶ
ἀξίους οὐ μόνον ὑπ' ἐμοῦ μισεῖσθαι, ἀλλὰ καὶ ὑφ'
ὑμῶν πάντων καὶ τῶν ἄλλων πολιτῶν τῆς δίκης
ἕνεκα ταυτησί.

34 Οὗτοι γὰρ τῇ μὲν πρώτῃ ἡμέρᾳ ᾗ ἀπέθανεν ὁ
παῖς, καὶ τῇ ὑστεραίᾳ[3] ᾗ προέκειτο, οὐδ' αὐτοὶ
ἠξίουν αἰτιᾶσθαι ἐμὲ [οὐδ'][4] ἀδικεῖν ἐν τῷ πράγματι
τούτῳ οὐδέν, ἀλλὰ συνῆσαν ἐμοὶ καὶ διελέγοντο·

---

[1] Verba οὗτοι . . . ᾐτιῶντο om. N.
[2] εἴ τι ἠδικοῦντο Blass, coll. § 26 : ἠδίκουν καὶ codd.
[3] ὑστεραίᾳ A : ὑστέρα N.
[4] οὐδ' del. Wilamowitz.

which is consistent with that account, with facts which are consistent with that evidence, with presumptions drawn immediately from those facts, and with two arguments of the greatest significance and weight in addition : the first, the circumstance that the prosecution have been proved impostors both by themselves and by me : and the second, the circumstance that I have been proved innocent both by the prosecution and by myself ; for in refusing to obtain proof of such injury as they had sustained when I was ready for an inquiry into the crime with which they were charging me, they were clearly acknowledging my innocence and testifying to the injustice and falsity of their own accusation. If I supplement the evidence of my own witnesses with that of my opponents in person, what other expedients, what other proofs are necessary to establish my entire freedom from the charge ?

I feel that both the arguments and proofs which I have put before you, gentlemen, would justify you in acquitting me ; you all know that the charge before the court does not concern me. However, to confirm you in that knowledge, I will go further. I will prove that my accusers here are the most reckless perjurors and the most godless scoundrels alive : that they have earned not only my own hatred, but the hatred of every one of you and of your fellow-citizens besides, by instituting this trial.

On the first day, the day of the boy's death, and on the second, when the body was laid out, not even the prosecution themselves thought of accusing me of having played any kind of criminal part in the accident : on the contrary, they avoided neither meeting

271

τῇ δὲ τρίτῃ ἡμέρᾳ ᾗ ἐξεφέρετο ὁ παῖς, ταύτῃ δὴ
πεπεισμένοι ἦσάν [τινες]¹ ὑπὸ τῶν ἐχθρῶν τῶν
ἐμῶν, καὶ παρεσκευάζοντο αἰτιᾶσθαι καὶ προαγορεύειν εἴργεσθαι τῶν νομίμων. τίνες οὖν ἦσαν οἱ
πείσαντες αὐτούς; καὶ τίνος ἕνεκα καὶ πρόθυμοι
ἐγένοντο πεῖσαι αὐτούς; δεῖ γάρ με καὶ ταῦτα
ὑμᾶς διδάξαι.

35 Κατηγορήσειν ἔμελλον Ἀριστίωνος καὶ Φιλίνου
καὶ Ἀμπελίνου καὶ τοῦ ὑπογραμματέως τῶν
θεσμοθετῶν, μεθ' οὗπερ συνέκλεπτον, περὶ ὧν
εἰσήγγειλα εἰς τὴν βουλήν. καὶ αὐτοῖς ἐκ μὲν τῶν
πεπραγμένων οὐδεμία ἦν ἐλπὶς ἀποφεύξεσθαι—τοιαῦτα ἄρ' ἦν τὰ ἠδικημένα—· πείσαντες δὲ τούτους
ἀπογράφεσθαι καὶ προαγορεύειν ἐμοὶ εἴργεσθαι
τῶν νομίμων, ἡγήσαντο ταύτην σφίσιν ἔσεσθαι σωτηρίαν καὶ ἀπαλλαγὴν τῶν πραγμάτων ἁπάντων.

36 ὁ γὰρ νόμος οὕτως ἔχει, ἐπειδάν τις ἀπογραφῇ
φόνου δίκην, εἴργεσθαι τῶν νομίμων· καὶ οὔτ' ἂν
ἐγὼ οἷός τ' ἦ ἐπεξελθεῖν εἰργόμενος τῶν νομίμων,
ἐκεῖνοί τε ἐμοῦ τοῦ εἰσαγγείλαντος καὶ ἐπισταμένου
τὰ πράγματα μὴ ἐπεξιόντος ῥᾳδίως ἔμελλον ἀποφεύξεσθαι καὶ δίκην οὐ δώσειν ὑμῖν² ὧν ἠδίκησαν.
καὶ τοῦτ' οὐκ ἐπ' ἐμοὶ πρῶτον ἐμηχανήσαντο
Φιλῖνος καὶ οἱ ἕτεροι, ἀλλὰ καὶ ἐπὶ Λυσιστράτῳ
πρότερον, ὡς αὐτοὶ ὑμεῖς ἠκούσατε.

¹ τινες del. Dobree.   ² ὑμῖν A corr. N.: ἐμοὶ A pr.

ᵃ The force of συνῆσαν καὶ διελέγοντο can best be conveyed
by a negative. The implication is, of course, that had the
prosecution believed the speaker guilty, they would have
avoided all contact with him for fear of being tainted with
the μίασμα which rested on him. *Cf. Tetr. I. a.* 10.

ᵇ τὸ εἴργεσθαι τῶν νομίμων was the immediate consequence
of a πρόρρησις. A suspected murderer had to withdraw from

272

me nor speaking to me.[a] It was only on the third day, the day of the boy's burial, that they yielded to my enemies and set about bringing a charge and proclaiming me to be under the usual disabilities.[b] Now who was it who instigated them? And what reason had those others for wanting to do such a thing? I must enlighten you on these further points.

I was about to prosecute Aristion, Philinus, Ampelinus, and the secretary to the Thesmothetae, with whose embezzlements they had been associated, on charges which I had presented to the Council in the form of an impeachment. As far as the facts of the case were concerned, they had no hope of an acquittal: their offences were too serious. On the other hand, could they but induce my accusers here to register a charge and proclaim that I was under the statutory ban, they would, they thought, be safely rid of the whole business. The law runs that the ban comes into force as soon as anyone has a charge of murder registered against him; and if placed under it, not only should I myself have been unable to proceed with my case, but once the party responsible for the impeachment and in possession of the facts failed to proceed, the four would gain an acquittal without difficulty, and the wrong which they had done you would go unpunished. I was not, I may say, the first against whom Philinus and his companions had employed this device; they had already done the same to Lysistratus, as you have heard for yourselves.[c]

intercourse with his fellows until his innocence had been established or his guilt expiated. *Cf. Herodes*, Introd.

[c] Nothing further is known of Lysistratus.

37 Καὶ οὗτοι τότε μὲν πρόθυμοι ἦσαν ἀπογράφεσθαί
με εὐθὺς τῇ ὑστεραίᾳ ᾗ ὁ παῖς ἐθάπτετο, πρὶν τὴν
οἰκίαν καθῆραι[1] καὶ τὰ νομιζόμενα ποιῆσαι, αὐτὴν
ταύτην φυλάξαντες τὴν ἡμέραν ἐν ᾗ ἔμελλεν ὁ
πρῶτος ἐκείνων κριθήσεσθαι, ὅπως μηδὲ καθ' ἑνὸς
αὐτῶν οἷός τε γενοίμην ἐπεξελθεῖν μηδ' ἐνδεῖξαι
38 τῷ δικαστηρίῳ τἀδικήματα· ἐπειδὴ δὲ αὐτοῖς ὁ
βασιλεὺς τούς τε νόμους ἀνέγνω, καὶ χρόνους
ἐπέδειξεν ὅτι[2] οὐκ ἐγχωροίη ἀπογράψασθαι καὶ τὰς
κλήσεις καλεῖσθαι ὅσας ἔδει, καὶ ἐγὼ τοὺς ταῦτα
μηχανωμένους εἰσάγων εἰς τὸ δικαστήριον εἷλον
ἅπαντας, καὶ ἐτιμήθη αὐτοῖς ὧν ὑμεῖς ἐπίστασθε,
καὶ οὗτοι ὧν ἕνεκα ἐλάμβανον χρήματα οὐδὲν
αὐτοῖς οἷοί τε ἦσαν ὠφελῆσαι, τότε δὴ προσιόντες
[146] αὐτῷ τ' ἐμοὶ καὶ τοῖς φίλοις ἐδέοντο διαλλαγῆναι,
καὶ δίκην ἕτοιμοι ἦσαν διδόναι τῶν ἡμαρτημένων.
39 καὶ ἐγὼ πεισθεὶς ὑπὸ τῶν φίλων διηλλάγην τούτοις
ἐν τῇ πόλει[3] ἐναντίον μαρτύρων, οἵπερ διήλλαττον
ἡμᾶς πρὸς τῷ νεῷ τῆς Ἀθηνᾶς· καὶ μετὰ τοῦτο
συνῆσάν μοι καὶ διελέγοντο ἐν τοῖς ἱεροῖς, ἐν τῇ
ἀγορᾷ, ἐν τῇ ἐμῇ οἰκίᾳ, ἐν τῇ σφετέρᾳ αὐτῶν[4]
40 καὶ ἑτέρωθι πανταχοῦ. τὸ τελευταῖον, ὦ Ζεῦ
καὶ θεοὶ πάντες, Φιλοκράτης αὐτὸς οὑτοσὶ ἐν τῷ
βουλευτηρίῳ ἐναντίον τῆς βουλῆς, ἑστὼς μετ' ἐμοῦ

---

[1] καθῆραι Sauppe: καθάραι A, καθᾶραι N.
[2] ὅτι Dobree: τί codd.
[3] ἐν τῇ πόλει] ἐν Διπολείοις Scheibe, coll. Harpocratione,
s.v. Διπόλεια.
[4] ἐν τῇ σφ. αὐτῶν A : καὶ ἐν σφ. ἑαυτῶν N.

---

[a] προσκλήσεις are writs summoning the witnesses for the
prosecution and defence.

The prosecution started by doing their utmost to register a charge at once, on the day after the burial, before the house had been purified or the proper rites performed ; they had taken care to choose the very day on which the first of the other four was to be tried, to make it impossible for me to proceed against a single one of them or present the court with any statement of their offences. However, the Basileus read them the law, and showed that there was not sufficient time to register a charge or issue the necessary writs[a] ; so I took the originators of the plot into court, and secured a conviction in every case—and you know the amount at which the damages were fixed. No sooner, however, did my accusers here find it impossible to give the help which they had been paid to give than they approached me and my friends with a request for a reconciliation, and offered to make amends for their past errors. I took my friends' advice, and was formally reconciled to them on the Acropolis[b] in the presence of witnesses, who performed the ceremony near the temple of Athena. Afterwards, they met me and spoke to me in temples, in the Agora, in my house, in their own—everywhere in fact. The crowning point was reached in the Council-chamber in front of the Council—heavens, to think of it !—when Philocrates here himself joined me on the tribune and conversed with

[b] Scheibe conjectured ἐν Διιπολείοις for ἐν τῇ πόλει, on the ground that Harpocration quotes the word Diipolcia as occurring in this speech. The Diipoleia (cf. Tetr. I. δ. 8) was an ancient festival celebrated annually in the first week of June on the Acropolis in honour of Zeus Polieus. Its date would suit the context; but the fact that the last part of the speech is apparently incomplete makes it possible that Harpocration is quoting from some lost passage.

ANTIPHON

ἐπὶ τοῦ βήματος, ἁπτόμενος ἐμοῦ διελέγετο, ὀνόματι οὗτος[1] ἐμὲ προσαγορεύων, καὶ ἐγὼ τοῦτον,
ὥστε δεινὸν δόξαι εἶναι τῇ βουλῇ, ἐπειδὴ ἐπύθετο
προειρημένον μοι εἴργεσθαι τῶν νομίμων ὑπὸ τούτων, οὓς ἑώρων[2] μοι τῇ προτεραίᾳ[3] συνόντας καὶ
διαλεγομένους.

41 Σκέψασθε δὲ καί μοι μνήσθητε, ὦ ἄνδρες· ταῦτα
γὰρ οὐ μόνον μάρτυσιν ὑμῖν ἀποδείξω, ἀλλὰ καὶ
ἐξ αὐτῶν τῶν ἔργων ἃ τούτοις πέπρακται, ῥᾳδίως
γνώσεσθε ὅτι ἀληθῆ λέγω. καὶ πρῶτον ἃ τοῦ
βασιλέως κατηγοροῦσι καὶ διὰ τὴν ἐμὴν σπουδὴν
οὔ φασιν ἐθέλειν αὐτὸν ἀπογράφεσθαι τὴν δίκην,
τοῦτο δὴ[4] κατ' αὐτῶν τούτων ἔσται τεκμήριον ὅτι
42 οὐκ ἀληθῆ λέγουσιν. ἔδει μὲν γὰρ τὸν βασιλέα,
ἐπειδὴ ἀπεγράψατο, τρεῖς προδικασίας[5] ποιῆσαι ἐν
τρισὶ μησί, τὴν δίκην δ' εἰσάγειν τετάρτῳ μηνί,
ὥσπερ νυνί· τῆς δ' ἀρχῆς αὐτῷ λοιποὶ δύο μῆνες
ἦσαν, Θαργηλιὼν καὶ Σκιροφοριών. καὶ οὔτ' εἰσάγειν δήπου οἷός τ' ἂν ἦν ἐφ' ἑαυτοῦ, οὔτε[6] παραδοῦναι φόνου δίκην[7] ἔξεστι, οὐδὲ παρέδωκεν οὐδεὶς
πώποτε βασιλεὺς ἐν τῇ γῇ ταύτῃ. ἥντινα οὖν μήτε
εἰσάγειν μήτε παραδοῦναι ἐξῆν αὐτῷ, οὐδ' ἀπο-
43 γράφεσθαι ἠξίου παρὰ τοὺς ὑμετέρους νόμους. καὶ

---

[1] οὗτος N : ὁ τοιοῦτος A.　　　　[2] ἑώρων N : ἑώρα A.
[3] προτεραίᾳ Baiter et Sauppe : προτέρᾳ codd.
[4] δὴ Baiter : δὲ codd.
[5] προδικασίας A pr. : προδιαδικασίας A corr. N.
[6] οὔτε Reiske : οὐδὲ codd.　　　[7] δίκην om. A.

---

[a] A reference to the sudden change of front shown by
Philocrates when he saw that the Choregus had discovered
his own activities.

[b] The dates are roughly as given in the Introduction.
The Βασιλεύς went out of office on 21st June : Philocrates

276

me, his hand on my arm, addressing me by my name as I addressed him by his. No wonder that the Council was astounded to learn that I had been proclaimed under the ban by the very persons whom they had seen in my company chatting to me on the previous day.[a]

And now I want your attention, gentlemen : I want you to cast your minds back ; for I shall not use witnesses alone to prove the facts to which I am now coming ; your own knowledge of how the prosecution have acted will itself show you at once that I am telling the truth. To begin with, they complain of the Basileus and attribute his refusal to register their charge to activities of mine. That complaint, however, will serve merely to damage their case by suggesting that their statements in general are untrue ; for after registering the action, the Basileus was obliged to hold three preliminary inquiries in the course of the three months following, only bringing the case into court during the fourth—as he has done to-day. Yet only two months of office remained to him, Thargelion and Scirophorion.[b] It would thus clearly have been impossible for him to bring the case into court during his own period of office ; and he is not allowed to hand on an action for murder to his successor ; such a thing has never been done by any Basileus in this country. So, as it was a case which he could neither bring into court nor hand on to his successor, he did not see why he should break your laws by registering it. There is, indeed, one very striking indication that

attempted to register his charge in the last week of April. Thargelion and Scirophorion were the last two months of the Attic year.

ὅτι οὐκ ἠδίκει¹ αὐτούς, μέγιστον σημεῖον· Φιλοκράτης γὰρ οὑτοσὶ ἑτέρους τῶν ὑπευθύνων ἔσειε
καὶ ἐσυκοφάντει, τούτου δὲ τοῦ βασιλέως, ὅν φασι
δεινὰ καὶ σχέτλια εἰργάσθαι, οὐκ ἦλθε κατηγορή-
σων εἰς τὰς εὐθύνας. καίτοι τί ἂν ὑμῖν μεῖζον τούτου τεκμήριον ἀποδείξαιμι, ὅτι οὐκ ἠδικεῖτο οὔθ᾽
ὑπ᾽ ἐμοῦ οὔθ᾽ ὑπ᾽ ἐκείνου;

44 Ἐπειδὴ δὲ² οὑτοσὶ ὁ βασιλεὺς εἰσῆλθεν, ἐξὸν
αὐτοῖς ἀπὸ τῆς πρώτης ἡμέρας³ ἀρξαμένοις τοῦ
Ἑκατομβαιῶνος μηνὸς τριάκονθ᾽ ἡμέρας συνεχῶς
τούτων ᾗτινι ἐβούλοντο ἀπογράφεσθαι, ἀπεγράφοντο οὐδεμιᾷ· καὶ αὖθις τοῦ Μεταγειτνιῶνος
μηνὸς ἀπὸ τῆς πρώτης ἡμέρας ἀρξαμένοις ἐξὸν
αὐτοῖς ἀπογράφεσθαι ⟨ᾗ⟩τινι⁴ ἐβούλοντο, οὐδ᾽ αὖ
πω⁵ ἐνταῦθα ἀπεγράψαντο, ἀλλὰ παρεῖσαν⁶ καὶ τούτου τοῦ μηνὸς εἴκοσιν ἡμέρας⁷· ὥστε αἱ σύμπασαι
ἡμέραι ἐγένοντο αὐτοῖς πλεῖν ἢ πεντήκοντα ἐπὶ
τούτου τοῦ βασιλέως, ἐν αἷς ἐξὸν αὐτοῖς ἀπο-
45 γράψασθαι οὐκ ἀπεγράψαντο. καὶ οἱ μὲν ἄλλοι
ἅπαντες ὅσοις⁸ ἐπὶ τοῦ αὐτοῦ βασιλέως ὁ χρόνος μὴ
ἐγχωρεῖ⁹ . . .¹⁰ οὗτοι δ᾽ ἐπιστάμενοι μὲν τοὺς
νόμους ἅπαντας, ὁρῶντες δ᾽ ἐμὲ βουλεύοντα καὶ

---

¹ ἠδίκει Reiske: ἀδικεῖ codd.   ² δὲ Gebauer: γὰρ codd.
³ ἡμέρας vulg.: ἡμέραι ὁ AN.   ⁴ ᾗ om. AN.
⁵ αὖ πω Blass: αὐτῷ codd.
⁶ παρεῖσαν N: παρῆσαν A.
⁷ ἡμέρας vulg.: ἡμέραις A corr. N, ἡμέραι A pr.
⁸ ὅσοις A pr.: ὅσοι A corr. N.
⁹ ἐγχωρεῖ Dobree: ἐχώρει N, ἐνεχώρει A.
¹⁰ Lacunam indicavit Dobree, qui sensum sic supplevit:
εὐθὺς εἰσελθόντος τοῦ διαδόχου ἀπογράφονται.

278

he did not rob the prosecution of their rights : whereas Philocrates yonder tormented other magistrates who had to render account of their office [a] with vexatious complaints, he failed to come forward with any grievance when this particular Basileus, whose conduct, we are told, had been so outrageously high-handed, was rendering account of his. What clearer indication could I present to you that Philocrates had suffered no injury from either myself or him ?

Moreover, after the present Basileus had come into office, there were thirty clear days from the first of Hecatombaeon onwards,[b] on any of which they could have registered their charge, had they wanted to ; yet they did not do so. Similarly, they could have registered it any day they liked from the first of Metageitnion onwards. But even then they did not do so : they let twenty days of this second month go by as well. Thus the total number of days in the present archonship on which they could have registered their charge, but failed to do so, was over fifty.[c] Ordinarily, anyone who has not time enough under one archon ⟨registers his charge as soon as he can under the next⟩. But the prosecution, who were perfectly familiar with the laws concerned and could see that I was a member of the Council and used the

[a] The εὔθυναι of a magistrate consisted of a public examination of his accounts and general conduct at the end of his period of office. There was a corresponding δοκιμασία, or preliminary investigation of his fitness, before his installation.

[b] Hecatombaeon was the first month of the official Attic year ; it extended from 22nd June to 21st July. Metageitnion followed it.

[c] The words " over fifty " look like a rhetorical exaggeration. For the bearing of this and the following section on the date of the speech, see Introd. p. 236.

εἰσιόντ᾽· ἐς τὸ βουλευτήριον—καὶ ἐν αὐτῷ τῷ
βουλευτηρίῳ Διὸς βουλαίου καὶ Ἀθηνᾶς βουλαίας
ἱερόν ἐστι καὶ εἰσιόντες οἱ βουλευταὶ προσεύχονται,
ὧν κἀγὼ εἷς ἦ, ὅς[1] ταῦτα πράττων, καὶ εἰς τἆλλα
ἱερὰ πάντα εἰσιὼν μετὰ τῆς βουλῆς, καὶ θύων καὶ
εὐχόμενος ὑπὲρ τῆς πόλεως ταύτης, καὶ πρὸς τούτοις πρυτανεύσας τὴν πρώτην πρυτανείαν ἅπασαν
πλὴν δυοῖν ἡμέραιν, καὶ ἱεροποιῶν καὶ θύων ὑπὲρ
τῆς δημοκρατίας, καὶ ἐπιψηφίζων καὶ λέγων
γνώμας περὶ τῶν μεγίστων καὶ πλείστου ἀξίων τῇ
46 πόλει φανερὸς ἦ· καὶ οὗτοι παρόντες καὶ ἐπιδη-
μοῦντες, ἐξὸν αὐτοῖς ἀπογράφεσθαι καὶ εἴργειν ἐμὲ
τούτων ἁπάντων, οὐκ ἠξίουν ἀπογράφεσθαι· καίτοι[2]
ἱκανά γ᾽ ἦν ὑπομνῆσαι καὶ ἐνθυμηθῆναι, εἴπερ
ἠδικοῦντο, ἀμφότερα καὶ σφῶν αὐτῶν ἕνεκα καὶ
τῆς πόλεως. διὰ τί οὖν οὐκ ἀπεγράφοντο;[3] δι᾽ ὅ
τι[4] συνῆσαν καὶ διελέγοντο· συνῆσάν τε γάρ μοι
[147] οὐκ ἀξιοῦντες φονέα εἶναι, καὶ οὐκ ἀπεγράφοντο
τούτου αὐτοῦ ἕνεκα, οὐχ ἡγούμενοί με ἀποκτεῖναι
τὸν παῖδα οὐδ᾽ ἔνοχον εἶναι τοῦ φόνου, οὐδὲ προσ-
ήκειν μοι τούτου τοῦ πράγματος οὐδέν.

47 Καίτοι πῶς ἂν ἄνθρωποι σχετλιώτεροι ἢ ἀνομώ-
τεροι γένοιντο; οἵτινες ἅπερ αὐτοὶ σφᾶς αὐτοὺς
οὐκ ἔπεισαν, ταῦθ᾽ ὑμᾶς ἀξιοῦσι πεῖσαι, καὶ ἃ αὐτοὶ

---

[1] ὅς Blass: ὁ codd.   ταῦτα Maetzner: ταὐτα codd.
[2] καίτοι Reiske: καὶ codd.
[3] οὖν οὐκ ἀπέγραφ. Reiske: ὅπου κατέγραφ. codd.
[4] δι᾽ ὅ τι Dobree: διὰ τί codd.

---

[a] The βουλή was divided into ten sections, each represent-
ing a tribe. Each section took it in turn to act as presidents
(πρυτάνεις) for a period known as a πρυτανεία (one tenth of the
year) at meetings of both the βουλή and the ἐκκλησία. The
πρυτάνεις themselves were under the presidency of one of their

Council-chamber—why, in that very chamber itself stands a shrine of Zeus the Councillor and Athena the Councillor, where members offer prayers as they enter; and I was one of those members: I did as they did: in their company I entered all our other sanctuaries: I offered sacrifices and prayers on behalf of this city: nay more, I acted as a Prytanis for the whole of the first Prytany save two days [a]: I was to be seen sacrificing and making offerings on behalf of our sovereign people: I was to be seen putting motions to the vote: I was to be seen voicing my opinion on the most momentous, the most vital public questions. And the prosecution were in Athens: they witnessed it: by registering their charge they could have debarred me from it all. In spite of that, they did not see fit to do so. Yet if their wrong was real, their duty to themselves and their duty to the state were alike enough to keep the memory of it fresh and to make it their constant thought. Then why did they fail to register a charge? Their reason was the same as their reason for not refusing to associate and converse with me. They associated with me because they did not think me a murderer: and they refused to register a charge for exactly the same reason: they did not think that I had either killed the boy, been concerned in his death, or had any part in the affair at all.

Where indeed could one find fewer scruples or a greater contempt for law? Here are men who expect to persuade you to believe what they have failed to

number known as an ἐπιστάτης who was selected by lot. It was he who put motions to the vote in the Assembly. The Choregus was clearly ἐπιστάτης during his Prytany.

ἔργῳ ἀπεδίκασαν, ταῦθ᾽ ὑμᾶς κελεύουσι κατα-
δικάσαι· καὶ οἱ μὲν ἄλλοι ἄνθρωποι τοῖς ἔργοις
τοὺς λόγους ἐξελέγχουσιν, οὗτοι δὲ τοῖς λόγοις
48 ζητοῦσι τὰ ἔργα ἄπιστα[1] καταστῆσαι. καίτοι εἰ
μηδὲν ἄλλο μήτε εἶπον μήτε ἀπέφηνα μήτε μάρτυρας παρεσχόμην, ἀλλὰ ταῦτα ὑμῖν ἀπέδειξα,
τούτους[2] ὅπου μὲν χρήματα λαμβάνοιεν ἐπ᾽ ἐμοί,
αἰτιωμένους καὶ προαγορεύοντας, ὅπου δὲ μὴ εἴη
ὁ δώσων, συνόντας καὶ διαλεγομένους, ἱκανὰ ἦν
καὶ αὐτὰ ταῦτα ἀκούσαντας ἀποψηφίσασθαι καὶ
τούτους νομίζειν ἐπιορκοτάτους καὶ ἀνοσιωτάτους
49 πάντων ἀνθρώπων. οὗτοι γὰρ ποίαν δίκην οὐ δικά-
σαιντ᾽ ἂν ἢ ποῖον δικαστήριον οὐκ ἐξαπατήσειαν
ἢ τίνας ὅρκους οὐκ ἂν τολμήσειαν παραβαίνειν;
οἵτινες καὶ νῦν τριάκοντα μνᾶς ἐπ᾽ ἐμοὶ λαβόντες παρὰ τῶν ποριστῶν καὶ τῶν πωλητῶν[3] καὶ
τῶν πρακτόρων καὶ τῶν ὑπογραμματέων οἱ τούτοις ὑπεγραμμάτευον, ἐξελάσαντές με ἐκ τοῦ
βουλευτηρίου, ὅρκους τοιούτους διωμόσαντο,[4] ὅτι
πρυτανεύων πυθόμενος αὐτοὺς δεινὰ καὶ σχέτλια
ἐργάζεσθαι εἰσῆγον εἰς τὴν βουλήν, καὶ ἐδίδαξα
50 ὡς χρὴ ζητοῦντας ἐπεξελθεῖν τῷ πράγματι. καὶ
νῦν δίκην διδόασιν ὧν ἠδικήκασιν αὐτοί τε καὶ οἱ
μεσεγγυησάμενοι καὶ παρ᾽ οἷς ἐτέθη τὰ χρήματα,
καὶ τὰ πραχθέντα φανερὰ γεγένηται, ὥστ᾽ οὐδ᾽ ἂν

---

[1] ἄπιστα Reiske : πιστὰ codd.
[2] τούτους Ald. : τούτοις codd.
[3] πωλητῶν Reiske : πολιτῶν codd.
[4] διωμόσαντο vulg. : διωμόσαντος N pr., διομόσαντος A
N corr.

---

[a] For an explanation of this see Introduction.
[b] Apparently it had come to light in the course of the
investigations into the activities of the Practores, etc. that

persuade themselves to believe, who bid you declare guilty the man whom they have themselves in fact declared innocent ; whereas everyone else uses the facts to prove the worth of mere assertion, they use mere assertion for the purpose of discrediting the facts. Indeed, if I had said nothing, established nothing, and produced evidence of nothing, but had proved to you the one fact that, whereas when paid to attack me the prosecution produced charges and proclamations, they frequented my society and were on speaking terms with me when there was no one to finance them, you would have heard enough to acquit me and treat the prosecution as the worst perjurors and the most impious scoundrels alive. What accusation would they hesitate to bring, what court would they hesitate to mislead, what oaths would they feel any compunction in breaking, after taking thirty minae, as they have, from the Poristae, the Poletae, the Practores, and the clerks attached to them, to bring me into court,[a] after driving me from the Council-chamber, and after swearing oaths so solemn, all because during my Prytany I learned of their scandalous malpractices, brought them before the Council, and showed that an inquiry should be instituted and the matter probed to the bottom. As it is, they themselves, those who struck the bargain with them, and the parties with whom the money was deposited are paying the price of their misdeeds [b] ; and the facts have been revealed so clearly that the

thirty minae had been promised Philocrates if his charge of homicide was successful. The money would be deposited with a third party, to be claimed by Philocrates when he had earned it.

οὗτοι βούλωνται ἀρνεῖσθαι ῥᾳδίως οἷοί τ' ἔσονται·
οὕτως αὐτοῖς πέπρακται τὰ πράγματα.

51 Ποῖον οὖν δικαστήριον οὐκ ἂν ἔλθοιεν ἐξαπατήσοντες, ἢ τίνας ὅρκους οὐκ ἂν τολμήσαιεν παραβαίνειν οὗτοι οἱ ἀνοσιώτατοι; οἵτινες καὶ ὑμᾶς
εἰδότες εὐσεβεστάτους τῶν Ἑλλήνων δικαστὰς καὶ
δικαιοτάτους καὶ ἐφ' ὑμᾶς ἥκουσιν ἐξαπατήσοντες
εἰ δύναιντο, ὅρκους τοσούτους διομοσάμενοι.

---

[a] The repetitions in these closing paragraphs, and the

prosecution will find it difficult to deny them, even if they wish to ; such is the lack of success which they have had.

What court, then, would they hesitate to invade with their lies, what oaths would they feel the slightest compunction in breaking ? The impious scoundrels ! They knew that you are the most conscientious and the fairest judges in this nation ; yet they come before you intent on deceiving even you, if they can, in spite of the solemn oaths which they have sworn.[a]

absence of the usual ἐπίλογος make it probable that the end of the speech, as we have it, is mutilated.

FRAGMENTS

FRAGMENTS

NOTE

ANTIPHON suffered no less than many classical authors during the late Roman and Byzantine periods. Whereas Caecilius of Calactê, writing under Augustus, was acquainted with thirty-five speeches which were certainly his, and twenty-five others falsely attributed to him, only fifteen were current by the thirteenth century, when our oldest existing manuscript was copied. These fifteen, the φονικοὶ λόγοι, presumably survived, as did the κληρικοί of Isaeus, because they were considered fairly to represent the qualities of their author, who was but little read in comparison with the more celebrated of the canon. But the titles and fragments of the other twenty, preserved by lexicographers and grammarians,[a] show that Antiphon was prepared to undertake cases of every description, whether a subject-state wished its grievances placed before the Assembly or a jury of dicasts had to have the intricacies of a mining-lease explained to them. The pages following contain a list of these lost speeches, classified according to their character,[b] together with such fragments as amount to something more than single words, quoted for their rarity or peculiarity.

[a] This does not of course include the papyrus fragments of the Περὶ Μεταστάσεως, q.v., pp. 294-299.
[b] I have followed the grouping of Blass (*Att. Beredsamkeit,* i. pp. 91-94) as being the most convenient.

A. ΛΟΓΟΙ ΔΗΜΗΓΟΡΙΚΟΙ

1. ΠΕΡΙ ΤΟΥ ΛΙΝΔΙΩΝ ΦΟΡΟΥ

Title known from Harpocration.

Like the speech which follows, this must have been written for the representatives of a subject-state who had come to Athens to seek a readjustment of tribute. It is known that Lindus, together with the rest of Rhodes, revolted from Athens in 412 B.C. The present speech, however, must have been delivered before 413,[a] when a 5 per cent tax on imports and exports was substituted for the φόρος.

2. ΠΕΡΙ ΤΟΥ ΣΑΜΟΘΡΑΙΚΩΝ ΦΟΡΟΥ

1. Ἡ γὰρ νῆσος, ἣν ἔχομεν, δήλη μὲν καὶ πόρρωθεν ⟨ὅτι⟩[1] ἐστὶν ὑψηλὴ καὶ τραχεῖα· καὶ τὰ μὲν χρήσιμα καὶ ἐργάσιμα μικρὰ αὐτῆς ἐστι, τὰ δ᾽ ἀργὰ πολλά, μικρᾶς αὐτῆς οὔσης. Demetrius, On Style 53.

2. Καὶ γὰρ οἱ τὴν ἀρχὴν οἰκίσαντες[2] τὴν νῆσον ἦσαν Σάμιοι, ἐξ ὧν ἡμεῖς ἐγενόμεθα. κατῳκίσθησαν δὲ ἀνάγκῃ, οὐκ ἐπιθυμίᾳ τῆς νήσου· ἐξέπεσον γὰρ ὑπὸ τυράννων ἐκ Σάμου καὶ τύχῃ

---

[1] ὅτι add. Sauppe.
[2] οἰκίσαντες Boeckh : οἰκήσαντες codd.

A. *Speeches written for delivery in the Ecclesia*

1. ON THE TRIBUTE OF LINDUS

The word ἐπίσκοπος, quoted by Harpocration as occurring in the speech, shows that there was at least some reference to Athenian supervision of the civil affairs of the subject-states.[b] The fact that Antiphon should have written a speech of this kind is not surprising, when it is remembered that it was a part of oligarchic policy to uphold the cause of the subject-states against the popular government. In the same way he supported the claims of Samothrace against Athens, and composed a defence for a native Lesbian, charged with the murder of an Athenian cleruch.

2. ON THE TRIBUTE OF SAMOTHRACE

1. For the island we inhabit is mountainous and rocky, as can be seen even from afar. It is but small; yet the productive and cultivable portion is small, and the unproductive large.

2. For those who originally occupied the island were Samians; and from them we are descended. They settled there from force of circumstances, not from any desire for the island; for they were driven

---

[a] Possibly as early as 425-424, when a general increase in the φόρος appears to have begun. But see further the work mentioned p. 293, note a.

[b] *Cf. I.G.* i². 10, Erythraean Decree.

ἐχρήσαντο ταύτῃ . . .¹ καὶ λείαν λαβόντες ἀπὸ
τῆς Θρᾴκης ἀφικνοῦνται εἰς τὴν νῆσον. Suidas,
s.v. Σαμοθρᾴκη.

3. Καίτοι οὐκ ἂν τῆς μὲν τῶν ἄλλων πολιτῶν
ταλαιπωρίας προὐσκέψαντο, τῆς δὲ σφετέρας
αὐτῶν σωτηρίας² οὐκ ἐνεθυμήθησαν. Priscian
18. 280.

4. Ἡιρέθησαν γὰρ ἐκλογῆς παρ' ἡμῖν οἷς πλεῖστα ἐδόκει χρήματα εἶναι. Harpocration, s.v. ἐκλογεῖς.

A speech of the same character as the preceding. The
evidence of the quota-lists ᵃ shows that in, or shortly before,
421 B.C. the arrangements for collecting the tribute of the island
of Samothrace were changed. Previously, for purposes of
taxation, Samothrace and the settlements under her control
on the Thracian coast opposite had been treated as a single
unit and appear in the quota-lists as Σαμοθρᾶκες. By
421, however, these coastal towns (e.g. Salê and Serrheion)
are mentioned separately, a fact which suggests that Samothrace had henceforward to pay independently; at the
same time, it is virtually certain that the Samothracian
assessment was increased. The present speech must have
been composed for a delegation from Samothrace which
had come to Athens to protest against the new arrange-
ment. The first fragment shows that the natural poverty
of the island was stressed, while the reference to tyrants in
the second, which comes from an account of the original
292

from Samos by tyrants and met with the following
adventures . . . and after a successful raid on
Thrace they reached the island.

3. Yet if they were concerned for the sufferings
of their fellows, they can hardly have failed to take
thought for their own lives.

4. Those of us were appointed Collectors who
were reputed the wealthiest.

settlement of Samothrace, was doubtless intended to conciliate Athenian feeling by implying that the sympathies of
the inhabitants had been democratic from the beginning.

That tradition connected Samothrace with Samos can also
be gathered from a statement of Apollodorus, who says that
Samothrace was " colonized by Ionians from Samos " [b];
but this may represent nothing more than a conjecture
based upon the similarity between the names of the two
islands. The reason given by Antiphon for the settlement
from Samos is difficult to accept at its face value ; the
tyranny to which he refers can only be that of Polycrates,
who ruled from *c.* 532 B.C. until shortly before 521, and
yet Samothrace was already inhabited in Homeric times.[c]
The Homeric Samothracians were probably " Pelasgians,"
it is true ; but Samothrace, which by the beginning of the
fifth century had numerous dependencies near the mouth
of the Hebrus, must have become Greek long before Polycrates rose to power. The fourth fragment is important as
containing one of the rare references in literature to the
system whereby the tribute was collected from the subject-
states. Native " Collectors " (ἐκλογεῖς) were appointed,
and these would be responsible to the Athenian government
for the total sum due, whether or not they had been successful
in collecting it.

[a] *Cf. I.G.* i². 212 and 64, and see also *Ath. Tribute Lists,*
Meritt, Wade-Gery and McGregor, vol. i. (1939), p. 158.
[b] Schol. *Il.* xiii. 12.
[c] *Il.* xxiv. 753.

---

[1] Lacunam indic. Sauppe.
[2] σωτηρίας Spengel : ἀτηριας, ἀτυριας, ἀγεριας codd.

ΑΝΤΙΦΩΝ

Β. ΛΟΓΟΙ ΔΙΚΑΝΙΚΟΙ

1. ΠΕΡΙ ΤΗΣ ΜΕΤΑΣΤΑΣΕΩΣ

1. Περὶ τοίνυν ὧν ᾿Απόληξις κατηγόρηκεν, ὡς
στασιώτης ἢ ⟨καὶ⟩[1] ἐγὼ καὶ ὁ πάππος ὁ ἐμός . . .
οὐκ ἂν τοὺς μὲν τυραννοῦντας ἐδυνήθησαν οἱ
πρόγονοι κολάσαι,[2] τοὺς δὲ δορυφόρους ἠδυνάτησαν.
Harpocration, s.v. στασιώτης.

2. Col. I. [ὡς αἱρεθεὶς][3] |[1] ἀρχ]ὴν ἄρξαι[4] |
χρ]ήματα πολ|λὰ] διεχείρισα | κ]αὶ εὔθυναί μοι |[5]
ἦσ]αν ἃς[5] ἐδεδοί|κε]ιν ἢ ἄτιμος | ἦ]ν ἢ κακόν | τι
ὑ]μᾶς εἰργα|σ]άμην ἢ δί|[10]κ]ην ἐπιρρέ|π]ουσαν
ἐδε|δοίκ]ειν; οὐ δῆ|τα τοῦ][6]τό γε ἐπεὶ | οὐδ]έν
μοι ἦν |[15] τού]των. ᾿Αλλ᾿ ὡς | χ]ρήματα ἀ|φεί]-
λεσθε ἐμοῦ; | ἀλ]λ᾿ ὡς[7] τῶν | πρ]ογόνων |[20] τῶν]
ἐμῶν κα|κόν] τι εἰργα|σμένων[8] ἐμὲ] | ἐτιμωρή-
σα]||σθε ;[9] τοιούτων] |[25] [γάρ τινες ἔνε]- Col. II.
κ]α[10] ἄλλης τινὸς | πολιτείας ἢ | τῆς καθεστη|κυίας
ἐπιθυ|[5]μοῦσιν, ἵνα | ἢ ὧν ἠδίκη|σαν δίκην μὴ |
δῶσιν ἢ ὧν ἔ|παθον τιμω|[10]ρῶνται καὶ αὖ|θις μηδὲν
π[ά]σχωσιν· ἀλλ᾿ ἐ|μοὶ τοιοῦτον | οὐδὲν ἦν. ᾿Αλ|[15]λὰ
μὲν δὴ λέ|γουσιν οἱ κα|τήγοροι ὡς συν|έγραφόν τε
δί|κας ἄλλοις καὶ |[20] τὸ ε΄ ἐκέρδαι|νον ἀπὸ τού|του.
Οὐκοῦν ἐν | μὲν τῆι ὀλι|γαρχίαι οὐκ ἂν |[25] ἦν μοι
[τ]οῦτο, Col. III. ἐ]ν δ[ὲ τῆι δη|μο]κρα[τίαι ἰ|δί]αι
ὁ κρ[ατῶν[11] | εἰμι ἐγώ, ἐκ [δὲ |[5] τοῦ λέγειν ἐν | μὲν

---

[1] ἢ καὶ Blass: ἦν codd. [2] κολάσαι Dobree : καλέσαι codd.
[3] Initium suppl. Thalheim et Pohl.
[4] ἀρχὴν ἄρξαι Nicole. [5] ἦσαν ἃς Wilamowitz.
[6] οὐ δῆτα suppl. Thalheim : οὐ δὲ τοῦτό γε Wilamowitz.
[7] ἀλλ᾿ ὡς Wilamowitz.
[8] εἰργασμένων Nicole.
[9] ἐμὲ ἐτιμωρήσασθε Crönert.

B. *Speeches delivered before a court of law*

1. ON THE REVOLUTION

1. As for the charge brought by Apolexis that I belonged to a political faction, like my grandfather before me . . . your forefathers can hardly have been powerless to punish the tyrants' bodyguard, when they were able to punish the tyrants.

2. ⟨Could it be said that I desired a revolution⟩ because I had handled large sums of money as a public magistrate, and was faced with an audit which I feared? Or because I had been disfranchised? Or because I had done you some wrong? Or because I feared an impending lawsuit? No, it could not, for the very good reason that I was not placed in any such situation. Then was it because you had taken my property from me? Or because you had visited me with punishment for some wrong done you by my forefathers? Those are reasons which lead some to desire a change of government, so that they may avoid paying for misdeeds which they have committed, or else gain redress for wrongs which they have suffered and prevent their recurrence. But no such motive was at work in my case. My accusers state, however, that I have been in the habit of composing speeches for others to deliver in court, and that the Four Hundred profited by this. I reply that, while under the oligarchy such a practice would have been forbidden me, under the democracy I am the one man who is all-powerful; and whereas

---

[10] τοιούτων γάρ τινες ἔνεκα suppl. Thalheim.
[11] ἰδίαι ὁ κρατῶν Thalheim: καὶ ὁ κρατῶν Jander.

τῆι ὀλι|γαρχίαι οὐδε|νὸς ἔμ[ελλον | ἄξιος ἔσεσθα[ι,
|[10] ἐν δὲ τῆι δη|μοκρατίαι | πολλοῦ; φέρ[ε | δὴ
πῶς εἰκό[ς | ἐστιν ἐμὲ ὀλ[ι|[15]γαρχίας ἐπι|θυμεῖν;
πότ[ε|ρον [ταῦτ]α[1] ἐκ|λογίζεσθαι | οὐχ οἶός τ᾽
εἰ[μι |[20] ἢ οὐ γιγνώ|σκειν τὰ λ[υσι|τελοῦντ[α[2]
ἐ]μαυτῶι [μόνος | ᾽Αθη[ναίων;[3]

3. Col. IV.[4] ξοις ἐδόκει μὰ | τοὺ]ς θεοὺς τοὺς |
᾽Ολυ]μπίους οὐ | . . . . ε]ἴ γε ὀρθῶς |[5] . . . σκοπεῖσθε
| . . ἐπ]ειδὴ Θηρα|μέ]νης, ὃς ἐμοῦ | κατ]ηγόρησεν
| . . . . . . εν ἐν |[10] τῆι βο]υλῆι ᾽Ε| . . . . . s οὑτοσὶ
| . . . . . . ρυς δι| . . . . . ν ἐκεῖ | κατηγ]ορήκει
|[15] . . . . . . οὑ]τοσὶ| . . . . . . στον | . . . . . . ων
| . . . . . . εινα ὁ πα- (desunt versus septem).

4. . . . καὶ τοὺς ἐμποδὼν ἐκολάσατε . . . Harpocration, s.v. ἐμποδών.

Of all that has come down to us under the name of
Antiphon nothing is more interesting than the fragments
of his own defence against a charge of high treason in the
year 411 B.C. Until recently only two inconsiderable
excerpts (nos. 1 and 4) were known, both from the lexico-
grapher Harpocration.[a] But in 1907 the remains of a
papyrus roll of the late second century A.D. came to light
containing additional fragments of some length.[b] Of the
seven columns of the papyrus which survive, the first three
admit of certain restoration, while the fourth, though more
seriously damaged, contains a few consecutive words of

---

[1] ταῦτα Wilamowitz: τἆλλα Nicole.
[2] λυσιτελοῦντα Wilamowitz.
[3] μόνος ᾽Αθηναίων Thalheim.
[4] Nicole in hunc modum restituebat: ἆρα οὕτως τοῖς ἐνδό⟩ξοις
ἐδόκει; μὰ τοὺς θεοὺς τοὺς ᾽Ολυμπίους οὐ⟨δενί⟩, εἴ γε ὀρθῶς
⟨δια⟩σκοπεῖσθε. ⟨ἀλλ᾽⟩ ἐπειδὴ Θηραμένης, ὃς ἐμοῦ κατηγόρησεν,
⟨ἡσύχαζ⟩εν ἐν τῇ βουλῇ, ᾽Ε. . . . . . s οὑτοσὶ ⟨ἀντικ⟩ρὺς δικώξας
ὢ⟩ν ἐκεῖ κατηγορήκει . . . . . . οὑτοσί, ⟨οὐ τὸ εἰκο⟩στὸν ⟨ἔλαβε
τῶν ψήφ⟩ων. ⟨ἐκ⟩εῖνα ὁ πα⟨τὴρ⟩. . .

under the oligarchy my powers as a speaker were
certain to count for nothing, under the democracy
they count for much. I ask you : what likelihood
is there that I should desire an oligarchic government ? Am I incapable of appreciating these facts
for myself ? Am I the one man in Athens who
cannot see where his own advantage lies ?

3. Did the . . . think so ? By all the gods upon
Olympus they did not, as you will see if you consider
the matter aright. When Theramenes, who accused
me . . . in the Council, E . . . s here . . . the
charges he had there made. . . .

4. . . . and you punished those who were at
hand . . .

some importance. All four are printed above in full.
The remaining three columns are unfortunately too incomplete to allow the sense to be elicited with any certainty,
although more than one restoration of the text has been
proposed ; they have therefore been omitted from the
present edition.

Even with the help of the papyrus fragments the remains
of the speech are too scanty to admit of a reconstruction of
its general plan. But it is at least clear that it must have
contained a detailed account of Antiphon's political activities
before and during the revolution of the Four Hundred ;
and that, in turn, makes it probable that it furnished a more ·
or less complete record of the constitutional changes of the
year 411. Indeed the suggestion has been made [c]—and it
is a plausible one—that the Περὶ Μεταστάσεως was the
principal source for the history of the revolution given by
Aristotle in chaps. xxix.-xxxii. of the 'Αθηναίων Πολιτεία.

[a] A third fragment (D. 1 *infra*) which some would assign
to the present speech, would have suited numerous other
occasions also, and must therefore be left among the
ἀπαράσημα.

[b] Published by J. Nicole, *L'Apologie d'Antiphon* (1907).

[c] See Ferguson, " The Condemnation of Antiphon," ap.
Mélanges Glotz, vol. i.

ANTIPHON

Aristotle is certainly not following Thucydides, as there are too many discrepancies between their narratives ; and the odd fact that Thucydides at one point seems deliberately to contradict Aristotle's source [a] makes it almost certain that Aristotle is using a source with which Thucydides was himself

2. ΠΡΟΣ ΤΗΝ ΔΗΜΟΣΘΕΝΟΥΣ ΓΡΑΦΗΝ ΑΠΟΛΟΓΙΑ

. . . ἵνα τοὺς κελέοντας κατέπηξεν. . . . Harpocration, *s.v.* κελέοντες.

According to the Pseudo-Plutarch one of Antiphon's most famous speeches. The Demosthenes in question was the general, and therefore the case must have been heard before 413 B.C., when he met his death in Sicily. The

3. ΠΡΟΣ ΤΗΝ ΚΑΛΛΙΟΥ ΕΝΔΕΙΞΙΝ ΑΠΟΛΟΓΙΑ

Title known from Harpocration.

4. ΠΡΟΣ ΝΙΚΟΚΛΕΑ ΠΕΡΙ ΟΡΩΝ

Title known from Harpocration.

5. ΠΑΡΑΝΟΜΩΝ ΚΑΤΗΓΟΡΙΑ

Title known from Suidas. Only the following hopelessly corrupt fragment survives :

†ναυμάχους ὡς περὶ δωρεῶν μὲν εἰπεῖν κατάγειν δεῦρο.†

---

[a] Thuc. viii. 67. 2 ; Ἀθ. Πολ. xxix. 5.

familiar, but which, from his own knowledge, he considered inaccurate. Such a source, as far as we can judge, is most likely to have been the present speech of Antiphon, which was certainly known to Thucydides and must have been widely read in the fourth century.

2. DEFENCE AGAINST AN INDICT- MENT BROUGHT BY DEMOSTHENES

. . . where he fixed the uprights of the loom. . . .

speaker is accused of having proposed an unconstitutional measure in the Ecclesia. It is not unlikely that he was a political ally of Antiphon who had come into conflict with the democratic party.

3. DEFENCE AGAINST AN INFORMATION LAID BY CALLIAS

Date and circumstances unknown.

4. PROSECUTION OF NICOCLES IN A SUIT RELATING TO BOUNDARIES

Known only from some half a dozen single words quoted by lexicographers. From these it has been conjectured with some probability that the dispute related to the de-limitation of mine-workings leased from the state at Laurium. A reference to Hyperbolus shows that the speech cannot have been written much before 425 B.C. at the earliest.

5. PROSECUTION FOR AN UNCON- STITUTIONAL PROPOSAL IN THE ECCLESIA

Date and circumstances unknown. Identified by some with No. 2 *supra*.

6. ΚΑΤΑ ΦΙΛΙΝΟΥ

. . . τούς τε θῆτας ἅπαντας ὁπλίτας ποιῆσαι.
Harpocration, *s.v.* θῆτες.

References in the *Choreutes* to the prosecution of Philinus
for embezzlement make it certain that the present speech
was delivered shortly before the *Choreutes*. It has been
argued [a] from the sole surviving fragment of the Κατὰ Φιλίνου
that both speeches must belong to the period immediately
following the disaster in Sicily, as only then could the

7. ΚΑΤΑ ΠΡΥΤΑΝΕΩΣ

Title known from Harpocration.

8. ΠΕΡΙ ΑΝΔΡΑΠΟΔΙΣΜΟΥ

Ἐπειδὴ γὰρ ἀπῳκίσθην Ἀθήναζε καὶ ἀπηλλάγην
τῆς κληρουχίας . . . Photius, *Lex.* 42, 12 R.

9. ΥΠΕΡ ΤΗΣ ΕΙΣ ΤΟΝ ΕΛΕΥΘΕΡΟΝ
ΠΑΙΔΑ ⟨ΥΒΡΕΩΣ⟩

Title known from Harpocration. The word ὕβρεως,
which is missing in the MSS., was first supplied in the edition
of Gronovius.

6. PROSECUTION OF PHILINUS

. . . and to make all the Thetes hoplites.

proposal to turn the Thetes into heavy infantry have been seriously put forward. But the chronological data in the *Choreutes* itself point rather to the year 419, and as Thucydides makes it clear that in 413–412 the shortage was one of rowers, not of infantry, it is hard to see why the one class of citizen which regularly manned the fleet should be transferred at such a moment to service on land. For further details see *Choreutes*, Introd. p. 234.

7. PROSECUTION OF A PRYTANIS

The genuineness of this speech was doubted by Harpocration. The title might also mean " Prosecution of Prytanis (-eus) "; but Prytanis does not occur as a proper name in the classical period. We have no means of discovering either the date or the circumstances of the speech.

8. IN A CASE OF ENSLAVEMENT

For when I removed to Athens and was finished with the cleruchy . . .

Date and circumstances unknown.

9. IN A CASE OF ASSAULT UPON A BOY OF FREE PARENTAGE

To be attributed to Lysias according to some MSS. and grammarians. Date and circumstances unknown. The title itself is doubtful. See crit. note.

---

^a *e.g.* by Gernet, Budé Antiphon.

ANTIPHON

10. ΕΠΙΤΡΟΠΙΚΟΣ ⟨ΚΑΤΑ⟩ ΚΑΛΛΙΣΤΡΑΤΟΥ

Title known from Harpocration. κατά was added by Sauppe.

11. ΕΠΙΤΡΟΠΙΚΟΣ ⟨ΚΑΤΑ⟩ ΤΙΜΟΚΡΑΤΟΥΣ

Title known from Harpocration. The mss. vary between τιμοκράτης and τιμοκράτω. I have corrected as in the text, adding κατά.

12. ΠΡΟΣ ΕΡΑΣΙΣΤΡΑΤΟΝ ΠΕΡΙ ΤΩΝ ΤΑΩΝ

1. Εἴ τις ἐθέλοι καταβαλεῖν εἰς πόλιν τοὺς ὄρνιθας, οἰχήσονται ἀναπτόμενοι· ἐὰν δὲ τῶν πτερύγων ἀποτέμῃ, τὸ κάλλος ἀφαιρήσεται· τὰ πτέρα γὰρ αὐτῶν τὸ κάλλος ἐστίν, ἀλλ' οὐ τὸ σῶμα. Athenaeus ix. 397 c-d.

2. Ἀλλὰ τὰς μὲν νουμηνίας ὁ βουλόμενος εἰσῄει· τὰς δ' ἄλλας ἡμέρας εἴ τις ἔλθοι βουλόμενος θεάσασθαι, οὐκ ἔστιν ὅστις ἔτυχε. καὶ ταῦτα οὐκ ἐχθὲς οὐδὲ πρώην, ἀλλ' ἔτη πλέον ἢ τριάκοντά ἐστιν. Ibid.

Said by the Pseudo-Plutarch to have been one of Antiphon's four finest speeches. Athenaeus, who has preserved the two fragments quoted above, gives a few further details : " There is a speech by the orator Antiphon entitled *On the Peacocks*. The word ' peacock ' nowhere occurs in the speech itself, though he frequently refers to ' many-coloured

302

10. PROSECUTION OF CALLISTRATUS IN A CASE RELATING TO GUARDIANSHIP

It was maintained in the course of the speech that an adopted son could not return to his family unless his adoptive father had sons of his own already. Date and circumstances unknown.

11. PROSECUTION OF TIMOCRATES IN A CASE RELATING TO GUARDIANSHIP

Date and circumstances unknown.

12. PROSECUTION OF ERASISTRATUS IN THE MATTER OF THE PEACOCKS

1. Should one think to set the birds loose in Athens, they will fly away. On the other hand, if one clips their wings, their beauty will be taken from them ; for their beauty lies in their plumage, not in their bodies.

2. On the first of the month all comers were admitted, whereas if anyone came to see them on any other day, he was invariably disappointed. Nor has this been the case only during the last day or two ; it has been going on for over thirty years.

birds,' saying that they were kept by Demus, son of Pyrilampes, and that many came from Sparta and Thessaly to see them and tried to obtain some of their eggs." Aelian adds that according to Antiphon the peacocks were valued at a thousand drachmae a pair.[a] Of the circumstances of

---

[a] *Hist. An.* v. 21.

the speech we are ignorant. Possibly Erasistratus had
attempted to steal either the birds or their eggs; but on
that point neither title nor fragments give any information.
Demus was still little more than a boy in 422, to judge
from an allusion in the *Wasps* [a]; and so it is reasonable to

13. ΚΑΤΑ ΙΠΠΟΚΡΑΤΟΥΣ

Title known from [Plut.], *Vita Antiphontis*, § 21: ἔγραψε
(*sc.* Antiphon) δὲ καὶ κατὰ Ἱπποκράτους τοῦ ἰατροῦ (other
MSS. στρατηγοῦ) λόγον καὶ εἷλεν αὐτὸν ἐξ ἐρήμου.

Known only from its title, which is quoted by the Pseudo-
Plutarch in his *Life of Antiphon*. The MSS. offer a choice
between Hippocrates the general, who fell at Delium in
424 B.C., and Hippocrates of Cos, the physician. As Blass

14. ΚΑΤΑ ΛΑΙΣΠΟΔΙΟΥ

Title known from Harpocration.

15. ΥΠΕΡ ΜΥΡΡΟΥ

1. Οὐ γὰρ πω[1] ἐπεπόνθη ταῦτα, ἅττα νῦν
πέπονθα ὑπὸ τούτου. Suidas, *s.v.* ἅττα.

2. Οἱ γὰρ ἄνθρωποι ἅττα ἂν ὁρῶσι τῇ ὄψει
πιστότερα ἡγοῦνται ἢ οἷς εἰς ἀφανὲς ἥκει ὁ ἔλεγχος
τῆς ἀληθείας. *Ibid.*

16. ΠΡΟΣ ΠΟΛΥΕΥΚΤΟΝ

Title known from the Antiatticistes, Bekker Anecdota
82. 29.

¹ οὐ γὰρ πω Cobet : οὐ γὰρ ἐγώ codd.

---

[a] *Wasps* 98. [b] Plut. *Per.* 13.
[c] *Birds* 1569. [d] Thuc. viii. 86. 9.

suppose that the speech was written some time later. The last sentence of the second fragment presumably contains a reference to the peacocks owned by Demus' father, Pyrilampes, renowned for his wealth and magnificence before the Peloponnesian War and a friend of Pericles in his younger days.[b]

13. PROSECUTION OF HIPPOCRATES

observes, the second is the more likely, since the Pseudo-Plutarch goes on to say that the defendant lost the suit by default. This is intelligible in the case of Hippocrates of Cos, who might well have been absent from Athens at the time. It is less likely that Hippocrates the general should have jeopardized his reputation by failing to appear in court.

14. PROSECUTION OF LAESPODIAS

Date and circumstances unknown. Laespodias was στρατηγός in 414 B.C. and is ridiculed as such in the *Birds*[c] of Aristophanes. Later he appears to have joined the oligarchs, and in 411 served on a deputation sent by the Four Hundred to Sparta.[d]

15. IN DEFENCE OF MYRRHUS

1. For I had not then been treated by my accuser as I have been since.

2. For men consider things which they see with their eyes more credible than things which cannot be established by ocular proof.

Date and circumstances unknown.

16. PROSECUTION OF POLYEUCTUS

Date and circumstances unknown.

17. ΠΡΟΣ ΦΙΛΙΠΠΟΝ ΑΠΟΛΟΓΙΑ

Title known from Harpocration.

C.

1. ΑΛΚΙΒΙΑΔΟΥ ΛΟΙΔΟΡΙΑΙ

Ἐπειδὴ ἐδοκιμάσθης ὑπὸ τῶν ἐπιτρόπων, παραλαβὼν παρ' αὐτῶν τὰ σαυτοῦ χρήματα, ᾤχου
ἀποπλέων εἰς Ἄβυδον, οὔτε χρέος ἴδιον σαυτοῦ
πραξόμενος οὐδὲν οὔτε προξενίας οὐδεμιᾶς ἕνεκα,
ἀλλὰ τῇ σαυτοῦ παρανομίᾳ καὶ ἀκολασίᾳ τῆς
γνώμης ὁμοίους ἔργων τρόπους μαθησόμενος παρὰ
τῶν ἐν Ἀβύδῳ γυναικῶν, ὅπως ἐν τῷ ἐπιλοίπῳ
βίῳ σαυτοῦ ἔχοις χρῆσθαι αὐτοῖς. Athenaeus xii.
525 b.

Probably a polemical pamphlet rather than a set speech.
An obvious parallel is the Κατ' Ἀλκιβιάδου, wrongly ascribed
to Andocides. Plutarch mentions two other anecdotes from

2. ΠΡΟΟΙΜΙΑ ΚΑΙ ΕΠΙΛΟΓΟΙ

1. Ἐγραψάμην ταύτην τὴν γραφὴν ἠδικημένος
ὑπὸ τούτου νὴ Δία πολλά, ἔτι δὲ καὶ πλείω ὑμᾶς
ᾐσθημένος ἠδικημένους καὶ τοὺς ἄλλους πολίτας.
Suidas, s.v. αἴσθεσθαι.

2. Ἀλλ' εἰ τό τε[1] πρᾶγμά μοι κρεῖττον φαίνεται
ἅμα τε μαρτυρίας ἀκριβεῖς[2] παρέχομαι[3] . . .
Suidas, s.v. ἅμα.

[1] τό τε Spengel : τότε codd.
[2] μαρτυρίας ἀκριβεῖς Sauppe : μαρτυρίᾳ ἀρετῆς codd.

17. DEFENCE AGAINST PHILIPPUS

Date and circumstances unknown. The genuineness of
the speech was doubted by Harpocration.

C. *Miscellaneous*

1. ABUSE OF ALCIBIADES

No sooner had you been presented to your deme
by your guardians than you took over your property
from them and were off to Abydos, not to recover
some personal debt or because you had any official
connexion with the place, but to take lessons from
the women of Abydos in the sort of behaviour which
befitted your natural wildness and depravity, so that
you might be able to put it into practice in later
life.

the Λοιδορίαι of the same type as the above. The most
likely date of publication is 418–417 B.C., when efforts
were being made to bring about the ostracism of Alcibiades.

2. PROEMS AND PERORATIONS

1. I brought this indictment because, heaven
knows, I had been deeply wronged by the defendant,
and because I saw that you and your fellows had been
wronged still more deeply.
2. But if the facts of the matter appear to favour
me, and if I am furnishing detailed confirmation of
them at the same time . . .

---

³ παρέχομαι scripsi : πράξομαι codd.

3. . . . κἀγὼ μὲν ὁ μοχθηρός, ὅντινα ἐχρῆν
τεθνηκέναι, ζῶ τοῖς ἐχθροῖς κατάγελως . . . Suidas,
s.v. μοχθηρός.

3. ΡΗΤΟΡΙΚΑΙ ΤΕΧΝΑΙ ΑΒΓ

1. Ἀντιφῶν τε ἐν ταῖς ῥητορικαῖς τέχναις τὸ
μὲν τὰ παρόντα ἔφη καὶ τὰ ὑπάρχοντα καὶ τὰ
παρακειμένα αἰσθάνεσθαι κατὰ φύσιν εἶναι ἡμῖν·
παρὰ φύσιν δὲ τὸ φυλάττειν αὐτῶν ἐκποδὼν γενομένων ἐναργῆ τὸν τύπον.[1] Longinus, ap. Rhet. Gr.,
Spengel, i. 318.

2. . . . τὰ μὲν[2] παροιχόμενα σημείοις πιστοῦσθαι, τὰ δὲ μέλλοντα τεκμηρίοις. . . . Am-
monius, Περὶ διαφ. λεξ. 127.

D. ΑΠΑΡΑΣΗΜΑ

1. Περὶ τοῦ μὴ ἐλεεῖν ὑμᾶς ἐμὲ ἐδεήθη, δείσας
μὴ ἐγὼ δάκρυσι καὶ ἱκετείαις πειρῶμαι ὑμᾶς
ἀναπείθειν. Suidas, s.v. ἱκετεία.

2. . . . τοῦτο δὲ τοὺς νόμους εἰδὼς πατρίους
καὶ παλαίους ὄντας ὑμῖν . . . Suidas, s.v. πατρῴων.

3. Τέως μὲν γὰρ ὁ πολὺς χρόνος τοῦ ὀλίγου
πιστότερος ἦν. Suidas, s.v. τέως.

---

[1] τύπον Finckh : πόθον codd.
[2] μὲν add. Eranius.

3. . . . and I, poor wretch, who should be dead, live on to be mocked by my foes . . .

Date unknown. The work must have consisted of a series of *loci communes* compiled by Antiphon for the benefit of pupils.

3. THE ART OF PUBLIC SPEAKING, IN THREE BOOKS

1. In his *Art of Public Speaking* Antiphon says: " We are naturally disposed to notice things present, to hand, and before us. But it is not natural to retain a clear image of them when they have gone from our sight."

2. . . . what has happened is confirmed by means of *tokens*, what will happen by means of *presumptions*.

Date unknown. At least one ancient authority was disposed to reject the work as spurious.

D. *Fragments of uncertain origin*

1. He besought you to have no pity on me, because he feared that I might try to move you by tears and entreaties.

2. . . . and knowing, on the other hand, that your laws were handed down to you from long ago by your forefathers . . .

3. For a while, you see, the long period seemed more plausible than the short.

APPENDIX

APPENDIX

NOTE

THE two following documents, which are known to-day from the Pseudo-Plutarch, who incorporates them in his life of Antiphon, can be traced back through Caecilius of Calactê to the σύνταγμα ψηφισμάτων or collection of Athenian historical inscriptions, compiled by Craterus, the brother of Antigonus Gonatas, in the third century B.C. The first is a resolution of the Boulê committing Antiphon, together with Archeptolemus and Onomacles, for trial in 411; the second, the official record of the sentence passed by the court upon Antiphon and Archeptolemus. As Craterus, to whom their first transcription was due, is known to have taken pains to be accurate, we need not doubt that both texts faithfully reproduce the fifth-century originals.

A

Ἔδοξε τῇ βουλῇ, μιᾷ καὶ εἰκοστῇ τῆς πρυτανείας,
Δημόνικος Ἀλωπεκῆθεν ἐγραμμάτευε, Φιλόστρατος
Παλληνεὺς[1] ἐπεστάτει, Ἄνδρων εἶπε· περὶ τῶν
ἀνδρῶν οὓς ἀποφαίνουσιν οἱ στρατηγοὶ πρεσβευο-
μένους εἰς Λακεδαίμονα ἐπὶ κακῷ τῆς πόλεως τῆς
Ἀθηναίων καὶ [ἐκ][2] τοῦ στρατοπέδου πλεῖν ἐπὶ
πολεμίας νεὼς καὶ πεζεῦσαι διὰ Δεκελείας, Ἀρχεπτόλεμον καὶ Ὀνομακλέα καὶ Ἀντιφῶντα συλ-
λαβεῖν καὶ ἀποδοῦναι εἰς τὸ δικαστήριον, ὅπως
δῶσι δίκην· παρασχόντων δ᾽ αὐτοὺς οἱ στρατηγοὶ
καὶ ἐκ τῆς βουλῆς οὕστινας ἂν δοκῇ[3] τοῖς στρατηγοῖς
προσελομένοις[4] μέχρι δέκα, ὅπως ἂν περὶ παρόντων
γένηται ἡ κρίσις· προσκαλεσάσθων δ᾽ αὐτοὺς οἱ
θεσμοθέται ἐν τῇ αὔριον ἡμέρᾳ, καὶ εἰσαγόντων,
ἐπειδὰν αἱ κλήσεις ἐξήκωσιν, εἰς τὸ δικαστήριον
περὶ προδοσίας. κατηγορεῖν ⟨δὲ⟩[5] τοὺς ᾑρημένους
συνηγόρους καὶ τοὺς στρατηγοὺς καὶ ἄλλος[6] ἄν
τις βούληται· ὅτου δ᾽ ἂν καταψηφίσηται τὸ δικα-

---

[1] Παλληνεὺς Taylor: Πελληνεὺς codd.
[2] ἐκ del. Reiske.   [3] δοκῇ Franke: δοκοῖ codd.
[4] προσελομένοις Reiske: προσελομένους codd.
[5] δὲ add. Emperius.
[6] ἄλλος Turnebus: ἄλλους codd.

---

[a] From the omission of the name of the tribe whose
Prytany it was, it has been argued that the opening words
314

A

RESOLVED by the Council on the twenty-first day of
the Prytany [a] : secretary, Demonicus of Alopecê :
president, Philostratus of Pallene : on the motion
of Andron. As touching those persons whom the
Generals show to have served as envoys to Sparta
with intent to harm the city of Athens and the
Athenian army, and to have taken passage for that
purpose in an enemy vessel and to have returned by
land through Decelea : Archeptolemus, Onomacles,
and Antiphon shall be arrested and handed over to
the court, to the end that they may be punished.
And the Generals and such members of the Council
as the Generals shall see fit to choose to assist them,
up to the number of ten, shall hold the accused in
readiness, to the end that they may stand their
trial in person. And on the day following this the
Thesmothetae shall issue to the accused a summons
to appear : and when the time allowed by the
summons shall have expired, they shall bring them
before the court on a charge of treason. And the
prosecutors appointed for the purpose, the Generals,
and anyone else who so desires shall accuse them.
And any of them who shall be found guilty by

of the decree are mutilated. Ferguson, however, shows
good reason for supposing it complete as it stands (see " The
Condemnation of Antiphon," **ap.** *Mélanges Glotz,* vol. i.).

στήριον, περὶ αὐτοῦ ποιεῖν κατὰ τὸν νόμον ὃς
κεῖται περὶ τῶν προδόντων.

B

Προδοσίας ὦφλον[1] Ἀρχεπτόλεμος Ἱπποδάμου
Ἀγρυλῆθεν παρών, Ἀντιφῶν Σοφίλου Ῥαμνούσιος
παρών. τούτοιν ἐτιμήθη τοῖς ἕνδεκα παραδοθῆναι
καὶ τὰ χρήματα δημόσια εἶναι καὶ τῆς θεοῦ τὸ
ἐπιδέκατον, καὶ τὼ οἰκία[2] κατασκάψαι αὐτοῖν,[3]
καὶ ὅρους θεῖναι ⟨ἐπὶ⟩[4] τοῖν οἰκοπέδοιν, ἐπιγρά-
ψαντας Ἀρχεπτολέμου καὶ Ἀντιφῶντος τοῖν
προδόταιν· τὼ δὲ δημάρχω[5] ἀποφῆναι τὴν οὐσίαν
αὐτοῖν[6]· καὶ μὴ ἐξεῖναι θάψαι Ἀρχεπτόλεμον καὶ
Ἀντιφῶντα Ἀθήνησι μηδ' ὅσης Ἀθηναῖοι κρα-
τοῦσι, καὶ ἄτιμον εἶναι Ἀρχεπτόλεμον καὶ Ἀντιφῶντα, καὶ γένος τὸ ἐκ τούτοιν, καὶ νόθους καὶ
γνησίους, καὶ ἐάν ⟨τις⟩[7] ποιήσηταί τινα τῶν ἐξ
Ἀρχεπτολέμου καὶ Ἀντιφῶντος, ἄτιμος ἔστω ὁ
ποιησάμενος. ταῦτα δὲ γράψαι ἐν στήλῃ χαλκῇ,
⟨καὶ⟩[8] ᾗπερ ἂν καὶ τὰ ψηφίσματα τὰ περὶ Φρυνίχου,
καὶ τοῦτο θέσθαι.

---

[1] ὦφλον Turnebus : ὦ φίλον codd.
[2] τὼ οἰκία Franke : τῷ οἰκίᾳ codd.
[3] αὐτοῖν Blass : αὐτῶν codd.   [4] ἐπὶ add. Blass.
[5] τὼ δὲ δημάρχω Meier : τῷ δὲ δημάρχῳ codd.

APPENDIX

the court shall be punished in accordance with the existing law which relates to traitors.

B

FOUND guilty of treason : Archeptolemus, son of Hippodamus, of Agrylê, being present : Antiphon, son of Sophilus, of Rhamnus, being present. The penalty was assessed as follows : the two prisoners shall be delivered to the Eleven : their goods shall be confiscated and a tithe given to the Goddess : their houses shall be rased to the ground and stones of record placed upon the sites of both, thus inscribed : " Here lived Archeptolemus and Antiphon, the traitors " : and the two Demarchs concerned shall make a return of their property. Furthermore it shall be unlawful to bury Archeptolemus and Antiphon at Athens or anywhere within the dominions of Athens. And Archeptolemus and Antiphon shall be disfranchised, and their issue likewise, whether born in wedlock or out of wedlock. And if any man shall adopt any of the issue of Archeptolemus or Antiphon, he who does so shall be disfranchised. This sentence to be inscribed upon a pillar of bronze and set up in the same place as the decrees concerning Phrynichus.

---

⁶ ἀποφῆναι τὴν οὐσίαν αὐτοῖν Westermann : ἀποφῆναί τε οἰκίαν ἐς τόν codd.
⁷ τις add. Blass.   ⁸ καὶ add. Reiske.

ANDOCIDES

LIFE OF ANDOCIDES

ANDOCIDES came of a family distinguished equally for its antiquity,[a] its wealth, and its record of public service. He himself was born shortly before the year 440 B.C.[b]; and, to judge from allusions in the comic poets [c] to his father's reputation as a *bon viveur*, he must have spent his early days in surroundings of elegance and comfort. Of his education nothing is known. Presumably, like most well-to-do young men of his time, he attached himself to one or more of the sophists who were generally to be found in Athens, and he may well have been acquainted with Socrates. But it is clear that his education was of a general kind, as befitted a man of leisure, and that his ability as a speaker was not the result of any elaborate course of study ; throughout his life, in fact, he always remained the talented amateur who regarded the professional rhetorician with disdain. By the time he had reached his twenties his political sympathies had already led him to join one of those ἑταιρεῖαι or " clubs " which were to play so important a part in the revolution

---

[a] It was said to have traced descent from Hermes.

[b] This date best suits the age of Andocides in 415, and is confirmed by [Lys.] vi. 46, where he is said to be " over forty " in 399.

[c] Ar. *Wasps* 1269 ; Plato Com. *Fr.* 106.

320

of 411 B.C. ; and it was to his fellow-members that
he delivered one of his first public speeches, the Πρὸς
τοὺς ἑταίρους, of which one or two fragments survive.
But it is by no means certain that his sympathies
were markedly oligarchic. A young aristocrat he
undoubtedly was, and as such he despised the up-
start demagogues who had succeeded Pericles ; but
he had none of Antiphon's remorseless hatred of
democracy. His references in later life to the
scandal of 415 which led to his exile, suggest, meagre
though they are, that at the age of twenty-five he
was merely a hot-headed young man-about-town
with more money than sense ; and when, after some
years of exile, he made his first two attempts to return
to Athens, it is significant that he appealed first to
the Four Hundred and then to the restored democracy. Indeed he seems to have been at heart a
moderate of the type of Theramenes, without his
political gifts, but with much of his astuteness.

Andocides' exile, his repeated efforts to return,
and his great struggle to prevent a second exile, or
worse, in 399, only four years after he had been
allowed to resume his rights as a citizen, are best
described by himself. After his acquittal in 399 he
was still vigorous and appears to have taken an
active part in public life. Thus we still possess a
speech which he delivered in the Ecclesia some eight
years later as a member of a delegation sent to
Sparta to arrange terms of peace ; in spite of their
possessing full authority, the delegates had preferred
to refer the Spartan proposals to the Ecclesia for
discussion, and Andocides explains their advantages
at length. The speech was clear and able ; but it
failed to carry conviction. We have it on the

authority of Philochorus that both he and his fellow-
delegates were banished from Attica upon the
motion of Callistratus. What became of him after
his second exile is unknown. He can still have been
little more than fifty ; but tradition preserves no
record of further attempts to return. We can only
surmise that he lived as he had in his younger days,
by his wits and the hospitality of his friends abroad.

I
ON THE MYSTERIES

INTRODUCTION

Andocides delivered his speech *On The Mysteries* in the year 399 B.C. He was pleading for his life, but he had a sympathetic audience and the facts upon which the case against him rested were by now remote enough to be half-forgotten. Given the necessary self-assurance, it was not difficult to construct a plausible defence, and the jury welcomed it—the men of the restored democracy were little inclined to unearth buried scandals. Andocides' explanations were accepted without too close a scrutiny, and he was acquitted.

In order to understand the circumstances which led to his appearance in court, it is necessary to go back some sixteen years. In 415, when the Sicilian expedition was about to leave Peiraeus, a double scandal came to light, with momentous effects not only upon the success of the expedition itself but upon the fortunes of Athens at large during the next two or three years. A certain Pythonicus stated before the Assembly that Alcibiades, one of the generals in command of the forces about to sail for the West, had recently parodied the Eleusinian Mysteries with a party of friends ; he produced an eyewitness to confirm his story. The result was a popular uproar ; Athens was an enlightened city, but she was not prepared to see a cult which gave

325

expression to her most intimate religious beliefs, exposed to deliberate ridicule. And the public indignation increased tenfold when it was further discovered that numbers of the stone images of Hermes scattered throughout Athens had been mutilated in a single night. A commission was hurriedly appointed to conduct an inquiry into both outrages, and rewards were offered for information.

The profanation of the Mysteries proved a simpler matter to investigate than the mutilation of the Hermae. Three informers came forward almost at once, each with a mock celebration to describe ; the names of the offenders were obtained ; and the few who had not already quitted the country were arrested and executed. Alcibiades, the first to be denounced, escaped ; and Athens had many occasions for regretting it in the troubled years which followed.

One of the three informers mentioned, a metic named Teucrus, also volunteered a statement with regard to the mutilation, and furnished the Council with a list of eighteen names. But almost immediately afterwards a certain Diocleides appeared with a much more elaborate story. Diocleides had, it seems, watched the criminals at work. There had been some three hundred in all, and as a preliminary he gave the names of forty-two. The result was a panic. An oligarchic plot was suspected, and precautions were hastily taken to prevent the possibility of an organized rising. Meanwhile the forty-two were arrested and thrown into prison.

Among them was Andocides, together with most of his family. Their situation looked desperate ; and Andocides adopted the only course open to him in the circumstances. He knew what the truth was ; so he offered to turn informer himself, on condition that he was guaranteed immunity. The offer was accepted ; and he had little difficulty in proving Diocleides' story a fabrication. There were actually only twenty-two criminals in all ; and eighteen of the twenty-two had been exposed by Teucrus.

Andocides was safe once more, in virtue of the immunity granted him by the Council. That he had had some connexion with the outrage is clear even from his words in the present speech ; from what he says elsewhere,[a] and from the remarks of Thucydides,[b] it is practically certain that he had taken an active part in it. But in spite of that, he was entitled to continue living in Athens under the protection of his ἄδεια. This state of affairs did not last long, however. During that same year a decree was proposed and carried by Isotimides to the effect that anyone who had committed impiety and confessed to it should be debarred from the temples of Attica and the Athenian Agora, whether he had been accorded an immunity or not. That is to say, his ἄδεια was still to hold good, in that his life and property were assured to him ; but the unexpiated defilement which lay upon him was to prevent him from participating in the political and religious life of the community.

The decree of Isotimides was clearly aimed at Andocides, and he found himself obliged to withdraw into exile. For over ten years he remained abroad, for the most part engaged in trade. Then, in 403, when the democracy was restored and a general amnesty proclaimed, he returned to Athens. He was accepted as a citizen without question,

<hr>

[a] *De Reditu*, §§ 7, 10. [b] vi. 60.

once more took up residence in the town-house of his family, and threw himself energetically into public life. But as time passed he made enemies. First he came into collision with a powerful syndicate of tax-farmers, headed by Agyrrhius, who had been drawing handsome profits until Andocides stepped in and outbid them for the contracts concerned ; then he earned the hatred of a certain Cephisius, who like himself had returned under the amnesty—possibly Andocides was urging the recovery of monies which Cephisius was known to have embezzled some years previously—; and finally he quarrelled with Callias, a distant relative of his by marriage and a member of what had once been one of the wealthiest families in Athens. This last feud came to a head when both Callias and Andocides claimed the right to one of the daughters of Andocides' uncle, Epilycus. Epilycus had died intestate ; and according to law his daughters had now to be given in marriage to the nearest surviving male relative, provided that he was not within the prohibited degrees. Andocides was a cousin : Callias the grandfather. Callias was debarred from marrying either of the daughters himself ; but he had a son for whom he thought the match would be eminently suitable.

There had been little love lost between Callias and Andocides even before this fresh dispute occurred ; and when Andocides intimated that he was about to bring the case into court, Callias decided to act. It was the beginning of October, the time of the Great Eleusinia. Andocides, who was an initiate, attended the celebration as he had been in the habit of doing since his return. But no sooner were the ceremonies at Eleusis over than he found that an information

ON THE MYSTERIES

had been lodged against him with the Basileus to the effect that he had taken part in rites from which he was automatically debarred by the decree of Isotimides. The information (ἔνδειξις) was due to Cephisius, who had received a thousand drachmae from Callias to bring the case, and with Cephisius were associated Agyrrhius and two others, Epichares and Meletus, both of whom had reasons for wishing Andocides out of the way.

To strengthen their position, the five went further. It was arranged that a suppliant's bough should be placed on the altar of the Eleusinium at Athens. Callias, acting in his official capacity as a member of the clan of the Heralds or Ceryces, would bring the matter to the notice of the Council, when it assembled there for its traditional meeting at the close of the Eleusinia; he would show that Andocides was responsible; and he would further declare that, according to Athenian religious law, the penalty for committing such an act during the festival was instant death.

The move proved unfortunate. On being questioned, Callias was unable to prove that Andocides was the offender; it was further pointed out that Callias was a Ceryx, not a Eumolpid, and had therefore no right to interpret the law; while in any event his interpretation was wrong—the penalty for the crime in question was not death, but a fine. Callias and Cephisius were thus forced to fall back upon their original ἔνδειξις ἀσεβείας. This came before the Heliaea in due course; the jury was composed of initiates, and the Basileus presided.

We can gain a reasonably accurate idea of the line of attack chosen by the prosecution, partly from the reply of Andocides himself and partly from the *In Andocidem*, wrongly attributed to Lysias. In all probability this last was actually delivered at the trial, although as a δευτερολογία or supporting speech. The prosecution set out to prove two things : first, that Andocides had been genuinely guilty of impiety in 415, and was therefore liable to the penalties prescribed by the decree of Isotimides : secondly, that he was not entitled to protection under the amnesty of 403. With regard to their first point, they produced evidence to show that Andocides had been concerned not only in the mutilation of the Hermae, but in the profanation of the Mysteries as well ; with regard to their second, they took the line that the amnesty was the result of an agreement between two specific parties, " the men of the City " and " the men of Peiraeus," and as such was intended to benefit them and them alone. Andocides had belonged to neither party ; and he was not entitled to protection.

Andocides replies to each of these points in turn. He first shows that he had no connexion whatsoever with the profanation of the Mysteries, and next to none with the mutilation, and that therefore the decree of Isotimides had never affected him. This of course misrepresents the facts ; had he not been guilty of impiety to at least some extent, he would have had no cause for withdrawing into exile after the passing of the decree. But luckily the prosecution had made the tactical error of introducing the profanation of the Mysteries, with which Andocides had in fact had nothing to do ; and the refutation of their charges in this connexion gives him ample opportunity for thrusting other awkward facts into the background.

Next he turns to the question of the amnesty, a crucial one. It mattered little whether he could clear himself completely with regard to the events of 415, provided that he could convince the court that there were no legal grounds for proceeding against him in 399. The position is examined in §§ 70-91.

First comes a detailed analysis of the various forms which disfranchisement could take. It is then shown that citizens suffering from the disabilities in question were reinstated by the decree of Patrocleides, passed after the battle of Aegospotami in 405. Next we have the general restoration of exiles in 404 at Spartan dictation, followed by the repeal of all laws earlier than the archonship of Eucleides (July 403), and the drafting of a fresh code to meet present circumstances. Lastly there is the oath taken by the City-party and the Peiraeus-party to bury all differences.

Strictly speaking, none of these facts were relevant to Andocides' case ; and the prosecution had touched upon a very real weakness in his position when they maintained that the amnesty was limited in its application. Andocides had suffered disfranchisement (ἀτιμία) owing to the defilement incurred for an act of impiety ; and in many respects his offence corresponded closely with homicide, which also brought defilement upon the guilty party. Now it is noteworthy that the decree of Patrocleides expressly excludes persons exiled for homicide in its definition of the classes of disfranchised citizens which it proposes to reinstate ; it is concerned solely with state-debtors and political offenders. Similarly, the restoration of exiles in 404 was a purely political move, as was the revision of the legal code which followed. And the oath taken by the two parties, although sweeping in its terms, was intended primarily to effect a reunion between hitherto hostile factions within the state. The truth is that exiles like Andocides formed too limited a class to attract attention among the graver issues of the moment ; and when a test-case such as the present came into court, there were, properly speaking, no legal precedents for deciding it. It is true that a decree was hurried through the Assembly in 403 by Archinus, stating that the terms of the amnesty were to be so interpreted as to forbid the re-opening of civil actions decided previously, and thus a number of those prosecuted for crimes committed before 403 were enabled to claim protection ; but there was still much room for doubt and perplexity. Everything must have depended upon individual cases and the personal likes and dislikes of jurors. In the present instance, Andocides, who had proved himself a useful member of the community since his return, found that the court was prepared to treat him generously. Its verdict was in his favour ; and his opponents were forced to accept their defeat with such grace as they could. No further attempt was made to recall to the public mind the scandal of 415.

――――――

NOTE.—The accompanying tables show (I) those members of the family of Andocides whose names appeared among the forty-two given by Diocleides, (II) the connexion between the families of Callias, Andocides, and Epilycus.

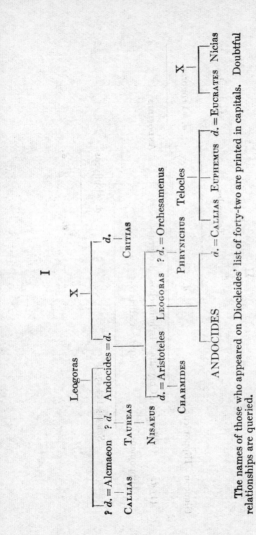

I

The names of those who appeared on Diocleides' list of forty-two are printed in capitals. Doubtful relationships are queried.

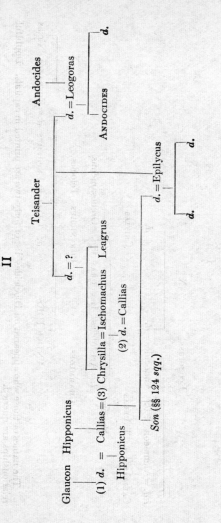

II

ANALYSIS

ΠΕΡΙ ΤΩΝ ΜΥΣΤΗΡΙΩΝ

Τὴν μὲν παρασκευήν, ὦ ἄνδρες, καὶ τὴν προθυμίαν τῶν ἐχθρῶν τῶν ἐμῶν, ὥστ' ἐμὲ κακῶς ποιεῖν ἐκ παντὸς τρόπου, καὶ δικαίως καὶ ἀδίκως, ἐξ ἀρχῆς ἐπειδὴ τάχιστα ἀφικόμην εἰς τὴν πόλιν ταυτηνί, σχεδόν τι πάντες ἐπίστασθε, καὶ οὐδὲν δεῖ περὶ τούτων πολλοὺς λόγους ποιεῖσθαι· ἐγὼ δέ, ὦ ἄνδρες, δεήσομαι ὑμῶν δίκαια καὶ ὑμῖν τε ῥᾴδια χαρίζεσθαι καὶ ἐμοὶ ἄξια πολλοῦ τυχεῖν παρ' 2 ὑμῶν. καὶ πρῶτον μὲν ἐνθυμηθῆναι ὅτι νῦν ἐγὼ ἥκω οὐδεμιᾶς μοι ἀνάγκης οὔσης παραμεῖναι, οὔτ' ἐγγυητὰς καταστήσας οὔθ' ὑπὸ δεσμῶν ἀναγκασθείς, πιστεύσας δὲ μάλιστα μὲν τῷ δικαίῳ, ἔπειτα δὲ καὶ ὑμῖν, γνώσεσθαι τὰ δίκαια καὶ μὴ περιόψεσθαί με ἀδίκως ὑπὸ τῶν ἐχθρῶν τῶν ἐμῶν διαφθαρέντα, ἀλλὰ πολὺ μᾶλλον σώσειν δικαίως κατά τε τοὺς νόμους τοὺς ὑμετέρους καὶ τοὺς ὅρκους οὓς ὑμεῖς ὀμόσαντες μέλλετε τὴν ψῆφον οἴσειν.

3 Εἰκότως δ' ἄν, ὦ ἄνδρες, τὴν αὐτὴν γνώμην

---

[a] Four years earlier, in 403.

[b] Much of §§ 1, 6, 7, and 9 consists of *loci communes* which recur in Lysias and Isocrates. Both they and Andocides were making use of the same handbook of proems.

ON THE MYSTERIES

THE systematic and untiring efforts of my enemies, gentlemen, to do me every possible injury, by fair means or by foul, from the very moment of my arrival in this city,[a] are known to almost all of you, and it is unnecessary for me to pursue the subject. Instead, I shall make a request of you, gentlemen, a fair request, which it is as easy for you to grant as it is valuable for me to gain.[b] First, I ask you to bear in mind that it is not because I have been forced to face my trial that I am here to-day—I have not been on bail, nor have I been kept in confinement.[c] I am here, first and foremost because I rely upon justice : and secondly because I rely upon you ; I believe that you will decide my case impartially and, far sooner than allow my enemies to defy justice by taking my life, will uphold justice by protecting me, as your laws and your oaths as jurors require you to do.

With defendants who face a trial of their own free

[c] This was not customary in a case of ἔνδειξις. The accused, if a citizen, was usually given the choice of furnishing sureties (ἐγγυηταί) or suffering imprisonment until the case came into court. Possibly it was felt that the conditions in the present instance were exceptional and that Andocides should be allowed the opportunity of quitting Attica if he so desired.

ἔχοιτε περὶ τῶν ἐθελοντῶν[1] εἰς τοὺς κινδύνους καθ-
ισταμένων, ἥνπερ[2] αὐτοὶ περὶ αὐτῶν ἔχουσιν.
ὁπόσοι μὲν γὰρ μὴ ἠθέλησαν ὑπομεῖναι καταγνόντες αὐτῶν ἀδικίαν, εἰκότως τοι καὶ ὑμεῖς
τοιαῦτα περὶ αὐτῶν γιγνώσκετε οἷά[3] περ καὶ αὐτοὶ
περὶ σφῶν αὐτῶν ἔγνωσαν· ὁπόσοι δὲ πιστεύσαντες
μηδὲν ἀδικεῖν ὑπέμειναν, δίκαιοί ἐστε καὶ ὑμεῖς
περὶ τούτων τοιαύτην ἔχειν τὴν γνώμην οἵαν περ
καὶ αὐτοὶ περὶ αὐτῶν ἔσχον, καὶ μὴ προκατα-
4 γιγνώσκειν ἀδικεῖν. αὐτίκα ἐγὼ πολλῶν μοι
ἀπαγγελλόντων ὅτι λέγοιεν οἱ ἐχθροὶ ὡς ἄρα ἐγὼ
οὔτ' ἂν ὑπομείναιμι οἰχήσομαί τε φεύγων,—" τί
γὰρ ἂν καὶ βουλόμενος Ἀνδοκίδης ἀγῶνα τοσοῦτον
ὑπομείνειεν, ᾧ ἔξεστι μὲν ἀπελθόντι ἐντεῦθεν ἔχειν
πάντα τὰ ἐπιτήδεια, ἔστι δὲ πλεύσαντι εἰς Κύπρον,
ὅθεν περ ἥκει, γῆ[4] πολλὴ καὶ ἀγαθὴ διδομένη καὶ
δωρεὰν[5] ὑπάρχουσα; οὗτος ἄρα βουλήσεται περὶ
τοῦ σώματος τοῦ ἑαυτοῦ κινδυνεῦσαι; εἰς τί
ἀποβλέψας; οὐχ ὁρᾷ τὴν πόλιν ἡμῶν ὡς διά-
5 κειται; " ἐγὼ δέ, ὦ ἄνδρες, πολὺ τὴν ἐναντίαν
τούτοις γνώμην ἔχω. ἄλλοθί τε γὰρ ὢν πάντα
τὰ ἀγαθὰ ἔχειν στερόμενος τῆς πατρίδος οὐκ ἂν
δεξαίμην· τῆς ⟨τε⟩[6] πόλεως οὕτω διακειμένης ὥσπερ
αὐτοὶ οἱ ἐχθροὶ λέγουσι, πολύ γ' ἂν[7] αὐτῆς μᾶλλον
ἐγὼ πολίτης δεξαίμην εἶναι ἢ ἑτέρων πόλεων, αἳ
ἴσως πάνυ μοι δοκοῦσιν ἐν τῷ παρόντι εὐτυχεῖν,
ἅπερ γιγνώσκων ἐπέτρεψα διαγνῶναι ὑμῖν περὶ
τοῦ σώματος τοῦ ἐμαυτοῦ.

---

[1] ἐθελοντῶν Bekker : ἐθελόντων codd.
[2] ἥνπερ Ald. : ἥπερ codd.   [3] οἷά Bekker : ὅσα codd.
[4] γῆ Valckenaer et Reiske : ἢ codd.
[5] δωρεὰν Reiske : δωρεᾶ codd.
[6] τε add. Sluiter.   [7] γ' ἂν Valckenaer : δ' ἂν codd.

will, gentlemen, it stands to reason that you should feel as convinced of their innocence as they do themselves. When a defendant admits himself guilty by refusing to await trial, you naturally endorse the verdict which he has passed upon himself; so it follows that if a man is prepared to face his trial because his conscience is clear, you should let his verdict upon himself determine your own in the same way, instead of presuming him guilty. Mine is a case in point. My enemies have been saying, or so I keep hearing, that I would take to my heels instead of standing my ground. "What motive could Andocides possibly have for braving so hazardous a trial?" they argue. "He can count upon a livelihood sufficient for all his needs, if he does no more than withdraw from Attica; while if he returns to Cyprus whence he has come,[a] an abundance of good land has been offered him and is his for the asking. Will a man in his position want to risk his life? What object could he have in doing so? Cannot he see the state of things in Athens?" That entirely misrepresents my feelings, gentlemen. I would never consent to a life abroad which cut me off from my country, whatever the advantages attached to it; and although conditions in Athens may be what my enemies allege, I would far sooner be a citizen of hers than of any other state which may appear to me to be just now at the height of prosperity. Those are the feelings which have led me to place my life in your hands.

[a] The *De Reditu* shows that Andocides had spent a considerable time in Cyprus during his years of exile. He was on very friendly terms with Evagoras, who had succeeded in regaining the throne of Salamis in 410. Evagoras was notoriously eager to attract likely Greek settlers.

6 Αἰτοῦμαι οὖν ὑμᾶς, ὦ ἄνδρες, εὔνοιαν πλείω
παρασχέσθαι ἐμοὶ τῷ ἀπολογουμένῳ ἢ τοῖς κατηγόροις, εἰδότας ὅτι κἂν ἐξ ἴσου ἀκροᾶσθε, ἀνάγκη
τὸν ἀπολογούμενον ἔλαττον ἔχειν. οἱ μὲν γὰρ ἐκ
πολλοῦ χρόνου ἐπιβουλεύσαντες καὶ συνθέντες,
αὐτοὶ ἄνευ κινδύνων ὄντες, τὴν κατηγορίαν ἐποιή-
σαντο· ἐγὼ δὲ μετὰ δέους καὶ κινδύνου καὶ διαβολῆς
τῆς μεγίστης τὴν ἀπολογίαν ποιοῦμαι. εἰκὸς οὖν
ὑμᾶς ἐστιν εὔνοιαν πλείω παρασχέσθαι ἐμοὶ ἢ τοῖς
κατηγόροις.

7 Ἔτι δὲ καὶ τόδε ἐνθυμητέον, ὅτι πολλοὶ ἤδη
πολλὰ καὶ δεινὰ κατηγορήσαντες παραχρῆμα
[2] ἐξηλέγχθησαν ψευδόμενοι οὕτω φανερῶς, ὥστε
ὑμᾶς πολὺ ἂν ἥδιον δίκην λαβεῖν παρὰ τῶν
κατηγόρων ἢ παρὰ τῶν κατηγορουμένων· οἱ δὲ αὖ,
μαρτυρήσαντες τὰ ψευδῆ ἀδίκως ἀνθρώπους ἀπολέσαντες, ἑάλωσαν παρ' ὑμῖν ψευδομαρτυρίων,
ἡνίκ' οὐδὲν ἦν ἔτι πλέον τοῖς πεπονθόσιν. ὁπότ'
οὖν ἤδη πολλὰ τοιαῦτα γεγένηται,[1] εἰκὸς ὑμᾶς
ἐστι μήπω τοὺς τῶν κατηγόρων λόγους πιστοὺς
ἡγεῖσθαι. εἰ μὲν γὰρ δεινὰ κατηγόρηται ἢ μή,
οἷόν τε γνῶναι ἐκ τῶν τοῦ κατηγόρου λόγων· εἰ
δὲ ἀληθῆ ταῦτά ἐστιν ἢ ψευδῆ, οὐχ οἷόν τε ὑμᾶς
πρότερον εἰδέναι πρὶν ἂν καὶ ἐμοῦ ἀκούσητε
ἀπολογουμένου.

8 Σκοπῶ μὲν οὖν ἔγωγε, ὦ ἄνδρες, πόθεν χρὴ
ἄρξασθαι τῆς ἀπολογίας, πότερον ἐκ τῶν τελευ-
ταίων λόγων, ὡς παρανόμως με ἐνέδειξαν, ἢ περὶ
τοῦ ψηφίσματος τοῦ Ἰσοτιμίδου, ὡς ἄκυρόν ἐστιν,
ἢ περὶ τῶν νόμων καὶ τῶν ὅρκων τῶν γεγενημένων,

---

[1] γεγένηται Dobree, coll. Lysias xix. 4: γεγένηνται codd.

I ask you, then, to show more sympathy to me, the defendant, gentlemen, than to my accusers, in the knowledge that even if you give us an impartial hearing, the defence is inevitably at a disadvantage. The prosecution have brought their charge in perfect safety, after elaborating their plans at leisure ; whereas I who am answering that charge am filled with fear ; my life is at stake, and I have been grossly misrepresented. You have good reason for showing more sympathy to me than you do to my accusers.

And there is another thing to be borne in mind. Serious charges have often before now been disproved at once, and so decisively that you would much rather have punished the accusers than the accused. Again, witnesses have caused the death of innocent men by giving false evidence, and have only been convicted of perjury when it was too late to be of help to the victims. When this kind of thing has been so common, you can hardly do less than refuse for the present to consider the prosecution's statement of the case trustworthy. You may use it to judge whether the charge is serious or not ; but you cannot tell whether the charge is true or false until you have heard my reply as well.

Now I am wondering at what point to begin my defence, gentlemen. Shall I start with what ought to be discussed last and prove that the prosecution disobeyed the law in lodging their information against me ?[a] Shall I take the decree of Isotimides and show that it has been annulled ? Shall I start with the laws which have been passed and the oaths which

---

[a] A reference, apparently, to the amnesty of 403. According to Andocides, it debarred the prosecution from reopening his case.

εἴτε καὶ ἐξ ἀρχῆς ὑμᾶς διδάξω τὰ γεγενημένα.
ὃ δέ με ποιεῖ μάλιστ' ἀπορεῖν, ἐγὼ ὑμῖν ἐρῶ, ὅτι
οὐ πάντες ἴσως ἐπὶ πᾶσι τοῖς κατηγορουμένοις
ὁμοίως ὀργίζεσθε, ἀλλ' ἕκαστός τι ὑμῶν ἔχει πρὸς
ὃ βούλοιτο ἄν με πρῶτον ἀπολογεῖσθαι· ἅμα δὲ
περὶ πάντων εἰπεῖν ἀδύνατον. κράτιστον οὖν μοι
εἶναι δοκεῖ ἐξ ἀρχῆς ὑμᾶς διδάσκειν πάντα τὰ
γενόμενα καὶ παραλείπειν μηδέν. ἂν γὰρ ὀρθῶς
μάθητε τὰ πραχθέντα, ῥᾳδίως γνώσεσθ' ἅ μου
κατεψεύσαντο οἱ κατήγοροι.

9 Τὰ μὲν οὖν δίκαια γιγνώσκειν ὑμᾶς ἡγοῦμαι
καὶ αὐτοὺς¹ παρεσκευάσθαι, οἷσπερ ἐγὼ πιστεύσας
ὑπέμεινα, ὁρῶν ὑμᾶς καὶ ἐν τοῖς ἰδίοις καὶ ἐν τοῖς
δημοσίοις περὶ πλείστου τοῦτο ποιουμένους, ψηφίζεσθαι κατὰ τοὺς ὅρκους· ὅπερ καὶ συνέχει
μόνον τὴν πόλιν, ἀκόντων τῶν οὐ βουλομένων
ταῦτα οὕτως ἔχειν. τάδε δὲ ὑμῶν δέομαι, μετ'
εὐνοίας μου τὴν ἀκρόασιν τῆς ἀπολογίας ποιήσασθαι, καὶ μήτ' ἐμοὶ ἀντιδίκους καταστῆναι μήτε
ὑπονοεῖν τὰ λεγόμενα μήτε ῥήματα θηρεύειν,
ἀκροασαμένους δὲ διὰ τέλους τῆς ἀπολογίας τότε
ἤδη ψηφίζεσθαι τοῦτο ὅ τι ἂν ὑμῖν αὐτοῖς ἄριστον
10 καὶ εὐορκότατον νομίζητε εἶναι. ὥσπερ δὲ καὶ
προεῖπον ὑμῖν, ὦ ἄνδρες, ἐξ ἀρχῆς περὶ πάντων
ποιήσομαι τὴν ἀπολογίαν, πρῶτον μὲν περὶ αὐτῆς
τῆς αἰτίας ὅθεν περ ἡ ἔνδειξις ἐγένετο, διόπερ εἰς
τὸν ἀγῶνα τόνδε κατέστην, περὶ τῶν μυστηρίων
ὡς οὔτ' ἐμοὶ ἠσέβηται οὐδὲν οὔτε μεμήνυται οὔθ'

¹ καὶ αὐτοὺς Emperius: καὶ λόγους codd.

have been taken ? Or shall I tell you the story right from the beginning ? I will explain the chief reason for my hesitation. Doubtless the different charges made have not moved you all to the same degree, and each of you has some one of them to which he would like me to reply first ; yet to answer them all simultaneously is impossible. On the whole, I think it best to tell you the entire story from the beginning, omitting nothing ; once you are properly acquainted with the facts, you will see immediately how unfounded are the charges which my accusers have brought against me.

Now to return a just verdict is already, I feel sure, your intention ; indeed, it was because I relied upon you that I stood my ground. I have observed that in suits public and private the one thing to which you attach supreme importance is that your decision should accord with your oath ; and it is that, and that alone, which keeps our city unshaken, in spite of those who would have things otherwise. I do, however, ask you to listen to my defence with sympathy ; do not range yourselves with my opponents ; do not view my story with suspicion ; do not watch for faults of expression. Hear my defence to the end : and only then return the verdict which you think best befits yourselves and best satisfies your oath. As I have already told you, gentlemen, my defence will begin at the beginning and omit nothing. I shall deal first with the actual charge which furnished grounds for the lodging of the information that has brought me into court to-day, profanation of the Mysteries. I shall show that I have committed no act of impiety, that I have never turned informer, that I have never admitted guilt, and that I do not

345

ὡμολόγηται, οὐδ' οἶδα[1] τοὺς μηνύσαντας ὑμῖν περὶ
αὐτῶν οὔτ' εἰ ψευδῆ οὔτ' εἰ ἀληθῆ ἐμήνυσαν· ταῦθ'
ὑμᾶς διδάξω.

11 Ἦν μὲν γὰρ ἐκκλησία τοῖς στρατηγοῖς τοῖς εἰς
Σικελίαν, Νικίᾳ καὶ Λαμάχῳ καὶ Ἀλκιβιάδῃ,
καὶ τριήρης ἡ στρατηγὶς ἤδη ἐξώρμει ἡ Λαμάχου·
ἀναστὰς δὲ Πυθόνικος ἐν τῷ δήμῳ εἶπεν '' ὦ
Ἀθηναῖοι, ὑμεῖς μὲν στρατιὰν ἐκπέμπετε καὶ
παρασκευὴν τοσαύτην, καὶ κίνδυνον ἀρεῖσθαι[2]
μέλλετε· Ἀλκιβιάδην δὲ τὸν στρατηγὸν ἀποδείξω
ὑμῖν τὰ μυστήρια ποιοῦντα ἐν οἰκίᾳ μεθ' ἑτέρων,
καὶ ἐὰν ψηφίσησθε ἄδειαν ⟨ᾧ⟩[3] ἐγὼ κελεύω,
θεράπων ὑμῖν ἑνὸς τῶν ἐνθάδε ἀνδρῶν[4] ἀμύητος
ὢν ἐρεῖ τὰ μυστήρια· εἰ δὲ μή, χρῆσθέ μοι[5] ὅ τι ἂν
12 ὑμῖν δοκῇ, ἐὰν μὴ τἀληθῆ λέγω.'' ἀντιλέγοντος
δὲ Ἀλκιβιάδου πολλὰ καὶ ἐξάρνου ὄντος ἔδοξε
τοῖς πρυτάνεσι τοὺς μὲν ἀμυήτους μεταστήσασθαι,
αὐτοὺς δ' ἰέναι ἐπὶ τὸ μειράκιον ὃ ὁ Πυθόνικος
ἐκέλευε. καὶ ᾤχοντο, καὶ ἤγαγον θεράποντα
Ἀρχεβιάδου ⟨τοῦ⟩ Πολεμάρχου[6]· Ἀνδρόμαχος αὐτῷ
ὄνομα ἦν. ἐπεὶ δὲ ἐψηφίσαντο αὐτῷ τὴν ἄδειαν,

---

[1] οὐδ' οἶδα Blass, coll. § 29 : οὔτ' οἶδα codd.
[2] ἀρεῖσθαι Bekker : αἱρεῖσθαι codd.
[3] ᾧ add. Bekker.
[4] ἐνθάδε ἑνὸς τῶν ἀνδρῶν Blass, ft. recte.
[5] χρῆσθέ μοι Hickie, coll. § 26 : χρῆσθ' ἐμοὶ codd.
[6] Ἀρχεβιάδου τοῦ Πολεμάρχου Marchant: Ἀρχεβιάδου πρὸς
τὸν πολέμαρχον Helbig : [ἀλκιβιάδου] Πολεμάρχου Bekker :
ἀλκιβιάδου πολέμαρχον codd.

---

[a] June, 415 B.C. Andocides is our only authority for this
last-minute meeting of the Assembly. It was probably
convened to make final arrangements for the expedition.

[b] The word ἄδεια is used in two slightly different senses.
(a) It is the immunity granted by the Assembly or Council

346

know whether the statements made to you by those who did turn informers were true or false. Of all this you shall have proof.

The Assembly had met *a* to give audience to Nicias, Lamachus, and Alcibiades, the generals about to leave with the Sicilian expedition—in fact, Lamachus' flag-ship was already lying off-shore—when suddenly Pythonicus rose before the people and cried : "Countrymen, you are sending forth this mighty host in all its array upon a perilous enterprise. Yet your commander, Alcibiades, has been holding celebrations of the Mysteries in a private house, and others with him ; I will prove it. Grant immunity *b* to him whom I indicate, and a non-initiate, a slave belonging to someone here present, shall describe the Mysteries to you. You can punish me as you will, if that is not the truth." Alcibiades denied the charge at great length ; so the Prytanes *c* decided to clear the meeting of non-initiates and themselves fetch the lad indicated by Pythonicus. They went off, and returned with a slave belonging to Archebiades, son of Polemarchus. His name was Andromachus. As soon as immunity had been voted him,

to persons who have a statement to make to them, but who are debarred from addressing them without special permission. This applied to slaves, metics, and women. Hence Andromachus, Teucrus, and Agariste all have to obtain an ἄδεια before lodging their information. (*b*) It is the immunity granted to a criminal who is prepared to turn informer. Often the two senses are combined, as here ; Andromachus was both debarred from addressing the Assembly in normal circumstances, and he was implicated in the crime which he was exposing. The same applies to Teucrus.

c That section of the βουλή which presided at meetings of the Ecclesia for the time being. For further details see Antiphon, *Choreutes*, p. 280, note *a*.

ἔλεγεν ὅτι ἐν τῇ οἰκίᾳ τῇ Πουλυτίωνος γίγνοιτο
μυστήρια· Ἀλκιβιάδην μὲν οὖν καὶ Νικιάδην καὶ
Μέλητον, τούτους μὲν αὐτοὺς εἶναι τοὺς ποιοῦντας,
συμπαρεῖναι δὲ καὶ ὁρᾶν τὰ γιγνόμενα καὶ ἄλλους,
παρεῖναι δὲ καὶ δούλους, ἑαυτόν τε καὶ τὸν ἀδελφὸν
καὶ Ἱκέσιον τὸν αὐλητὴν καὶ τὸν Μελήτου δοῦλον.

13   Πρῶτος[1] μὲν οὗτος ταῦτα ἐμήνυσε, καὶ ἀπέγραψε
[3] τούτους· ὧν Πολύστρατος μὲν συνελήφθη καὶ
ἀπέθανεν, οἱ δὲ ἄλλοι φεύγοντες ᾤχοντο, καὶ
αὐτῶν ὑμεῖς θάνατον κατέγνωτε. καί μοι λαβὲ
καὶ ἀνάγνωθι αὐτῶν τὰ ὀνόματα.

   ONOMATA.—Τούσδε Ἀνδρόμαχος ἐμήνυσεν· Ἀλκιβιάδην, Νικιάδην, Μέλητον, Ἀρχεβιάδην, Ἄρχ-
   ιππον, Διογένη, Πολύστρατον, Ἀριστομένη, Οἰωνίαν,[2]
   Παναίτιον.

14   Πρώτη μέν, ὦ ἄνδρες, μήνυσις ἐγένετο αὕτη
ὑπὸ Ἀνδρομάχου κατὰ τούτων τῶν ἀνδρῶν. καί
μοι κάλει Διόγνητον.

   Ἦσθα ζητητής, ὦ Διόγνητε, ὅτε Πυθόνικος εἰσ-
   ήγγειλεν ἐν τῷ δήμῳ περὶ Ἀλκιβιάδου ;
   Ἦ.[3]
   Οἶσθα οὖν μηνύσαντα Ἀνδρόμαχον τὰ ἐν τῇ οἰκίᾳ τῇ
   Πουλυτίωνος γιγνόμενα ;
   Οἶδα.

---

[1] πρῶτος A corr.: πρῶτον A pr.
[2] Οἰωνίαν Kirchoff e titulis poletarum : ἰωνίαν codd.
[3] ἦ Blass: ἦν codd.

---

[a] The names of a number of those whose goods were
confiscated and sold after the mutilation of the Hermae have
survived on a fragmentary inscription (*I.G.* i². 327, 332).
They confirm the lists given by Andocides. Oeonias,

348

he stated that Mysteries had been celebrated in Pulytion's house. Alcibiades, Niciades, and Meletus —those were the actual celebrants ; but others had been present and had witnessed what took place. The audience had also included slaves, namely, himself, his brother, the flute-player Hicesius, and Meletus' slave.

Such was the statement of Andromachus, the first of the informers. He gave the following list of persons concerned,[a] all of whom, save Polystratus, fled the country and were sentenced to death by you in their absence ; Polystratus was arrested and executed. Take the list, please, and read out their names.[b]

NAMES.—The following were denounced by Andromachus: Alcibiades, Niciades, Meletus, Archebiades, Archippus, Diogenes, Polystratus, Aristomenes, Oeonias, Panaetius.

This was the first information, gentlemen ; it was due to Andromachus, and implicated the persons mentioned. Now call Diognetus, please.

You were on the commission of inquiry,[c] Diognetus, when Pythonicus impeached Alcibiades before the Assembly ?
Yes.
You recollect that Andromachus laid an information as to what was going on in Pulytion's house ?
Yes.

Panaetius, and Polystratus are mentioned from the list of Andromachus : Axiochus, Adeimantus, Cephisodorus, and Euphiletus from the later lists of Teucrus and Andocides himself.

[b] Addressed to the γραμματεύς or clerk of the court.

[c] An extraordinary board of ζητηταί was set up to investigate both the profanation of the Mysteries and the mutilation of the Hermae ; they would act as an advisory committee to the βουλή. Peisander and Charicles were also members (§ 36).

Τὰ ὀνόματα οὖν τῶν ἀνδρῶν ἐστι ταῦτα, καθ' ὧν
ἐκεῖνος ἐμήνυσεν;

Ἔστι ταῦτα.

15 Δευτέρα τοίνυν μήνυσις ἐγένετο. Τεῦκρος ἦν
ἐνθάδε μέτοικος, ὃς ᾤχετο Μέγαράδε ὑπεξελθών,
ἐκεῖθεν δὲ ἐπαγγέλλεται τῇ βουλῇ, εἴ οἱ ἄδειαν
δοῖεν, μηνύσειν περὶ ⟨τε⟩[1] τῶν μυστηρίων, συνεργὸς
ὤν, καὶ τοὺς ἄλλους τοὺς ποιοῦντας μεθ' ἑαυτοῦ,
καὶ περὶ τῶν Ἑρμῶν τῆς περικοπῆς ἃ ᾔδει.
ψηφισαμένης δὲ τῆς βουλῆς—ἦν γὰρ αὐτοκράτωρ—
ᾤχοντο ἐπ' αὐτὸν Μέγαράδε· καὶ κομισθείς,
ἄδειαν εὑρόμενος, ἀπογράφει τοὺς μεθ' ἑαυτοῦ.
καὶ οὗτοι κατὰ τὴν Τεύκρου μήνυσιν ᾤχοντο
φεύγοντες. καί μοι λαβὲ καὶ ἀνάγνωθι τὰ
ὀνόματα αὐτῶν.

ΟΝΟΜΑΤΑ.—Τούσδε Τεῦκρος ἐμήνυσε· Φαῖδρον, Γνι-
φωνίδην, Ἰσόνομον, Ἡφαιστόδωρον, Κηφισόδωρον,
ἑαυτόν, Διόγνητον, Σμινδυρίδην, Φιλοκράτη, Ἀντιφῶντα, Τείσαρχον, Παντακλέα.

Μέμνησθε δέ, ὦ ἄνδρες, ὅτι[2] καὶ ταῦθ' ὑμῖν
προσομολογεῖται ἅπαντα.

16 Τρίτη μήνυσις ἐγένετο. ἡ γυνὴ Ἀλκμεωνίδου,[3]
γενομένη δὲ καὶ Δάμωνος—Ἀγαρίστη ὄνομα
αὐτῇ—αὕτη ἐμήνυσεν ἐν τῇ οἰκίᾳ τῇ Χαρμίδου
τῇ παρὰ τὸ Ὀλύμπιεῖον[4] μυστήρια ποιεῖν Ἀλκι-

---

[1] τε add. Blass, coll. § 34.   [2] ὅτι om. A pr.
[3] Ἀλκμεωνίδου Blass: ἀλκμαιονίδου codd.
[4] Ὀλύμπιεῖον Reiske: ὀλύμπιον codd.

And these are the names of those implicated by that information ?

Yes.

A second information followed. An alien named Teucrus, resident in Athens, quietly withdrew to Megara. From Megara he informed the Council that if immunity were granted him, he was prepared not only to lodge an information with regard to the Mysteries—as one of the participants, he would reveal the names of his companions—but he would also tell what he knew of the mutilation of the Hermae. The Council, which had supreme powers at the time, voted acceptance ; and messengers were sent to Megara to fetch him. He was brought to Athens, and on being granted immunity, furnished a list of his associates. No sooner had Teucrus denounced them than they fled the country. Take the list, please, and read out their names.

NAMES.—The following were denounced by Teucrus Phaedrus, Gniphonides, Isonomus, Hephaestodorus, Cephisodorus, himself, Diognetus, Smindyrides, Philocrates, Antiphon,[a] Teisarchus, Pantacles.

Let me remind you, gentlemen, that you are receiving confirmation of these further facts in every detail.[b]

A third information followed. According to the wife of Alcmaeonides—she had previously been married to Damon and was named Agariste—according, as I say, to Alcmaeonides' wife, Alcibiades, Axiochus, and Adeimantus celebrated Mysteries in Charmides'

---

[a] Not, of course, the orator.

[b] i.e. Diognetus, who had first-hand knowledge, had listened to the recital in silence.

βιάδην καὶ ᾿Αξίοχον καὶ ᾿Αδείμαντον· καὶ ἔφυγον[1]
οὗτοι πάντες ἐπὶ ταύτῃ τῇ μηνύσει.

17 Ἔτι μήνυσις ἐγένετο μία. Λυδὸς ὁ Φερεκλέους
τοῦ Θημακέως ἐμήνυσε μυστήρια γίγνεσθαι ἐν τῇ
οἰκίᾳ Φερεκλέους τοῦ δεσπότου τοῦ ἑαυτοῦ, ἐν
Θημακῷ· καὶ ἀπογράφει τούς τε ἄλλους, καὶ τὸν
πατέρα ἔφη τὸν ἐμὸν παρεῖναι μέν, καθεύδειν δὲ
ἐγκεκαλυμμένον. Σπεύσιππος δὲ βουλεύων[2] παραδίδωσιν αὐτοὺς τῷ δικαστηρίῳ. κἄπειτα ὁ πατὴρ
καταστήσας ἐγγυητὰς ἐγράψατο τὸν Σπεύσιππον
παρανόμων, καὶ ἠγωνίσατο ἐν ἑξακισχιλίοις
᾿Αθηναίων, καὶ μετέλαβε δικαστῶν τοσούτων
οὐδὲ διακοσίας ψήφους ὁ Σπεύσιππος. ὁ δὲ
πείσας καὶ δεόμενος μεῖναι τὸν πατέρα ἐγὼ ἦν
18 μάλιστα, εἶτα δὲ καὶ οἱ ἄλλοι συγγενεῖς. καί μοι
κάλει Καλλίαν καὶ Στέφανον[3]—κάλει δὲ καὶ Φίλιππον καὶ ᾿Αλέξιππον· οὗτοι γάρ εἰσιν ᾿Ακουμενοῦ
καὶ Αὐτοκράτορος συγγενεῖς, οἳ ἔφυγον[4] ἐπὶ τῇ
Λυδοῦ μηνύσει· τοῦ μὲν ἀδελφιδοῦς ἐστιν Αὐτοκράτωρ, τοῦ δὲ θεῖος ᾿Ακουμενός· οἷς προσήκει
μισεῖν μὲν τὸν ἐξελάσαντα ἐκείνους, εἰδέναι δὲ

---

[1] ἔφυγον Blass, coll. §§ 26, 35, etc.: ἔφευγον codd.
[2] βασιλεύων malunt Sluiter et Bekker.
[3] ΜΑΡΤΥΡΕΣ add. Radermacher post Στέφανον.
[4] ἔφυγον Blass: ἔφευγον codd.

---

[a] Lydus gave his information before the βουλή. Speusippus at once proposed that the offenders named be tried by
the Heliaea in the usual way. Leogoras protested against
his inclusion in the list (a) because he had never been near
Themacus and (b) because even Lydus did not go so far as to
assert that he had had any part in the celebration. He then
blocked Speusippus' proposal by a γραφὴ παρανόμων which
had to be settled before the proposal could take effect.

house, next to the Olympieum. No sooner had the information been lodged than those concerned left the country to a man.

There was still one more information. According to Lydus, a slave of Pherecles of Themacus, Mysteries were celebrated at the house of his master, Pherecles, at Themacus. He gave a list of those concerned, including my father among them ; my father had been present, so Lydus said, but asleep with his head under his cloak. Speusippus, one of the members of the Council, was for handing them all over to the proper court ; whereupon my father furnished sureties and brought an action against Speusippus for making an illegal proposal.[a] The case was tried before six thousand citizens.[b] There were six thousand jurors, I repeat ; yet Speusippus failed to gain the votes of two hundred. I may add that my father was induced to stay in the country partly by the entreaties of his relatives in general, but principally by my own. Kindly call Callias and Stephanus—yes, and call Philippus and Alexippus. Philippus and Alexippus are related to Acumenus and Autocrator, who fled in consequence of the information lodged by Lydus ; Autocrator is a nephew of the one, and Acumenus is the other's uncle. They have little reason to love the man who drove the two from the country, and they should also know better than anyone who it was who caused their exile in the

The γραφή came before the Heliaea in the usual way ; and Leogoras obtained a verdict in his favour. He had, of course, to furnish sureties for his own appearance in the event of his losing his case against Speusippus.

[b] This represents the whole of the Heliasts for the year. A jury of this size occurs nowhere else ; but there are no good grounds for doubting Andocides' figures.

μάλιστα δι᾽ ὅντινα ἔφυγον.[1] βλέπετε εἰς τούτους,
καὶ μαρτυρεῖτε εἰ ἀληθῆ λέγω.

19 Τὰ μὲν γενόμενα[2] ἠκούσατε, ὦ ἄνδρες, καὶ ὑμῖν[3]
οἱ μάρτυρες μεμαρτυρήκασιν· ἃ δὲ οἱ κατήγοροι
ἐτόλμησαν εἰπεῖν, ἀναμνήσθητε. οὕτω[4] γὰρ καὶ
δίκαιον ἀπολογεῖσθαι, ἀναμιμνήσκοντα[5] τοὺς τῶν
κατηγόρων λόγους ἐξελέγχειν. ἔλεξαν γὰρ ὡς ἐγὼ
μηνύσαιμι περὶ τῶν μυστηρίων, ἀπογράψαιμί τε
τὸν πατέρα τὸν ἐμαυτοῦ παρόντα, καὶ γενοίμην
μηνυτὴς κατὰ τοῦ πατρὸς τοῦ ἐμαυτοῦ, λόγον
οἶμαι πάντων δεινότατόν τε[6] καὶ ἀνοσιώτατον
λέγοντες. ὁ μὲν γὰρ ἀπογράψας αὐτὸν Λυδὸς ἦν
ὁ Φερεκλέους, ὁ δὲ πείσας ὑπομεῖναι καὶ μὴ
οἴχεσθαι φεύγοντα ἐγώ, πολλὰ ἱκετεύσας καὶ
20 λαμβανόμενος τῶν γονάτων. καίτοι τί ἐβουλόμην,
εἰ ἐμήνυσα μὲν κατὰ τοῦ πατρός, ὡς οὗτοί φασιν,
[4] ἱκέτευον δὲ τὸν πατέρα μείναντά τι παθεῖν ὑπ᾽
ἐμοῦ; καὶ ὁ πατὴρ ἐπείσθη ἀγῶνα τοιοῦτον
ἀγωνίσασθαι, ἐν ᾧ δυοῖν τοῖν μεγίστοιν κακοῖν οὐκ
ἦν αὐτῷ ἁμαρτεῖν· ἢ γὰρ ἐμοῦ δόξαντος τὰ ὄντα
μηνῦσαι κατ᾽ ἐκείνου ὑπ᾽ ἐμοῦ ἀποθανεῖν, ἢ αὐτῷ
σωθέντι ἐμὲ ἀποκτεῖναι. ὁ γὰρ νόμος οὕτως εἶχεν·
εἰ μὲν τἀληθῆ μηνύσειέ τις, εἶναι τὴν ἄδειαν, εἰ

---

[1] ἔφυγον Blass : ἔφευγον codd.
[2] γενόμενα Bekker : γινόμενα codd.
[3] ὑμῖν apogr. : ἡμῖν A.   [4] οὕτω Reiske : οὐ codd.
[5] ἀναμιμνήσκοντα Reiske : ἀναμιμνήσκοντας codd.
[6] τε om. A pr.

---

[a] i.e. (1) Speusippus, who had initiated proceedings

354

first instance.[a] Face the court, gentlemen. and state
whether I have been telling the truth.

Witnesses

Now that you have heard the facts, gentlemen, and
the witnesses have confirmed them for you, let me
remind you of the version of those facts which the
prosecution had the effrontery to give—for after all,
the right way to conduct a defence is to recall the statements of the prosecution and disprove them. According to the prosecution, I myself gave information in
the matter of the Mysteries and included my own
father in my list of those present : yes, turned
informer against my own father. I cannot imagine
a more outrageous, a more abominable suggestion.
My father was denounced by Pherecles' slave,
Lydus : it was I who persuaded him to remain in
Athens instead of escaping into exile—and it was
only after numberless entreaties and by clinging to
his knees that I did so. What, pray, was I about
in informing against my father, as we are asked to
believe that I did, when at the same time I was begging him to remain in Athens—begging him, that is,
to let me be guilty of the consequences to himself ?
Again, we are to suppose that my father himself
consented to face a trial which was bound to have one
or other of two terrible results for him ; if my information against him was deemed true, his blood would be
upon my hands : if he himself was acquitted, mine
would be upon his ; because the law ran that whereas
an informer's claim to immunity should be allowed
if his information were true, he should be put to death,

against them, and (2) Lydus, from whom the information
had originated.

δὲ τὰ[1] ψευδῆ, τεθνάναι. καὶ μὲν δὴ τοῦτό γε
ἐπίστασθε πάντες, ὅτι ἐσώθην καὶ ἐγὼ καὶ ὁ ἐμὸς
πατήρ· οἷόν τε δ᾽ οὐκ ἦν, εἴπερ ἐγὼ μηνυτὴς
ἐγενόμην περὶ τοῦ πατρός, ἀλλ᾽ ἢ ἐμὲ ἢ ἐκεῖνον
ἔδει ἀποθανεῖν.

21 Φέρε δὴ τοίνυν, εἰ καὶ ὁ πατὴρ ἐβούλετο ὑπομένειν, τοὺς φίλους ἂν οἴεσθε ἢ ἐπιτρέπειν αὐτῷ
μένειν ἢ ἐγγυήσασθαι, ἀλλ᾽ οὐκ ἂν παραιτεῖσθαι
καὶ δεῖσθαι ἀπιέναι ὅπου [ἂν][2] ἔμελλεν αὐτὸς[3]
σωθήσεσθαι ἐμέ τε οὐκ ἀπολεῖν;

22 Ἀλλὰ γὰρ καὶ ὅτε Σπεύσιππον ἐδίωκεν ὁ πατὴρ
τῶν παρανόμων, αὐτὰ ταῦτα ἔλεγεν, ὡς οὐδεπώποτε ἔλθοι[4] εἰς Θημακὸν ὡς Φερεκλέα· ἐκέλευε δὲ
βασανίσαι τὰ ἀνδράποδα, καὶ μὴ τοὺς μὲν παρα-
διδόντας μὴ ἐθέλειν ἐλέγχειν, τοὺς δὲ μὴ θέλοντας
ἀναγκάζειν. ταῦτα δὲ λέγοντος τοῦ πατρὸς τοῦ
ἐμοῦ, ὡς ἅπαντες ἴστε, τί ὑπελείπετο τῷ Σπευσ-
ίππῳ λέγειν, εἰ ἀληθῆ οἶδε λέγουσιν, ἀλλ᾽ ἢ
" Ὦ Λεωγόρα, τί βούλῃ περὶ θεραπόντων λέγειν;
οὐχ ὁ υἱὸς οὑτοσὶ μεμήνυκε κατὰ σοῦ, καί φησί σε
παρεῖναι ἐν Θημακῷ; ἔλεγχε σὺ τὸν πατέρα, ἢ
οὐκ ἔστι σοι ἄδεια." ταυτὶ ἔλεγεν ἂν ὁ Σπεύσ-

23 ιππος, ὦ ἄνδρες, ἢ οὔ; ἐγὼ μὲν οἶμαι. εἰ τοίνυν
ἀνέβην ἐπὶ δικαστήριον, ἢ λόγος τις περὶ ἐμοῦ
ἐγένετο, ἢ μήνυσίς τις ἐμή ἐστιν ἢ[5] ἀπογραφή, μὴ
ὅτι ἐμὴ καθ᾽ ἑτέρου, ἀλλ᾽ εἰ καὶ ἄλλου τινὸς κατ᾽
ἐμοῦ, ἐλεγχέτω με ὁ βουλόμενος ἐνταῦθα ἀναβάς.

---

[1] τὰ om. A pr.   [2] ἂν del. Dobree.
          [3] αὐτὸς om. A pr.
[4] ἔλθοι apogr.: ἔλθη A.   [5] ἢ Reiske: ἡ codd.

---

[a] For the torturing of slaves cf. p 70. note.

if it were not. Yet if there is one thing of which you are all certain, it is the fact that my father and I both escaped with our lives. That could not have happened, if I had informed against my father ; either he or I would have had to die.

Then again, assume that he actually desired to stay. Do you imagine that his friends would have let him do so ? Would they have gone bail for him ? Would they not have urged him to change his mind ? Would they not have begged him to find some place of refuge abroad, where he would be out of harm's way himself and would avoid causing my death also ?

But to return to facts : when prosecuting Speusippus for making an illegal proposal, one thing upon which my father insisted repeatedly was that he had never visited Pherecles at Themacus in his life ; and he offered the defence the opportunity of examining his slaves under torture *a* ; those who were ready to hand over their slaves, he said, ought not to meet with a refusal of the test which they were proposing, when those who were not ready to hand them over were forced to do so. You all know my father's challenge to be a fact. Now if there is any truth in the prosecution's assertion, what had Speusippus to reply but : " Why talk of slaves, Leogoras ? Has not your son here informed against you ? Does not he say that you were at Themacus ? Andocides, prove your father guilty, or your chance of a pardon is gone." Was that Speusippus' natural retort or not, gentlemen ? I for one think so. In fact, if I ever entered a court, if I was ever mentioned in connexion with the affair, or if there is any recorded information or list containing my name, let alone any for which I was myself responsible, anyone who wishes is welcome to step

ἀλλὰ γὰρ λόγον ἀνοσιώτερον καὶ ἀπιστότερον[1]
οὐδένας πώποτ' ἐγὼ εἰπόντας οἶδα, οἳ τοῦτο μόνον
ἡγήσαντο δεῖν, τολμῆσαι κατηγορῆσαι· εἰ δ' ἐλεγχθήσονται ψευδόμενοι, οὐδὲν αὐτοῖς ἐμέλησεν.

24 ὥσπερ οὖν, εἰ ἀληθῆ ἦν ταῦτα ἅ μου[2] κατηγόρησαν,
ἐμοὶ ἂν ὠργίζεσθε καὶ ἠξιοῦτε δίκην τὴν μεγίστην
ἐπιτιθέναι, οὕτως ἀξιῶ ὑμᾶς, γιγνώσκοντας ὅτι
ψεύδονται, πονηρούς τε αὐτοὺς νομίζειν, χρῆσθαί
τε τεκμηρίῳ ὅτι εἰ τὰ δεινότατα τῶν κατηγορηθέντων περιφανῶς ἐλέγχονται ψευδόμενοι, ᾗ που
τά γε πολλῷ φαυλότερα ῥᾳδίως ὑμῖν ἀποδείξω
ψευδομένους αὐτούς.

25 Αἱ μὲν μηνύσεις ὧδε περὶ τῶν μυστηρίων αὗται
ἐγένοντο τέτταρες· οἳ δὲ ἔφυγον[3] καθ' ἑκάστην
μήνυσιν, ἀνέγνων ὑμῖν τὰ ὀνόματα αὐτῶν, καὶ οἱ
μάρτυρες μεμαρτυρήκασιν. ἔτι δὲ πρὸς τούτοις
ἐγὼ πιστότητος ὑμῶν ἕνεκα, ὦ ἄνδρες, τάδε
ποιήσω. τῶν γὰρ φυγόντων[4] ἐπὶ τοῖς[5] μυστηρίοις
οἱ μέν τινες ἀπέθανον φεύγοντες, οἱ δ' ἥκουσι καὶ
εἰσὶν ἐνθάδε καὶ πάρεισιν ὑπ' ἐμοῦ κεκλημένοι.

26 ἐγὼ οὖν ἐν τῷ ἐμῷ λόγῳ δίδωμι τῷ βουλομένῳ
ἐμὲ ἐλέγξαι[6] ὅτι ἔφυγέ τις αὐτῶν δι' ἐμὲ ἢ ἐμήνυσα
κατά του,[7] ἢ οὐχ ἕκαστοι ἔφυγον κατὰ τὰς μηνύσεις
ταύτας ἃς ἐγὼ ὑμῖν ἀπέδειξα. καὶ ἐάν τις ἐλέγξῃ

---

[1] ἀνοσιώτερον καὶ ἀπιστότερον Reiske: ἀνοσιώτατον καὶ ἀπιστότατον codd.
[2] μου Dobree: με codd.   [3] ἔφυγον Blass: ἔφευγον codd.
[4] φυγόντων Blass: φευγόντων codd.
[5] ἐπὶ τοῖς Reiske: ἐν τοῖς codd.
[6] ἐλέγξαι A pr.: ἐξελέγξαι A corr.
[7] κατά του Sluiter: κατ' αὐτοῦ codd.

---

[a] The time allowed for the speeches of the prosecution

up here and prove it against me. For my own part, I have never known anyone tell so outrageous or so unconvincing a story. All that was necessary, they imagined, was sufficient effrontery to bring a charge ; the possibility of their being refuted did not disturb them in the least. Be consistent, then. Had this accusation of theirs been true, your anger would have fallen upon me, and you would have considered the severest penalty justified. So now that you see them to be lying, I demand that you look upon them instead as scoundrels—and with good reason too : for if the worst of their charges are shown to be conspicuously false, I shall hardly find it difficult to prove the same of those which are less serious.

Such, then, were the informations lodged in connexion with the Mysteries ; they were, as I say, four in number. I have read you the names of those who went into exile after each, and the witnesses have given their evidence. I shall now do something more to convince you, gentlemen. Of those who went into exile as a result of the profanation of the Mysteries, some died abroad ; but others have returned and are living in Athens. These last are present in court at my request. Any of them who wishes is welcome to prove, in the time now allotted to me,[a] that I was responsible for the exile of any of their number, that I informed against any of them, or that the various groups did not go into exile in consequence of the particular informations which I have described to you.

and defence in an Athenian court of law was limited. It was measured by a water-clock (κλεψύδρα) which varied in size according to the nature of the case. The outflow of water was stopped during the reading of documents, depositions, etc. Here Andocides offers to stand aside with the clock still running.

με ὅτι ψεύδομαι, χρήσασθέ μοι ὅ τι βούλεσθε.
καὶ σιωπῶ, καὶ παραχωρῶ, εἴ τις ἀναβαίνειν
βούλεται.

27 Φέρε δή, ὦ ἄνδρες, μετὰ ταῦτα τί ἐγένετο;
ἐπειδὴ αἱ μηνύσεις ἐγένοντο, περὶ τῶν μηνύτρων
—ἦσαν γὰρ κατὰ τὸ Κλεωνύμου ψήφισμα χίλιαι
δραχμαί, κατὰ δὲ τὸ Πεισάνδρου μύριαι—περὶ
δὲ τούτων ἠμφεσβήτουν¹ οὗτοί τε οἱ μηνύσαντες
καὶ Πυθόνικος, φάσκων πρῶτος εἰσαγγεῖλαι, καὶ
28 Ἀνδροκλῆς ὑπὲρ τῆς βουλῆς. ἔδοξεν οὖν τῷ
δήμῳ ἐν τῷ τῶν θεσμοθετῶν δικαστηρίῳ τοὺς
μεμνημένους, ἀκούσαντας τὰς μηνύσεις² ἃς ἕκαστος
ἐμήνυσε, διαδικάσαι. καὶ ἐψηφίσαντο πρώτῳ μὲν
Ἀνδρομάχῳ, δευτέρῳ δὲ Τεύκρῳ, καὶ ἔλαβον
Παναθηναίων τῷ ἀγῶνι Ἀνδρόμαχος μὲν μυρίας
δραχμάς, Τεῦκρος δὲ χιλίας. καί μοι κάλει
τούτων τοὺς μάρτυρας.

ΜΑΡΤΥΡΕΣ

¹ ἠμφεσβήτουν Lipsius: ἠμφισβήτουν codd.
² μηνύσεις vulg.: μυήδεις A pr.: μυνήδεις A corr.

ᵃ The question of offering rewards for information probably arose when the commission of inquiry was being appointed. After Cleonymus' thousand drachmae was found
to be producing insufficient results, it would be supplemented
by the much more substantial sum proposed by Peisander.
For Peisander see p. 366, note.
ᵇ i.e. Andromachus, Teucrus, Agariste, and Lydus.
Pythonicus' claim was based on the fact that he had been
originally responsible for bringing the matter to the notice
of the Assembly. Androcles is here mentioned for the first
time. From Thucydides viii. 65 and Plutarch, Alcib. 19 it is
clear that he played an important part in the investigations;
probably it was through his agency that Teucrus, the first
informer to approach the βουλή, was induced to come forward. ὑπὲρ τῆς βουλῆς here cannot possibly mean " on the

If I am shown not to be speaking the truth, you may punish me as you will. I shall now interrupt my defence and give place to anyone who wishes to step up here.

And now, gentlemen, what followed ? After the various informations had been laid, the question of rewards arose : for Cleonymus' decree had offered one thousand drachmae, and Peisander's ten.[a] Conflicting claims were made by the informers I have mentioned,[b] by Pythonicus, on the ground that he had first brought the matter before the Assembly, and by Androcles, who urged the part played by the Council. It was therefore publicly resolved that such members of the court of the Thesmothetae [c] as were initiates should be presented with the informations of the several claimants and decide between them. As a result the principal reward was voted to Andromachus, the second to Teucrus ; and at the festival of the Panathenaea [d] Andromachus received ten thousand drachmae and Teucrus one thousand. Kindly call witnesses to confirm this.

Witnesses

Council's behalf " ; there was no question of rewarding the βουλευταί. It is more like " in view of the Council's part in the affair " ; *i.e.* Androcles maintained that the Council had been of more importance throughout than the Assembly, and that therefore, as the person responsible for the first disclosures made to it, he himself deserved the principal reward.

[c] *i.e.* the Heliaea. As with Leogoras' γραφὴ παρανόμων the jury is an exceptionally large one, although here the special circumstances make its size more easily intelligible. The case would take the form of a διαδικασία.

[d] The Panathenaea was held every year, beginning on the 17th of Hecatombaeon (July 8th), and with extra pomp every four years, when the πέπλος of Athena was carried in procession.

29 Περὶ μὲν τῶν μυστηρίων, ὦ ἄνδρες, ὧν ἕνεκα
[5] ἡ ἔνδειξις ἐγένετο καὶ περὶ ὧν ὑμεῖς οἱ μεμυημένοι
εἰσεληλύθατε, ἀποδέδεικταί μοι ὡς οὔτε ἠσέβηκα
οὔτε μεμήνυκα[1] περὶ οὐδενὸς οὔτε ὡμολόγηκα περὶ
αὐτῶν, οὐδὲ ἔστι μοι ἁμάρτημα περὶ τὼ θεώ οὔτε
μεῖζον οὔτ' ἔλαττον οὐδὲ ἕν. ὅπερ ἐμοὶ περὶ
πλείστου ἐστὶν ὑμᾶς πεῖσαι. καὶ γὰρ οἱ λόγοι τῶν
κατηγόρων, ⟨οἳ⟩[2] ταῦτα τὰ δεινὰ καὶ φρικώδη
ἀνωρθίαζον, καὶ λόγους εἶπον ὡς πρότερον ἑτέρων
ἁμαρτόντων καὶ ἀσεβησάντων περὶ τὼ θεώ, οἷα
ἕκαστος αὐτῶν ἔπαθε καὶ ἐτιμωρήθη—τούτων οὖν
30 ἐμοὶ τῶν λόγων ἢ τῶν ἔργων τί προσήκει; ἐγὼ
γὰρ πολὺ μᾶλλον ἐκείνων κατηγορῶ, καὶ δι' αὐτὸ
τοῦτό φημι δεῖν ἐκείνους μὲν ἀπολέσθαι, ὅτι
ἠσέβησαν, ἐμὲ δὲ σώζεσθαι, ὅτι οὐδὲν ἡμάρτηκα.
ἢ δεινόν γ' ἂν εἴη, εἰ ἐμοὶ ὀργίζοισθε ἐπὶ τοῖς
ἑτέρων ἁμαρτήμασι, καὶ τὴν εἰς ἐμὲ διαβολὴν
εἰδότες ὅτι ὑπὸ τῶν ἐχθρῶν τῶν ἐμῶν λέγεται,
κρείττω τῆς ἀληθείας ἡγήσαισθε.[3] δῆλον γὰρ ὅτι[4]
τοῖς μὲν ἡμαρτηκόσι τὰ τοιαῦτα ἁμαρτήματα οὐκ
ἔστιν ἀπολογία ὡς οὐκ ἐποίησαν· ἡ γὰρ βάσανος
δεινὴ παρὰ τοῖς εἰδόσιν· ἐμοὶ δὲ ὁ ἔλεγχος ἥδιστος,
ἐν οἷς ὑμῶν οὐδέν με δεῖ δεόμενον οὐδὲ παραιτού-
μενον σωθῆναι ἐπὶ τῇ τοιαύτῃ αἰτίᾳ, ἀλλ' ἐλέγ-

---

[1] μεμήνυκα vulg.: μεμήηκα A pr.: μεμήνηκα A corr.
[2] Locus vexatus. οἳ add. Blass: καὶ λόγους εἶπον del.
Helbig: alii alia.
[3] ἡγήσαισθε Reiske: ἡγήσεσθε codd.
[4] δῆλον γὰρ ὅτι Naber: δηλονότι γὰρ codd.

---

[a] Demeter and Korê, the central figures of the Eleusis-cult.

362

So much for the profanation of the Mysteries, gentlemen, on which the information lodged against me is based and which you are here as initiates to investigate. I have shown that I have committed no act of impiety, that I have never turned informer, that I have never admitted guilt, and that I have not a single offence against the Two Goddesses [a] upon my conscience, whether serious or otherwise. And it is vitally important for me to convince you of this ; for the stories told you by the prosecution, who treated you to so shrill a recital of blood-curdling horrors, with their descriptions of past offenders who have made mock of the Two Goddesses and of the fearful end to which they have been brought as a punishment—what, I ask you, have such tales and such crimes to do with me ? It is I, in fact, who am much more truly the accuser, and they the accused. They have been guilty of impiety ; and therefore, I maintain, they deserve death. I, on the other hand, have done no wrong, and therefore I deserve to go unharmed. It would be nothing less than monstrous to vent upon me the wrath which the misdeeds of others have aroused in you, or to let the malicious attack to which I have been subjected weigh more with you than the truth, when you know that it is my enemies who are responsible for it. Obviously anyone who was guilty of an offence such as that with which we are concerned could not clear himself by denying that he had committed it : for the scrutiny to which a defendant's statements are subjected is formidable indeed when the court already knows the truth. But to me the inquiry into the facts is the very opposite of embarrassing ; I have no need to resort to entreaties or appeals for mercy to gain an

χοντα τοὺς τῶν κατηγόρων λόγους καὶ ὑμᾶς
31 ἀναμιμνήσκοντα[1] τὰ γεγενημένα, οἵ τινες ὅρκους
μεγάλους ὀμόσαντες οἴσετε τὴν ψῆφον περὶ ἐμοῦ,
καὶ ἀρασάμενοι[2] τὰς μεγίστας ἀρὰς ὑμῖν τε αὐτοῖς
καὶ παισὶ τοῖς ὑμετέροις αὐτῶν, ἦ μὴν ψηφιεῖσθαι
περὶ ἐμοῦ τὰ δίκαια, πρὸς δὲ τούτοις μεμύησθε καὶ
ἑοράκατε τοῖν θεοῖν τὰ ἱερά, ἵνα τιμωρήσητε μὲν
τοὺς ἀσεβοῦντας, σῴζητε δὲ τοὺς μηδὲν ἀδικοῦντας.
32 νομίσατε τοίνυν ἀσέβημα οὐδὲν ἔλαττον εἶναι
τῶν μηδὲν ἠδικηκότων[3] ἀσεβεῖν καταγνῶναι ἢ τοὺς
ἠσεβηκότας μὴ τιμωρεῖσθαι. ὥστ' ἐγὼ ὑμῖν πολὺ
μᾶλλον τῶν κατηγόρων πρὸς τοῖν θεοῖν ἐπισκήπτω,
ὑπέρ τε τῶν ἱερῶν ἃ εἴδετε, καὶ ὑπὲρ τῶν Ἑλλήνων
οἳ τῆς ἑορτῆς ἕνεκα ἔρχονται δεῦρο· εἰ μέν τι
ἠσέβηκα ἢ ὡμολόγηκα ἢ ἐμήνυσα κατά τινος
ἀνθρώπων, ἢ ἄλλος τις περὶ ἐμοῦ, ἀποκτείνατέ
33 με· οὐ παραιτοῦμαι· εἰ δὲ οὐδὲν ἡμάρτηταί μοι,
καὶ τοῦτο ὑμῖν ἀποδείκνυμι σαφῶς, δέομαι ὑμῶν
αὐτὸ φανερὸν τοῖς Ἕλλησι πᾶσι ποιῆσαι, ὡς
ἀδίκως εἰς τόνδε τὸν ἀγῶνα κατέστην. ἐὰν γὰρ
μὴ μεταλάβῃ τὸ πέμπτον μέρος τῶν ψήφων καὶ
ἀτιμωθῇ ὁ ἐνδείξας ἐμὲ Κηφίσιος οὑτοσί, οὐκ
ἔξεστιν αὐτῷ εἰς τὸ ἱερὸν τοῖν θεοῖν εἰσιέναι, ἢ
ἀποθανεῖται. εἰ οὖν ὑμῖν δοκῶ ἱκανῶς περὶ

---

[1] ἀναμιμνήσκοντα Reiske : ἀναμιμνήσκω codd.
[2] ἀρασάμενοι A corr. : ἀράμενοι vel ἀσάμενοι A pr.
[3] τῶν μηδὲν ἠδικηκότων Lipsius : τοὺς μηδὲν ἠδικηκότας codd.

---

[a] The prosecutor who failed to gain one-fifth of the votes
of the jury was condemned to a fine of one thousand drachmae
and debarred from bringing a similar action in future. In a
case of ἀσεβεία, such as the present, he was further deprived
of the right of entering the temples of the gods against whom
the alleged act of impiety had been committed. Thus

acquittal upon a charge such as this: I have merely to show the absurdity of the statements of my accusers by reminding you of what actually occurred. And you yourselves have taken solemn oaths as the jurors who are to decide my fate : as jurors you have sworn to see that that decision is a fair one, under pain of causing the most terrible of curses to fall upon yourselves and your children ; and at the same time you are here as initiates who have witnessed the rites of the Two Goddesses, in order that you may punish those who are guilty of impiety and protect those who are innocent. Understand, then, that to condemn the innocent for impiety is no less an act of impiety than to acquit the guilty. Indeed, in the name of the Two Goddesses I repeat yet more sternly the charge laid upon you by my accusers, for the sake both of the rites which you have witnessed and of the Greeks who are coming to this city for the festival. If I have committed any act of impiety, if I have admitted guilt, if I have informed against another, or if another has informed against me, then put me to death; I ask no mercy. But if, on the other hand, I have committed no offence, and completely satisfy you of the fact, then I ask you to let the whole nation see that I have been brought to trial wrongfully. Should Cephisius here, who was responsible for the information laid against me, fail to gain one-fifth of your votes and so lose his rights as a citizen, he is forbidden to set foot within the sanctuary of the Two Goddesses under pain of death.[a] And now, if you think my defence satisfactory up to

---

[a] Cephisius stands to suffer partial ἀτιμία ; the fine will not trouble him, as Callias has indemnified him in advance (§ 121).

τούτων ἀπολελογῆσθαι, δηλώσατέ μοι, ἵνα προ-
θυμότερον περὶ τῶν ἄλλων ἀπολογῶμαι.

34 Περὶ δὲ τῶν ἀναθημάτων τῆς περικοπῆς καὶ τῆς
μηνύσεως, ὥσπερ καὶ ὑπεσχόμην ὑμῖν, οὕτω καὶ
ποιήσω· ἐξ ἀρχῆς γὰρ ὑμᾶς διδάξω ἅπαντα τὰ
γεγενημένα. ἐπειδὴ Τεῦκρος ἦλθε Μεγαρόθεν,
ἄδειαν εὑρόμενος μηνύει περί τε τῶν μυστηρίων
ἃ ᾔδει καὶ ἐκ τῶν περικοψάντων τὰ ἀναθήματα
ἀπογράφει¹ δυοῖν δέοντας εἴκοσιν ἄνδρας. ἐπειδὴ
δὲ οὗτοι ἀπεγράφησαν, οἱ μὲν αὐτῶν φεύγοντες
ᾤχοντο, οἱ δὲ συλληφθέντες ἀπέθανον κατὰ τὴν
Τεύκρου μήνυσιν. καί μοι ἀνάγνωθι αὐτῶν τὰ
ὀνόματα.

35 ΟΝΟΜΑΤΑ.—Τεῦκρος ἐπὶ τοῖς Ἑρμαῖς ἐμήνυσεν Εὐ-
κτήμονα, Γλαύκιππον, Εὐρύμαχον, Πολύευκτον,
Πλάτωνα, Ἀντίδωρον, Χάριππον, Θεόδωρον,
Ἀλκισθένη, Μενέστρατον, Ἐρυξίμαχον, Εὐφίλητον,
Εὐρυδάμαντα, Φερεκλέα, Μέλητον, Τιμάνθη,
Ἀρχίδαμον, Τελένικον.

Τούτων τοίνυν τῶν ἀνδρῶν οἱ μὲν ἥκουσι καὶ
εἰσὶν ἐνθάδε, τῶν δὲ ἀποθανόντων εἰσὶ πολλοὶ
προσήκοντες· ὧν ὅστις βούλεται, ἐν τῷ ἐμῷ λόγῳ
ἀναβὰς με ἐλεγξάτω ἢ ὡς ἔφυγέ τις δι' ἐμὲ τούτων
τῶν ἀνδρῶν ἢ ὡς ἀπέθανεν.

36 Ἐπειδὴ δὲ ταῦτα ἐγένετο, Πείσανδρος καὶ

---

¹ καὶ ἐκ τῶν . . . ἀπογράφει Lipsius : καὶ τῶν . . . καὶ
ἀπογράφει Aldina, quem Bekker et Blass secuti sunt. ἐκ
τῶν . . . καὶ ἀπογράφει codd.

ᵃ Came into prominence once more during the struggles
of 412–411. By the end of 412 he had identified himself with
the oligarchic cause, and was active in trying to procure

the present, show your approval, so that I may present what remains with increased confidence.

Next comes the mutilation of the images and the denunciation of those responsible. I will do as I promised and tell you the whole story from the beginning. On his return from Megara Teucrus was guaranteed his immunity. Hereupon, besides communicating what he knew about the Mysteries, he gave a list of eighteen of those responsible for the mutilation of the images. Of these eighteen, a number fled the country upon being denounced ; the remainder were arrested and executed upon the information lodged by Teucrus. Kindly read their names.

NAMES.—In the matter of the Hermae Teucrus denounced : Euctemon, Glaucippus, Eurymachus, Polyeuctus, Plato, Antidorus, Charippus, Theodorus, Alcisthenes, Menestratus, Eryximachus, Euphiletus, Eurydamas, Pherecles, Meletus, Timanthes, Archidamus, Telenicus.

A number of these men have returned to Athens and are present in court, as are several of the relatives of those who have died. Any of them is welcome to step up here, during the time now allotted me, and prove against me that I caused either the exile or the death of a single one.

And now for what followed. Peisander [a] and

the return of Alcibiades. He was largely responsible for the installation of the Four Hundred at Athens in 411, and did his utmost to have Andocides put to death when he attempted to return to Athens during that year (*cf. De Reditu*, §§ 13-15). After the fall of the Four Hundred Peisander fled to Decelea ; he was condemned to death *in absentia* and his property was confiscated. Nothing more is heard of him. Throughout he was a bitter personal enemy of Andocides.

ANDOCIDES

Χαρικλῆς, ὄντες μὲν τῶν ζητητῶν, δοκοῦντες δ᾽
[6] ἐν ἐκείνῳ τῷ χρόνῳ εὐνούστατοι εἶναι τῷ δήμῳ,
ἔλεγον ὡς εἴη τὰ ἔργα τὰ γεγενημένα οὐκ ὀλίγων
ἀνδρῶν ἀλλ᾽ ἐπὶ τῇ τοῦ δήμου καταλύσει, καὶ
χρῆναι ἐπιζητεῖν[1] καὶ μὴ παύσασθαι. καὶ ἡ πόλις
οὕτω διέκειτο, ὥστ᾽ ἐπειδὴ τὴν βουλὴν εἰς τὸ
βουλευτήριον ὁ κῆρυξ ἀνείποι[2] ἰέναι καὶ τὸ σημεῖον
καθέλοι, τῷ αὐτῷ σημείῳ ἥ μὲν βουλὴ εἰς τὸ
βουλευτήριον ᾔει, οἱ δ᾽ ἐκ τῆς ἀγορᾶς ἔφευγον,[3]
δεδιότες εἷς ἕκαστος μὴ συλληφθείη.

37 Ἐπαρθεὶς οὖν τοῖς τῆς πόλεως κακοῖς εἰσ-
αγγέλλει Διοκλείδης[4] εἰς τὴν βουλήν, φάσκων εἰδέναι
τοὺς περικόψαντας τοὺς Ἑρμᾶς, καὶ εἶναι αὐτοὺς
εἰς τριακοσίους· ὡς δ᾽ ἴδοι καὶ περιτύχοι τῷ πράγματι, ἔλεγε. καὶ τούτοις, ὦ ἄνδρες, δέομαι ὑμῶν
προσέχοντας τὸν νοῦν ἀναμιμνήσκεσθαι, ἐὰν ἀληθῆ
λέγω, καὶ διδάσκειν ἀλλήλους· ἐν ὑμῖν γὰρ ἦσαν
οἱ λόγοι, καί μοι ὑμεῖς τούτων μάρτυρές ἐστε.

38 Ἔφη γὰρ εἶναι μὲν ἀνδράποδόν οἱ ἐπὶ Λαυρείῳ,

---

[1] ἐπιζητεῖν A pr.: ἔτι ζητεῖν A corr.
[2] ἀνείποι Bekker: ἀνείπη codd.
[3] ἔφευγον Baiter: ἔφυγον codd.
[4] Διοκλείδης Ald.: δίο καὶ δὶς codd.

---

[a] Another turncoat, who started as an extreme radical and then became a member of the Four Hundred. Like Peisander, he escaped to Decelea after their collapse ; but he succeeded in effecting his return in 404 when Sparta ordered the restoration of exiles. He became a member of the Thirty, and was responsible for some of their worst excesses. After their fall nothing more is heard of him. For a sketch of his conduct at this later period see § 101.

[b] There is some doubt about the meaning of this statement. (a) According to Suidas, a flag was hoisted in the Agora before meetings of the Ecclesia and lowered when they were

Charicles,[a] who were regarded in those days as the
most fervent of democrats, were members of the
commission of inquiry. These two maintained that
the outrage was not the work of a small group of
criminals, but an organized attempt to overthrow the
popular government : and that therefore inquiries
ought still to be pursued as vigorously as ever. As
a result, Athens reached such a state that the lowering of the flag by the Herald, when summoning a
meeting of the Council, was quite as much a signal
for citizens to hurry from the Agora, each in terror of
arrest, as it was for the Council to proceed to the
Council-chamber.[b]

The general distress encouraged Diocleides to
bring an impeachment before the Council. He
claimed that he knew who had mutilated the Hermae,
and gave their number as roughly three hundred.
He then went on to explain how he had come to
witness the outrage. Now I want you to think carefully here, gentlemen ; try to remember whether I
am telling the truth, and inform your companions ;
for it was before you that Diocleides stated his case,
and you are my witnesses of what occurred.

Diocleides' tale was that he had had to fetch the

concluded. If this is the flag referred to here, the meeting
of the βουλή is the meeting held immediately after the adjourn-
ment of the Ecclesia. The Agora would then be thronged
with citizens coming from the Pnyx. (*b*) Possibly a flag was
flown from the roof of the βουλευτήριον and taken down
when the Council was sitting. There is no evidence for this,
however; and it is a possible objection that this lowering of
the flag *during* a meeting is precisely the opposite of the
custom followed in the case of the Ecclesia. If the first
explanation be accepted we must assume that Andocides
is referring only to those meetings of the βουλή which occurred
after a sitting of the Ecclesia ; the βουλή in fact met daily.

δεῖν δὲ κομίσασθαι ἀποφοράν. ἀναστὰς δὲ πρῷ
ψευσθεὶς τῆς ὥρας βαδίζειν· εἶναι δὲ πανσέληνον.
ἐπεὶ δὲ παρὰ τὸ προπύλαιον τοῦ Διονύσου ἦν, ὁρᾶν
ἀνθρώπους πολλοὺς ἀπὸ τοῦ ᾠδείου καταβαίνοντας
εἰς τὴν ὀρχήστραν· δείσας δὲ αὐτούς, εἰσελθὼν
ὑπὸ τὴν σκιὰν καθέζεσθαι μεταξὺ τοῦ κίονος καὶ
τῆς στήλης ἐφ' ᾗ ὁ στρατηγός ἐστιν ὁ χαλκοῦς.
ὁρᾶν δὲ ἀνθρώπους τὸν μὲν ἀριθμὸν μάλιστα[1]
τριακοσίους, ἑστάναι δὲ κύκλῳ ἀνὰ πέντε καὶ
δέκα ἄνδρας, τοὺς δὲ ἀνὰ εἴκοσιν· ὁρῶν δὲ αὐτῶν
πρὸς τὴν σελήνην τὰ πρόσωπα τῶν πλείστων[2]
39 γιγνώσκειν. καὶ πρῶτον μέν, ὦ ἄνδρες, τοῦθ'
ὑπέθετο, δεινότατον πρᾶγμα, οἶμαι, ὅπως ἐν
ἐκείνῳ εἴη ὅντινα βούλοιτο Ἀθηναίων φάναι τῶν
ἀνδρῶν τούτων εἶναι, ὅντινα δὲ μὴ βούλοιτο, λέγειν
ὅτι οὐκ ἦν. ἰδὼν δὲ ταῦτ' ἔφη ἐπὶ Λαύρειον ἰέναι, καὶ
τῇ ὑστεραίᾳ ἀκούειν ὅτι οἱ Ἑρμαῖ εἶεν περικεκομ-
μένοι· γνῶναι οὖν εὐθὺς ὅτι τούτων εἴη τῶν ἀνδρῶν
40 τὸ ἔργον. ἥκων δὲ εἰς ἄστυ ζητητάς τε ἤδη
ᾑρημένους καταλαμβάνειν καὶ μήνυτρα κεκηρυγ-
μένα ἑκατὸν μνᾶς. ἰδὼν δὲ Εὔφημον τὸν Καλλίου
τοῦ Τηλοκλέους ἀδελφὸν ἐν τῷ χαλκείῳ καθήμενον,
ἀναγαγὼν αὐτὸν εἰς τὸ Ἡφαιστεῖον λέγειν ἅπερ
ὑμῖν ἐγὼ εἴρηκα, ὡς ἴδοι ἡμᾶς[3] ἐν ἐκείνῃ τῇ νυκτί·
οὔκουν δέοιτο παρὰ τῆς πόλεως χρήματα λαβεῖν

---

[1] Verba μὲν et μάλιστα ex Galeno xviii. A, p. 450 addidit
Sluiter.
[2] τῶν πλείστων A corr. : τὰ πλεῖστα A pr.
[3] ἡμᾶς Ald. : ὑμᾶς codd.

---

[a] The mines of Laurium in S. Attica were leased by the
state to private individuals. These in their turn hired slaves
to work them, if they had not enough of their own. The
slave's earnings were paid to his master.

earnings of a slave of his at Laurium.*a* He arose at an early hour, mistaking the time, and started off on his walk by the light of a full moon. As he was passing the gateway of the theatre of Dionysus, he noticed a large body of men coming down into the orchestra from the Odeum.*b* In alarm, he withdrew into the shadow and crouched down between the column and the pedestal with the bronze statue of the general upon it. He then saw some three hundred men standing about in groups of five and ten and, in some cases, twenty. He recognized the faces of the majority, as he could see them in the moonlight. Now to begin with, gentlemen, Diocleides gave his story this particular form simply to be in a position to say of any citizen, according as he chose, that he was or was not one of the offenders—a monstrous proceeding. However, to continue his tale: after seeing what he had, he went on to Laurium; and when he learned next day of the mutilation of the Hermae, he knew at once that it was the work of the men he had noticed. On his return to Athens he found a commission already appointed to investigate, and a reward of one hundred minae offered for information *c*; so seeing Euphemus, the brother of Callias, son of Telocles, sitting in his smithy, he took him to the temple of Hephaestus. Then, after describing, as I have described to you, how he had seen us on the night in question, he said that he would rather take

---

b The theatre of Dionysus lay on the S.E. slopes of the Acropolis. Adjoining it was the Odeum of Pericles, a rectangular hall with a conical roof, the remains of which have been brought to light in recent years ; it was used for musical festivals.

c *i.e.* the second, larger reward proposed by Peisander (§ 27).

μᾶλλον ἢ παρ' ἡμῶν, ὥσθ' ἡμᾶς ἔχειν φίλους.
εἰπεῖν οὖν τὸν Εὔφημον ὅτι καλῶς ποιήσειεν
εἰπών, καὶ νῦν ἥκειν[1] κελεῦσαί οἱ εἰς τὴν Λεωγόρου
οἰκίαν, " ἵν' ἐκεῖ συγγένη μετ' ἐμοῦ 'Ανδοκίδη
41 καὶ ἑτέροις οἷς δεῖ." ἥκειν ἔφη τῇ ὑστεραίᾳ, καὶ
δὴ κόπτειν τὴν θύραν· τὸν δὲ πατέρα τὸν ἐμὸν
τυχεῖν ἐξιόντα, καὶ εἰπεῖν αὐτῷ[2]· " ἆρά γε σὲ οἵδε
περιμένουσι; χρὴ μέντοι μὴ ἀπωθεῖσθαι τοιούτους
φίλους." εἰπόντα δὲ αὐτὸν ταῦτα οἴχεσθαι. καὶ
τούτῳ μὲν τῷ τρόπῳ τὸν πατέρα μου ἀπώλλυε,
συνειδότα ἀποφαίνων. εἰπεῖν δὲ ἡμᾶς ὅτι δεδογ-
μένον ἡμῖν εἴη δύο μὲν τάλαντα ἀργυρίου διδόναι
οἱ ἀντὶ τῶν ἑκατὸν μνῶν τῶν ἐκ τοῦ δημοσίου, ἐὰν
δὲ κατάσχωμεν ἡμεῖς ἃ βουλόμεθα, ἕνα αὐτὸν[3] ἡμῶν
εἶναι, πίστιν δὲ τούτων δοῦναί τε καὶ δέξασθαι.
42 ἀποκρίνασθαι δὲ αὐτὸς πρὸς ταῦτα ὅτι βουλεύσοιτο·
ἡμᾶς δὲ κελεύειν αὐτὸν ἥκειν εἰς Καλλίου τοῦ
Τηλοκλέους, ἵνα κἀκεῖνος παρείη. τὸν δ' αὖ
κηδεστήν μου οὕτως ἀπώλλυεν. ἥκειν ἔφη εἰς
Καλλίου, καὶ καθομολογήσας ἡμῖν πίστιν δοῦναι
ἐν ἀκροπόλει, καὶ ἡμᾶς συνθεμένους οἱ τὸ ἀργύριον εἰς τὸν ἐπιόντα[4] μῆνα δώσειν διαψεύδεσθαι καὶ
οὐ διδόναι· ἥκειν οὖν μηνύσων τὰ γενόμενα.
43 Ἡ μὲν εἰσαγγελία αὐτῷ,[5] ὦ ἄνδρες, τοιαύτη·
ἀπογράφει δὲ τὰ ὀνόματα τῶν ἀνδρῶν ὧν ἔφη

---

[1] Verba καὶ νῦν ἥκειν vix sana.   καὶ συνήκειν Emperius.
[2] αὐτῷ Lipsius : αὐτόν codd.
[3] αὐτὸν Reiske : αὐτῶν codd.
[4] ἐπιόντα Emperius : εἰσιόντα codd.
[5] αὐτῷ Reiske : αὐτῶν codd.

---

[a] i.e. twenty minae more.
[b] Implying that the mutilation of the Hermae was defin-

our money than the state's, as he would thereby avoid making enemies of us. Euphemus thanked Diocleides for confiding in him. " And now," he added, " be good enough to come to Leogoras' house, so that you and I can see Andocides and the others who must be consulted." According to his story, Diocleides called next day. My father happened to be coming out just as he was knocking at the door. " Are you the man they are expecting in there ? " he asked. " Well, well, we must not turn friends like you away." And with these words he went off. This was an attempt to bring about my father's death by showing that he was in the secret.

We informed Diocleides, or so he alleged, that we had decided to offer him two talents of silver, as against the hundred minae from the Treasury,[a] and promised that he should become one of ourselves, if we achieved our end.[b] Both sides were to give a guarantee of good faith. Diocleides replied that he would think it over ; and we told him to meet us at Callias' house, so that Callias, son of Telocles, might be present as well. This was a similar attempt to bring about the death of my brother-in-law.

Diocleides said that he went to Callias' house, and after terms had been arranged, pledged his word on the Acropolis.[c] We on our side agreed to give him the money the following month ; but we broke our promise and did not do so. He had therefore come to reveal the truth.

Such was the impeachment brought by Diocleides, gentlemen. He gave a list of forty-two persons whom

itely part of a plot to overthrow the democracy. Diocleides is promised a place in the oligarchic government which is to follow.

[c] In one of the temples (cf. § 40).

γνῶναι, δύο καὶ τετταράκοντα, πρώτους μὲν
Μαντίθεον καὶ ᾿Αψεφίωνα, βουλευτὰς ὄντας καὶ
καθημένους ἔνδον, εἶτα δὲ καὶ τοὺς ἄλλους.
ἀναστὰς δὲ Πείσανδρος ἔφη χρῆναι λύειν τὸ ἐπὶ
Σκαμανδρίου ψήφισμα καὶ ἀναβιβάζειν ἐπὶ τὸν
τροχὸν τοὺς ἀπογραφέντας, ὅπως μὴ πρότερον
νὺξ ἔσται πρὶν πυθέσθαι τοὺς ἄνδρας ἅπαντας.

44 ἀνέκραγεν ἡ βουλὴ ὡς εὖ λέγει. ἀκούσαντες δὲ
[7] ταῦτα Μαντίθεος καὶ ᾿Αψεφίων ἐπὶ τὴν ἑστίαν
ἐκαθέζοντο, ἱκετεύοντες μὴ στρεβλωθῆναι ἀλλ᾿
ἐξεγγυηθέντες[1] κριθῆναι. μόλις δὲ τούτων τυχόντες,
ἐπειδὴ τοὺς ἐγγυητὰς κατέστησαν, ἐπὶ τοὺς ἵππους
ἀναβάντες ᾤχοντο εἰς τοὺς πολεμίους αὐτομολή-
σαντες, καταλιπόντες τοὺς ἐγγυητάς, οὓς ἔδει ⟨ἐν⟩[2]
τοῖς αὐτοῖς ἐνέχεσθαι ἐν οἷσπερ οὓς ἠγγυήσαντο.

45 Ἡ δὲ βουλὴ ἐξελθοῦσα ἐν ἀπορρήτῳ συνέλαβεν
ἡμᾶς καὶ ἔδησεν ἐν τοῖς ξύλοις. ἀνακαλέσαντες
δὲ τοὺς στρατηγοὺς ἀνειπεῖν ἐκέλευσαν ᾿Αθηναίων
τοὺς μὲν ἐν ἄστει οἰκοῦντας ἰέναι εἰς τὴν ἀγορὰν
τὰ ὅπλα λαβόντας, τοὺς δ᾿ ἐν μακρῷ τείχει εἰς τὸ
Θησεῖον, τοὺς δ᾿ ἐν Πειραιεῖ εἰς τὴν Ἱπποδαμείαν
ἀγοράν, τοὺς δ᾿ ἱππέας ἔτι ⟨πρὸ⟩[3] νυκτὸς σημῆναι
τῇ σάλπιγγι ἥκειν εἰς τὸ ᾿Ανάκειον, τὴν δὲ βουλὴν
εἰς ἀκρόπολιν ἰέναι κἀκεῖ καθεύδειν, τοὺς δὲ

---

[1] ἐξεγγυηθέντες Bekker : ἐξεγγυηθέντας codd.
[2] ἐν add. Weidner.   [3] πρὸ add. Blass, coll. § 48.

---

[a] The decree forbade the examination of citizens under
torture. The βουλή had been empowered to act entirely at its
own discretion during the crisis (cf. § 15), and so could suspend
the ψήφισμα in question if it thought fit.

he claimed to have recognized, and at the head of the forty-two appeared Mantitheus and Apsephion who were members of the Council and present at that very meeting. Peisander hereupon rose and moved that the decree passed in the archonship of Scamandrius *a* be suspended and all whose names were on the list sent to the wheel, to ensure the discovery of everyone concerned before nightfall. The Council broke into shouts of approval. At that Mantitheus and Apsephion took sanctuary on the hearth, and appealed to be allowed to furnish sureties and stand trial, instead of being racked. They finally managed to gain their request ; but no sooner had they provided their sureties than they leapt on horseback and deserted to the enemy,*b* leaving the sureties to their fate, as they were now liable to the same penalties as the prisoners for whom they had gone bail.

The Council adjourned for a private consultation and in the course of it gave orders for our arrest and close confinement.*c* Then they summoned the Generals and bade them proclaim that citizens resident in Athens proper were to proceed under arms to the Agora ; those between the Long Walls to the Theseum ; and those in Peiraeus to the Agora of Hippodamus. The Knights were to be mustered at the Anaceum *d* by trumpet before nightfall, while the Council would take up its quarters on the Acropolis

---

b They would probably make for the Boeotian frontier (*cf.* § 45 *infr.*), though Thucydides states that there was also a Spartan force at the Isthmus at this time (vi. 61).

c Lit. "made us fast in the stocks." These were in the gaol itself.

d The Agora of Hippodamus was the Agora of Peiraeus: the Anaceum, a temple of the Dioscuri to the N.W. of the Acropolis.

πρυτάνεις ἐν τῇ θόλῳ. Βοιωτοὶ δὲ πεπυσμένοι
τὰ πράγματα ἐπὶ τοῖς ὁρίοις ἦσαν ἐξεστρατευμένοι.
τὸν δὲ τῶν κακῶν τούτων αἴτιον Διοκλείδην ὡς
σωτῆρα ὄντα τῆς πόλεως ἐπὶ ζεύγους ἦγον εἰς τὸ
πρυτανεῖον στεφανώσαντες,[1] καὶ ἐδείπνει ἐκεῖ.

46 Πρῶτον μὲν οὖν ταῦτα, ὦ ἄνδρες, ὁπόσοι ὑμῶν
παρῆσαν, ἀναμιμνήσκεσθε καὶ τοὺς ἄλλους δι-
δάσκετε· εἶτα δέ μοι τοὺς πρυτάνεις κάλει τοὺς
τότε πρυτανεύσαντας, Φιλοκράτη καὶ τοὺς ἄλλους.

ΜΑΡΤΥΡΕΣ

47 Φέρε δή, καὶ τὰ ὀνόματα ὑμῖν ἀναγνώσομαι τῶν
ἀνδρῶν ὧν ἀπέγραψεν, ἵν' εἰδῆτε ὅσους μοι τῶν
συγγενῶν ἀπώλλυεν, πρῶτον μὲν τὸν πατέρα, εἶτα
δὲ τὸν κηδεστήν, τὸν μὲν συνειδότα ἀποδεικνύς,
τοῦ δ' ἐν τῇ οἰκίᾳ φάσκων τὴν σύνοδον γενέσθαι.
τῶν δ' ἄλλων ἀκούσεσθε τὰ ὀνόματα. καὶ αὐτοῖς
ἀναγίγνωσκε.

Χαρμίδης Ἀριστοτέλους.

οὗτος ἀνεψιὸς ἐμός· ἡ μήτηρ ⟨ἡ⟩[2] ἐκείνου καὶ ὁ
πατὴρ ὁ ἐμὸς ἀδελφοί.

Ταυρέας.

οὑτοσὶ ἀνεψιὸς τοῦ πατρός.

Νισαῖος.

υἱὸς Ταυρέου.

---

[1] στεφανώσαντες Bekker : στεφανώσοντες codd.
[2] ἡ add. Bekker.

[a] The θόλος was a circular building with a domed roof
situated in the Agora ; it was sometimes known as the σκιάς.
It is the same as the Prytaneum mentioned a few lines below.

for the night, and the Prytanes in the Tholus.[a] In the meantime, the Boeotians, who had heard the news, had taken the field and were on the frontier; while Diocleides, the author of all the mischief, was hailed as the saviour of Athens : a garland was placed upon his head, and he was driven upon an ox-cart to the Prytaneum, where he was entertained.

Now first of all I want those of you who witnessed all this to picture it once more and describe it to those who did not. Next I will ask the clerk to call the Prytanes in office at the time, Philocrates and his colleagues.

Witnesses

And now I am also going to read you the names of those denounced by Diocleides, so that you may see how many relatives of mine he tried to ruin. First there was my father, and then my brother-in-law; my father he had represented as in the secret, while he had alleged that my brother-in-law's house was the scene of the meeting. The names of the rest you shall hear. Read them out to the court.

Charmides, son of Aristoteles.

That is a cousin of mine ; his mother and my father were brother and sister.

Taureas.

That is a cousin of my father's.

Nisaeus.

A son of Taureas.

The Prytanes and their γραμματεύς dined there daily, and distinguished foreign visitors were often entertained at the Tholus at the public cost. Diocleides was accorded this privilege.

377

Καλλίας ὁ 'Αλκμέωνος.

ἀνεψιὸς τοῦ πατρός.

Εὔφημος.

Καλλίου τοῦ Τηλοκλέους ἀδελφός.

Φρύνιχος ὁ 'Ορχησαμενοῦ.[1]

ἀνεψιός.

Εὐκράτης.

ὁ Νικίου ἀδελφός.[2] κηδεστὴς οὗτος Καλλίου.

Κριτίας.

ἀνεψιὸς[3] καὶ οὗτος τοῦ πατρός· αἱ μητέρες ἀδελφαί.

Τούτους πάντας ἐν τοῖς τετταράκοντα ἀνδράσιν ἀπέγραψεν.[4]

48 'Επειδὴ δὲ ἐδεδέμεθα πάντες ἐν τῷ αὐτῷ καὶ νύξ τε ἦν καὶ τὸ δεσμωτήριον συνεκέκλητο, ἦκον δὲ τῷ μὲν μήτηρ τῷ δὲ ἀδελφὴ τῷ δὲ γυνὴ καὶ παῖδες, ἦν δὲ βοὴ καὶ οἶκτος κλαόντων καὶ ὀδυρομένων τὰ παρόντα κακά, λέγει πρός με Χαρμίδης, ὧν μὲν ἀνεψιός, ἡλικιώτης δὲ καὶ συνεκτραφεὶς ἐν τῇ οἰκίᾳ τῇ ἡμετέρᾳ ἐκ παιδός,

[1] 'Ορχησαμενοῦ Wilhelm: ὀρχησάμενος codd.
[2] Verba ὁ Νικίου ἀδελφός quae in codd. cum Εὐκράτης coniuncta sunt ita distinxi.
[3] Post ἀνεψιὸς habent codd. Εὐκρατίας ὁ Νικίου ἀδελφὸς e praecedentibus male iterata. Eiecit Reiske. Hunc indicem turbatum esse ex § 68 satis liquet.
[4] ἀπέγραψεν Stephanus: ἐπέγραψεν codd.

---

[a] The ms. reading is retained by some and translated "the

Callias, son of Alcmaeon.

A cousin of my father's.

Euphemus.

A brother of Callias, son of Telocles.

Phrynichus, son of Orchesamenus.[a]

A cousin.

Eucrates.

The brother of Nicias.[b] He is Callias' brother-in-law.

Critias.

Another cousin of my father's ; their mothers were sisters.

All of these appeared among the last forty on Diocleides' list.

We were all thrown into one prison. Darkness fell, and the gates were shut. Mothers, sisters, wives, and children had gathered. Nothing was to be heard save the cries and moans of grief-stricken wretches bewailing the calamity which had overtaken them. In the midst of it all, Charmides, a cousin of my own age who had been brought up with me in my own home

ex-dancer," on the ground that a famous dancer named Phrynichus was living in Athens at this period (*cf.* Ar. *Wasps* 1302). But no true parallel can be produced for such a use of the aorist participle. It is preferable to emend as in the text, as proper names with a participial form were not uncommon ; *cf.* 'Ακεσαμενός, 'Αλεξαμενός, Τεισαμενός, 'Ακουμενός.

[b] The words ὁ Νικίου ἀδελφός are misplaced in the MSS. Andocides is clearly quoting from an official list ; and in such documents a man would be referred to by his father's name, not by his brother's. The reference to the brother is part of the commentary of Andocides which follows. The Nicias in question is the general.

49 ὅτι '' 'Ανδοκίδη, τῶν μὲν παρόντων κακῶν ὁρᾷς
τὸ μέγεθος, ἐγὼ δ' ἐν μὲν τῷ παρελθόντι χρόνῳ
οὐδὲν ἐδεόμην λέγειν οὐδέ σε λυπεῖν, νῦν δὲ ἀναγ-
κάζομαι διὰ τὴν παροῦσαν ἡμῖν συμφοράν. οἷς
γὰρ ἐχρῶ καὶ οἷς συνῆσθα ἄνευ ἡμῶν τῶν συγγενῶν, οὗτοι ἐπὶ ταῖς αἰτίαις δι' ἃς ἡμεῖς ἀπο-
λλύμεθα οἱ μὲν αὐτῶν τεθνᾶσιν, οἱ δὲ οἴχονται
50 φεύγοντες, σφῶν αὐτῶν καταγνόντες ἀδικεῖν[1] . . .
εἰ ἤκουσάς τι τούτου τοῦ πράγματος τοῦ γενομένου,
εἰπέ, καὶ πρῶτον μὲν σεαυτὸν σῶσον, εἶτα δὲ τὸν
πατέρα, ὃν εἰκός ἐστί σε μάλιστα φιλεῖν, εἶτα δὲ
τὸν κηδεστὴν ὃς ἔχει σου τὴν ἀδελφὴν ἥπερ σοι
μόνη ἐστίν, ἔπειτα δὲ τοὺς ἄλλους συγγενεῖς καὶ
ἀναγκαίους τοσούτους ὄντας, ἔτι δὲ ἐμέ, ὃς ἐν
ἅπαντι τῷ βίῳ ἠνίασα μέν σε οὐδὲν πώποτε,
προθυμότατος δὲ εἰς σὲ καὶ τὰ σὰ πράγματά εἰμι,
ὅ τι ἂν δέῃ[2] ποιεῖν.''

51 Λέγοντος δέ, ὦ ἄνδρες, Χαρμίδου ταῦτα, ἀντι-
βολούντων δὲ τῶν ἄλλων καὶ ἱκετεύοντος ἑνὸς
ἑκάστου, ἐνεθυμήθην πρὸς ἐμαυτόν, '' Ὦ πάντων
ἐγὼ δεινοτάτῃ συμφορᾷ περιπεσών, πότερα περιίδω
τοὺς ἐμαυτοῦ συγγενεῖς ἀπολλυμένους ἀδίκως, καὶ
αὐτούς τε ἀποθανόντας καὶ τὰ χρήματα αὐτῶν
δημευθέντα, πρὸς δὲ τούτοις ἀναγραφέντας ἐν
στήλαις ὡς ὄντας ἀλιτηρίους τῶν θεῶν τοὺς
οὐδενὸς αἰτίους τῶν γεγενημένων, ἔτι δὲ τρια-
[8] κοσίους 'Αθηναίων μέλλοντας ἀδίκως ἀπολεῖσθαι,[3]

---

[1] Habet A lacunam duodecim litterarum post ἀδικεῖν.
τούτων τοίνυν add. Sauppe, ἀλλὰ δέομαι σοῦ Reiske.
[2] δέῃ Bekker : δέοι codd.
[3] ἀπολεῖσθαι Stephanus : ἀπολέσθαι codd.

since boyhood, said to me : " You see the utter hopelessness of our position, Andocides. I have never yet wished to say anything which might distress you : but now our plight leaves me no choice. Your friends and associates outside the family have all been subjected to the charges which are now to prove our own undoing : and half of them have been put to death, while the other half have admitted their guilt by going into exile.[a] I beg of you : if you have heard anything concerning this affair, disclose it. Save yourself : save your father, who must be dearer to you than anyone in the world : save your brother-in-law, the husband of your only sister : save all those others who are bound to you by ties of blood and family : and lastly, save me, who have never vexed you in my life and who am ever ready to do anything for you and your good."

At this appeal from Charmides, gentlemen, which was echoed by the rest, who each addressed their entreaties to me in turn, I thought to myself : " Never, oh, never has a man found himself in a more terrible strait than I. Am I to look on while my own kindred perish for a crime which they have not committed : while they themselves are put to death and their goods are confiscated : nay more, while the names of persons entirely innocent of the deed which has been done are inscribed upon stones of record as the names of men accursed in the sight of heaven ? Am I to pay no heed to three hundred Athenians who are to be wrongfully put to death, to the desperate

---

[a] Charmides' argument seems to be that, as Andocides' friends have already been exposed, he can do no harm to them by any revelations he may choose to make. On the other hand, he will be able to save his family from certain death.

τὴν δὲ πόλιν ἐν κακοῖς οὖσαν τοῖς μεγίστοις καὶ
ὑποψίαν εἰς ἀλλήλους ἔχοντας, ἢ εἴπω Ἀθηναίοις
ἅπερ ἤκουσα Εὐφιλήτου αὐτοῦ τοῦ ποιήσαντος;"

52 Ἔτι δὲ ἐπὶ τούτοις καὶ τόδε ἐνεθυμήθην, ὦ
ἄνδρες, καὶ ἐλογιζόμην πρὸς ἐμαυτὸν τοὺς ἐξημαρτηκότας καὶ τὸ ἔργον εἰργασμένους, ὅτι οἱ
μὲν αὐτῶν ἤδη ἐτέθνασαν ὑπὸ Τεύκρου μηνυθέντες,
οἱ δὲ φεύγοντες ᾤχοντο καὶ αὐτῶν θάνατος κατέγνωστο, τέτταρες δὲ ἦσαν ὑπόλοιποι οἳ οὐκ ἐμηνύθησαν ὑπὸ Τεύκρου τῶν πεποιηκότων, Παναίτιος,

53 Χαιρέδημος, Διάκριτος, Λυσίστρατος· οὓς εἰκὸς
ἦν ἁπάντων μάλιστα δοκεῖν εἶναι τούτων τῶν
ἀνδρῶν οὓς ἐμήνυσε Διοκλείδης, φίλους ὄντας τῶν
ἀπολωλότων ἤδη. καὶ τοῖς μὲν οὐδέπω βέβαιος
ἦν ἡ σωτηρία, τοῖς δὲ ἐμοῖς οἰκείοις φανερὸς ⟨ὁ⟩[1]
ὄλεθρος, εἰ μή τις ἐρεῖ Ἀθηναίοις τὰ γενόμενα.
ἐδόκει οὖν μοι κρεῖττον εἶναι τέτταρας ἄνδρας
ἀποστερῆσαι τῆς πατρίδος δικαίως, οἳ νῦν ζῶσι
καὶ κατεληλύθασι καὶ ἔχουσι τὰ σφέτερα αὐτῶν,
ἢ ἐκείνους ἀποθανόντας ἀδίκως περιιδεῖν.

54 Εἰ οὖν τινι ὑμῶν, ὦ ἄνδρες, ⟨ἢ⟩[2] τῶν ἄλλων
πολιτῶν γνώμη τοιαύτη παρειστήκει πρότερον
περὶ ἐμοῦ, ὡς ἄρα ἐγὼ ἐμήνυσα κατὰ τῶν ἑταίρων
τῶν ἐμαυτοῦ, ὅπως ἐκεῖνοι μὲν ἀπόλοιντο, ἐγὼ
δὲ σωθείην—ἃ ἐλογοποίουν οἱ ἐχθροὶ περὶ ἐμοῦ,
βουλόμενοι διαβάλλειν με—σκοπεῖσθε ἐξ αὐτῶν

55 τῶν γεγενημένων. νῦν γὰρ ἐμὲ μὲν λόγον δεῖ
δοῦναι[3] τῶν ἐμοὶ πεπραγμένων μετὰ τῆς ἀληθείας,
αὐτῶν παρόντων οἵπερ ἥμαρτον καὶ ἔφυγον ταῦτα
ποιήσαντες, ἴσασι δὲ ἄριστα εἴτε ψεύδομαι εἴτε

---

[1] ὁ add. Reiske.   [2] ἢ add. Sluiter.
[3] δεῖ δοῦναι Dobree : διδόναι codd.

plight of Athens, to the suspicions of citizen for citizen ? Or am I to reveal to my countrymen the story told me by the true criminal, Euphiletus ? " [a]

Then a further thought struck me, gentlemen. I reminded myself that a number of the offenders responsible for the mutilation had already been executed upon the information lodged by Teucrus, while yet others had escaped into exile and been sentenced to death in their absence. In fact, there remained only four of the criminals whose names had not been divulged by Teucrus : Panaetius, Chaeredemus, Diacritus, and Lysistratus ; and it was only natural to assume that they had been among the first to be denounced by Diocleides, as they were friends of those who had already been put to death. It was thus still doubtful whether they would escape : but it was certain that my own kindred would perish, unless Athens learned the truth. So I decided that it was better to cut off from their country four men who richly deserved it—men alive to-day and restored to home and property—than to let those others go to a death which they had done nothing whatever to deserve.

If, then, any of you yourselves, gentlemen, or any of the public at large has ever been possessed with the notion that I informed against my associates with the object of purchasing my own life at the price of theirs—a tale invented by my enemies, who wished to present me in the blackest colours—use the facts themselves as evidence ; for to-day not only is it incumbent upon me to give a faithful account of myself—I am in the presence, remember, of the actual offenders who went into exile after committing the

[a] Already denounced by Teucrus (§ 35).

ἀληθῆ λέγω, ἔξεστι δὲ αὐτοῖς ἐλέγχειν με ἐν τῷ
ἐμῷ λόγῳ· ἐγὼ γὰρ ἐφίημι· ὑμᾶς δὲ δεῖ μαθεῖν τὰ
56 γενόμενα. ἐμοὶ γάρ, ὦ ἄνδρες, τοῦδε τοῦ ἀγῶνος
τουτ᾽ ἔστι μέγιστον, σωθέντι μὴ δοκεῖν κακῷ εἶναι,
⟨ἀλλὰ πρῶτον μὲν ὑμᾶς,[1]⟩ εἶτα δὲ καὶ τοὺς ἄλλους
ἅπαντας μαθεῖν ὅτι οὔτε μετὰ κακίας οὔτε μετ᾽
ἀνανδρίας οὐδεμιᾶς τῶν γεγενημένων πέπρακται
ὑπ᾽ ἐμοῦ οὐδέν, ἀλλὰ διὰ συμφορὰν γεγενημένην
μάλιστα μὲν τῇ πόλει, εἶτα ⟨δὲ⟩[2] καὶ ἡμῖν, εἶπον δὲ
ἃ ἤκουσα Εὐφιλήτου προνοίᾳ μὲν τῶν συγγενῶν καὶ
τῶν φίλων, προνοίᾳ δὲ τῆς πόλεως ἁπάσης, μετ᾽
ἀρετῆς ἀλλ᾽ οὐ μετὰ κακίας, ὡς ἐγὼ νομίζω. εἰ
οὖν οὕτως ἔχει ταῦτα, σῴζεσθαί τε ἀξιῶ καὶ
δοκεῖν ὑμῖν εἶναι μὴ κακός.

57 Φέρε δή—χρὴ γάρ, ὦ ἄνδρες, ἀνθρωπίνως περὶ
τῶν πραγμάτων ἐκλογίζεσθαι, ὥσπερ ἂν αὐτὸν
ὄντα ἐν τῇ συμφορᾷ—τί ἂν ὑμῶν ἕκαστος ἐποίησεν;
εἰ μὲν γὰρ ἦν δυοῖν τὸ ἕτερον ἑλέσθαι, ἢ καλῶς
ἀπολέσθαι ἢ αἰσχρῶς σωθῆναι, ἔχοι ἄν τις εἰπεῖν
κακίαν εἶναι τὰ γενόμενα[3]· καίτοι πολλοὶ ἂν καὶ
τοῦτο εἵλοντο, τὸ ζῆν περὶ πλείονος ποιησάμενοι
58 τοῦ καλῶς ἀποθανεῖν· ὅπου δὲ τούτων τὸ ἐναν-
τιώτατον ἦν, σιωπήσαντι μὲν αὐτῷ τε αἴσχιστα
ἀπολέσθαι μηδὲν ἀσεβήσαντι, ἔτι δὲ τὸν πατέρα
περιιδεῖν ἀπολόμενον καὶ τὸν κηδεστὴν καὶ τοὺς
συγγενεῖς καὶ ἀνεψιοὺς τοσούτους, οὓς οὐδεὶς

---

[1] Nonnihil excidisse videtur. ἀλλὰ πρῶτον μὲν ὑμᾶς add.
Blass: alii alia.
[2] δὲ add. Reiske: lacunam duarum litterarum habent
codd.
[3] γενόμενα Reiske: λεγόμενα codd.

crime which we are discussing ; they know better than anyone whether I am lying or not, and they have my permission to interrupt me and prove that what I am saying is untrue—but it is no less incumbent upon you to discover what truly happened. I say this, gentlemen, because the chief task confronting me in this trial is to prevent anyone thinking the worse of me on account of my escape : to make first you and then the whole world understand that the explanation of my behaviour from start to finish lay in the desperate plight of Athens and, to a lesser degree, in that of my own family, not in any lack of principles or courage : to make you understand that, in disclosing what Euphiletus had told me, I was actuated solely by my concern for my relatives and friends and by my concern for the state as a whole, motives which I for one consider not a disgrace but a credit. If this proves to be the truth of the matter, I think it only my due that I should be acquitted with my good name unimpaired.

Come now, in considering a case, a judge should make allowances for human shortcomings, gentlemen, as he would do, were he in the same plight himself. What would each of you have done ? Had the choice lain between dying a noble death and preserving my life at the cost of my honour, my behaviour might well be described as base—though many would have made exactly the same choice ; they would rather have remained alive than have died like heroes. But the alternatives before me were precisely the opposite. On the other hand, if I remained silent, I myself died in disgrace for an act of impiety which I had not committed, and I allowed my father, my brother-in-law, and a host of my relatives and cousins to perish

385

ἄλλος ἀπώλλυεν ἢ ἐγὼ μὴ εἰπὼν ὡς ἕτεροι ἥμαρτον.
Διοκλείδης μὲν γὰρ ψευσάμενος ἔδησεν αὐτούς,
σωτηρία δὲ αὐτῶν ἄλλη οὐδεμία ἦν ἢ πυθέσθαι
Ἀθηναίους πάντα τὰ πραχθέντα· φονεὺς οὖν
αὐτῶν ἐγιγνόμην ἐγὼ μὴ εἰπὼν ὑμῖν ἃ ἤκουσα.
ἔτι δὲ τριακοσίους Ἀθηναίων ἀπώλλυον, καὶ ἡ
59 πόλις ἐν κακοῖς τοῖς μεγίστοις ἐγίγνετο. ταῦτα
μὲν οὖν ἦν ἐμοῦ μὴ εἰπόντος· εἰπὼν δὲ τὰ ὄντα
αὐτός τε ἐσῳζόμην καὶ τὸν πατέρα ἔσῳζον καὶ
τοὺς ἄλλους συγγενεῖς, καὶ τὴν πόλιν ἐκ φόβου
καὶ κακῶν τῶν μεγίστων ἀπήλλαττον. φυγάδες
δὲ δι' ἐμὲ τέτταρες ἄνδρες ἐγίγνοντο, οἵπερ καὶ
ἥμαρτον· τῶν δ' ἄλλων, οἳ πρότερον[1] ὑπὸ Τεύκρου
ἐμηνύθησαν, οὔτε δήπου οἱ τεθνεῶτες δι' ἐμὲ
μᾶλλον ἐτέθνασαν, οὔτε οἱ φεύγοντες μᾶλλον
ἔφευγον.

60 Ταῦτα δὲ πάντα σκοπῶν ηὕρισκον, ὦ ἄνδρες,
τῶν παρόντων κακῶν ταῦτα ἐλάχιστα εἶναι, εἰπεῖν
τὰ γενόμενα ὡς τάχιστα καὶ ἐλέγξαι Διοκλείδην
ψευσάμενον, καὶ τιμωρήσασθαι ἐκεῖνον, ὃς ἡμᾶς
[9] μὲν ἀπώλλυεν ἀδίκως, τὴν δὲ πόλιν ἐξηπάτα, ταῦτα
δὲ ποιῶν μέγιστος εὐεργέτης ἐδόκει εἶναι καὶ
61 χρήματα ἐλάμβανε. διὰ ταῦτα εἶπον τῇ βουλῇ
ὅτι εἰδείην τοὺς ποιήσαντας, καὶ ἐξήλεγξα τὰ
γενόμενα, ὅτι εἰσηγήσατο μὲν πινόντων ἡμῶν
ταύτην τὴν βουλὴν [γενέσθαι][2] Εὐφίλητος, ἀντεῖπον
δὲ ἐγώ, καὶ τότε μὲν οὐ γένοιτο δι' ἐμέ, ὕστερον
δ' ἐγὼ μὲν ἐν Κυνοσάργει ἐπὶ πωλίον ὅ μοι ἦν
ἀναβὰς ἔπεσον καὶ τὴν κλεῖν συνετρίβην καὶ τὴν

---

[1] τῶν δ' ἄλλων, οἳ πρότερον Dobree: τῶν δ' ἄλλων οἱ λοιποὶ
πρότερον codd.
[2] γενέσθαι delevit Bekker.

in addition. Yes, I, and I alone, was sending them
to their death, if I refused to say that others were to
blame ; for Diocleides had thrown them into prison
by his lies, and they could only be rescued if their
countrymen were put in full possession of the facts ;
therefore I became their murderer if I refused to tell
what I had heard. Besides this, I was causing three
hundred citizens to perish ; while the plight of
Athens was growing desperate. That is what silence
meant. On the other hand, by revealing the truth I
saved my own life, I saved my father, I saved the rest
of my family, and I freed Athens from the panic
which was working such havoc. True, I was sending
four men into exile ; but all four were guilty. And
as for the others, who had already been denounced
by Teucrus, I am sure that none of them, whether
dead or in exile, was one whit the worse off for any
disclosures of mine.

Taking all this into consideration, gentlemen, I
found that the least objectionable of the courses open
to me was to tell the truth as quickly as possible, to
prove that Diocleides had lied, and so to punish the
scoundrel who was causing us to be put to death
wrongfully and imposing upon the public, while in
return he was being hailed as a supreme benefactor
and rewarded for his services. I therefore informed
the Council that I knew the offenders, and showed
exactly what had occurred. The idea, I said, had
been suggested by Euphiletus at a drinking-party ;
but I opposed it, and succeeded in preventing its
execution for the time being. Later, however, I was
thrown from a colt of mine in Cynosarges [a] ; I broke

---

[a] A gymnasium sacred to Heracles on the eastern outskirts
of Athens, near the Diomean Gate.

κεφαλὴν κατεάγην, φερόμενός τε ἐπὶ κλίνης
62 ἀπεκομίσθην οἴκαδε· αἰσθόμενος δ᾽ Εὐφίλητος ὡς
ἔχοιμι, λέγει πρὸς αὐτοὺς ὅτι πέπεισμαι ταῦτα
συμποιεῖν καὶ ὡμολόγηκα αὐτῷ[1] μεθέξειν τοῦ
ἔργου καὶ περικόψειν τὸν Ἑρμῆν τὸν παρὰ τὸ
Φορβαντεῖον. ταῦτα δ᾽ ἔλεγεν ἐξαπατῶν ἐκείνους·
καὶ διὰ ταῦτα ὁ Ἑρμῆς ὃν ὁρᾶτε πάντες, ὁ παρὰ
τὴν πατρῴαν οἰκίαν τὴν ἡμετέραν, ὃν ἡ Αἰγῇς
ἀνέθηκεν, οὐ περιεκόπη μόνος τῶν Ἑρμῶν τῶν
Ἀθήνησιν, ὡς ἐμοῦ τοῦτο ποιήσοντος,[2] ὡς ἔφη
πρὸς αὐτοὺς Εὐφίλητος.
63   Οἱ δ᾽ αἰσθόμενοι δεινὰ ἐποίουν, ὅτι εἰδείην μὲν τὸ
πρᾶγμα, πεποιηκὼς δὲ οὐκ εἴην. προσελθόντες
δέ μοι τῇ ὑστεραίᾳ Μέλητος καὶ Εὐφίλητος ἔλεγον
ὅτι " γεγένηται, ὦ Ἀνδοκίδη, καὶ πέπρακται ἡμῖν
ταῦτα. σὺ μέντοι εἰ μὲν ἀξιοῖς ἡσυχίαν ἔχειν καὶ
σιωπᾶν, ἕξεις ἡμᾶς ἐπιτηδείους ὥσπερ καὶ πρό-
τερον· εἰ δὲ μή, χαλεπώτεροί σοι ἡμεῖς ἐχθροὶ ἐσό-
64 μεθα ἢ ἄλλοι τινὲς δι᾽ ἡμᾶς φίλοι." εἶπον αὐτοῖς
ὅτι νομίζοιμι μὲν διὰ τὸ πρᾶγμα Εὐφίλητον
πονηρὸν εἶναι, ἐκείνοις δὲ οὐκ ἐμὲ δεινὸν εἶναι,
ὅτι οἶδα, ἀλλὰ μᾶλλον αὐτὸ τὸ ἔργον πολλῷ, ὅτι
πεποίηται.
    Ὡς οὖν ἦν ταῦτ᾽ ἀληθῆ, τόν τε παῖδα τὸν ἐμὸν
παρέδωκα βασανίσαι, ὅτι ἔκαμνον καὶ οὐδ᾽ ἀν-
ιστάμην ἐκ τῆς κλίνης, καὶ τὰς θεραπαίνας ἔλαβον
οἱ πρυτάνεις, ὅθεν ὁρμώμενοι ταῦτ᾽ ἐποίουν

---

[1] αὐτῷ A corr. : αὐτῶν A pr.
[2] ποιήσοντος Valckenaer : ποιήσαντος codd.

---

[a] One of the many ἥρωα scattered over the city.   Phorbas
was an Attic hero ; he had been the charioteer of Theseus.

my collar-bone and fractured my skull, and had to be taken home on a litter. When Euphiletus saw my condition, he informed the others that I had consented to join them and had promised him to mutilate the Hermes next to the shrine of Phorbas *a* as my share in the escapade. He told them this to hoodwink them ; and that is why the Hermes which you can all see standing close to the home of our family, the Hermes dedicated by the Aegeïd tribe, was the only one in Athens unmutilated, it being understood that I would attend to it as Euphiletus had promised.

When the others learned the truth, they were furious to think that I was in the secret without having taken any active part ; and the next day I received a visit from Meletus *b* and Euphiletus. "We have managed it all right, Andocides," they told me. "Now if you will consent to keep quiet and say nothing, you will find us just as good friends as before. If you do not, you will find that you have been much more successful at making enemies of us than at making fresh friends by turning traitor to us." I replied that I certainly thought Euphiletus a scoundrel for acting as he had ; although he and his companions had far less to fear from my being in the secret than from the mere fact that the deed was done.

I supported this account by handing over my slave for torture, to prove that I was ill at the time in question and had not even left my bed ; and the Prytanes arrested the women-servants in the house which the criminals had used as their base. The

b Meletus had also been connected with the profanation of the Mysteries; his name appears on Andromachus' list (§ 13). Like Euphiletus, he was denounced by Teucrus for mutilation of the Hermae (§ 35).

ANDOCIDES

65 ἐκεῖνοι. ἐξελέγχοντες δὲ τὸ πρᾶγμα ἥ τε βουλὴ
καὶ οἱ ζητηταί, ἐπειδὴ ἦν ᾗ ἐγὼ ἔλεγον καὶ
ὡμολογεῖτο πανταχόθεν, τότε δὴ καλοῦσι τὸν
Διοκλείδην· καὶ οὐ πολλῶν λόγων ἐδέησεν, ἀλλ᾽
εὐθὺς ὡμολόγει ψεύδεσθαι, καὶ ἐδεῖτο σῴζεσθαι
φράσας τοὺς πείσαντας αὐτὸν λέγειν ταῦτα· εἶναι
δὲ Ἀλκιβιάδην τὸν Φηγούσιον καὶ Ἀμίαντον τὸν
66 ἐξ Αἰγίνης. καὶ οὗτοι μὲν δείσαντες ᾤχοντο
φεύγοντες· ὑμεῖς δὲ ἀκούσαντες ταῦτα Διοκλείδην
μὲν τῷ δικαστηρίῳ παραδόντες ἀπεκτείνατε, τοὺς
δὲ δεδεμένους καὶ μέλλοντας ἀπολεῖσθαι ἐλύσατε,
τοὺς ἐμοὺς συγγενεῖς, δι᾽ ἐμέ, καὶ τοὺς φεύγοντας
κατεδέξασθε, αὐτοὶ δὲ λαβόντες τὰ ὅπλα ἀπῇτε,[1]
67 πολλῶν κακῶν καὶ κινδύνων ἀπαλλαγέντες. ἐν
οἷς ἐγώ, ὦ ἄνδρες, τῆς μὲν τύχης ᾗ ἐχρη-
σάμην δικαίως ἂν ὑπὸ πάντων ἐλεηθείην, τῶν
δὲ γενομένων ἕνεκα εἰκότως ⟨ἂν⟩[2] ἀνὴρ ἄριστος
δοκοίην εἶναι, ὅστις εἰσηγησαμένῳ μὲν Εὐφιλήτῳ
πίστιν τῶν ἐν ἀνθρώποις ἀπιστοτάτην ἠναντιώθην
καὶ ἀντεῖπον καὶ ἐλοιδόρησα ἐκεῖνον[3] ὧν ἦν ἄξιος,
ἁμαρτόντων δ᾽ ἐκείνων τὴν ἁμαρτίαν αὐτοῖς
συνέκρυψα, καὶ μηνύσαντος κατ᾽ αὐτῶν Τεύκρου
οἱ μὲν αὐτῶν ἀπέθανον οἱ δ᾽ ἔφυγον, πρὶν ἡμᾶς
ὑπὸ Διοκλείδου δεθῆναι καὶ μέλλειν ἀπολεῖσθαι.
τότε δὲ ἀπέγραψα τέτταρας ἄνδρας, Παναίτιον,
68 Διάκριτον, Λυσίστρατον, Χαιρέδημον· οὗτοι μὲν
ἔφυγον δι᾽ ἐμέ, ὁμολογῶ· ἐσώθη δέ γε ὁ πατήρ,

---

[1] ἀπῇτε Weidner : ἀπίητε codd.
[2] ἂν add. Reiske.
[3] ἐκεῖνον Naber : ἐκείνῳ codd. : secl. Weidner.

Council and the commission of inquiry went into the matter closely, and when at length they found that it was as I said and that the witnesses corroborated me without exception, they summoned Diocleides. He, however, made a long cross-examination unnecessary by admitting at once that he had been lying, and begged that he might be pardoned if he disclosed who had induced him to tell his story ; the culprits, he said, were Alcibiades of Phegus [a] and Amiantus of Aegina. Alcibiades and Amiantus fled from the country in terror ; and when you heard the facts yourselves, you handed Diocleides over to the court and put him to death. You released the prisoners awaiting execution—my relatives, who owed their escape to me alone—you welcomed back the exiles, and yourselves shouldered arms [b] and dispersed, freed from grave danger and distress.

Not only do the circumstances in which I here found myself entitle me to the sympathy of all, gentlemen, but my conduct can leave you in no doubt about my integrity. When Euphiletus suggested that we pledge ourselves to what was the worst possible treachery, I opposed him, I attacked him, I heaped on him the scorn which he deserved. Yet once his companions had committed the crime, I kept their secret ; it was Teucrus who lodged the information which led to their death or exile, before we had been thrown into prison by Diocleides or were threatened with death. After our imprisonment I denounced four persons : Panaetius, Diacritus, Lysistratus, and Chaeredemus. I was responsible for the exile of these four, I admit ; but I saved my father, my brother-in-

---

[a] A deme in the neighbourhood of Marathon.
[b] *Cf.* § 45.

ὁ κηδεστής, ἀνεψιοὶ τρεῖς, τῶν ἄλλων συγγενῶν
ἑπτά, μέλλοντες ἀποθανεῖσθαι ἀδίκως· οἳ νῦν
ὁρῶσι τοῦ ἡλίου τὸ φῶς δι' ἐμέ, καὶ αὐτοὶ ὁμο-
λογοῦσιν· ὁ δὲ τὴν πόλιν ὅλην συνταράξας καὶ εἰς
τοὺς ἐσχάτους κινδύνους καταστήσας ἐξηλέγχθη,
ὑμεῖς δὲ ἀπηλλάγητε μεγάλων φόβων καὶ τῶν εἰς
ἀλλήλους ὑποψιῶν.

69 Καὶ ταῦτ' εἰ ἀληθῆ λέγω, ὦ ἄνδρες, ἀναμιμνήσκεσθε, καὶ οἱ εἰδότες[1] διδάσκετε τοὺς ἄλλους.
σὺ δέ μοι αὐτοὺς κάλει τοὺς λυθέντας δι' ἐμέ·
ἄριστα γὰρ ἂν εἰδότες τὰ γενόμενα λέγοιεν εἰς
τούτους. οὑτωσὶ δὲ ἔχει, ὦ ἄνδρες· μέχρι τούτου
ἀναβήσονται καὶ λέξουσιν ὑμῖν, ἕως ἂν ἀκροᾶσθαι
[10] βούλησθε, ἔπειτα δ' ἐγὼ περὶ τῶν ἄλλων ἀπολογήσομαι.

⟨ΜΑΡΤΥΡΕΣ⟩[2]

70 Περὶ μὲν οὖν τῶν τότε γενομένων ἀκηκόατε
πάντα καὶ ἀπολελόγηταί μοι ἱκανῶς, ὥς γ' ἐμαυτὸν
πείθω· εἰ δέ τίς τι ὑμῶν ποθεῖ ἢ νομίζει τι μὴ
ἱκανῶς εἰρῆσθαι ἢ παραλέλοιπά τι, ἀναστὰς ὑπο-
μνησάτω, καὶ ἀπολογήσομαι καὶ πρὸς τοῦτο· περὶ
δὲ τῶν νόμων ἤδη ὑμᾶς διδάξω.

71 Κηφίσιος γὰρ οὑτοσὶ ἐνέδειξε μέν με κατὰ τὸν
νόμον τὸν κείμενον, τὴν δὲ κατηγορίαν ποιεῖται
κατὰ ψήφισμα πρότερον γενόμενον, ὃ εἶπεν

---

[1] εἰδότες Reiske: ἰδόντες codd.
[2] ΜΑΡΤΥΡΕΣ add. Reiske.

---

[a] The figures given here do not correspond with the list
of § 47, where the father, the brother-in-law, two cousins,
and five other relatives only are mentioned. The faulty ms.
tradition of § 47 (see app. crit. ad loc.) makes it more probable

law, three cousins, and seven other relatives,[a] all of whom were about to be put to death wrongfully; they owe it to me that they are still looking on the light of day, and they are the first to acknowledge it. In addition, the scoundrel who had thrown the whole of Athens into chaos and endangered her very existence was exposed; and your own suspense and suspicions of one another were at an end.

Now recollect whether what I have been saying is true, gentlemen; and if you know the facts, make them clear to those who do not. Next I will ask the clerk to call the persons who owed their release to me; no one knows what happened better than they, and no one can give the court a better account of it. The position, then, is this, gentlemen: they will address you from the platform for as long as you care to listen to them; then, when you are satisfied, I will proceed to the remainder of my defence.

⟨*Witnesses*⟩

You now know exactly what took place at the time and I for one think that I have given all the explanations necessary. However, should any of you wish to hear more or think that any point has not been dealt with satisfactorily, or should I have omitted anything, he has only to rise and mention it, and I will reply to his inquiry as well. Otherwise, I will proceed to explain the legal position to you.

Admittedly, Cephisius here conformed with the law as it stands in lodging his information against me; but he is resting his case upon an old decree, that it is the list which is incorrect; and alteration of the numerals given in the present passage is not a satisfactory solution of the difficulty.

Ἰσοτιμίδης, οὗ¹ ἐμοὶ προσήκει οὐδέν. ὁ μὲν γὰρ
εἶπεν εἴργεσθαι τῶν ἱερῶν τοὺς ἀσεβήσαντας καὶ
ὁμολογήσαντας, ἐμοὶ δὲ τούτων οὐδέτερα πε-
72 ποίηται· οὔτε ἠσέβηται οὔτε ὡμολόγηται. ὡς δὲ
καὶ τοῦτο τὸ ψήφισμα λέλυται καὶ ἄκυρόν ἐστιν,
ἐγὼ ὑμᾶς διδάξω. καίτοιγε τοιαύτην ἀπολογίαν
περὶ αὐτοῦ ποιήσομαι, ὅπου μὴ πείθων μὲν ὑμᾶς
αὐτὸς ζημιώσομαι, πείσας δὲ ὑπὲρ τῶν ἐχθρῶν
ἀπολελογημένος ἔσομαι. ἀλλὰ γὰρ τἀληθῆ εἰρή-
σεται.

73 Ἐπεὶ γὰρ αἱ νῆες διεφθάρησαν καὶ ἡ πολιορκία
ἐγένετο, ἐβουλεύσασθε περὶ ὁμονοίας, καὶ ἔδοξεν
ὑμῖν τοὺς ἀτίμους ἐπιτίμους ποιῆσαι, καὶ εἶπε τὴν
γνώμην Πατροκλείδης. οἱ δὲ ἄτιμοι τίνες ἦσαν,
καὶ τίνα τρόπον ἕκαστοι; ἐγὼ ὑμᾶς διδάξω.
οἱ μὲν ἀργύριον ὀφείλοντες τῷ δημοσίῳ, ὁπόσοι
εὐθύνας ὦφλον² ἄρξαντες ἀρχάς, ἢ ἐξούλας ἢ
γραφὰς ἢ ἐπιβολὰς³ ὦφλον, ἢ ὠνὰς πριάμενοι ἐκ
τοῦ δημοσίου μὴ κατέβαλον τὰ χρήματα, ἢ ἐγγύας
ἠγγυήσαντο⁴ πρὸς τὸ δημόσιον, τούτοις ἡ μὲν

¹ Ἰσοτιμίδης, οὗ Reiske : εἰς ὅτι μηδ' ἴσου codd.
² ὦφλον Reiske : ὤφειλον codd.
³ ἐπιβολὰς Stephanus : ἐπιβουλὰς codd.
⁴ ἠγγυήσαντο Stephanus : ἐγγυήσαντο codd., unde ἐγγυησά-
μενοι Schoell.

───────────────

ᵃ In 415 B.C.
ᵇ i.e. if Andocides can prove that he is protected by the
amnesty, he will eo ipso create a precedent whereby his
accusers will themselves be able to claim exemption from
punishment for the various offences which they committed
before 403. The nature of these is explained in detail later
(§ 92 et sqq.).

moved by Isotimides,[a] which does not concern me at all. Isotimides proposed to exclude from temples all who had committed an act of impiety and admitted their guilt. I have done neither : I have not committed any act of impiety, nor have I admitted guilt. Further, I will prove to you that the decree in question has been repealed and is void. I shall be adopting a dangerous line of defence here, I know ; if I fail to convince you, I shall myself be the sufferer, and if I succeed in convincing you, I shall have cleared my opponents.[b] However, the truth shall be told.

After the loss of your fleet and the investment of Athens [c] you discussed ways and means of re-uniting the city. As a result you decided to reinstate those who had lost their civic rights, a resolution moved by Patrocleides. Now who were the disfranchised, and what were their different disabilities ? I will explain.[d]

First, state-debtors. All who had been condemned on their accounts when vacating a public office, all who had been condemned as judgement-debtors,[e] all those fined in a public action or under the summary jurisdiction of a magistrate, all who farmed taxes and then defaulted or were liable to the state as sureties

---

[c] The fleet was lost at Aegospotami, Sept. 405 ; this disaster was followed by the siege of Athens, which finally capitulated in April 404. The decree of Patrocleides was passed in the autumn of 405.

[d] For the relevance of the following paragraphs see Introd. pp. 331-332.

[e] Persons against whom judgement had been given in a civil action, but who refused (a) to pay the damages awarded to the plaintiff by the court, (b) to cede to the plaintiff property to which he had established his claim, were liable to a δίκη ἐξούλης. Such suits were common at Athens, where the machinery for ensuring that a judgement was enforced was lamentably defective.

ἔκτεισις ἦν ἐπὶ τῆς ἐνάτης πρυτανείας, εἰ δὲ μή,
διπλάσιον ὀφείλειν καὶ τὰ κτήματα αὐτῶν πε-
πρᾶσθαι.

74 Εἷς μὲν τρόπος οὗτος ἀτιμίας ἦν, ἕτερος δὲ ὧν
τὰ μὲν¹ σώματα ἄτιμα ἦν, τὴν δ᾽ οὐσίαν εἶχον² καὶ
ἐκέκτηντο· οὗτοι δ᾽ αὖ ἦσαν ὁπόσοι κλοπῆς ἢ
δώρων ὄφλοιεν· τούτους ἔδει καὶ αὐτοὺς καὶ τοὺς
ἐκ τούτων ἀτίμους εἶναι· καὶ ὁπόσοι λίποιεν τὴν
τάξιν, ἢ ἀστρατείας ἢ δειλίας ἢ ἀναυμαχίου³
ὄφλοιεν, ἢ τὴν ἀσπίδα ἀποβάλοιεν, ἢ τρὶς ψευδομαρτυρίων ἢ τρὶς ψευδοκλητείας ὄφλοιεν, ἢ τοὺς
γονέας κακῶς ποιοῖεν, οὗτοι πάντες ἄτιμοι ἦσαν
τὰ σώματα, τὰ δὲ χρήματα εἶχον.

75 Ἄλλοι αὖ κατὰ προστάξεις, οἵτινες οὐ παντάπασιν ἄτιμοι ἦσαν, ἀλλὰ μέρος τι αὐτῶν, οἷον
οἱ στρατιῶται, οἷς, ὅτι ἐπέμειναν ἐπὶ τῶν τετρα-
κοσίων⁴ ἐν τῇ πόλει, τὰ μὲν ἄλλα ἦν ἅπερ τοῖς
ἄλλοις πολίταις, εἰπεῖν δ᾽ ἐν τῷ δήμῳ οὐκ ἐξῆν

---

¹ ὧν τὰ μὲν Ald.: ὧν μὲν τὰ codd.
² εἶχον Bekker: ἔσχον codd.
³ ἀναυμαχίου Suidas, s.v.: ναυμαχίου codd.
⁴ τετρακοσίων Dobree, coll. psephismate quod sequitur:
τυράννων codd.

ᵃ Tax-farmers usually formed themselves into companies
headed by an ἀρχώνης who personally contracted with the
state for the purchase of the right to collect a given tax. The
agreed sum was not paid until the tax had been collected;
and so the ἀρχώνης had to furnish sureties, who became liable
if he himself defaulted. It was the practice to auction the
various taxes, the highest bidder obtaining the right to farm
them, cf. § 133.

ᵇ The six classes of state-debtor here enumerated suffered
disfranchisement only so long as their debt remained unpaid.
They were allowed eight Prytanies (i.e. roughly nine months)
in which to find the money; at the end of that time their

for a defaulter,[a] had to pay within eight Prytanies ; otherwise, the sum due was doubled and the delinquent's property distrained upon.[b]

Such was one form of disfranchisement. According to a second, delinquents lost all personal rights, but retained possession of their property. This class included all persons convicted of theft or of accepting bribes—it was laid down that both they and their descendants should lose their personal rights. Similarly, all who deserted on the field of battle, who were found guilty of evasion of military service, of cowardice, or of withholding a ship from action,[c] all who threw away their shields, or were thrice convicted of giving perjured evidence or of falsely endorsing a summons,[d] or who were found guilty of maltreating their parents, were deprived of their personal rights, while retaining possession of their property.

Others again had their rights curtailed in specified directions ; they were only partially, not wholly, disfranchised. The soldiers who remained in Athens under the Four Hundred are a case in point.[e] They enjoyed all the rights of ordinary citizens, except that they were forbidden to speak in the Assembly or

property was distrained upon for double the original amount. Should the confiscation fail to produce the requisite sum, they remained ἄτιμοι until the balance was forthcoming.

[c] When Trierarchs.

[d] Whenever a plaintiff had to serve a summons in person, the law required that he should do so in the presence of witnesses. The names of these witnesses were entered on the writ. If the plaintiff secured the witnesses' names without serving the summons and so won the case by default, the defendant had the right to bring a γραφὴ ψευδοκλητείας against the witnesses (κλητῆρες) concerned.

[e] This penalty appears to have been inflicted in 410, after the restoration of the democracy.

αὐτοῖς οὐδὲ βουλεῦσαι. τούτων ἦσαν οὗτοι ἄτιμοι
76 αὕτη γὰρ ἦν τούτοις πρόσταξις. ἑτέροις οὐκ ἦν
γράψασθαι, τοῖς δὲ ἐνδεῖξαι, τοῖς δὲ μὴ ἀναπλεῦσαι
εἰς Ἑλλήσποντον, ἄλλοις δ' εἰς Ἰωνίαν· τοῖς δ'
εἰς τὴν ἀγορὰν μὴ εἰσιέναι πρόσταξις ἦν.

Ταῦτ' οὖν ἐψηφίσασθε ἐξαλεῖψαι πάντα τὰ ψηφίσματα, καὶ αὐτὰ καὶ εἴ πού τι ἀντίγραφον ἦν,
καὶ πίστιν ἀλλήλοις περὶ ὁμονοίας δοῦναι ἐν
ἀκροπόλει. καί μοι ἀνάγνωθι τὸ ψήφισμα τὸ
Πατροκλείδου, καθ' ὃ ταῦτα ἐγένετο.

77 ΨΗΦΙΣΜΑ. — Πατροκλείδης εἶπεν· ἐπειδὴ ἐψηφίσαντο Ἀθηναῖοι τὴν ἄδειαν περὶ ⟨τῶν ἀτίμων καὶ⟩[1]
τῶν ὀφειλόντων, ὥστε λέγειν ἐξεῖναι καὶ ἐπιψηφίζειν-
ψηφίσασθαι τὸν δῆμον ταῦτὰ ἅπερ ὅτε ἦν τὰ Μηδικά,
καὶ συνήνεγκεν Ἀθηναίοις ἐπὶ τὸ ἄμεινον. περὶ δὲ
τῶν ἐγγεγραμμένων[2] εἰς τοὺς πράκτορας ἢ τοὺς ταμίας
τῆς θεοῦ καὶ τῶν ἄλλων θεῶν ἢ τὸν βασιλέα [ἢ][3] εἰ
τις μὴ ἐξεγράφη μέχρι τῆς ἐξελθούσης βουλῆς ἐφ'
78 ἧς Καλλίας ἦρχεν, ὅσοι ἄτιμοι ἦσαν [ἢ][4] ὀφείλοντες,
καὶ ὅσων εὔθυναί τινές εἰσι κατεγνωσμέναι ἐν τοῖς
λογιστηρίοις ὑπὸ τῶν εὐθύνων καὶ[5] τῶν παρέδρων, ἢ
μήπω εἰσηγμέναι εἰς τὸ δικαστήριον γραφαί τινές
εἰσι περὶ τῶν εὐθυνῶν, ἢ προστάξεις . . .,[6] ἢ ἐγγύαι

---

[1] τῶν ἀτίμων καὶ add. Sauppe e Dem. *Timocr.* § 46.
[2] ἐγγεγραμμένων Emperius: ἐπιγεγραμμένων codd.
[3] ἢ del. Emperius.   [4] ἢ secl. Reiske.
[5] καὶ Boeckh: ἢ codd.
[6] Lacunam ind. Droysen.

---

[a] The decree reinstates (a) public debtors whose names
were still on the official registers in June-July 405, (b) political
offenders who had suffered ἀτιμία in 410 after the downfall
of the Four Hundred and the restoration of the full democracy. These include both members of the Four Hundred

become members of the Council. They lost their
rights in these two respects, because in their case the
limited disability took this particular form. Others
were deprived of the right of bringing an indictment,
or of lodging an information : others of sailing up the
Hellespont, or of crossing to Ionia : while yet others
were specifically debarred from entering the Agora.

You enacted, then, that both the originals and all
extant copies of these several decrees should be cancelled, and your differences ended by an exchange
of pledges on the Acropolis. Kindly read the decree
of Patrocleides whereby this was effected.[a]

DECREE.—On the motion of Patrocleides : whereas the
Athenians have enacted that persons disfranchised and public
debtors may speak and propose measures in the Assembly
with impunity, the People shall pass the decree which was
passed at the time of the Persian Wars and which proved of
benefit to Athens. As touching such of those registered with
the Superintendents of Revenue, the Treasurers of Athena
and the other Deities, or the Basileus, as had not been
removed from the register before the last sitting of the Council
in the archonship of Callias [b] : all who before that date had
been disfranchised as debtors : or had been found guilty of
maladministration by the Auditors and their assessors at the
Auditors' offices : or had been indicted for maladministration, but had not as yet been publicly tried : or ⟨had been
condemned to suffer⟩ specific disabilities : or had been con-

---

and their supporters. An exception is made, however, of
those oligarchs who fled to Decelea (*e.g.* Peisander and
Charicles), and of persons in exile for homicide, massacre,
or attempted tyranny. The last two crimes are only mentioned because Patrocleides is here quoting from a law of
Solon's and wishes to be complete. Trials for massacre or
attempted tyranny had long been unheard of. For the text
of the Solonian law see Plut. *Solon* 19.

[b] Callias was Archon from 406 to 405. His year of office
terminated in June-July 405, and the Decree of Patrocleides
followed during the autumn.

τινές εἰσι κατεγνωσμέναι εἰς τὸν αὐτὸν τοῦτον χρόνον·
καὶ ὅσα ὀνόματα τῶν τετρακοσίων τινὸς ἐγγέγραπται,
ἢ ἄλλο τι περὶ τῶν ἐν τῇ ὀλιγαρχίᾳ πραχθέντων ἐστί
που γεγραμμένον· πλὴν ὁπόσα ἐν στήλαις γέγραπται
τῶν μὴ ἐνθάδε μεινάντων, ἢ ἐξ Ἀρείου πάγου ἢ τῶν
ἐφετῶν ἢ ἐκ πρυτανείου ἢ Δελφινίου δικασθεῖσιν[1] [ἢ][2]

[11] ὑπὸ τῶν βασιλέων [ἢ][3] ἐπὶ φόνῳ τίς ἐστι φυγῇ ἢ
79 θάνατος κατεγνώσθη, ἢ σφαγεῦσιν ἢ τυράννοις[4]· τὰ
δὲ ἄλλα πάντα ἐξαλεῖψαι τοὺς πράκτορας καὶ τὴν
βουλὴν κατὰ τὰ εἰρημένα πανταχόθεν, ὅπου τι ἔστιν
ἐν τῷ δημοσίῳ, καὶ εἴ ⟨τι⟩[5] ἀντίγραφόν που ἔστι,
παρέχειν τοὺς θεσμοθέτας καὶ τὰς ἄλλας ἀρχάς.
ποιεῖν δὲ ταῦτα τριῶν ἡμερῶν, ἐπειδὰν δόξῃ τῷ
δήμῳ. ἃ δ' εἴρηται ἐξαλεῖψαι, μὴ κεκτῆσθαι ἰδίᾳ
μηδενὶ ἐξεῖναι μηδὲ μνησικακῆσαι μηδέποτε· εἰ δὲ μή,
ἔνοχον εἶναι τὸν παραβαίνοντα ταῦτα ἐν τοῖς αὐτοῖς
ἐν οἷσπερ οἱ ἐξ Ἀρείου πάγου φεύγοντες, ὅπως ἂν
ὡς πιστότατα ἔχῃ[6] Ἀθηναίοις καὶ νῦν καὶ εἰς τὸν
λοιπὸν χρόνον.

80 Κατὰ μὲν τὸ ψήφισμα τουτὶ τοὺς ἀτίμους ἐπιτίμους ἐποιήσατε· τοὺς δὲ φεύγοντας οὔτε Πατροκλείδης εἶπε κατιέναι οὔθ' ὑμεῖς ἐψηφίσασθε.
ἐπεὶ δ' αἱ σπονδαὶ πρὸς Λακεδαιμονίους ἐγένοντο,

---

[1] δικασθεῖσιν Lipsius: ἐδικάσθη codd.
[2] ἢ del. Luzac.   [3] ἢ seclusit Droysen.
[4] ἢ σφαγαῖσιν ἢ τυραννίδι Kirchhoff.
[5] τι add. Blass.   [6] ἔχῃ G. Hermann: ἔχει, ἔχοι codd.

[a] The Areopagus tried cases of wilful murder. The fifty-
one Ephetae sat in different courts according to the nature of
the offence which they were trying, but always in the open
air for religious reasons. Sitting ἐπὶ Πρυτανείῳ, in the pre-

demned as sureties for a defaulter ; and all who were recorded
as members of the Four Hundred : or who had recorded
against them any act performed under the oligarchy—always
excepting those publicly recorded as fugitives : those who
have been tried for homicide by the Areopagus, or by the
Ephetae, whether sitting at the Prytaneum or the Delphinium,
under the presidency of the Basileus, and are now in
exile or under sentence of death *a* : and those guilty of
massacre or attempted tyranny—shall one and all have their
names everywhere cancelled by the Superintendents of
Revenue and by the Council in accordance with the fore-
going, wherever any public record of their offence be
found ; and any copies of such records which anywhere exist
shall be produced by the Thesmothetae and other magistrates.
This shall be done within three days after the consent of the
People has been given. And no one shall secretly retain a
copy of those records which it has been decided to cancel,
nor shall he at any time make malicious reference to the past.
He who does so shall be liable to the punishment of fugitives
from the court of the Areopagus *b* : to the end that the
Athenians may live in all security both now and hereafter.

By this decree you reinstated those who had lost
their rights ; but neither the proposal of Patrocleides
nor your own enactment contained any reference to a
restoration of exiles. However, after you had come

cincts of the Prytaneum, they heard cases of justifiable homicide (φόνος δίκαιος) : sitting ἐπὶ Δελφινίῳ, in the precincts of
the temple of Apollo Delphinius, they heard cases of homicide where the criminal was a person or persons unknown or
where death had been caused by an inanimate instrument.
They further met ἐπὶ Παλλαδίῳ to try cases of φόνος ἀκούσιος
and βούλευσις φόνου ἀκουσίου (*cf.* Antiphon, *Choreutes*, Introd.) ;
and in Phreatto, a quarter of Peiraeus on the sea-shore, to try
persons already in exile for homicide and charged with a
second murder, committed before they quitted Attica. The
accused pleaded from a boat. These last two courts are not
mentioned here. See also Antiphon, *Tetralogies*, Gen. Introd.
p. 41.

b *i.e.* be put to death, if he is ever apprehended within the
dominions of Athens.

καὶ τὰ τείχη καθείλετε, καὶ τοὺς φεύγοντας κατεδέξασθε, καὶ κατέστησαν οἱ τριάκοντα, καὶ μετὰ
ταῦτα Φυλή τε κατελήφθη Μουνυχίαν τε κατ-
ελάβον, ἐγένετό ⟨θ'⟩[1] ὑμῖν ὧν ἐγὼ οὐδὲν δέομαι
μεμνῆσθαι οὐδ' ἀναμιμνήσκειν ὑμᾶς τῶν γεγενη-
81 μένων κακῶν. ἐπειδὴ δ' ἐπανήλθετε ἐκ Πειραιῶς,
γενόμενον ἐφ' ὑμῖν τιμωρεῖσθαι ἔγνωτε ἐᾶν τὰ
γεγενημένα, καὶ περὶ πλείονος ἐποιήσασθε σῴζειν
τὴν πόλιν ἢ τὰς ἰδίας τιμωρίας, καὶ ἔδοξε μὴ
μνησικακεῖν ἀλλήλοις τῶν γεγενημένων. δόξαντα
δὲ ὑμῖν ταῦτα εἵλεσθε ἄνδρας εἴκοσι· τούτους δὲ
ἐπιμελεῖσθαι τῆς πόλεως, ἕως [ἂν][2] οἱ νόμοι
τεθεῖεν· τέως δὲ χρῆσθαι τοῖς Σόλωνος νόμοις καὶ
82 τοῖς Δράκοντος θεσμοῖς. ἐπειδὴ δὲ βουλήν τε
ἀπεκληρώσατε νομοθέτας τε εἵλεσθε, εὑρίσκοντες[3]
τῶν νόμων τῶν τε Σόλωνος καὶ τῶν Δράκοντος
πολλοὺς ὄντας οἷς πολλοὶ τῶν πολιτῶν ἔνοχοι ἦσαν
τῶν πρότερον ἕνεκα γενομένων,[4] ἐκκλησίαν ποιήσαντες ἐβουλεύσασθε περὶ αὐτῶν, καὶ ἐψηφίσασθε,
δοκιμάσαντες πάντας τοὺς νόμους, εἶτ' ἀναγράψαι

[1] θ' add. Reiske. [2] ἂν secl. Dobree.
[3] εὑρίσκοντες Reiske: εὑρίσκον codd.
[4] γενομένων Reiske: γινομένων codd.

---

[a] In April, 404. The Thirty were installed by the following summer on the motion of Dracontides, which the presence
of the Spartan garrison made it difficult to reject. In the
winter of 404 a number of the exiled democrats under
Thrasybulus seized Phyle on the northern frontier of Attica;
then they moved on Peiraeus and fortified Munychia. By
February 403 they were strong enough to crush the Thirty,
the remnants of whom fled to Eleusis, whence they were
finally extirpated in 401.
[b] February 403.

to terms with Sparta and demolished your walls, you
allowed your exiles to return too.[a] Then the Thirty
came into power, and there followed the occupation
of Phylê and Munychia, and those terrible struggles
which I am loath to recall either to myself or to you.
After your return from Peiraeus[b] you resolved to
let bygones be bygones, in spite of the opportunity
for revenge. You considered the safety of Athens
of more importance than the settlement of private
scores ; so both sides, you decided, were to forget
the past. Accordingly, you elected a commission of
twenty to govern Athens until a fresh code of laws
had been authorized ; during the interval the code
of Solon and the statutes of Draco were to be in force.
However, after you had chosen a Council by lot and
elected Nomothetae,[c] you began to discover that there
were not a few of the laws of Solon and Draco under
which numbers of citizens were liable, owing to
previous events. You therefore called a meeting of
the Assembly to discuss the difficulty, and as a result
enacted that the whole of the laws should be revised

[c] Further details are given in the decree which follows.
The ordinary Nomothetae were chosen by lot from the
Heliasts of each year to revise the existing laws and examine
proposed additions. The Nomothetae here mentioned are
an entirely distinct body. They were 500 in number and
elected by the demes. In conjunction with the Council they
were to revise the laws. It was found, however, that the
anarchy of the previous year had rendered a vast number of
citizens technically liable to punishment. This meant that
a very extensive modification of the existing legal code was
necessary. A committee was therefore selected from the
500 Nomothetae by the Council to draft a fresh body of laws.
Its recommendations were to be submitted to the Council
and the remaining Nomothetae for approval. In the
interval the laws of Solon and the θεσμοί of Draco dealing
with homicide were to be in force.

ἐν τῇ στοᾷ τούτους τῶν νόμων οἳ ἂν δοκιμασθῶσι.
καί μοι ἀνάγνωθι τὸ ψήφισμα.

83   (ΨΗΦΙΣΜΑ.)[1]—Ἔδοξε τῷ δήμῳ, Τεισαμενὸς εἶπε·
πολιτεύεσθαι Ἀθηναίους κατὰ τὰ πάτρια, νόμοις δὲ
χρῆσθαι τοῖς Σόλωνος, καὶ μέτροις καὶ σταθμοῖς,
χρῆσθαι δὲ καὶ τοῖς Δράκοντος θεσμοῖς, οἷσπερ
ἐχρώμεθα ἐν τῷ πρόσθεν χρόνῳ. ὁπόσων δ' ἂν
προσδέῃ,[2] οἵδε ᾑρημένοι νομοθέται ὑπὸ τῆς βουλῆς
ἀναγράφοντες ἐν σανίσιν ἐκτιθέντων πρὸς τοὺς ἐπω-
νύμους, σκοπεῖν τῷ βουλομένῳ, καὶ παραδιδόντων
84   ταῖς ἀρχαῖς ἐν τῷδε τῷ μηνί. τοὺς δὲ παραδιδομένους
νόμους δοκιμασάτω πρότερον ἡ βουλὴ καὶ οἱ νομοθέται
οἱ πεντακόσιοι, οὓς οἱ δημόται εἵλοντο, ἐπειδὰν ὀμωμόκωσιν[3]· ἐξεῖναι δὲ καὶ ἰδιώτῃ τῷ βουλομένῳ, εἰσιόντι
εἰς τὴν βουλὴν συμβουλεύειν ὅ τι ἂν ἀγαθὸν ἔχῃ
περὶ τῶν νόμων. ἐπειδὰν δὲ τεθῶσιν οἱ νόμοι, ἐπι-
μελείσθω ἡ βουλὴ ἡ ἐξ Ἀρείου πάγου τῶν νόμων,
ὅπως ἂν αἱ ἀρχαὶ τοῖς κειμένοις νόμοις χρῶνται.
τοὺς δὲ κυρουμένους τῶν νόμων ἀναγράφειν εἰς τὸν
τοῖχον, ἵνα περ πρότερον ἀνεγράφησαν, σκοπεῖν τῷ
βουλομένῳ.

85   Ἐδοκιμάσθησαν μὲν οὖν οἱ νόμοι, ὦ ἄνδρες,
κατὰ τὸ ψήφισμα τουτί, τοὺς δὲ κυρωθέντας
ἀνέγραψαν εἰς τὴν στοάν. ἐπειδὴ ⟨δ'⟩[4] ἀνεγράφησαν, ἐθέμεθα νόμον, ᾧ πάντες χρῆσθε. καί μοι
ἀνάγνωθι τὸν νόμον.

ΝΟΜΟΣ.—Ἀγράφῳ δὲ νόμῳ τὰς ἀρχὰς μὴ χρῆσθαι
μηδὲ περὶ ἑνός.

86   Ἆρά γε ἔστιν ἐνταυθοῖ ὅ τι[5] περιελείπετο περὶ
ὅτου οἷόν τε ἢ ἀρχὴν εἰσάγειν ἢ ὑμῶν πρᾶξαί τινι,

---

[1] Titulum add. Ald.
[2] προσδέῃ Bekker : προσδέοι codd.

and that such as were approved should be inscribed in the Portico.[a] Kindly read the decree.

⟨DECREE.⟩—On the motion of Teisamenus [b] the People decreed that Athens be governed as of old, in accordance with the laws of Solon, his weights and his measures, and in accordance with the statutes of Draco, which we used aforetime. Such further laws as may be necessary shall be inscribed upon tables by the Nomothetae elected by the Council and named hereafter, exposed before the Tribal Statues for all to see, and handed over to the magistrates during the present month. The laws thus handed over, however, shall be submitted beforehand to the scrutiny of the Council and the five hundred Nomothetae elected by the Demes, when they have taken their oath. Further, any private citizen who so desires may come before the Council and suggest improvements in the laws. When the laws have been ratified, they shall be placed under the guardianship of the Council of the Areopagus, to the end that only such laws as have been ratified may be applied by magistrates. Those laws which are approved shall be inscribed upon the wall, where they were inscribed aforetime, for all to see.

There was a revision of the laws, gentlemen, in obedience to this decree, and such as were approved were inscribed in the Portico. When this had been done, we passed a law which is universally enforced. Kindly read it.

LAW.—In no circumstances shall magistrates enforce a law which has not been inscribed.

Is any loophole left here? Can a single suit be brought before a jury by a magistrate or set in

---

[a] The στοὰ βασίλειος in the Agora.
[b] One of the 500 Nomothetae.

---

[3] ἐπειδὰν ὀμωμόκωσιν Dobree: ἐπειδὴ ὀμωμόκασιν codd.
[4] δ' add. Stephanus.
[5] ἔστιν ἐνταυθοῖ ὅ τι Dobree, coll. § 89: ἐστι τοῦτο ὅτι codd.

ἀλλ' ἢ κατὰ τοὺς ἀναγεγραμμένους νόμους; ὅπου
οὖν ἀγράφῳ νόμῳ οὐκ ἔξεστι χρήσασθαι, ἢ που
ἀγράφῳ γε ψηφίσματι παντάπασιν οὐ δεῖ [γε]¹
χρήσασθαι. ἐπειδὴ τοίνυν ἑωρῶμεν ὅτι πολλοῖς
τῶν πολιτῶν εἶεν συμφοραί, τοῖς μὲν κατὰ νόμους,
τοῖς δὲ κατὰ ψηφίσματα [τὰ]² πρότερον γενόμενα,
τουτουσὶ τοὺς νόμους ἐθέμεθα, αὐτῶν ἕνεκα τῶν
νυνὶ ποιουμένων, ἵνα τούτων μηδὲν γίγνηται μηδὲ
ἐξῇ συκοφαντεῖν μηδενί. καί μοι ἀνάγνωθι τοὺς
νόμους.

87   ΝΟΜΟΙ.—Ἀγράφῳ δὲ νόμῳ τὰς ἀρχὰς μὴ χρῆσθαι
      μηδὲ περὶ ἑνός. ψήφισμα δὲ μηδὲν μήτε βουλῆς
[12] μήτε δήμου νόμου κυριώτερον εἶναι. μηδὲ ἐπ' ἀνδρὶ
      νόμον ἐξεῖναι θεῖναι, ἐὰν μὴ τὸν αὐτὸν ἐπὶ πᾶσιν
      Ἀθηναίοις, ἐὰν μὴ ἑξακισχιλίοις δόξῃ κρύβδην
      ψηφιζομένοις.

Τί οὖν ἦν ἐπίλοιπον; οὑτοσὶ ὁ νόμος. καί μοι
ἀνάγνωθι τοῦτον.

⟨ΝΟΜΟΣ.⟩³—Τὰς δὲ δίκας καὶ τὰς διαίτας κυρίας
εἶναι, ὁπόσαι ἐν δημοκρατουμένῃ τῇ πόλει ἐγένοντο.
τοῖς δὲ νόμοις χρῆσθαι ἀπ' Εὐκλείδου ἄρχοντος.

88   Τὰς μὲν δίκας, ὦ ἄνδρες, καὶ τὰς διαίτας ἐποιήσατε κυρίας εἶναι, ὁπόσαι ἐν δημοκρατουμένῃ τῇ
πόλει ἐγένοντο, ὅπως μήτε χρεῶν ἀποκοπαὶ εἶεν
μήτε δίκαι ἀνάδικοι γίγνοιντο, ἀλλὰ τῶν ἰδίων
συμβολαίων αἱ πράξεις εἶεν· τῶν δὲ δημοσίων
⟨ἐφ'⟩⁴ ὁπόσοις ἢ γραφαί εἰσιν ἢ φάσεις ἢ ἐνδείξεις
ἢ ἀπαγωγαί, τούτων ἕνεκα τοῖς νόμοις ἐψηφίσασθε
89   χρῆσθαι ἀπ' Εὐκλείδου ἄρχοντος. ὅπου⁵ οὖν ἔδοξεν

---

¹ γε secl. Gebauer.   ² τὰ secl. Lipsius.
³ Titulum add. Ald.   ⁴ ἐφ' add. Blass.
                    ⁵ ὅπου Lipsius: ὅποτ' codd.

motion by one of you, save under the laws inscribed ? Then if it is illegal to enforce a law which has not been inscribed, there can surely be no question of enforcing a decree which has not been inscribed.

Now when we saw that a great many citizens had been placed in a serious position either by previous laws or by previous decrees, we enacted the laws which follow as a safeguard against the very thing which is now going on ; we wished to prevent anything of the kind happening, that is to say, and to make it impossible for anyone to prosecute from malice. Kindly read the laws.

LAWS.—In no circumstances shall magistrates enforce a law which has not been inscribed. No decree, whether of the Council or Assembly, shall override a law. No law shall be directed against an individual without applying to all citizens alike, unless an Assembly of six thousand so resolve by secret ballot.[a]

What was needed to complete the list ? Only the following law, which I will ask the clerk to read to you.

LAW.—All decisions given in private suits and by arbitrators under the democracy shall be valid. But of the laws only those passed since the archonship of Eucleides [b] shall be enforced.

The validity of decisions given in private suits and by arbitrators under the democracy you upheld, gentlemen ; and you did so to avoid the cancelling of debts and the reopening of such suits, and to ensure the enforcement of private contracts. On the other hand, in the matter of public offences dealt with by indictment, denunciation, information, or arrest, you enacted that only such laws should be enforced as had been passed since the archonship of Eucleides.

[a] A reference to ostracism.
[b] *i.e.* later than midsummer, 403.

ὑμῖν δοκιμάσαι μὲν τοὺς νόμους, δοκιμάσαντας
δὲ ἀναγράψαι, ἀγράφῳ δὲ νόμῳ τὰς ἀρχὰς μὴ
χρῆσθαι μηδὲ περὶ ἑνός, ψήφισμα δὲ ⟨μηδὲν⟩[1]
μήτε βουλῆς μήτε δήμου ⟨νόμου⟩[2] κυριώτερον εἶναι,
μηδ' ἐπ' ἀνδρὶ νόμον ⟨ἐξεῖναι⟩[3] τιθέναι ἐὰν μὴ τὸν
αὐτὸν ἐπὶ πᾶσιν Ἀθηναίοις, τοῖς δὲ νόμοις τοῖς
κειμένοις χρῆσθαι ἀπ' Εὐκλείδου ἄρχοντος, ἐνταυθοῖ ἔστιν ὅ τι ὑπολείπεται ἢ μεῖζον ἢ ἔλαττον
τῶν γενομένων[4] πρότερον ψηφισμάτων, πρὶν Εὐ-
κλείδην ἄρξαι, ὅπως κύριον ἔσται; οὐκ οἶμαι
ἔγωγε, ⟨ὦ⟩[5] ἄνδρες. σκοπεῖτε δὲ καὶ αὐτοί.

90 Φέρε δὴ τοίνυν, οἱ ὅρκοι ὑμῖν πῶς ἔχουσιν; ὁ
μὲν κοινὸς τῇ πόλει ἁπάσῃ, ὃν ὀμωμόκατε πάντες
μετὰ τὰς διαλλαγάς, " καὶ οὐ μνησικακήσω τῶν
πολιτῶν οὐδενὶ πλὴν τῶν τριάκοντα ⟨καὶ τῶν
δέκα⟩[6] καὶ τῶν ἕνδεκα· οὐδὲ τούτων ὃς ἂν
ἐθέλῃ εὐθύνας διδόναι τῆς ἀρχῆς ἧς ἦρξεν."
ὅπου τοίνυν αὐτοῖς τοῖς τριάκοντα ὤμνυτε[7] μὴ
μνησικακήσειν, τοῖς μεγίστων κακῶν αἰτίοις, εἰ
διδοῖεν εὐθύνας, ἦ που σχολῇ τῶν γε ἄλλων
πολιτῶν τινι ἠξιοῦτε μνησικακεῖν. ἡ δὲ βουλὴ αὖ[8]

91 ἡ ἀεὶ βουλεύουσα τί ὄμνυσι; " καὶ οὐ δέξομαι
ἔνδειξιν οὐδὲ ἀπαγωγὴν ἕνεκα τῶν πρότερον γεγενημένων, πλὴν τῶν φυγόντων[9]." ὑμεῖς δ' αὖ,
ὦ Ἀθηναῖοι, τί ὀμόσαντες δικάζετε; " καὶ οὐ

---

[1] μηδὲν add. Blass.
[2] νόμου add. Reiske.
[3] ἐξεῖναι add. Sauppe.
[4] γενομένων Baiter et Sauppe : γινομένων codd.
[5] ὦ add. Blass.
[6] καὶ τῶν δέκα add. de Valois, coll. Ἀθ. Πολ. xxxix. 6.
[7] ὤμνυτε Ald. : ὤμνυται codd.
[8] αὖ ἡ Reiske : αὕτη codd.
[9] φυγόντων Sauppe : φευγόντων codd.

Now you decided that the laws were to be revised and afterwards inscribed : that in no circumstances were magistrates to enforce a law which had not been inscribed : that no decree, whether of the Council or the Assembly, was to override a law : that no law might be directed against an individual without applying to all citizens alike : and that only such laws as had been passed since the archonship of Eucleides were to be enforced. In view of this, can any decree passed before the archonship of Eucleides, whatever its importance or unimportance, still remain in force ? I for one think not, gentlemen. Just consider the matter for yourselves.

And now, what of your oaths ? First, the oath in which the whole city joined, the oath which you swore one and all after the reconciliation : ". . . and I will harbour no grievance against any citizen, save only the Thirty, the Ten,[a] and the Eleven : and even of them against none who shall consent to render account of his office." After swearing to forgive even the Thirty, whom you had to thank for sufferings untold, provided that they rendered account of themselves, you can have been in very little hurry to harbour grievances against the ordinary citizen. Again, what is the oath sworn by the Council when it takes office ? ". . . and I will allow no information or arrest arising out of past events, save only in the case of those who fled from Athens."[b] And what is your own oath as jurors, gentlemen ?

[a] The board of ten set up by Lysander in Peiraeus. It was overthrown by Thrasybulus at the end of 404. The Eleven are, of course, the ordinary police-magistrates who had been compelled by the Thirty to do their bidding.

[b] i.e. to Eleusis, with the surviving members of the Thirty, after their downfall in February 403.

μνησικακήσω, οὐδὲ ἄλλῳ πείσομαι, ψηφιοῦμαι δὲ
κατὰ τοὺς κειμένους νόμους." ἃ χρὴ σκοπεῖν, εἰ
δοκῶ ὀρθῶς ὑμῖν λέγειν ὡς ὑπὲρ ὑμῶν λέγω καὶ
τῶν νόμων.

92 Σκέψασθε τοίνυν, ὦ ἄνδρες, καὶ τοὺς νόμους
καὶ τοὺς κατηγόρους, τί αὐτοῖς ὑπάρχον[1] ἑτέρων
κατηγοροῦσι. Κηφίσιος μὲν οὑτοσὶ πριάμενος
ὠνὴν ἐκ τοῦ δημοσίου, τὰς ἐκ ταύτης ἐπικαρπίας
τῶν ἐν τῇ γῇ γεωργούντων ἐνενήκοντα μνᾶς
ἐκλέξας, οὐ κατέβαλε τῇ πόλει καὶ ἔφυγεν· εἰ γὰρ
93 ἦλθεν, ἐδέδετ' ἂν ἐν τῷ ξύλῳ. ὁ γὰρ νόμος οὕτως
εἶχε, κυρίαν εἶναι τὴν [τε][2] βουλήν, ὃς ἂν πριάμενος
τέλος μὴ καταβάλῃ, δεῖν εἰς τὸ ξύλον. οὗτος
τοίνυν, ὅτι τοῖς νόμοις ἐψηφίσασθε ἀπ' Εὐκλείδου
ἄρχοντος χρῆσθαι, ἀξιοῖ ἃ ἔχει ὑμῶν ἐκλέξας μὴ
ἀποδοῦναι, καὶ νῦν γεγένηται ἀντὶ μὲν φυγάδος
πολίτης, ἀντὶ δὲ ἀτίμου συκοφάντης, ὅτι τοῖς
νόμοις τοῖς νῦν κειμένοις χρῆσθε.

94 Μέλητος δ' αὖ οὑτοσὶ ἀπήγαγεν ἐπὶ τῶν τριάκοντα Λέοντα, ὡς ὑμεῖς ἅπαντες ἴστε, καὶ ἀπέθανεν
ἐκεῖνος ἄκριτος. καί⟨τοι⟩[3] οὗτος ὁ νόμος καὶ
πρότερον ἦν ⟨καὶ⟩[4] ὡς καλῶς ἔχων καὶ νῦν ἔστι,
καὶ χρῆσθε αὐτῷ, τὸν βουλεύσαντα ἐν τῷ αὐτῷ
ἐνέχεσθαι καὶ τὸν τῇ χειρὶ ἐργασάμενον. Μέλητον
τοίνυν τοῖς παισὶ τοῖς τοῦ Λέοντος οὐκ ἔστι φόνου

---

[1] ὑπάρχον Emperius : ὑπάρχον τῶν Bekker ; ὑπαρχόντων codd.
[2] τε del. Bekker : τήν τε βουλὴν καὶ . . . Rosenberg.
[3] καίτοι Sluiter : καὶ codd.
[4] καὶ add. Baiter.

---

[a] The Leon here mentioned is almost certainly the Leon
of Salamis whom Socrates, at the risk of his own life, re-

410

". . . and I will harbour no grievance and submit to no influence, but will give my verdict in accordance with the laws in force at the present time." Let those oaths help you to decide whether I am right when I say that I am championing yourselves and the laws.

And now, gentlemen, consider how my accusers stand with regard to the laws. They are prosecuting others; but what is their own position? Cephisius here purchased from the state the right to collect certain public rents, and obtained thereby a return of ninety minae from the farmers occupying the lands concerned. He then defaulted; and since he would have been placed in close confinement had he appeared in Athens—it being laid down by law that any defaulting tax-farmer may be so punished by the Council—he retired into exile. Owing, however, to the fact that you decided to apply only those laws passed since the archonship of Eucleides, Cephisius considers himself entitled to keep his profits from your lands. He is no longer an exile, but a citizen: no longer an outcast without rights, but an informer—and all because you are applying only the revised laws.

Then there is Meletus here. Meletus arrested Leon [a] under the Thirty, as you all know; and Leon was put to death without a trial. But we find it laid down that there shall be no distinction between the principal who plans a crime and the agent who commits it; the law not only existed in the past, but still exists and is still enforced because of its fairness. Quite so; but Leon's sons cannot prosecute Meletus for murder, because only laws passed since the

fused to arrest when ordered to do so by the Thirty. Some 1500 persons were executed without a trial during the reign of terror (Isocr. vii. 67).

411

διώκειν, ὅτι τοῖς νόμοις δεῖ χρῆσθαι ἀπ' Εὐκλείδου
ἄρχοντος, ἐπεὶ ὥς γε οὐκ ἀπήγαγεν, οὐδ' αὐτὸς
ἀντιλέγει.

95 Ἐπιχάρης δ' οὑτοσί,[1] ὁ πάντων πονηρότατος
καὶ βουλόμενος εἶναι τοιοῦτος, ὁ μνησικακῶν
αὐτὸς αὑτῷ,—οὗτος γὰρ ἐβούλευεν ἐπὶ τῶν τριά-
κοντα· ὁ δὲ νόμος τί κελεύει, ὃς ἐν τῇ στήλῃ
ἔμπροσθέν ἐστι τοῦ βουλευτηρίου; " ὃς ἂν ἄρξῃ
ἐν τῇ πόλει τῆς δημοκρατίας καταλυθείσης,
νηποινεὶ τεθνάναι, καὶ τὸν ἀποκτείναντα ὅσιον
εἶναι καὶ τὰ χρήματα ἔχειν τοῦ ἀποθανόντος."
ἄλλο τι[2] οὖν, ὦ Ἐπίχαρες, ἢ νῦν ὁ ἀποκτείνας σε
[13] καθαρὸς τὰς χεῖρας ἔσται, κατά γε τὸν Σόλωνος
96 νόμον; καί μοι ἀνάγνωθι τὸν νόμον τὸν ἐκ τῆς
στήλης.

ΝΟΜΟΣ.—Ἔδοξε τῇ βουλῇ καὶ τῷ δήμῳ. Αἰαντὶς
ἐπρυτάνευε, Κλειγένης ἐγραμμάτευε, Βοηθὸς ἐπεστάτει. τάδε Δημόφαντος συνέγραψεν. ἄρχει χρόνο-
τοῦδε τοῦ ψηφίσματος ἡ βουλὴ οἱ πεντακόσιοι ⟨οἱ⟩[3]
λαχόντες τῷ κυάμῳ, οἷς[4] Κλειγένης πρῶτος ἐγραμ-
μάτευεν. ἐάν τις δημοκρατίαν καταλύῃ τὴν
Ἀθήνησιν, ἢ ἀρχήν τινα ἄρχῃ καταλελυμένης τῆς
δημοκρατίας, πολέμιος ἔστω[5] Ἀθηναίων καὶ νηποινεὶ
τεθνάτω, καὶ τὰ χρήματα αὐτοῦ δημόσια ἔστω, καὶ
97 τῆς θεοῦ τὸ ἐπιδέκατον· ὁ δὲ ἀποκτείνας τὸν ταῦτα

---

[1] οὑτοσί Blass : οὗτος codd.
[2] ἄλλο τι . . . ἢ Reiske : ἀλλ' ὅτι . . . εἰ codd.
[3] οἱ add. Bekker.
[4] οἷς Droysen, coll. *I.G.* i[2]. 304 : ὅτε codd.
[5] ἔστω Steph. : ἔσται codd.

---

[a] The argument of this paragraph is not stated as clearly
as it might be. Andocides means : (*a*) after the amnesty
special legal measures were taken to ensure against prose-

archonship of Eucleides can be enforced. The fact of the arrest, of course, is not denied, even by Meletus himself.[a]

Then Epichares here, an utter blackguard, and proud of it, a man who does his best not to let his own bygones be bygones—friend Epichares served on the Council under the Thirty. And yet what does the law upon the stone in front of the Council-chamber say ? "Whosoever shall hold a public office after the suppression of the democracy may be slain with impunity. No taint shall rest upon his slayer, and he shall possess the goods of the slain." Thus as far as Solon's law is concerned, Epichares, it is clear that anyone can kill you here and now without defiling his hands. Kindly read the law from the stone.

LAW.[b]—Enacted by the Council and People. Prytany of the tribe Aeantis. Secretary: Cleigenes. President: Boethus. The enactment following was framed by Demophantus and his colleagues. The date of this decree is the first sitting of the Council of Five Hundred, chosen by lot, at which Cleigenes acted as Secretary.

If anyone shall suppress the democracy at Athens or hold any public office after its suppression, he shall become a public enemy and be slain with impunity; his goods shall be confiscated and a tithe given to the Goddess. No sin

cution for crimes committed before 403; therefore, although (b) the principle that βούλευσις φόνου ἑκουσίου deserves the same punishment as φόνος ἑκούσιος itself has always been, and still is, recognized as valid, Meletus cannot be accused of having caused Leon's death.

[b] The decree was passed after the restoration of the full democracy in 410. Demophantus is a member of the board of συγγραφεῖς ("compilers") appointed to revise the laws. The revision was not completed until the appointment of the 500 Nomothetae in 403 for a similar purpose. The decree was based on a Solonian law (§ 95 ad fin.); hence the reference in it to tyranny.

413

ποιήσαντα καὶ ὁ συμβουλεύσας ὅσιος ἔστω καὶ εὐαγής.
ὀμόσαι δ' Ἀθηναίους ἅπαντας καθ' ἱερῶν τελείων,
κατὰ φυλὰς καὶ κατὰ δήμους, ἀποκτενεῖν¹ τὸν ταῦτα
ποιήσαντα. ὁ δὲ ὅρκος ἔστω ὅδε· "κτενῶ καὶ λόγῳ
καὶ ἔργῳ καὶ ψήφῳ καὶ² τῇ ἐμαυτοῦ χειρί, ἂν δυνατὸς
ὦ, ὃς ἂν καταλύσῃ τὴν δημοκρατίαν τὴν Ἀθήνησι,
καὶ ἐάν τις ἄρξῃ τιν³ ἀρχὴν καταλελυμένης τῆς
δημοκρατίας τὸ λοιπόν, καὶ ἐάν τις τυραννεῖν
ἐπαναστῇ ἢ τὸν τύραννον συγκαταστήσῃ· καὶ ἐάν
τις ἄλλος ἀποκτείνῃ, ὅσιον αὐτὸν νομιῶ εἶναι καὶ
πρὸς θεῶν καὶ δαιμόνων, ὡς πολέμιον κτείναντα τὸν
Ἀθηναίων, καὶ τὰ κτήματα τοῦ ἀποθανόντος πάντα
ἀποδόμενος ἀποδώσω τὰ ἡμίσεα τῷ ἀποκτείναντι, καὶ
98   οὐκ ἀποστερήσω οὐδέν. ἐὰν δέ τις κτείνων τινὰ
τούτων ἀποθάνῃ ἢ ἐπιχειρῶν, εὖ ποιήσω αὐτόν τε
καὶ τοὺς παῖδας τοὺς ἐκείνου καθάπερ Ἁρμόδιόν τε
καὶ Ἀριστογείτονα καὶ τοὺς ἀπογόνους αὐτῶν. ὁπόσοι
δὲ ὅρκοι ὀμώμονται Ἀθήνησιν ἢ ἐν τῷ στρατοπέδῳ
ἢ ἄλλοθί που ἐναντίοι τῷ δήμῳ τῷ⁴ Ἀθηναίων, λύω
καὶ ἀφίημι." ταῦτα δὲ ὀμοσάντων Ἀθηναῖοι πάντες
καθ' ἱερῶν τελείων, τὸν νόμιμον ὅρκον, πρὸ Διονυσίων·
καὶ ἐπεύχεσθαι εὐορκοῦντι μὲν εἶναι πολλὰ καὶ ἀγαθά,
ἐπιορκοῦντι δ' ἐξώλη αὐτὸν εἶναι καὶ γένος.

99   Πότερον, ὦ συκοφάντα καὶ ἐπίτριπτον κίναδος,
κύριος ὁ νόμος ὅδε ἐστὶν ἢ οὐ κύριος; ⟨οὐ κύριος·⟩⁵
διὰ τοῦτο δ' οἶμαι γεγένηται ἄκυρος, ὅτι τοῖς
νόμοις δεῖ χρῆσθαι ἀπ' Εὐκλείδου ἄρχοντος. καὶ
σὺ ζῇς καὶ περιέρχῃ τὴν πόλιν ταύτην, οὐκ ἄξιος
ὤν· ὃς ἐν δημοκρατίᾳ μὲν συκοφαντῶν ἔζης, ἐν
ὀλιγαρχίᾳ δέ, ὡς μὴ ἀναγκασθείης τὰ χρήματα

---

¹ ἀποκτενεῖν Droysen : ἀποκτείνειν codd.
² καὶ λόγῳ καὶ ἔργῳ καὶ ψήφῳ καὶ huc transt. Sauppe,

shall he commit, no defilement shall he suffer who slays such an one or who conspires to slay him. And all the Athenians shall take oath by tribes and by demes over a sacrifice without blemish to slay such an one. And this shall be the oath : " If it be in my power, I will slay by word and by deed, by my vote and by my hand, whosoever shall suppress the democracy at Athens, whosoever shall hold any public office after its suppression, and whosoever shall attempt to become tyrant or shall help to instal a tyrant. And if another shall slay such an one, I will deem him to be without sin in the eyes of the gods and powers above, as having slain a public enemy. And I will sell all the goods of the slain and will give over one half to the slayer, and will withhold nothing from him. And if anyone shall lose his life in slaying such an one or in attempting to slay him, I will show to him and to his children the kindness which was shown to Harmodius and Aristogeiton and to their children. And all oaths sworn at Athens or in the army [a] or elsewhere for the overthrow of the Athenian democracy I annul and abolish." All the Athenians shall take this oath over a sacrifice without blemish, as the law enjoins, before the Dionysia. And they shall pray that he who observes this oath may be blessed abundantly : but that he who observes it not may perish from the earth, both he and his house.

Well, Mr. Informer, is this law in force ? Yes or no, you practised villain ? [b] No ; and the reason for that is of course that only laws passed after the archonship of Eucleides can be applied. That is how you come to be walking about this city alive—hardly the fate which you deserved after making a living as a common informer under the democracy, and becoming the tool of the Thirty under the oligarchy

[a] At Samos in 411, where Peisander had at first successfully intrigued for the overthrow of the democracy at home.
[b] An echo of Soph. *Ajax* 103.

---

coll. Lycurg. § 127.   In codd. post τῷ ἀποκτείναντι inveniuntur.
[3] τιν' Reiske : τὴν codd.   [4] τῷ Spengel : τῶν codd.
[5] οὐ κύριος addidi auct. Reiske.

ANDOCIDES

ἀποδοῦναι ὅσα συκοφαντῶν ἔλαβες, ἐδούλευες τοῖς
100 τριάκοντα. εἶτα σὺ περὶ ἑταιρείας ἐμοὶ μνείαν
ποιῇ καὶ κακῶς τινας λέγεις; ὃς ἑνὶ μὲν οὐχ
ἡταίρησας (καλῶς γὰρ ἄν σοι εἶχε), πραττόμενος
δ' οὐ πολὺ ἀργύριον τὸν βουλόμενον ἀνθρώπων,
ὡς οὗτοι ἴσασιν, ἐπὶ τοῖς αἰσχίστοις ἔργοις ἔζης,
καὶ ταῦτα οὕτω μοχθηρὸς ὢν τὴν ἰδέαν.
101 Ἀλλ' ὅμως οὗτος ἑτέρων[1] τολμᾷ[2] κατηγορεῖν, ᾧ
κατὰ τοὺς νόμους τοὺς ὑμετέρους οὐδ' αὐτῷ ὑπὲρ
αὐτοῦ ἔστιν ἀπολογεῖσθαι. ἀλλὰ γάρ, ὦ ἄνδρες,
καθήμενος ἡνίκα μου κατηγόρει, βλέπων εἰς αὐτὸν
οὐδὲν ἄλλο ἢ ὑπὸ τῶν τριάκοντα συνειλημμένος
ἔδοξα κρίνεσθαι. εἰ γὰρ τότε ἠγωνιζόμην, τίς
ἄν μου κατηγόρει; οὐχ οὗτος ὑπῆρχεν, εἰ μὴ
ἐδίδουν ἀργύριον; καὶ γὰρ νῦν. ἀνέκρινε δ' ἄν
με τίς ἄλλος ἢ Χαρικλῆς, ἐρωτῶν, Εἰπέ μοι, ὦ
Ἀνδοκίδη, ἦλθες εἰς Δεκέλειαν, καὶ ἐπετείχισας
τῇ πατρίδι τῇ σεαυτοῦ; Οὐκ ἔγωγε. Τί δέ;
ἔτεμες τὴν χώραν, καὶ ἐλήσω ἢ κατὰ γῆν ἢ κατὰ
θάλατταν τοὺς πολίτας τοὺς σεαυτοῦ; Οὐ δῆτα.
Οὐδ' ἐναυμάχησας ἐναντία τῇ πόλει, οὐδὲ συγ-
κατέσκαψας τὰ τείχη, οὐδὲ συγκατέλυσας τὸν
δῆμον, οὐδὲ βίᾳ κατῆλθες εἰς τὴν πόλιν; Οὐδὲ
τούτων[3] πεποίηκα οὐδέν. Δοκεῖς οὖν χαιρήσειν καὶ[4]
οὐκ ἀποθανεῖσθαι, ὡς ἕτεροι πολλοί;

[1] ἑτέρων Reiske : ἑταιρῶν codd.
[2] τολμᾷ Blass : ἐτόλμα codd.
[3] οὐδὲ τούτων Muretus : οὐδὲν τούτων codd.
[4] καὶ Dobree : ἢ codd.

[a] i.e. political intrigues. A reference to Andocides'
membership of an oligarchic club (ἑταιρεία).
[b] Because of his immorality.
[c] Cf. § 36, note.

416

to avoid having to disgorge your profits. But that is not enough. You actually talk to me of my intrigues ! [a] You actually hold others up to censure— you, who had not the decency to confine your own intrigues to but a single admirer, but welcomed the entire world for next to nothing, as the court knows, and supported yourself by vice, your villainous appearance notwithstanding.

But yet, although your laws deny him even the right of defending himself,[b] the fellow has the impudence to accuse others. Really, gentlemen, as I sat watching him make his speech for the prosecution, I quite thought that I had been arrested and put on trial by the Thirty. Who would have prosecuted, if I had found myself in court in those days ? Epichares, none other. There he would have been, ready with a charge, unless I bought him off. And here he is once more. Who, again, but Charicles [c] would have cross-examined me ? " Tell me Andocides," he would have asked, " did you go to Decelea [d] and occupy it as a menace to your country ? " " I did not." "Well, did you lay Attica waste and pillage your fellow-Athenians by land or by sea ? " " No." " Then at least you fought Athens at sea,[e] or helped to demolish her walls or put down her democracy, or reinstalled yourself by force ? "[f] " No, I have done none of those things either." " Then do you expect to escape the fate of so many others ? "

[d] In 411, with the Four Hundred when they were overthrown.

[e] At Aegospotami, 405 B.C. Possibly this is a reference to the treachery of the pro-Spartan elements in the Athenian navy during the battle. More probably Charicles is thinking of Athenian exiles who served with the Spartan forces.

[f] In 403 B.C.

102 Ἆρ᾽ ⟨ἂν⟩¹ οἴεσθε, ὦ ἄνδρες, ἄλλων τινῶν τυχεῖν
με δι᾽ ὑμᾶς,² εἰ ἐλήφθην ὑπ᾽ αὐτῶν; οὐκ οὖν δεινόν,
εἰ ὑπὸ μὲν τούτων διὰ τοῦτ᾽ ἂν ἀπωλόμην, ὅτι εἰς
τὴν πόλιν οὐδὲν ἥμαρτον, ὥσπερ καὶ ἑτέρους
ἀπέκτειναν, ἐν ὑμῖν δὲ κρινόμενος, οὓς οὐδὲν
κακὸν πεποίηκα, οὐ σωθήσομαι; πάντως δήπου·
ἢ σχολῇ γέ τις ἄλλος ἀνθρώπων.

103 Ἀλλὰ γάρ, ὦ ἄνδρες, τὴν μὲν ἔνδειξιν ἐποιήσαντό
[14] μου κατὰ νόμον κείμενον, τὴν δὲ κατηγορίαν κατὰ
τὸ ψήφισμα τὸ πρότερον γεγενημένον περὶ ἑτέρων.
εἰ οὖν ἐμοῦ καταψηφιεῖσθε, ὁρᾶτε μὴ οὐκ ἐμοὶ
μάλιστα τῶν πολιτῶν προσήκει λόγον δοῦναι τῶν
γεγενημένων, ἀλλὰ πολλοῖς ἑτέροις μᾶλλον, τοῦτο
μὲν οἷς ὑμεῖς ἐναντία μαχεσάμενοι διηλλάγητε
καὶ ὅρκους ὠμόσατε, τοῦτο δὲ οὓς φεύγοντας
κατηγάγετε, τοῦτο δὲ οὓς ἀτίμους ὄντας ἐπιτίμους
ἐποιήσατε· ὧν ἕνεκα καὶ στήλας ἀνείλετε καὶ
νόμους ἀκύρους ἐποιήσατε καὶ ψηφίσματα ἐξ-
ηλείψατε· οἳ νυνὶ μένουσιν ἐν τῇ πόλει πιστεύοντες

104 ὑμῖν, ὦ ἄνδρες. εἰ οὖν γνώσονται ὑμᾶς ἀπο-
δεχομένους τὰς κατηγορίας τῶν πρότερον γεγενημένων, τίνα αὐτοὺς οἴεσθε γνώμην ἕξειν περὶ σφῶν
αὐτῶν; ἢ τίνα αὐτῶν ἐθελήσειν εἰς ἀγῶνας καθ-
ίστασθαι ἕνεκα τῶν πρότερον γεγενημένων; φανή-
σονται γὰρ πολλοὶ μὲν ἐχθροὶ πολλοὶ δὲ συκοφάνται,
οἳ καταστήσουσιν αὐτῶν ἕκαστον εἰς ἀγῶνα.

105 ἥκουσι δὲ νυνὶ ἀκροασόμενοι ἀμφότεροι, οὐ τὴν
αὐτὴν γνώμην ἔχοντες ἀλλήλοις, ἀλλ᾽ οἱ μὲν
εἰσόμενοι εἰ χρὴ πιστεύειν τοῖς νόμοις τοῖς κειμένοις καὶ τοῖς ὅρκοις οὓς ὠμόσατε ἀλλήλοις,

---

¹ ἂν add. Dobree.
² δι᾽ ὑμᾶς Reiske : δι᾽ ἡμᾶς codd.

Do you not agree, gentlemen, that that is just how I would have been treated for remaining loyal to you, had I fallen into the clutches of the Thirty ? Then will it not be a travesty of justice if a man whom the Thirty would have put to death, as they did others, for failing to commit any act of disloyalty to Athens, is not to be acquitted when tried before you whom he refused to wrong ? Such a thing would be an outrage. It would make acquittal next to impossible in any case whatsoever.

The truth is, gentlemen, that although the prosecution may have availed themselves of a perfectly valid law in lodging their information against me, they based their charge upon that old decree which is concerned with an entirely different matter. So if you condemn me, beware ; you will find that a host of others ought to be answering for their past conduct with far more reason than I. First there are the men who fought you, with whom you swore oaths of reconciliation : then there are the exiles whom you restored : and finally there are the citizens whose rights you gave back to them. For their sakes you removed stones of record, annulled laws, and cancelled decrees ; and it is because they trust you that they are still in Athens, gentlemen. What, do you imagine, will they presume their own position to be, if they find that you are allowing prosecutions for past conduct ? Will any of them be ready to stand trial for his past conduct ? Yet enemies and informers will spring up right and left, ready to bring every man of them into court. To-day both parties have come to listen, but from very different motives. One side wants to know whether they are to rely upon the laws as they now stand and on the oaths which you and they swore to

οἱ δὲ ἀποπειρώμενοι τῆς ὑμετέρας γνώμης, εἰ
αὐτοῖς ἐξέσται ἀδεῶς συκοφαντεῖν καὶ γράφεσθαι,
τοὺς δὲ ἐνδεικνύναι, τοὺς δὲ ἀπάγειν. οὕτως οὖν
ἔχει, ὦ ἄνδρες· ὁ μὲν ἀγὼν ἐν τῷ σώματι τῷ ἐμῷ
καθέστηκεν, ἡ δὲ ψῆφος ἡ ὑμετέρα δημοσίᾳ κρινεῖ,[1]
πότερον χρὴ τοῖς νόμοις τοῖς ὑμετέροις πιστεύειν,
ἢ τοὺς συκοφάντας παρασκευάζεσθαι, ἢ φεύγειν
αὐτοὺς ἐκ τῆς πόλεως καὶ ἀπιέναι ὡς τάχιστα.

106 Ἵνα δὲ εἰδῆτε, ὦ ἄνδρες, ὅτι τὰ πεποιημένα
ὑμῖν εἰς ὁμόνοιαν οὐ κακῶς ἔχει, ἀλλὰ τὰ προσ-
ήκοντα καὶ τὰ συμφέροντα ὑμῖν αὐτοῖς ἐποιήσατε,
βραχέα βούλομαι καὶ περὶ τούτων εἰπεῖν. οἱ γὰρ
πατέρες οἱ ὑμέτεροι γενομένων τῇ πόλει κακῶν
μεγάλων, ὅτε οἱ τύραννοι μὲν εἶχον τὴν πόλιν,
ὁ δὲ δῆμος ἔφευγε,[2] νικήσαντες μαχόμενοι τοὺς
τυράννους ἐπὶ Παλληνίῳ, στρατηγοῦντος Λεωγόρου
τοῦ προπάππου τοῦ ἐμοῦ καὶ Χαρίου[3] οὗ ἐκεῖνος
τὴν θυγατέρα εἶχεν, ἐξ ἧς ὁ ἡμέτερος ἦν πάππος,
κατελθόντες εἰς τὴν πατρίδα τοὺς μὲν ἀπέκτειναν,
τῶν δὲ φυγὴν κατέγνωσαν, τοὺς δὲ μένειν ἐν τῇ
πόλει ἐάσαντες ἠτίμωσαν.

107 Ὕστερον δὲ ἡνίκα βασιλεὺς ἐπεστράτευσεν ἐπὶ
τὴν Ἑλλάδα, γνόντες τῶν συμφορῶν τῶν ἐπιουσῶν
τὸ μέγεθος καὶ τὴν παρασκευὴν τὴν[4] βασιλέως,
ἔγνωσαν τούς τε φεύγοντας[5] καταδέξασθαι καὶ τοὺς
ἀτίμους ἐπιτίμους ποιῆσαι καὶ κοινὴν τήν τε σωτη-

---

[1] κρινεῖ Stephanus : κρίνει codd.
[2] ἔφευγε Sauppe : ἔφυγε codd.
[3] Καλλίου maluit Sluiter, coll. Hdt. vi. 121.
[4] τὴν Bekker : τοῦ codd.
[5] φεύγοντας Baiter et Sauppe : φυγόντας codd.

[a] Andocides was a poor historian (cf. Peace with Sp.,
Introd.). Here he confuses the battle of Pallene (Hdt. i. 62),

one another ; while the others have come to sound
your feelings, to find out whether they will be given
complete licence to fill their pockets by indictments,
or informations, maybe, or arrests. Thus the truth
of the matter is, gentlemen, that although it is my
life alone which is at stake in this trial, your verdict
will decide for the public at large whether they are
to put faith in your laws, or whether, on the other
hand, they must choose between buying off informers
or fleeing and quitting Athens as fast as they can.

Your measures for re-uniting Athens, gentlemen,
have not been wasted ; they were appropriate, and
they were sound policy. To convince you of this, I
wish to say a few words with regard to them. Those
were dark days for Athens when the tyrants ruled
her and the democrats were in exile. But, led by
Leogoras, my own great-grandfather, and Charias,
whose daughter bore my grandfather to Leogoras,
your ancestors crushed the tyrants near the temple
at Pallene,[a] and came back to the land of their birth.
Some of their enemies they put to death, some they
exiled, and some they allowed to live on in Athens
without the rights of citizens.

Later the Great King invaded Greece. As soon
as our fathers saw what an ordeal faced them and
what vast forces the King was assembling, they
decreed that exiles should be restored and disfranchised citizens reinstated, that these too should take

by which Peisistratus regained his tyranny for the third time
(c. 546), and the battle of Sigeum which resulted in the final
expulsion of his son Hippias, the last of the dynasty (510).
Leogoras and Charias were not as prominent on this occasion
as Andocides would have the jury believe. The fall of
Hippias was mainly due to the energy of the Alcmaeonidae
and the substantial help provided by Sparta.

ρίαν καὶ τοὺς κινδύνους ποιήσασθαι. πράξαντες
δὲ ταῦτα, καὶ δόντες ἀλλήλοις πίστεις καὶ ὅρκους
μεγάλους, ἠξίουν σφᾶς αὐτοὺς προτάξαντες πρὸ
τῶν Ἑλλήνων ἁπάντων ἀπαντῆσαι τοῖς βαρβά-
ροις Μαραθῶνάδε, νομίσαντες τὴν σφετέραν
αὐτῶν ἀρετὴν ἱκανὴν εἶναι τῷ πλήθει τῷ ἐκείνων
ἀντιτάξασθαι· μαχεσάμενοί τε ἐνίκων, καὶ τήν
τε Ἑλλάδα ἠλευθέρωσαν καὶ τὴν πατρίδα ἔσωσαν.

108 ἔργον δὲ τοιοῦτον ἐργασάμενοι οὐκ ἠξίωσάν τινι
τῶν πρότερον γενομένων μνησικακῆσαι. τοιγάρτοι
διὰ ταῦτα, τὴν πόλιν ἀνάστατον παραλαβόντες
ἱερά τε κατακεκαυμένα τείχη τε καὶ οἰκίας κατα-
πεπτωκυίας, ἀφορμήν τε οὐδεμίαν ἔχοντες, διὰ
τὸ ἀλλήλοις ὁμονοεῖν τὴν ἀρχὴν τῶν Ἑλλήνων
κατηργάσαντο καὶ τὴν πόλιν ὑμῖν τοιαύτην καὶ

109 τοσαύτην παρέδοσαν. ὑμεῖς οὖν καὶ αὐτοὶ ὕστερον,
κακῶν οὐκ ἐλαττόνων ἢ ἐκείνοις γεγενημένων,
ἀγαθοὶ ἐξ ἀγαθῶν ὄντες ἀπέδοτε τὴν ὑπάρχουσαν
ἀρετήν· ἠξιώσατε γὰρ τούς τε φεύγοντας καταδέξασθαι καὶ τοὺς ἀτίμους ἐπιτίμους ποιῆσαι. τί
οὖν ὑμῖν ὑπόλοιπόν ἐστι τῆς ἐκείνων ἀρετῆς; μὴ
μνησικακῆσαι, εἰδότας, ὦ ἄνδρες, ὅτι ἡ πόλις ἐκ
πολὺ ἐλάττονος ἀφορμῆς ἐν τῷ ἔμπροσθεν χρόνῳ
μεγάλη καὶ εὐδαίμων ἐγένετο· ἃ ⟨καὶ⟩[1] νῦν αὐτῇ
ὑπάρχει, εἰ ἐθέλοιμεν οἱ πολῖται σωφρονεῖν τε καὶ
ὁμονοεῖν ἀλλήλοις.

[15]
110 Κατηγόρησαν δέ μου καὶ περὶ τῆς ἱκετηρίας, ὡς

---

[1] καὶ add. Blass.

their part in the perilous struggle for deliverance. After passing this decree, and exchanging solemn pledges and oaths, they fearlessly took up their stand as the protectors of the whole of Greece, and met the Persians at Marathon ; for they felt that their own valour was itself a match for the enemy hordes. They fought, and they conquered. They gave back Greece her freedom, and they delivered Attica, the land of their birth. After their triumph, however, they refused to revive old quarrels. And that is how men who found their city a waste, her temples burnt to the ground, and her walls and houses in ruins, men who were utterly without resources,[a] brought Greece under their sway and handed on to you the glorious and mighty Athens of to-day—by living in unity. Long afterwards you in your turn had to face a crisis just as great [b] ; and by deciding to restore your exiles and give back their rights to the citizens who had lost them you showed that you still had the noble spirit of your forefathers. What, then, have you still to do to equal them in generosity ? You must refuse to cherish grievances, gentlemen, remembering that Athens had far less in the old days upon which to build her greatness and prosperity. The same greatness and prosperity are hers still, were only we, her citizens, ready to control our passions and live in unity.

The prosecution have also accused me in connexion with the suppliant's bough. They allege that it was

[a] Another gross historical error. Andocides fails to distinguish between the first Persian invasion, which ended with the Athenian victory at Marathon (490 B.C.) and the second (480 B.C.), in the course of which Athens was sacked by the enemy.

[b] After Aegospotami.

καταθείην ἐγὼ ἐν τῷ Ἐλευσινίῳ, νόμος δ' εἴη[1]
πάτριος, ὃς ἂν θῇ ἱκετηρίαν μυστηρίοις, τεθνάναι.
καὶ οὕτως εἰσὶ τολμηροὶ ὥσθ' ἃ αὐτοὶ κατ-
εσκεύασαν, οὐκ ἀρκεῖ αὐτοῖς ὅτι οὐ κατέσχον ἃ
ἐπεβούλευσαν, ἀλλὰ καὶ κατηγορίαν ἐμοῦ ποιοῦνται
ὡς ἀδικοῦντος.

111 Ἐπειδὴ γὰρ ἤλθομεν Ἐλευσινόθεν καὶ ἡ ἔνδειξις
ἐγεγένητο, προσῄει ⟨τοῖς πρυτάνεσιν⟩[2] ὁ βασιλεὺς
περὶ τῶν γεγενημένων Ἐλευσῖνι κατὰ τὴν τελε-
τήν, ὥσπερ ἔθος ἐστίν· οἱ δὲ πρυτάνεις προσάξειν
ἔφασαν αὐτὸν πρὸς τὴν βουλήν, ἐπαγγεῖλαί[3] τ'
ἐκέλευον ἐμοί τε καὶ Κηφισίῳ παρεῖναι εἰς τὸ
Ἐλευσίνιον· ἡ γὰρ βουλὴ ἐκεῖ καθεδεῖσθαι ἔμελλε
κατὰ τὸν Σόλωνος νόμον, ὃς κελεύει τῇ ὑστεραίᾳ
τῶν μυστηρίων ἕδραν ποιεῖν ἐν τῷ Ἐλευσινίῳ.

112 καὶ παρῆμεν κατὰ τὰ προειρημένα. καὶ ἡ βουλὴ
ἐπειδὴ ἦν πλήρης, ἀναστὰς Καλλίας ὁ Ἱππονίκου
τὴν σκευὴν ἔχων λέγει ὅτι ἱκετηρία κεῖται ἐπὶ τοῦ
βωμοῦ, καὶ ἔδειξεν αὐτοῖς. κᾆθ' ὁ κῆρυξ ἐκήρυττε
τίς τὴν ἱκετηρίαν καταθείη, καὶ οὐδεὶς ὑπήκουεν.
ἡμεῖς δὲ παρέσταμεν, καὶ οὗτος ἡμᾶς ἑώρα.
ἐπειδὴ δὲ οὐδεὶς ὑπήκουεν καὶ ᾤχετο εἰσιὼν ⟨ὁ⟩[4]

---

[1] δ' εἴη Bekker: δὲ ἦν codd.
[2] τοῖς πρυτάνεσιν add. Blass.
[3] ἐπαγγεῖλαι Bekker: ἀπαγγεῖλαι codd.
[4] ὁ add. Blass. Post εἰσίων interpungunt alii, inter prae-
conem Euclemque distinguentes.

---

[a] This stood near the Acropolis and was probably the
starting-point for the procession along the Sacred Way to
Eleusis during the Eleusinia.
[b] i.e. after Cephisius had lodged his ἔνδειξις ἀσεβείας with
the Basileus. The Basileus would report this to the βουλή

424

I who placed it in the Eleusinium,[a] and that under an ancient law the penalty for doing such a thing during the Mysteries is death. The impudence of it! They resort to a ruse for my undoing, but will not leave well alone when their plot proves a failure. They proceed to bring a formal accusation against me in spite of it.

It was on our return from Eleusis, after the information had already been lodged against me.[b] The Basileus appeared before the Prytanes to give the usual report on all that had occurred during the performance of the ceremonies there. The Prytanes said that they would bring him before the Council, and told him to give Cephisius and myself notice to attend at the Eleusinium, as it was there that the Council was to sit in conformity with a law of Solon's, which lays down that a sitting shall be held in the Eleusinium on the day after the Mysteries. We duly attended; and when the Council had assembled, Callias, son of Hipponicus, who was wearing his ceremonial robes,[c] rose and announced that a suppliant's bough had been placed on the altar. He displayed this bough to the Council. Thereupon the herald[d] called for the person responsible. There was no reply, although I was standing close by and in full view of Cephisius. When no one replied, and Eucles

when it met in the Eleusinium, and both Cephisius and Andocides would have to attend.

[c] As δαδοῦχος (Torch-bearer), the hereditary office of his family, who belonged to the ancient clan of the κήρυκες. The torch was symbolic of Demeter's search through the world for her daughter.

[d] Eucles, mentioned below. He was the official town-crier of Athens (cf. § 36), and appears in various inscriptions (cf. I.G. ii². 73). The insertion of ὁ before ἐπεξελθών is the simplest correction of the MS. reading in the next sentence but one. Others wish to distinguish between ὁ κῆρυξ and Eucles.

ἐπεξελθὼν Εὐκλῆς οὑτοσί,—καί μοι κάλει αὐτόν.
πρῶτα μὲν οὖν ταῦτα εἰ ἀληθῆ λέγω, μαρτύρησον,
Εὔκλεις.

⟨ΜΑΡΤΥΡΙΑ⟩[1]

113 'Ως μὲν ἀληθῆ λέγω, μεμαρτύρηται· πολὺ δέ μοι
δοκεῖ τὸ ἐναντίον εἶναι ἢ οἱ κατήγοροι εἶπον.
ἔλεξαν γάρ, εἰ μέμνησθε, ὅτι αὐτώ με τὼ θεὼ
παραγάγοιεν[2] ὥστε θεῖναι τὴν ἱκετηρίαν μὴ εἰδότα
τὸν νόμον, ἵνα δῶ δίκην. ἐγὼ δέ, ὦ ἄνδρες, εἰ
ὡς μάλιστα ἀληθῆ λέγουσιν οἱ κατήγοροι, ὑπ'
114 αὐτοῖν με[3] φημὶ τοῖν θεοῖν σεσῶσθαι. εἰ γὰρ
ἔθηκα μὲν τὴν ἱκετηρίαν, ὑπήκουσα δὲ μή, ἄλλο
τι ἢ αὐτὸς μὲν αὐτὸν ἀπώλλυον τιθεὶς τὴν ἱκετηρίαν,
ἐσῳζόμην δὲ τῇ τύχῃ διὰ τὸ μὴ ὑπακοῦσαι, δῆλον
ὅτι διὰ τὼ θεώ; εἰ γὰρ ἐβουλέσθην με ἀπολλύναι
τὼ θεώ, ἐχρῆν δήπου καὶ μὴ θέντα με τὴν ἱκετηρίαν
ὁμολογῆσαι. ἀλλ' οὔτε ὑπήκουσα οὔτ' ἔθηκα.

115 'Επειδὴ δ' ἔλεγε τῇ βουλῇ Εὐκλῆς ὅτι οὐδεὶς
ὑπακούοι, πάλιν ὁ Καλλίας ⟨ἀνα⟩στὰς[4] ἔλεγεν ὅτι
εἴη νόμος πάτριος, εἴ τις ἱκετηρίαν θείη ἐν τῷ
'Ελευσινίῳ, ἄκριτον ἀποθανεῖν, καὶ ὁ πατήρ ποτ'
αὐτοῦ 'Ιππόνικος ἐξηγήσαιτο[5] ταῦτα 'Αθηναίοις,
ἀκούσειε δὲ ὅτι ἐγὼ θείην τὴν ἱκετηρίαν. ἐντεῦθεν
116 ἀναπηδᾷ Κέφαλος οὑτοσὶ καὶ λέγει· " ὦ Καλλία,
πάντων ἀνθρώπων ἀνοσιώτατε, πρῶτον μὲν ἐξηγῇ

---

[1] ΜΑΡΤΥΡΙΑ add. Ald.
[2] παραγάγοιεν Dobree: περιαγάγοιεν codd.
[3] με Reiske: μὲν codd.
[4] ἀναστὰς Baiter: στὰς codd.
[5] ἐξηγήσαιτο Dobree: ἐξηγήσατο codd.

here, who had come out to inquire, had disappeared inside once more—but call him. Now, Eucles, testify whether these facts are correct to start with.

⟨*Evidence*⟩

The truth of my account has been attested ; and it seems to me to contradict the prosecution's story flatly. The prosecution, you may remember, alleged that the Two Goddesses themselves infatuated me and made me place the bough on the altar in ignorance of the law, in order that I might be punished. But I maintain, gentlemen, that even if every word of the prosecution's story is true, it was the Goddesses themselves who saved my life. Suppose that I laid the bough there, and then failed to answer the Herald. Was it not I myself who was bringing about my doom by putting the bough on the altar ? And was it not a piece of good fortune, my silence, that saved me, a piece of good fortune for which I clearly had the Two Goddesses to thank ? Had the Goddesses desired my death, I ought surely to have confessed that I had laid the bough there, even though I had not done so. As it was, I did not answer, nor had I placed the bough on the altar.

When Eucles informed the Council that there had been no response, Callias rose once more and said that under an ancient law, as officially interpreted on a former occasion by his father, Hipponicus, the penalty for placing a bough in the Eleusinium during the Mysteries was instant death. He added that he had heard that it was I who had put it there. Thereupon Cephalus here leapt to his feet and cried : " Callias, you impious scoundrel, first you are giving interpretations, when you have no right to do such

427

Κηρύκων ὤν,[1] οὐχ ὅσιον ⟨ὄν⟩[2] σοι ἐξηγεῖσθαι·
ἔπειτα δὲ νόμον πάτριον λέγεις, ἡ δὲ στήλη παρ'
ᾗ ἕστηκας χιλίας δραχμὰς κελεύει ὀφείλειν, ἐάν
τις ἱκετηρίαν θῇ ἐν τῷ Ἐλευσινίῳ. ἔπειτα δὲ τίνος
ἤκουσας ὅτι Ἀνδοκίδης θείη τὴν ἱκετηρίαν;
κάλεσον αὐτὸν τῇ βουλῇ, ἵνα καὶ ἡμεῖς ἀκούσωμεν.''
ἐπειδὴ δὲ ἀνεγνώσθη ἡ στήλη κἀκεῖνος οὐκ εἶχεν
εἰπεῖν ὅτου ἤκουσε, καταφανὴς ἦν τῇ βουλῇ αὐτὸς
θεὶς τὴν ἱκετηρίαν.

117 Φέρε δὴ τοίνυν, ὦ ἄνδρες—τάχα γὰρ ἂν αὐτὸ
βούλοισθε[3] πυθέσθαι—, ὁ δὲ Καλλίας τί βουλόμενος
ἐτίθη τὴν ἱκετηρίαν; ἐγὼ δὲ ὑμῖν διηγήσομαι
ὧν ὑπ' αὐτοῦ ἕνεκα ἐπεβουλεύθην. Ἐπίλυκος ἦν
ὁ Τεισάνδρου θεῖός μοι, ἀδελφὸς τῆς μητρὸς τῆς
ἐμῆς· ἀπέθανε δὲ ἐν Σικελίᾳ ἄπαις ἀρρένων παίδων,
θυγατέρας δὲ δύο καταλιπών, αἳ ἐγίγνοντο εἴς τε
118 ἐμὲ καὶ Λέαγρον. τὰ δὲ πράγματα τὰ οἴκοι
πονήρως εἶχε· τὴν μὲν γὰρ φανερὰν οὐσίαν οὐδὲ
δυοῖν ταλάντοιν κατέλιπε, τὰ δὲ ὀφειλόμενα πλέον
ἦν ἢ πέντε τάλαντα. ὅμως δ' ἐγὼ καλέσας
Λέαγρον ἐναντίον τῶν φίλων ἔλεγον ὅτι ταῦτ'
εἴη ἀνδρῶν ἀγαθῶν, ἐν τοῖς τοιούτοις δεικνύναι
119 τὰς οἰκειότητας ἀλλήλοις. ''ἡμᾶς γὰρ οὐ δίκαιόν
ἐστιν οὔτε χρήματα ἕτερα[4] οὔτ' εὐτυχίαν ἀνδρὸς
ἑλέσθαι, ὥστε καταφρονῆσαι τῶν Ἐπιλύκου θυγα-

---

[1] Κηρύκων ὤν Reiske: κηρύκων ὤν codd.
[2] ὄν add. Frohberger.
[3] βούλοισθε Dobree: βούλεσθε codd.
[4] ἑτέρου Richards. Post ἀνδρὸς add. ἑτέρου Lipsius.

---

[a] ἐξήγησις was the prerogative of the Eumolpidae alone.
[b] For the family relationships described here and in the
following §§ see p. 334.

428

a thing as a member of the Ceryces.[a] Then you talk of an ' ancient law,' when the stone at your side lays down that the penalty for placing a bough in the Eleusinium shall be a fine of a thousand drachmae. And lastly, who told you that Andocides had put the bough there ? Summon him before the Council, so that we too may hear what he has to say." The stone was read, and Callias could not say who his informant was. It was thus clear to the Council that he had put the bough there himself.

And now, gentlemen, you would perhaps like to know what motive Callias had in putting the bough on the altar. I will explain why he tried to trap me. Epilycus, son of Teisander, was my uncle, my mother's brother.[b] He died in Sicily without male issue, but left two daughters who ought now to have passed to Leagrus and myself.[c] His private affairs were in confusion. The tangible property which he left did not amount to two talents, while his debts came to more than five. However, I arranged a meeting with Leagrus [d] before our friends and told him that this was the time for decent men to show their respect for family ties. " We have no right to prefer a wealthy or successful alliance and look down upon the daughters of Epilycus," I argued: " for if Epilycus

---

[c] If a citizen died intestate, leaving daughters, but no sons, the daughters became heiresses (ἐπίκληροι) and shared the estate between them. They were then obliged by law to marry their nearest male relatives, but not in the ascending line. The relatives concerned put in a claim before the Archon (ἐπιδικασία), and if it was not disputed, the Archon adjudged the daughters to them severally according to their degrees of relationship. If, however, as here, rival claimants appeared, a διαδικασία was held and the ἐπίκληροι were allotted accordingly.

[d] Leagrus, like Andocides, must have been a cousin.

τέρων. καὶ γὰρ εἰ ἔζη Ἐπίλυκος ἢ τεθνεὼς πολλὰ
κατέλιπε χρήματα, ἠξιοῦμεν ἂν γένει ὄντες ἐγγυ-
τάτω ἔχειν τὰς παίδας. τοιγάρτοι ἐκεῖνα μὲν δι'
Ἐπίλυκον ἂν ἦν ἢ διὰ τὰ χρήματα· νῦν δὲ διὰ τὴν
[16] ἡμετέραν ἀρετὴν τάδε ἔσται. τῆς μὲν οὖν σὺ
ἐπιδικάζου, τῆς δὲ ἐγώ.''

120 Ὡμολόγησέ μοι, ὦ ἄνδρες. ἐπεδικασάμεθα
ἄμφω κατὰ τὴν πρὸς ἡμᾶς ὁμολογίαν. καὶ ἧς
μὲν ἐγὼ ἐπεδικασάμην, ἡ παῖς τύχῃ χρησαμένη
καμοῦσα ἀπέθανεν· ἡ δ' ἑτέρα ἔστιν ἔτι. ταύτην
Καλλίας ἔπειθε Λέαγρον, χρήματα ὑπισχνούμενος,
ἐὰν αὐτὸν λαβεῖν· αἰσθόμενος δ' ἐγὼ εὐθὺς ἔθηκα
παράστασιν, καὶ ἔλαχον προτέρῳ μὲν Λεάγρῳ,
ὅτι '' εἰ μὲν σὺ βούλῃ ἐπιδικάζεσθαι, ἔχε τύχῃ
121 ἀγαθῇ, εἰ δὲ μή, ἐγὼ ἐπιδικάσομαι.'' γνοὺς ταῦτα
Καλλίας λαγχάνει τῷ υἱεῖ τῷ ἑαυτοῦ τῆς ἐπικλήρου,
τῇ δεκάτῃ ἱσταμένου, ἵνα μὴ ἐπιδικάσωμαι ἐγώ.
ταῖς δ' εἰκάσι, μυστηρίοις τούτοις, δοὺς Κηφισίῳ
χιλίας δραχμὰς ἐνδείκνυσί με καὶ εἰς τὸν ἀγῶνα
τοῦτον καθίστησιν. ἐπειδὴ δ' ἑώρα με ὑπο-
μένοντα, τίθησι τὴν ἱκετηρίαν, ὡς ἐμὲ μὲν ἀπο-
κτενῶν ἄκριτον ἢ ἐξελῶν,[1] αὐτὸς δὲ πείσας[2] Λέαγρον
χρήμασι συνοικήσων τῇ Ἐπιλύκου θυγατρί.

122 Ἐπειδὴ δ' οὐδ' ὡς[3] ἄνευ ἀγῶνος ἑώρα ἐσόμενα
τὰ πράγματα, τότε δὴ προσιὼν Λυσίστρατον,

[1] ἐξελῶν Valckenaer: ἐξελὼν codd.
[2] πείσας Scaliger: πείσων codd.
[3] οὐδ' ὡς Bekker: οὕτως codd.

---

[a] Callias was actually claiming the girl on his son's behalf
(§ 121); as her grandfather, he was forbidden by law to
marry her himself.

[b] The παράστασις was a fee of one drachma, paid by anyone
disputing the claim of a relative to an ἐπίκληρος.

were alive, or had died a rich man, we should be claiming the girls as their next of kin. We should have married them then either because of Epilycus himself or because of his money ; we will do the same now because we are men of honour. Do you obtain an order of the court for the one, and I will do the same for the other."

He assented, gentlemen ; so in accordance with our agreement we both applied for an order of the court. The girl claimed by me happened to fall ill, and died ; the other is still alive. Now Callias tried to bribe Leagrus into letting him have this second daughter.[a] Directly I heard of it, I deposited a fee,[b] and began by obtaining leave to proceed against Leagrus, to this effect : " If you will claim the girl for yourself, take her and good luck to you. If not, I will claim her myself."[c] As soon as Callias learned of this, he entered a claim for the girl in his son's name, on the tenth of the month, to prevent me from obtaining an order. Soon after the twentieth,[d] during the Mysteries which are just over, he gives Cephisius a thousand drachmae, gets an information lodged against me, and involves me in to-day's trial. Then, when he saw that I was standing my ground, he put the bough on the altar, intending to have me either put to death without a trial or banished, and then to marry the daughter of Epilycus himself by bribing Leagrus.

However, he saw that even thus he would not get his way without coming into court ; so he ap-

[c] If Leagrus stood aside, Andocides would have a prior claim to Callias' son in the eyes of the law. See stemma, Introd. p. 334.

[d] εἰκάδες. The last ten days of the month.

Ἡγεμόνα, Ἐπιχάρη, ὁρῶν φίλους ὄντας ἐμοὶ καὶ
χρωμένους, εἰς τοῦτο βδελυρίας ἦλθε καὶ παρανομίας ὥστ᾽ ἔλεγε πρὸς τούτους ὡς εἰ ἔτι καὶ νῦν
βουλοίμην ἀποστῆναι τῆς Ἐπιλύκου θυγατρός,
ἕτοιμος εἴη παύσασθαί με κακῶς ποιῶν, ἀπαλλάξαι
δὲ Κηφίσιον, δίκην δ᾽ ἐν τοῖς φίλοις δοῦναί μοι
123 τῶν πεποιημένων. εἶπον αὐτῷ καὶ κατηγορεῖν
καὶ παρασκευάζειν ἄλλους· εἰ δ᾽ ἐγὼ αὐτὸν ἀποφεύξομαι[1] καὶ γνώσονται Ἀθηναῖοι περὶ ἐμοῦ τὰ
δίκαια, ἐγὼ αὐτὸν οἶμαι περὶ τοῦ σώματος τοῦ
ἑαυτοῦ ἐν τῷ μέρει κινδυνεύσειν. ἅπερ αὐτὸν οὐ
ψεύσομαι, ἐὰν ὑμῖν, ὦ ἄνδρες, δοκῇ. ὡς δ᾽
ἀληθῆ λέγω, κάλει μοι τοὺς μάρτυρας.

MAPTYPEΣ

124 Ἀλλὰ γὰρ τὸν υἱὸν αὐτοῦ τοῦτον, ᾧ λαχεῖν
ἠξίωσε τῆς Ἐπιλύκου θυγατρός, σκέψασθε πῶς
γέγονε καὶ πῶς ἐποίησατ᾽ αὐτόν· ταῦτα γὰρ καὶ
ἄξιον ἀκοῦσαι, ὦ ἄνδρες. γαμεῖ μὲν Ἰσχομάχου
θυγατέρα· ταύτῃ δὲ συνοικήσας οὐδ᾽ ἐνιαυτὸν
τὴν μητέρα αὐτῆς ἔλαβε, καὶ συνῴκει ὁ πάντων
σχετλιώτατος ἀνθρώπων τῇ μητρὶ καὶ τῇ θυγατρί,
ἱερεὺς ὢν τῆς μητρὸς καὶ τῆς θυγατρός, καὶ εἶχεν
ἐν τῇ οἰκίᾳ ἀμφοτέρας.

125 Καὶ οὗτος μὲν οὐκ ᾐσχύνθη οὐδ᾽ ἔδεισε τὼ θεώ·
ἡ δὲ τοῦ Ἰσχομάχου θυγάτηρ τεθνάναι νομίσασα
λυσιτελεῖν ἢ ζῆν ὁρῶσα τὰ γιγνόμενα, ἀπαγχομένη
μεταξὺ κατεκωλύθη,[2] καὶ ἐπειδὴ ἀνεβίω, ἀποδρᾶσα[3]
ἐκ τῆς οἰκίας ᾤχετο, καὶ ἐξήλασεν ἡ μήτηρ τὴν

---

[1] ἀποφεύξομαι Bekker : ἀποφεύξαιμι codd.
[2] κατεκωλύθη Sluiter : κατεκλίθη codd.
[3] ἀποδρᾶσα Bekker : ἀποδράσασα.

proached Lysistratus, Hegemon, and Epichares, whom he saw to be intimate friends of mine. He had insolence enough, he had contempt enough for the law to inform them that if I was prepared even now to relinquish my claims to the daughter of Epilycus, he was ready to stop persecuting me, to call off Cephisius, and to make amends for his behaviour with our friends as arbitrators. I told him to proceed with his case and hire still more help. "But if the people of Athens return a true verdict and I escape you," I warned him, "you will find that it is your turn, I think, to fight for your life." And with your permission, gentlemen, I will not disappoint him. Kindly call witnesses to confirm what I have been saying.

Witnesses

But you must let me tell you how the son to whom Callias tried to have the daughter of Epilycus awarded was born and acknowledged by his father; it is quite worth hearing, gentlemen. Callias married a daughter of Ischomachus; but he had not been living with her a year before he made her mother his mistress. Was ever man so utterly without shame? He was the priest of the Mother and the Daughter; yet he lived with mother and daughter and kept them both in his house together.

The thought of the Two Goddesses may not have awoken any shame or fear in Callias; but the daughter of Ischomachus thought death better than an existence where such things went on before her very eyes. She tried to hang herself: but was stopped in the act. Then, when she recovered, she ran away from home; the mother drove out the

433

θυγατέρα. ταύτης δ᾽ αὖ διαπεπλησμένος ἐξέβαλε
καὶ ταύτην. ἡ δ᾽ ἔφη κυεῖν ἐξ αὐτοῦ· καὶ ἐπειδὴ
ἔτεκεν υἱόν, ἔξαρνος ἦν μὴ εἶναι ἐξ αὐτοῦ τὸ
126 παιδίον. λαβόντες δὲ οἱ προσήκοντες τῇ γυναικὶ
τὸ παιδίον ἧκον ἐπὶ τὸν βωμὸν Ἀπατουρίοις,
ἔχοντες ἱερεῖον, καὶ ἐκέλευον κατάρξασθαι τὸν
Καλλίαν. ὁ δ᾽ ἠρώτα τίνος εἴη τὸ παιδίον· ἔλεγον
" Καλλίου τοῦ Ἱππονίκου." " ἐγώ εἰμι οὗτος."
" καὶ ἔστι γε σὸν τὸ παιδίον." λαβόμενος τοῦ
βωμοῦ ὤμοσεν ἦ μὴν μὴ εἶναί ⟨οἱ⟩[1] υἱὸν ἄλλον
μηδὲ γενέσθαι πώποτε, εἰ μὴ Ἱππόνικον ἐκ τῆς
Γλαύκωνος θυγατρός· ἦ ἐξώλη εἶναι καὶ αὐτὸν
καὶ τὴν οἰκίαν, ὥσπερ ἔσται.

127 Μετὰ ταῦτα τοίνυν, ὦ ἄνδρες, ὑστέρῳ πάλιν
χρόνῳ τῆς γραὸς τολμηροτάτης γυναικὸς ἀνηράσθη,
καὶ κομίζεται αὐτὴν εἰς τὴν οἰκίαν, καὶ τὸν παῖδα
ἤδη μέγαν ὄντα εἰσάγει εἰς Κήρυκας, φάσκων
εἶναι υἱὸν αὐτοῦ.[2] ἀντεῖπε μὲν Καλλιάδης[3] μὴ
εἰσδέξασθαι, ἐψηφίσαντο δὲ οἱ Κήρυκες κατὰ τὸν
νόμον ὅς ἐστιν αὐτοῖς, τὸν πατέρα ὀμόσαντα
εἰσάγειν ἦ μὴν υἱὸν ὄντα ἑαυτοῦ εἰσάγειν. λαβόμενος τοῦ βωμοῦ ὤμοσεν ἦ μὴν τὸν παῖδα ἑαυτοῦ
εἶναι γνήσιον, ἐκ Χρυσίλλης[4] γεγονότα· ὃν ἀπώμοσε.
καί μοι τούτων ἁπάντων τοὺς μάρτυρας κάλει.

⟨ΜΑΡΤΥΡΕΣ⟩[5]

[1] οἱ add. Muretus.
[2] αὐτοῦ Baiter: αὑτοῦ codd.
[3] Καλλιάδης Valckenaer: καλλίδης codd.
[4] Χρυσίλλης Jernstedt: χρυσιάδης codd.
[5] ΜΑΡΤΥΡΕΣ add. Ald.

daughter. Finally Callias grew tired of the mother as well, and drove her out in her turn. She then said she was pregnant by him ; but when she gave birth to a son, Callias denied that the child was his. At that, the woman's relatives came to the altar at the Apaturia *a* with the child and a victim for sacrifice, and told Callias to begin the rites. He asked whose child it was. "The child of Callias, son of Hipponicus," they replied. "But I am he." "Yes, and the child is yours." Callias took hold of the altar and swore that the only son he had or had ever had was Hipponicus, and the mother was Glaucon's daughter. If that was not the truth, he prayed that he and his house might perish from the earth—as they surely will.

Now some time afterwards, gentlemen, he fell in love with the abandoned old hag once more and welcomed her back into his house, while he presented the boy, a grown lad by this time, to the Ceryces, asserting that he was his own son. Calliades opposed his admission ; but the Ceryces voted in favour of the law which they have, whereby a father can introduce his son, if he swears that it is his own son whom he is introducing. So Callias took hold of the altar and swore that the boy was his legitimate son by Chrysilla. Yet he had disowned that same son. Call witnesses to confirm all this, please.

⟨*Witnesses*⟩

---

a Held for three days in Pyanepsion (Oct.-Nov.). The citizens assembled κατὰ φρατρίας, and on the third day (κουρεῶτις) newly born children were registered in the official list of φράτορες. A sacrifice accompanied the registration. The father had to swear that the child was the legitimate offspring of free-born parents, both of whom were citizens.

128 Φέρε δὴ τοίνυν, ὦ ἄνδρες, σκεψώμεθα εἰ πώποτε
ἐν τοῖς Ἕλλησι πρᾶγμα τοιοῦτον ἐγένετο, ὅπου
γυναῖκά τις γήμας ἐπέγημε τῇ θυγατρὶ τὴν μητέρα
καὶ ἐξήλασεν ἡ μήτηρ τὴν θυγατέρα· ταύτῃ δὲ
[17] συνοικῶν βούλεται τὴν Ἐπιλύκου θυγατέρα λαβεῖν,
ἵν' ἐξελάσῃ τὴν τήθην ἡ θυγατριδῆ. ἀλλὰ γὰρ τῷ
129 παιδὶ αὐτοῦ τί χρὴ τοὔνομα θέσθαι; οἶμαι γὰρ
ἔγωγε οὐδένα οὕτως ἀγαθὸν εἶναι λογίζεσθαι,
ὅστις ἐξευρήσει τοὔνομα αὐτοῦ. τριῶν γὰρ οὐσῶν
γυναικῶν αἷς συνῳκηκὼς ἔσται ὁ πατὴρ αὐτοῦ,
τῆς μὲν υἱός ἐστιν, ὥς φησι, τῆς δὲ ἀδελφός, τῆς
δὲ θεῖος. τίς ἂν εἴη οὗτος; Οἰδίπους, ἢ Αἴγισθος·
ἢ τί χρὴ αὐτὸν ὀνομάσαι;

130 Ἀλλὰ γάρ, ὦ ἄνδρες, βραχύ τι ὑμᾶς ἀναμνῆσαι
περὶ Καλλίου βούλομαι. εἰ γὰρ μέμνησθε, ὅτε ἡ
πόλις ἦρχε τῶν Ἑλλήνων καὶ ηὐδαιμόνει μάλιστα,
Ἱππόνικος δὲ ἦν πλουσιώτατος τῶν Ἑλλήνων,
τότε μέντοι πάντες ἴστε ὅτι παρὰ τοῖς παιδαρίοις
τοῖς μικροτάτοις καὶ τοῖς γυναίοις κληδὼν ἐν
ἁπάσῃ τῇ πόλει κατεῖχεν,[1] ὅτι Ἱππόνικος ἐν τῇ οἰκίᾳ
ἀλιτήριον τρέφει, ὃς αὐτοῦ τὴν τράπεζαν ἀνατρέπει.
131 μέμνησθε ταῦτα, ὦ ἄνδρες. πῶς οὖν ἡ φήμη ἡ
τότε οὖσα δοκεῖ ὑμῖν ἀποβῆναι; οἰόμενος γὰρ
Ἱππόνικος υἱὸν τρέφειν ἀλιτήριον αὑτῷ ἔτρεφεν,
ὃς ἀνατέτροφεν ἐκείνου τὸν πλοῦτον, τὴν σωφρο-
σύνην, τὸν ἄλλον βίον ἅπαντα. οὕτως οὖν χρὴ
περὶ τούτου γιγνώσκειν, ὡς ὄντος Ἱππονίκου
ἀλιτηρίου.

132 Ἀλλὰ γάρ, ὦ ἄνδρες, διὰ τί ποτε τοῖς ἐμοὶ νυνὶ
ἐπιτιθεμένοις μετὰ Καλλίου καὶ συμπαρασκευάσασι

---

[1] κατεῖχεν Blass: κατέσχεν codd.

Let us just see, gentlemen, whether anything of this kind has ever happened in Greece before. A man marries a wife, and then marries the mother as well as the daughter. The mother turns the daughter out. Then, while living with the mother, he wants to marry the daughter of Epilycus, so that the grand-daughter can turn the grandmother out. Why, what ought his child to be called? Personally, I do not believe that there is anyone ingenious enough to find the right name for him. There are three women with whom his father will have lived : and he is the alleged son of one of them, the brother of another, and the uncle of the third. What ought a son like that to be called? Oedipus, Aegisthus, or what?

As a matter of fact, I want to remind you briefly, gentlemen, of a certain incident connected with Callias. As you may remember, when Athens was mistress of Greece and at the height of her pro-sperity, and Hipponicus was the richest man in Greece, a rumour with which you are all familiar was on the lips of little children and silly women throughout the city : "Hipponicus," they said, "has an evil spirit in his house, and it upsets his books." [a] You remember it, gentlemen. Now in what sense do you think that the saying current in those days proved true? Why, Hipponicus imagined that he had a son in his house ; but that son was really an evil spirit, which has upset his wealth, his morals, and his whole life. So it is as Hipponicus' evil spirit that you must think of Callias.

Now take my other accusers, Callias' partners, who have helped to institute this trial and have financed

---

[a] Lit. "his table," with a play on τράπεζα meaning a "bank." The pun cannot be rendered exactly in English.

τὸν ἀγῶνα καὶ χρήματα εἰσενεγκοῦσιν ἐπ' ἐμοὶ
τρία μὲν ἔτη ἐπιδημῶν καὶ ἥκων ἐκ Κύπρου οὐκ
ἀσεβεῖν ἐδόκουν αὐτοῖς, μυῶν μὲν 'Α. . . Δελφόν,[1]
ἔτι δὲ ἄλλους ξένους ἐμαυτοῦ, καὶ εἰσιὼν εἰς τὸ
Ἐλευσίνιον καὶ θύων, ὥσπερ ἐμαυτὸν ἄξιον νομίζω
εἶναι· ἀλλὰ τοὐναντίον λῃτουργεῖν οὗτοι προὐ-
βάλλοντο, πρῶτον μὲν γυμνασίαρχον Ἡφαιστίοις,
ἔπειτα ἀρχεθέωρον εἰς Ἰσθμὸν καὶ Ὀλυμπίαζε,
εἶτα δὲ ταμίαν ἐν πόλει τῶν ἱερῶν χρημάτων. νῦν
δὲ ἀσεβῶ καὶ ἀδικῶ εἰσιὼν εἰς τὰ ἱερά.

133   Ἐγὼ ὑμῖν ἐρῶ διότι οὗτοι ταῦτα νῦν γιγνώ-
σκουσιν. Ἀγύρριος γὰρ οὑτοσί, ὁ καλὸς κἀγαθός,
ἀρχώνης[2] ἐγένετο τῆς πεντηκοστῆς τρίτον ἔτος,
καὶ ἐπρίατο τριάκοντα ταλάντων, μετέσχον δ'
αὐτῷ[3] οὗτοι πάντες οἱ παρασυλλεγέντες ὑπὸ τὴν
λεύκην, οὓς[4] ὑμεῖς ἴστε οἷοί εἰσιν· οἳ διὰ τοῦτο
ἔμοιγε δοκοῦσι συλλεγῆναι ἐκεῖσε, ἵν' αὐτοῖς

---

[1] 'Α. . . Δελφόν Bekker : ἀδελφόν codd.
[2] ἀρχώνης Valckenaer : ἄρχων εἰς codd.
[3] αὐτῷ Reiske : αὐτοὶ codd.
[4] λεύκην, οὓς Muretus : λευκὴν τὸ πόσους codd.

---

[a] One of the ἐγκύκλιοι λῃτουργίαι which recurred annually.
Citizens owning property to the value of three talents or over
were liable to them. Other such liturgies were the χορηγία,
λαμπαδαρχία, ἀρχεθεωρία, ἑστίασις. The various tribes selected
suitable persons to perform them from among their members.
The γυμνασιαρχία is practically identical with the λαμπαδαρχία.
It involved the provision of torches for the great torch-race
at the festival of Hephaestus and the training of the runners.
The expense was considerable; Isaeus classes the γυμνασιαρχία
with the χορηγία, and puts the cost at twelve minae.

[b] Another regular liturgy. State deputations were always
sent to the great games (Olympian, Isthmian, Pythian,

the prosecution. Why, I ask, did it never strike them that I was committing sacrilege during the three years which I have spent in Athens since my return from Cyprus? I initiated A—— from Delphi and other friends of mine besides from outside Attica, and I frequented the Eleusinium and offered sacrifices, as I consider I have a perfect right to do. Yet so far from prosecuting, they actually proposed me for public services, first as Gymnasiarch *a* at the Hephaestia, then as head of the state deputation to the Isthmus and to Olympia,*b* and finally as Treasurer of the Sacred Monies on the Acropolis.*c* To-day, on the other hand, I commit a sacrilege and a crime by entering a temple.

I will tell you the reason for this change of front. Last year and the year before our honest Agyrrhius here was chief contractor for the two per cent customs duties.*d* He farmed them for thirty talents, and the friends he meets under the poplar *e* all took shares with him. You know what *they* are like; it is my belief that they met there for a double purpose: to be paid for

Nemean). These were headed by an ἀρχεθέωρος who was responsible for their management. He also bore a considerable part of the expense. The state contributed a certain amount; but the ἀρχεθέωρος was expected to see that the deputation was as impressive as possible. Andocides must have gone to Olympia in 400, as this was the first year in which the games were held after his return to Athens. The ἀρχεθεωρία to the Isthmian Games will then fall in 402.

c There were ten ταμίαι τῆς θεοῦ, and ten ταμίαι τῶν ἄλλων θεῶν, chosen annually by lot from the wealthiest class of citizens. The treasury of both boards was in the Opisthodomus of the Parthenon. Andocides may have been a member of either.

d Levied on all imports and exports at Peiraeus.

e Apparently a well-known spot. It is not mentioned elsewhere.

ἀμφότερα ᾖ, καὶ μὴ ὑπερβάλλουσι[1] λαβεῖν ἀργύριον
134 καὶ ὀλίγου πραθείσης μετασχεῖν. κερδήναντες δὲ
ἐξ[2] τάλαντα, γνόντες τὸ πρᾶγμα οἷον εἴη, [ὡς
πολλοῦ ἄξιον,][3] συνέστησαν πάντες, καὶ μεταδόντες
τοῖς ἄλλοις ἐωνοῦντο πάλιν τριάκοντα ταλάντων.
ἐπεὶ δ' οὐκ ἀντεωνεῖτο οὐδείς, παρελθὼν ἐγὼ εἰς
τὴν βουλὴν ὑπερέβαλλον, ἕως ἐπριάμην ἓξ καὶ
τριάκοντα ταλάντων. ἀπελάσας δὲ τούτους καὶ
καταστήσας ὑμῖν ἐγγυητὰς ἐξέλεξα τὰ χρήματα
καὶ κατέβαλον τῇ πόλει καὶ αὐτὸς οὐκ ἐζημιώθην,
ἀλλὰ καὶ βραχέα ἀπεκερδαίνομεν οἱ μετασχόντες·
τούτους δ' ἐποίησα τῶν ὑμετέρων μὴ διανείμασθαι
ἓξ τάλαντα ἀργυρίου.

135 Ἃ οὗτοι γνόντες ἔδοσαν σφίσιν αὐτοῖς λόγον,
ὅτι '' ἄνθρωπος[4] οὑτοσὶ οὔτε αὐτὸς λήψεται τῶν
κοινῶν χρημάτων οὔθ' ἡμᾶς ἐάσει, φυλάξει δὲ καὶ
ἐμποδὼν ἔσται διανείμασθαι τὰ κοινά· πρὸς δὲ
τούτοις, ὃν ἂν ἡμῶν ἀδικοῦντα λάβῃ, εἰσάξει εἰς
τὸ πλῆθος τὸ[5] Ἀθηναίων καὶ ἀπολεῖ. δεῖ οὖν
τοῦτον ἐκποδὼν ἡμῖν[6] εἶναι καὶ δικαίως καὶ
136 ἀδίκως.'' ταῦτα μὲν οὖν, ὦ ἄνδρες δικασταί, τούτοις ποιητέα ἦν, ὑμῖν δέ γε ⟨τὸ⟩[7] ἐναντίον τούτων·
ὡς[8] γὰρ πλείστους εἶναι ὑμῖν[9] ἤθελον ἂν τοιούσδε
οἷόσπερ ἐγώ, τούτους δὲ μάλιστα ⟨μὲν⟩[10] ἀπολωλέναι, εἰ δὲ μή, εἶναι τοὺς μὴ ἐπιτρέψαντας
αὐτοῖς, οἷς καὶ προσήκει ἀνδράσιν εἶναι καὶ ἀγαθοῖς καὶ δικαίοις περὶ τὸ πλῆθος τὸ ὑμέτερον,
καὶ βουλόμενοι δυνήσονται εὖ ποιεῖν ὑμᾶς. ἐγὼ

---

[1] ὑπερβάλλουσι Stephanus : ὑπερβάλλωσι codd.
[2] ἐξ Reiske : τρία codd.
[3] ὡς πολλοῦ ἄξιον del. Sluiter.
[4] ἄνθρωπος Blass : ἄνθρωπος codd.

not raising the bidding, and to take shares in taxes
which have been knocked down cheap. After making
a profit of six talents, they saw what a gold-mine
the business was; so they combined, gave rival
bidders a percentage, and again offered thirty talents.
There was no competition; so I went before the
Council and outbid them, until I purchased the
rights for thirty-six talents. I had ousted them. I
then furnished you with sureties, collected the tax,
and settled with the state. I did not lose by it, as
my partners and I actually made a small profit. At
the same time I stopped Agyrrhius and his friends
from sharing six talents which belonged to you.

They saw this themselves, and discussed the situation. "This fellow will not take any of the public
money himself," they argued, "and he will not let
us take any either. He will be on the watch and
stop our sharing what belongs to the state; and
furthermore, if he catches any of us acting dis-
honestly, he will bring him into the public courts and
ruin him. He must be got rid of at all costs." The
prosecution were bound to behave thus, gentlemen;
but you must do the opposite: for I should be happy
to see you with as many men as possible like myself
and to see my accusers stamped out of existence, or
at least confronted by those who will not countenance
their activities. Such men should show themselves
staunch and impartial champions of your interests,
and they will be able to serve you well, if they are
willing to do so. I for one promise you either to put

---

[5] τὸ Fuhr : τῶν codd.
[6] ἡμῖν Reiske : ὑμῖν codd.
[7] τὸ add. Sluiter.
[8] ὡς Blass : τοὺς codd.
[9] ὑμῖν Reiske : ἡμῖν codd.
[10] μὲν add. Bekker.

οὖν ὑμῖν ὑπισχνοῦμαι ἢ παύσειν τούτους ταῦτα
ποιοῦντας καὶ βελτίους παρέξειν, ἢ εἰς ὑμᾶς εἰσ-
αγαγὼν κολάσειν τοὺς ἀδικοῦντας αὐτῶν.

137 Κατηγόρησαν δέ μου καὶ περὶ τῶν ναυκληριῶν
[18] καὶ περὶ τῆς ἐμπορίας, ὡς ἄρα οἱ θεοὶ διὰ τοῦτό
με ἐκ τῶν κινδύνων σώσαιεν, ἵνα ἐλθὼν δεῦρο, ὡς
ἔοικεν, ὑπὸ Κηφισίου ἀπολοίμην. ἐγὼ δέ, ὦ
Ἀθηναῖοι, οὐκ ἀξιῶ τοὺς θεοὺς τοιαύτην γνώμην
ἔχειν, ὥστ᾽ εἰ ἐνόμιζον ὑπ᾽ ἐμοῦ ἀδικεῖσθαι, λαμ-
βάνοντάς με ἐν τοῖς μεγίστοις κινδύνοις μὴ τιμωρεῖσθαι. τίς γὰρ κίνδυνος μείζων ἀνθρώποις ἢ
χειμῶνος ὥρᾳ πλεῖν τὴν θάλατταν; ἐν οἷς ἔχοντες
μὲν τὸ σῶμα τοὐμόν, κρατοῦντες δὲ τοῦ βίου καὶ
138 τῆς οὐσίας τῆς ἐμῆς, εἶτα ἔσῳζον; οὐκ ἐξῆν[1]
αὐτοῖς ποιῆσαι μηδὲ ταφῆς τὸ σῶμα ἀξιωθῆναι;
ἔτι δὲ πολέμου γενομένου καὶ τριήρων ἀεὶ κατὰ
θάλατταν οὐσῶν καὶ λῃστῶν, ὑφ᾽ ὧν πολλοὶ
ληφθέντες, ἀπολέσαντες τὰ ὄντα, δουλεύοντες τὸν
βίον διετέλεσαν, οὔσης δὲ χώρας βαρβάρου, εἰς
ἣν πολλοὶ ἤδη ἐκπεσόντες αἰκείαις ταῖς μεγίσταις
περιέπεσον καὶ τὰ σφέτερα αὐτῶν σώματα αἰκι-
139 σθέντες ἀπέθανον,—εἶτα οἱ μὲν θεοὶ ἐκ τοσούτων
κινδύνων ἔσῳζόν με, σφῶν δὲ αὐτῶν προὐστήσαντο
τιμωρὸν γενέσθαι Κηφίσιον τὸν πονηρότατον
Ἀθηναίων, ὃν οὗτός φησι πολίτης εἶναι οὐκ ὤν,
ᾧ οὐδ᾽ ὑμῶν τῶν καθημένων οὐδεὶς ἂν ἐπιτρέψειεν
οὐδὲν τῶν ἰδίων, εἰδὼς τοῦτον οἷός ἐστιν; ἐγὼ
μὲν οὖν, ὦ ἄνδρες, ἡγοῦμαι χρῆναι νομίζειν τοὺς

---

[1] οὐκ ἐξῆν Stephanus: οὐ πεζῆν codd.

a stop to the practices of the prosecution and render them better citizens, or to bring such of them as are guilty of criminal behaviour into court and have them punished.

The prosecution have also found grounds for attacking me in the fact that I am a merchant who owns ships. We are asked to believe that the only object of the gods in saving me from the dangers of the sea was, apparently, to let Cephisius put an end to me when I reached Athens. No, gentlemen. I for one cannot believe that if the gods considered me guilty of an offence against them, they would have been disposed to spare me when they had me in a situation of the utmost peril—for when is man in greater peril than on a winter sea-passage ? Are we to suppose that the gods had my person at their mercy on just such a voyage, that they had my life and my goods in their power, and that in spite of it they kept me safe ? Why, could they not have caused even my corpse to be denied due burial ? Furthermore, it was war-time ; the sea was infested with triremes and pirates, who took many a traveller prisoner, and after robbing him of his all, sent him to end his days in slavery. And there were foreign shores on which many a traveller had been wrecked, to be put to death after meeting with shameful indignities and maltreatment. Is it conceivable that the gods saved me from perils of that nature, only to let themselves be championed by Cephisius, the biggest scoundrel in Athens, whose citizen he claims to be when he is nothing of the kind, and whom every one of you sitting in this court knows too well to trust with anything belonging to him ? No, gentlemen ; to my mind the dangers of a trial like the present are to be

τοιούτους κινδύνους ἀνθρωπίνους, τοὺς δὲ κατὰ
θάλατταν θείους. εἴπερ οὖν δεῖ τὰ τῶν θεῶν
ὑπονοεῖν, πάνυ¹ ἂν αὐτοὺς οἶμαι ἐγὼ ὀργίζεσθαι
καὶ ἀγανακτεῖν, εἰ τοὺς ὑφ' ἑαυτῶν σῳζομένους
ὑπ' ἀνθρώπων² ἀπολλυμένους ὁρῷεν.

140 Καὶ μὲν δὴ καὶ τάδε ὑμῖν ἄξιον, ὦ ἄνδρες, ἐνθυμηθῆναι, ὅτι νυνὶ πᾶσι τοῖς Ἕλλησιν ἄνδρες
ἄριστοι καὶ εὐβουλότατοι δοκεῖτε γεγενῆσθαι, οὐκ
ἐπὶ τιμωρίαν τραπόμενοι τῶν γεγενημένων, ἀλλ'
ἐπὶ σωτηρίαν τῆς πόλεως καὶ ὁμόνοιαν τῶν
πολιτῶν. συμφοραὶ μὲν γὰρ ἤδη καὶ ἄλλοις
πολλοῖς ἐγένοντο οὐκ ἐλάττους ἢ καὶ ἡμῖν· τὸ δὲ
τὰς γενομένας διαφορὰς πρὸς ἀλλήλους θέσθαι
καλῶς, τοῦτ' εἰκότως ἤδη δοκεῖ ἀνδρῶν ἀγαθῶν
καὶ σωφρόνων ἔργον εἶναι. ἐπειδὴ τοίνυν παρὰ
πάντων ὁμολογουμένως ταῦθ' ὑμῖν ὑπάρχει, καὶ
εἴ τις φίλος ὢν τυγχάνει καὶ εἴ τις ἐχθρός, μὴ
μεταγνῶτε, μηδὲ βούλεσθε³ τὴν πόλιν ἀποστερῆσαι
ταύτης τῆς δόξης, μηδὲ αὐτοὶ δοκεῖν τύχῃ ταῦτα
μᾶλλον ἢ γνώμῃ ψηφίσασθαι.

141 Δέομαι οὖν ἁπάντων ⟨ὑμῶν⟩⁴ περὶ ἐμοῦ τὴν
αὐτὴν γνώμην ἔχειν, ἥνπερ καὶ περὶ τῶν ἐμῶν
προγόνων, ἵνα κἀμοὶ ἐγγένηται ἐκείνους μιμήσασθαι, ἀναμνησθέντας αὐτῶν ὅτι ὅμοιοι τοῖς
πλείστων καὶ μεγίστων ἀγαθῶν αἰτίοις τῇ πόλει
γεγένηνται, πολλῶν ἕνεκα σφᾶς αὐτοὺς παρέχοντες
τοιούτους, μάλιστα δὲ τῆς εἰς ὑμᾶς εὐνοίας, καὶ
ὅπως, εἴ ποτέ τις αὐτοῖς ἢ τῶν ἐξ ἐκείνων τινὶ
κίνδυνος γένοιτο⁵ ἢ συμφορά, σῴζοιντο συγγνώμης
παρ' ὑμῶν τυγχάνοντες. εἰκότως δ' ἂν αὐτῶν

regarded as the work of man, and the dangers of the sea as the work of God. So if we must perforce speculate about the gods, I for one am sure that they would be moved to the deepest wrath and indignation to see those whom they had themselves preserved brought to destruction by mortal men.

There is yet another thing worth your consideration, gentlemen. At the moment the whole of Greece thinks that you have shown the greatest generosity and wisdom in devoting yourselves, not to revenge, but to the preservation of your city and the reuniting of its citizens. Many before now have suffered no less than we ; but it is very rightly recognized that the peaceable settlement of differences requires generosity and self-control. Now it is acknowledged on all sides, by friend and foe alike, that you possess those gifts. So do not change your ways : do not hasten to rob Athens of the glory which she has gained thereby, or allow it to be supposed that you authorized your decree more by chance than by intention.

I beg you one and all, then, to hold towards me the feelings which you hold towards my ancestors, so that I may have the opportunity of imitating them. They rank, remember, among the most tireless and the greatest benefactors of our city ; and foremost among the many motives which inspired them came devotion to your welfare and the hope that if they or any of their children were ever in danger or distress, they would find protection in your sympathy. You have good reason, indeed, for remembering them;

¹ πάνυ Reiske : πολὺ codd.
² ἀνθρώπων Hertlein : ἄλλων codd.
³ βούλεσθε Reiske : βουλεύεσθε codd.
⁴ ὑμῶν add. Reiske.   ⁵ γένοιτο Dobree : γένηται codd.

445

142 μεμνῆσθε· καὶ γὰρ τῇ πόλει ἁπάσῃ αἱ τῶν ὑμετέρων¹
προγόνων ἀρεταὶ πλείστου ἄξιαι ἐγένοντο. ἐπειδὴ
γάρ, ὦ ἄνδρες, αἱ νῆες διεφθάρησαν, πολλῶν
βουλομένων τὴν πόλιν ἀνηκέστοις συμφοραῖς
περιβαλεῖν, Λακεδαιμόνιοι ἔγνωσαν ὅμως τότε
ἐχθροὶ ὄντες σῴζειν τὴν πόλιν διὰ τὰς ἐκείνων τῶν
ἀνδρῶν ἀρετάς, οἳ ὑπῆρξαν τῆς ἐλευθερίας ἁπάσῃ
143 τῇ Ἑλλάδι. ἐπειδὴ τοίνυν καὶ ἡ πόλις ἐσώθη
δημοσίᾳ διὰ τὰς τῶν προγόνων τῶν ὑμετέρων²
ἀρετάς, ἀξιῶ κἀμοὶ διὰ τὰς τῶν προγόνων τῶν
ἐμῶν ἀρετὰς σωτηρίαν γενέσθαι. καὶ γὰρ αὐτῶν
τῶν ἔργων, δι' ἅπερ ἡ πόλις ἐσώθη, οὐκ ἐλάχιστον
μέρος οἱ ἐμοὶ πρόγονοι συνεβάλοντο· ὧν ἕνεκα
καὶ ἐμοὶ δίκαιον ὑμᾶς μεταδοῦναι τῆς σωτηρίας,
ἧσπερ καὶ αὐτοὶ παρὰ τῶν Ἑλλήνων ἐτύχετε.

144   Σκέψασθε τοίνυν καὶ τάδε, ἄν με σώσητε, οἷον
ἕξετε πολίτην· ὃς πρῶτον μὲν ἐκ πολλοῦ πλούτου,
ὅσον ὑμεῖς ἴστε, οὐ δι' ἐμαυτὸν ἀλλὰ διὰ τὰς τῆς
πόλεως συμφορὰς εἰς πενίαν πολλὴν καὶ ἀπορίαν
κατέστην, ἔπειτα δὲ καινὸν³ βίον ἠργασάμην ἐκ
τοῦ δικαίου, τῇ γνώμῃ καὶ τοῖν χεροῖν τοῖν
ἐμαυτοῦ⁴· ἔτι δὲ εἰδότα μὲν οἷόν ἐστι πόλεως
τοιαύτης πολίτην εἶναι, εἰδότα δὲ οἷόν ἐστι ξένον
[19] εἶναι καὶ μέτοικον ἐν τῇ τῶν πλησίον, ἐπιστάμενον
145 δὲ οἷον τὸ σωφρονεῖν καὶ ὀρθῶς βουλεύεσθαι,
ἐπιστάμενον δ' οἷον τὸ ἁμαρτόντα πρᾶξαι κακῶς,
πολλοῖς συγγενόμενος καὶ πλείστων πειραθείς,
ἀφ' ὧν ἐμοὶ ξενίαι καὶ φιλότητες πρὸς πολλοὺς
καὶ βασιλέας καὶ πόλεις καὶ ἄλλους ἰδίᾳ ξένους

---

¹ ὑμετέρων Reiske: ἡμετέρων codd.
² ὑμετέρων Reiske: ἡμετέρων codd.
³ καινὸν Emperius: καὶ codd.

for from the heroic deeds of your own forefathers Athens as a whole received inestimable benefit. After the loss of our fleet, when there was a general desire to cripple Athens for ever, the Spartans, although our enemies at the time, decided to spare her because of the valiant exploits of those heroes who had led the whole of Greece to freedom.[a] Now since Athens as a city was spared because of the brave exploits of your forefathers, I likewise claim to be spared because of the brave deeds of mine ; for my own forefathers themselves played no small part in those very exploits to which Athens owed her salvation, and I therefore have the right to expect from you the mercy shown to you yourselves by the Greeks.

Think, furthermore, what a citizen you will have in me, if you give me your protection. I was once, as you know, a man of great wealth. Then to begin with, through no fault of my own, but through the disasters which overtook Athens, I was plunged into utter penury and want. I then started life afresh, a life of honest toil, with my brains and my hands to help me. Nay more, I not only know what it is to be the citizen of a city such as this ; I know what it is to be an alien sojourning in the lands of neighbouring peoples ; I have learnt the meaning of self-control and good sense ; I have learnt what it is to suffer for one's mistakes.[b] I have been on terms of familiarity with many, and I have had dealings with still more. In consequence, I have formed ties and friendships with kings, with states, and with individuals too, in

---

[a] Cf. Peace with Sparta, § 21.
[b] An interesting admission. Cf. Return, § 7.

---

⁴ τοῖν χεροῖν τοῖν ἐμ. Marchant: ταῖν χ. ταῖν ἐμ. codd.

γεγένηνται, ὧν ἐμὲ σώσαντες μεθέξετε, καὶ ἔσται[1]
ὑμῖν χρῆσθαι τούτοις, ὅπου ἂν ἐν καιρῷ τι ὑμῖν
γίγνηται.

146 Ἔχει δὲ καὶ ὑμῖν, ὦ ἄνδρες, οὕτως· ἐάν με νυνὶ
διαφθείρητε, οὐκ ἔστιν ὑμῖν ἔτι λοιπὸς τοῦ γένους
τοῦ ἡμετέρου οὐδείς, ἀλλ᾽ οἴχεται πᾶν πρόρριζον.
καίτοι οὐκ ὄνειδος ὑμῖν ἐστιν ἡ Ἀνδοκίδου καὶ
Λεωγόρου οἰκία οὖσα, ἀλλὰ πολὺ μᾶλλον τότ᾽ ἦν
ὄνειδος, ὅτ᾽ ἐμοῦ φεύγοντος Κλεοφῶν αὐτὴν ὁ
λυροποιὸς ᾤκει.   οὐ γὰρ ἔστιν ὅστις πώποτε
ὑμῶν παριὼν τὴν οἰκίαν τὴν ἡμετέραν ἀνεμνήσθη
147 ἢ ἰδίᾳ τι ἢ δημοσίᾳ κακὸν παθὼν ὑπ᾽ ἐκείνων, οἳ
πλείστας μὲν στρατηγήσαντες στρατηγίας πολλὰ
τρόπαια τῶν πολεμίων καὶ κατὰ γῆν καὶ κατὰ
θάλατταν ὑμῖν ἀπέδειξαν, πλείστας δὲ ἄλλας ἀρχὰς
ἄρξαντες καὶ χρήματα διαχειρίσαντες τὰ ὑμέτερα
οὐδένα[2] πώποτε ὦφλον, οὐδ᾽ ἡμάρτηται οὐδὲν οὔτε
ἡμῖν εἰς ὑμᾶς οὔτε ὑμῖν εἰς ἡμᾶς, οἰκία δὲ πασῶν
ἀρχαιοτάτη καὶ κοινοτάτη ἀεὶ τῷ δεομένῳ.   οὐδ᾽
ἔστιν ὅπου ἐκείνων τις τῶν ἀνδρῶν καταστὰς εἰς
ἀγῶνα ἀπήτησεν ὑμᾶς χάριν τούτων τῶν ἔργων.
148 μὴ τοίνυν, εἰ αὐτοὶ τεθνᾶσι, καὶ περὶ τῶν πεπραγμένων αὐτοῖς ἐπιλάθησθε, ἀλλ᾽ ἀναμνησθέντες τῶν
ἔργων νομίσατε τὰ σώματα αὐτῶν ὁρᾶν αἰτουμένων
ἐμὲ παρ᾽ ὑμῶν σῶσαι.   τίνα γὰρ καὶ ἀναβιβάσωμαι[3]
δεησόμενον ὑπὲρ ἐμαυτοῦ; τὸν πατέρα; ἀλλὰ
τέθνηκεν.   ἀλλὰ τοὺς ἀδελφούς; ἀλλ᾽ οὐκ εἰσίν.

---

[1] ἔσται Stephanus : ἔστιν codd.
[2] οὐδένα Blass : οὐδὲν ἂν codd.
[3] ἀναβιβάσωμαι Blass : ἀναβιβάσομαι codd.

---

[a] An extreme democrat who first came into prominence
after the collapse of the oligarchic movement of 411.   He

plenty. Acquit me, and you will share in them all, and be able to make use of them whenever occasion may arise.

The position is in fact this, gentlemen. If you sentence me to death to-day, you leave not a single member of our family alive ; it perishes root and branch. Yet the home of Andocides and Leogoras does not disgrace you by its presence. It was far more truly a disgrace during my exile, when Cleophon [a] the lyre-maker occupied it. Not one of you, in passing our house, was ever reminded of an injury done him by its owners whether privately or publicly. They have held countless commands, and have won you many a victory over your foes on land and sea. They have held countless other offices and handled public monies ; yet not once have they been found guilty of fraud. We have not wronged you, and you have not wronged us. Our house is the oldest in Athens, and has always been the first to open its doors to those in need. Yet never once has any member of my family appeared on trial before you and asked you to show your gratitude for these services. So although they are dead, at least do not forget what they did. Remember their achievements : imagine that you can see them in the flesh, begging you for my life. For after all, whom can I produce here to plead for me ? My father ? He is dead. My brothers ? I

interested himself in finance, and was responsible for the dole of two obols a day paid to the poorer classes after 410. After the battle of Cyzicus he succeeded in getting the Spartan peace proposals rejected, and he did the same after Aegospotami (405). He was finally put to death during the siege of Athens through the agency of the pro-Spartan party in the city. With his execution active resistance to Sparta practically came to an end.

ANDOCIDES

149 ἀλλὰ τοὺς παῖδας; ἀλλ' οὔπω γεγένηνται. ὑμεῖς
τοίνυν καὶ ἀντὶ πατρὸς ἐμοὶ καὶ ἀντὶ ἀδελφῶν καὶ
ἀντὶ παίδων γένεσθε· εἰς ὑμᾶς καταφεύγω καὶ
ἀντιβολῶ καὶ ἱκετεύω· ὑμεῖς με παρ' ὑμῶν αὐτῶν
αἰτησάμενοι σώσατε, καὶ μὴ βούλεσθε Θετταλοὺς
καὶ 'Ανδρίους πολίτας ποιεῖσθαι δι' ἀπορίαν
ἀνδρῶν, τοὺς δὲ ὄντας πολίτας ὁμολογουμένως,
οἷς προσήκει ἀνδράσιν ἀγαθοῖς εἶναι καὶ βουλόμενοι δυνήσονται, τούτους δὲ ἀπόλλυτε. μὴ δῆτα.
ἔπειτα καὶ ταῦθ' ὑμῶν δέομαι, εὖ ποιῶν ὑμᾶς
ὑφ' ὑμῶν τιμᾶσθαι. ὥστ' ἐμοὶ μὲν πειθόμενοι
οὐκ ἀποστερεῖσθε εἴ τι ἐγὼ δυνήσομαι ὑμᾶς εὖ
ποιεῖν· ἐὰν δὲ τοῖς ἐχθροῖς τοῖς ἐμοῖς πεισθῆτε,
οὐδ' ἂν ὑστέρῳ χρόνῳ ὑμῖν μεταμελήσῃ, οὐδὲν
150 ἔτι πλέον ποιήσετε. μὴ τοίνυν μήθ' ὑμᾶς αὐτοὺς
τῶν ἀπ' ἐμοῦ ἐλπίδων ἀποστερήσητε μήτ' ἐμὲ
τῶν εἰς ὑμᾶς.

'Αξιῶ δ' ἔγωγε τούτους οἵτινες ὑμῖν ἀρετῆς ἤδη
τῆς μεγίστης εἰς τὸ πλῆθος τὸ ὑμέτερον ἔλεγχον
ἔδοσαν, ἀναβάντας ἐνταυθοῖ συμβουλεύειν ὑμῖν
ἃ γιγνώσκουσι περὶ ἐμοῦ. δεῦρο "Ανυτε, Κέφαλε,
ἔτι δὲ καὶ οἱ φυλέται οἱ ᾑρημένοι[1] μοι συνδικεῖν,
Θράσυλλος καὶ οἱ ἄλλοι.

---

[1] ᾑρημένοι Valckenaer: εἰρημένοι codd.

---

[a] Very influential at this time. He had taken a leading
part with Thrasybulus in overthrowing the Thirty and re-

have none. My children ? They are still unborn.
It is you who must act as my father and my brothers
and my children. It is with you that I seek refuge.
It is to you that I turn with my entreaties and my
prayers. You must plead with yourselves for my
life, and save it. When you are ready to extend
civic rights to Thessalians and Andrians on the ground
that men are scarce, you cannot but refuse to put
acknowledged citizens to death, men who should serve
you well, and who will have the opportunity of doing
so, if they are willing. You cannot but refuse, gentlemen. Again, I ask you to show your appreciation of
my services to you. Then, if you listen to me, you will
not rob yourselves of such further services as I may
be able to render. On the other hand, if you listen
to my opponents, even repentance later on will avail
you nothing. So do not deprive yourselves of what
you can reasonably expect from me, and do not
deprive me of what I can reasonably expect from you.

And now I will ask men who have given public
proof of their outstanding worth to take my place
here and give you their opinion of me. Come,
Anytus [a] and Cephalus [b] : come, Thrasyllus and you
others of my tribe who have been chosen to support me.

storing the democracy in 403. He was one of the accusers
of Socrates in 399.

[b] A democrat who came into prominence after 403. He is
referred to by Demosthenes (*De Cor.* § 219) and Aeschines
(*In Ctes.* § 194) in complimentary terms.

II

ON HIS RETURN

INTRODUCTION

In point of time the speech *On His Return*, or the *De Reditu Suo* as it is commonly called, precedes the *Mysteries* by a number of years. It belongs to the period of Andocides' exile, and allows us to see at close quarters something of the bitter party-feeling which successfully prevented his reinstatement at Athens until the general amnesty of 403.

Its date has been disputed. It was certainly delivered after the fall of the Four Hundred in September 411; but how long afterwards it is impossible to be sure. The facts to be taken into consideration are these. Andocides is endeavouring to purchase the repeal of the decree of Isotimides, which had caused his withdrawal into exile in 415, by an offer of corn from Cyprus at a moment of threatened famine. Now a scarcity of corn at Athens meant that the supplies from Pontus, upon which she largely relied, had been partially or totally cut off; and such a situation can only have arisen when she had lost control of the Hellespont and Bosporus. This did in fact happen in September 411. Abydos and Byzantium had revolted during the summer; they were rapidly followed by Cyzicus and Chalcedon; and when Mindarus concentrated the Spartan naval forces in the north-east Aegean in the September, the grain-route was seriously endangered. The battle of Cynossema during the same month retrieved the position on the Hellespont for the moment, and Athens was successful in a second engagement off Abydos a few weeks later; but the Spartans recovered Cyzicus early in 410, and it was not until their complete defeat in the battle of Cyzicus (April 410) that Athens regained control of the Propontis. Alcibiades spent most of 410 consolidating his gains; and it was only in 409 that he made a determined effort to recover the Bosporus. Byzantium finally fell in 408.

It is clear from this that Athens was in greatest danger of famine in September 411 and the months following. The victories of Cynossema and Abydos must have brought relief; but it was not until the crushing defeat of Sparta off Cyzicus in April 410 that a free passage from the Euxine was assured; for the remainder of the year there can have been no real fear of a shortage of grain. However, Sparta made one more effort to close the route from the north-west during the winter which followed. Clearchus was sent out with a fleet to strengthen the defences of Byzantium and Chalcedon; and he successfully resisted all Athenian efforts to dislodge him until the autumn of B.C. 408. Thus there must have been considerable difficulty in ensuring an adequate food-supply for something like eighteen months after the beginning of 409.

From this it would appear that there were two periods in the years following the fall of the Four Hundred during which Athens found her main food-supply endangered, the first from September 411 to April 410, and the second from approximately January 409 to September 408. Throughout either of these

455

two periods Andocides might reasonably expect to find an offer of extra corn welcome.

The speech itself makes it clear that this was Andocides' second attempt to return since his exile in 415. The first had been made while the Four Hundred were in power, and thanks to the efforts of his bitter enemy Peisander, had resulted in his immediate imprisonment. How long this imprisonment lasted Andocides does not state ; but it is probable that he was released only when the Four Hundred were finally overthrown in the September. He then quitted Athens once again. Now if his second attempt to reinstate himself was made during the first of the periods of grain-shortage mentioned above, he must have begun working for it almost immediately after his escape from the Four Hundred. And this is the view held by a number of modern editors.[a] Andocides, according to them, went straight to Cyprus, loaded as many merchantmen as he could with corn, and returned without delay to Athens, where he made his second plea for reinstatement.

This is possible ; but when certain other facts are taken into consideration, improbable. Thus it is at least clear that the De Reditu was addressed to the restored democracy (see, for instance, §§ 26 ff.)— having failed with the oligarchs Andocides is trying his fortune with their opponents. But the democracy was not restored until April 410, after the battle of Cyzicus. We have therefore to suppose that immediately Athens won a victory which removed all danger of famine,[b] Andocides set about making preparations for relieving her want. And when he

[a] e.g. Jebb and Marchant.
[b] Xen. Hell. i. 1. 35.

arrived from Cyprus, he not only brought corn with
him, but communicated to the Council a scheme
which he had elaborated for ensuring a steady supply
in future.

It may be objected that Andocides started on his
way from Cyprus before the battle of Cyzicus was
fought, and therefore while distress at Athens was
still acute. But if he did so, it was with the intention
of trying to placate, not the democracy, but the Five
Thousand, into whose hands the government passed
between September 411 and April 410 ; and such a
move on his part seems doubtful. It must be remembered that he had already found to his cost what kind
of a reception an oligarchic administration was likely
to give him ; and he could hardly be sure that he
would be any the more welcome to the Five Thousand
than he had been to the Four Hundred. A certain
delay before his second attempt to return seems far
more probable.

There would thus seem to be fairly weighty objections against dating the *De Reditu* to the first of
the two periods of food-shortage at Athens. On the
other hand, these objections disappear if it is assumed
that Andocides came back for the second time during
the later period (*c.* January 409–September 408).
There would then be a real need for any corn that he
could supply, and he would have allowed a reasonable
interval to elapse since his first appearance. Further,
his reference in his speech to the " victory which alone
saved Athens," [a] a victory which he had himself made
possible by supplying equipment to the Athenian
fleet, can then be taken to point to the battle of
Cyzicus, which did indeed mark a turning-point in

[a] § 12.

Athenian fortunes both at home and abroad. On the other hypothesis it will have to be assumed that Andocides is talking of Cynossema, the engagement of the previous September.

There is one further indication that the later date for the speech is the correct one. In describing the victory mentioned, Andocides implies that it had been won a considerable time before (*cf.* ἐν τῷ τότε χρόνῳ, § 12). This is not what we should expect, were he reminding the Assembly early in 410 of a victory won in the autumn of 411. It seems far more likely that Cyzicus is the battle which he has in mind, and that he is speaking well over a year after it had been fought, *i.e.* late in 409 or in the first half of 408.

The *De Reditu* was delivered before the Ecclesia, and therefore differs considerably in manner from the *De Mysteriis*, which was composed for a court of law and could afford to be more diffuse. It is an abrupt speech, abrupt in its phrasing and abrupt in its argument. Andocides had little need to describe in detail the scandal which had led to his exile ; it was still only too familiar to the majority of his audience. Still less did he feel the moment suitable for any such passionate assertion of his innocence as that in which he indulged ten years later, when the facts at issue were already passing into oblivion. He therefore has no hesitation in admitting his guilt. What concerns him is his patriotic energy since 415. He has materially aided Athens to win a great naval victory, and he has averted a famine by bringing corn from Cyprus. It is on this that he rests his appeal for the removal of the disabilities inflicted upon him since 415.

Unfortunately the appeal failed. Even before Andocides rose to speak there was a good deal of noisy opposition ; and the somewhat insolent tone with which he opened [a] can hardly have helped him. He spoke forcibly and plausibly ; but the restored democracy was not readily tolerant of those whose sympathies had been in former days confessedly oligarchic. Andocides left Athens an exile once again.

[a] § 1, l. 5.

ANALYSIS

§ 26. The services of his ancestor, Leogoras, to the democracy. This affords a presumption that he himself will behave in the same way, if given the opportunity.

§§ 27-28. He feels no ill-will for the treatment which he has received at the hands of the Athenian people in the past.

ΠΕΡΙ ΤΗΣ ΕΑΥΤΟΥ ΚΑΘΟΔΟΥ

1 Εἰ μέν, ὦ ἄνδρες, ἐν ἑτέρῳ τῳ πράγματι οἱ
παριόντες μὴ τὴν αὐτὴν γνώμην ἔχοντες πάντες
ἐφαίνοντο, οὐδὲν ἂν θαυμαστὸν ἐνόμιζον· ὅπου
μέντοι δεῖ τὴν πόλιν ἐμέ τι ποιῆσαι ἀγαθόν, ἢ εἴ τις
ἕτερος[1] βούλοιτο ἐμοῦ κακίων, δεινότατον ἁπάντων
χρημάτων ἡγοῦμαι, εἰ τῷ μὲν δοκεῖ ταῦτα τῷ δὲ
μή, ἀλλὰ μὴ πᾶσιν ὁμοίως. εἴπερ γὰρ ἡ πόλις
ἁπάντων τῶν πολιτευομένων κοινή ἐστι, καὶ τὰ
γιγνόμενα δήπου ἀγαθὰ τῇ πόλει κοινά ἐστι.

2 Τουτὶ τοίνυν τὸ μέγα καὶ δεινὸν πάρεστιν ὑμῖν
ὁρᾶν τοὺς μὲν ἤδη πράττοντας, τοὺς δὲ τάχα μέλ-
λοντας· καί μοι μέγιστον θαῦμα παρέστηκε, τί
[20] ποτε οὗτοι οἱ ἄνδρες δεινῶς οὕτω περικάονται, εἴ
τι ὑμᾶς χρὴ ἀγαθὸν ἐμοῦ ἐπαυρέσθαι. δεῖ γὰρ
αὐτοὺς ἤτοι ἀμαθεστάτους εἶναι πάντων ἀνθρώπων,
ἢ τῇ πόλει ταύτῃ δυσμενεστάτους. εἰ μέν γε
νομίζουσι τῆς πόλεως εὖ πραττούσης καὶ τὰ ἴδια
σφῶν αὐτῶν ἄμεινον ἂν φέρεσθαι, ἀμαθέστατοί
εἰσι τὰ ἐναντία νῦν τῇ ἑαυτῶν ὠφελείᾳ σπεύδοντες·

3 εἰ δὲ μὴ ταῦτα ἡγοῦνται σφίσι τε αὐτοῖς συμφέρειν
καὶ τῷ ὑμετέρῳ κοινῷ, δυσμενεῖς ἂν τῇ πόλει
εἶεν· οἵτινες εἰσαγγείλαντός μου ἀπόρρητα εἰς τὴν
βουλὴν περὶ τῶν πραγμάτων, ὧν ἀποτελεσθέντων

---

[1] ἕτερος Reiske : ἑτέρως codd.

ON HIS RETURN

HAD some other matter been at issue, gentlemen, I should have felt no surprise at finding a difference of opinion among the speakers who addressed you. But when the question is whether or not I, or anyone less worthy who so desires, should do this state a service, nothing seems to me more extraordinary than that contrary views should be held, instead of there being complete unanimity; for if the state is common to all who enjoy civic rights, the benefits which the state receives are likewise, I presume, common benefits.

Such disagreement is a matter for alarm and astonishment; yet, as you can see, it has already been expressed by some, and will shortly be expressed by others. Indeed, I am completely at a loss to understand why the question of your receiving a benefit from me should cause such excitement among our friends here. They must either be the most stupid of mankind or the worst of public enemies. If they hold that when the state is prospering they are better off individually, they are showing extreme stupidity in advocating to-day a policy which directly conflicts with their own interests; while if they do not identify their interests as individuals with yours as a community, they can only be public enemies. Indeed when I secretly communicated to the Council a proposal which would be of the very greatest service

οὐκ εἰσὶ τῇ πόλει ταύτῃ μείζονες ὠφέλειαι, καὶ
τούτων ἀποδεικνύντος μου τοῖς βουλευταῖς σαφεῖς
τε καὶ βεβαίους τὰς ἀποδείξεις, ἐκεῖ μὲν οὔτε
τούτων τῶν ἀνδρῶν οἱ παραγενόμενοι ἐλέγχοντες[1]
οἷοί τ᾽ ἦσαν ἀποδεῖξαι εἴ τι μὴ ὀρθῶς ἐλέγετο, οὔτ᾽
ἄλλος οὐδείς, ἐνθάδε δὲ νῦν πειρῶνται διαβάλλειν.
4 σημεῖον οὖν τοῦτο ὅτι οὗτοι οὐκ ἀφ᾽ αὑτῶν ταῦτα
πράττουσιν—εὐθὺς γὰρ ἂν τότε ἠναντιοῦντο—ἀλλ᾽
ἀπ᾽ ἀνδρῶν ἑτέρων, οἷοί εἰσιν ἐν τῇ πόλει ταύτῃ,
οὐδενὸς ἂν χρήματος δεξάμενοι ὑμᾶς τι ἀγαθὸν ἐξ
ἐμοῦ πρᾶξαι. καὶ αὐτοὶ μὲν οὗτοι οἱ ἄνδρες οὐ
τολμῶσι σφᾶς αὐτοὺς εἰς τὸ μέσον καταστήσαντες
διισχυρίζεσθαι περὶ τούτων, φοβούμενοι ἔλεγχον
διδόναι εἴ τι εἰς ὑμᾶς τυγχάνουσι μὴ εὖ φρονοῦντες·
ἑτέρους δὲ εἰσπέμπουσι, τοιούτους ἀνθρώπους οἷς
εἰθισμένοις ἤδη ἀναισχυντεῖν οὐδὲν διαφέρει εἰπεῖν
5 τε καὶ ἀκοῦσαι τὰ μέγιστα τῶν κακῶν. τὸ δ᾽
ἰσχυρὸν τοῦτο μόνον εὕροι τις ἂν αὐτῶν ἐν τοῖς
λόγοις, τὰς ἐμὰς συμφορὰς ἐπὶ παντὶ ὀνειδίζειν,
καὶ ταῦτα ἐν εἰδόσι δήπου κάλλιον ὑμῖν, ὥστε
μηδὲν ἂν τούτων δικαίως τιμὴν αὐτοῖς τινα
φέρειν.

Ἐμοὶ δέ, ὦ ἄνδρες, καὶ τῷ πρώτῳ τοῦτο εἰπόντι
ὀρθῶς δοκεῖ εἰρῆσθαι, ὅτι πάντες ἄνθρωποι
γίγνονται ἐπὶ τῷ εὖ καὶ κακῶς πράττειν, μεγάλη
6 δὲ δήπου καὶ τὸ ἐξαμαρτεῖν δυσπραξία ἐστί, καὶ
εἰσὶν εὐτυχέστατοι μὲν οἱ ἐλάχιστα ἐξαμαρτάνοντες,
σωφρονέστατοι δὲ οἳ ἂν τάχιστα μεταγιγνώσκωσι.
καὶ ταῦτα οὐ διακέκριται τοῖς μὲν γίγνεσθαι τοῖς
δὲ μή, ἀλλ᾽ ἔστιν ἐν τῷ κοινῷ πᾶσιν ἀνθρώποις
καὶ ἐξαμαρτεῖν τι καὶ κακῶς πρᾶξαι. ὧν ἕνεκα,

---

[1] ἐλέγχοντες Emperius: ἐλέγξοντες codd.

to this city if carried into effect, and proved as much clearly and conclusively to the members present, such of my present critics as were among my audience found it as impossible as anyone else to show by argument that any of my statements was incorrect ; yet they are now trying to impugn those statements. This proves, then, that they are acting not on their own initiative—or they would have had no hesitation in opposing me originally—but on the instigation of others, of men such as are to be found in this city, who would not allow you to receive a benefit from me for all the money in the world. These others have not the courage to come into the open and make good their assertions in person, as they are afraid of letting their own possible shortcomings as patriots be examined too closely. Instead, they send substitutes to address you, men to whom effrontery is second nature, men who will utter or face the bitterest abuse with complete indifference. The entire strength of their case against me, one finds, lies in their taunting me at every turn with my misfortunes ; and that too when their listeners know better than they, so that not a word which they have uttered can bring them any true credit.

To my mind, gentlemen, he was a wise man who first said that every human being is born to meet with good fortune and with bad : that to make a mistake is to meet with great ill fortune : and that while those who make the fewest mistakes are the luckiest, those who repent of them soonest show most good sense. Nor is this the peculiar lot of some men only ; it is the common fate of humanity to make mistakes and suffer misfortune. So do but remember the frailty

ὦ Ἀθηναῖοι, εἰ ἀνθρωπίνως περὶ ἐμοῦ γιγνώσκοιτε,
εἴητε ἂν ἄνδρες εὐγνωμονέστεροι. οὐ γὰρ φθόνου
7 μᾶλλον ἢ οἴκτου ἄξιά μοί ἐστι τὰ γεγενημένα· ὃς
εἰς τοσοῦτον ἦλθον δυσδαιμονίας, εἴτε χρὴ εἰπεῖν
νεότητί τε καὶ ἀνοίᾳ τῇ ἐμαυτοῦ,[1] εἴτε καὶ δυνάμει
τῶν πεισάντων με ἐλθεῖν εἰς τοιαύτην συμφορὰν
τῶν φρενῶν, ὥστ' ἀνάγκην μοι γενέσθαι δυοῖν
κακοῖν τοῖν μεγίστοιν θάτερον ἑλέσθαι, ἢ μὴ
βουληθέντι[2] κατειπεῖν τοὺς ταῦτα ποιήσαντας οὐ
περὶ ἐμοῦ μόνου ὀρρωδεῖν, εἴ τι ἔδει παθεῖν, ἀλλὰ
καὶ τὸν πατέρα οὐδὲν ἀδικοῦντα σὺν ἐμαυτῷ
ἀποκτεῖναι—ὅπερ ἀνάγκη παθεῖν ἦν αὐτῷ, εἰ ἐγὼ
μὴ ἐβουλόμην ταῦτα ποιῆσαι—ἢ κατειπόντι τὰ
γεγενημένα αὐτὸν μὲν ἀφεθέντα μὴ τεθνάναι, τοῦ
δὲ ἐμαυτοῦ πατρὸς μὴ φονέα γενέσθαι. τί δ' ἂν
οὐ πρό γε τούτου τολμήσειεν ἄνθρωπος ποιῆσαι;
8   Ἐγὼ τοίνυν ἐκ τῶν παρόντων εἱλόμην ταῦτα, ἃ
ἐμοὶ μὲν λύπας ἐπὶ χρόνον πλεῖστον οἴσειν ἔμελλεν,
ὑμῖν δὲ ταχίστην τοῦ παρόντος τότε κακοῦ μετά-
στασιν. ἀναμνήσθητε δὲ ἐν οἵῳ κινδύνῳ τε καὶ
ἀμηχανίᾳ καθέστατε, καὶ ὅτι οὕτω σφόδρα σφᾶς
αὐτοὺς ἐπεφόβησθε, ὥστ' οὐδ' εἰς τὴν ἀγορὰν ἔτι
ἐξῇτε, ἕκαστος ὑμῶν οἰόμενος συλληφθήσεσθαι.
ταῦτα τοίνυν ὥστε μὲν γενέσθαι τοιαῦτα, πολ-
λοστὸν δή τι ἐγὼ μέρος τῆς αἰτίας ηὑρέθην ἔχων,
ὥστε μέντοι παυθῆναι, ἐγὼ εἷς ὢν μόνος αἴτιος.
9 καὶ ὅμως τό γε δυστυχέστατος εἶναι ἀνθρώπων
οὐδαμῇ ἐκφεύγω, ὅτε δὴ προαγομένης μὲν τῆς

---

[1] τῇ ἐμαυτοῦ Frohberger, qui huc transtulit. Ante δυσδαιμονίας habent τῆς ἐμαυτοῦ codd.

of man in passing judgement upon me, gentlemen, and your feelings for me will be more kindly. Indeed I do not deserve ill-will so much as sympathy for the past. Owing to—shall I say my own youthful folly, or the influence of others who persuaded me into such a piece of madness ? [a]—I was luckless enough to be forced to choose between two of the most painful alternatives imaginable. On the one hand, I could refuse to disclose the authors of the outrage. In that case I not only trembled for my own fate, but caused the death of my father, who was entirely innocent, as well as my own—he was inevitably doomed, if I refused to speak. On the other hand, I could purchase my own life and liberty and avoid becoming my father's murderer—and what would a man not bring himself to do to escape that ?—but only by turning informer.

Of the alternatives before me, then, I chose that which meant years of sorrow for myself, but immediate release for you from the distress of the moment. Remember your peril : remember your helplessness : remember how you stood in such fear of one another that you ceased going abroad even into the Agora, because you each expected arrest.[b] That such a state of things should have occurred at all proved to be due only in small part to me ; that it ended, on the other hand, proved to be due to me alone. Notwithstanding, I have never succeeded in being anything save the unluckiest man alive ; for when

[a] A clear indication that Andocides had been concerned to at least some extent in the mutilation of the Hermae.

[b] Cf. Myst. § 36.

---

[2] βουληθέντι Ald. : βουληθέντα codd.

πόλεως ἐπὶ ταύτας τὰς συμφορὰς οὐδεὶς ἐμοῦ
ἤρχετο γίγνεσθαι δυσδαιμονέστερος, μεθισταμένης
δὲ πάλιν εἰς τὸ ἀσφαλὲς ἁπάντων ἐγὼ ἀθλιώτατος.
ὄντων γὰρ κακῶν τοσούτων τῇ πόλει ἀδύνατον
[21] ἦν ταῦτα ἰαθῆναι ἄλλως ἢ τῷ ἐμῷ αἰσχρῷ, ὥστ᾽
ἐν αὐτῷ[1] ᾧ ἐγὼ κακῶς ἔπραττον, ἐν τούτῳ ὑμᾶς
σῴζεσθαι. χάριν οὖν εἰκός με, οὐ μῖσος τῷ δυσ-
τυχήματι τούτῳ φέρεσθαι παρ᾽ ὑμῶν.

10 Καίτοι ἐγὼ τότ᾽ αὐτὸς γνοὺς τὰς ἐμαυτοῦ συμ-
φοράς, ᾧ τινι κακῶν τε καὶ αἰσχρῶν οὐκ οἶδ᾽ εἴ
τι ἀπεγένετο, τὰ μὲν παρανοίᾳ τῇ ἐμαυτοῦ, τὰ δ᾽
ἀνάγκῃ τῶν παρόντων πραγμάτων, ἔγνων ἥδιστον
εἶναι πράττειν τε τοιαῦτα καὶ διαιτᾶσθαι ἐκεῖ,
ὅπου ἥκιστα μέλλοιμι ὀφθήσεσθαι ὑφ᾽ ὑμῶν.
ἐπειδὴ δὲ χρόνῳ ὕστερον[2] εἰσῆλθέ μοι, ὥσπερ εἰκός,
ἐπιθυμία τῆς τε μεθ᾽ ὑμῶν πολιτείας ἐκείνης καὶ
διαίτης, ἐξ ἧς δευρὶ μετέστην, ἔγνων λυσιτελεῖν
μοι ἢ τοῦ βίου ἀπηλλάχθαι, ἢ τὴν πόλιν ταύτην
ἀγαθόν τι τοσοῦτον ἐργάσασθαι, ὥστε ὑμῶν ἑκόν-
των εἶναί ποτέ μοι πολιτεύσασθαι μεθ᾽ ὑμῶν.

11 Ἐκ δὲ τούτου οὐ πώποτε οὔτε τοῦ σώματος
οὔτε τῶν ὄντων ἐμοὶ ἐφεισάμην, ὅπου ἔδει παρα-
κινδυνεύειν· ἀλλ᾽ αὐτίκα μὲν τότε εἰσήγαγον εἰς
στρατιὰν ὑμῶν οὖσαν ἐν Σάμῳ κωπέας, τῶν τετρακοσίων ἤδη τὰ πράγματα ἐνθάδε κατειληφότων,
ὄντος μοι Ἀρχελάου ξένου πατρικοῦ καὶ διδόντος
τέμνεσθαί[3] τε καὶ ἐξάγεσθαι ὁπόσους ἐβουλόμην.

---

[1] αὐτῷ ante τούτῳ ponit Sluiter.
[2] ὕστερον delent nonnulli.
[3] τέμνεσθαί Dobree: γενέσθαι codd.

468

Athens was heading for this disaster, no one came near suffering the sorrows which I suffered : and when she was once more regaining her security, I was of all men the most to be pitied. The desperate distress of Athens could be remedied only at the cost of my good name : so that your deliverance meant my own ruin. It is your gratitude, therefore, not your scorn that I deserve for my sufferings.

At the time I needed none to remind me of my plight—partly through my own folly, partly through the force of circumstances, nothing was wanting to complete my misery and my disgrace—and I saw that you would be best pleased were I to adopt that mode of life and that place of residence which would enable me to remain furthest from your sight.[a] Eventually, however, as was only natural, I was seized with a longing for the old life as a citizen among you which I had abandoned for my present place of exile ; and I decided that I should be best advised either to have done with life or to render this city such a service as would dispose you to let me at last resume my rights as your fellow.

From that moment I have been reckless of both life and goods when called upon for a perilous venture. In fact, I at once proceeded to supply your forces in Samos with oar-spars—this was after the Four Hundred had seized power at Athens [b]—since Archelaus [c] had hereditary connexions with my family and offered me the right of cutting and exporting as many as

[a] Andocides was not exiled under the actual terms of the decree of Isotimides. The decree made life at Athens so intolerable for him that he found it better to withdraw of his own accord.
[b] *i.e.* in 411.
[c] King of Macedon from 413 to 399 B.C.

τούτους τε εἰσήγαγον τοὺς κωπέας, καὶ παρόν μοι
πέντε δραχμῶν τὴν τιμὴν αὐτῶν δέξασθαι οὐκ
ἠθέλησα πράξασθαι πλέον ἢ ὅσου¹ ἐμοὶ κατέστησαν·
12 εἰσήγαγον δὲ σῖτόν τε καὶ χαλκόν. καὶ οἱ ἄνδρες
ἐκεῖνοι ἐκ τούτων παρεσκευασμένοι ἐνίκησαν μετὰ
ταῦτα Πελοποννησίους ναυμαχοῦντες, καὶ τὴν
πόλιν ταύτην μόνοι ἀνθρώπων ἔσωσαν ἐν τῷ τότε
χρόνῳ. εἰ τοίνυν μεγάλων ἀγαθῶν αἴτια² ὑμᾶς
ἠργάσαντο ἐκεῖνοι, μέρος ἐγὼ οὐκ ἂν ἐλάχιστον
δικαίως ταύτης τῆς αἰτίας ἔχοιμι. εἰ γὰρ τοῖς
ἀνδράσιν ἐκείνοις τότε τὰ ἐπιτήδεια μὴ εἰσήχθη,
οὐ περὶ τοῦ σῶσαι τὰς Ἀθήνας ὁ κίνδυνος ἦν
αὐτοῖς μᾶλλον ἢ περὶ τοῦ μηδ' αὐτοὺς σωθῆναι.
13 Τούτων τοίνυν οὕτως ἐχόντων οὐκ ὀλίγῳ μοι
παρὰ γνώμην ηὑρέθη τὰ ἐνταῦθα πράγματα ἔχοντα.
κατέπλευσα μὲν γὰρ ὡς ἐπαινεθησόμενος ὑπὸ
τῶν ἐνθάδε προθυμίας τε ἕνεκα καὶ ἐπιμελείας
τῶν ὑμετέρων πραγμάτων· πυθόμενοι δέ τινές με
ἥκοντα τῶν τετρακοσίων ἐζήτουν τε παραχρῆμα,
14 καὶ λαβόντες ἤγαγον εἰς τὴν βουλήν. εὐθὺς δὲ
παραστάς μοι Πείσανδρος "ἄνδρες" ἔφη "βουλευταί, ἐγὼ τὸν ἄνδρα τοῦτον ἐνδεικνύω ὑμῖν σῖτόν
τε εἰς τοὺς πολεμίους εἰσαγαγόντα καὶ κωπέας."
καὶ τὸ πρᾶγμα ἤδη πᾶν διηγεῖτο ὡς ἐπέπρακτο.
ἐν δὲ τῷ τότε τὰ ἐναντία φρονοῦντες δῆλοι ἦσαν
ἤδη οἱ ἐπὶ στρατιᾶς ὄντες τοῖς τετρακοσίοις.
15 Κἀγώ—θόρυβος γὰρ δὴ τοιοῦτος ἐγίγνετο τῶν

¹ ὅσου A corr. : ὅσον A pr.
² αἴτια Blass : ἄξια codd.

ᵃ The text of an Attic decree honouring Archelaus for
supplying ξύλα καὶ κωπέας still survives (*I.G.* i². 105). It may
be consulted best in the restored version of B. D. Meritt ;

I wished.[a]   And not only did I supply the spars ; I
refused to charge more for them than they had
cost me, although I might have obtained a price of
five drachmae apiece.   In addition, I supplied corn
and bronze.   Thus equipped, the forces in Samos
went on to defeat the Peloponnesians at sea [b] ; and
it was they, and they alone who saved Athens at the
time.   Now if those heroes rendered you true service
by their deed, I may fairly claim that that service was
in no small degree due to me.   Had that army not
been furnished with supplies just then, they would
have been fighting not so much to save Athens as to
save their own lives.

In these circumstances, I was not a little surprised
at the situation which I found at Athens.   I returned
thither fully expecting the congratulations of the city
on the active way in which I had displayed my devotion to your interests.   Instead, directly they learned
of my arrival, certain of the Four Hundred sought me
out, arrested me, and brought me before the Council.[c]
Whereupon Peisander [d] at once came up, took his
stand beside me, and cried : " Gentlemen, I hereby
denounce this man as having supplied corn and
oar-spars to the enemy."   Then he went on to tell
the whole story.   By this time, of course, it was
clear that there had been a complete estrangement
between the men on service and the Four Hundred.

I saw the uproar into which the meeting was

see *Classical Studies presented to Edward Capps*, Princeton,
1936.   Meritt would date it to 407-406 B.C.

[b] Most probably the battle of Cyzicus, April 410.   See
Introd.

[c] *i.e.* their fellow-members of the Four Hundred.   The
Council proper had been superseded.

[d] For the career of Peisander see *Mysteries*, § 36 note.

βουλευτῶν—[καὶ]¹ ἐπειδὴ ἐγίγνωσκον ἀπολούμενος,
εὐθὺς προσπηδῶ πρὸς τὴν ἑστίαν καὶ λαμβάνομαι
τῶν ἱερῶν. ὅπερ μοι καὶ πλείστου ἄξιον ἐγένετο²
ἐν τῷ τότε· εἰς γὰρ τοὺς θεοὺς ἔχοντα ὀνείδη οὗτοί
με³ μᾶλλον τῶν ἀνθρώπων ἐοίκασι κατελεῆσαι,
βουληθέντων τε αὐτῶν ἀποκτεῖναί με οὗτοι ἦσαν
οἱ διασώσαντες. δεσμά τε ὕστερον καὶ κακὰ ὅσα
τε καὶ οἷα τῷ σώματι ἠνεσχόμην, μακρὸν ἂν εἴη
16 μοι λέγειν. οὗ δὴ καὶ μάλιστ' ἐμαυτὸν ἀπωλο-
φυράμην· ὅστις τοῦτο μὲν ἐν ᾧ ἐδόκει ὁ δῆμος
κακοῦσθαι, ἐγὼ ἀντὶ τούτου κακὰ εἶχον, τοῦτο δὲ
ἐπειδὴ ἐφαίνετο ⟨εὖ⟩⁴ ὑπ' ἐμοῦ πεπονθώς, πάλιν
αὖ καὶ διὰ τοῦτ' ἐγὼ ἀπωλλύμην.⁵ ὥστε ὁδόν τε
καὶ πόρον μηδαμῇ ἔτι εἶναί μοι εὐθαρσεῖν· ὅποι⁶
γὰρ τραποίμην, πάντοθεν κακόν τί μοι ἐφαίνετο
ἑτοιμαζόμενον. ἀλλ' ὅμως καὶ ἐκ τούτων τοιούτων ὄντων ἀπαλλαγεὶς οὐκ ἔστιν ὅ τι ἕτερον ἔργον
περὶ πλείονος ἐποιούμην ἢ τὴν πόλιν ταύτην
ἀγαθόν τι ἐργάσασθαι.

17 Ὁρᾶν δὲ χρή, ὦ Ἀθηναῖοι, ὅσῳ τὰ τοιαῦτα
τῶν ὑπουργημάτων διαφέρει. τοῦτο μὲν γὰρ ὅσοι
τῶν πολιτῶν τὰ ὑμέτερα πράγματα διαχειρίζοντες
ἀργύριον ὑμῖν ἐκπορίζουσιν, ἄλλο τι ἢ τὰ ὑμέτερα
ὑμῖν διδόασι; τοῦτο δὲ ὅσοι στρατηγοὶ γενόμενοι
καλόν τι τὴν πόλιν κατεργάζονται, τί ἄλλο ἢ μετὰ
[22] τῆς τῶν ὑμετέρων σωμάτων ταλαιπωρίας τε καὶ
κινδύνων, καὶ ἔτι τῶν κοινῶν χρημάτων δαπάνης,

---

¹ καὶ del. Reiske. Verbum post καὶ excidisse putat Fuhr.
² ἐγένετο Emperius : ἐγίνετο codd.
³ ἔχοντα ὀνείδη οὗτοί με Sauppe : εἶχον τὰ ὀνείδη οὗτοι, οἳ
με codd. ⁴ εὖ add. Ald.
⁵ ἀπωλλύμην ci. Bekker : ἀπολοίμην codd.
⁶ ὅποι Reiske : ὅπου codd.

breaking, and knew that I was lost ; so I sprang at
once to the hearth and laid hold of the sacred
emblems. That act, and that alone, was my salvation
at the time ; for although I stood disgraced in the
eyes of the gods,[a] they, it seems, had more pity on
me than did men ; when men were desirous of putting
me to death, it was the gods who saved my life. My
subsequent imprisonment and the extent and nature
of the bodily suffering to which I was subjected would
take too long to describe. It was then that I bewailed
my lucklessness more bitterly than ever. When the
people appeared to be hardly used, it was I who
suffered in their stead ; on the other hand, when they
had been manifestly benefited by me, that act of
service likewise threatened me with ruin.[b] Indeed I
no longer had either ways or means of sustaining my
hopes ; everywhere I turned I saw woe in store for
me. However, disheartening though my reception
had been, I was no sooner a free man than my every
thought was again directed to the service of this city.

You must understand, gentlemen, how far such
services as mine surpass ordinary services. When
citizens who hold public office add to your revenues,
are they not in fact giving you what is yours already ?
And when those who hold military command benefit
their country by some fine exploit, is it not by exposing your persons to fatigue and danger and by spend-
ing public money in addition that they render you

[a] Owing to his participation in the mutilation of the
Hermae four years before.

[b] *i.e.* (a) Andocides put an end to the reign of terror which
followed the mutilation of the Hermae, but at the cost of his
own happiness. (b) He had helped Athens win a victory
over Sparta at sea, but had again suffered for it by imprisonment at the hands of the Four Hundred.

ποιοῦσιν ὑμᾶς εἴ τι τυγχάνουσιν ἀγαθόν; ἐν ᾧ
καὶ ἄν τι ἐξαμάρτωσιν, οὐκ αὐτοὶ τῆς σφετέρας
αὐτῶν ἁμαρτίας δίκην διδόασιν, ἀλλ' ὑμεῖς ὑπὲρ
18 τῶν ἐκείνοις ἡμαρτημένων. ἀλλ' ὅμως οὗτοι
στεφανοῦνταί γε ὑφ' ὑμῶν καὶ ἀνακηρύττονται ὡς
ὄντες ἄνδρες ἀγαθοί. καὶ οὐκ ἐρῶ ὡς οὐ δικαίως·
μεγάλη γάρ ἐστιν ἀρετή, ὅστις τὴν ἑαυτοῦ πόλιν
ὁτῳοῦν δύναται τρόπῳ ἀγαθόν τι ἐργάζεσθαι.
ἀλλ' οὖν γιγνώσκειν γε χρὴ ὅτι ἐκεῖνος ἂν εἴη πολὺ
πλείστου ἄξιος ἀνήρ, ὅστις τοῖς ἑαυτοῦ παρα-
κινδυνεύων χρήμασί τε καὶ σώματι τολμῴη
ἀγαθόν τι ποιεῖν τοὺς ἑαυτοῦ πολίτας.

19 Ἐμοὶ τοίνυν τὰ μὲν ἤδη εἰς ὑμᾶς πεπραγμένα
σχεδόν τι ἅπαντες ἂν εἰδεῖτε, τὰ δὲ μέλλοντά τε
καὶ ἤδη πραττόμενα ἄνδρες ὑμῶν πεντακόσιοι ἐν
ἀπορρήτῳ ἴσασιν [ἡ βουλή]¹· οὓς πολλῷ δήπου εἰκὸς²
ἧττον ἄν τι ἐξαμαρτεῖν, ἢ εἰ ὑμᾶς δέοι ἀκούσαντάς
τι ἐν τῷ παραχρῆμα νῦν διαβουλεύσασθαι. οἱ μέν
γε σχολῇ περὶ τῶν εἰσαγγελλομένων σκοποῦνται,
ὑπάρχει τε αὐτοῖς, ἐάν τι ἐξαμαρτάνωσιν, αἰτίαν
ἔχειν καὶ λόγον αἰσχρὸν ἐκ τῶν ἄλλων πολιτῶν·
ὑμῖν δὲ οὐκ εἰσὶν ἕτεροι ὑφ' ὧν αἰτίαν ⟨ἂν⟩³ ἔχοιτε·
20 τὰ γὰρ ὑμέτερα αὐτῶν ἐφ' ὑμῖν δικαίως ἐστὶ καὶ
εὖ καὶ κακῶς, ἐὰν βούλησθε, διαθέσθαι. ἅ γε
μέντοι ἔξω τῶν ἀπορρήτων οἷόν τέ⁴ μοί ἐστιν
εἰπεῖν εἰς ὑμᾶς ἤδη πεπραγμένα, ἀκούσεσθε.
ἐπίστασθε γάρ που ὡς ἠγγέλθη ὑμῖν⁵ ὅτι οὐ

---

¹ ἡ βουλή del. Valckenaer.   ² εἰκὸς Ald. : εἰς codd.
³ ἂν add. Dobree. Ante αἰτίαν Lipsius.
⁴ οἷόν τέ Stephanus : οἷόν γέ codd.
⁵ ὑμῖν Valckenaer : ἡμῖν codd.

such service as they do? Again, if they make a
mistake at some point, it is not they themselves who
pay for their mistake; it is you who pay for the error
which was due to them. Yet you bestow crowns on
such persons and publicly proclaim them as heroes.
And I will not deny that they deserve it; it is proof
of signal merit to be able to render one's country a
service in any way whatsoever. But you must see
that that man is far the worthiest who has the courage
to expose his own life and his own goods to danger in
order to confer a benefit on his fellow-countrymen.

My past services must be known to almost all of
you. But the services which I am about to render,
which I have, in fact, already begun to render, have
been revealed in secret to only five hundred of you
[, to the Council, that is to say [a]]; they, I think, are
likely to make far fewer mistakes than you would
be, had you to debate the matter here and now immediately after listening to my explanations. Those
five hundred are considering at leisure the proposal
placed before them, and they are liable to be called
to account and censured by the rest of you for any
mistake which they may make; whereas you have
none to hold you to blame, as you very rightly
have the power of ordering your affairs wisely or
foolishly at will. However, I will disclose to you such
services as I can, such services as are not a secret,
because they have already been performed.

I need not remind you, I imagine, how you received

[a] The words ἡ βουλή were rightly bracketed by Valckenaer
as a gloss upon what precedes. The "secret proposal"
placed before the Council must have been connected with
the future corn-supply of Athens. Andocides was doubtless
to use his influence in Cyprus to ensure that it should not
be interrupted.

μέλλει ἐκ Κύπρου σῖτος ἥξειν ἐνταῦθα· ἐγὼ τοίνυν
τοιοῦτός τε καὶ τοσοῦτος ἐγενόμην, ὥστε τοὺς
ἄνδρας τοὺς ταῦτα βουλεύσαντας ἐφ᾽ ὑμῖν καὶ
21 πράξαντας ψευσθῆναι τῆς αὑτῶν[1] γνώμης. καὶ ὡς
μὲν ταῦτα διεπράχθη, οὐδὲν προὔργου ἀκοῦσαι
ὑμῖν· τάδε ⟨δὲ⟩[2] νυνὶ βούλομαι ὑμᾶς εἰδέναι, ὅτι αἱ
μέλλουσαι νῆες ἤδη σιταγωγοὶ καταπλεῖν εἰς τὸν
Πειραιᾶ εἰσιν ὑμῖν τέτταρες καὶ δέκα, αἱ δὲ λοιπαὶ
τῶν ἐκ Κύπρου ἀναχθεισῶν ἥξουσιν ἀθρόαι οὐ πολὺ
ὕστερον. ἐδεξάμην δ᾽ ⟨ἂν⟩[3] ἀντὶ πάντων χρημάτων
εἶναι ἐν ἀσφαλεῖ φράσαι πρὸς ὑμᾶς ἃ καὶ τῇ βουλῇ
ἐν ἀπορρήτῳ εἰσήγγειλα, ὅπως αὐτόθεν προῄδετε.[4]
22 νῦν δὲ ἐκεῖνα μὲν τότε ὅταν ἀποτελεσθῇ γνώσεσθε
ἅμα καὶ ὠφελήσεσθε[5]· νῦν δέ, ὦ Ἀθηναῖοι, εἰ
μοι βουληθεῖτε δοῦναι χάριν μικράν τε καὶ ἄπονον
ὑμῖν καὶ ἅμα δικαίαν, πάνυ ἄν μοι τοῦτο ἐν μεγάλῃ
ἡδονῇ γένοιτο. ὡς δὲ καὶ δικαία ἐστίν, εἴσεσθε. ἃ
γάρ μοι αὐτοὶ γνόντες τε καὶ ὑποσχόμενοι ἔδοτε,
ὕστερον δὲ ἑτέροις πειθόμενοι ἀφείλεσθε, ταῦθ᾽
ὑμᾶς, εἰ μὲν βούλεσθε, αἰτῶ, εἰ δὲ μὴ[6] βούλεσθε,
23 ἀπαιτῶ. ὁρῶ δὲ ὑμᾶς πολλάκις καὶ δούλοις ἀνθρώποις καὶ ξένοις παντοδαποῖς[7] πολιτείαν τε διδόντας[8] καὶ εἰς χρήματα μεγάλας δωρείας, οἳ ἂν
ὑμᾶς φαίνωνται ποιοῦντές τι ἀγαθόν. καὶ ταῦτα
μέντοι ὀρθῶς ὑμεῖς φρονοῦντες δίδοτε· οὕτω γὰρ
ἂν ὑπὸ πλείστων ἀνθρώπων εὖ πάσχοιτε. ἐγὼ
τοίνυν τοσοῦτον ὑμῶν μόνον δέομαι· τὸ ψήφισμα

---

[1] αὑτῶν Baiter et Sauppe: αὐτῶν codd.
[2] τάδε δὲ Gebauer: τὰ δὲ codd.
[3] ἂν add. Dobree.
[4] προῄδετε Blass: προειδῆτε codd.
[5] ὠφελήσεσθε Fuhr: ὠφεληθήσεσθε codd.
[6] μὴ ante βούλεσθε del. Reiske.

news that no grain was to be exported to Athens from Cyprus. Now I was able to handle the situation with such effect that the persons who had formed the plot and put it into execution were frustrated. It is of no importance that you should know how this was done ; what I do wish you to know is that the ships on the point of putting in to the Peiraeus at this moment with a cargo of grain number no less than fourteen ; while the remainder of the convoy which sailed from Cyprus will arrive in a body shortly after them.

I would have given all the money in the world to be able to reveal to you with safety the secret proposal which I have placed before the Council, so that you might know at once what to expect. Instead, you will only learn what it is when you begin to benefit by it, and that will not be until it is put into effect. However, if you would consent even as it is, gentlemen, to bestow on me what is only a small token of gratitude, and one which is both easily granted and just, nothing would give me more delight. That I am entitled to it you will see at once. I am asking of you only what you yourselves gave me in fulfilment of a solemn promise, but were afterwards persuaded to withdraw. If you are prepared to restore it, I ask it as a favour ; if you are not, I claim it as my due. I often see you bestowing civic rights and substantial grants of money upon both slaves and foreigners from every part of the world, if they prove to have done you some service. And you are acting wisely in making such gifts ; they engender the greatest possible willingness to serve you. Now my own request is merely this. You decreed on the

---

[7] παντοδαποῖς Stephanus : παντοδαπῆς codd.
[8] πολιτείαν τε διδόντας Reiske : πολιτείας διδόντας τε codd.

ὃ Μενίππου εἰπόντος ἐψηφίσασθε, εἶναί μοι ἄδειαν,
πάλιν ἀπόδοτε. ἀναγνώσεται δὲ ὑμῖν αὐτό· ἔτι
γὰρ καὶ νῦν ἐγγέγραπται ἐν τῷ βουλευτηρίῳ.

ΨΗΦΙΣΜΑ

24 Τουτὶ τὸ ψήφισμα ὃ ἠκούσατε ψηφισάμενοί μοι,
ὦ 'Αθηναῖοι, ὕστερον ἀφείλεσθε χάριν ἑτέρῳ φέ-
ροντες. πείθεσθε οὖν μοι, καὶ ἤδη παύσασθε
εἴ τῳ ὑμῶν διάβολόν τι ἐν τῇ γνώμῃ περὶ ἐμοῦ
παρέστηκεν. εἰ γὰρ ὅσα οἱ ἄνθρωποι γνώμῃ
ἁμαρτάνουσι, τὸ σῶμα αὐτῶν μὴ αἴτιόν ἐστιν,
ἐμοῦ[1] τὸ μὲν σῶμα τυγχάνει ταὐτὸν ἔτι ὄν,[2] ὅπερ
τῆς αἰτίας ἀπήλλακται, ἡ δὲ γνώμη ἀντὶ τῆς
προτέρας ἑτέρα νυνὶ παρέστηκεν. οὐδὲν οὖν ἔτι
ὑπολείπεται ὅτῳ ἄν μοι δικαίως διαβεβλῆσθε.[3]
25 ὥσπερ δὲ τῆς τότε ἁμαρτίας τὰ ἀπὸ τῶν ἔργων
σημεῖα ἔφατε χρῆναι πιστότατα ποιούμενοι κακόν
με ἄνδρα ἡγεῖσθαι, οὕτω καὶ ἐπὶ τῇ νῦν εὐνοίᾳ μὴ
ζητεῖτε ἑτέραν βάσανον ἢ τὰ ἀπὸ τῶν νυνὶ ἔργων
σημεῖα ὑμῖν γιγνόμενα.
26 Πολὺ δέ μοι προσήκει ταῦτα μᾶλλον ἐκείνων
καὶ τῷ γένει συνηθέστερά ἐστι. τάδε γὰρ οὐ
ψευσαμένῳ μοι λαθεῖν οἷόν τ' ἐστι τούς γε πρεσβυτέρους ὑμῶν, ὅτι ὁ τοῦ ἐμοῦ πατρὸς πάππος[4]
Λεωγόρας στασιάσας πρὸς τοὺς τυράννους ὑπὲρ
τοῦ δήμου, ἐξὸν αὐτῷ διαλλαχθέντι τῆς ἔχθρας καὶ

[23]

---

[1] ἐμοῦ Reiske : ὁμοῦ codd.
[2] ταὐτὸν ἔτι ὄν Bekker : τοῦτ' ἀναίτιον codd.
[3] διαβεβλῆσθε Bekker : διαβεβλῆσθαι codd.
[4] πάππος Valckenaer, coll. Myst. § 106 : πρόπαππος codd.

[a] i.e. Peisander. Andocides meant that the decree of

motion of Menippus that I should be granted immunity ; restore me my rights under that decree. The herald shall read it to you, as it is lying even now among the records in the Council-chamber.

Decree

This decree to which you have been listening, gentlemen, was passed by you in my favour, but afterwards revoked to oblige another.[a] Be advised by me, then. If any of you feels prejudiced against me, let him rid himself of that prejudice. You will admit that men's persons are not to blame for the mistakes which spring from their opinions. Now my own person is still unchanged, and is free from guilt ; whereas different opinions have replaced the old. Thus you are left without any just ground for prejudice.[b] In the case of my old blunder you maintained that you had to treat the indications furnished by conduct as decisive, and that therefore you were obliged to regard me as a criminal. Be consistent, then ; use only the indications furnished by my present conduct to prove the genuineness of my present desire to serve you.

Furthermore, my behaviour to-day is much more in keeping with my character than my behaviour then, just as it accords far more with the traditions of my family. I am not lying — no lie of this sort could deceive my older listeners — when I say that my father's grandfather, Leogoras, led a revolt of the people against the tyrants,[c] and in spite of the oppor-

Menippus was effectively stultified by the decree of Isotinides, passed shortly afterwards at Peisander's instigation.

[b] A sophistry worthy of the *Tetralogies*.

[c] *Cf. Mysteries*, § 106 and footnote.

γενομένῳ κηδεστῇ ἄρξαι μετ᾽ ἐκείνων τῶν ἀνδρῶν
τῆς πόλεως, εἵλετο μᾶλλον ἐκπεσεῖν μετὰ τοῦ
δήμου καὶ φεύγων κακοπαθεῖν μᾶλλον ἢ προδότης
αὐτῶν καταστῆναι. ὥστ᾽ ἔμοιγε καὶ διὰ τὰ τῶν
προγόνων ἔργα εἰκότως ὑπάρχει δημοτικῷ εἶναι,
εἴπερ τι ἀλλὰ νῦν γε[1] φρονῶν τυγχάνω. ὧν καὶ
ἕνεκα εἰκὸς ὑμᾶς, ἐὰν χρηστὸς ὢν ἀνὴρ εἰς ὑμᾶς
φαίνωμαι, προθυμότερόν μου ἀποδέχεσθαι τὰ
πραττόμενα.

27 Τὸ δὲ δόντας ἐμοὶ τὴν ἄδειαν ἀφελέσθαι ὑμᾶς,
εὖ ἴστε ὅτι οὐδεπώποτε ἠγανάκτησα· ὅπου γὰρ
ὑπὸ τῶν ἀνδρῶν τούτων αὐτοὶ εἰς ὑμᾶς αὐτοὺς
ἐπείσθητε τὰ μέγιστα ἐξαμαρτεῖν, ὥστε ἀντὶ τῆς
ἀρχῆς δουλείαν ἀλλάξασθαι, ἐκ δημοκρατίας δυνα-
στείαν καταστήσαντες, τί ἄν τις ὑμῶν θαυμάζοι
28 καὶ εἰς ἐμὲ εἴ τι ἐπείσθητε ἐξαμαρτεῖν; βουλοίμην
μέντ᾽ ἄν, ὥσπερ ἐν τοῖς ὑμετέροις αὐτῶν πράγ-
μασιν, ἐπειδὴ ἐξουσίαν ἐλάβετε, τὰς τῶν ἐξαπατη-
σάντων ὑμᾶς ἀκύρους ἔθετε βουλάς, οὕτω καὶ ἐν
ᾧ περὶ ἐμοῦ ἐπείσθητε γνῶναί τι ἀνεπιτήδειον,
ἀτελῆ τὴν γνώμην αὐτῶν ποιῆσαι, καὶ μήτε ἐν
τούτῳ μήτε ἐν ἑτέρῳ τῳ τοῖς ὑμῶν αὐτῶν ἐχθίστοις
ὁμόψηφοί ποτε γένησθε.

---

[1] ἀλλὰ νῦν γε Schneider : ἄλλο νῦν γε codd.

tunity of coming to terms with them, marrying into
their house, and ruling the people of Athens at their
side, chose to share the exile of the democrats and
suffer the hardships of banishment rather than turn
traitor to them. Thus the behaviour of my forefathers should be an additional inspiration to me
to show affection for the people, if I have indeed
regained my senses at last; and it also gives you
a natural reason for accepting my services the more
readily, if you see me to have your interests at
heart.

The fact that you deprived me of the pardon which
you had given me has never, I assure you, caused me
to feel aggrieved. After those scoundrels had induced
you to wrong your own selves so grossly as to exchange empire for slavery, and to replace democracy
by despotism,[a] why should it surprise any of you that
you were induced to wrong me likewise? However,
I could wish that after reversing the policy of those
who duped you in those matters which concern yourselves,—as you did as soon as you were able—you
would similarly render their purposes ineffective in
the matter of that unfortunate measure which you
were persuaded to pass with regard to me. Refuse,
in fact, to side, on this or any other question, with
those who are your worst enemies.

[a] *i.e.* the Four Hundred.

481

III
ON THE PEACE WITH SPARTA

INTRODUCTION

THE authenticity of the speech which follows has been doubted more than once. As long ago as the first century B.C. Dionysius of Halicarnassus gave it as his considered opinion that it was not the work of Andocides ; and in modern times his verdict has been upheld by more than one critic. Thus Eduard Meyer regarded the *De Pace* as a party-pamphlet issued in vindication of Andocides and others who had advocated peace with Sparta in 391 B.C. and suffered exile in consequence. The opposite view, however, has also received strong support, and at the present time it is held generally that the speech was delivered by Andocides himself on the occasion in question. The problem is one that can be better appreciated after a brief survey of the political situation at the end of the first decade of the fourth century.

After the final collapse of Athens in 404 B.C. Sparta was the foremost power in the Greek world. To all appearances she could easily step into the place vacated by Athens, establish a Spartan empire on the lines of the Delian League, and enjoy the material prosperity of her old rival. In fact, however, this was not to be, largely for three reasons : (1) Sparta had no naval tradition and would never make a first-class sea-power : (2) she had made an unfortunate agreement with Persia under the terms of which the

Greek cities of Asia Minor were to be surrendered to Artaxerxes in return for Persian support in the war with Athens : (3) the Greek allies, notably Thebes and Corinth, who had helped her to victory were demanding, perfectly justly, a share in the spoils.

Of (1) nothing further need be said. As a result of (2) Sparta found herself in a dilemma ; if she kept her promise, she was not only depriving herself of the material of empire, but was also turning traitor to her countrymen across the Aegean ; if, on the other hand, she dishonoured the agreement, she made a foe of Persia, and she lost her name for honest dealing at the same time. In consequence she failed to follow either the one course or the other and ended by losing both the goodwill of Persia and the control of the Asiatic seaboard. She started by conceding Ionia to Cyrus ; but when his successor, Tissaphernes, attempted the forcible recovery of the other cities claimed by Persia (400 B.C.), she sent Thibron to oppose him. In 398 Thibron was superseded by Dercyllidas ; and during the years 396–395 Agesilaus himself conducted a series of brilliant predatory raids into Persian territory. In 394, however, he was recalled owing to the serious turn taken by home affairs; and just after he left for Greece the Spartan fleet commanded by his brother-in-law was annihilated off Cnidus by the Persians, who had engaged the services of the Athenian Conon. By 393 Sparta had lost her footing and her prestige in the eastern Aegean and Asia Minor. An abrupt change of policy followed. Proposals of peace were made to Persia, Sparta offering to recognize her right to the Greek seaboard in exchange for an undertaking that Persia would do nothing to interfere with the autonomy of the states of the Aegean and Greece proper, *i.e.* that she would henceforward cease helping Athens, as she had been doing of late, to rebuild something of her shattered empire. The proposals came to nothing; so in 391 Thibron was sent east once again. The expedition was a complete failure. Thibron lost his life and most of his men were cut to pieces by the Lydian satrap. Sparta never again attempted an Asiatic campaign.

The result of (3) was domestic war which effectively destroyed Spartan hegemony in Greece proper. The claims of Thebes and Corinth in 404 were coolly set aside and no attempt was made to conciliate either state; hence both were estranged and ready to oppose Sparta, should occasion offer. In 396 Persia, desirous of putting an end to the activities of Agesilaus in Asia Minor, sent Timocrates, a Rhodian, to Greece with a liberal supply of money to foment anti-Spartan feeling. By 395 Thebes, Corinth, Athens, and Sparta's ancient enemy, Argos, were ranged against her. The struggle was precipitated by a Spartan invasion of Boeotia in answer to an appeal from Phocis. Little was achieved save the establishment of Orchomenus as an independent state; and in the following year the allies replied by carrying the war into the Peloponnese. Meanwhile Agesilaus had been duly recalled. The allied forces were intercepted at Nemea by a hastily assembled Spartan army and heavily defeated (July 394). Sixteen days later they fought a second engagement at Coronea to prevent the passage through Boeotia of Agesilaus who had hastened homewards through Thrace and Macedonia. They were again defeated;

but Ágesilaus judged it prudent to push on to the Peloponnese. Henceforward the war centred round the elaborate fortifications of Corinth, and something of a stalemate had been reached when Conon and Tiribazus suddenly appeared off the Isthmus with the Persian fleet (393). The demonstration was followed by a conference between Tiribazus and the allies which made the hostility of Persia towards Sparta plain ; and immediately afterwards Conon sailed across to Peiraeus and superintended the rebuilding of the walls of Athens which had been razed by Lysander in 404.

It was in these circumstances that Sparta deemed it wise to come to an understanding with Persia, and accordingly Antalcidas was sent to Sardis with the proposals of peace already mentioned (393). As has been said, nothing came of his mission. It seems to have been followed by a congress at Sparta itself, where terms were discussed by representatives of Athens, Thebes, Corinth, and Argos. Among the Athenian delegates was Andocides who, with his fellows, decided to refer the suggestions of Sparta to the Ecclesia. The present speech purports to have been delivered in the course of the debate which took place in the Assembly upon their return.

We must now turn for a moment to the evidence for the history of the last two years (393-392) of the period outlined above. The sources, apart from the *De Pace* itself, are two, Xenophon and Philochorus.[a] Xenophon describes the mission of Antalcidas in some detail, but says not a word of the congress at Sparta. Philochorus, quoted by Didymus in his

---

[a] Athenian historian, *d.* 260 B.C.

commentary on the *Philippics* of Demosthenes,[a] mentions both in the following words: καὶ τὴν εἰρήνην τὴν ἐπ' Ἀνταλκίδου κατέπεμψεν ὁ βασιλεύς, ἣν Ἀθηναῖοι οὐκ ἐδέξαντο, διότι ἐγέγραπτο ἐν αὐτῇ τοὺς τὴν Ἀσίαν οἰκοῦντας Ἕλληνας ἐν βασιλέως οἴκῳ πάντας εἶναι συννενεμημένους. ἀλλὰ καὶ τοὺς πρέσβεις τοὺς ἐν Λακεδαίμονι συγχωρήσαντας ἐφυγάδευσαν, Καλλιστράτου γράψαντος, καὶ οὐχ ὑπομείναντας τὴν κρίσιν, Ἐπικράτην Κηφισιέα, Ἀνδοκίδην Κυδαθηναιέα, Κρατῖνον . . . ἵστιον, Εὐβουλίδην Ἐλευσίνιον, *i.e.* " . . . and the king sent down the Peace of Antalcidas, which the Athenians refused to accept because it was therein laid down that the Greeks living in Asia were one and all part of the king's household. Nay more, on the motion of Callistratus, they exiled the delegates who came to terms at Sparta and who did not abide their trial, namely, Epicrates of Cephisia Andocides of Cydathenaeum, Cratinus of . . ., and Eubulides of Eleusis." The date of the banishment of the four is given by Philochorus as the archonship of Philocles (392–391).

From this two things are clear. First, Andocides represented Athens at a congress held at Sparta shortly after the failure of Antalcidas to arrange a permanent peace at Sardis in 393. Secondly, he and his colleagues acquiesced in the proposals put forward by Sparta at this congress, and suffered for it on returning home. Philochorus does not mention the debate which must have taken place in the Athenian Assembly, when the delegates reported upon their mission and sought to justify themselves;

[a] Papyrus fragments of the commentary of Didymus on Demosthenes were discovered in 1901. Ed. Diehls-Schubart, Teubner, 1904. I give the text as it has been (with certainty) restored.

but his narrative is quite sufficient to show that the circumstances presupposed by the *De Pace* are historical. What, however, of the business transacted at the congress? What were the terms to which Andocides and his fellows assented? Again Philochorus gives no direct information; but the very fact that he speaks of these terms in the same breath as the proposals of peace made at Sardis and emphasizes the rejection by Athens of both alike, shows that he regarded them as largely the same in character. His language, in fact, suggests that at this second congress Sparta once more sought a general settlement by proposing that the Greeks of Asia Minor should pass under Persian control, although it would be natural to suppose that she was now prepared to modify her previous demand for the complete autonomy of the remaining Greek states, in view of the opposition of Athens, Thebes, and Argos. This is, admittedly, mere conjecture; but it may be of interest to compare it with what the *De Pace* has to say of the same congress. Andocides makes it quite clear that the proposals made at Sparta had been, at least in part, similar to those made the year before at Sardis; that is to say, the basis of the peace is to be the autonomy of the Greek states. But exceptions are now to be allowed; Athens herself, for example, will retain Lemnos, Imbros, and Scyros, together with her walls and fleet. On the other hand, there is no hint of any proposal to hand over the Greeks of Asia Minor to Persia. Yet we should have expected some attempt to justify such a step, if, as Philochorus appears to suggest, it had formed an important part of the Spartan programme at the later congress as well as in 393. Can such a discrepancy be explained, or have we after all placed too strained an interpretation upon the words of Philochorus ?

The answer is perhaps to be found by comparing what Philochorus and Andocides have to say with the parallel account of Xenophon. Xenophon, it will be remembered, does not mention the conference at Sparta, but gives a detailed account of the mission of Antalcidas to Sardis in 393.[a] Antalcidas, he says, tells Tiribazus that " the Spartans do not contest the king's claim to the Greek cities in Asia, but will be satisfied if all the islands and the remaining states are independent." Tiribazus favours a peace on such terms ; but the representatives from Athens, Thebes, and Argos refuse to have anything to do with it. " For the Athenians were afraid to consent to an agreement which allowed the islands their independence, lest they should lose Lemnos, Imbros, and Scyros ; the Thebans feared that they would be compelled to recognize the independence of the cities of Boeotia ; and the Argives thought that once an armistice was concluded on such terms, it would become impossible for them to achieve the one thing for which they longed, the inclusion of Corinth within the Argive state."

It will be observed that this differs from the account of the negotiations given by Philochorus. Philochorus, in fact, disagrees with Xenophon over the congress at Sardis exactly as he appears to disagree with Andocides over the later congress at Sparta. He says nothing of the Athenian fears for the loss of their Aegean possessions, but gives as their one reason for the rejection of the proposals of Antalcidas

[a] *Hell.* iv. 8. 14.

the threat to the cities of Asia Minor. This is in itself less probable than the account given by Xenophon. Ever since 404 Athens had been thinking regretfully of her lost empire, and the rebuilding of her walls by Conon was symbolic of her reviving ambition. It is known that about this time (393) she had contracted fresh alliances with Rhodes, Cos, Carpathus, Cnidus, and Eretria,[a] while her cleruchies in Lemnos, Imbros, and Scyros had already been recovered. When, therefore, she refused to sign a treaty of peace which guaranteed the autonomy of every state in the Aegean and on the Greek mainland, while it transferred those on the Asiatic coast to Persia, her first reason must have been that acquiescence in such terms would mean her own immediate extinction as an imperial power. Thus Philochorus would seem to state only half the truth when he says that " the Athenians refused to accept the peace because it was therein laid down that the Greeks living in Asia were one and all part of the king's household." Their refusal was not to be attributed solely to a sentimental reluctance to see Greeks governed by barbarians.

If then, as seems certain, Philochorus oversimplifies the motives of Athens in 393, he is doubtless doing the same when he implies that it was the acquiescence of the delegates in the abandonment of the Asiatic Greeks which caused their exile in 392–391. Thus his evidence is not so much contradicted as supplemented by that of the *De Pace*. Whereas the congress at Sparta must in fact have discussed two proposals, one which concerned the Greeks of Asia Minor, and another which concerned

[a] *C.A.H.* vi. p. 50.

the autonomy of the other communities of the Greek world, Philochorus hints only at the first and Andocides talks only of the second. That the *De Pace* should contain no reference to the Asiatic Greeks is intelligible, if it be remembered that Andocides is concerned throughout with the effects which the peace will have upon Athens herself. He has a difficult case to plead, as the imperialists, headed by Callistratus, will certainly wish to know how Athenian expansion in the future can be anything more than a dream, if Athens is to guarantee the autonomy of every state in Greece and the Aegean ; and to introduce any mention of the proposal to place the Greeks of Asia Minor under Persian control would hardly make matters easier.[a] It is not therefore surprising that Andocides should give such prominence to the positive advantages which Athens herself will gain from the peace, the right to maintain a fleet, to continue to enjoy the protection of her newly rebuilt walls, and to possess the three islands of Lemnos, Imbros, and Scyros, while passing over in silence those other conditions which could not be presented so attractively.

But although Andocides says nothing of the proposal to recognize the claims of Persia to the Asiatic seaboard, it is none the less of the greatest importance as evidence of the purpose of this second peace conference. It is generally assumed that Sparta summoned the conference in order to put an end to the Corinthian War and leave her hands free for operations

---

[a] It should be remembered how many other deliberate omissions and how much false emphasis the speech contains. See especially the account of relations between Sparta and Athens since 404, §§ 21-23.

against Persia, who had rejected her advances of the previous year. But in the light of what Philochorus says it would seem that this explanation will not quite do. If Sparta's intention in 392–391 was simply the settlement of domestic difficulties, what need was there to introduce the question of the Asiatic Greeks ? Once again Xenophon's account of the mission of Antalcidas is suggestive. After giving the reasons for the rejection of his proposals in 393 by Athens, Thebes, and Argos, Xenophon goes on to describe the behaviour of Tiribazus.[a] Tiribazus had been attracted by the Spartan offer ; but he could do nothing without consulting his master. He therefore made the Spartans a secret grant of money for the equipment of a fleet, threw Conon into prison, and " went up to the king to inform him of the Spartan proposals and of the arrest of Conon for treachery and to inquire of him what course of action should be taken in the whole affair." When he had reached Susa and explained matters, " the king sent down Struthas to take control of the coast. Struthas, however, remembering the harm which the king's domains had suffered at the hands of Agesilaus, showed strong sympathy towards the Athenians and their allies." In consequence, the Spartans dispatched Thibron to Asia Minor.

Xenophon does not mention how long an interval elapsed between the departure of Tiribazus and the arrival of Struthas. But if Tiribazus left for Susa towards the end of 393 and his successor did not reach the coast until seven or eight months later,[b] it is

[a] *Hell.* iv. 8. 16.

[b] From Xenophon's narrative of the events of 393, it is in fact necessary to suppose that Tiribazus did not leave for Susa until the end of the year. On the other hand, the

possible to see why the Asiatic Greeks should have
been mentioned at the conference at Sparta. Sparta,
still imagining that Tiribazus will bring back a favourable answer from Susa, has called a meeting of the
allies in order to overcome their objections to the
peace before his return. She places modified proposals before them : Athens is to keep Lemnos,
Imbros, and Scyros, and Boeotia is to remain under
Theban control with the exception of Orchomenus.
The Asiatic cities are still to be handed over to Persia.
If this is what lies behind the words of Philochorus, the
congress of 392 will represent, not an attempt on the
part of Sparta to clear up the domestic situation in
order to attack Persia, but an attempt to clear it up
in order to conciliate her. The proposals came to
nothing, however ; and subsequently Persia revealed
herself as still pro-Athenian. Reaction followed at
Sparta, and Thibron left for the east.

To return to the *De Pace*. It has been seen that
there is excellent evidence to show that Andocides
was a delegate to Sparta in 392-391 B.C., and that
he favoured the Spartan proposals for peace. Further,
the character of those proposals, although not fully
stated by Philochorus, can be deduced with some
probability from Xenophon's account of the negotiations conducted at Sardis by Antalcidas during the
previous year ; and it is proposals of precisely this
type which are outlined in the present speech.
Lastly, if the *De Pace* contains no reference to the
fate of the Asiatic Greeks, such silence can be satis-

archonship of Philocles, during which the conference at
Sparta took place, began in the July of 392. Thus if Struthas
did not appear until the autumn, it might well have been
held before his arrival.

factorily explained. On the other hand, one difficulty remains. As has often been pointed out, the brief sketch of fifth century history which occupies the opening paragraphs is hopelessly muddled. To take a single instance, the speaker talks of the ostracism of Miltiades, son of Cimon, and of the fifty years' peace which he arranged between Sparta and Athens upon his return from exile. He is presumably thinking of the ostracism of Cimon, son of Miltiades, who remained in exile *c.* 461–451 B.C., and who was largely responsible for the five years' truce with Sparta negotiated shortly after his return. The five years' truce itself has become confused with the thirty years' peace of 445 B.C., which Cimon did not live to see. Do inaccuracies of this kind make against the authenticity of the *De Pace* ? Would Andocides have been incapable of such confusion ? Fortunately the answer to such questions is less difficult than might appear. It must be remembered in the first place that Aeschines accepted the historical summary of the *De Pace* without hesitation and inserted it in his own *De Falsa Legatione*, delivered in 362 B.C. ; secondly that Andocides himself shows elsewhere how hazy was his recollection of times, persons, and places. In the *Mysteries* his version of the fall of the Peisistratidae by no means accords with the facts, while in the same speech he goes so far as to confuse the battles of Marathon and Plataea. If he was capable of forgetting his history to this extent, it is hardly surprising that the intricacies of the Pentecontaetia should prove too much for him.

factorily explained. On the other hand, one difficulty remains. As has often been pointed out, the
Athens upon his return from exile. He is presum

ANALYSIS

§§ 1-12. It is held that peace with Sparta will
endanger the democracy. This can
easily be disproved by the facts of
history.

  (a) The peace negotiated by Miltiades,
  son of Cimon. The resulting benefits. §§ 3-5.

  (b) The peace which ended the Aeginetan
  War. The resulting benefits. §§ 6-7.

  (c) The peace of Nicias. Its benefits.
  §§ 8-9.

  (d) The truce after Aegospotami is not a
  case in point, as Sparta dictated her own
  terms. §§ 10-12.

§§ 13-16. Examination of possible motives for continuing war with Sparta. None of these
will bear criticism.

§§ 17-23. What are the other powers gaining from
the peace as compared with Athens?

  (a) Sparta. §§ 17-19.

  (b) Boeotia. § 20.

  (c) Athens. §§ 21-23.

§§ 24-27. Corinth and Argos are refusing peace.
But to what will Athens find herself
committed if she sides with them?

§§ 28-32. Folly of rejecting powerful friendships and

496

making alliances with those who are weak and treacherous. Historical illustrations.

(a) The episode of Amorges. § 29.
(b) The Segestan alliance. § 30.
(c) The Argive alliance of 420. § 31.

§§ 33-36. Justification of the action of the delegates in referring the Spartan proposals to the Ecclesia.

§§ 37-39. The terms of peace do not restore to Athens her foreign possessions. But they restore her walls and fleet, and it was from these that the empire sprang.

§§ 40-41. Any citizen who wishes can suggest improvements in the terms presented to the Assembly, thanks to the delegates, who refused to commit themselves finally at Sparta.

ΠΕΡΙ ΤΗΣ ΠΡΟΣ ΛΑΚΕΔΑΙΜΟΝΙΟΥΣ ΕΙΡΗΝΗΣ

1 Ὅτι μὲν εἰρήνην ποιεῖσθαι δικαίαν ἄμεινόν ἐστιν
ἢ πολεμεῖν, δοκεῖτέ μοι, ὦ Ἀθηναῖοι, πάντες
γιγνώσκειν· ὅτι δὲ οἱ ῥήτορες τῷ μὲν ὀνόματι τῆς
εἰρήνης συγχωροῦσι, τοῖς δ' ἔργοις ἀφ' ὧν ἂν ἡ
εἰρήνη[1] γένοιτο ἐναντιοῦνται, τοῦτο δὲ οὐ πάντες
αἰσθάνεσθε. λέγουσι γὰρ ὡς ἔστι δεινότατον τῷ
δήμῳ, γενομένης εἰρήνης, ἡ νῦν οὖσα πολιτεία μὴ
καταλυθῇ.

2 Εἰ μὲν οὖν μηδεπώποτε πρότερον ὁ δῆμος ὁ
[τῶν][2] Ἀθηναίων εἰρήνην ἐποιήσατο πρὸς Λακεδαιμονίους, εἰκότως ἂν ἐφοβούμεθα αὐτὸ διά τε τὴν
ἀπειρίαν τοῦ ἔργου διά τε τὴν ἐκείνων ἀπιστίαν·
ὅπου δὲ πολλάκις ἤδη πρότερον εἰρήνην ἐποιήσασθε[3]
δημοκρατούμενοι, πῶς οὐκ εἰκὸς ὑμᾶς πρῶτον
ἐκεῖνα σκέψασθαι τὰ τότε γενόμενα; χρὴ γάρ,
ὦ Ἀθηναῖοι, τεκμηρίοις χρῆσθαι τοῖς πρότερον
γενομένοις περὶ τῶν μελλόντων ἔσεσθαι.

3 Ἡνίκα τοίνυν ἦν μὲν ὁ πόλεμος ἡμῖν ἐν Εὐβοίᾳ,

---

[1] ἂν ἡ εἰρήνη Lipsius : ἂν εἰρήνη Q, ἡ εἰρήνη A.
[2] τῶν del. Spengel.
[3] ἐποιήσασθε Reiske : ἐποιήσατε codd.

ON THE PEACE WITH SPARTA

I THINK you all understand, gentlemen, that it is better to make peace on fair terms than to continue fighting. But some of you fail to see that although our political leaders have no objection to peace in the abstract, they are opposed to such measures as would lead to it, on the ground that the people would be in very grave danger of seeing the existing constitution overthrown once peace was concluded.

Now had the Athenian people never made peace with Sparta in the past, our lack of previous experience and the untrustworthy character of the Spartans might have justified such fears. But you have done so on a number of occasions since the establishment of the democracy; and it is therefore only logical that you should first of all consider the results which followed at the time; one must use the past as a guide to the future, gentlemen.

[a] Now take the days when we were fighting in

---

[a] §§ 3-12 of this speech were inserted by Aeschines, with slight alterations, in his *De Falsa Legatione* (§§ 172-176), an interesting example of the plagiarism which is known to have been common in ancient times. The *De Falsa Legatione* was delivered in 343, almost fifty years after this.

ANDOCIDES

Μέγαρα δὲ εἴχομεν καὶ Πηγὰς καὶ Τροζῆνα,
εἰρήνης ἐπεθυμήσαμεν, καὶ Μιλτιάδην τὸν Κίμωνος
ὠστρακισμένον καὶ ὄντα ἐν Χερρονήσῳ κατεδεξά-
μεθα δι' αὐτὸ τοῦτο, πρόξενον ὄντα Λακεδαιμονίων,
ὅπως πέμψαιμεν[1] εἰς Λακεδαίμονα προκηρυκευσό-
4 μενον περὶ σπονδῶν. καὶ τότε ἡμῖν εἰρήνη ἐγένετο
[24] πρὸς Λακεδαιμονίους ἔτη πεντήκοντα,[2] καὶ ἐνεμείναμεν ἀμφότεροι ταύταις ταῖς σπονδαῖς ἔτη
τριακαίδεκα. ἐν δὴ τοῦτο, ὦ Ἀθηναῖοι, πρῶτον
σκεψώμεθα. ἐν ταύτῃ τῇ εἰρήνῃ ὁ δῆμος ὁ [τῶν][3]
Ἀθηναίων ἔσθ' ὅπου κατελύθη; οὐδεὶς ἀποδείξει.
ἀγαθὰ δὲ ὅσα ἐγένετο διὰ ταύτην τὴν εἰρήνην, ἐγὼ
5 ὑμῖν[4] φράσω. πρῶτον μὲν τὸν Πειραιᾶ[5] ἐτειχίσαμεν
ἐν τούτῳ τῷ χρόνῳ, εἶτα τὸ μακρὸν τεῖχος τὸ
βόρειον· ἀντὶ δὲ τῶν τριήρων αἳ τότε ἡμῖν ἦσαν
παλαιαὶ καὶ ἄπλοι, αἷς βασιλέα καὶ τοὺς βαρβάρους[6]
καταναυμαχήσαντες ἠλευθερώσαμεν τοὺς Ἕλληνας,
ἀντὶ τούτων τῶν νεῶν ἑκατὸν τριήρεις ἐναυπηγη-

---

[1] πέμψαιεν Α : πέμψωμεν Q.
[2] πεντήκοντα cum Aeschine Meursius: πέντε codd., quod
retinet Dobree, verbis καὶ ἐνεμείναμεν . . . τριακαίδεκα post ἔτη
τριάκοντα § 6 collocatis.   [3] τῶν del. Spengel.
[4] ἐγὼ ὑμῖν edd. : ἐγὼ ἡμῖν Α : ἡμῖν ἐγὼ Q.
[5] τότε post Πειραιᾶ add. Α.
[6] τοὺς βαρβάρους Q : βαρβάρους Α.

---

[a] Andocides is confused in his history here. He is referring to the revolt of Euboea which occurred in 446 B.C. and
which was followed by a *thirty* years' peace with Sparta. He
is also inaccurate in stating that Athens was still holding
Megara ; Megara revolted at the same time as Euboea, and
Athens was left only with the two ports of Pegae and Nisaea.
The peace marked the end of her effort to acquire an empire
on land. See Thucyd. i. 112.

Euboea[a] and controlled Megara, Pegae, and Troezen.
We were seized with a longing for peace ; and, in
virtue of his being Sparta's representative at Athens,
we recalled Cimon's son, Miltiades,[b] who had been
ostracized and was living in the Chersonese, for the
one purpose of sending him to Sparta to make overtures for an armistice. On that occasion we secured
a peace of fifty years with Sparta ; and both sides
kept the treaty in question for thirteen. Let us consider this single instance first, gentlemen. Did the
Athenian democracy ever fall during this peace ?
No one can show that it did. On the contrary, I will
tell you how much you benefited by this peace. To
begin with, we fortified Peiraeus in the course of this
period[c] : secondly, we built the Long Wall to the
north[d] : then the existing fleet of old, unseaworthy
triremes with which we had won Greece her independence by defeating the king of Persia and his barbarians—these existing vessels were replaced by a

---

[b] A double historical error. (a) Andocides means Cimon,
son of Miltiades. (b) Cimon had been dead three years
when the thirty years' peace was negotiated. A. is thinking
of the truce of five years with Sparta arranged by Cimon
in 451 immediately upon his return from exile. It was at
the time of its expiry that the revolt of Euboea occurred.
Cimon had been ostracized in 461 after his ignominious
dismissal by the Spartans from Ithome. His exile marked
the triumph of the advanced democrats headed by Ephialtes
and Pericles.

[c] Again an error. Peiraeus was fortified by Themistocles
immediately after the repulse of the Persians in 480.

[d] The northern Long Wall, connecting Athens with
Peiraeus, was in fact built in 457, over ten years before the
negotiation of the peace which Andocides is discussing.
Nothing is said of the wall to the south, running between
Athens and Phalerum, which was constructed at the same
time.

σάμεθα, καὶ πρῶτον τότε τριακοσίους ἱππέας
κατεστησάμεθα καὶ τοξότας τριακοσίους Σκύθας
ἐπριάμεθα. [καὶ]¹ ταῦτα ἐκ τῆς εἰρήνης τῆς πρὸς
Λακεδαιμονίους ἀγαθὰ τῇ πόλει καὶ δύναμις τῷ
δήμῳ τῷ² Ἀθηναίων ἐγένετο.

6 Μετὰ δὲ ταῦτα δι' Αἰγινήτας εἰς πόλεμον
κατέστημεν, καὶ πολλὰ κακὰ παθόντες πολλὰ δὲ
ποιήσαντες ἐπεθυμήσαμεν πάλιν τῆς εἰρήνης, καὶ
ᾑρέθησαν³ δέκα ἄνδρες ἐξ Ἀθηναίων ἁπάντων πρέσβεις εἰς Λακεδαίμονα περὶ εἰρήνης αὐτοκράτορες,
ὧν ἦν καὶ Ἀνδοκίδης ὁ πάππος ὁ ἡμέτερος.
οὗτοι ἡμῖν⁴ εἰρήνην ἐποίησαν⁵ πρὸς Λακεδαιμονίους
ἔτη τριάκοντα. καὶ ἐν τοσούτῳ χρόνῳ ἔστιν ὅπου,
ὦ Ἀθηναῖοι, ὁ δῆμος κατελύθη; τί δέ; πράτ-
τοντές τινες δήμου κατάλυσιν ἐλήφθησαν; οὐκ
ἔστιν ὅστις ἀποδείξει. ἀλλ' αὐτὸ τὸ ἐναντιώτατον·
7 αὕτη γὰρ ἡ εἰρήνη τὸν δῆμον τὸν Ἀθηναίων⁶
ὑψηλὸν ἦρε καὶ κατέστησεν ἰσχυρὸν οὕτως ὥστε
πρῶτον μὲν ἐν τούτοις τοῖς ἔτεσιν εἰρήνην λαβόντες⁷
ἀνηνέγκαμεν χίλια τάλαντα εἰς τὴν ἀκρόπολιν, καὶ

¹ καὶ del. Blass, coll. §§ 7, 9. ² τῷ Spengel : τῶν codd.
³ ᾑρέθησαν Q : εὑρέθησαν A. ⁴ ἡμῖν Q : ὑμῖν A.
⁵ ἐποίησαν Bekker : ἐποιήσαντο codd.
⁶ τὸν Ἀθ. Bekker : τῶν Ἀθ. codd.
⁷ λαβόντες] ἄγοντες Reiske.

ᵃ An obvious inaccuracy. The Athenian fleet had been growing steadily since the Persian Wars and the institution of the Delian League.

ᵇ Cavalry had been in existence since at least the seventh century. Solon, at the beginning of the sixth, formed his second property class of Ἱππεῖς, citizens wealthy enough to provide themselves with a horse in time of war. Archers (τοξόται) were imported for the first time shortly after Salamis (480 B.C.).

hundred new ones [a] : and it was at this time that we first enrolled three hundred cavalry and purchased three hundred Scythian archers.[b] Such were the benefits which Athens derived from the peace with Sparta, such the strength which was added thereby to the Athenian democracy.

Later we went to war on account of Aegina [c] ; and after both sides had suffered heavily, we were seized once more with a desire for peace. So a deputation of ten — among them my grandfather, Andocides—was chosen from the whole citizen body and dispatched to Sparta with unlimited powers to negotiate a peace. They arranged a thirty years' peace with Sparta for us. That is a long period, gentlemen ; yet did the democracy ever fall in the course of it ? Was any party, I ask you, ever caught plotting a revolution ? No one can point to an instance. In fact just the opposite happened. The peace in question exalted the Athenian democracy ; it rendered it so powerful that during the years after we gained peace we first of all deposited a thousand talents on the Acropolis and passed a law which set

[c] There is bad confusion here. Aegina lost her independence and was incorporated in the Athenian empire in 457. Under the Thirty Years' Peace of 446 she was guaranteed autonomy on condition that she continued to pay tribute. In 432 she made secret overtures to Sparta, alleging that her autonomy had not been respected. Thus Andocides may be thinking of her share in precipitating the Archidamian War. On the other hand, the peace which follows is not the Peace of Nicias ; when talking of the benefits which ensued from it, Andocides seems to be referring once again to the Thirty Years' Peace (see § 3). Probably he is thinking of the peace of 446, and assumes that because the status of Aegina figured prominently in the negotiations, it was Aegina which had originally sent Athens to war.

νόμῳ κατεκλήσαμεν ἐξαίρετα εἶναι τῷ δήμῳ, τοῦτο
δὲ τριήρεις ἄλλας ἑκατὸν ἐναυπηγησάμεθα, καὶ
ταύτας ἐξαιρέτους ἐψηφισάμεθα εἶναι, νεωσοίκους
τε ᾠκοδομησάμεθα, χιλίους τε καὶ διακοσίους
ἱππέας καὶ τοξότας τοσούτους ἑτέρους κατεστή-
σαμεν, καὶ τὸ τεῖχος τὸ μακρὸν τὸ νότιον ἐτειχίσθη.
ταῦτα ἐκ τῆς[1] εἰρήνης τῆς πρὸς Λακεδαιμονίους
ἀγαθὰ τῇ πόλει καὶ δύναμις τῷ δήμῳ τῷ[2] Ἀθηναίων ἐγένετο.

8   Πάλιν δὲ διὰ Μεγαρέας πολεμήσαντες καὶ τὴν
χώραν τμηθῆναι προέμενοι, πολλῶν ἀγαθῶν στερη-
θέντες αὖθις τὴν εἰρήνην ἐποιησάμεθα, ἣν ἡμῖν
Νικίας ὁ Νικηράτου κατηργάσατο. οἶμαι δ' ὑμᾶς
ἅπαντας εἰδέναι τοῦτο, ὅτι διὰ ταύτην τὴν εἰρήνην
ἑπτακισχίλια μὲν τάλαντα νομίσματος εἰς τὴν
9 ἀκρόπολιν ἀνηνέγκαμεν, ναῦς δὲ πλείους ἢ τριακοσίας[3] ἐκτησάμεθα, καὶ φόρος προσῄει κατ'
ἐνιαυτὸν πλέον ἢ διακόσια καὶ χίλια τάλαντα, καὶ

---

[1] ἐκ ταύτης τῆς QL.   [2] τῷ Spengel : τῶν codd.
[3] τριακοσίας cum Aeschine Markland (cf. Thucyd. ii. 13. 8):
τετρακοσίας codd.

---

[a] For Athenian finance between 446 and 432 see *I.G.* i[2].
91. According to Thucydides a reserve of 6000 talents had
been accumulated on the Acropolis by the end of the period.
One thousand were specially set apart against a naval crisis.
It was forbidden to use this sum for any other purpose under
pain of death. Andocides appears to be confusing the money
earmarked for ships with the ships themselves.

[b] Inaccurate. The docks had been built by Themistocles
in the decade following the Persian Wars.

[c] *i.e.* the Middle Wall, running parallel to the wall on the
north and connecting Athens with Peiraeus by a narrow
corridor. It was built during the Thirty Years' Peace.

[d] The famous Megarian decree which excluded Megara
from the markets of Attica and the ports of the Athenian
empire was passed in 432. It brought Peloponnesian

504

them apart as a state reserve [a]; in addition to that we built a hundred triremes, and decreed that they should be kept in reserve likewise : we laid out docks,[b] we enrolled twelve hundred cavalry and as many archers, and the Long Wall to the south was constructed.[c] Such were the benefits which Athens derived from the peace with Sparta, such the strength which was added thereby to the Athenian democracy.

Then we went to war again on account of Megara,[d] and allowed Attica to be laid waste ; but the many privations which we suffered led us to make peace once more, this time through Nicias, the son of Niceratus.[e] As you are all aware, I imagine, this peace enabled us to deposit seven thousand talents of coined silver on the Acropolis and to acquire over three hundred ships [f] : an annual tribute of more than twelve hundred talents was coming in [g] : we

discontent to a head, and the Archidamian War followed (431–421). See Thucyd. i. 139.

[e] In 421 B.C. It was a Fifty Years' Peace ; but in 420 Athens allied herself with Argos, Elis, and Mantinea, who were aggressively anti-Spartan. By 418 she was at war again.

[f] The MSS. give four hundred. Markland's correction, based on the corresponding passage in Aeschines and Thucydides ii. 13, is now universally accepted.

[g] According to Thucydides (ii. 13) the revenue from tribute at the beginning of the Archidamian War was 600 talents yearly. In 425 there was a re-assessment (known from *I.G.* i². 63) which increased the total annual contribution of the allies to just over 960 talents. There is no good evidence to show that this figure was ever exceeded : and Andocides' 1200 must be treated as an exaggeration.

The mention of a reserve of 7000 talents is suspicious. Athens did, it is true, recover remarkably from the effects of the Archidamian War during the period between 421 and the Sicilian Expedition of 415. But Andocides is here talking of the years 421–419 only. He may be basing his figures on the financial reserve of Athens before the Archidamian War.

Χερρόνησόν τε εἴχομεν καὶ Νάξον καὶ Εὐβοίας
πλέον ἢ τὰ δύο μέρη· τάς τε ἄλλας ἀποικίας καθ'
ἕκαστον διηγεῖσθαι μακρὸς ἂν εἴη λόγος. ταῦτα
δ' ἔχοντες τὰ ἀγαθὰ πάλιν κατέστημεν εἰς πόλεμον πρὸς Λακεδαιμονίους, πεισθέντες καὶ τότε ὑπ'
Ἀργείων.

10 Πρῶτον μὲν οὖν, ὦ Ἀθηναῖοι, τούτου ἀναμνήσθητε, τί ὑμῖν ἐξ ἀρχῆς ὑπεθέμην τῷ λόγῳ.
ἄλλο τι ἢ τοῦτο, ὅτι διὰ τὴν εἰρήνην οὐδεπώποτε
ὁ δῆμος ὁ [τῶν]¹ Ἀθηναίων κατελύθη; οὐκοῦν
ἀποδέδεικται. καὶ οὐδεὶς ἐξελέγξει² με ὡς οὐκ
ἔστι ταῦτα ἀληθῆ. ἤδη δέ τινων ἤκουσα λεγόντων
ὡς ἐκ τῆς τελευταίας εἰρήνης τῆς πρὸς Λακεδαιμονίους οἵ τε τριάκοντα κατέστησαν πολλοί τε
Ἀθηναίων κώνειον πιόντες ἀπέθανον, οἱ δὲ φεύ-
11 γοντες ᾤχοντο. ὁπόσοι οὖν ταῦτα λέγουσιν, οὐκ
ὀρθῶς γιγνώσκουσιν· εἰρήνη γὰρ καὶ σπονδαὶ πολὺ
διαφέρουσι σφῶν αὐτῶν. εἰρήνην μὲν γὰρ ἐξ ἴσου
ποιοῦνται πρὸς ἀλλήλους ὁμολογήσαντες περὶ ὧν
ἂν διαφέρωνται· σπονδὰς δέ, ὅταν κρατήσωσι κατὰ
τὸν πόλεμον, οἱ κρείττους τοῖς ἥττοσιν ἐξ ἐπιταγμάτων ποιοῦνται, ὥσπερ ἡμῶν κρατήσαντες
Λακεδαιμόνιοι τῷ πολέμῳ ἐπέταξαν ἡμῖν καὶ ⟨τὰ⟩³
τείχη καθαιρεῖν καὶ τὰς ναῦς παραδιδόναι καὶ τοὺς
12 φεύγοντας καταδέχεσθαι. τότε μὲν οὖν σπονδαὶ
κατ' ἀνάγκην ἐξ ἐπιταγμάτων ἐγένοντο· νῦν δὲ
[25] περὶ εἰρήνης βουλεύεσθε. σκέψασθε δὲ ἐξ αὐτῶν
τῶν γραμμάτων, ἅ τε ἡμῖν ἐν τῇ στήλῃ γέγραπται,

¹ τῶν del. Spengel.
² ἐξελέγξει Taylor : ἐξελέγχει codd.   ³ τὰ add. Reiske.

ᵃ Argos invaded the territory of Epidaurus in 419, thereby
bringing about an open breach with Sparta. Athens, at the

506

controlled the Chersonese, Naxos, and over two-thirds
of Euboea : while to mention our other settlemenst
abroad individually would be tedious. But in spiet
of all these advantages we went to war with Sparta
afresh, then as now at the instigation of Argos.[a]

Now first of all, gentlemen, call to mind what I
originally said that I was setting out to show. It
was, was it not, that peace has never yet caused the
fall of the Athenian democracy. That has now been
proved against all possible arguments to the contrary.
However, I have heard some people saying before
now that the result of our last peace with Sparta[b]
was the instalment of the Thirty, the death of many
citizens by the hemlock-cup, and the exile of others.
Those who talk in this fashion misapprehend matters.
There is a wide difference between a peace and a
truce. A peace is a settlement of differences between
equals : a truce is the dictation of terms to the conquered by the conquerors after victory in war, exactly
as the Spartans laid down after their victory over us
that we should demolish our walls, surrender our fleet,
and restore our exiles. The agreement made then
was a forced truce upon dictated terms : whereas
to-day you are considering a peace. Why, look at
the actual provisions of the two as they stand recorded ; contrast the conditions of the truce inscribed

instance of Alcibiades, gave Argos her support in virtue of
the alliance of the previous year.

" Then as now at the instigation of Argos," *i.e.* Argive
representatives are again present, while Andocides is speak-
ing, to urge Athens to continue war with Sparta (*cf.* §§ 24 ff.).
This seems more probable than the other possible rendering :
" Once again at the instigation of Argos," referring to the
Athenian alliance with Argos in 462 B.C.

[b] In 404, after Aegospotami.

ἐφ᾽ οἷς τε νῦν ἔξεστι τὴν εἰρήνην ποιεῖσθαι. ἐκεῖ
μὲν γὰρ¹ γέγραπται τὰ τείχη καθαιρεῖν, ἐν δὲ
τοῖσδε ἔξεστιν οἰκοδομεῖν· ναῦς ἐκεῖ μὲν δώδεκα
κεκτῆσθαι, νῦν δ᾽ ὁπόσας ἂν βουλώμεθα· Λῆμνον
δὲ καὶ Ἴμβρον καὶ Σκῦρον τότε μὲν ἔχειν τοὺς
ἔχοντας, νῦν δὲ ἡμετέρας εἶναι· καὶ φεύγοντας νῦν
μὲν οὐκ ἐπάναγκες οὐδένα καταδέχεσθαι, τότε δ᾽
ἐπάναγκες, ἐξ ὧν ὁ δῆμος κατελύθη. τί ταῦτα
ἐκείνοις ὁμολογεῖ; τοσοῦτον οὖν ἔγωγε, ὦ Ἀθηναῖοι, διορίζομαι περὶ τούτων, τὴν μὲν εἰρήνην
σωτηρίαν εἶναι τῷ δήμῳ καὶ δύναμιν, τὸν δὲ
πόλεμον δήμου² κατάλυσιν γίγνεσθαι. περὶ μὲν οὖν
τούτων ταῦτα λέγω.

13 Φασὶ δέ τινες ἀναγκαίως νῦν ἡμῖν ἔχειν πολεμεῖν·
σκεψώμεθα οὖν πρῶτον, ὦ ἄνδρες Ἀθηναῖοι, διὰ
τί καὶ πολεμήσωμεν. οἶμαι γὰρ ἂν πάντας ἀνθρώπους ὁμολογῆσαι διὰ τάδε δεῖν πολεμεῖν, ἢ ἀδικου-
μένους³ ἢ βοηθοῦντας ἀδικουμένοις.⁴ ἡμεῖς τοίνυν
αὐτοί τε ἠδικούμεθα Βοιωτοῖς τε ἀδικουμένοις
ἐβοηθοῦμεν. εἰ τοίνυν ἡμῖν τέ ἐστι τοῦτο παρὰ
Λακεδαιμονίων, τὸ μηκέτι ἀδικεῖσθαι, Βοιωτοῖς
τε δέδοκται ποιεῖσθαι τὴν εἰρήνην ἀφεῖσιν⁵ Ὀρχομενὸν αὐτόνομον, τίνος ἕνεκα πολεμήσωμεν;

14 ἵνα ἡ πόλις ἡμῶν ἐλευθέρα ᾖ; ἀλλὰ τοῦτό γε
αὐτῇ ὑπάρχει. ἀλλ᾽ ὅπως ἡμῖν⁶ τείχη γένηται;
ἔστι καὶ ταῦτα ἐκ τῆς εἰρήνης. ἀλλ᾽ ἵνα τριήρεις

¹ γὰρ om. Q.　　　　² δήμου Schiller : δήπου codd
³ ἀδικουμένους A corr. : ἠδικημένους A pr. : ἀδικοῦντας Q.
⁴ ἀδικουμένοις Q : ἠδικημένοις A.
⁵ ἀφεῖσιν Reiske : ἀφήσειν codd.
⁶ ἡμῖν om. Q.

508

upon the stone [a] with the conditions on which you can make peace to-day. On the stone it is laid down that we shall demolish our walls : whereas under the present terms we can rebuild them. The truce allows us twelve ships : the peace as many as we like. Under the truce Lemnos, Imbros, and Scyros remained in the possession of their occupants : under the peace they are to be ours. Nor is there to-day any obligation upon us to restore our exiles, as there was then, with the fall of the democracy as its consequence. Where is the similarity between the one and the other ? Thus the general conclusion which I reach in the matter is this, gentlemen : peace means safety and power for the democracy, whereas war means its downfall. So much for that aspect of the question.

Now it is argued by some that present circumstances oblige us to continue fighting. Let us begin, then, gentlemen, by considering exactly why we are to fight. Everyone would agree, I think, that war is justified only so long as one is either suffering a wrong oneself or supporting the cause of another who has been wronged. Now we were both suffering a wrong ourselves and also supporting the cause of the Boeotians who had been wronged. If, then, Sparta guarantees that our wrongs shall cease, and if the Boeotians have decided to allow Orchomenus its independence and make peace, why are we to continue fighting ? To free Athens ? She is free already. To be able to build ourselves walls ? The peace gives us that right also. To be allowed to

[a] It was customary to inscribe treaties, etc., upon upright slabs of stone ($\sigma\tau\hat{\eta}\lambda\alpha\iota$). At Athens such $\sigma\tau\hat{\eta}\lambda\alpha\iota$ would stand for the most part on the Acropolis.

ἐξῇ ναυπηγεῖσθαι καὶ τὰς οὔσας ἐπισκευάζειν καὶ
κεκτῆσθαι; καὶ τοῦτο ὑπάρχει· τὰς γὰρ πόλεις
αὐτονόμους αἱ συνθῆκαι ποιοῦσιν. ἀλλ᾽ ὅπως
τὰς νήσους κομισώμεθα, Λῆμνον καὶ Σκῦρον καὶ
Ἴμβρον; οὐκοῦν διαρρήδην γέγραπται ταύτας
15 Ἀθηναίων εἶναι. φέρε, ἀλλὰ Χερρόνησον καὶ τὰς
ἀποικίας καὶ τὰ ἐγκτήματα¹ καὶ τὰ χρέα ἵνα
ἀπολάβωμεν;² ἀλλ᾽ οὔτε βασιλεὺς οὔτε οἱ σύμμαχοι συγχωροῦσιν ἡμῖν, μεθ᾽ ὧν αὐτὰ δεῖ πο-
λεμοῦντας κτήσασθαι. ἀλλὰ νὴ Δία ἕως ἂν
Λακεδαιμονίους καταπολεμήσωμεν καὶ τοὺς συμμάχους αὐτῶν, μέχρι τούτου δεῖ πολεμεῖν; ἀλλ᾽
οὔ μοι δοκοῦμεν³ οὕτω παρεσκευάσθαι. ἐὰν δ᾽
ἄρα κατεργασώμεθα, τί ποτε αὐτοὶ πείσεσθαι
δοκοῦμεν ὑπὸ τῶν βαρβάρων, ὅταν ταῦτα πράξω-
16 μεν; εἰ τοίνυν περὶ τούτου μὲν ἔδει πολεμεῖν,
χρήματα δὲ ὑπῆρχεν ἡμῖν⁴ ἱκανά, τοῖς δὲ σώμασιν
ἦμεν δυνατοί, οὐδὲ οὕτως ἔδει πολεμεῖν. εἰ δὲ
μήτε δι᾽ ὅ τι μήτε ὅτοισι μήτε ἀφ᾽ ὅτου πολεμήσωμεν ἔστι, πῶς οὐκ ἐκ παντὸς τρόπου τὴν εἰρήνην
ποιητέον ἡμῖν;
17 Σκέψασθε δέ, ὦ Ἀθηναῖοι, καὶ τόδε, ὅτι νυνὶ
πᾶσι τοῖς Ἕλλησι κοινὴν εἰρήνην καὶ ἐλευθερίαν
πράττετε, καὶ μετέχειν ἅπασι πάντων ἐξουσίαν
ποιεῖτε. ἐνθυμήθητε οὖν τῶν⁵ πόλεων τὰς μεγίστας,
τίνι τρόπῳ τὸν πόλεμον καταλύονται. πρῶτον
μὲν Λακεδαιμονίους, οἵτινες ἀρχόμενοι μὲν ἡμῖν
καὶ τοῖς συμμάχοις πολεμεῖν ἦρχον καὶ κατὰ γῆν
καὶ κατὰ θάλατταν, νῦν δ᾽ αὐτοῖς ἐκ τῆς εἰρήνης

---

¹ ἐγκτήματα Valckenaer : ἐγκλήματα codd.
² ἀπολάβωμεν Q : ἀπολαύωμεν A.
³ δοκοῦμεν Q : δοκεῖ A.

build new triremes, and refit and keep our old ones ?
That is assured us as well, since the treaty affirms the
independence of each state. To recover the islands,
Lemnos, Scyros, and Imbros ? It is expressly laid
down that these shall belong to Athens. Well then,
is it to get back the Chersonese, our colonies, our
landed property abroad, and the debts owed us ? [a]
A war for their recovery needs the support of the
king of Persia and our allies, and they refuse that
support. Or shall I be told that we must continue
fighting until we have crushed Sparta and her allies ?
We are not adequately equipped, in my opinion, for
a campaign on such a scale ; and if we are successful,
what must we ourselves expect from Persia afterwards ? No, even if this were a justifiable ground
for war, and we had sufficient money and the necessary men, we ought not to continue it. So if we
have no reasons for prolonging the war, no enemy
to fight, and no resources, why should we not make
every effort to secure peace ?

Do not overlook another thing, gentlemen ; you
are negotiating to-day for the peace and independence
of all Greeks alike : you are giving them all the
opportunity of sharing in every advantage. Think
of the circumstances in which the leading powers
are ceasing hostilities. To begin with, take Sparta.
When she first went to war with us and our allies,[b] she
controlled both land and sea ; but the peace is leaving

[a] *i.e.* all that had been lost when the empire collapsed
in 404.

[b] In 395, when Pausanias and Lysander invaded Boeotia.
This began the " Corinthian War."

---

[4] ὑπῆρχεν ἡμῖν A : ὑπῆρχε μὲν Q.   [5] τῶν om. Q.

18 οὐδέτερον τούτων ὑπάρχει. καὶ οὐχ ὑφ᾽ ἡμῶν[1]
ἀναγκαζόμενοι ταῦτ᾽ ἀφιᾶσιν, ἀλλ᾽ ἐπ᾽ ἐλευθερίᾳ
πάσης τῆς Ἑλλάδος. νενικήκασι γὰρ τρὶς ἤδη
μαχόμενοι, τότε μὲν ἐν Κορίνθῳ πάντας πανδημεὶ
τοὺς συμμάχους παρόντας, οὐχ ὑπολιπόντες πρόφασιν οὐδεμίαν, ἀλλ᾽ ἐν τῷ κρατιστεύειν μόνοι
πάντων, αὖθις δ᾽ ἐν Βοιωτοῖς,[2] ὅτ᾽ αὐτῶν Ἀγησί-
λαος ἡγεῖτο, τὸν αὐτὸν τρόπον καὶ τότε[3] τὴν νίκην
ἐποιήσαντο, τρίτον δ᾽ ἡνίκα Λέχαιον ἔλαβον,
Ἀργείους μὲν ἅπαντας καὶ Κορινθίους, ἡμῶν δὲ
19 καὶ Βοιωτῶν τοὺς παρόντας. τοιαῦτα δ᾽ ἔργα
ἐπιδειξάμενοι [τοῖς Ἕλλησι][4] τὴν εἰρήνην εἰσὶν
ἕτοιμοι ποιεῖσθαι τὴν ἑαυτῶν ἔχοντες, οἳ ἐνίκων
μαχόμενοι, καὶ τὰς πόλεις αὐτονόμους εἶναι καὶ
τὴν θάλατταν κοινὴν ἐῶντες τοῖς ἡττημένοις.
καίτοι ποίας τινὸς ἂν ἐκεῖνοι παρ᾽ ἡμῶν εἰρήνης
ἔτυχον, εἰ μίαν μόνον μάχην ἡττήθησαν;
20 Βοιωτοὶ δ᾽ αὖ πῶς τὴν εἰρήνην ποιοῦνται;
οἵτινες τὸν μὲν[5] πόλεμον ἐποιήσαντο ἕνεκα Ὀρχο-
μενοῦ, ὡς οὐκ ἐπιτρέψοντες αὐτόνομον εἶναι, νῦν
[26] δὲ τεθνεώτων μὲν αὐτοῖς ἀνδρῶν τοσούτων τὸ
πλῆθος, τῆς δὲ γῆς ἐκ μέρους τινὸς τετμημένης,

---

[1] ἡμῶν Q : ὑμῶν A.
[2] δ᾽ ἐν Βοιωτοῖς Sauppe : δὲ Βοιωτούς Bekker : δὲ Βοιωτοῖς
codd.   [3] τότε Sluiter : ὅτε codd.
[4] τοῖς Ἕλλησι add. QL.   [5] μὲν om. Q.

---

[a] July 394. The Spartans met the allied forces of Thebes,
Athens, Corinth, and Argos at Nemea, between Corinth and
Sicyon, and heavily defeated them. The battle was fought
before Agesilaus, who had been recalled from Asia Minor,
had reached Greece.

[b] The battle of Coronea, fought a fortnight or so after
Nemea. The allied forces attempted to block the passage
of Agesilaus as he marched southwards through Boeotia on

her mistress of neither. And she is sacrificing this
supremacy, not because we forced her to do so, but
in order to give the whole of Greece its independence.
The Spartans have now won three battles : the first
at Corinth [a] against the full allied forces, who were
left with no excuse for their defeat, save only that
the Spartans, with none to aid them, fought more
bravely than all the rest together ; the second in
Boeotia under Agesilaus,[b] when they once more
gained a similar victory ; and the third at the capture
of Lechaeum,[c] against the full Argive and Corinthian
forces, together with the Athenians and Boeotians
present. But in spite of these amazing successes
they, the victors in the field, are ready for a peace
which will leave them with nothing save their own
territory : they are recognizing the independence
of the Greek states, and they are allowing their
defeated opponents to share the freedom of the
seas. Yet what terms of peace would they have
gained from us, had they met with but a single
defeat ?

Again, what are the conditions under which Boeotia
is making peace ? Boeotia went to war because she
refused to allow Orchomenus its independence.[d]
To-day, after the loss of thousands of lives, after the
devastation of a large part of her territory, after

his homeward journey from Asia Minor. The Spartans were
victorious, but sustained heavy losses ; and Agesilaus was
content to continue his march without halting.

[c] Corinth was now fortified by Long Walls on the Athenian
plan. In 393 Sparta made a determined effort to break
through the fortifications. She succeeded, and seized the
Corinthian port of Lechaeum on the west and Sidus and
Crommyon on the east in spite of strong opposition from the
allied forces.

[d] See Introduction.

χρήματα δ' εἰσενηνοχότες πολλὰ καὶ ἰδίᾳ καὶ
δημοσίᾳ, ὧν στέρονται, πολεμήσαντες δὲ ἔτη
τέτταρα, ὅμως Ὀρχομενὸν ἀφέντες αὐτόνομον τὴν
εἰρήνην ποιοῦνται καὶ ταῦτα[1] μάτην πεπόνθασιν·
ἐξῆν γὰρ αὐτοῖς καὶ τὴν ἀρχὴν ἐῶσιν Ὀρχομενίους
αὐτονόμους εἰρήνην ἄγειν. οὗτοι δ' αὖ τούτῳ ⟨τῷ⟩[2]
τρόπῳ τὸν πόλεμον καταλύονται.

21 Ἡμῖν δέ, ὦ Ἀθηναῖοι, πῶς ἔξεστι τὴν εἰρήνην
ποιήσασθαι; ποίων τινῶν Λακεδαιμονίων τυγχά-
νοντας; καὶ γὰρ εἴ τις ὑμῶν ἀχθεσθήσεται παρ-
αιτοῦμαι· ⟨τὰ⟩[3] γὰρ ὄντα λέξω. πρῶτον μὲν γὰρ
ἡνίκα ἀπωλέσαμεν τὰς ναῦς ἐν Ἑλλησπόντῳ καὶ
τειχήρεις ἐγενόμεθα, τίνα γνώμην ἔθεντο περὶ
ἡμῶν οἱ νῦν μὲν ἡμέτεροι τότε δὲ Λακεδαιμονίων
ὄντες σύμμαχοι; οὐ τὴν πόλιν ἡμῶν ἀνδραποδίζε-
σθαι καὶ τὴν χώραν ἐρημοῦν; οἱ δὲ διακωλύσαντες
ταῦτα μὴ γενέσθαι τίνες ἦσαν; οὐ Λακεδαιμόνιοι,
τοὺς μὲν συμμάχους ἀποτρέψαντες τῆς γνώμης,
αὐτοὶ δ' οὐδ' ἐπιχειρήσαντες διαβουλεύσασθαι περὶ
22 τοιούτων ἔργων; μετὰ δὲ τοῦτο ὅρκους ὀμόσαντες
αὐτοῖς καὶ τὴν στήλην εὑρόμενοι ⟨παρ'⟩[4] αὐτῶν
στῆσαι, κακὸν ἀγαπητὸν ἐν ἐκείνῳ τῷ χρόνῳ,
σπονδὰς ἤγομεν ἐπὶ ῥητοῖς. εἶτα δὲ συμμαχίαν
ποιησάμενοι Βοιωτοὺς καὶ Κορινθίους ἀποστή-
σαντες αὐτῶν, Ἀργείους δὲ ἀγαγόντες εἰς τὴν ποτὲ
φιλίαν, αἴτιοι τῆς ἐν Κορίνθῳ μάχης ἐγενόμεθα
αὐτοῖς. τίνες δὲ βασιλέα πολέμιον αὐτοῖς ἐποίησαν,
καὶ Κόνωνι τὴν ναυμαχίαν παρεσκεύασαν, δι' ἣν

---

[1] ταῦτα om. Q.   [2] τῷ om. AQ, add. apographa.
[3] τὰ add. Ald.   [4] παρ' add. Ald.

heavy public and private expenditure, which is now a dead loss, after four years of fighting, Boeotia is recognizing the independence of Orchomenus and making peace, thereby rendering her sufferings useless, as by acknowledging the independence of Orchomenus at the outset she need never have gone to war at all. Those are the circumstances in which Boeotia is ceasing hostilities.

Now what are the terms available to ourselves, gentlemen ? How is Sparta disposed to us ? Here, if I am about to cause distress to any of you, I ask his forgiveness, as I shall be stating nothing but the facts. To begin with, when we lost our fleet on the Hellespont and were shut within our walls,[a] what did our present allies,[b] who were then on the Spartan side, propose to do with us ? They proposed, did they not, to sell our citizens as slaves and make Attica a waste. And who was it who prevented this ? The Spartans ; they dissuaded the allies, and for their own part refused even to contemplate such measures. Later we gave them our oath, were allowed to erect the column, and accepted a truce upon dictated terms, a hardship which was welcome enough at the time. Nevertheless we then proceeded, by means of an alliance, to detach Boeotia and Corinth from Sparta, and to resume friendly relations with Argos, thereby involving Sparta in the battle of Corinth.[c] Who, again, turned the king of Persia against Sparta ? Who enabled Conon to fight the engagement at sea which lost her her maritime

[a] The siege of Athens, which followed immediately after Aegospotami, lasted from September 405 to April 404.
[b] Notably the Thebans and Corinthians.
[c] i.e. Nemea in 394.

23 ἀπώλεσαν τὴν ἀρχὴν τῆς θαλάττης; ὅμως τοίνυν
ταῦτα πεπονθότες ὑφ' ἡμῶν συγχωροῦσι ταῦτα[1]
ἅπερ οἱ σύμμαχοι, καὶ διδόασιν ἡμῖν τὰ τείχη καὶ
τὰς ναῦς καὶ τὰς νήσους ἡμῶν εἶναι. ποίαν τίν'
οὖν χρὴ εἰρήνην πρεσβεύοντας ἥκειν; οὐ ταῦτα[1]
παρὰ τῶν πολεμίων εὑρομένους ἅπερ οἱ φίλοι
διδόασι, καὶ δι' ἅπερ ἠρξάμεθα πολεμεῖν, ἵνα ἡμῶν
γένηται τῇ πόλει ταῦτα; οἱ μὲν τοίνυν ἄλλοι τὴν
εἰρήνην ποιοῦνται τῶν ὑπαρχόντων ἀφιέντες, ἡμεῖς
δὲ προσλαμβάνοντες αὐτὰ ὧν μάλιστα δεόμεθα.

24 Τί οὖν ἐστιν ὑπόλοιπον περὶ ὅτου δεῖ
βουλεύεσθαι; περὶ Κορίνθου[2] καὶ περὶ ὧν [ἂν][3]
ἡμᾶς Ἀργεῖοι προκαλοῦνται.[4] πρῶτον μὲν
περὶ Κορίνθου διδαξάτω μέ τις, Βοιωτῶν μὴ
συμπολεμούντων, εἰρήνην δὲ ποιουμένων πρὸς
Λακεδαιμονίους, τίνος ἐστὶν ἡμῖν ἀξία Κόρινθος.

25 ἀναμνήσθητε γάρ, ὦ Ἀθηναῖοι, τῆς ἡμέρας ἐκείνης
ὅτε Βοιωτοῖς τὴν συμμαχίαν ἐποιούμεθα, τίνα
γνώμην ἔχοντες ταῦτα ἐπράττομεν. οὐχ ὡς ἱκανὴν
οὖσαν τὴν Βοιωτῶν δύναμιν μεθ' ἡμῶν γενομένην
κοινῇ πάντας ἀνθρώπους ἀμύνασθαι; νῦν δὲ βουλευόμεθα,[5] Βοιωτῶν εἰρήνην ποιουμένων πῶς δυνα-
τοὶ Λακεδαιμονίοις πολεμεῖν ἐσμεν ἄνευ Βοιωτῶν.

26 ναί, φασί τινες, ἂν Κόρινθόν τε φυλάττωμεν καὶ
συμμάχους ἔχωμεν Ἀργείους. ἰόντων[6] δὲ Λακεδαιμονίων εἰς Ἄργος πότερον βοηθήσομεν[7] αὐτοῖς
ἢ οὔ; πολλὴ γὰρ ἀνάγκη ὁπότερον τούτων ἑλέσθαι. μὴ βοηθούντων μὲν οὖν ἡμῶν οὐδὲ λόγος

---

[1] ταῦτα Baiter : ταῦτα codd.
περὶ Κορίνθου add. QL.   [3] ἂν del. Dobree.
[4] προκαλοῦνται apographa : προσκαλοῦνται AQ.
[5] βουλευόμεθα Q : βουλευώμεθα A.

supremacy ? [a] Yet in spite of all that she has suffered
at our hands, she agrees to the same concessions as
those made us by our allies, and offers us our walls,
our fleet, and our islands. What terms of peace do you
expect representatives to bring you back, may I ask ?
Can they do better than obtain the same advantages
from the enemy as our friends are offering us, the
very advantages which we went to war to secure for
Athens ? Whereas others make peace at a loss to
themselves, we gain precisely what we most want.

What, then, remains to be considered ? Corinth,
and the appeal which Argos is making to us. First
as to Corinth. I should like to be informed of the
value of Corinth to us, if Boeotia leaves our ranks and
makes peace with Sparta. Recall the day on which
we concluded our alliance with Boeotia, gentlemen :
recall the assumption on which we acted. We imagined, did we not, that once Boeotia joined forces
with us we could face the whole world. Yet here we
are considering how we can continue fighting Sparta
without her help, now that she is making peace.
" Perfectly well," say some, " provided that we protect Corinth and are allied with Argos." But if
Sparta attacks Argos, shall we go to her help or not ?
For we shall assuredly have no choice but to follow
the one course or the other. Yet should we withhold
our help, we are left without a single argument where-

[a] After Aegospotami Conon, the Athenian admiral, fled
to the court of Evagoras of Salamis in Cyprus. Through his
influence he ultimately won the confidence of the satrap
Pharnabazus. In 397 he was put in charge of the Persian
fleet, and in 394 utterly routed the Spartans under Peisander
off Cnidus.

---

[6] ἰόντων Ald. : ὄντων codd.
[7] βοηθήσομεν A : βοηθήσωμεν Q.

ὑπολείπεται μὴ οὐκ ἀδικεῖν καὶ ποιεῖν Ἀργείους[1]
ὁποῖον ἄν τι βούλωνται δικαίως· βοηθούντων δὲ
ἡμῶν εἰς Ἄργος οὐχ ἕτοιμον μάχεσθαι Λακεδαιμονίοις; ἵνα ἡμῖν τί γένηται; ἵνα ἡττώμενοι μὲν
καὶ τὴν οἰκείαν χώραν ἀπολέσωμεν πρὸς τῇ Κορινθίων, νικήσαντες δὲ τὴν Κορινθίων Ἀργείων
27 ποιήσωμεν.[2] οὐχ ἕνεκα τούτων πολεμήσομεν;[3]

Σκεψώμεθα δὴ καὶ τοὺς Ἀργείων λόγους. κελεύουσι γὰρ ἡμᾶς κοινῇ μετὰ σφῶν καὶ μετὰ
Κορινθίων πολεμεῖν, αὐτοὶ δ᾽ ἰδίᾳ εἰρήνην ποιησάμενοι τὴν χώραν οὐ παρέχουσιν ἐμπολεμεῖν. καὶ
μετὰ μὲν πάντων τῶν συμμάχων τὴν εἰρήνην
ποιουμένους[4] οὐκ ἐῶσιν ἡμᾶς οὐδὲν πιστεύειν
Λακεδαιμονίοις· ἃ δὲ πρὸς τούτους μόνους ἐκεῖνοι
συνέθεντο, ταῦτα δ᾽[5] οὐδεπώποτ᾽ αὐτούς φασι
παραβῆναι. πατρίαν τε εἰρήνην ὀνομάζοντες ᾗ
χρῶνται, τοῖς [δὲ][6] ἄλλοις Ἕλλησιν οὐκ ἐῶσι
[27] πατρίαν γενέσθαι τὴν εἰρήνην· ἐκ γὰρ τοῦ πολέμου
χρονισθέντος Κόρινθον ἑλεῖν προσδοκῶσι, κρατήσαντες δὲ τούτων ὑφ᾽ ὧν ἀεὶ κρατοῦνται, καὶ τοὺς
συννικῶντας ἐλπίζουσι παραστήσεσθαι.[7]

28 Τοιούτων δ᾽ ἐλπίδων μετασχόντας ἡμᾶς δεῖ δυοῖν
θάτερον ἑλέσθαι, ἢ πολεμεῖν μετὰ Ἀργείων Λακεδαιμονίοις, ἢ μετὰ Βοιωτῶν κοινῇ τὴν εἰρήνην
ποιεῖσθαι. ἐγὼ μὲν οὖν ἐκεῖνο δέδοικα μάλιστα,[8]

---

[1] ἀδικεῖν καὶ ποιεῖν Ἀργείους Sluiter : ἀδικεῖν ἀργείους καὶ
ποιεῖν AQ.

[2] ποιήσωμεν apographa : ποιήσομεν AQ.

[3] πολεμήσομεν Ald. : πολεμήσωμεν AQ.

[4] ποιουμένους Reiske : ποιουμένοις codd.

[5] ταῦτα δ᾽ QL : ταῦτ᾽ A.   [6] δὲ del. Reiske.

[7] παραστήσεσθαι Reiske : ἀποστήσεσθαι codd.

[8] μάλιστα om. Q.

with to justify ourselves or to show that Argos has
not the right to act as she pleases. On the other
hand, should we give her our aid, is not a conflict with
Sparta inevitable ? And to what end ? To enable
us to lose our own territory as well as that of Corinth
in the event of defeat, and to secure Corinth for Argos
in the event of victory. Will not that prove to be
our object in fighting ?

Now let us examine the Argive proposals in their
turn. Argos urges us to join Corinth and herself in
maintaining the war ; yet in virtue of a private peace
which she has negotiated,[a] she has withdrawn her
own territory from the field of hostilities. She forbids us to place the least trust in Sparta, although all
our allies are joining us in making peace ; yet she
admits that Sparta's treaty with herself, which was
made without any such support, has been faithfully
observed. Again, Argos calls her own peace traditional, but forbids the other Greeks to secure a
traditional peace for themselves : the reason being
that she expects to annex Corinth by prolonging
the war, and after gaining control of the state which
has always controlled her, she hopes to extend her
influence over her partners in victory as well.

Such are the prospects to which we are committed ; and we have a choice between two alternatives, that of joining Argos in fighting Sparta,
and that of joining Boeotia in making common peace
with her. Now what alarms me above all else,

---

[a] Possibly a reference to the Argive trick of celebrating a
ἱερομηνία, or "sacred month," when Sparta was about to
invade their territory. The ἱερομηνία was taken up with the
festival of the Carneia, and it was traditional among Dorians
that war could not be waged in the course of it. See Xen.
Hell. iv. 7. 2.

ὦ 'Αθηναῖοι, τὸ εἰθισμένον κακόν, ὅτι τοὺς κρείττους φίλους ἀφιέντες ἀεὶ τοὺς ἥττους αἱρούμεθα,
καὶ πόλεμον ποιούμεθα δι' ἑτέρους, ἐξὸν δι' ἡμᾶς
29 αὐτοὺς εἰρήνην ἄγειν· οἵτινες πρῶτον μὲν βασιλεῖ
τῷ μεγάλῳ—χρὴ γὰρ ἀναμνησθέντας τὰ γεγενημένα
καλῶς βουλεύσασθαι—σπονδὰς ποιησάμενοι καὶ
συνθέμενοι φιλίαν εἰς τὸν ἅπαντα χρόνον, ἃ ἡμῖν
ἐπρέσβευσεν Ἐπίλυκος Τεισάνδρου, τῆς μητρὸς τῆς
ἡμετέρας ἀδελφός, ⟨μετὰ⟩[1] ταῦτα Ἀμόργῃ πειθόμενοι τῷ δούλῳ τοῦ βασιλέως καὶ φυγάδι τὴν μὲν
βασιλέως δύναμιν ἀπεβαλόμεθα[2] ὡς οὐδενὸς[3] οὖσαν
ἀξίαν, τὴν δὲ Ἀμόργου φιλίαν εἱλόμεθα, κρείττω
νομίσαντες εἶναι· ἀνθ' ὧν βασιλεὺς ὀργισθεὶς ἡμῖν,
σύμμαχος γενόμενος Λακεδαιμονίοις, παρέσχεν
αὐτοῖς εἰς τὸν πόλεμον πεντακισχίλια τάλαντα,
ἕως κατέλυσεν ἡμῶν τὴν δύναμιν. ἐν μὲν βούλευμα
30 τοιοῦτον ἐβουλευσάμεθα· Συρακόσιοι δ' ὅτε ἦλθον
ἡμῶν δεόμενοι, φιλότητα μὲν ἀντὶ διαφορᾶς
ἐθέλοντες εἰρήνην δ' ἀντὶ πολέμου ποιεῖσθαι, τήν
τε συμμαχίαν ἀποδεικνύντες ὅσῳ κρείττων ἡ
σφετέρα εἴη τῆς[4] Ἐγεσταίων καὶ Καταναίων, εἰ

---

[1] μετὰ add. Reiske.
[2] ἀπεβαλόμεθα A : ἀπεβαλλόμεθα Q.
[3] οὐδενὸς Reiske : οὐδὲν codd.
[4] τῆς Ἐγ. καὶ Κατ. Francke : τῶν Ἐγ. καὶ τῶν Κατ. codd.

---

[a] Epilycus is not mentioned elsewhere. The last formal
peace negotiated between Athens and Persia had been the
Peace of Callias, c. 462-460 B.C. Andocides may have in
mind the deputation which was sent to the Persian Court in
424 (Thucyd. iv. 50).

[b] Amorges was the son of a rebel satrap of Lydia named

gentlemen, is our old, old fault of invariably abandoning powerful friends in preference for weak, and of going to war for the sake of others when, as far as we ourselves are concerned, we could perfectly well remain at peace. Thus—and it is only by calling the past to mind that one can properly determine policy—we began by making a truce with the Great King and establishing a permanent accord with him, thanks to the diplomacy of my mother's brother, Epilycus, the son of Teisander.[a] But later the king's runaway slave, Amorges,[b] induced us to discard the powerful support of his master as worthless. We chose instead what we imagined to be a more advantageous understanding with Amorges himself. The king in his anger replied by allying himself with Sparta,[c] and furnished her with five thousand talents with which to prosecute the war ; nor was he satisfied until he had overthrown our empire. That is one instance of such policy.

Again, an urgent request came to us from Syracuse; she was ready to end our differences by a pact of friendship, to end war by peace and she pointed out the advantages of an alliance with herself, if only we would consent to it, over those of the existing

Pissuthnes. After the recovery of Lydia by Tissaphernes Amorges took refuge in Caria. He was given shelter by Iasus, a member of the Athenian Confederacy. Iasus was stormed by the Spartans in 412 on the instigation of Tissaphernes, and Amorges was handed over to the Persians (Thucyd. viii. 5, 5).

[c] In 413. The sum mentioned is an exaggeration. From 413 to 407 Tissaphernes made it a point of policy to withhold subsidies from the Spartans as far as possible in order to prolong the war and weaken both combatants. In 407 he was superseded by Cyrus, who brought with him 500 talents for the improvement of the Spartan navy.

ANDOCIDES

βουλοίμεθα¹ πρὸς αὐτοὺς ποιεῖσθαι, ἡμεῖς τοίνυν
εἱλόμεθα καὶ τότε πόλεμον μὲν ἀντὶ εἰρήνης,
Ἐγεσταίους δὲ ἀντὶ Συρακοσίων, στρατεύεσθαι
δ' εἰς Σικελίαν ἀντὶ τοῦ μένοντες οἴκοι συμμάχους
ἔχειν Συρακοσίους· ἐξ ὧν πολλοὺς μὲν Ἀθηναίων
ἀπολέσαντες ἀριστίνδην καὶ τῶν συμμάχων, πολλὰς
δὲ ναῦς καὶ χρήματα καὶ δύναμιν ἀποβαλόντες,
αἰσχρῶς διεκομίσθησαν οἱ σωθέντες αὐτῶν.

31 Ὕστερον δ' ὑπ' Ἀργείων ἐπείσθημεν, οἵπερ νῦν
ἥκουσι πείθοντες² πολεμεῖν, πλεύσαντες ἐπὶ τὴν
Λακωνικὴν εἰρήνης ἡμῖν οὔσης πρὸς Λακεδαιμονίους ἐντεῖναι³ ⟨ἐκείνων⟩ τὸν θυμόν, ἀρχὴν πολλῶν
κακῶν· ἐξ οὗ πολεμήσαντες ἠναγκάσθημεν τὰ
τείχη κατασκάπτειν καὶ τὰς ναῦς παραδιδόναι
καὶ τοὺς φεύγοντας καταδέχεσθαι. ταῦτα δὲ πα-
σχόντων ἡμῶν οἱ πείσαντες ἡμᾶς πολεμεῖν Ἀργεῖοι
τίνα ὠφέλειαν παρέσχον ἡμῖν; τίνα δὲ κίνδυνον
ὑπὲρ [τῶν]⁴ Ἀθηναίων ἐποιήσαντο;

32 Νῦν οὖν τοῦτο ὑπόλοιπόν ἐστιν ἡμῖν,⁵ πόλεμον μὲν⁵
ἑλέσθαι καὶ νῦν ἀντ' εἰρήνης, τὴν δὲ συμμαχίαν τὴν
Ἀργείων ἀντὶ τῆς Βοιωτῶν, Κορινθίων δὲ τοὺς νῦν
ἔχοντας τὴν πόλιν ἀντὶ Λακεδαιμονίων. μὴ δῆτα,
ὦ Ἀθηναῖοι, μηδεὶς ἡμᾶς ταῦτα πείσῃ⁶· τὰ γὰρ
παραδείγματα τὰ γεγενημένα τῶν ἁμαρτημάτων
ἱκανὰ τοῖς σώφροσι τῶν ἀνθρώπων ὥστε μηκέτι
ἁμαρτάνειν.

---

¹ βουλοίμεθα Reiske: βουλόμεθα codd.
² ἥκουσι πείθοντες A: ἥκοντες πείθουσι Q.
³ ἐντεῖναι ⟨ἐκείνων⟩ scripsi: ἐντεῖναι ⟨αὐτῶν⟩ Lipsius: ἐκτεῖναι codd. ΄τῶν del. Pertz.
⁵ Verba ἡμῖν, μὲν om. Q. πείσῃ A: πείσει Q.

522

alliance with Segesta and Catana.[a] But once more we chose war instead of peace, Segesta instead of Syracuse ; instead of staying at home as the allies of Syracuse, we chose to send an armament to Sicily. The result was the loss of a large part of the Athenian and allied forces, the bravest being the first to fall : a reckless waste of ships, money, and resources : and the return of the survivors in disgrace.

Later,[b] the same Argives who are here to-day to persuade us to continue the war, induced us to arouse Sparta's anger by making a naval descent upon Laconia while at peace with her, an act which was responsible for endless disasters ; from it sprang a war which ended with our being forced to demolish our walls, to surrender our fleet, and to restore our exiles. Yet what help did we receive in our misfortunes from Argos who had drawn us into the war ? What danger did she brave for Athens ?

To-day, then, it remains for us to choose war instead of peace once again, the Argive instead of the Boeotian alliance, the present masters of Corinth instead of Sparta. Gentlemen, I trust that no one will induce us to choose such a course. The examples furnished by our past mistakes are enough to prevent men of sense from repeating them.

[a] Athens had formed an alliance with Segesta as early as 453 (*I.G.* i². 19-20). It was renewed in 424 by Laches. In 416 Segesta found herself ranged against the combined forces of Selinus and Syracuse. She appealed to Athens for help, and the disastrous Syracusan expedition resulted.

[b] Actually in 419. Andocides is thinking of Alcibiades' descent on Epidaurus in support of the Argives, who had already invaded her territory by land. The expedition was made in virtue of the alliance of the previous year between Athens, Argos, Elis, and Mantinea.

33 Εἰσὶ δέ τινες ὑμῶν[1] οἳ τοσαύτην ὑπερβολὴν τῆς
ἐπιθυμίας ἔχουσιν εἰρήνην ὡς τάχιστα γενέσθαι·
φασὶ γὰρ καὶ τὰς τετταράκονθ᾽ ἡμέρας ἐν αἷς
ὑμῖν[2] ἔξεστι βουλεύεσθαι περίεργον εἶναι, καὶ τοῦτο ἀδικεῖν ἡμᾶς· αὐτοκράτορας γὰρ πεμφθῆναι εἰς
Λακεδαίμονα διὰ ταῦθ᾽,[3] ἵνα μὴ πάλιν ἐπανα-
φέρωμεν. τήν τε ἀσφάλειαν ἡμῶν τῆς ἐπαναφορᾶς
δέος ὀνομάζουσι, λέγοντες ὡς οὐδεὶς πώποτε τὸν
δῆμον τὸν[4] Ἀθηναίων ἐκ τοῦ φανεροῦ πείσας
ἔσωσεν, ἀλλὰ δεῖ λαθόντας ἢ ἐξαπατήσαντας αὐτὸν
εὖ ποιῆσαι.

34 Τὸν λόγον οὖν τοῦτον οὐκ ἐπαινῶ. φημὶ γάρ, ὦ
Ἀθηναῖοι, πολέμου μὲν ὄντος ἄνδρα στρατηγὸν τῇ
πόλει τε εὔνουν εἰδότα τε ὅ τι πράττῃ,[5] λανθάνοντα
δεῖν τοὺς πολλοὺς τῶν ἀνθρώπων καὶ ἐξαπατῶντα
ἄγειν ἐπὶ[6] τοὺς κινδύνους, εἰρήνης δὲ πέρι πρεσβεύοντας[7] κοινῆς τοῖς Ἕλλησιν, ἐφ᾽ οἷς ὅρκοι τε
ὀμοσθήσονται στῆλαί τε σταθήσονται γεγραμμέναι,
ταῦτα δὲ οὔτε λαθεῖν οὔτε ἐξαπατῆσαι δεῖν, ἀλλὰ
πολὺ μᾶλλον ἐπαινεῖν ἢ ψέγειν, εἰ πεμφθέντες
[28] αὐτοκράτορες ἔτι[8] ἀποδώσομεν ὑμῖν[9] περὶ αὐτῶν[10]
σκέψασθαι. βουλεύσασθαι μὲν οὖν ἀσφαλῶς[11] χρὴ
κατὰ δύναμιν, οἷς δ᾽ ἂν ὀμόσωμεν καὶ συνθώμεθα,
τούτοις ἐμμένειν.

35 Οὐ γὰρ μόνον, ὦ Ἀθηναῖοι, πρὸς γράμματα τὰ
γεγραμμένα δεῖ βλέποντας πρεσβεύειν ἡμᾶς, ἀλλὰ
καὶ πρὸς τοὺς τρόπους τοὺς ὑμετέρους. ὑμεῖς γὰρ
περὶ μὲν τῶν ἑτοίμων ὑμῖν ὑπονοεῖν εἰώθατε καὶ

---

¹ ὑμῶν A : ἡμῶν Q.   ² ὑμῖν Bekker : ἡμῖν codd.
          ³ ταῦθ᾽ Reiske : ταύτην codd.
          ⁴ τὸν Spengel : τῶν codd.
          ⁵ πράττῃ Yдén : πράττοι codd.
⁶ ἐπὶ A : παρὰ Q.   ⁷ πρεσβεύοντας A : πρεσβεύοντα Q.

A number of you are extremely anxious to see peace concluded as quickly as possible. In fact, according to those in question, the forty days allowed you for consideration are a waste of time and a concession which we delegates have done wrong to obtain, as the one object of our being sent to Sparta with full powers was to avoid any further reference of the matter to the Assembly. Our desire to secure our position by such a reference they call nervousness, since no one, they argue, has ever yet saved the Athenian people by open persuasion : measures for its good must be secret or disguised.

Now I cannot praise this reasoning. I admit, gentlemen, that in time of war a patriotic and experienced general should employ secrecy or deception in leading the majority of men into danger ; but when a peace to include the entire nation is being negotiated, an agreement to which sworn assent will be given and which will be recorded on public monuments, I deny that the negotiators should practise secrecy or deception. I maintain that we deserve praise much more than blame, if, in spite of our full powers of discretion, we still refer the question to you for consideration. Decisions should be reached with all the caution possible ; then, once we have made our sworn compact, we should abide by it.

As delegates, we must be guided not only by your written instructions, but by your character, gentlemen. You have a way of suspecting and being dissatisfied with a thing if you can have it : while if

---

[8] ἔτι Reiske : τι codd.
[9] ὑμῖν apogr. : ἡμῖν AQ.
[10] περὶ αὑτῶν A : περὶ τῶν αὑτῶν Q.
[11] ἀσφαλῶς om. Q.

δυσχεραίνειν, τὰ δ' οὐκ ὄντα λογοποιεῖν ὡς ἔστιν
ὑμῖν ἕτοιμα· κἂν μὲν πολεμεῖν δέῃ, τῆς εἰρήνης
ἐπιθυμεῖτε, ἐὰν δέ τις ὑμῖν[1] τὴν εἰρήνην πράττῃ,
λογίζεσθε τὸν πόλεμον ὅσα ἀγαθὰ ὑμῖν κατ-
36 ηργάσατο. ὅπου καὶ νῦν ἤδη τινὲς λέγουσιν οὐ
γιγνώσκειν τὰς διαλλαγὰς αἵτινές εἰσιν, τείχη καὶ
νῆες εἰ γενήσονται τῇ πόλει· τὰ γὰρ ἴδια τὰ σφέτερ'
αὐτῶν ἐκ τῆς ὑπερορίας οὐκ ἀπολαμβάνειν, ἀπὸ δὲ
τῶν τειχῶν οὐκ εἶναι σφίσι τροφήν. ἀναγκαίως
οὖν ἔχει καὶ πρὸς ταῦτ' ἀντειπεῖν.

37 Ἦν γάρ ποτε χρόνος, ὦ Ἀθηναῖοι, ὅτε τείχη
καὶ ναῦς οὐκ ἐκεκτήμεθα[2]· γενομένων δὲ τούτων
τὴν ἀρχὴν ἐποιησάμεθα τῶν ἀγαθῶν. ὧν εἰ καὶ
νῦν ἐπιθυμεῖτε, ταῦτα κατεργάσασθε. ταύτην δὲ
λαβόντες ἀφορμὴν οἱ πατέρες ἡμῶν κατηργάσαντο
τῇ πόλει δύναμιν τοσαύτην ὅσην οὔπω τις ἄλλη
πόλις ἐκτήσατο, τὰ μὲν πείσαντες τοὺς Ἕλληνας,
τὰ δὲ λαθόντες, τὰ δὲ πριάμενοι, τὰ δὲ βιασάμενοι.

38 πείσαντες μὲν οὖν Ἀθήνησι ποιήσασθαι τῶν κοινῶν χρημάτων Ἑλληνοταμίας, καὶ τὸν σύλλογον
τῶν νεῶν παρ' ἡμῖν γενέσθαι, ὅσαι δὲ τῶν πόλεων
τριήρεις μὴ κέκτηνται, ταύταις ἡμᾶς παρέχειν·
λαθόντες δὲ Πελοποννησίους τειχισάμενοι[3] τὰ τεί-
χη· πριάμενοι δὲ παρὰ Λακεδαιμονίων μὴ δοῦναι
τούτων δίκην· βιασάμενοι δὲ τοὺς ἐναντίους τὴν
ἀρχὴν τῶν Ἑλλήνων κατηργασάμεθα. καὶ ταῦτα
τὰ ἀγαθὰ ἐν ὀγδοήκοντα καὶ πέντε ἡμῖν ἔτεσιν

[1] ὑμῖν Q : ἡμῖν A.
[2] ἐκεκτήμεθα Hirschig : ἐκτήμεθα Bekker : κεκτήμεθα AQ.
[3] τειχισάμενοι Emperius : ἐτειχίσαμεν codd.

---

[a] According to Thucydides (i. 96) the Hellenotamiae were
Athenian officials from the very start. But the evidence of

there is anything which you have not, you airily talk
as though it lay ready to your hand. If it is your
duty to go to war, you want peace ; if peace is
arranged for you, you count up the benefits which
war has brought you. Thus there are those who are
already complaining that they cannot see the meaning of the treaty, if it is walls and ships which Athens
is to recover. They are not recovering their own
private property from abroad : and walls cannot feed
them. This objection also requires an answer.

There was once a time, gentlemen, when we had
no walls or fleet : but it was when we acquired them
that our prosperity began. If you have a similar
desire for prosperity to-day, then make sure of your
walls and your ships. It was with them that our forefathers started ; and, partly by persuasion, partly by
stealth, partly by bribery, and partly by force, they
won for Athens a greater empire than any other state
has ever gained. Persuasion we used in arranging
that Hellenotamiae should be appointed at Athens to
control the joint funds,ᵃ that the allied fleet should
assemble in our own harbour, and that such states as
possessed no ships should be supplied with them by
us : stealth in building our walls unknown to the
Peloponnesians ᵇ : bribery in purchasing Sparta's
acquiescence : and force in crushing our enemies ;
thus it was that we built up an empire over the whole
nation. All these successes were achieved in eighty-

the Quota-lists rather indicates that the office first became
purely Athenian in 454, after the transference of the treasury
of the League from Delos to Athens.

ᵇ Apparently a reference to the famous trick of Themistocles when rebuilding the walls of Athens in the winter of
479 (Thucyd. i. 90). Thucydides, however, does not suggest
that there was any danger of war from Sparta in consequence.

39 ἐγένετο. κρατηθέντες δὲ τῷ πολέμῳ τά τε ἄλλα[1]
ἀπωλέσαμεν, καὶ τὰ τείχη καὶ τὰς ναῦς ἔλαβον
ἡμῶν ἐνέχυρα Λακεδαιμόνιοι, τὰς[2] μὲν παραλαβόντες, τὰ δὲ καθελόντες, ὅπως μὴ πάλιν ταύτην[3]
ἔχοντες ἀφορμὴν δύναμιν τῇ πόλει κατασκευά-
σαιμεν. πεισθέντες τοίνυν ὑφ' ἡμῶν Λακεδαιμόνιοι
πάρεισι νυνὶ πρέσβεις αὐτοκράτορες, τά τε ἐνέχυρα
ἡμῖν ἀποδιδόντες, καὶ τὰ τείχη καὶ ⟨τὰς⟩[4] ναῦς
ἐῶντες κεκτῆσθαι, τάς τε νήσους ἡμετέρας εἶναι.

40 Τὴν αὐτὴν τοίνυν ἀρχὴν ἀγαθῶν λαμβάνοντας
ἥνπερ ἡμῶν ἐλάμβανον οἱ πρόγονοι, ταύτην οὐκ
ἀκτέον φασὶ τὴν εἰρήνην τινὲς εἶναι. παριόντες
οὖν αὐτοὶ διδασκόντων ὑμᾶς[5]—ἐξουσίαν δ' αὐτοῖς
ἡμεῖς ἐποιήσαμεν, προσθέντες τετταράκοντα ἡμέρας
βουλεύσασθαι—τοῦτο μὲν τῶν γεγραμμένων εἴ τι[6]
τυγχάνει μὴ καλῶς ἔχον· ἔξεστι γὰρ ἀφελεῖν· τοῦτο
δ' εἴ τίς ⟨τι⟩[7] προσθεῖναι βούλεται, πείσας ὑμᾶς[8]
προσγραψάτω. πᾶσί τε τοῖς γεγραμμένοις χρω-

41 μένοις ἔστιν εἰρήνην ἄγειν. εἰ δὲ μηδὲν ἀρέσκει
τούτων, πολεμεῖν ἕτοιμον. καὶ ταῦτ' ἐφ' ὑμῖν[9]
πάντ' ἐστίν, ὦ Ἀθηναῖοι· τούτων ὅ τι ἂν βούλησθε
ἕλεσθε.[10] πάρεισι μὲν γὰρ Ἀργεῖοι καὶ Κορίνθιοι
διδάξοντες ὡς ἄμεινόν ἐστι πολεμεῖν, ἥκουσι δὲ
Λακεδαιμόνιοι πείσοντες ὑμᾶς εἰρήνην ποιήσασθαι.
τούτων δ' ἐστὶ τὸ τέλος παρ' ὑμῖν, ἀλλ' οὐκ ἐν
Λακεδαιμονίοις, δι' ἡμᾶς.[11] πρεσβευτὰς οὖν πάντας

---

[1] ἄλλα A : ἄλλα πάντα QL.
[2] τὰς Reiske : τὰ codd.
[3] ταύτην Hirschig ex § 37. 2 : ταῦτ' codd.
[4] τὰς add. Fuhr, coll. § 23. 3.
[5] ὑμᾶς Q : ἡμᾶς A.

five years.[a] Then came defeat ; and not only did we lose our empire : our walls and our fleet were also seized as securities by Sparta. The fleet she confiscated, and the walls she demolished, to prevent our using them as the foundations of a fresh Athenian dominion. Thanks to the efforts of us delegates, representatives have to-day come from Sparta with full powers, offering to restore those securities to us, to concede us our walls and our fleet, and to recognize the islands as ours.

Now although we hold the very same key to prosperity as our forefathers, it is maintained by some that we must not acquiesce in this peace. Let such critics come forward in person, then,—we have ourselves made it possible for them to do so by securing a further forty days for discussion—and let them tell you on the one hand whether any of the clauses drafted is undesirable : if it is, it can be excised ; on the other hand, if anyone wishes to make any additions, let him gain your approval and make them. If you accept all the clauses drafted, you can live in peace. If you are satisfied with none of them, war is inevitable. The decision rests entirely with you, gentlemen ; make your choice. Argives and Corinthians are here to show you that war is preferable : while Spartans have come to gain your consent to a peace. The final word in the matter rests with you instead of with Sparta—thanks to us. Thus we

---

[a] *i.e.* between 490 and 405, Marathon and Aegospotami.

---

[6] εἴ τι Ald. : ἔτι codd.

[7] τι add. Blass.　　　　　　[8] ὑμᾶς Q : ἡμᾶς A.

[9] ὑμῖν Q : ἡμῖν A.

[10] ἕλεσθε vulg. : ἑλέσθαι codd.

[11] δι' ἡμᾶς Q : δι' ὑμᾶς A.

ὑμᾶς ἡμεῖς οἱ πρέσβεις ποιοῦμεν· ὁ γὰρ τὴν χεῖρα
μέλλων ὑμῶν[1] αἴρειν, οὗτος ὁ πρεσβεύων ἐστίν,
ὁπότερ' ἂν αὑτῷ δοκῇ, καὶ τὴν εἰρήνην καὶ τὸν
πόλεμον ποιεῖν. μέμνησθε μὲν οὖν, ὦ Ἀθηναῖοι,
τοὺς ἡμετέρους λόγους, ψηφίσασθε δὲ τοιαῦτα ἐξ
ὧν ὑμῖν[2] μηδέποτε μεταμελήσει.

[1] ὑμῶν A: ἡμῶν Q. [2] ὑμῖν A: ἡμῖν Q.

delegates are making delegates of you all ; every man of you who is about to raise his hand to vote is a delegate whose business is peace and war, no matter which he prefers. So bear in mind all that I have said, gentlemen : and vote for that alternative which will never cause you regrets.

IV

AGAINST ALCIBIADES

INTRODUCTION

THIS is a speech which is curiously different from the other three attributed to Andocides. It is an attack upon Alcibiades, consisting partly of political criticism, partly of personal abuse; and the occasion is an extraordinary meeting of the Athenian Assembly, held for the purpose of easing the political tension of the moment by the ostracism of one of three men, Nicias, Alcibiades, and the speaker.

Even in antiquity doubts were felt and expressed about the authorship of the *In Alcibiadem*; and it is now universally recognized that Andocides himself cannot have written it. To take only one objection, if we suppose for the moment that the speech was actually delivered, it must have been delivered before 415 B.C., when Nicias and Alcibiades sailed for Sicily; and at that time Andocides was a young man in his early twenties. Yet the writer states that he has had a distinguished public career, serving on no less than six official deputations to states in western Greece and Sicily. This cannot have been true of Andocides. Apart from the fact that he would have been far too young to discharge public duties of this kind, he says not a word of them in those passages of the *Return* and the *Mysteries* where he is giving as detailed an account as he can of the services which he has rendered Athens in the past.

AGAINST ALCIBIADES

But even if someone other than Andocides is the author, it is impossible to believe that the speech was ever delivered before the Assembly. As the speaker himself points out in his opening remarks, the procedure in a case of ostracism differed from that in a court of law. There were no speeches for the prosecution and none for the defence, because there was no question of voting upon the guilt or innocence of a given individual. In theory the Demos had recourse to an ὀστρακοφορία when it was felt that the political influence of party-leaders was becoming excessive and that Athens would be better without one or other of them ; and, although in practice it was doubtless well known beforehand upon whom the blow was likely to fall, it was open to the voters to write upon their potsherds the name of any citizen whatsoever, if they considered that his removal would be of advantage to the community. It is therefore all the more strange that the writer of the *In Alcibiadem*, who has some acquaintance with the purpose of ostracism and the procedure followed at an ὀστρακοφορία, should proceed to compose an elaborate attack upon a particular individual, or, indeed, that he should state in so many words that the judgement of the Demos is to be given against one of three persons, Nicias, Alcibiades, and himself.

It seems, then, that the speech is not the work of Andocides, and that it was not delivered before the Assembly on the occasion of an ὀστρακοφορία which was to decide whether Nicias, Alcibiades, or the writer himself most deserved exile. It has, indeed, been suggested that the *In Alcibiadem* was composed for delivery at the preliminary meeting of the

Assembly at which the people were asked whether they desired to resort to ostracism that year. But it is impossible to accept such a solution of the difficulty. The whole tone of the speech itself makes against it —the author assumes throughout that his audience are on the point of voting as between Nicias, Alcibiades, and himself—; and, furthermore, we have no evidence that such an attack would have been permitted even at the preliminary meeting, where proceedings were confined to the purely general question : " Shall an ὀστρακοφορία be held ? "

We cannot, however, dismiss the circumstances presupposed by the speech as entirely unhistorical. The political situation is clearly intended to be that of the year 417, when an ὀστρακοφορία was held to decide between the two rivals, Alcibiades and Nicias. Alcibiades had gained prominence in 420 by his tireless advocacy of an anti-Spartan policy in the Peloponnese, and it was largely through his efforts that the Quadruple Alliance between Athens, Argos, Elis, and Mantinea was formed, ostensibly for defensive purposes, but in reality as a means of bringing the North Peloponnese under Athenian influence and prosecuting the war with Sparta on her own ground. In 418, however, Alcibiades temporarily lost his hold upon the Assembly, and was not re-elected to the Strategia. Nicias, who was thoroughly opposed to any policy which would lead to a fresh outbreak of hostilities with Sparta, seized the opportunity to undo what he could of Alcibiades' work ; Athens became dilatory in her support of her allies, with the result that Sparta won a decisive victory at Mantinea (418), and the Quadruple Alliance came to an end. Political feeling ran high

AGAINST ALCIBIADES

at Athens in consequence ; and the demagogue
Hyperbolus thought the moment an excellent one
for removing one or other of the two men who stood
in the way of his own supremacy. At his instigation
it was decided to hold an ὀστρακοφορία. But Alcibiades
was too clever for him. By arranging a truce with
Nicias and combining the latter's following with his
own, he succeeded in bringing about the ostracism
of Hyperbolus himself (spring, 417).

Our chief source of information for the intrigues
which led to the ostracism of Hyperbolus is Plutarch,
who mentions the affair more than once. On two
occasions he speaks only of Nicias, Alcibiades, and
Hyperbolus. But in the *Life of Alcibiades* [a] he refers
also to a certain Phaeax. His words are as follows :
ἀγῶνα δ' εἶχε [*i.e.* Alcibiades] πρός τε Φαίακα τὸν
Ἐρασιστράτου καὶ Νικίαν τὸν Νικηράτου . . . ἐπεὶ δὲ
δῆλον ἦν ὅτι ἑνὶ τῶν τριῶν τὸ ὄστρακον ἐποίσουσι,
συνήγαγε τὰς στάσεις εἰς ταὐτὸν ὁ Ἀλκιβιάδης καὶ
διαλεχθεὶς πρὸς τὸν Νικίαν κατὰ τοῦ Ὑπερβόλου τὴν
ὀστρακοφορίαν ἔτρεψεν. Phaeax would thus seem to
be the leader of a third political party, and himself
in danger of ostracism. We know something of him
from Aristophanes and Thucydides. He had been
sent as Athenian representative to Sicily in 425, he
had at least once been on trial for his life, and his
politics were conservative enough to satisfy Aristophanes, who criticizes him with some geniality in the
Knights. [b] From Eupolis we learn further that he was
too conversational to make a good orator. [c] As to his
relations with Nicias and Alcibiades we cannot be

[a] *Alc.* 13.
[b] 1375 ff.
[c] λαλεῖν ἄριστος, ἀδυνατώτατος λέγειν. Kock, fr. 7.

537

completely certain ; but it has been argued plausibly enough from the words of Plutarch and the other references to him that his sympathies were with Nicias, who may well have tried to use him as a shield when threatened with ostracism. Phaeax himself would thus be exposed to the danger of exile ; but this would be averted by the coalition effected by Alcibiades.

Clearly Phaeax bears a strong resemblance to the speaker who delivers the present attack upon Alcibiades ; and there is evidence that the ancients themselves were struck by it. Plutarch at least appears to have held that the *In Alcibiadem* was the work of Phaeax, if we are to accept Xylander's correction of the words λόγος τις κατ᾽ Ἀλκιβιάδου καὶ Φαίακος γεγραμμένος in the *Alcibiades* to ὑπὸ Φ. γεγραμμένος; and some such correction is certainly necessary. But in spite of the fact that the speaker in the *In Alcibiadem* and Phaeax had both represented Athens in Sicily, had both been on trial for their lives, and were both involved in the political struggle between Nicias and Alcibiades in 417, we cannot go so far as to maintain that we have here a speech written and delivered by Phaeax in that year. In the first place, as we have seen, it is highly improbable that the speech was ever delivered ; in the second, the reference in § 22 to the capture of Melos proves that it must have been written after 416. The most likely explanation is that it is a literary exercise, written long enough after the final disappearance of ostracism for the author to be uncertain of the procedure followed at an ὀστρακοφορία, but written in the character of Phaeax. Blass would assign it on grounds of style to the early fourth century, when literary forgeries of this kind were common enough, if we are to believe Isocrates. As parallels we have the two spurious speeches included in our MSS. of Lysias, which also belong to the first ten years of the fourth century and which are also concerned with Alcibiades.

          Betters. He has never been convicted,
          and therefore his integrity is sufficiently
          proved.
§§ 10-13. The public conduct of Alcibiades. He has
          attacked the subject-states of the Empire
          in doubling their tribute, and has in
          addition been guilty of embezzlement.
§§ 14-33. The private conduct of Alcibiades.
          (1) §§ 14-15. His marriage and divorce.
          (2) §§ 16-17. Agatharchus the painter.
          (5) §§ 22-23. His treatment of Diomedes
                         at Olympia.

ANALYSIS

[ΑΝΔΟΚΙΔΟΥ]
ΚΑΤΑ ΑΛΚΙΒΙΑΔΟΥ

[29]   Οὐκ ἐν τῷ παρόντι μόνον γιγνώσκω τῶν πο-
λιτικῶν πραγμάτων ὡς σφαλερόν ἐστιν ἅπτεσθαι,
ἀλλὰ καὶ πρότερον χαλεπὸν ἡγούμην, πρὶν τῶν
κοινῶν ἐπιμελεῖσθαί τινος. πολίτου δὲ ἀγαθοῦ
νομίζω[1] προκινδυνεύειν ἐθέλειν τοῦ πλήθους, καὶ μὴ
καταδείσαντα τὰς ἔχθρας τὰς ἰδίας ὑπὲρ τῶν
δημοσίων ἔχειν ἡσυχίαν· διὰ μὲν γὰρ τοὺς τῶν
ἰδίων ἐπιμελουμένους οὐδὲν αἱ πόλεις μείζους καθίστανται, διὰ δὲ τοὺς τῶν κοινῶν μεγάλαι καὶ
2 ἐλεύθεραι γίγνονται. ὧν [τῶν ἀγαθῶν][2] εἷς ἐγὼ
βουληθεὶς ἐξετάζεσθαι μεγίστοις περιπέπτωκα[3]
κινδύνοις, προθύμως μὲν καὶ ἀγαθῶν ἀνδρῶν ὑμῶν
τυγχάνων, δι' ὅπερ σῴζομαι, πλείστοις δὲ καὶ
δεινοτάτοις ἐχθροῖς χρώμενος, ὑφ' ὧν διαβάλλομαι.
ὁ μὲν οὖν ἀγὼν ὁ παρὼν οὐ στεφανηφόρος, ἀλλ' εἰ
χρὴ μηδὲν ἀδικήσαντα τὴν πόλιν δέκα ἔτη φεύγειν·
οἱ δ' ἀνταγωνιζόμενοι περὶ τῶν ἄθλων τούτων
ἐσμὲν ἐγὼ καὶ Ἀλκιβιάδης καὶ Νικίας, ὧν ἀναγκαῖον ἕνα τῇ συμφορᾷ περιπεσεῖν.

---

¹ νομίζω om. Q.   ² τῶν ἀγαθῶν del. Valckenaer.
³ περιπέπτωκα Α : περιπίπτω Q.

AGAINST ALCIBIADES

THIS is not the first occasion upon which the perils
of engaging in politics have come home to me ; I
regarded it as no less hazardous in the past, before I
had concerned myself in any way with affairs of state.
Yet I consider it the duty of the good citizen, not to
withhold himself from public life for fear of making
personal enemies, but to be ready to face danger for
the benefit of the community. Those who think only
of themselves contribute nothing to a state's advance-
ment ; it is to those who think of the state that its
greatness and its independence are due. I myself
desired to be included in this number : and consequently I now find myself in the utmost peril. True,
in yourselves I have an audience actively devoted to
the public good, and that circumstance makes for
my salvation ; but I have innumerable enemies of
the most dangerous kind, and by them I am being
misrepresented. Nor is the contest in which I am
engaged for the winning of a crown ; it is to decide
whether one who has done the state no wrong is to
spend ten years in exile. The competitors for that
prize are Alcibiades, Nicias, and myself. Upon one
of us the blow must fall.

543

3 Ἄξιον δὲ μέμψασθαι τὸν θέντα τὸν νόμον, ὃς
ἐναντία τῷ ὅρκῳ τοῦ δήμου καὶ τῆς βουλῆς ἐνο-
μοθέτησεν· ἐκεῖ μὲν γὰρ ὄμνυτε μηδένα μήτε
ἐξελᾶν μήτε δήσειν μήτε ἀποκτενεῖν¹ ἄκριτον, ἐν
δὲ τῷδε τῷ καιρῷ οὔτε κατηγορίας γενομένης οὔτε
ἀπολογίας ἀποδοθείσης [οὔτε]² διαψηφισαμένων
κρύβδην τὸν ὀστρακισθέντα τοσοῦτον χρόνον δεῖ
4 στερηθῆναι τῆς πόλεως. εἶτα ἐν τοῖς τοιούτοις οἱ
τοὺς ἑταίρους καὶ συνωμότας κεκτημένοι πλέον
φέρονται τῶν ἄλλων· οὐ γὰρ ὥσπερ ἐν τοῖς δικαστηρίοις οἱ λαχόντες κρίνουσιν, ἀλλὰ τούτου τοῦ
πράγματος ἅπασιν Ἀθηναίοις μέτεστι. πρὸς δὲ
τούτοις τῷ μὲν ἐλλείπειν τῷ δ' ὑπερβάλλειν ὁ
νόμος μοι³ δοκεῖ· τῶν μὲν γὰρ ἰδίων ἀδικημάτων
μεγάλην τιμωρίαν ταύτην νομίζω, τῶν δὲ δημοσίων
μικρὰν καὶ οὐδενὸς ἀξίαν ἡγοῦμαι ζημίαν,⁴ ἐξὸν
5 κολάζειν χρήμασι καὶ δεσμῷ καὶ θανάτῳ. ἔτι δ'
εἴ τις διὰ τοῦτο μεθίσταται ὅτι ⟨πονηρὸς⟩⁵ πολίτης
ἐστίν, οὗτος οὐδ' ἀπελθὼν ἐνθένδε⁶ παύσεται, ἀλλ'
ὅπου ἂν οἰκῇ, ταύτην τὴν πόλιν διαφθερεῖ,⁷ καὶ τῇδε
οὐδὲν ἧττον ἐπιβουλεύσει, ἀλλὰ καὶ μᾶλλον ⟨καὶ⟩⁸
δικαιότερον ἢ πρὶν ἐκβληθῆναι. οἶμαι δὲ καὶ τοὺς
φίλους ὑμῶν⁹ ἐν ταύτῃ μάλιστα τῇ ἡμέρᾳ λυπεῖσθαι
καὶ τοὺς ἐχθροὺς ἥδεσθαι, συνειδότας ὡς ἂν ἀγ-
νοήσαντες ἐξελάσητε τὸν βέλτιστον, δέκα ἐτῶν ἡ
πόλις οὐδὲν ἀγαθὸν ὑπὸ¹⁰ τούτου τοῦ ἀνδρὸς πείσεται.

---

¹ ἀποκτενεῖν Stephanus : ἀποκτείνειν codd.
² οὔτε del. Schleiermacher.
³ μοι om. Q.   ⁴ ζημίαν ἡγοῦμαι Q.
⁵ πονηρὸς add. Emperius : πολίτης codd. κακὸς addebat
Reiske.   ⁶ ἐνθένδε A corr.: ἐνθάδε A et Q.
⁷ διαφθερεῖ Ald.: διαφθείρῃ A, διαφθείρει Q.
⁸ καὶ add. Reiske.

Now the legislator [a] responsible for this deserves censure ; for the law which he framed violates the oath of the People and Council. Under the terms of that oath you swear to exile no one, to imprison no one, to put no one to death, without trial ; whereas on this present occasion, when the person ostracized is to be cut off from his country for so long, no accusation has been made, no defence allowed, and the voting is secret. Moreover, at a time like this those who have political associates and confederates have an advantage over the rest, because the judges are not appointed by lot as in courts of law : in the present decision every member of the community has a voice. And not only that : the law appears to me to go both too far and not far enough ; for wrongs done to individuals I consider such redress as this excessive : for wrongs done to the state I regard it as an insufficient and useless penalty, when you have the right to punish by fine, imprisonment, or death. Furthermore, if a man is exiled because he is a bad citizen, his leaving Athens will not cure him ; wherever he lives, he will do this city harm and intrigue against her no less than hitherto—nay more so and with more justification than before his banishment. To-day, too, above all days, your friends, I feel, are filled with sorrow and your enemies with joy, because they know that if you unwittingly banish your best citizen, Athens will derive no benefit from him for

[a] Cleisthenes, in 510 B.C., cf. 'Aθ. Πολ. xxii. καὶ γὰρ συνέβη τοὺς μὲν Σόλωνος νόμους ἀφανίσαι τὴν τυραννίδα διὰ τὸ μὴ χρῆσθαι, καινοὺς δ' ἄλλους θεῖναι τὸν Κλεισθένην στοχαζόμενον τοῦ πλήθους, ἐν οἷς ἐτέθη καὶ ὁ περὶ τοῦ ὀστρακισμοῦ νόμος. For the procedure cf. Philochorus frag. 79b, F.G.H. i. 396.

⁹ ὑμῶν Stephanus : ἡμῶν codd.
¹⁰ ὑπὸ Bekker : ἀπὸ codd.

6 ῥᾴδιον δὲ καὶ ἐντεῦθεν γνῶναι τὸν νόμον πονηρὸν
ὄντα· μόνοι γὰρ αὐτῷ τῶν Ἑλλήνων χρώμεθα, καὶ
οὐδεμία τῶν ἄλλων πόλεων ἐθέλει μιμήσασθαι.
καίτοι ταῦτα διέγνωσται ἄριστα τῶν δογμάτων, ἃ
καὶ τοῖς πολλοῖς καὶ τοῖς ὀλίγοις ἁρμόττοντα
μάλιστα τυγχάνει καὶ πλείστους ἐπιθυμητὰς ἔχει.

7 Περὶ μὲν οὖν τούτων οὐκ οἶδ' ὅ τι δεῖ μακρότερα
λέγειν· πάντως γὰρ οὐδὲν[1] ἂν πλεῖον εἰς τὸ παρὸν
ποιήσαιμεν· δέομαι δ' ὑμῶν τῶν λόγων ἴσους καὶ
κοινοὺς ἡμῖν ἐπιστάτας γενέσθαι, καὶ πάντας ἄρ-
χοντας περὶ τούτων καταστῆναι, καὶ μήτε τοῖς
[30] λοιδορουμένοις μήτε τοῖς ὑπὲρ καιρὸν χαριζομένοις
ἐπιτρέπειν, ἀλλὰ τῷ μὲν θέλοντι λέγειν καὶ ἀκούειν
εὐμενεῖς εἶναι, τῷ δὲ ἀσελγαίνοντι καὶ θορυβοῦντι
χαλεπούς. ἀκούσαντες γὰρ ἕκαστον[2] τῶν ὑπαρχόντων ἄμεινον βουλεύσεσθε περὶ ἡμῶν.

8 Ἔστι δὲ περὶ τῆς μισοδημίας καὶ τῆς στασιωτείας[3] βραχύς μοι λόγος καταλελειμμένος. εἰ μὲν
γὰρ ἄκριτος ἦν, εἰκότως ἂν τῶν κατηγορούντων
ἠκροᾶσθε καὶ ἐμοὶ ἀναγκαῖον ἦν ἀπολογεῖσθαι περὶ
τούτων· ἐπειδὴ δὲ τετράκις ἀγωνιζόμενος ἀπέφυγον, οὐκέτι δίκαιον ἡγοῦμαι λόγον οὐδένα περὶ

---

[1] γὰρ οὐδὲν Reiske : οὐδὲν γὰρ codd.
[2] ἕκαστον scripsi : ἑκάστου AQ. περὶ add. Reiske.
[3] στασιωτείας Ald. : στασιωτίας A, ἀσωτίας Q.

---

[a] The evidence on the subject of ostracism in Greece at
large is too inconclusive to enable us either to accept or to
reject this statement with confidence. It is known that the
institution existed for a time at least at Argos (Arist. *Pol.*
viii. 3, 1302 b 18), at Miletus (Schol. Ar. *Eq.* 855), at Megara
(*ibid.*), and at Syracuse (Diod. Sic. xi. 87. 6). It was

ten years. Then still another fact makes it easy to
see that the law is a bad one : we are the only
Greeks to observe it, and no other state is prepared
to imitate us.[a] Yet it is recognized that the best
institutions are those which have proved most suited
to democracy and oligarchy alike and which are the
most generally favoured.

I see no reason for dwelling further on this subject,
as, whatever the outcome, I should achieve nothing
of immediate advantage. But I do ask you to preside
over our speeches in a fair and impartial manner, and
one and all to act as Archons.[b] Do not countenance
abuse or undue flattery. Show yourselves kindly
to him who desires to speak and to listen : show yourselves stern to him who is insolent and disorderly ;
for you will decide our fate all the better, if each of
the cases to be laid before you is given a hearing.

It remains for me to make a brief reference to my
hostility to the democracy and my membership of a
political faction. Had I never appeared in court, you
would have had some reason for listening to my
accusers, and it would have been necessary for me
to answer them on these points. But since I have
been tried and acquitted four times, I do not consider

introduced at Syracuse in 454 B.C. under the name of
πεταλισμός, definitely in imitation of Athens.

[b] Dalmeyda (Andoc., ed. Budé) is probably right in explaining this as a reference to the procedure observed when
an ὀστρακισμός was held. According to the Scholiast on Ar.
Eq. 855, the people met under the presidency of the Archons
and the Boulê, *i.e.* the Archons together with the Prytanes in
office for the time being. These last would have one of their
members as ἐπιστάτης or president for the day. The speaker
is therefore urging his audience to regard themselves as
placed in the same responsible position as the Archons and
ἐπιστάτης τῶν πρυτανέων.

τούτου γίγνεσθαι. πρὶν μὲν γὰρ κριθῆναι οὐ
ῥᾴδιον [ἦν]¹ εἰδέναι τὰς αἰτίας, οὔτ᾽ εἰ ψευδεῖς εἰσιν
οὔτ᾽ εἰ ἀληθεῖς· ἀποφυγόντος² δὲ ἢ καταγνωσθέντος
τέλος ἔχει καὶ διώρισται τούτων ὁπότερόν ἐστιν.
9 ὥστε³ δεινὸν νομίζω τοὺς μὲν ἁλόντας μιᾷ ψήφῳ
μόνον ἀποθνήσκειν, καὶ τὰ χρήματα δημεύεσθαι⁴
αὐτῶν, τοὺς δὲ νικήσαντας⁵ πάλιν τὰς αὐτὰς κατηγορίας ὑπομένειν, καὶ τοὺς δικαστὰς ἀπολέσαι μὲν
κυρίους εἶναι, σῶσαι δ᾽ ἀκύρους καὶ ἀτελεῖς φαίνε-
σθαι, ἄλλως τε καὶ τῶν νόμων ἀπαγορευόντων δὶς
περὶ τῶν αὐτῶν⁶ πρὸς τὸν αὐτὸν μὴ ἐξεῖναι δικάζε-
σθαι, καὶ ὑμῶν⁷ ὀμωμοκότων χρῆσθαι τοῖς νόμοις.
10 Ὧν ἕνεκα περὶ ἐμαυτοῦ παραλιπὼν Ἀλκιβιάδου
τὸν βίον ἀναμνῆσαι βούλομαι. καίτοι ἀπορῶ γε
διὰ τὸ πλῆθος τῶν ἁμαρτημάτων πόθεν ἄρξωμαι,⁸
ἐμποδὼν ἁπάντων ὄντων. περὶ μὲν οὖν μοιχείας
καὶ γυναικῶν ἀλλοτρίων ἁρπαγῆς καὶ τῆς ἄλλης
βιαιότητος καὶ παρανομίας καθ᾽ ἕκαστον εἰ δεήσειε⁹
λέγειν, οὐκ ἂν ἐξαρκέσειεν ὁ παρὼν χρόνος, ἅμα δὲ
καὶ πολλοῖς ἀπεχθοίμην τῶν πολιτῶν, φανερὰς τὰς
συμφορὰς ποιῶν αὐτῶν. ἃ δὲ περὶ τὴν πόλιν
εἴργασται καὶ τοὺς προσήκοντας καὶ τῶν ἄλλων
ἀστῶν καὶ ξένων τοὺς ἐντυγχάνοντας, ἀποδείξω.
11 Πρῶτον μὲν οὖν πείσας ὑμᾶς¹⁰ τὸν φόρον ταῖς
πόλεσιν ἐξ ἀρχῆς τάξαι τὸν ὑπ᾽ Ἀριστείδου πάντων

¹ ἦν secl. Blass.
² ἀποφυγόντος Ald. : ἀποφεύγοντος codd.
³ ὥστε Stephanus : ὡς codd.
⁴ δημεύεσθαι Muretus : δημεύειν codd.
⁵ τοὺς δὲ νικήσαντας Muretus : τῶν δὲ νικησάντων codd.
⁶ τῶν αὐτῶν Q : τοῦ αὐτοῦ A.
⁷ ὑμῶν A : ἡμῶν Q.
⁸ ἄρξωμαι Blass : ἄρξομαι codd.
⁹ δεήσειε Baiter : δεήσει codd.
¹⁰ ὑμᾶς A : ἡμᾶς Q.

any further discussion of the subject justified. Before a man is tried, it is difficult to know whether the charges made against him are false or true ; but after his acquittal or conviction the matter is decided, and it is settled whether they are the one or the other. Hence I cannot but think it strange that while defendants who are convicted by but a single vote[a] are put to death and have their property confiscated by you, those who win their case should have to face the same charges again : that while the court has the power to take away life, it should so clearly lack the authority to save it once and finally, especially as the laws forbid the same charge to be brought twice against the same defendant, and you have sworn to observe those laws.

I shall therefore say nothing of myself. I wish instead to remind you of the past of Alcibiades—although such is the multitude of his misdeeds that I am at a loss where to begin : there is not one of them that does not press for mention. Were I faced with the task of describing at length his career as an adulterer, as a stealer of the wives of others, as a perpetrator of acts of lawless violence in general, the time at my disposal would be all too short, and I should furthermore earn the ill-will of many of my fellows for making public the injuries which they have suffered. Of his conduct towards the state, however, and towards the members of his family and such citizens and foreigners as have crossed his path, I will give you some account.

To begin with, he persuaded you to revise the assessment of the tribute of the subject-states made

---

[a] *i.e.* by a majority of one. If the jury was equally divided, the accused was acquitted. *Cf.* Antiphon, *Herodes*, § 51.

δικαιότατα τεταγμένον, αἱρεθεὶς ἐπὶ τούτῳ δέκατος
αὐτὸς μάλιστα διπλάσιον αὐτὸν ἑκάστοις[1] τῶν
συμμάχων ἐποίησεν, ἐπιδείξας δ' αὐτὸν φοβερὸν
καὶ μέγα δυνάμενον ἰδίας ἀπὸ τῶν κοινῶν προσ-
όδους κατεσκευάσατο. σκέψασθε δὲ πῶς ἄν τις
κακὰ μείζω τούτων κατασκευάσειεν, εἰ τῆς σωτηρίας ἡμῖν πάσης διὰ τῶν συμμάχων οὔσης,
ὁμολογουμένως νῦν κάκιον ἢ πρότερον πραττόντων,
12 τὸν φόρον ἑκάστοις[2] διπλασιάσειεν. ὥστ' εἴπερ
ἡγεῖσθε πολίτην ἀγαθὸν Ἀριστείδην καὶ δίκαιον
γεγονέναι, τοῦτον προσήκει κάκιστον νομίζειν, ὡς
τἀναντία περὶ τῶν πόλεων[3] ἐκείνῳ γιγνώσκοντα.
τοιγάρτοι διὰ ταῦτα πολλοὶ τὴν πατρίδα τὴν αὑτῶν
ἀπολιπόντες[4] φυγάδες γίγνονται καὶ εἰς Θουρίους
οἰκήσοντες ἀπέρχονται. δηλώσει δὲ ἡ τῶν συμμάχων ἔχθρα, ὅταν πρῶτον[5] ἡμῖν καὶ Λακεδαιμονίοις γένηται ναυτικὸς πόλεμος. ἐγὼ δὲ νομίζω
τὸν τοιοῦτον πονηρὸν εἶναι προστάτην, ὅστις τοῦ
παρόντος χρόνου ἐπιμελεῖται, ἀλλὰ μὴ καὶ τοῦ

---

[1] ἑκάστοις Blass : ἑκάστω codd.
[2] ἑκάστοις Baiter et Sauppe : ἑκάστης codd.
[3] περὶ τῶν πόλεων om. Q.
[4] ἀπολιπόντες A : καταλιπόντες Q.
[5] ὅταν πρῶτον Reiske : πρῶτον ὅταν codd.

---

[a] In 478 B.C., at the formation of the Confederacy of Delos.
According to Thucydides (i. 96), the tribute as assessed by
Aristeides amounted to 460 talents. It is difficult to accept
this statement, as the existing quota-lists show that even
between 450 B.C. and 436 B.C., when the Confederacy was
far larger and contributions of money had almost entirely
superseded those of ships, the total sum collected never

with the utmost fairness by Aristeides.[a] Chosen with nine others to perform the task,[b] he practically doubled the contribution of each member of the alliance, while by showing how formidable he was and how influential, he made the revenues of the state a means of procuring revenue for himself.[c] Now just consider : when our safety depends entirely upon our allies and those allies are acknowledged to be worse off to-day than in the past, how could anyone do greater mischief than by doubling the tribute of each ? In fact, if you hold that Aristeides was a good Athenian and a just one, you can only regard Alcibiades as a scoundrel, since his policy towards the subject-states is the exact opposite of that of Aristeides. Indeed, because of his behaviour, many are leaving their homes as exiles and going off to settle at Thurii[d] ; while the bitter feeling of the allies will manifest itself directly there is a war at sea between Sparta and ourselves. In my own opinion, he is a worthless statesman who considers only the present without also giving thought to the future, who advocates the

exceeded 455 talents. The original assessment of Aristeides cannot have produced much more than 250 talents.

[b] Nothing is known of this re-assessment. In 425 B.C. the existing tribute had been practically doubled, probably at the instigation of Cleon (*I.G.* i¹. 63) ; and the speaker may conceivably be making a mistaken reference to this, although Alcibiades would have been only about twenty-five at the time, and therefore too young to be concerned in it. A second attempt to increase the revenue was made *c.* 413, when a 5 per cent toll on maritime commerce was instituted in lieu of tribute (Thucyd. vii. 28).

[c] *i.e.* he used his position to extort blackmail, under threat of an excessive assessment.

[d] A colony founded in 443 B.C. on the site of Sybaris in S. Italy. The bulk of the settlers were Athenian, although numbers came from all parts of the Greek world.

μέλλοντος προνοεῖται, καὶ τὰ ἥδιστα τῷ πλήθει,
παραλιπὼν τὰ βέλτιστα, συμβουλεύει.

13 Θαυμάζω δὲ τῶν πεπεισμένων Ἀλκιβιάδην δημοκρατίας ἐπιθυμεῖν, τοιαύτης πολιτείας ἣ μάλιστα
κοινότητα δοκεῖ ᾑρῆσθαι,[1] οἳ οὐδ' ἀπὸ τῶν ἰδίων
αὐτὸν θεῶνται, ὁρῶντες τὴν πλεονεξίαν καὶ τὴν
ὑπερηφανίαν, ὃς τὴν Καλλίου γήμας ἀδελφὴν ἐπὶ
δέκα ταλάντοις, τελεύτησαντος Ἱππονίκου στρατηγοῦντος ἐπὶ Δηλίῳ ἕτερα τοσαῦτα προσεπράξατο,
λέγων ὡς ὡμολόγησεν ἐκεῖνος, ὁπότε παῖς αὐτῷ ἐκ
14 τῆς θυγατρὸς[2] γένοιτο, προσθήσειν ταῦτα. λαβὼν[3]
δὲ τοσαύτην προῖκα ὅσην οὐδεὶς τῶν Ἑλλήνων,
οὕτως ὑβριστὴς ἦν, ἐπεισάγων εἰς τὴν αὐτὴν οἰκίαν
ἑταίρας, καὶ δούλας καὶ ἐλευθέρας, ὥστ' ἠνάγκασε
τὴν γυναῖκα σωφρονεστάτην οὖσαν ἀπολιπεῖν, ἐλ-
θοῦσαν πρὸς τὸν ἄρχοντα κατὰ τὸν νόμον. οὗ δὴ
μάλιστα τὴν αὑτοῦ δύναμιν ἐπεδείξατο· παρακα-
λέσας γὰρ τοὺς ἑταίρους, ἁρπάσας ἐκ τῆς ἀγορᾶς
τὴν γυναῖκα ᾤχετο βίᾳ, καὶ πᾶσιν ἐδήλωσε καὶ τῶν
ἀρχόντων καὶ τῶν νόμων καὶ τῶν ἄλλων πολιτῶν
[31] καταφρονῶν. οὐ τοίνυν ταῦτα μόνον ἐξήρκεσεν,
15 ἀλλὰ καὶ λαθραῖον θάνατον ἐπεβούλευσε Καλλίᾳ,
ἵνα τὸν οἶκον τὸν Ἱππονίκου[4] κατάσχοι, ὡς ἐναντίον
πάντων ὑμῶν ἐν τῇ ἐκκλησίᾳ κατηγόρει[5]· καὶ τὰ
χρήματα τῷ δήμῳ ἔδωκεν, εἴ πως τελευτήσειεν
ἄπαις, φοβούμενος μὴ διὰ τὴν οὐσίαν[6] ἀπόλοιτο.

---

[1] ᾑρῆσθαι Valckenaer : εὑρῆσθαι codd.
[2] θυγατρὸς αὑτοῦ γένοιτο Q.
[3] λαβὼν A : παραλαβὼν Q.
[4] τὸν Ἱππονίκου A : τοῦ Ἱππ. Q.
[5] κατηγόρει Stephanus : κατηγορεῖ codd.
[6] οὐσίαν A : ἀπουσίαν Q.

---

[a] For Hipponicus and Callius cf. *Mysteries*, §§ 115, 130.

policy which will best please the people and says nothing of that which their true interests require.

I am astonished, furthermore, at those who are persuaded that Alcibiades is a lover of democracy, that form of government which more than any other would seem to make equality its end. They are not using his private life as evidence of his character, in spite of the fact that his greed and his arrogance are plain to them. On his marriage with the sister of Callias he received a dowry of ten talents; yet after Hipponicus[a] had lost his life as one of the generals at Delium,[b] he exacted another ten, on the ground that Hipponicus had agreed to add this further sum as soon as Alcibiades should have a child by his daughter. Then, after obtaining a dowry such as no Greek had ever obtained before, he behaved in so profligate a fashion, bringing mistresses, slave and free, into the bridal house, that he drove his wife, who was a decent woman, to present herself before the Archon, as she was legally entitled to do, and divorce him. At that he gave conspicuous proof of his power. He called in his friends, and carried off his wife from the Agora by force, showing the whole world his contempt for the magistrates, the laws, and his fellow Athenians in general. Nor was this one outrage enough for him. He went further. In order to possess himself of Hipponicus' estate, he planned the assassination of Callias. Callias himself accused him of it before you all in the Assembly, and, for fear that his wealth would cost him his life, made over his property to the state

---

[b] In 424 B.C. Demosthenes and Hippocrates planned a joint invasion of Boeotia. The scheme miscarried; and the Athenians were heavily defeated at Delium.

ἀλλὰ μὴν οὐδ' ἔρημος οὐδ' εὐαδίκητός ἐστιν, ἐπεὶ
διὰ τὸν πλοῦτον ἔχει πολλοὺς τοὺς βοηθήσοντας.[1]
καίτοι ὅστις ὑβρίζει γυναῖκα τὴν ἑαυτοῦ καὶ τῷ
κηδεστῇ θάνατον ἐπιβουλεύει, τί χρὴ προσδοκᾶν
τοῦτον περὶ τοὺς ἐντυχόντας τῶν πολιτῶν διαπράτ-
τεσθαι; πάντες γὰρ ἄνθρωποι τοὺς οἰκείους τῶν
ἀλλοτρίων ποιοῦνται περὶ πλείονος.

16 Ὁ δὲ πάντων δεινότατόν ἐστι, τοιοῦτος ὢν ὡς
εὔνους τῷ δήμῳ τοὺς λόγους ποιεῖται, καὶ τοὺς[2]
ἄλλους ὀλιγαρχικοὺς καὶ μισοδήμους ἀποκαλεῖ.
καὶ ὃν ἔδει[3] τεθνάναι διὰ τὰ ἐπιτηδεύματα, κατήγορος τῶν διαβεβλημένων ὑφ' ὑμῶν[4] αἱρεῖται,
καί φησι φύλαξ εἶναι τῆς πολιτείας, οὐδενὶ τῶν
ἄλλων Ἀθηναίων οὔτ' ἴσον οὔτ' ὀλίγῳ πλέον ἀξιῶν
ἔχειν· ἀλλ' οὕτω σφόδρα καταπεφρόνηκεν ὥστε
διατετέλεκεν ἀθρόους μὲν ὑμᾶς κολακεύων, ἕνα δ'
17 ἕκαστον προπηλακίζων. ὃς εἰς τοσοῦτον ἐλήλυθε
τόλμης, ὥστε πείσας Ἀγάθαρχον τὸν γραφέα[5]
συνεισελθεῖν [οἴκαδε][6] τὴν οἰκίαν ἐπηνάγκασε γράφειν, δεομένου δὲ καὶ προφάσεις ἀληθεῖς λέγοντος,
ὡς οὐκ ἂν δύναιτο ταῦτα πράττειν ἤδη διὰ τὸ
συγγραφὰς ἔχειν παρ' ἑτέρων, προεῖπεν αὐτῷ
δήσειν, εἰ μὴ πάνυ ταχέως γράφοι. ὅπερ ἐποίησε·
καὶ οὐ πρότερον ἀπηλλάγη, πρὶν ἀποδρὰς ᾤχετο
τετάρτῳ μηνί, τοὺς φύλακας λαθών, ὥσπερ παρὰ
βασιλέως. οὕτω δ' ἀναίσχυντός ἐστι, ὥστε

---

[1] Verba ἀλλὰ μὴν . . . βοηθήσοντας, quae post περὶ πλείονος
(§ 15 ad fin.) habent codd., huc transposuit Fuhr.
[2] καὶ τοὺς Dobree: αὐτὸς codd.
[3] ἔδει Dobree: δεῖ codd.
[4] ὑμῶν Emperius: ἡμῶν codd.
[5] τὸν γραφέα om. Q.
[6] οἴκαδε del. Hirschig.

in the event of his dying without issue. However, Callias neither lacks friends nor is he an easy victim. Thanks to his riches he can be sure of protection in plenty. None the less, when a man offers violence to his own wife and plots the death of his brother-in-law, how is he to be expected to behave towards such of his fellow-citizens as cross his path ? Everyone has more regard for members of his own family than he has for strangers.

But most monstrous of all is the fact that a man of his character should talk as though he were a friend of the people, and call others oligarchs and foes of the democracy. Yes, although he himself deserves death for behaving as he does, he is chosen by you to proceed against any whose sympathies conflict with yours ; and he poses as guardian of the constitution, in spite of the fact that he refuses to be the equal of, or but little superior to, his fellows. So completely, indeed, does he despise you that he spends his time flattering you in a body and insulting you individually. Why, there are no limits to his impudence. He persuaded Agatharchus, the artist, to accompany him home,[a] and then forced him to paint ; and when Agatharchus appealed to him, stating with perfect truth that he could not oblige him at the moment because he had other engagements, Alcibiades threatened him with imprisonment, unless he started painting straight away. And he carried out his threat. Agatharchus only made his escape three months later, by slipping past his guards and running away as he might have done from the king of Persia. But so shameless is Alcibiades that

---

[a] Plutarch also mentions this episode (*Alcib.* 16) ; but adds that Alcibiades sent Agatharchus away with a reward.

προσελθὼν[1] ἐνεκάλει αὐτῷ ὡς ἀδικούμενος, καὶ οὐχ
ὧν ἐβιάσατο μετέμελεν αὐτῷ, ἀλλ' ὅτι κατέλιπε τὸ
ἔργον ἠπείλει, καὶ οὔτε τῆς δημοκρατίας οὔτε τῆς
ἐλευθερίας οὐδὲν ἦν ὄφελος· οὐδὲν γὰρ ἧττον
18 ἐδεδέκει[2] τῶν ὁμολογουμένων δούλων. ἀγανακτῶ
δ' ἐνθυμούμενος ὑμῖν μὲν[3] οὐδὲ τοὺς κακούργους
ἀσφαλὲς εἰς τὸ δεσμωτήριον ὂν ἀπάγειν, διὰ τὸ
χιλίας δραχμὰς τετάχθαι ἀποτεῖσαι ὃς ἂν τὸ πέμπτον μέρος μὴ μεταλάβῃ τῶν ψήφων· ὁ δὲ τοσοῦτον χρόνον εἴρξας καὶ ἐπαναγκάζων γράφειν
οὐδὲν κακὸν πέπονθεν, ἀλλὰ διὰ ταῦτα σεμνότερος
δοκεῖ καὶ φοβερώτερος εἶναι. καὶ πρὸς μὲν τὰς
ἄλλας πόλεις ἐν τοῖς συμβόλοις συντιθέμεθα μὴ
ἐξεῖναι μήθ' εἶρξαι μήτε δῆσαι τὸν ἐλεύθερον· ἐὰν
δέ τις παραβῇ, μεγάλην ζημίαν ἐπὶ τούτοις, ἔθεμεν·
τούτου δὲ τοιαῦτα πράξαντος οὐδεμίαν οὐδεὶς οὔτ'
19 ἰδίαν οὔτε δημοσίαν τιμωρίαν ποιεῖται. νομίζω δὲ
ταύτην εἶναι σωτηρίαν ἅπασι, πείθεσθαι τοῖς ἄρχουσι καὶ τοῖς νόμοις· ὅστις δὲ ὑπερορᾷ ταῦτα, τὴν
μεγίστην φυλακὴν ἀνῄρηκε τῆς πόλεως. δεινὸν
μὲν οὖν ἐστι καὶ ὑπὸ τῶν ἀγνοούντων τὰ δίκαια
πάσχειν κακῶς, πολὺ δὲ χαλεπώτερον, ὅταν τις
ἐπιστάμενος τὰ διαφέροντα παραβαίνειν τολμᾷ·
φανερῶς[4] γὰρ ἐνδείκνυται, ὥσπερ οὗτος, οὐκ αὐτὸς
τοῖς νόμοις τοῖς τῆς[5] πόλεως, ἀλλ' ὑμᾶς τοῖς αὑτοῦ[6]
τρόποις ἀκολουθεῖν ἀξιῶν.
20 Ἐνθυμήθητε δὲ Ταυρέαν, ὃς ἀντιχορηγὸς ἦν Ἀλ-

---

[1] προσελθὼν A : προελθὼν Q.
[2] ἐδεδέκει Emperius : ἐδεδοίκει codd.
[3] ὑμῖν μὲν οὐδὲ A corr. : ὑμῖν οὐδὲ A pr. Q.
[4] φανερῶς Q : φανερὸς A.
[5] τοῖς τῆς πόλεως Q : τοῖς πόλεως A.
[6] αὑτοῦ Baiter et Sauppe : αὐτοῦ codd.

he went to Agatharchus and accused him of doing
him a wrong ; instead of apologizing for his violence,
he uttered threats against him for leaving his work
unfinished.   Democracy, freedom went for nothing :
Agatharchus had been put in chains exactly like any
acknowledged slave.   It makes me angry to think
that while you yourselves cannot place even malefactors under arrest without risk, because it is enacted
that anyone who fails to gain one-fifth of the votes
shall be liable to a fine of a thousand drachmae,
Alcibiades, who imprisoned a man for so long and
forced him to paint, went unpunished—nay, increased
thereby the awe and the fear in which he is held.   In
our treaties with other states *a* we make it a condition
that no free man shall be imprisoned or placed in
durance, and a heavy fine is prescribed as the penalty
for so doing. Yet when Alcibiades behaved as he did,
no one sought satisfaction, whether for himself or for
the state. Obedience to the magistrates and the laws
is to my mind the one safeguard of society ; and anyone who sets them at nought is destroying at one
blow the surest guarantee of security which the state
possesses.   It is hard enough to be made to suffer
by those who have no conception of right and wrong ;
but it is far more serious when a man who knows what
the public interest requires, acts in defiance of it.
He shows clearly, as Alcibiades has done, that instead
of holding that he ought himself to conform with the
laws of the state, he expects you to conform with his
own way of life.

Then again, remember Taureas *b* who competed

a For σύμβολα see p. 215, note *d*.
b *Cf.* Dem. xxi. 147.

κιβιάδη[1] παισί. κελεύοντος δὲ τοῦ νόμου τῶν
χορευτῶν ἐξάγειν ὃν ἄν τις βούληται ξένον ἀγωνιζό-
μενον, οὐκ ἐξὸν ἐπιχειρήσαντα κωλύειν, ἐναντίον
ὑμῶν καὶ τῶν ἄλλων Ἑλλήνων τῶν θεωρούντων
καὶ τῶν ἀρχόντων ἁπάντων παρόντων ⟨τῶν⟩[2] ἐν
τῇ πόλει τύπτων ἐξήλασεν αὐτόν, καὶ τῶν θεατῶν
συμφιλονικούντων ἐκείνῳ καὶ μισούντων τοῦτον,
ὥστε τῶν χορῶν τὸν μὲν ἐπαινούντων, τοῦ δ᾽
ἀκροάσασθαι οὐκ ἐθελόντων, οὐδὲν πλέον ἔπραξεν·
21 ἀλλὰ τῶν κριτῶν οἱ μὲν φοβούμενοι οἱ δὲ χαριζό-
μενοι νικᾶν ἔκριναν αὐτόν, περὶ ἐλάττονος ποιούμενοι τὸν ὅρκον ἢ τοῦτον. εἰκότως δέ μοι δοκοῦσιν
οἱ κριταὶ ὑπέρχεσθαι Ἀλκιβιάδην, ὁρῶντες Ταυρέαν
μὲν τοσαῦτα[3] χρήματα ἀναλώσαντα προπηλακιζό-
[32] μενον, τὸν δὲ τοιαῦτα παρανομοῦντα μέγιστον
δυνάμενον. αἴτιοι δ᾽ ὑμεῖς,[4] οὐ τιμωρούμενοι τοὺς
ὑβρίζοντας, καὶ τοὺς μὲν λάθρᾳ ἀδικοῦντας κολά-
ζοντες, τοὺς δὲ φανερῶς ἀσελγαίνοντας θαυμά-
22 ζοντες. τοιγάρτοι τῶν νέων αἱ διατριβαὶ οὐκ ἐν
τοῖς γυμνασίοις, ἀλλ᾽ ἐν τοῖς δικαστηρίοις εἰσί, καὶ
στρατεύονται μὲν οἱ πρεσβύτεροι, δημηγοροῦσι δὲ
οἱ νεώτεροι, παραδείγματι τούτῳ χρώμενοι, ὃς
τηλικαύτας ποιεῖται τῶν ἁμαρτημάτων ὑπερβολάς,

---

[1] Ἀλκιβιάδη A : Ἀλκιβιάδου Q.
[2] τῶν add. Blass. Idem tamen παρόντων secludit.
[3] μὲν τοσαῦτα Q : τοσαῦτα μὲν A.
[4] ὑμεῖς A : ἡμεῖς Q.

against Alcibiades as Choregus of a chorus of boys.[a]
The law allows the ejection of any member whatsoever of a competing chorus who is not of Athenian
birth, and it is forbidden to resist any attempt at
such ejection. Yet in your presence, in the presence
of the other Greeks who were looking on, and before
all the magistrates in Athens, Alcibiades drove off
Taureas with his fists.[b] The spectators showed their
sympathy with Taureas and their hatred of Alcibiades by applauding the one chorus and refusing
to listen to the other at all. Yet Taureas was none
the better off for that. Partly from fear, partly
from subservience, the judges pronounced Alcibiades
the victor, treating him as more important than
their oath. And it seems to me only natural that
the judges should thus seek favour with Alcibiades,
when they could see that Taureas, who had spent
so vast a sum, was being subjected to insults, while
his rival, who showed such contempt for the law,
was all-powerful. The blame lies with you. You
refuse to punish insolence ; and while you chastise
secret wrongdoing, you admire open effrontery. That
is why the young spend their days in the courts instead
of in the gymnasia ; that is why our old men fight
our battles, while our young men make speeches—
they take Alcibiades as their model, Alcibiades who
carries his villainy to such unheard-of lengths that,

[a] For the duties of such a Choregus see Antiphon, *Choreutes*, §§ 11-13. Choruses of boys selected from each of the
ten tribes competed against one another at all the major
festivals of the Attic year.

[b] The speaker is not very clear. Apparently Taureas
attempted to secure the ejection of a member of Alcibiades'
chorus, but met with violent resistance from Alcibiades
himself. *Cf.* Dem. xxi. 147 Ταυρέαν ἐπάταξε χορηγοῦντ' ἐπὶ
κόρρης.

ὥστε περὶ τῶν Μηλίων γνώμην ἀποφηνάμενος
ἐξανδραποδίζεσθαι, πριάμενος γυναῖκα τῶν αἰχ-
μαλώτων υἱὸν ἐξ αὐτῆς πεποίηται, ὃς τοσούτῳ
παρανομωτέρως¹ Αἰγίσθου γέγονεν, ὥστ' ἐκ τῶν
ἐχθίστων ἀλλήλοις πέφυκε, καὶ τῶν οἰκειοτάτων
ὑπάρχει αὐτῷ τὰ ἔσχατα τοὺς μὲν πεποιηκέναι
23 τοὺς δὲ πεπονθέναι. ἄξιον δὲ τὴν τόλμαν αὐτοῦ
σαφέστερον ἔτι διελθεῖν. ἐκ ταύτης γὰρ² παιδο-
ποιεῖται τῆς γυναικός, ἣν ἀντ' ἐλευθέρας δούλην
κατέστησε, καὶ ἧς τὸν πατέρα καὶ τοὺς προσήκοντας ἀπέκτεινε, καὶ [ἧς]³ τὴν πόλιν ἀνάστατον
πεποίηκεν, ὡς ἂν μάλιστα τὸν υἱὸν ἐχθρὸν ἑαυτῷ
καὶ τῇ πόλει ποιήσειε· τοσαύταις ἀνάγκαις κατεί-
ληπται μισεῖν. ἀλλ' ὑμεῖς ἐν μὲν ταῖς τραγῳδίαις
τοιαῦτα θεωροῦντες δεινὰ νομίζετε, γιγνόμενα δ'
ἐν τῇ πόλει ὁρῶντες οὐδὲν φροντίζετε. καίτοι
ἐκεῖνα μὲν οὐκ ἐπίστασθε πότερον οὕτω γεγένηται
ἢ πέπλασται ὑπὸ τῶν ποιητῶν· ταῦτα δὲ σαφῶς
εἰδότες οὕτω παρανόμως πεπραγμένα⁴ ῥᾳθύμως
φέρετε.

24 Πρὸς δὲ τούτοις τολμῶσί τινες περὶ αὐτοῦ λέγειν
ὡς οὐδὲ γεγένηται οὐδεὶς πώποτε τοιοῦτος. ἐγὼ
δὲ νομίζω μέγιστα κακὰ τὴν πόλιν ὑπὸ τούτου
πείσεσθαι, καὶ τηλικούτων πραγμάτων εἰς τὸν
λοιπὸν χρόνον αἴτιον δόξειν, ὥστε μηδένα τῶν

---

¹ παρανομωτέρως Reiske: παρανομώτατος A : -ώτερος Q.
² γὰρ A : δὲ Q.
³ ἧς om. A pr.
⁴ παρανόμως πεπραγμένα Q: πεπρ. παρανόμως A.

ᵃ In 425 B.C. Melos refused to pay the increased tribute
demanded of her, and during the years which followed
displayed a general defiance of Athens. Athens finally

after recommending that the people of Melos *a* be sold into slavery, he purchased a woman from among the prisoners and has since had a son by her, a child whose birth was more unnatural than that of Aegisthus,*b* since he is sprung from parents who are each other's deadliest enemies, and of his nearest kin the one has committed and the other has suffered the most terrible of wrongs. Indeed it would be well to make such shamelessness still plainer. He got himself a child by the very woman whom he had turned from a free citizen into a slave, whose father and kinsfolk he had put to death and whose city he had made a waste, that he might thereby make his son the deadly enemy of himself and of this city ; so inevitably is the boy driven to hate both. When you are shown things of this kind on the tragic stage, you regard them with horror ; but when you see them taking place in Athens, you remain unmoved—and yet you are uncertain whether the tales of tragedy are founded on the truth or spring merely from the imagination of the poets ; whereas you well know that these other lawless outrages, which you accept with indifference, have occurred in fact.

In addition to all this, some dare to say that the like of Alcibiades has never been before. For my part, I believe that Athens will meet with terrible calamities at his hands, that he will be deemed responsible hereafter for disasters so awful that no

---

acted in the summer of 416. A fleet attacked the island, the male population was massacred, and the women and children sold as slaves. See Thucyd. v.

b Son of Thyestes by his own daughter, Pelopeia. He was exposed as a child, but saved by shepherds. His uncle, Atreus, then brought him up as his own son. Later he murdered Atreus and placed Thyestes on his throne.

προτέρων ἀδικημάτων μεμνῆσθαι· ἀνέλπιστον γὰρ
οὐδέν, τὸν τὴν ἀρχὴν τοῦ βίου τοιαύτην κατα-
σκευασάμενον καὶ τὴν τελευτὴν ὑπερβάλλουσαν
ποιήσασθαι. ἔστι δὲ σωφρόνων ἀνδρῶν φυλάτ-
τεσθαι τῶν πολιτῶν τοὺς ὑπεραυξανομένους, ἐν-
θυμουμένους ὑπὸ τῶν τοιούτων τὰς τυραννίδας
καθισταμένας.

25 Ἡγοῦμαι δ' αὐτὸν πρὸς ταῦτα[1] μὲν οὐδὲν ἀντ-
ερεῖν, λέξειν δὲ περὶ τῆς νίκης τῆς Ὀλυμπιάσι,
καὶ περὶ πάντων μᾶλλον ἢ τῶν κατηγορηθέντων
ἀπολογήσεσθαι.[2] ἐξ αὐτῶν δὲ τούτων ἐπιδείξω
αὐτὸν ἐπιτηδειότερον τεθνάναι μᾶλλον ἢ σῴζεσθαι.
διηγήσομαι δ' ὑμῖν.

26 Διομήδης ἦλθε ζεῦγος ἵππων ἄγων Ὀλυμπίαζε,
κεκτημένος μὲν οὐσίαν μετρίαν, στεφανῶσαι δὲ ἀπὸ
τῶν ὑπαρχόντων τὴν πόλιν καὶ τὴν οἰκίαν βουλόμενος, λογιζόμενος τοὺς ἀγῶνας τοὺς ἱππικοὺς
τύχῃ[3] τοὺς πλείστους κρινομένους. τοῦτον Ἀλκιβιάδης πολίτην ὄντα καὶ ⟨οὐ⟩[4] τὸν ἐπιτυχόντα,
δυνάμενος παρὰ τοῖς ἀγωνοθέταις τῶν Ἠλείων,
⟨τὸ ζεῦγος⟩[5] ἀφελόμενος αὐτὸς ἠγωνίζετο. καίτοι
τί ἂν ἐποίησεν, εἴ τις τῶν συμμάχων τῶν ὑμετέρων[6]

27 ἀφίκετο ζεῦγος ἵππων ἔχων; ἦ που ταχέως ἐπ-
έτρεψεν ἂν ἀνταγωνίζεσθαι ἑαυτῷ, ὃς Ἀθηναῖον[7]
ἄνδρα βιασάμενος τοῖς ἀλλοτρίοις ἐτόλμησεν ἵπποις
ἁμιλλᾶσθαι, δηλώσας τοῖς Ἕλλησι μηδὲν θαυμάζειν

---

[1] ταῦτα Meier : τοῦτο codd.
[2] ἀπολογήσεσθαι Ald. : ἀπολογήσασθαι codd.
[3] τύχῃ] τέχνῃ Schiller, Cobet : τιμῇ Sluiter.
[4] οὐ add. Stephanus.   [5] τὸ ζεῦγος add. Scaliger.
[6] ὑμετέρων A : ἡμετέρων Q.
[7] Ἀθηναῖον Q : Ἀθηναίων A.

[a] Cf. Plutarch, Alc. 13 ff.

one will remember his past misdeeds ; for it is only to be expected that one who has begun his life in such a fashion will make its close no less portentous. Men of sense should beware of those of their fellows who grow too great, remembering that it is such as they who set up tyrannies.

I imagine that Alcibiades will make no reply to this, but will talk instead of his victory at Olympia,[a] and that he will seek to defend himself on any grounds rather than those on which he has been charged. But I will use the very facts upon which he relies to prove that he deserves death rather than acquittal. Let me explain.

Diomedes took a chariot-team to Olympia. He was a man of moderate means, but desired to win a garland for Athens and for his family with such resources as he had, since he held that the chariot-races were for the most part decided by chance. Diomedes was no casual competitor, but a citizen of Athens.[b] Yet thanks to his influence with the Masters of the Games [c] at Elis, Alcibiades deprived him of his team and competed with it himself. What would he have done, may we ask, had one of your allies arrived with a team ? I imagine he would have been all eagerness to let him compete against himself, considering that he had forcibly ousted an Athenian rival and then had the impudence to contest the race with another man's horses—after he had, in fact, warned the Greeks in general that they must not be

---

[b] Or possibly : " Diomedes was a citizen of Athens and a person of some distinction."

[c] Properly known as Ἑλλανοδίκαι. In the time of Pausanias they numbered eight. They were appointed by lot from the whole body of Eleans and had the general superintendence of the Games.

ἄν τινα αὐτῶν βιάσηται, ἐπεὶ καὶ τοῖς πολίταις οὐκ
ἐξ ἴσου χρῆται, ἀλλὰ τοὺς μὲν ἀφαιρούμενος, τοὺς
δὲ τύπτων, τοὺς δὲ εἰργνύων, τοὺς δὲ χρήματα
πραττόμενος, οὐδενὸς ἀξίαν τὴν δημοκρατίαν ἀποφαίνει,¹ τοὺς μὲν λόγους δημαγωγοῦ τὰ δ' ἔργα
τυράννου παρέχων, καταμαθὼν ὑμᾶς τοῦ μὲν
ὀνόματος φροντίζοντας, τοῦ δὲ πράγματος ἀμε-
28 λοῦντας. τοσοῦτον δὲ διαφέρει Λακεδαιμονίων,
ὥστ' ἐκεῖνοι μὲν καὶ ὑπὸ τῶν συμμάχων ἀντ-
αγωνιζομένων² ἀνέχονται ἡττώμενοι, οὗτος δὲ οὐδ'
ὑπὸ τῶν πολιτῶν, ἀλλὰ φανερῶς εἴρηκεν οὐκ ἐπι-
τρέψειν τοῖς ἀντεπιθυμοῦσί τινος. εἶτ' ἐκ τῶν
τοιούτων ἀναγκαῖον τὰς πόλεις τῶν ἡμετέρων
πολεμίων ἐπιθυμεῖν, ἡμᾶς δὲ μισεῖν.

29 Ἵνα δὲ μὴ μόνον Διομήδην, ἀλλὰ καὶ τὴν πόλιν
ὅλην ὑβρίζων ἐπιδείξειε,³ τὰ πομπεῖα παρὰ τῶν
[33] ἀρχιθεώρων αἰτησάμενος, ὡς εἰς τἀπινίκια⁴ τῇ
προτεραίᾳ⁵ τῆς θυσίας⁶ χρησόμενος, ἐξηπάτησε καὶ
ἀποδοῦναι οὐκ ἤθελε, βουλόμενος τῇ ὑστεραίᾳ πρότερος τῆς πόλεως χρήσασθαι τοῖς χρυσοῖς χερνιβ-
βίοις⁷ καὶ θυμιατηρίοις. ὅσοι μὲν οὖν τῶν ξένων
μὴ ἐγίγνωσκον ἡμέτερα ὄντα, τὴν πομπὴν τὴν
κοινὴν ὁρῶντες ὑστέραν οὖσαν τῆς Ἀλκιβιάδου τοῖς
τούτου πομπείοις χρῆσθαι ἐνόμιζον ἡμᾶς· ὅσοι δὲ
ἢ παρὰ τῶν πολιτῶν ἤκουον ἢ καὶ ἐπεγίγνωσκον

---

¹ ἀποφαίνει Reiske: ἀποφαίνων codd.
² ἀνταγωνιζομένων A: ἀγωνιζομένων Q.
³ ὑβρίζων ἐπιδείξειε Emperius (ἐπιδείξαιτο Reiske): ὑβρίζων
(-ειν) ἐπιδόξειε codd.
⁴ τἀπινίκια Meursius: τὰ πινάκια codd.
⁵ προτεραίᾳ Canter: προτέρα codd.

surprised at his offering violence to any of them, seeing
that he does not treat his own fellow-Athenians as
his equals, but robs them, strikes them, throws them
into prison, and extorts money from them, yes, shows
the democracy to be nothing better than a sham, by
talking like a champion of the people and acting like
a tyrant, since he has found out that while the word
"tyranny" fills you with concern, the thing for which
it stands leaves you undisturbed.   Indeed, so different
is he from the Spartans that whereas the Spartans
accept defeat even at the hands of their allies, when
they compete against them, Alcibiades will not endure
it even at the hands of his fellow-citizens ; in fact, he
has openly stated that he will brook no rivals.   It
is inevitable that such behaviour should cause the
states within our confederacy to feel sympathy for
our enemies and loathing for us.

In order to make it clear, however, that he was
insulting Athens as a whole in addition to Diomedes,
he asked the leaders of the Athenian deputation to
lend him the processional vessels, alleging that he
intended to use them for a celebration of his victory
on the day before the sacrifice ; he then abused the
trust placed in him and refused to return them, as
he wanted to use the golden basins and censers next
day before Athens did so.   Naturally, when those
strangers who did not know that they belonged to
us saw the state-procession taking place after that of
Alcibiades, they imagined that we were using his
vessels : while those who had either heard the truth
from the Athenians present or else knew the ways of

---

⁶ θυσίας Scaliger : οὐσίας codd.
⁷ χερνιβίοις Valckenaer ex Athen. ix. 408 c : χερνίβοις codd.

τὰ τούτου, κατεγέλων ἡμῶν, ὁρῶντες ἕνα ἄνδρα
μεῖζον ἁπάσης[1] τῆς πόλεως δυνάμενον.

30 Σκέψασθε δὲ καὶ τὴν ἄλλην ἀποδημίαν τὴν εἰς
Ὀλυμπίαν ὡς διέθετο. τούτῳ[2] σκηνὴν μὲν Περ-
σικὴν Ἐφέσιοι διπλασίαν τῆς δημοσίας ἔπηξαν,
ἱερεῖα δὲ καὶ τοῖς ἵπποις ἐφόδια Χῖοι παρεσκεύασαν,
οἶνον δὲ καὶ τὰ ἄλλα ἀναλώματα Λεσβίοις προσ-
έταξε. καὶ οὕτως εὐτυχής ἐστιν, ὥστε τοὺς
Ἕλληνας τῆς παρανομίας καὶ τῆς δωροδοκίας
μάρτυρας κεκτημένος οὐδεμίαν δέδωκε δίκην, ἀλλὰ
ὁπόσοι μὲν ἄρχοντες ἐν μιᾷ πόλει γεγένηνται,
31 ὑπεύθυνοί εἰσιν, ὁ δὲ πάντων τῶν συμμάχων
⟨ἄρχων⟩[3] καὶ χρήματα λαμβάνων οὐδενὸς τούτων
ὑπόδικός ἐστιν, ἀλλὰ τοιαῦτα διαπεπραγμένος
σίτησιν ἐν Πρυτανείῳ ἔλαβε, καὶ προσέτι πολλῇ τῇ
νίκῃ χρῆται, ὥσπερ οὐ πολὺ μᾶλλον ἠτιμακὼς ἢ
ἐστεφανωκὼς τὴν πόλιν. εἰ δὲ βούλεσθε σκοπεῖν,
εὑρήσετε τῶν πολλάκις τούτῳ[4] πεπραγμένων ἕκαστον ὀλίγον χρόνον πράξαντάς τινας ἀναστάτους τοὺς
οἴκους ποιήσαντας· οὗτος δ' ἐπιτηδεύων ἅπαντα
32 πολυτελέστατα διπλασίαν οὐσίαν κέκτηται. καίτοι
ὑμεῖς γε νομίζετε τοὺς φειδομένους καὶ τοὺς ἀκριβῶς διαιτωμένους φιλοχρημάτους εἶναι, οὐκ ὀρθῶς
γιγνώσκοντες· οἱ γὰρ μεγάλα δαπανώμενοι πολλῶν
δεόμενοι αἰσχροκερδέστατοί εἰσιν. αἴσχιστον δὲ
φανήσεσθε ποιοῦντες, εἰ τοῦτον μὲν ἀγαπᾶτε τὸν ἀπὸ

---

[1] μεῖζον ἁπάσης Sluiter: μείζονα πάσης codd.
[2] διέθετο. τούτῳ Reiske: διέθετο τούτῳ. Stephanus: διέθετο
(διετίθετο) τοῦτο. codd.   [3] ἄρχων add. Meier.
[4] τῶν πολλάκις τούτῳ Lipsius: πολλὰ τῶν τούτῳ codd.

---

[a] σίτησις ἐν Πρυτανείῳ was the usual reward for a victory
at the games or signal service to the state. The same

Alcibiades, laughed at us when they saw one man showing himself superior to our entire community.

Then again, look at the arrangements which he made for his stay at Olympia as a whole. For Alcibiades the people of Ephesus erected a Persian pavilion twice as large as that of our official deputation : Chios furnished him with beasts for sacrifice and with fodder for his horses : while he requisitioned wine and everything else necessary for his maintenance from Lesbos. And so lucky is he that although the Greek people at large can testify to his lawlessness and corruption, he has gone unpunished. While those who hold office within a single city have to render account of that office, Alcibiades, whose authority extends over all our allies and who receives monies from them, is not liable to answer for any of his public acts ; on the contrary, after behaving as I have described, he was rewarded with free entertainment in the Prytaneum *a* ; and not content with that, he is for ever taking credit for his victory, as though he had not so much brought Athens into disgrace as won her a garland of honour. Only reflect, and you will find that men who have given way even temporarily to any single one of the excesses in which Alcibiades has indulged time and again, have brought ruin upon their houses ; yet Alcibiades, whose entire life is devoted to extravagance, has doubled his wealth. You regard as misers those who are niggardly and close-fisted ; but you are mistaken. It is the spendthrift, with his endless wants, who stoops lowest to fill his pockets. In fact, it will be a public disgrace, if you show tolerance towards a man who has achieved

privilege was granted Diocleides in 415, after his information in the matter of the Hermae. *Cf. Mysteries,* § 45.

τῶν ὑμετέρων¹ χρημάτων ταῦτα κατεργασάμενον,²
Καλλίαν δὲ τὸν Διδυμίου, τῷ σώματι νικήσαντα
πάντας τοὺς στεφανηφόρους ἀγῶνας, ἐξωστρακί-
σατε πρὸς τοῦτο³ οὐδὲν ἀποβλέψαντες, ὃς ἀπὸ
τῶν ἑαυτοῦ πόνων ἐτίμησε τὴν πόλιν.

33 Ἀναμνήσθητε δὲ καὶ τοὺς προγόνους, ὡς ἀγαθοὶ
καὶ σώφρονες ἦσαν, οἵτινες ἐξωστράκισαν Κίμωνα
διὰ παρανομίαν, ὅτι τῇ ἀδελφῇ τῇ ἑαυτοῦ συνῴκησε.
καίτοι οὐ μόνον⁴ αὐτὸς ὀλυμπιονίκης ἦν, ἀλλὰ καὶ
ὁ πατὴρ αὐτοῦ Μιλτιάδης. ἀλλ' ὅμως οὐδὲν
ὑπελογίζοντο τὰς νίκας· οὐ γὰρ ἐκ τῶν ἀγώνων
ἀλλ' ἐκ τῶν ἐπιτηδευμάτων ἔκρινον⁵ αὐτόν.

34 Ἀλλὰ μὴν εἰ δεῖ κατὰ γένος σκοπεῖν, ἐμοὶ μὲν
οὐδαμόθεν προσήκει τούτου τοῦ πράγματος—οὐδὲ
ἔστιν οὐδεὶς ὅστις ἂν ἀποδείξειε τῶν ἡμετέρων
οὐδένα τῇ συμφορᾷ ταύτῃ χρησάμενον—Ἀλκιβιάδῃ⁶
δὲ μάλιστα πάντων Ἀθηναίων. καὶ γὰρ ὁ τῆς
μητρὸς πατὴρ Μεγακλῆς καὶ ὁ πάππος Ἀλκιβιάδης
⟨δὶς⟩⁷ ἐξωστρακίσθησαν ἀμφότεροι, ὥστ' οὐδὲν
θαυμαστὸν οὐδ' ἄτοπον πείσεται τῶν αὐτῶν τοῖς
προγόνοις ἀξιούμενος. καὶ μὴν οὐδ' ἂν αὐτὸς
ἐπιχειρήσειεν ἀντειπεῖν, ὡς οὐ τῶν ἄλλων ἐκεῖνοι
παρανομώτατοι ὄντες τούτου σωφρονέστεροι καὶ
δικαιότεροι⁸ ἦσαν, ἐπεὶ τῶν γε τούτῳ πεπραγμένων
οὐδ' ἂν εἷς ἀξίως κατηγορῆσαι δύναιτο.

---

¹ ὑμετέρων Α : ἡμετέρων Q.
² κατεργασάμενον Α : κατειργασμένον Q.
τοῦτο Stephanus : τούτων Reiske : τοῦτον codd.
⁴ οὐ μόνον Α : μὴ μόνος Q.
⁵ ἔκρινον Α : ἔκριναν Q.
⁶ Ἀλκιβιάδῃ Valckenaer : ἀλκιβιάδης Α, -δην Q.
⁷ δὶς add. Markland, coll. Lys. § 14. 39.
⁸ καὶ δικαιότεροι om. Q.

his success only with the help of your money, when in ostracizing Callias, son of Didymius, who won victories at all the great games by his personal prowess, you took no account whatsoever of his achievement, although it was by his own efforts that he brought glory to Athens.

Then again, remember how steadfast, how true to their principles your fathers showed themselves, when they ostracized Cimon for breaking the law by taking his own sister to wife *a* ; and yet not only was Cimon himself an Olympic victor ; his father, Miltiades, had been one likewise. Nevertheless, they took no account of his victories ; for it was not by his exploits at the games, but by his manner of life that they judged him.

Furthermore, if account is to be taken of our families, I on my side cannot claim any acquaintance with ostracism. No one could show that any kinsman of mine has ever had the misfortune to suffer it. Alcibiades, on the other hand, knows more of it than any other member of the community. His mother's father, Megacles, and his father's father, Alcibiades, were both ostracized twice ; so it will be neither surprising nor unnatural if he receives the same treatment as his ancestors. Indeed, not even Alcibiades himself would venture to maintain that they, the worst miscreants of their time though they were, did not have more regard for decency and honesty than he himself ; for no one in the world could frame an accusation which would do justice to his misdeeds.

a The story is mentioned by Plutarch (*Cim.* 15), who, however, gives the correct reason for C.'s ostracism—the failure of his pro-Spartan policy. He was ostracized almost immediately after his return in disgrace from Ithome in 461.

35 Νομίζω δὲ καὶ τὸν θέντα τὸν νόμον ταύτην τὴν
διάνοιαν ἔχειν· ἀποβλέψαντα τῶν πολιτῶν πρὸς
τοὺς κρείττους τῶν ἀρχόντων καὶ τῶν νόμων,
ἐπειδὴ παρὰ τῶν τοιούτων οὐκ ἔστιν ἰδίᾳ δίκην
λαβεῖν, δημοσίαν τιμωρίαν ὑπὲρ τῶν ἀδικουμένων
κατασκευάσαι. ἐγὼ ⟨μὲν⟩[1] τοίνυν ἔν τε τῷ κοινῷ
κέκριμαι τετράκις, ἰδίᾳ τε οὐδένα διεκώλυσα δι-
κάζεσθαι βουλόμενον· Ἀλκιβιάδης δὲ τοιαῦτα
ἐργασάμενος[2] οὐδεμίαν πώποτε δίκην ὑποσχεῖν
36 ἐτόλμησεν. οὕτω γὰρ χαλεπός ἐστιν, ὥστε οὐ περὶ
τῶν παρελ-.λυθότων ἀδικημάτων αὐτὸν τιμωροῦν-
ται, ἀλλ᾽ ὑπὲρ τῶν μελλόντων φοβοῦνται, καὶ τοῖς
μὲν πεπονθόσι κακῶς ἀνέχεσθαι λυσιτελεῖ, τούτῳ
δὲ οὐκ ἐξαρκεῖ, εἰ μὴ καὶ τὸ λοιπὸν ὅ τι ἂν βούλη-
[34] ται διαπράξεται.[3] καίτοι οὐ δήπου, ὦ Ἀθηναῖοι,
ὀστρακισθῆναι μὲν ἐπιτήδειός εἰμι, τεθνάναι δὲ οὐκ
ἄξιος, οὐδὲ κρινόμενος μὲν ἀποφυγεῖν, ἄκριτος δὲ
φεύγειν, οὐδὲ τοσαυτάκις ἀγωνιζόμενος [καὶ] νικήσας δικαίως[4] ⟨ἂν⟩ πάλιν δόξαιμι δι᾽ ἐκεῖνα ἐκπεσεῖν.

37 Ἀλλὰ γὰρ ἴσως μετὰ μικρᾶς διαβολῆς ἢ φαύλων
κατηγόρων ἢ διὰ τῶν ἐπιτυχόντων ἐχθρῶν ἐκινδύ-
νευον, ἀλλ᾽ οὐ διὰ τῶν ἐρρωμενεστάτων καὶ λέγειν
καὶ πράττειν, οἵ τινες δύο τῶν τὴν αὐτὴν αἰτίαν
ἐχόντων ἐμοὶ ἀπέκτειναν. οὔκουν τοὺς τοιούτους
δίκαιον ἐκβάλλειν, οὓς πολλάκις ἐλέγχοντες εὑ-

---

[1] μὲν ci. Bekker.
[2] ἐργασάμενος A : εἰργασμένος Q.
[3] διαπράξεται Bekker : διαπράξηται codd.
[4] ἀγ. [καὶ] νικήσας δικαίως Bekker, ἂν add. Baiter et Sauppe:
ἀγ. δικαίως καὶ νικήσας codd.

---

[a] A quibble. The speaker tries to argue that if he was

570

Moreover, the legislator who instituted ostracism appears to me to have had the following intention. Observing that whenever members of the community are more powerful than the magistrates and the laws, it is impossible for an individual to obtain redress from them, he arranged that punishment for their misdeeds should be exacted by the state. Now I myself have been publicly tried four times, and have never prevented any private person who so desired from bringing me to justice. On the other hand, Alcibiades, who has worked such mischief, has never yet dared to answer for it in any way whatsoever. So forbidding is he that instead of punishing him for the wrongs which he has done already, men fear him for what he will do hereafter ; and while it pays his victims to suffer in silence, he himself is not satisfied unless he can work his will in the future also. Yet I hardly deserve to be ostracized, gentlemen, if I do not deserve to be put to death [a] ; and if I was acquitted when brought to trial, I cannot deserve to be sent into exile when no trial has taken place ; nor after vindicating myself so many times in court can I be thought to merit banishment on the same grounds of accusation again.

It may be objected that when I was prosecuted, the attack made upon me was a weak one, that my accusers were unimpressive, or that the case was conducted by casual enemies instead of by those who excel both as speakers and as men of action and who, in fact, brought about the death of two of the persons charged with the same offences as myself. I answer that justice requires you to banish, not those

acquitted when tried for his life, he must similarly be acquitted when the penalty in question is exile for ten years.

ρίσκετε μηδὲν ἀδικοῦντας, ἀλλὰ τοὺς μὴ θέλοντας
38 ὑποσχεῖν τῇ πόλει περὶ τοῦ βίου λόγον. δεινὸν δέ
μοι δοκεῖ εἶναι, εἰ μέν τις ἀπολογεῖσθαι ἀξιώσειεν
ὑπὲρ τῶν ἀποθανόντων ὡς ἀδίκως ἀπολώλασιν, οὐκ
⟨ἂν⟩ ἀνασχέσθαι τῶν ἐπιχειρούντων· εἰ δέ τις τῶν
ἀποφυγόντων πάλιν περὶ τῆς αὐτῆς αἰτίας κατηγορεῖ, πῶς οὐ δίκαιον περὶ τοὺς ζῶντας καὶ τοὺς
τεθνηκότας τὴν αὐτὴν γνώμην[1] ἔχειν;
39 Ἔστι μὲν οὖν[2] Ἀλκιβιάδου μήτε αὐτὸν[3] τῶν
νόμων καὶ τῶν ὅρκων φροντίζειν, ὑμᾶς τε παραβαίνειν ἐπιχειρεῖν διδάσκειν, καὶ τοὺς μὲν ἄλλους
ἐκβάλλειν καὶ ἀποκτείνειν ἀνηλεῶς, αὐτὸν δὲ ἱκε-
τεύειν καὶ δακρύειν οἰκτρῶς. καὶ ταῦτα μὲν οὐ
θαυμάζω· πολλῶν γὰρ αὐτῷ κλαυμάτων ἄξια
εἴργασται· ἐνθυμοῦμαι δὲ τίνας ποτὲ καὶ πείσει
δεόμενος, πότερα τοὺς νεωτέρους, οὓς πρὸς τὸ
πλῆθος διαβέβληκεν ἀσελγαίνων καὶ τὰ γυμνάσια
καταλύων καὶ παρὰ τὴν ἡλικίαν πράττων, ἢ τοὺς
πρεσβυτέρους, οἷς οὐδὲν ὁμοίως βεβίωκεν, ἀλλὰ
τῶν ἐπιτηδευμάτων αὐτῶν καταπεφρόνηκεν;
40 Οὐ μόνον δὲ αὐτῶν ἕνεκα τῶν παρανομούντων,
ἵνα δίκην διδῶσιν, ἐπιμελεῖσθαι ἄξιον, ἀλλὰ καὶ τῶν
ἄλλων, ὅπως τούτους ὁρῶντες δικαιότεροι καὶ
σωφρονέστεροι γίγνωνται. ἐμὲ μὲν τοίνυν ἐξελά-
σαντες τοὺς βελτίστους περιδεεῖς καταστήσετε,

whom, after repeated inquiry, you have found to
be innocent, but those who refuse to render to the
state an account of their past. Indeed what seems
strange to me is this. If one sought to vindicate
persons who have been put to death by showing that
they met their end unjustly, such an attempt would
not be tolerated. If, on the other hand, those who
have been declared innocent should once more be
accused on the same charge—is it not only right
that you should behave in the case of the living as
you would in the case of the dead ?

It is characteristic of Alcibiades to pay no attention to laws or oaths himself, and to try to teach you
to disregard them as well, and while he is ruthless
in bringing about the banishment and the death of
others, to have recourse to heart-rending tears and
appeals for mercy on his own account. Nor does
such behaviour surprise me—he has done much that
calls for tears. But whose goodwill will he gain by
his entreaties, I wonder ? That of the young, upon
whom he has brought the disfavour of the people by
his insolence, by his emptying of the gymnasia,
and by behaviour which his years do not warrant ?
Or that of the old, whose ways are the exact opposite
of his own, and whose mode of life he has treated with
contempt ?

However, it is not the mere exaction of punishment from wrongdoers themselves that should be
your object ; you should seek also to render everyone else more upright and more self-controlled by
the sight of that punishment. If, then, you send
me into exile, you will strike fear into all men of

---

[1] τὴν αὐτὴν γνώμην post δίκαιον habet Q.
[2] οὖν om. Q.   [3] αὐτὸν A : αὐτῶν Q.

τοῦτον δὲ κολάσαντες τοὺς ἀσελγεστάτους¹ νομι-
μωτέρους ποιήσετε.

41 Βούλομαι δ' ὑμᾶς ἀναμνῆσαι τῶν ἐμοὶ πεπραγμένων. ἐγὼ γὰρ πρεσβεύσας εἰς Θετταλίαν καὶ εἰς²
Μακεδονίαν καὶ εἰς Μολοσσίαν καὶ εἰς Θεσπρωτίαν
καὶ εἰς Ἰταλίαν καὶ εἰς Σικελίαν τοὺς μὲν διαφόρους
ὄντας διήλλαξα, τοὺς δ' ἐπιτηδείους ἐποίησα, τοὺς
δ' ἀπὸ τῶν ἐχθρῶν ἀπέστησα. καίτοι εἰ τῶν
πρεσβευόντων³ ἕκαστος τὰ⁴ αὐτὰ ἐποίησεν, ὀλίγους
ἂν πολεμίους εἴχετε καὶ πολλοὺς συμμάχους ἐκέ-
κτησθε.

42 Περὶ δὲ τῶν λῃτουργιῶν οὐκ ἀξιῶ μεμνῆσθαι,
πλὴν κατὰ τοσοῦτον, ὅτι τὰ προσταττόμενα δαπανῶ
οὐκ ἀπὸ τῶν κοινῶν ἀλλ' ἀπὸ τῶν⁵ ἰδίων. καίτοι
τυγχάνω νενικηκὼς εὐανδρίᾳ καὶ λαμπάδι καὶ
τραγῳδοῖς, οὐ τύπτων τοὺς ἀντιχορηγοῦντας, οὐδ'
αἰσχυνόμενος εἰ τῶν νόμων ἔλαττον δύναμαι. τοὺς
οὖν τοιούτους τῶν πολιτῶν πολὺ μᾶλλον ἐπιτηδείους
ἡγοῦμαι μένειν ἢ φεύγειν.

---

¹ ἀσελγεστάτους Emperius : ἀσελγεστέρους codd.
² εἰς om. A.
³ πρεσβευόντων Luzac : πρωτευόντων codd.
⁴ τὰ om. Q.   ⁵ τῶν om. Q.

worth. If, on the other hand, you punish Alcibiades, you will inspire a greater respect for the law in those whose insolence is uncontrolled.

I wish, further, to remind you of what I have done. I have been sent on missions to Thessaly, to Macedonia, to Molossia, to Thesprotia, to Italy, and to Sicily. In the course of them I have reconciled such as had quarrelled with you, others I have won over to friendship, others I have detached from your enemies. If every representative of yours had done the same, you would have few foes, and you would have gained many an ally.

Of my public services I do not intend to speak. I will say only this : the expenditure required of me I meet, not from monies belonging to the state, but from my own pocket. And yet I have in fact gained victories in the contest of physique,[a] in the torch-race, and at the tragic competitions—without striking rival Choregi, and without feeling shame at my possessing less power than the laws. Citizens of this kind, it seems to me, deserve to remain in Athens far more than to be sent into exile.

[a] See Harpocration, *s.v.*, and Athenaeus xiii. 565 f. The ἀγὼν εὐανδρίας was held at the Panathenaea.

FRAGMENTS

FRAGMENTS

NOTE

Unlike Antiphon, Andocides never made oratory his profession. If he spoke in public, the occasion was one which directly concerned himself. In addition, his career was interrupted by an enforced absence from Athens of over ten years. It is thus no matter for surprise that his published speeches should have been few in number. The three which survive, together with one other, dating from the days when he was still a young aristocrat dabbling in politics, probably represent all that their author ever left behind him. The scanty remains of this fourth speech are printed in the following pages.

I. ΣΥΜΒΟΥΛΕΥΤΙΚΟΣ

Title known from the Antiatticistes (Bekker, Anecdota 94. 21) and Photius.

II. ΠΡΟΣ ΤΟΥΣ ΕΤΑΙΡΟΥΣ

Καὶ τάφον μὲν αὐτοῦ λαμπρὸν ἐν τῇ ἀγορᾷ
Μάγνητες ἔχουσι· περὶ δὲ τῶν λειψάνων οὔτ'
'Ανδοκίδῃ προσέχειν ἄξιον ἐν τῷ πρὸς τοὺς ἑταίρους λέγοντι φωράσαντας τὰ λείψανα διαρρῖψαι
τοὺς 'Αθηναίους· ψεύδεται γὰρ ἐπὶ τὸν δῆμον
παροξύνων τοὺς ὀλιγαρχικούς.—Plut. Themist. 32.

Of the date of this speech we have no exact indication. Its title suggests that it was composed and delivered before the exile of Andocides in 415 B.C., when his active membership of an oligarchic ἑταιρεία came to an end, and if the second of the two fragments printed below also belongs to the Πρὸς τοὺς ἑταίρους, it must be placed before 417, as in that year Hyperbolus was ostracized. Its theme seems to have been a vituperative attack upon the existing demo-

I. DELIBERATIVE SPEECH

Only two isolated words, quoted by lexicographers, survive. The subject and date of the speech, if it is in fact distinct from that which follows, are unknown. Its title, however, which is unusually vague, may well be the abbreviation of some such MS. rubric as ΠΡΟΣ ΤΟΥΣ ΕΤΑΙΡΟΥΣ. ΣΥΜΒΟΥΛΕΥΤΙΚΟΣ.

II. TO THE MEMBERS OF HIS PARTY

THE people of Magnesia have a splendid tomb bearing the name of Themistocles in their Agora. As to his remains, Andocides deserves no credit when he says in his speech *To the Members of his Party* : " The Athenians removed his remains by stealth and scattered them to the winds." He is lying, in order to incite the oligarchs against the democracy.

cratic government ; and if, as Plutarch suggests, Andocides did not mind distorting his facts to encourage his companions, we need not suppose that we have lost a document which might have illumined much that is dark in the history of Athens during the fifth century. As evidence, however, of party polemics at the close of the Archidamian War, its interest would have been great. The fragment preserved by Plutarch is apparently concerned with the fickleness of the Demos, which insults without scruple the ashes of one of its greatest leaders.

ANDOCIDES

III. ΑΠΑΡΑΣΗΜΑ

1. Μὴ γὰρ ἴδοιμέν ποτε πάλιν ἐκ τῶν ὁρῶν τοὺς ἀνθρακευτὰς καὶ τὰς ἀμάξας εἰς τὸ ἄστυ ἤκοντας, καὶ πρόβατα καὶ βοῦς καὶ γύναια, καὶ πρεσβυτέρους ἄνδρας καὶ ἐργάτας ἐξοπλιζομένους· μηδὲ ἄγρια λάχανα καὶ σκάνδικας ἔτι φάγοιμεν.—Suidas, *s.v.* σκάνδιξ.

The reading of the mss., τοὺς ἀνθρακευτὰς ἤκοντας καὶ πρόβατα καὶ βοῦς καὶ τὰς ἀμάξας εἰς τὸ ἄστυ, is clearly faulty. I have made what seems the simplest correction. Sluiter's suggestion, τοὺς ἀνθρακευτὰς ἤκοντας εἰς τὸ ἄστυ, καὶ γύναια ⟨καὶ παῖδας⟩ καὶ πρόβατα καὶ βοῦς καὶ τὰς ἀμάξας ⟨ἄγοντας⟩, καὶ πρεσβυτέρους ἄνδρας κτλ., involves unnecessary changes, which the phrase βοῦς καὶ τὰς ἀμάξας ἄγοντας remains unconvincing. With some hesitation I print a comma after γύναια. It would be equally possible to read πρόβατα καὶ βοῦς, καὶ γύναια πρεσβ. κτλ.; but there is no evidence that Athens was forced to arm women in its defence during the Archidamian War.

2. Περὶ Ὑπερβόλου λέγειν αἰσχύνομαι, οὗ ὁ μὲν πατὴρ ἐστιγμένος ἔτι καὶ νῦν ἐν τῷ ἀργυροκοπείῳ δουλεύει τῷ δημοσίῳ, αὐτὸς δὲ ξένος ὢν καὶ βάρβαρος λυχνοποιεῖ.—Schol. Arist. *Vesp.* 1007.

Almost certainly a passage from the Πρὸς τοὺς ἑταίρους The reference to Hyperbolus as still living in Athens shows that it must have been written before 417 B.C., the year of

FRAGMENTS

III. FRAGMENTS OF UNCERTAIN ORIGIN

1. May we never again see the charcoal-burners and their waggons arriving in Athens from the mountains, nor sheep and cattle and helpless women, no, nor old men and labourers arming for battle. May we never again eat wild herbs and chervil.

It has been conjectured with probability that this fragment, like the following, belongs to the Πρὸς τοὺς ἑταίρους. Andocides is clearly referring to the hardship felt in Athens during the Archidamian War, when the city was crowded with countryfolk and the Spartan forces were regularly destroying the produce of the farms and olive-yards of Attica. It is not difficult to see how a passage such as this formed part of an attack upon the democratic and imperialist party, whose policy, in the eyes of the oligarchs, had led directly to the conflict with Sparta.

2. Hyperbolus I blush to mention. His father, a branded slave, still works at the public mint ; while he himself, a foreign interloper, makes lamps for a living.

his ostracism ; and the tone of the speaker well represents the feelings of the oligarchic minority towards the radical leaders of the democratic party.

INDEX OF PROPER NAMES

An. = *Antiphon,* *As.* = *Andocides,* *fr.* = *fragments,* *app.* = *appendix* (*pp. 314-317*). *References are to the speeches as numbered. It is hoped to add an index of subjects to the second volume.*

584

INDEX OF PROPER NAMES

585

INDEX OF PROPER NAMES

INDEX OF PROPER NAMES

INDEX OF PROPER NAMES

Printed in Great Britain by R. & R. Clark, Limited, *Edinburgh*

THE LOEB CLASSICAL LIBRARY

VOLUMES ALREADY PUBLISHED

LATIN AUTHORS

AMMIANUS MARCELLINUS. J. C. Rolfe. 3 Vols.

APULEIUS : THE GOLDEN ASS (METAMORPHOSES). W. Adlington (1566). Revised by S. Gaselee.

ST. AUGUSTINE : CITY OF GOD. 7 Vols. Vol. I. G. E. McCracken.

ST. AUGUSTINE, CONFESSIONS OF. W. Watts (1631). 2 Vols.

ST. AUGUSTINE : SELECT LETTERS. J. H. Baxter.

AUSONIUS. H. G. Evelyn White. 2 Vols.

BEDE. J. E. King. 2 Vols.

BOETHIUS : TRACTS AND DE CONSOLATIONE PHILOSOPHIAE. Rev. H. F. Stewart and E. K. Rand.

CAESAR : ALEXANDRIAN, AFRICAN AND SPANISH WARS. A. G. Way.

CAESAR : CIVIL WARS. A. G. Peskett.

CAESAR : GALLIC WAR. H. J. Edwards.

CATO AND VARRO : DE RE RUSTICA. H. B. Ash and W. D. Hooper.

CATULLUS. F. W. Cornish ; TIBULLUS. J. B. Postgate ; and PERVIGILIUM VENERIS. J. W. Mackail.

CELSUS : DE MEDICINA. W. G. Spencer. 3 Vols.

CICERO : BRUTUS AND ORATOR. G. L. Hendrickson and H. M. Hubbell.

CICERO : DE FINIBUS. H. Rackham.

CICERO : DE INVENTIONE, etc. H. M. Hubbell.

CICERO : DE NATURA DEORUM AND ACADEMICA. H. Rackham.

CICERO : DE OFFICIIS. Walter Miller.

1

THE LOEB CLASSICAL LIBRARY

CICERO : DE ORATORE, etc. 2 Vols. Vol. I : DE ORATORE, Books I and II. E. W. Sutton and H. Rackham. Vol. II : DE ORATORE, Book III ; DE FATO ; PARADOXA STOI- CORUM ; DE PARTITIONE ORATORIA. H. Rackham.

CICERO : DE REPUBLICA, DE LEGIBUS, SOMNIUM SCIPIONIS. Clinton W. Keyes.

CICERO : DE SENECTUTE, DE AMICITIA, DE DIVINATIONE. W. A. Falconer.

CICERO : IN CATILINAM, PRO MURENA, PRO SULLA, PRO FLACCO. Louis E. Lord.

CICERO : LETTERS TO ATTICUS. E. O. Winstedt. 3 Vols.

CICERO : LETTERS TO HIS FRIENDS. W. Glynn Williams. 3 Vols.

CICERO : PHILIPPICS. W. C. A. Ker.

CICERO : PRO ARCHIA, POST REDITUM, DE DOMO, DE HA- RUSPICUM RESPONSIS, PRO PLANCIO. N. H. Watts.

CICERO : PRO CAECINA, PRO LEGE MANILIA, PRO CLUENTIO, PRO RABIRIO. H. Grose Hodge.

CICERO : PRO CAELIO, DE PROVINCIIS CONSULARIBUS, PRO BALBO. R. Gardner.

CICERO : PRO MILONE, IN PISONEM, PRO SCAURO, PRO FONTEIO, PRO RABIRIO POSTUMO, PRO MARCELLO, PRO LIGARIO, PRO REGE DEIOTARO. N. H. Watts.

CICERO : PRO QUINCTIO, PRO ROSCIO AMERINO, PRO ROSCIO COMOEDO, CONTRA RULLUM. J. H. Freese.

CICERO : PRO SESTIO, IN VATINIUM. R. Gardner.

[CICERO] : RHETORICA AD HERENNIUM. H. Caplan.

CICERO : TUSCULAN DISPUTATIONS. J. E. King.

CICERO : VERRINE ORATIONS. L. H. G. Greenwood. 2 Vols.

CLAUDIAN. M. Platnauer. 2 Vols.

COLUMELLA : DE RE RUSTICA ; DE ARBORIBUS. H. B. Ash, E. S. Forster, E. Heffner. 3 Vols.

CURTIUS, Q.: HISTORY OF ALEXANDER. J. C. Rolfe. 2 Vols.

FLORUS. E. S. Forster ; and CORNELIUS NEPOS. J. C. Rolfe.

FRONTINUS : STRATAGEMS AND AQUEDUCTS. C. E. Bennett and M. B. McElwain.

FRONTO : CORRESPONDENCE. C. R. Haines. 2 Vols.

GELLIUS. J. C. Rolfe. 3 Vols.

HORACE : ODES AND EPODES. C. E. Bennett.

HORACE : SATIRES, EPISTLES, ARS POETICA. H. R. Fairclough.

JEROME : SELECT LETTERS. F. A. Wright.

JUVENAL AND PERSIUS. G. G. Ramsay.

THE LOEB CLASSICAL LIBRARY

LIVY. B. O. Foster, F. G. Moore, Evan T. Sage, A. C. Schlesinger and R. M. Geer (General Index). 14 Vols.

LUCAN. J. D. Duff.

LUCRETIUS. W. H. D. Rouse.

MARTIAL. W. C. A. Ker. 2 Vols.

MINOR LATIN POETS: from PUBLILIUS SYRUS to RUTILIUS NAMATIANUS, including GRATTIUS, CALPURNIUS SICULUS, NEMESIANUS, AVIANUS, with " Aetna," " Phoenix " and other poems. J. Wight Duff and Arnold M. Duff.

OVID: THE ART OF LOVE AND OTHER POEMS. J. H. Mozley.

OVID: FASTI. Sir James G. Frazer.

OVID: HEROIDES AND AMORES. Grant Showerman.

OVID: METAMORPHOSES. F. J. Miller. 2 Vols.

OVID: TRISTIA AND EX PONTO. A. L. Wheeler.

PETRONIUS. M. Heseltine; SENECA: APOCOLOCYNTOSIS. W. H. D. Rouse.

PLAUTUS. Paul Nixon. 5 Vols.

PLINY: LETTERS. Melmoth's translation revised by W. M. L. Hutchinson. 2 Vols.

PLINY: NATURAL HISTORY. 10 Vols. Vols. I-V and IX. H. Rackham. Vols. VI and VII. W. H. S. Jones.

PROPERTIUS. H. E. Butler.

PRUDENTIUS. H. J. Thomson. 2 Vols.

QUINTILIAN. H. E. Butler. 4 Vols.

REMAINS OF OLD LATIN. E. H. Warmington. 4 Vols. Vol. I (Ennius and Caecilius). Vol. II (Livius, Naevius, Pacuvius, Accius). Vol. III (Lucilius, Laws of the XII Tables). Vol. IV (Archaic Inscriptions).

SALLUST. J. C. Rolfe.

SCRIPTORES HISTORIAE AUGUSTAE. D. Magie. 3 Vols.

SENECA: APOCOLOCYNTOSIS. Cf. PETRONIUS.

SENECA: EPISTULAE MORALES. R. M. Gummere. 3 Vols.

SENECA: MORAL ESSAYS. J. W. Basore. 3 Vols.

SENECA: TRAGEDIES. F. J. Miller. 2 Vols.

SIDONIUS: POEMS AND LETTERS. W. B. Anderson. 2 Vols.

SILIUS ITALICUS. J. D. Duff. 2 Vols.

STATIUS. J. H. Mozley. 2 Vols.

SUETONIUS. J. C. Rolfe. 2 Vols.

TACITUS: DIALOGUS. Sir Wm. Peterson: and AGRICOLA AND GERMANIA. Maurice Hutton.

TACITUS: HISTORIES AND ANNALS. C. H. Moore and J. Jackson. 4 Vols.

THE LOEB CLASSICAL LIBRARY

TERENCE. John Sargeaunt. 2 Vols.
TERTULLIAN: APOLOGIA AND DE SPECTACULIS. T. R. Glover,
MINUCIUS FELIX. G. H. Rendall.
VALERIUS FLACCUS. J. H. Mozley.
VARRO: DE LINGUA LATINA. R. G. Kent. 2 Vols.
VELLEIUS PATERCULUS AND RES GESTAE DIVI AUGUSTI.
F. W. Shipley.
VIRGIL. H. R. Fairclough. 2 Vols.
VITRUVIUS: DE ARCHITECTURA. F Granger. 2 Vols.

GREEK AUTHORS

ACHILLES TATIUS. S. Gaselee. (2nd Imp.)
AELIAN: ON THE NATURE OF ANIMALS. A. F. Scholfield.
3 Vols. Vols. I and II.
AENEAS TACTICUS, ASCLEPIODOTUS AND ONASANDER. The
Illinois Greek Club.
AESCHINES. C. D. Adams.
AESCHYLUS. H. Weir Smyth. 2 Vols.
ALCIPHRON, AELIAN AND PHILOSTRATUS: LETTERS. A. R.
Benner and F. H. Fobes.
APOLLODORUS. Sir James G. Frazer. 2 Vols.
APOLLONIUS RHODIUS. R. C. Seaton.
THE APOSTOLIC FATHERS. Kirsopp Lake. 2 Vols.
APPIAN'S ROMAN HISTORY. Horace White. 4 Vols.
ARATUS. Cf. CALLIMACHUS.
ARISTOPHANES. Benjamin Bickley Rogers. 3 Vols. Verse
trans.
ARISTOTLE: ART OF RHETORIC. J. H. Freese.
ARISTOTLE: ATHENIAN CONSTITUTION, EUDEMIAN ETHICS,
VIRTUES AND VICES. H. Rackham.
ARISTOTLE: GENERATION OF ANIMALS. A. L. Peck.
ARISTOTLE: METAPHYSICS. H. Tredennick. 2 Vols.
ARISTOTLE: METEOROLOGICA. H. D. P. Lee.
ARISTOTLE: MINOR WORKS. W. S. Hett. "On Colours,"
"On Things Heard," "Physiognomics," "On Plants,"
"On Marvellous Things Heard," "Mechanical Problems,"
"On Indivisible Lines," "Situations and Names of
Winds," "On Melissus, Xenophanes, and Gorgias."
ARISTOTLE: NICOMACHEAN ETHICS. H. Rackham.

4

Dio Cassius : Roman History. E. Cary. 9 Vols.

Dio Chrysostom. 5 Vols. Vols. I and II. J. W. Cohoon. Vol. III. J. W. Cohoon and H. Lamar Crosby. Vols. IV and V. H. Lamar Crosby.

Diodorus Siculus. 12 Vols. Vols. I-VI. C. H. Oldfather. Vol. VII. C. L. Sherman. Vols. IX and X. Russel M. Geer. Vol. XI. F. R. Walton.

Diogenes Laertius. R. D. Hicks. 2 Vols.

Dionysius of Halicarnassus : Roman Antiquities. Spelman's translation revised by E. Cary. 7 Vols.

Epictetus. W. A. Oldfather. 2 Vols.

Euripides. A. S. Way. 4 Vols. Verse trans.

Eusebius : Ecclesiastical History. Kirsopp Lake and J. E. L. Oulton. 2 Vols.

Galen : On the Natural Faculties. A. J. Brock.

The Greek Anthology. W. R. Paton. 5 Vols.

The Greek Bucolic Poets (Theocritus, Bion, Moschus). J. M. Edmonds.

Greek Elegy and Iambus with the Anacreontea. J. M. Edmonds. 2 Vols.

Greek Mathematical Works. Ivor Thomas. 2 Vols.

Herodes. Cf. Theophrastus : Characters.

Herodotus. A. D. Godley. 4 Vols.

Hesiod and the Homeric Hymns. H. G. Evelyn White.

Hippocrates and the Fragments of Heracleitus. W. H. S. Jones and E. T. Withington. 4 Vols.

Homer : Iliad. A. T. Murray. 2 Vols.

Homer : Odyssey. A. T. Murray. 2 Vols.

Isaeus. E. S. Forster.

Isocrates. George Norlin and LaRue Van Hook. 3 Vols.

St. John Damascene : Barlaam and Ioasaph. Rev. G. R. Woodward and Harold Mattingly.

Josephus. H. St. J. Thackeray and Ralph Marcus. 9 Vols. Vols. I-VII.

Julian. Wilmer Cave Wright. 3 Vols.

Longus : Daphnis and Chloe. Thornley's translation revised by J. M. Edmonds ; and Parthenius. S. Gaselee.

Lucian. A. M. Harmon. 8 Vols. Vols. I-V.

Lycophron. Cf. Callimachus.

Lyra Graeca. J. M. Edmonds. 3 Vols.

Lysias. W. R. M. Lamb.

THE LOEB CLASSICAL LIBRARY

MANETHO. W. G. Waddell; PTOLEMY: TETRABIBLOS. F. E. Robbins.

MARCUS AURELIUS. C. R. Haines.

MENANDER. F. G. Allinson.

MINOR ATTIC ORATORS. 2 Vols. K. J. Maidment and J. O. Burtt.

NONNOS: DIONYSIACA. W. H. D. Rouse. 3 Vols.

OPPIAN, COLLUTHUS, TRYPHIODORUS. A. W. Mair.

PAPYRI. NON-LITERARY SELECTIONS. A. S. Hunt and C. C. Edgar. 2 Vols. LITERARY SELECTIONS (Poetry). D. L. Page.

PARTHENIUS. *Cf.* LONGUS.

PAUSANIAS: DESCRIPTION OF GREECE. W. H. S. Jones. 5 Vols. and Companion Vol. arranged by R. E. Wycherley.

PHILO. 10 Vols. Vols. I-V. F. H. Colson and Rev. G. H. Whitaker; Vols. VI-IX. F. H. Colson.
Two Supplementary Vols. Translation only from an Armenian Text. Ralph Marcus.

PHILOSTRATUS: THE LIFE OF APOLLONIUS OF TYANA. F. C. Conybeare. 2 Vols.

PHILOSTRATUS: IMAGINES; CALLISTRATUS: DESCRIPTIONS. A. Fairbanks.

PHILOSTRATUS AND EUNAPIUS: LIVES OF THE SOPHISTS. Wilmer Cave Wright.

PINDAR. Sir J. E. Sandys.

PLATO I: EUTHYPHRO, APOLOGY, CRITO, PHAEDO, PHAEDRUS. H. N. Fowler.

PLATO II: THEAETETUS AND SOPHIST. H. N. Fowler.

PLATO III: STATESMAN, PHILEBUS. H. N. Fowler: ION. W. R. M. Lamb.

PLATO IV: LACHES, PROTAGORAS, MENO, EUTHYDEMUS. W. R. M. Lamb.

PLATO V: LYSIS, SYMPOSIUM, GORGIAS. W. R. M. Lamb.

PLATO VI: CRATYLUS, PARMENIDES, GREATER HIPPIAS, LESSER HIPPIAS. H. N. Fowler.

PLATO VII: TIMAEUS, CRITIAS, CLITOPHO, MENEXENUS, EPISTULAE. Rev. R. G. Bury.

PLATO VIII: CHARMIDES, ALCIBIADES, HIPPARCHUS, THE LOVERS, THEAGES, MINOS AND EPINOMIS. W. R. M. Lamb.

PLATO: LAWS. Rev. R. G. Bury. 2 Vols.

PLATO: REPUBLIC. Paul Shorey. 2 Vols.

PLUTARCH: MORALIA. 15 Vols. Vols. I-V. F. C. Babbitt;

THE LOEB CLASSICAL LIBRARY

Vol. VI. W. C. Helmbold ; Vol. VII. P. H. De Lacy and
B. Einarson ; Vol. X. H. N. Fowler ; Vol. XII. H.
Cherniss and W. C. Helmbold.

PLUTARCH : THE PARALLEL LIVES. B. Perrin. 11 Vols.

POLYBIUS. W. R. Paton. 6 Vols.

PROCOPIUS : HISTORY OF THE WARS. H. B. Dewing. 7 Vols.

PTOLEMY : TETRABIBLOS. *Cf.* MANETHO.

QUINTUS SMYRNAEUS. A. S. Way. Verse trans.

SEXTUS EMPIRICUS. Rev. R. G. Bury. 4 Vols.

SOPHOCLES. F. Storr. 2 Vols. Verse trans.

STRABO : GEOGRAPHY. Horace L. Jones. 8 Vols.

THEOPHRASTUS : CHARACTERS. J. M. Edmonds : HERODES.
etc. A. D. Knox.

THEOPHRASTUS : ENQUIRY INTO PLANTS. Sir Arthur Hort.
2 Vols.

THUCYDIDES. C. F. Smith. 4 Vols.

TRYPHIODORUS. *Cf.* OPPIAN.

XENOPHON : CYROPAEDIA. Walter Miller. 2 Vols.

XENOPHON : HELLENICA, ANABASIS, APOLOGY, AND SYMPO-
SIUM. C. L. Brownson and O. J. Todd. 3 Vols.

XENOPHON : MEMORABILIA AND OECONOMICUS. E. C. Marchant.

XENOPHON : SCRIPTA MINORA. E. C. Marchant.

VOLUMES IN PREPARATION

GREEK AUTHORS

ARISTOTLE : HISTORY OF ANIMALS. A. L. Peck.

PLOTINUS. A. H. Armstrong.

LATIN AUTHORS

BABRIUS AND PHAEDRUS. B. E. Perry.

DESCRIPTIVE PROSPECTUS ON APPLICATION

LONDON   CAMBRIDGE, MASS.
WILLIAM HEINEMANN LTD   HARVARD UNIV. PRESS